Grammar and Writing

AUTHORS AND ADVISERS

Walter Loban
General Adviser
Professor of Education
University of California
at Berkeley

Donald C. Freeman
Specialist, Linguistics
Temple University
Philadelphia, Pennsylvania

James Harkness
Specialist, Libraries and Information
State University of New York
Albany, New York

Vicki Jacobs
Specialist, Vocabulary
Holbrook Public Schools
Holbrook, Massachusetts

Robert J. Jones
Specialist, Test Taking
Educational Testing Service
Princeton, New Jersey

Patricia Laurence
Specialist, Composition
The City College, C.U.N.Y.
New York, New York

Robert W. Reising
Specialist, Grammar and Composition
Pembroke State University
Pembroke, North Carolina

Norman Rudnick
Specialist, Argumentation and Logic
Miramonte High School
Orinda, California

Sandra Stotsky
Specialist, Vocabulary
Curry College
Milton, Massachusetts

Norman Unrau
Specialist, Argumentation and Logic
Miramonte High School
Orinda, California

CONSULTANTS

Martha Brooks, Abilene Independent School District, Abilene, Texas
Leslie MacIntyre, Homestead High School, Mequon, Wisconsin
Henry F. Mooney, Danvers Public Schools, Danvers, Massachusetts
Norman Rudnick, Miramonte High School, Orinda, California
Milton Schaeffer, Maplewood - South Orange School District, New Jersey
Mary Jo Wagner, Leland High School, San Jose, California

Grammar and Writing

Macmillan Publishing Co., Inc.
New York
Collier Macmillan Publishers
London

WALTER LOBAN, General Adviser, has been active in English education for many years. Among his scholarly publications in the area of language is *Teaching Language and Literature: Grades 7–12,* of which he is co-author. Dr. Loban's landmark study *Language Development: Kindergarten Through Grade 12* (NCTE: 1976) has provided unique and valuable information about the acquisition of syntactic elements by student writers.

DONALD C. FREEMAN, who is special adviser on grammar, is professor of English and chairman of the committee on linguistics at Temple University, Philadelphia. His examination of student writing has made him a leader in error analysis.

ROBERT W. REISING, who is adviser on grammar and composition, is professor of communicative arts at Pembroke State University, Pembroke, North Carolina. He has led workshops in English, notably at the University of North Carolina, at Charlotte.

PATRICIA LAURENCE, who is adviser on composition and who wrote the "Patterns of Thinking and Writing" section, teaches basic writing, literature, and linguistics at The City College of the City University of New York.

SANDRA STOTSKY, who developed the vocabulary section, is associated with Curry College, Milton, Massachusetts, and Harvard University. She works extensively with teachers in the Holbrook, Massachusetts, public schools.

1982 Printing

Macmillan Publishing Co., Inc.
866 Third Avenue, New York, New York 10022
Collier Macmillan Canada, Ltd.

Printed in the United States of America
Student Edition ISBN 0-02-246090-X
Teacher's Edition ISBN 0-02-246100-0
987654

ACKNOWLEDGMENTS

Grateful acknowledgment is given authors and publishers for permission to reprint the following:

We are indebted to Mary S. Lawrence for significant contributions in the form of ideas and exercises that appear in Sections 10 and 12 of this text. This material is from *Writing As a Thinking Process* by Mary S. Lawrence, published by the University of Michigan Press, copyright © by The University of Michigan 1972.

"Aaron Hits 715th, Passes Babe Ruth" by Joseph Durso, 4/9/74. © 1974 The New York Times Company. Selection reprinted by permission.

ABC of Reading and "Ts'ai Chi'h" from *Personae*. Copyright © 1934 and copyright © 1926 by Ezra Pound. Selections reprinted by permission of New Directions and Faber and Faber Ltd.

"The Airport World" by William Safire, 11/20/78. © 1978 by The New York Times Company. Selection reprinted by permission.

Anne Frank: The Diary of a Young Girl by Anne Frank. Copyright © 1952 by Otto H. Frank. Selection reprinted by permission of Doubleday and Company, Inc. Vallentine, Mitchell & Co., Ltd.

Articles, 7/16/78, 12/5/78, 4/15/79 (by Erica Brown), and Editorial 1/16/72. © 1972/78/79 The New York Times Company. Selections reprinted by permission.

"Baseball Briefs: Oakland 2, Texas 1" by Robert Creamer. Reprinted by permission of the author.

"Checklist" from *The Nixon Poems* by Eve Merriam. Copyright © 1970. Reprinted by permission of Eve Merriam c/o International Creative Management.

The Children Are Gone by Arthur Cavanaugh. Copyright © 1966 by Arthur Cavanaugh. Selection reprinted by permission of Simon and Schuster a division of Gulf and Western Corporation and by International Creative Management.

The Child's Conception of Physical Causality by Jean Piaget. Selection reprinted by permission of Humanities Press, Inc., N.J.

Errors and Expectations: A Guide for the Teacher of Basic Writing by Mina P. Shaughnessy. Copyright © 1977 by Mina P. Shaughnessy. Material adapted by permission of Oxford University Press, Inc.

Fodor's Old West by Eugene Fodor and Robert C. Fisher. Copyright © 1976 by Fodor's Modern Guides. Selection reprinted by permission of the David McKay Company, Inc.

The Great Railway Bazaar by Paul Theroux. Copyright © 1975 by Paul Theroux. Selection reprinted by permission of Houghton Mifflin Company and Hamish Hamilton Ltd.

"History in Art" by Ariane Ruskin. Selection reprinted by permission of the author.

Holt Life Science by Ramsey et al. Copyright © 1978 by Holt, Rinehart, and Winston, Inc. Selection reprinted by permission of the publisher.

"How the City Grew" by Blanche R. Brown from *Natural History*, April, 1979. Copyright © 1979 the American Museum of Natural History. Selection reprinted by permission of *Natural History*.

The Illustrated Encyclopedia of Butterfly World. Copyright © 1976 Salamander Books Ltd. Selection reprinted by permission.

Information Please Almanac 1979. Copyright © 1978 Information Please Publishing, Inc. Selections adapted by permission of the publisher.

In the Shadow of Man by Jane van Lawick-Goodall. Copyright © 1971 by Hugo and Jane van Lawick-Goodall. Selection reprinted by permission of Houghton Mifflin Company and William Collins Sons and Co., Ltd.

John Keats's Porridge: Favorite Recipes by American Poets by Paul Zimmer. Selection reprinted by permission of the University of Iowa Press.

"Lineage" from *For My People* by Margaret Walker Alexander. Reprinted by permission of the author.

The Long-Legged House by Wendell Berry. Selection reprinted by permission of the author.

Macmillan Dictionary. William D. Halsey, Editorial Director. Copyright © 1977, 1973 Macmillan Publishing Co., Inc. Selections reprinted by permission of the publisher.

Nisei Daughter by Monica Sone. Copyright © 1953 by Monica Sone. Selection adapted by permission of Little, Brown and Co. in association with Atlantic Monthly Press and by Brandt and Brandt.

"The Nose That Weighs Scales" by Lewis Grossberger. Copyright © 1975, New York Post Corporation. Selection reprinted by permission of the New York Post.

"Other People: How Do You Respond to Those Who Are Different" by Barbara Lang Stern from *Vogue*, March 1979. Copyright © 1979 by the Condé Nast Publications Inc. Selections adapted and reprinted by permission.

Pilgrim at Tinker's Creek by Annie Dillard. Copyright © 1974 by Annie Dillard. Selection reprinted by permission of Harper and Row, Publishers, Inc. and by the author and her agent, Blanche C. Gregory, Inc.

"Prisons and Funerals" by Jessica Mitford, 9/15/73, Op-ed. © 1973 The New York Times Company. Selection reprinted by permission.

"A Provincial in New York: Living in the Big Cave" by Willie Morris. Copyright © 1967 by Willie Morris. Selection reprinted by permission of Joan Daves.

Readers' Guide to Periodical Literature. Copyright © 1978, 1979 by The H. W. Wilson Company. Selection reproduced by permission of the publisher.

Review of Joyce Butler's *Wildfire Loose* by Irene Keegan. Appeared in the Boston Globe, July 1, 1979. Selection reprinted courtesy of the Boston Globe.

Running for Health and Beauty by Kathryn Lance, copyright © 1977 by the Bobbs Merrill Company, Inc. and Proteus (Publishing) Limited. Selection reprinted by permission of the publishers.

"Safety of Common Food Additives" adapted from "Chemical Cuisine." Poster available from the Center for Science in the Public Interest, 755 S. Street, N.W., Washington, D.C. 20009 for $2.00. Selection adapted by permission of the publisher.

San Francisco: A Guide to the Bay and Its Cities, copyright © 1973 Hastings House, Publishers. Selection reprinted by permission of the publisher.

"Shakespearean Staging Techniques" by Elizabeth Dakelman. Reprinted by permission of the author.

The Shorter Oxford English Dictionary. Selection reprinted by permission of Oxford University Press.

Taking the ACT Assessment, 1979-80 edition: brief selection from the English Usage sample test appearing on page 19. Copyright © 1979 by the American College Testing Program. Selection reprinted by permission.

"Tea." Copyright © 1977 by Consumers Union of United States, Inc., Mount Vernon, NY 10550. Excerpted by permission from Consumer Reports, September 1977.

"To Build a Fire" by Jack London. Selection reprinted by permission of Irving Shepard.

"An Unknown Beauty" by Tom Wicker, 12/1/78. © 1978 The New York Times Company. Selection reprinted by permission.

A Way of Seeing by Margaret Mead and Rhoda Metraux. Published by William Morrow and Company, Inc. Selection reprinted by permission of the publisher and by Dr. Rhoda Metraux.

Webster's New Collegiate Dictionary © 1979 by G.&C. Merriam Co., Publishers of the Merriam-Webster Dictionaries. Selections reprinted by permission of the publisher.

Webster's New World Dictionary, Second College Edition. Copyright © 1978 by William Collins + World Publishing Co., Inc. Selections reprinted by permission of the publisher.

The Wide Net and Other Stories by Eudora Welty. Selection reprinted by permission of Harcourt Brace Jovanovich, Inc. and Russell and Volkening, Inc.

CONTENTS

Writing Aids

Special Section

Composition

1

PARTS OF SPEECH

Parts of Speech

There are good practical reasons for knowing about the different *kinds* of words—*parts of speech*, as they are called—that you use every day.

The more that you know about parts of speech, the fewer errors you will make in writing. You must guard against certain errors with nouns, other kinds of errors with verbs, and still others with adjectives. The more you know about these and other parts of speech, the better able you will be to understand how they work together and to guard against those errors that cause poor grades, lost jobs, and general embarrassment. Be sure to study the "Avoiding Errors" pages in this section.

Your education, your work, and your enjoyment of language and of life in general all benefit from a strong, useful vocabulary. Part of the meaning of any word lies in the kind of word it is. Part of the meaning of the word *cat*, for example, lies in the fact that it names a kind of living thing, that it is a noun. In other words, your vocabulary is made up of parts of speech. The more you know about what a particular part of speech can do, the more likely you are to build up your vocabulary of that kind of word. You will see that you can keep adding nouns, verbs, adjectives, and adverbs. (It may surprise you to learn that you probably already know all the words that make up the other parts of speech.)

Knowing the parts of speech will help you to use this book and to learn about and talk about ways of improving your writing.

The following pages explain how to recognize each part of speech—and how to use it. Writers have many questions about parts of speech as they put words on paper. Some of the questions below—and many more—are answered in this section:

- How do I show the possessive form for a noun that ends in *s*?
- Should I write "would have gone" or "had gone"?
- What is the comparative form of *narrow* —"narrower" or "more narrow"?
- Is *everyone* a singular or a plural indefinite pronoun?
- Should I write *good* or *well*? Are both adverbs?
- How should *like* be used? Is it a preposition?
- Instead of saying "the gypsies are traveling," what if I say "the traveling gypsies"?

Use this section to learn details that you may not know. Also use it to refer to whenever you have questions of grammar that need quick, simple answers with examples.

DIAGNOSTIC TEST. Number your paper from 1 to 50. After each numeral write the corresponding italicized word from the paragraph below. Decide which part of speech the word is as it is used in the paragraph. Then write the name of the part of speech after the word. You may abbreviate the parts of speech as follows:

noun, *n.*
verb, *v.*
adjective, *adj.*
adverb, *adv.*
pronoun, *pron.*
preposition, *prep.*
conjunction, *conj.*

I looked at the (1) *route* ahead. This next piece was not going to be easy. Our rock ledge (2) *was perched* right on top of the (3) *enormous* bluff running down (4) *into* the hollow. In fact, almost under my feet, I could see the (5) *dirty* patch on the (6) *floor* of the hollow, (7) *which* I (8) *knew* was Camp Four. In a sudden urge to escape our (9) *isolation* I waved and (10) *shouted*, and then as (11) *suddenly* stopped (12) *as* I (13) *realized* my foolishness. (14) *Against* the (15) *vast* expanse of Everest, eight thousand feet above them, (16) *we* would be quite invisible to the (17) *best* binoculars. (18) *I* turned back (19) *to* the (20) *problem* that was (21) *ahead.* The rock (22) *was* far too

(23) *steep* to attempt to drop down and go (24) *around* this pitch. The only thing to do was to try to shuffle (25) *along* the ledge (26) *and* cut (27) *handholds* in the bulging ice that was trying to push (28) *me* off it. Held on a tight rope by (29) *Tenzing*, I (30) *cut* a few handholds and (31) *then* (32) *thrust* my ice-axe as hard as I could (33) *into* the (34) *solid* snow and (35) *ice*. Using (36) *this* to take my (37) *weight*, I moved (38) *quickly* along the ledge. (39) *It* proved easier (40) *than* I (41) *had anticipated*. A few more handholds, another (42) *quick* swing across (43) *them*, (44) *and* I was able to cut a line of (45) *steps* up on to a (46) *safe* slope and chop out a (47) *roomy* terrace from which to belay Tenzing as (48) *he* (49) *climbed* up to (50) *me*.

—Edmund Hillary, *Summit*

1.a NOUNS

A **noun** is a word that names a person, place, thing, or idea.

The "thing" may be living (like an insect) or nonliving (like a car). It may be something concrete (like a crayon) or something abstract (like beauty).

EXAMPLES

PERSON: woman, man, boy, girl, baby, parent
ANIMAL: dolphin, parrot, kangaroo, mammal
PLACE: planet, island, farm, kitchen
OBJECT: book, calendar, telephone, stapler
GROUP OR ORGANIZATION: team, club, society, army, orchestra, class, troop, flock, herd
ACTION: the laughter, a smile, a walk, a ride, a cry
TIME: today, yesterday, tomorrow, week, month
EVENT: exam, meeting, assembly, game, party
IDEA OR QUALITY: beauty, sadness, gravity, philosophy

A noun that names a group, such as *team* or *club*, is called a **collective noun**.

A noun that names an idea or a quality is called an **abstract noun**.

You cannot look, listen, smell, taste, or touch without perceiving a noun. Every *thing* in the world is a noun. As people discover or invent new things and develop new ideas, more nouns are added to the language.

EXERCISE 1. In which column or columns does each of the twenty italicized nouns belong? (Some nouns can fit in more than one column.)

person	animal	place	object	group

action	time	event	idea or quality

1. the *city*
2. the *umbrella*
3. the *niece*
4. the *barbecue*
5. the *morning*
6. the *navy*
7. the *roughness*
8. the *coyote*
9. the *lake*
10. a *swim*
11. the *dance*
12. the *swarm*
13. the *president*
14. the *crowd*
15. the *hammock*
16. the *chimpanzee*
17. the *evening*
18. the *race*
19. a *transition*
20. a *wall*

APPLICATION. Pick five nouns from the preceding table. Each noun should be from a different column. Write five original sentences. In each, use one of the five nouns you have selected from the table.

1.a.1 Proper nouns and common nouns

A **proper noun** is the name of a particular thing—not just *some* thing. A proper noun is capitalized. All the nouns in Exercise 1 above are common nouns. **Common nouns** are the common – not the particular – names of things. The word *proper* comes from the Latin word *proprius*, which means "one's own." Therefore, a word that is "one's own"—such as a person's name—is considered *proper.*

EXAMPLES

PERSON: Robert Gonzalez, Dr. Beck, Aunt Shirley, Richard the Lion-Hearted

ANIMAL: Rover, Black Beauty, Smokey the Bear

PLACE: Mars, the Atlantic Ocean, the Bar-R Ranch, the Empire State Building

OBJECT: Flako soap, *Wuthering Heights*, the *New York Times*, the *Mona Lisa*, *Voyager I*

GROUP OR ORGANIZATION: Modern Publishing Company, New Idea Society, the Red Cross

TIME: Monday, March, the Dark Ages, the Renaissance, the Fourth of July

EVENT: Thanksgiving Day Parade, the War Between the States, the Boston Marathon

(For more rules on capitalization, see 7.a.)

EXERCISE 2. Match the numbered proper nouns on the left with the lettered common nouns on the right.

1. Nashville	a. automobile
2. *National Geographic*	b. continent
3. Wheaties	c. national landmark
4. Shakespeare	d. magazine
5. Barbra Streisand	e. restaurant
6. Cadillac	f. author
7. Africa	g. fighter
8. the Grand Canyon	h. city
9. MacDonald's	i. cereal
10. Muhammad Ali	j. singer

1.a.2 Compound nouns

A **compound noun** is a noun that is made up of more than one word.

EXAMPLES

housekeeper	ice cream	mother-in-law
bookmark	high school	great-grandfather
necklace	dining room	kilowatt-hour

Sometimes the two words are written as one word; sometimes they are written as two separate words; sometimes they are written with hyphens.

EXERCISE 3. For each of the following categories, list at least four common nouns. Then give one proper noun, real or imagined, for each category. You may use compound nouns.

1. nouns that can grow—for example, *tree*
2. nouns that can paint a sign—for example, *artist*
3. nouns that can bark—for example, *dog*
4. nouns that can be salty—for example, *eggplant*
5. nouns that you can hold in your hand—for example, *pebble*
6. nouns that you can feed—for example, *show dog, fire*
7. nouns that you can visit—for example, *lake*
8. nouns that you can study—for example, *textbook*
9. nouns that you can empty—for example, *glass*
10. nouns that you can polish—for example, *diamond*

1.a.3 Singular nouns and plural nouns

In grammar the word *singular* means "one," a single item. When a noun means "more than one," it is a **plural noun**.

EXAMPLES

I have one **car**. [singular]
I have two **cars**. [plural]
I have a number of **cars**. [plural]

Some nouns that are singular look or sound plural because they end in *s*. The following nouns identify *one* thing; they are singular nouns.

SINGULAR NOUNS THAT END IN *S*

MUMPS: Mumps **is** a childhood disease.
MEASLES: Measles **is** annoying.
MATHEMATICS: Mathematics **is** a required subject.

Some other nouns that end in s and identify one thing are treated as plural. These nouns include *scissors, pants, binoculars,* and *eyeglasses.*

PLURAL NOUNS THAT IDENTIFY ONE THING

These scissors **are** not sharp.
His pants **were** torn.
The binoculars **are** heavy.
My eyeglasses **were** broken in the accident.

The chart below summarizes the rules for making the plural forms of nouns. (See 5.b.1 for more details.)

SINGULAR AND PLURAL NOUNS

most nouns		***nouns ending in* s, ss, sh, ch, x, z, zz**		***nouns ending in* y *preceded by a consonant***	
desk	desks	gas	gases	sky	skies
carrot	carrots	kiss	kisses	baby	babies
		brush	brushes		
		bench	benches		
		tax	taxes		
		waltz	waltzes		
		buzz	buzzes		
nouns ending in* y *preceded by a vowel		***most nouns ending in* f *or* fe**		***some nouns ending in* f *or* fe**	
play	plays	roof	roofs	loaf	loaves
donkey	donkeys	giraffe	giraffes	wife	wives
most nouns ending in* o *preceded by a consonant		***nouns ending in* o *preceded by a vowel***		***proper nouns***	
potato	potatoes	radio	radios	Smith	the Smiths
				Jones	the Joneses
				Velez	the Velezes
				Quincy	the Quincys
irregular nouns		***no-change plurals***		***compound nouns***	
child	children	deer	deer	handful	handfuls
mouse	mice	sheep	sheep	mailbox	mailboxes
tooth	teeth	trout	trout	sister-in-law	sisters-in-law
ox	oxen	species	species	attorney general	attorneys general
woman	women	series	series		
man	men				

EXERCISE 4. Give the plural form of each of the following singular nouns. Use a dictionary if in doubt.

1. comb
2. glass
3. dolly
4. journey
5. calf
6. cuff
7. tomato
8. cameo
9. library
10. ox
11. blitz
12. deer
13. record player
14. mother-in-law
15. lunch
16. dictionary
17. pulley
18. teaspoonful
19. inch
20. hex
21. bus
22. sheep
23. money
24. knife
25. foot

APPLICATION. Pick five of the preceding nouns. Write two original sentences for each noun. In the first sentence use the singular form of the noun. In the second sentence use the plural form.

APPLICATION. Pick another five of the preceding nouns. For each noun write *one* sentence that uses *both* the singular and the plural forms of the noun.

1.a.4 Collective nouns

A **collective noun** names a group.

EXAMPLES

army	the public
committee	a pride (of lions)
the clergy	the staff (of a company)

A collective noun may be considered either singular or plural. You consider the collective noun singular when you talk about the group as a whole. You consider the collective noun plural when you talk about the individual members of the group.

COLLECTIVE NOUNS

The **committee** wants our attention. [singular: the committee as a whole]

The **committee** have gone their separate ways. [plural: the committee as separate members]

1.a.5 Numbers as nouns

Sometimes numbers and numerals (especially dates) and expressions of quantity can be considered nouns because they name something that is living or something that is abstract.

EXAMPLES

We are curious about **1984**.

Hundreds attended the meeting.

We ordered one **dozen**.

EXERCISE 5. For each of the following sentences, indicate whether the italicized noun is singular or plural. Remember that some nouns can have either a singular or a plural meaning, depending on how they are used. Read each sentence carefully.

1. The *people* of southern California are somewhat interested in the motion-picture industry.
2. The *revenues* collected from film companies there are enormous.
3. In addition, each film *company* provides thousands of jobs.
4. The *staff* of each company is made up of local citizens.
5. A typical film *crew* has fewer than a hundred people.
6. The *crew* have specialized talents.
7. The *cast* of a medium-sized film, however, often includes hundreds of people.
8. The *cast* often have come to southern California specifically to work in films.
9. The Los Angeles *public* hopes that Hollywood stays strong.
10. *Hundreds*, maybe thousands, of people depend on a strong film industry for their living.

1.a.6 The possessive form of nouns

The **possessive form** is used to show possession, ownership, or the relationship between two nouns.

POSSESSIVE USE	ALTERNATE USE
my aunt's pen	the pen of my aunt; the pen that belongs to my aunt
the crowd's cheer	the cheer made by the crowd
a day's wages	the wages earned during a day
two dollars' worth	the amount bought for two dollars
this morning's paper	the paper published this morning
in today's world	in the world of today

The following chart summarizes the rules for making the possessive forms of nouns (see 5.b.2 and 7.k.1).

POSSESSIVE FORMS OF NOUNS

***singular nouns not ending in* s**	***singular nouns of one syllable ending in* s *or* s *sound***	***singular nouns of more than one syllable ending in* s *or* s *sound***
the girl's coat the emperor's crown	the kiss's meaning the prince's crown	the witness' account the princess' crown
***plural nouns not ending in* s**	***plural nouns ending in* s**	***compound nouns***
the children's coats the people's choice	the girls' coats the witnesses' accounts	sister-in-law's job attorney general's job

EXERCISE 6. Rephrase each of the following expressions, using a possessive form of a noun.

EXAMPLE a wait that took a day
ANSWER *a day's wait*

1. a house that belongs to Mr. Morgan
2. a house that belongs to the Morgans
3. an opinion that the girl has
4. an opinion that the girls have

5. the magic of the kiss
6. the magic of the princess
7. the strength of the voters
8. the strength of the oxen
9. the book that belongs to my brother
10. the book that belongs to my brother-in-law

APPLICATION. Pick five of the phrases that you formed above. Write five original sentences. In each, use one of the phrases that you have selected.

REVIEW EXERCISE A. Identify each *common noun* in the following sentences. Each sentence has more than one noun. Remember that a common noun can be singular or plural; it can also be compound.

1. The practice of acupuncture has won increasing acceptance by the public in this country.
2. Recent research by a committee notes successful applications of the ancient Chinese art.
3. The technique has gained widespread popularity as an alternative to expensive face lifts.
4. Adam Lewenberg, an internist, uses the method for the removal of wrinkles on the surface of the skin.
5. Like many practitioners, Lewenberg uses modern electrical devices for the treatment.
6. Dr. Y. Ching Ting prefers more classical methods.
7. Michael O. Smith claims success with acupuncture in his work with smokers.
8. Luke S. W. Chu uses acupuncture on patients with ulcers and asthma.
9. A. Brandwein, a dentist, employs the technique for relief of pain during dental procedures.
10. The use of acupuncture has even been extended to animals—to dogs, cats, racehorses, cows, and giraffes.

On the following page you will find the first of a number of "Avoiding Errors" boxes. These are designed to help you as a writer in applying the grammar that you are studying and as an editor in reviewing your writing. (See also Section 9.)

AVOIDING ERRORS WITH NOUNS

1. Remember to change a noun to its plural form when you mean "more than one." The most common way to make a noun plural is to add *s* or *es* to the noun.

   NOT ~~two car~~ ~~many car~~
   BUT two car**s** many car**s**

   Show "more than one" by adding *s* (or *es*) to the noun whenever you use a word such as "two" or "many" before the noun.

2. Do not use an apostrophe with a noun to show "more than one."

   NOT The baby has two ~~hair's~~ on his head.
   BUT The baby has two hair**s** on his head.

3. Use the apostrophe to express "belongs to" or other relationships between nouns.

   NOT That is ~~John~~ book.
   BUT That is John**'s** book.

   It may be easier to remember to make *John* possessive in this case if you think about a related sentence:

   NOT That book is ~~John~~. [John is not a book; John is a person.]
   BUT That book is John**'s**.

4. Do not misplace the apostrophe in a proper noun that ends in *s*. Look at the following sentences, keeping in mind that the author's name is Charles Dicken*s*:

   NOT I read all Charles ~~Dicken's~~ books.
   BUT I read all Charles Dicken**s'** books.
   OR I read all Charles Dickens**'s** books.

   In adding an apostrophe to a proper noun, you must not forget a final *s* that belongs with the name.

1.b VERBS

A **verb** is a word that expresses action or that helps to make a statement.

There are two main kinds of verbs. **Action verbs** are words that tell what someone or something does. They tell that someone or something acts. **Linking verbs** basically tell that someone or something *is*, not what someone or something *does.*

ACTION VERBS	LINKING VERBS
Business people **work**.	Business people **are** busy.
Artists **paint**.	Artists **are** creative.
Entertainers **perform**.	Entertainers **seem** glamorous.
Officials **govern**.	Officials **appear** important.

Action verbs and linking verbs are the life of language. Without them, your efforts to say something would look like the following:

In a city, business people, artists, entertainers, and officials...

When you add action and linking verbs, you tell what these people do or tell what they are. You thus give life and meaning to your words. You form a sentence.

In a city, business people **work**, artists **paint**, entertainers **perform**, and officials **govern**.

EXERCISE 7. Identify the action verb in each of the following sentences.

1. Frisbee discs soar through the air as gracefully as birds.
2. Their path and speed depend on the player's grip, the force of the throw, and the wind.
3. The designer and the manufacturer make Frisbee discs in different weights and sizes.
4. The lighter ones fly farther and faster than heavier ones.
5. Players still prefer the heavier ones for team sports.
6. Heavier ones keep a steadier course on windy days.
7. The lighter discs cost slightly less than the others.
8. In general, customers pay less than five dollars for any disc, however.

9. Players practice their tosses anywhere and anytime.
10. Players need only the disc, an open space, and a partner.
11. In state and local championships, contestants follow formal rules.
12. Ordinarily, though, players set their own rules.
13. Players ignore the seasons.
14. They chase their discs through heat and through snow.
15. Night and darkness present no problems.
16. Factories also produce a line of nighttime discs.
17. The daytime colors change to a bright green glow at night.
18. Frisbee disc games provide a great deal of exercise.
19. Some players teach their dogs the game.
20. Dogs compete in championships, too.

EXERCISE 8. Decide which of the following words can be action verbs.

1. remember
2. peanut
3. kneel
4. nibble
5. elephant
6. purple
7. memory
8. never
9. forget
10. search
11. relax
12. outside
13. observe
14. mouse
15. company
16. playful
17. accompany
18. preposterous
19. sneeze
20. envy

APPLICATION. Pick five of the action verbs that you have identified above. Write five original sentences. In each, use one of the action verbs that you have selected.

1.b.1 Action verbs: physical and mental

Some action verbs express physical action—lively physical action or quiet physical action. Some action verbs express mental action.

EXAMPLES

In football the huge linemen **lead** the charge through the defense. [physical action]

Before each play the offensive players **huddle** around the quarterback for directions. [physical action]

During the game the coaches **consider** their team's strategy. [mental action]

Good quarterbacks **think** fast under pressure and in the midst of confusion. [mental action]

1.b.2 Transitive and intransitive verbs

An action verb that is followed by a word that answers the question *what?* or *whom?* is called a **transitive verb**. The word that actually answers the question *what?* or *whom?* after the action verb is called the **direct object**, or the **object of the verb** (see 2.j).

TRANSITIVE VERBS

Fleas **bite** people. [action verb + word that answers *whom?*]

Hawks **see** their prey from far away. [action verb + word that answers *what?*]

Mountain goats **climb** craggy rocks with ease. [action verb + word that answers *what?*]

An action verb that simply tells what someone or something does or an action verb that is followed only by words that tell *when, where,* or *how* is called an **intransitive verb**. That is, a verb that does not have a direct object is said to be an intransitive—*not* transitive—verb.

INTRANSITIVE VERBS

Fleas **bite**. [action verb alone = intransitive verb]

Hawks **see** well. [action verb + word that tells *how*]

Mountain goats **climb** in all weather conditions. [action verb + words that tell *when*]

Most action verbs can be either transitive (with a direct object) or intransitive (without a direct object), as you can see by comparing the two preceding sets of examples.

Some verbs can be *only* transitive. They must always be followed by a direct object.

EXAMPLES
Stars **emit** light.
Astronomers **view** Neptune by telescope.
The clouds of Jupiter **contain** ammonia.

Some verbs can be *only* intransitive. They cannot take a direct object.

EXAMPLES
Occasionally, large meteorites **fall** to earth.
Meteoroids **glow** brightly and briefly.

EXERCISE 9. Identify the action verb in each of the following sentences. Indicate whether it is used as a transitive or an intransitive verb in that sentence.

1. Anteaters prefer the warmer regions of the world.
2. Anteaters possess no teeth whatsoever.
3. On the whole, anteaters live rather peacefully.
4. Like other toothless animals, anteaters often hide from their enemies.
5. When fearful, though, anteaters act fiercely.
6. In general, they attack only insects.
7. With the razor-sharp claws of their front legs, they slash the nests of ants and termites.
8. Long, sticky tongues dart from their dime-sized mouths at the ends of their twelve-inch noses.
9. Within seconds their tubelike noses capture hundreds of insects.
10. In captivity some anteaters reach an age of fourteen years.

1.b.3 Be: a linking verb

Linking verbs are special kinds of verbs. A **linking verb** links, or joins, a noun or pronoun (the subject of a sentence) with a word or expression that identifies it.

EXAMPLES

The singer **is** an artist.
The insects **are** mosquitoes.
The days **were** hot.

Most commonly used as linking verbs are forms of *be*—for example, *am, is, are, was, were, has been, was being.* Other linking verbs include *seem, become,* and *remain* (see 1.b.4).

A linking verb can also help to state a condition, including the condition of *where* or *when.*

EXAMPLES

Summer **is** here.
Ice **is** on the lake.
Vacation **is** over.

As the examples above show, linking verbs help to tell *who, what,* or *when* or *where* about the subject of a sentence.

EXERCISE 10. Identify the linking verb in each of the following sentences.

1. "I am just a reporter."
2. The quotation above is a statement by Winslow Homer about his own role as a painter.
3. Homer (1836–1910) is famous for his portrayals of life in the New England countryside.
4. Ordinary people, the land, and the choppy ocean beyond it are the main subjects of Homer's paintings.
5. Homer's people are natural, active, and informal.
6. In his painting *The Country School* some of the older children in the classroom are barefoot.
7. In Homer's day one-room schools such as the one in his picture were common in rural America.
8. Americans were mostly rural dwellers then.
9. For most of his life, Homer was a resident of Boston or the New England countryside.
10. At the front during the Civil War, Homer was an artist and war correspondent for *Harper's Weekly.*

1.b.4 Other linking verbs

Other words besides forms of *be* can link one word with another word or expression that describes or identifies it.

EXAMPLES

LOOK: Week by week, tadpoles **look** less like fish and more like frogs.

GROW: Tadpoles **grow** more froglike each week.

FEEL: Some frog species **feel** at home on land and in the water.

REMAIN: In cold weather and during long dry spells, frogs and toads **remain** inactive.

APPEAR: Water creatures by night and land creatures by day, natterjack toads **appear** quite tame.

SEEM: Bullfrogs **seem** noisy for their size.

SOUND: A few bullfrogs in good voice **sound** to us like a herd of cattle.

BECOME: After visits to French restaurants, some people **become** quite fond of frogs' legs.

TASTE: Frogs' legs **taste** rather like the white meat of chicken.

STAY: Indian tiger frogs **stay** safe from enemies by means of poison glands in their backs.

SMELL: The poisonous secretions from these glands **smell** pleasant to humans.

1.b.5 Linking or action?

Except for forms of *be* and *seem*, all the words listed above (1.b.4) as linking verbs can also be action verbs. Each of the following sentence pairs shows a word first used as a linking verb and then as an action verb:

EXAMPLES

LINKING: Bird lovers **look** overjoyed upon spotting rare species.

ACTION: Bird lovers **look** for nearly extinct bald eagles.

LINKING: Farmers **grow** concerned about taxes.

ACTION: Farmers **grow** corn.

LINKING: Patients with no cavities **feel** relieved.

ACTION: Cavity-prone patients often **feel** holes in their teeth.

LINKING: Fans **remain** loyal to hometown teams.
ACTION: World Series fans usually **remained** after the game to congratulate the winners.

LINKING: Some companies **appear** responsive to consumer complaints.
ACTION: Consumer specialists **appear** on news shows [make an appearance].

LINKING: Trucks and planes **sound** noisy to city dwellers.
ACTION: Trucks and fire engines **sound** their horns.

LINKING: People **become** interested in their appearance during adolescence.
ACTION: Healthy skin and clear eyes **become** everyone.

LINKING: Earl Grey tea and oolong tea **taste** different.
ACTION: Tea tasters **taste** tea.

If you are unsure about whether a word is a linking verb, substitute the word *seem* in the sentence. If the sentence still makes sense, the word in question is probably a linking verb.

EXAMPLES

Small airplanes **grow** [seem] more popular. [Here, *grow* is a linking verb.]
Some pilots **grow** beards. [Here, *grow* is not a linking verb. *Seem* cannot be substituted for *grow*.]

EXERCISE 11. In each of the following sentences, identify the verb. Then indicate whether it is an action verb or a linking verb.

1. People often grow sick of insects.
2. In China, however, people keep insects such as crickets in cages as pets.
3. To Chinese people, crickets sound cheerful.
4. Most Americans eat insects only by accident.
5. Nevertheless, some insects probably taste good.
6. In certain places people regularly taste grasshoppers.
7. Insects look fragile.
8. Insects' bodies actually feel hard.
9. More than 700,000 species of insects live in the world today.

10. Insects vastly outnumber other animal species.
11. Insects appear entirely adaptable to climates.
12. Explorers find insects at the equator and in the Arctic.
13. Some insects develop in stages.
14. Caterpillars change into butterflies or moths.
15. Animal fossils answer questions about the past.
16. Fossils appear in rock, coal, or amber.
17. Insect fossils provide a great deal of information.
18. Many insect varieties in fossils seem like insects of today.
19. These ancient fossils prove the incredibly long history of some insects.
20. Insects remain the most durable and most widespread creatures on earth.

APPLICATION. Look again at the words that are linking verbs in the preceding sentences. For each of the first five, write an original sentence using the word as an *action verb.*

1.b.6 Agreement in number

A verb, action or linking, must **agree in number** with the person or thing that it is talking about (its **subject**).

With every verb except *be,* you have to worry about this rule only in the present tense and only with a singular third-person subject (see below). In the present tense, with a *singular* third-person subject, an *-s* is added to the basic form of the verb. In this situation the **number** is singular.

EXAMPLE

	Singular	Plural
1ST PERSON:	I walk.	We walk.
2ND PERSON:	You walk.	You walk.
3RD PERSON:	One robot walk**s**.	Two robots walk.
	The robot walk**s**.	They walk.
	A robot walk**s**.	
	He walk**s**.	
	She walk**s**.	
	It walk**s**.	
	One walk**s**.	

The linking verb *be* is irregular, with three forms in the present tense. It is the only verb that has two forms in the past tense.

Present	Past
I **am** happy.	I **was** happy.
You **are** happy.	You **were** happy.
He/She/It **is** happy.	He/She/It **was** happy.

The verb **have** is also irregular. It does not add an *-s* to the third-person singular in the present tense; *have* changes to *has*.

I **have** a book.
You **have** a book.
He/She/It **has** a book.

Verbs that end in *s, o, z, ch,* or *sh* add an *-es* to indicate the singular in the present tense, as with *harass* in the following sentence:

The storm harass**es** the town.

The best way to remember when to use the -*s* for present-tense verbs is to think about the following rule:

In general, an s *appears on a noun* or *on the verb—but not on both.*

EXAMPLE

The robot**s** walk.
The robot walk**s**.

1.b.7 Principal parts of verbs

All verbs have four **principal parts** as follows:

Basic verb	Present participle	Simple past tense	Past participle
sail	sailing	sailed	sailed
soar	soaring	soared	soared
work	working	worked	worked
sing	singing	sang	sung
be	being	was/were	been
hit	hitting	hit	hit

EXAMPLES

Eagles **soar**. [present tense]

Eagles **soared**. [past tense]

Eagles are **soaring**. [present participle used to form present progressive]

Eagles have **soared**. [past participle used to form present perfect tense]

Sometimes the past tense and the past participle of a verb are the same. Sometimes these parts are different. When both the past tense and the past participle end in *-ed* (as in *soared*), the verb is called a **regular verb**. When the past tense and the past participle do not end in *-ed* (such as *sang* and *sung*), the verb is called an **irregular verb**. A list of some common irregular verbs follows.

1.b.8 Irregular verbs

A great many of the most common action verbs and linking verbs in English are irregular verbs. An **irregular verb** forms its past and past participle in some other way than a regular verb does. Instead of just adding an *-ed* to the basic verb, an irregular verb requires some other spelling change or takes no change at all.

COMMON IRREGULAR VERBS

Basic verb	Simple past tense	Past participle
be	was	been
bear	bore	borne
beat	beat	beaten *or* beat
become	became	become
begin	began	begun
bite	bit	bitten
blow	blew	blown
break	broke	broken
bring	brought	brought
burst	burst	burst

Basic verb	Simple past tense	Past participle
cast	cast	cast
catch	caught	caught
choose	chose	chosen
come	came	come
creep	crept	crept
dive	dived *or* dove	dived
do	did	done
draw	drew	drawn
drink	drank	drunk
drive	drove	driven
eat	ate	eaten
fall	fell	fallen
feel	felt	felt
fling	flung	flung
fly	flew	flown
freeze	froze	frozen
get	got	got *or* gotten
give	gave	given
go	went	gone
grow	grew	grown
hang	hanged *or* hung[1]	hanged *or* hung
have	had	had
know	knew	known
lay[2]	laid	laid
lead	led	led
lend	lent	lent
lie[2]	lay	lain
lose	lost	lost
put	put	put
ride	rode	ridden
ring	rang	rung
rise[2]	rose	risen
run	ran	run
say	said	said
see	saw	seen

[1] People are *hanged*; pictures are *hung*.

[2] For more detailed instruction on *lay* vs. *lie*, *raise* vs. *rise*, and *sit* vs. *set* (top of following page), see Section 8, "Glossary of Usage Problems."

Basic verb	Simple past tense	Past participle
set	set	set
shake	shook	shaken
shine	shone *or* shined	shone *or* shined
sing	sang	sung
sink	sank *or* sunk	sunk
sit	sat	sat
slay	slew	slain
smell	smelled	smelt
speak	spoke	spoken
spring	sprang *or* sprung	sprung
steal	stole	stolen
sting	stung	stung
swear	swore	sworn
swim	swam	swum
swing	swung	swung
take	took	taken
tear	tore	torn
think	thought	thought
throw	threw	thrown
tie	tied	tied
try	tried	tried
wear	wore	worn
win	won	won
write	wrote	written

1.b.9 Auxiliary verbs

Auxiliary verbs are used with the present participle or past participle of verbs (see 1.b.7) to form certain tenses. The auxiliary verbs—or helping verbs, as they are often called—and the participle are used to form a **verb phrase**.

There are only two auxiliary, or helping, verbs: *be* and *have.* (Both *be* and *have,* as you know, can be used independently as a linking and an action verb, respectively; both are irregular. See 1.b.3 and 1.b.5.)

As auxiliary verbs, the forms of *be* are used to express continuing action.

EXAMPLES

I **am** walking.
I **was** walking.
I **have been** walking.
I **had been** walking.

The auxiliary verb *have*, as you can see from the above examples, can be used along with the auxiliary verb *be*. In addition, the auxiliary verb *have* can simply be used with a past participle.

EXAMPLES

I **have** walked.
I **had** walked.

Remember to make the auxiliary *have* and the auxiliary *be* agree in number with the person or thing that you are talking about, just as the verbs *have* and *be* when they are used alone must agree in number (see 1.b.6).

1.b.10 Modals

Modals are sometimes regarded as a kind of auxiliary verb, but, unlike auxiliary verbs, they are not used to form the tense of a verb. Each modal functions differently, as shown on the following pages. With the exception of *do*, each modal is used either (1) before a basic verb or (2) before the auxiliary *have* or the auxiliary *be*. The modal, the auxiliaries, and the basic verb together also form what is often called a **verb phrase**.

■ do, does, did

The three forms of *do* are used for three purposes:

1. to form questions

PRESENT: **Does** he walk?
PAST: **Did** he walk?

2. to help express the negative

PRESENT: He **does** not walk.
PAST: He **did** not walk.

3. to show emphasis

PRESENT: He **does** walk slowly.
PAST: He **did** walk yesterday.

Remember to make *do* agree in number with the person or thing that you are talking about. *Do* is for more than one or for *I* or *you*. *Does* is for one. *Do, does*, or *did* is always followed by the basic form of the verb.

■ can, could

PRESENT: She **can** walk.
PAST: She **could** walk.

Notice that *could* (and all the following modals) can be used not only with the basic verb but also with *have* and *be: She **could** have walked; She **could** be walking.*

■ may, might

She **may** walk again very soon.
She **might** walk again.

Most people feel that *might* carries with it a little more sense of doubt. No shift in time or tense is involved when choosing between *may* and *might.*

■ must

He **must** walk.
She **must** be finished.

Use *must* to express the idea of strong obligation or the idea of certainty.

■ will

The modal *will* is one of the most common ways of telling about the future.

He **will** walk again.

■ shall

Shall is really not a useful substitute for *will* in writing. You can do very well as a writer without ever using *shall.* In conversation *shall* is used to form questions that are really invitations.

Shall we dance?

If one were to say, ***Will*** *we dance?* it would be a straightforward question, not in any way a suggestion or invitation.

would

The modal *would* is often shown as the past tense of *will*, but actually it usually expresses a condition, an *if*.

He **would** walk if he were able to.

Would can also be used to ask a question that is really a request.

Would you please give this to her?

Will you please give this to her? works just as well, perhaps, but only because the word *please* makes it a request. *Will you give it to her?* is not a request. It is a question. It raises an element of doubt.

should

Should shows obligation.

She **should** walk more.

The example above is the equivalent of *She ought to walk more.*

Most modals can be used with *be* and *have* in addition to being used with the basic verb. *Do, does,* and *did* are notable exceptions.

MODAL	MODAL + *HAVE*
He **could** walk.	He **could** have walked.
may	**may**
might	**might**
must	**must**
will	**will**
shall	**shall**
would	**would**
should	**should**

MODAL + *BE*	**MODAL + *HAVE* + *BE***
He **could** be walking.	He **could** have been walking.
may	**may**
might	**might**
must	**must**
will	**will**
shall	**shall**
would	**would**
should	**should**

EXERCISE 12. Identify the verb phrase in each of the following sentences. Indicate the part of the verb phrase that is (a) an auxiliary or (b) a modal. (Words that interrupt a verb phrase are not considered part of the verb phrase.)

1. For a long time now, the April Fiesta has been the highlight of the year in San Antonio, Texas.
2. The Fiesta may be the world's most enchanting party.
3. For years now, people have crammed the area for Spanish and Mexican food and music.
4. Tourists can often hear country swing, country rock, and Dixieland.
5. The Fiesta must begin in front of the Alamo on a Saturday.
6. The Fiesta may last ten days.
7. Always the highlight, the Battle of Flowers parade has been attracting people since 1891.
8. All San Antonio's diverse cultures can brilliantly display themselves during the Fiesta.
9. The pomp and lavishness of the Fiesta could have humbled the royalty of Europe.
10. Tourists will long remember the lights, the flowers, the costumes, and the music.

1.b.11 Time and tense

The **tenses** of a verb are forms that help to show time.

A verb helps to tell *when*. Depending on which principal part of a verb you use and which if any auxiliary verbs you put before it, you can tell your readers such times as "now," "always," "ago," "later," or "since then until now." There are, of course, three basic categories of time—past, present, and future—and a number of ways of expressing each.

1.b.12 Present time: the present tense

There are several ways to talk or write about present time, or "now" time. One way is to use the **present tense** of a verb. The present tense of a linking verb tells that someone or something *exists* at the present moment. The present tense of an action verb tells that something *happens* at the present moment.

PRESENT TENSE OF VERB

	Singular	Plural
1ST PERSON:	I play.	We play.
2ND PERSON:	You play.	You play.
3RD PERSON:	He play**s**.	They play.
	She play**s**.	Children play.
	It play**s**.	
	One play**s**.	

Notice that in the forms of the third-person singular, the verb, *in this tense only*, adds an *-s*. *Be* has three forms in the present tense.

SPELLING PRESENT-TENSE VERBS

In the present tense of the verb *play*, one form of the action verb is *play* and the other form is *plays*. Remember that you must add *-es* (not just *-s*) to change the form of a verb that ends in *s, o, x, z, ch,* or *sh* (for example, *kiss***es**, *echo***es**, *crunch***es**, *waltz***es**). Remember, too, that if a verb ends in a consonant + *y*, you must change the *y* to *i* and add *-es* (for example, *hurr***ies**, *carr***ies**).

In addition to *be*, there is one other verb that has a unique change: *have* becomes *has*.

I **have** money.   She **has** money.

PRESENT TENSE OF *BE*

	Singular	Plural
1ST PERSON:	I **am** happy.	We **are** happy.
2ND PERSON:	You **are** happy.	You **are** happy.
3RD PERSON:	He **is** happy. She **is** happy. It **is** happy. One **is** happy.	They **are** happy. The children **are** happy.

The present tense often communicates more than simply present time. It can communicate habitual, or "ongoing," time or a general truth.

EXAMPLES

The United States Congress **has** two houses. [not just at this moment but throughout history]

Uranium **is** radioactive. [not just now but always – a general scientific truth]

The present tense is often used in historical writing and in some reporting, especially in sports reporting, to convey a sense of "being there" to the reader.

EXAMPLE

After divorcing his first wife, King Henry VIII **marries** Anne Boleyn. Boleyn **is** the first of his wives to be put to death.

EXERCISE 13. This exercise will help you practice using singular present-tense action verbs, those that take *-s*, *-es*, or *-ies* as an ending. For each of the following questions, answer in a complete sentence, beginning with *Yes*.

EXAMPLE Does the wholesaler supply goods?

ANSWER *Yes, the wholesaler supplies goods.*

1. Does a physical therapist have good job opportunities?
2. Does the police force expect expansion?
3. Does an urban planner have a chance in the new market?
4. Does a bank officer anticipate a good future?
5. Does new technology multiply chances for a computer technician?
6. Does the future carry hope for a petroleum engineer?

7. Does the job market impress dental hygienists?
8. Does the world search for more geologists?
9. Does the business world have room for more secretaries?
10. Does the nursing profession attract new people?

1.b.13 Present time: the present progressive

Another common way to express present time is to use the present progressive. Instead of saying *She* ***listens*** *to the radio now* (present tense), you can say *She* ***is listening*** *to the radio now* (present progressive). The **present progressive** tells that an action or a state of being is going on right now.

You form the present progressive by using a present-tense form of *be* (*am, is,* or *are*) and the present participle of a verb (for example, *listening*).

PRESENT PROGRESSIVE

I **am listening**.
You **are listening**.
He **is listening**.
She **is listening**.
It **is listening**.
We **are listening**.
They **are listening**.

AVOIDING ERRORS WITH THE PRESENT PROGRESSIVE

Do not overuse *is.* Remember to use *am* (for *I*) and *are* (for *you, we, they,* and any reference to two or more people or things).

NOT We ~~is~~ listening. They ~~is~~ listening.
BUT We **are** listening. They **are** listening.

SPELLING PRESENT PARTICIPLES

Ordinarily, you just add *-ing* to the basic form of a verb to form the present participle.

look + -ing	=	**looking**
carry + -ing	=	**carrying**

If the basic verb ends in *e*, drop the *e* before adding *-ing*.

manage + -ing	=	**managing**

If the basic verb is one syllable and ends in a single vowel + a single consonant, double the consonant before adding *-ing*.

fit + -ing	=	**fitting**

If the basic verb is more than one syllable, ends in a single vowel + a single consonant, and has its accent on the last syllable, double the consonant before adding *-ing*.

omit + -ing	=	**omitting**

EXERCISE 14. Revise each of the following sentences, changing the present tense to the present progressive.

EXAMPLE Computers become more popular.

ANSWER *Computers are becoming more popular.*

1. Electronics companies make some computers the size of calculators.
2. Travelers in foreign countries use mini-computers to translate foreign words and phrases into English.
3. Larger computers actually teach foreign languages.
4. Some American universities experiment with computer-assisted instruction in the classroom.
5. Many students enjoy their computer instruction.
6. Video terminals aid visual memory of words.
7. The computer helps students with individual problems.
8. The computer allows students to move at their own pace.
9. With this help, instructors check students' pronunciation.
10. Computer-assisted language study saves money for schools.

1.b.14 Past time: the past tense

One way to express past time is to use the past tense of an action or linking verb. The **past tense** tells that something happened or existed in the past. All verbs—except *be*—have just one past-tense form. When you use *be*, you must use the form that agrees with the person or thing you are talking about.

PAST TENSE OF *BE*

I **was** happy.	We **were** happy.
You **were** happy.	You **were** happy.
He **was** happy.	They **were** happy.
She **was** happy.	
It **was** happy.	

SPELLING PAST-TENSE VERBS

For regular verbs, you usually simply add *-ed* to the basic form of the verb to form the past.

listen + -ed = **listened**

If the basic verb ends in *e*, drop the *e* before adding *-ed.*

manage + -ed = **managed**

If the basic verb ends in a consonant + *y*, change the *y* to *i* before adding *-ed.*

bury + -ed = **buried**

If the basic verb is one syllable and ends in a single vowel + a single consonant, double the consonant before adding *-ed.*

pat + -ed = **patted**

If the basic verb is more than one syllable, ends in a single vowel + a single consonant, and has its accent on the last syllable, double the consonant before adding *-ed*

omit + -ed = **omitted**

Irregular verbs spell their past-tense form in different ways. See the chart on pages 23–25.

EXERCISE 15. For each of the following sentences, give the simple past-tense form of the action verb that is in parentheses.

1. In 1976 Californians __________ more patents than residents of any other state. (obtain)
2. Residents of New York State __________ second place that year. (take)
3. In 1836 Senator John Ruggles of Maine __________ the first patent ever issued. (receive)
4. Edwin Land __________ the Polaroid Land Camera in 1947. (patent)
5. In 1925 Clarence Birdseye __________ the fast-frozen food process. (perfect)
6. In 1960 a nine-year-old girl and her eight-year-old sister __________ a patent. (win)
7. They __________ a solar tepee, called a Wigwarm, for a science fair. (develop)
8. A twelve-year-old Ohio girl __________ about writing in the dark. (think)
9. The idea __________ to her "glow-in-the-dark writing board," patented in 1974. (lead)
10. This exercise __________ only a handful of patents. (recap)

EXERCISE 16. For each of the following sentences, give the simple past-tense form of the action verb that is in parentheses.

1. In 1949 Zoe Ann Olsen of Oakland, California, __________ her national diving record with her right arm and hand in a cast. (defend)
2. Quarterback Bob Waterfield once __________ a football 60 feet at a speed of 68.18 mph. (throw)
3. In 1937 Ted Terry __________ a bull from Ketchum, Idaho, to Times Square, New York. (ride)
4. The 1927 New York Giants __________ only three touchdowns all season. (allow)
5. Some of Jack Dempsey's punches __________ at an estimated 135 mph. (travel)
6. Joseph Arenault, of Prince Edward Island, __________ his last speed-skating trophy at age ninety-three. (win)

7. In 1900 Johann Huslinger __________ from Vienna to Paris, 871 miles, on his hands. (walk)
8. In 1876 Boston's Arthur Leonard __________ eight errors in one baseball game. (make)
9. A racing pigeon owned by E. S. Peterson __________ 803 miles in 24 hours to win a 1941 championship. (fly)
10. On April 12, 1915, Noah Young __________ a mile in 8 minutes carrying a 150-pound man on his back. (run)

EXERCISE 17. For each of the following sentences, give the past-tense form of the action verb that is in parentheses.

1. Ambrose Bierce __________ as a journalist in San Francisco in the 1860s. (begin)
2. He __________ his work to those "enlightened souls who prefer... clean English to slang." (address)
3. Bierce __________ a reputation for his cutting humor. (gain)
4. He once __________ a young writer to "cultivate the good opinion of squirrels." (advise)
5. In 1906 he __________ *The Cynic's Word Book.* (publish)
6. He later __________ the title of that book to *The Devil's Dictionary.* (change)
7. Bierce __________ *alone* as "in bad company." (define)
8. A *coward,* he __________, was "one who in a perilous emergency thinks with his legs." (say)
9. He __________ a *bore* "a person who talks when you wish him to listen." (call)
10. Bierce __________ *discussion* as "a method of confirming others in their errors." (interpret)

1.b.15 Past time: the past progressive

The **past progressive** tells that some action began in the past, went on for some time, and then ended in the past. Instead of saying *She **listened** to the radio* (past), you may say *She **was listening** to the radio* (past progressive).

You form the past progressive by using a past-tense form of *be* (*was* or *were*) and the present participle of an action or linking verb (for example, *listening* or *being*).

Often you will write a sentence that has one verb in the past progressive and one verb in the simple past tense. In that way, you can tell about a second action that began and ended while a first action was still going on.

EXAMPLE

I **was living** in North Dakota when the job **became** available.
past progressive — past

The skies **darkened** as we **were struggling** up the hill.
past — past progressive

1.b.16 Past time: *used*

Another way to express past time is to include the word *used*. *She listened* is sometimes not enough. You may want to say *She **used to listen***.

> **AVOIDING ERRORS WITH *USED***
>
> Do not write *use* when you mean *used*.
>
> NOT I ~~use~~ to watch only Westerns.
> BUT I **used** to watch only Westerns.

1.b.17 Past time: the present perfect

The **present-perfect** tense can also be used to express past time. It tells that an action occurred at *some* time—rather than at a *specific* time—in the past. It can be used to communicate the idea that an action *began* in the past even though it may still be going on in the present.

You form the present perfect by using the auxiliary *has* or *have* plus the past participle of the verb. You must use *has* when you talk about one person or thing. You must use *have* when you talk about more than one person or thing (or about *you* or *I*).

PRESENT PERFECT

He **has listened.**	I **have listened.**
She **has listened.**	You **have listened.**
It **has listened.**	We **have listened.**
One person **has listened.**	They **have listened.**
	Two people **have listened.**

Notice that you can also form the **present perfect progressive**: *I have been listening.*

> **AVOIDING ERRORS WITH THE PRESENT PERFECT**
>
> Do not forget to use the past participle form of the verb after *have* or *has.*
>
> NOT I have ~~watch~~ television for years.
> BUT I have **watched** television for years.
>
> NOT I have ~~drop~~ the dish.
> BUT I have **dropped** the dish.
>
> Notice that this error occurs with regular verbs.

1.b.18 Past time: the past perfect

The **past-perfect** tense is used to show that one past action began *and* ended before another past action began.

You form the past perfect by using *had* plus the past participle of the verb.

EXAMPLES

She **had worked** (past perfect) as manager before I **took** (past) the job.

[She worked; she stopped; I worked.]

Before I **arrived** (past), several actors **had auditioned** (past perfect).

[They auditioned; they finished; I arrived.]

Notice that you can also form the **past perfect progressive**: *I had been working.*

AVOIDING ERRORS WITH THE PAST PERFECT

1. Do not forget to use the past perfect for the earlier of two past actions.

   NOT Everything you said is something I ~~heard~~ before.
   BUT Everything you said is something I **had heard** before. [The hearing preceded the saying; it should be in past perfect.]

2. Do not use *would have* to express the earlier of two past actions. Use the past perfect.

   NOT If she ~~would have~~ practiced more, she would have been a better pianist.
   BUT If she **had practiced** more, she would have been a better pianist.

EXERCISE 18. Identify each present-perfect verb or past-perfect verb in the following sentences.

1. For too long, people have blamed their problems on birds, beasts, and insects.
2. Writers from the earliest times to the present have given animals imaginary human traits.
3. After people had attributed to animals the defects of the human race, animals were forever subjected to insults.
4. One says, for example, that the beast in a person has awakened.
5. People have associated wildcats with strikes, crocodiles with tears, and kangaroos with courts.
6. After people had insulted the beasts of the land, they directed their criticism to birds.
7. Cowardice has brought chickens to mind, and stupidity has reminded people of turkeys.
8. Sometimes, however, animals have received praise.
9. People respect a colleague who has worked as hard as a beaver and who has been as busy as a bee.
10. Throughout history a person who had outfoxed another was thought of as wise as an owl.

1.b.19 Future time

There are several ways to express future time, as shown here.

1. Using *will* or *shall*
   Brad **will mail** the application.
2. Using *going to*
   Brad **is going to mail** the application.
3. Using *about to*
   Brad **is about to mail** the applications.
4. Using the present tense and an adverb or prepositional phrase that shows future time.
   Brad **sails tomorrow**.
   Brad **sails on the fifteenth of the month**.

One more way to express future time is to use the future perfect. The future perfect tells that one future event will not only start but will also end before another future event begins.

You form the future perfect by using *will* plus *have* plus the past participle of the verb.

EXAMPLES

By June, I **will have worked** here ten months. [The ten months will be up by the time June – another future event – begins.]

By the time they reach high school, those children **will have watched** years' worth of television.

You can also form the **future progressive** *(I will be working)* and the **future perfect progressive** *(I will have been working)*.

EXERCISE 19. Explain the difference in meaning between the sentences in each of the following pairs. (The sentences are all correct and are labeled for time and tense.)

1. Did she live in Washington long? [past]
   Has she lived in Washington long? [present perfect]
2. They went to Utah for two weeks. [past]
   They have gone to Utah for two weeks. [present perfect]

3. He said that his parents had been in Virginia for three months. [past; past perfect]
   He said that his parents have been in Virginia for three months. [past; present perfect]
4. What happened in Oklahoma when you arrived? [past; past]
   What had happened in Oklahoma when you arrived? [past perfect; past]
5. She was working in New Mexico. [past progressive]
   She worked in New Mexico. [past]
6. What has she seen in Texas? [present perfect]
   What had she seen in Texas? [past perfect]
7. He will have traveled through Colorado when the summer is over. [future perfect; present with future meaning]
   He will travel through Colorado when the summer is over. [future; present with future meaning]
8. We took the children to Arizona. [past]
   We have taken the children to Arizona. [present perfect]
9. Have the students been to Hawaii? [present perfect]
   Had the students been to Hawaii? [past perfect]
10. How long has he been in Indiana? [present perfect]
    How long was he in Indiana? [past]

1.b.20 The passive voice

A sentence can be either in the **active voice** or in the **passive voice**. Notice the difference between the following two sentences. They mean the same thing, but they are different.

The trainer **teased** the lion. [active voice]
The lion **was teased** by the trainer. [passive voice]

Both sentences say the same thing, but in the first sentence the *trainer* (the subject of the sentence) performs the action. In the second sentence the *lion* (now the subject of the sentence) takes center stage, and the trainer is reduced to something called an **agent**.

As a writer, you often have a choice between using a verb in the active voice or a verb in the passive voice. It is often a question of to whom you want to give center stage – to the trainer or to the lion, for example.

It is generally suggested that the active voice is stronger, but there are times when the passive voice is preferred or, in fact, necessary. If you do not want to call attention to the performer or if you do not know the performer, use the passive voice (as in the first sentence of this paragraph).

EXAMPLES

The milk **was spilled**. [You may not want to identify the culprit.]
The diamond **was stolen**. [You may not know by whom.]

You form the passive voice by using a form of *be* plus the past participle of the verb. The verb phrase expressing the passive can actually be quite long.

EXAMPLES

The lion **is teased** by the trainer.
The lion **was being teased** by the trainer.
The lion **was going to be teased** by the trainer.

The doer, the performer of the action (often called the *agent*), may be stated and is the object of the preposition *by*.

EXERCISE 20. In each of the following sentences, change the active voice to the passive or the passive voice to the active.

1. Some of today's drive-in movie theaters have been changed by new technology.
2. In the earliest drive-ins the sound was transmitted by loudspeakers above the screen.
3. Those speakers were replaced by smaller window receivers.
4. Now, "radio sound" replaces the window receivers.
5. In this new system the car radio transmits the sound.
6. The sound is greatly improved by the new system.
7. Theater owners expect drive-in audiences to grow.
8. One other big advantage is offered by the radio systems: channels with two languages.
9. An audience in Los Angeles can choose an English or a Spanish sound track.
10. Drive-in owners see a great future for bilingual sound.

1.b.21 The subjunctive

The **subjunctive** is one of three moods that English has. The subjunctive mood expresses *possibility.* (A mood making a *statement*—the indicative mood—and a mood *expressing command*—the imperative mood—are the two others.)

The subjunctive is used quite seldom, usually in formal situations, but you should be aware of its purposes and of the form of the verb used to express the subjunctive.

There are three basic uses for the subjunctive. Only two noticeable changes in a verb are necessary to form the subjunctive.

THE USES AND FORMS OF THE SUBJUNCTIVE

uses	*examples*	*forms*
1. To express, indirectly, a demand, recommendation, suggestion, or statement of necessity	We demand that he **explains** his financial situation. We recommend that he **leaves** town. We suggest that she **runs** for office. It is necessary that one of us **speaks** French.	Drop the *-s* from the third-person singular.
2. To express, directly, a hope	Heaven **forbids**. May the better player **wins**. (May) God **saves** the Queen.	Drop the *-s* from the third-person singular.
3. To state a condition or a wish that is contrary to fact	If he **were** smart, he would buy that car. [not *was*: Apparently, he is not smart.] They spoke to me as if I **were** an imbecile. [not *was*: I am not an imbecile.] I wish that I **were** President. [not *was*: I am not President.]	Use *were*, not *was*. (Notice that this use of the subjunctive always requires the past tense.)

REVIEW EXERCISE B. Each of the following sentences uses an incorrect form of a verb. Write the correct form.

1. American scientists is studying Jupiter to find out more about the solar system.
2. In March 1979 an American spacecraft named *Voyager I* flied to the planet Jupiter.

3. Because of the distance between the earth and Jupiter, American scientists received signals that were transmitted thirty-eight minutes earlier.
4. American scientists studied the planet itself, and its four major moons were photographed.
5. Scientists have determine that the moons Europa, Callisto, and Ganymede are composed of water, ice, and rock.
6. The orange and white moon named Io have active volcanoes that disrupt its surface.
7. *Voyager I* has discover that Jupiter has a ring of rock fragments around it like the planet Saturn's.
8. If the rings would have been as large as Saturn's, astronomers would have discovered them earlier.
9. The ring of rock fragments use to be whole moons circling Jupiter.
10. Jupiter's apparent size is deceptive; the planet consist primarily of clouds of gases.
11. The gas clouds of Jupiter is brilliantly colored; *Voyager I*'s pictures showed shades of pink, deep red, and light blue.
12. One of the mysteries of Jupiter has been name the Red Spot.
13. The Red Spot is apparently a mammoth hurricane that consisted of swirling gases.
14. The Red Spot don't shift position or die out, as do hurricanes on earth.
15. The Red Spot has bewilder astronomers for many years.
16. An unknown force (buried beneath layers of gases) hold the Red Spot in place.
17. If astronauts walked on Jupiter's surface, they will weigh six hundred pounds.
18. American scientists speculate that if there was life on Jupiter, it would consist of froglike creatures.
19. By 1980 *Voyager I* had reach the planet Saturn.
20. After studying Saturn and Uranus, the spacecraft leaved the solar system for a tour of the universe.

REVIEW EXERCISE C. Each of the following sentences uses an incorrect form of a verb. Write the correct form. Some sentences may have to be rephrased.

1. Every word in every language possess a root and a history of its meaning.
2. Most words in our language have underwent a change in spelling or in meaning.
3. If you were to examine the original meaning of a word, it will provide an interesting clue to its present meaning.
4. The word *father* originate from the root word *Pa*, meaning "to feed."
5. The ancient root *LEUQ*, meaning "to shine," can be finded in the words *illuminate*, *lucid*, and *luminous*.
6. The words *cemetery* and *coma* once were connect in their common root *KEI*, meaning "to lie down."
7. *Green* originally meaned "growing."
8. It don't seem logical, but a direct relative of the word *blue* is a word meaning "yellow."
9. Oddly enough, the word *girl* use to mean "a boy."
10. The Chinese word *ketchup* use to refer to a sauce for fish!
11. Raising the eyebrows is characteristic of supercilious people; *supercilious* actually have its origin in a word meaning "eyebrow."
12. An ancient word meaning "blood" has came down as the word *red*.
13. The word *infant* has came from two Latin words meaning "not speaking."
14. The proper name *Barbara* mean "foreign."
15. The name *John* don't sound the same in all languages; it has taken the forms of *Jean*, *Giovanni*, *Juan*, *Johann*, *Hans*, *Jan*, and *Ivan*.
16. Long ago people had chose their last names from their professions; *Miller*, *Taylor*, and *Smith* were often chosen.
17. When people selected their last names, they use *Mac* and *Fitz* to mean "son of."
18. If you would have named your son *Paul Li*, he would translate his name as "little pear."
19. Today Americans is using words that come directly from the Spanish, such as *brocade*, *mosquito*, and *vanilla*.
20. English-speaking people learned Native American words after they have lived here for some time.

1.c ADJECTIVES

An **adjective** is a word that tells more about a noun or pronoun.

An adjective gives information about a noun or pronoun by stating a *quality* or a *condition* of the noun or pronoun. When an adjective appears with a noun, it is often said to *modify* the noun.[1] "Qualities" refer to a noun's size, shape, color, texture, speed, temperature, and so on. "Conditions" include such words as *safe, ready, healthy.*

An adjective can state a quality or a condition that you perceive through your senses or that you judge in your mind.

SENSORY ADJECTIVES	JUDGMENT ADJECTIVES
a **white** building	an **angelic** child
a **loud** song	an **ambitious** student
a **sweet** dessert	a **powerful** argument
a **salty** peanut	a **scary** experience
a **hot** stove	a **ridiculous** joke

Adjectives that express judgments often demand the most thought by writers. Most people would agree that a certain building is white (or a shade of white), but not everyone would agree about the quality of a book, a friend, a television show, or a painting. To one person a book may be *enjoyable.* To another person, it may be *dull.* To a third, it may be somewhere in between—say, *worthwhile.*

EXERCISE 21. Decide whether the italicized adjective in each item below states a quality or condition that (a) can be perceived through the senses and that most people would agree on or (b) calls for a value judgment.

1. a *green* giant
2. a *helpful* library
3. an *easy* test
4. a *valiant* firefighter
5. a *cool* breeze
6. a *wooden* desk
7. a *strong* personality
8. a *greasy* spoon
9. a *dismal* future
10. a *wonderful* opportunity

[1] Adjectives also modify pronouns (a *silly* someone) and gerunds (*steady* traveling). For the sake of simplicity, we talk only about nouns here.

11. a *golden* chain
12. a *peppery* taco
13. a *tearful* eye
14. a *sad* story
15. a *clever* plan
16. a *dull* speaker
17. a *dull* pencil
18. a *sharp* mind
19. *turquoise* ink
20. *true* love

APPLICATION. Pick ten adjectives from the preceding list. Write ten original sentences. In each, use one of the adjectives.

EXERCISE 22. Each sentence below is followed by two choices. Indicate the adjective that is more appropriate for the sentence.

1. Many women of the Old West were__________ campaigners for education and reform. (a) influential (b) itchy
2. Elizabeth Ordway, the first public school teacher in Seattle, was an__________ fighter for women's suffrage. (a) obsolete (b) active
3. Allie B. Wallace was an__________ educator. (a) important (b) elastic
4. Mary Adeline Vaughan, wife of an Arkansas antislavery activist, was certainly__________. (a) brave (b) circular
5. After her husband died, Vaughan walked all the way to Kansas in__________ snow to escape persecution. (a) profound (b) heavy
6. Zerelda Samuels remained__________ when her sons, Frank and Jesse James, turned to crime. (a) honest (b) authentic
7. Living through the Civil War, Samuels was a __________ member of her community. (a) respiratory (b) respectable
8. The exploits of Belle Starr and Etta Place are, of course, __________. (a) legendary (b) local
9. Other__________ outlaws include Cattle Annie and Rose of the Cimarron. (a) compound (b) colorful
10. These famous – or__________ – figures are only a handful of the heroines of the Old West. (a) infamous (b) internal

APPLICATION. Look again at the adjective that you did *not* pick for each item above. Write one original sentence for each. (Use a dictionary if necessary.)

1.c.1 Positions of adjectives in sentences

Adjectives may be used in various positions and in various ways within a sentence.

EXAMPLES

1. How **beautiful** the flower is!
2. The **beautiful** flower is a tulip.
3. The tulip is **beautiful**.
4. The florist considered the tulip **beautiful**.
5. The tulips **visible** from here seem to dance in the wind.
6. The tulips, **red** and **yellow**, danced in the wind.

In the first example an adjective appears in an exclamatory sentence. In Sentence 2 an adjective comes before a noun. In Sentences 3–6 adjectives are used in various ways after nouns.

Even though there are many ways in which adjectives can be used in a sentence, the most common uses are illustrated by Sentences 2 and 3.

1.c.2 Properties of adjectives

There are three important properties, or characteristics, of words that can be adjectives.

1. The vast majority of adjectives can be used either before a noun or after a noun and linking verb. That is, the vast majority of adjectives can logically fit in both slots in the following sentence:

   The ________ table is very ________ .

   Some adjectives can be used only before a noun and others only after a noun and a linking verb. For example, you can say *an **utter** mess*, but you cannot say *The mess is very utter*. You can also say, *The child is very **afraid***, but you cannot say *the afraid child*.

2. Most adjectives can be preceded by the word *very* as in the following examples. (For important exceptions, see "Avoiding Errors," page 53.)

How **very beautiful** the flower is!
The **very bright** flower is a tulip.
The tulip is **very tall**.

3. Most adjectives can take comparative and superlative forms as illustrated in 1.c.3.

EXERCISE 23. Identify each adjective in the following sentences.

1. The Everglades are full of birds both familiar and unfamiliar to the average visitor.
2. Native species form only a small part of the splendid array.
3. Birds observable from time to time often have migrated from cold regions.
4. Visitors find the birds colorful and extraordinary.
5. Birds that live on or near the water are a common sight.
6. Herons, stately and elegant, wade in shallow pools.
7. Pelicans, lazy and clever, often eye a visitor as they hope for free handouts.
8. The strange darter lifts its neck and swims like a snake. How bizarre!
9. The attractive spoonbill has a peculiar way of fishing.
10. It swings its long bill through the water and separates edible food from lifeless material.

1.c.3 Forms of adjectives: comparison

Most adjectives have three **degrees** – the regular form, the **comparative**, and the **superlative**. An adjective that shows two things being compared is called comparative. An adjective that shows three or more things being compared is called superlative.

You often want to compare things. Adjectives allow you to do so, but you must use adjectives in special ways when making comparisons. You have a number of ways to express comparison with adjectives:

1. the use of *-er* and *-est*
2. the use of *more* and *most*
3. the use of *as*
4. the use of *less* and *least*

Notice the alternative wordings available for comparing either two things or more than two things.

COMPARATIVE ADJECTIVES	SUPERLATIVE ADJECTIVES
John is **taller** (than Mary).	John is **tallest.**
John is **the taller**.	John is **the tallest.**
Mary is **more athletic** (than John).	Mary is **most athletic**.

Some adjectives use *-er* and *-est*, and some use *more* and *most*. The following chart illustrates preferred usage. Usage, you will see, is divided on many two-syllable adjectives. You must use your own judgment.

COMPARATIVE AND SUPERLATIVE FORMS OF ADJECTIVES

-er, -est		more, most
one-syllable adjectives	***two-syllable adjectives; two syllables and prefix***	***more-than-two-syllable adjectives***
loud	***narrow***	***fanatic***
loud**er**, loud**est**	narrow**er**, **more** narrow narrow**est**, the **most** narrow	**more** fanatic the **most** fanatic
sweet	***unhappy***	***powerful***
sweet**er**, sweet**est**	unhappi**er**, **more** unhappy unhappi**est**, the **most** unhappy	**more** powerful the **most** powerful

1.c.4 Irregular adjectives: comparison

A small group of common adjectives have special forms for the comparative and superlative.

There are complicated reasons – but reasons, nevertheless – that explain why the comparative and superlative forms of the following adjectives are so different from the basic forms. In short, the basic form came into modern English from one word and the comparative and superlative forms from another word that had the same meaning.

	COMPARATIVE FORM	SUPERLATIVE FORM
good	better	(the) best
well (health)[1]	better	(the) best
bad	worse	(the) worst
ill	worse	(the) worst
far (distance)	farther	farthest
far (degree)	further	furthest

The use of *-er* and *-est* sometimes involves a spelling change. The following chart summarizes the spelling rules that apply. (For more detailed instructions, see 5.c.3.)

SPELLING COMPARATIVE AND SUPERLATIVE FORMS OF ADJECTIVES

characteristic of adjective	first	then add
1. ends in consonant + *y* **happy**	drop *y*	add *i* + *-er*, *i* + *-est* **happier, happiest**
2. ends in silent *e* **wise**	drop *e*	add *-er, -est* **wiser, wisest**
3. ends in *ey* **dopey**	drop *ey*	add *i* + *-er*, *i* + *-est* **dopier, dopiest**
4. one-syllable adjective ending in single vowel + single consonant **sad**	double the consonant	add *-er, -est* **sadder, saddest**

[1]See 1.f.6 for a discussion of when to use *good* and *well*.

EXERCISE 24. Spell correctly the comparative and superlative forms for each adjective below. (Three of the adjectives require *more* and *most.*)

1. dry	6. good
2. gray	7. nice
3. slippery	8. ridiculous
4. mad	9. intelligent
5. bad	10. homey

APPLICATION. Pick five adjectives from Exercise 24. Write five original sentences. In each sentence use the comparative form of one of the adjectives.

1.c.5 Adjective or noun?

Often, a word can be labeled as a particular part of speech only when it is observed functioning in a sentence. Some items can be adjectives *or* nouns, depending on how they are used in a sentence.

EXAMPLES

The **criminal** had nothing to say. [noun]
Their **criminal** behavior must be punished. [adjective][1]

The couple pledged their **love** to each other. [noun]
They read a **love** poem. [adjective]

The wall was made of **concrete**. [noun]
They built a **concrete** wall. [adjective]

Some combinations of adjective and noun become so common that they are often thought of, to varying extents, as compound nouns (see 1.a.2).

EXAMPLES

city council	dog biscuit
summer squash	ice cream

[1] The words identified as adjectives in the second sentence of each of these pairs do not have all the properties of adjectives discussed in 1.c.2. As stated there, those properties are found in most—but not all—adjectives.

AVOIDING ERRORS WITH ADJECTIVES FOR COMPARISON

1. Do not make a double comparison. (A **double comparison** incorrectly uses both *-er* or *-est* and *more* or *most.*)

   NOT Wall Street is ~~more narrower~~ than Canal Street.
   BUT Wall Street is **more narrow** than Canal Street.
   OR Wall Street is **narrower** than Canal Street.

2. Do not make an incomplete comparison. Remember to use *other* or *else* when comparing one thing with the other members of the group to which it belongs.

   NOT Some claim that Eleanor Roosevelt was more active than ~~any~~ First Lady in America.
   BUT Some claim that Eleanor Roosevelt was more active than **any other** First Lady in America.

   Use two *as*'s in a comparison with adjectives.

   NOT Chris Evert Lloyd is as ~~steady~~, if not steadier than, Billie Jean King.
   BUT Chris Evert Lloyd is **as steady as**, if not steadier than, Billie Jean King.

3. Do not try to make comparative or superlative forms for adjectives that logically can have only an absolute form. Sometimes you hear comparative or superlative forms for these adjectives, but avoid those forms in writing.

   NOT Yours was the ~~most perfect~~ serve.
   BUT Yours was the **perfect** serve.

   Some other adjectives that cannot logically take a comparative or superlative form are *unique, complete, right, dead, open.* Furthermore, it is also considered illogical to use the adverb *very* before any of these adjectives.

EXERCISE 25. In each of the following sentences, indicate whether the italicized word is acting as a noun or as an adjective.

1. a) When she was only three, Belle Silverman performed on a *radio* program.
   b) She continued to work on *radio* throughout her childhood.
2. a) As a teen-ager, Belle Silverman made various *film* appearances.
   b) In more than one *film* she was listed in the opening credits.
3. a) At seventeen Belle Silverman made her debut in an *opera*—as Beverly Sills.
   b) After touring the nation, she became a leading *opera* singer in San Francisco and New York.
4. a) Sills has made *guest* appearances in many opera houses throughout Europe and South America.
   b) She has also been a *guest* on various major television programs.
5. a) On *television* or on stage, Beverly Sills is a popular performer.
   b) She has even hosted her own *television* series, a talk show that had little to do with opera.

AVOIDING ERRORS WITH ADJECTIVES

Do not use the adjectives *real* and *sure* when you should use the adverbs *very, really,* or *surely.*

NOT The President's wife is a ~~real~~ effective First Lady.
BUT The President's wife is a **very** effective First Lady.
OR The President's wife is a **really** effective First Lady.

NOT The President's wife is ~~sure~~ interested in equal rights for women.
BUT The President's wife is **surely** interested in equal rights for women.

1.c.6 Proper adjectives

A **proper adjective** is related to a proper noun (see 1.a.1). Like all adjectives, a proper adjective is used to state a quality or a condition of a noun.

Sometimes a proper adjective has the same form as the proper noun to which it is related. More often, the proper noun and proper adjective have different forms. Like proper nouns, proper adjectives are capitalized.

EXAMPLES

John F. Kennedy went to **Harvard**.
proper noun

John F. Kennedy was a **Harvard** graduate.
proper adjective

Ohio was buried by snow in **January**.
proper noun

The **January** snow buried Ohio.
proper adjective

A woman from Wisconsin went to **Israel**.
proper noun

Golda Meir became an **Israeli** leader.
proper adjective

Queen Victoria reigned from 1837 to 1901.
proper noun

The **Victorian** Age refers to her reign.
proper adjective

Some adjectives derived from proper nouns are not capitalized in special cases. For example, you always capitalize the *t* when you write *the ambassador from* ***T****urkey* and *the* ***T****urkish ambassador*, but you may write *the* ***t****urkish towel*. Check the list below or your dictionary if you are in doubt about the capitalization of particular adjectives.

EXAMPLES

china doll
diesel engine
morocco leather
venetian blinds

(For more information on the capitalization of proper adjectives, see 7.a.5.)

EXERCISE 26. Identify each proper adjective in each of the following sentences. (Some proper adjectives here have the same form as proper nouns.) One sentence does not have any proper adjectives.

1. Hawaii is a vital trade center as well as a strategic United States military outpost.
2. The Pacific chain links the American continents with Asia and Australia.
3. The Hawaiian Islands include Maui, Kahoolawe, Lanai, Molokai, Oahu, Kauai, Niihau, and Hawaii.
4. Pearl Harbor, on the Oahu coastline, is one of the largest natural harbors in the Pacific.
5. The Oahu harbor houses the United States naval fleet for the Pacific area.
6. Travelers to and from Asian countries often stop to relax on Waikiki Beach.
7. The first Hawaiian settlers were Polynesian seafarers.
8. The islands' European discoverer was James Cook, a captain in the British navy.
9. The Hawaiian "melting pot" includes people of Chinese, Philippine, Japanese, and Portuguese descent.
10. Both geographically and culturally, Hawaii is a bridge between eastern and western lands.

1.c.7 Sequence of adjectives

Often two or more adjectives are used together before a noun. At times, included in the sequence will be a participle used as an adjective (see 1.k). As you can see from the chart on the next page, it is possible to have a sequence of many adjectives preceding a noun. There is no special virtue to having a long string of adjectives before a noun. Use as many as seem natural to you.

Although the chart on the next page indicates the *order* in which kinds of adjectives usually appear in sequence, your own instinct and "ear" are your best guides.

You can use a sequence of adjectives in the predicate after a linking verb, but then you will usually separate them with coordinating conjunctions (see 1.h.1).

EXAMPLES

Before a noun

The **big, red, lazy** moon filled the sky.

In the predicate

The moon that night was **big and red and lazy**.

ORDER OF ADJECTIVES

general subjective →	***general objective*** →	***age*** →	***color*** →	***material*** →
beautiful	small	ageless	red	silk
horrible	squeaky	old	black	tin

proper adjective →	***participle*** →	***nounlike*** →	***NOUN***
Italian	handwoven	head	scarf
Japanese		transistor	radio

EXERCISE 27. From the Adjective Bank below, choose two adjectives that can be used together before each of the numbered nouns. You can use an adjective more than once. See page 58 to decide if you need a comma.

ANSWERS *big purple **computer*** [no comma needed]
*big, intricate **computer*** [comma needed]

1. computer
2. ship
3. suit
4. traveler
5. television
6. journey
7. bomb
8. debate
9. machine
10. room

In at least three of your phrases, use two adjectives from the first column below.

ADJECTIVE BANK

general	***age***	***color***	***proper***	***often nouns***
big	old	purple	Martian	time
long	new	chartreuse	American	space
intricate	ancient	white		life
portable				control
precious				

COMMAS WITH ADJECTIVES IN SERIES

In a sequence of adjectives before a noun, use a comma between two adjectives if the word *and* would sound right between them or if you could reverse their order.

NOT a horrible squeaky old black tin clock radio
BUT a horrible, squeaky, old, black tin clock radio

Commas were placed in the above sequence because you could say *a horrible and squeaky and old and black tin clock radio.* Notice that you could not reverse the order of *black* and *tin* or of *clock* and *radio*; the expression *a tin black clock radio* makes no sense. Therefore, commas should not be used between these words in the original sentence.

REVIEW EXERCISE D. For each of the following adjectives, suggest two nouns that the adjective can precede.

EXAMPLE richest
ANSWERS *richest person; richest dessert*

1. richest
2. silver
3. Alaskan
4. lofty
5. gaunt
6. rarer
7. muggy
8. shaggy
9. hypnotic
10. perfect

1.d PRONOUNS

A **pronoun** is a word that takes the place of a noun.

In the English language there are about seventy-five pronouns, all of which are listed on pages 62–63. You are familiar with all of them.

You use pronouns in a sentence in the same way that you use nouns and proper nouns. In general, a pronoun takes the place of a noun or nouns. English has the following kinds of pronouns:

- personal pronouns, including possessive pronouns and reflexive pronouns
- demonstrative pronouns
- interrogative pronouns
- relative pronouns
- indefinite pronouns

1.d.1 Personal pronouns

Personal pronouns refer to people or to things that can generally be identified.

■ Case

Personal pronouns have something called **case**. Personal pronouns have different forms depending on whether they are (1) the subject of a sentence or (2) the object of a verb or of a preposition.

EXAMPLES

I becomes *me:*
I hit the ball.
The ball hit **me**.
The ball sailed to **me**.

He becomes *him:*
He hit the ball.
The ball hit **him**.
The ball sailed to **him**.

She becomes *her:*
She hit the ball.
The ball hit **her**.
The ball sailed to **her**.

We becomes *us:*
We hit the ball.
The ball hit **us**.
The ball sailed to **us**.

They becomes *them:*
They hit the ball.
The ball hit **them**.
The ball sailed to **them**.

Pronouns used as objects of verbs or as objects of prepositions are in the **objective case**. Pronouns used as subjects are sometimes said to be in the **subjective**, or the **nominative**, **case**. Be especially careful of case when writing compound subjects and compound objects with one proper noun and one pronoun.

EXAMPLES

John and **I** hit the ball. [compound subject: pronoun in nominative case]

The ball hit John and **me**. [compound object: pronoun in objective case]

You will always be safe if you use a nominative pronoun after a form of *be* except when a possessive is called for, as in *It is mine.*

EXAMPLES

The writer is **she**. [or **he**]
Could it be **they**? [or **she** or **he**]

In speaking, it is perfectly acceptable to use *me* (rather than *I*) after a form of *be: It's **me**.* It is still more acceptable to write *It is **I***.

Gender

When you refer to a male person, use *he* or *him.* When you refer to a female person, use *she* or *her.* When you refer to an animal, use either *he/him* or *she/her* or the neuter pronoun *it.* For some reason, English speakers have often referred to ships as *she/her,* although people may consider such references sexist. In general, the pronoun *it* refers to an animal, a ship, a car, or some other nonhuman entity.

Number and person

Like most nouns, personal pronouns have number. They are either singular or plural.

I/me; we/us: When you use the personal pronoun *I* or *me,* there is seldom any doubt about who is speaking or writing. These are the words that the English language has for referring to ourselves. From the words *I* and *me* spring the plurals *we* and *us*; the possessives *my, mine, our, ours*; and the reflexives *myself* and *ourselves.* These pronouns are in the **first person**, the person(s) doing the speaking or writing.

You: When you hear or see the personal pronoun *you,* you can identify the person or persons whom the speaker or writer has in mind—yourself, or a group that includes you. The pronoun *you* has the possessive forms *your* and *yours* and the reflexive forms *yourself* and *yourselves*. These "you" pronouns are in the **second person**, the person(s) being addressed.

He/him; she/her; it; they/them: When you see the personal pronouns *he/him*, *she/her*, *it*, and *they/them*, you cannot identify the persons and things being referred to without looking back to find the nouns (or other words) that the pronouns are replacing. We call the noun (or other word) to which a pronoun refers the **antecedent**. The antecedent may be in an earlier part of the sentence or even in a preceding sentence. The antecedent may be a noun or any element that can be used as a noun: a proper noun, a gerund, an infinitive, a prepositional phrase, a noun clause, or another pronoun. Pronouns that refer not to me or to you but to a third person or thing, singular or plural, are said to be in the **third person**.

■ Pronoun-antecedent agreement

An **antecedent** is the noun (or other word) to which a pronoun refers. A personal pronoun must agree with its antecedent both in number and in gender. The pronoun is singular when the antecedent is singular and plural when the antecedent is plural. If the antecedent is male, the pronoun is masculine. If the antecedent is female, the pronoun is feminine. If the antecedent is neither male nor female, the pronoun is neuter—*it* or *its*.

EXAMPLES

Mr. Smith autographed **his** book. [singular male antecedent: singular masculine personal pronoun]

Ms. Velez autographed **her** book. [singular female antecedent: singular feminine personal pronoun]

The **auditorium** was filled to **its** capacity. [singular antecedent, neither male nor female: singular neuter personal pronoun]

When the antecedent may be *either* male or female—that is, when its gender is unknown—convention calls for a masculine personal pronoun in most writing.

EXAMPLE

The **owner** must move **his** car. [singular antecedent, gender unknown: singular masculine personal pronoun]

PERSONAL PRONOUNS

	nominative case singular	*nominative case plural*	*objective case singular*	*objective case plural*
first person	I	we	me	us
second person	you	you	you	you
third person	he	they	him	them
	she		her	
	it		it	

POSSESSIVE FORMS

	singular		*plural*	
	used as determiners	*used alone*	*used as determiners*	*used alone*
first person	my	mine	our	ours
second person	your	yours	your	yours
third person	his	his	their	theirs
	her	hers		
	its	its		

REFLEXIVE FORMS

Reflexive pronouns have no case.

	singular	*plural*
first person	myself	ourselves
second person	yourself	yourselves
third person	himself	themselves
	herself	
	itself	

RELATIVE PRONOUNS

Relative pronouns have no distinction between singular and plural.

Who is the only relative pronoun that has an objective case and a possessive form.

people only	*nonpeople*	*nonpeople in formal usage; people in informal*
who	which	that
whom		
whose		

INTERROGATIVE PRONOUNS

Interrogative pronouns have no distinction between singular and plural.

Who is the only interrogative pronoun that has an objective case and a possessive form.

people only	***nonpeople***	***people and nonpeople***
who? whom? whose?	what?	which?

Compounds: whoever, whomever, whatever

DEMONSTRATIVE PRONOUNS

Demonstrative pronouns have no case or person.

	singular	***plural***
near	this	these
far	that	those

INDEFINITE PRONOUNS

	universal	*"some"*	*"any"*	*negative*
always singular[1]	everybody everyone everything each either	somebody someone something somewhere another	anybody anyone anything anywhere	nobody no one nothing neither nowhere
always plural		both few many several		
singular or plural	all	some enough more most such	any	none

[1]By "always singular" we mean that the verb will have a singular form (usually adding *-s* to third-person present tense).

In speaking you may substitute two pronouns (to cover both males and females), but this solution does not produce smooth-sounding prose. If you object to using a masculine pronoun when the antecedent may be female, consider rephrasing your statement in the plural.

EXAMPLES

IN SPEAKING: The **owner** must move **his or her** car.

PLURAL, IN WRITING: The **owners** must move **their** cars.

(For advice on agreement between personal pronouns and antecedents that are *indefinite pronouns*, see 1.d.7.)

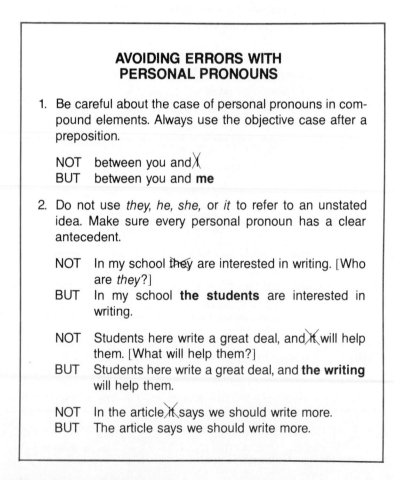

AVOIDING ERRORS WITH PERSONAL PRONOUNS

1. Be careful about the case of personal pronouns in compound elements. Always use the objective case after a preposition.

   NOT between you and ~~I~~
   BUT between you and **me**

2. Do not use *they, he, she,* or *it* to refer to an unstated idea. Make sure every personal pronoun has a clear antecedent.

   NOT In my school ~~they~~ are interested in writing. [Who are *they*?]
   BUT In my school **the students** are interested in writing.

   NOT Students here write a great deal, and ~~it~~ will help them. [What will help them?]
   BUT Students here write a great deal, and **the writing** will help them.

   NOT In the article ~~it~~ says we should write more.
   BUT The article says we should write more.

Continued

3. Do not use a personal pronoun that might refer to more than one antecedent. Revise the sentence if necessary.

   NOT Sue told Mary that ~~she~~ would be late. [Who would be late?]
   BUT Sue, who knew that she would be late, told Mary not to expect her on time.
   OR Sue knew that Mary would be late and told her so.

4. Be careful of case after *than* or *as*. The pronoun often determines the meaning of the sentence.

   NOT Mary plays the piano better than ~~him~~.
   BUT Mary plays the piano better than **he**. [better than he plays]

   Consider this situation: Mary likes Tom but she prefers Mike; Mike does not know Tom.

   NOT Mary likes Mike more than ~~he~~.
   BUT Mary likes Mike more than **him**. [more than Tom]

   Now, consider this situation: Tom likes Mike, but Mary likes Mike even more; Mary does not know Tom.

   NOT Mary likes Mike more than ~~him~~.
   BUT Mary likes Mike more than **he**. [more than Tom likes Mike]

EXERCISE 28. Adjust each of the following sentences according to the instructions in parentheses.

1. The top competitors in the race were *Frank Shorter and Bill Rodgers*. (Rewrite the sentence using a plural personal pronoun to replace the italicized words.)
2. Shorter and *Rodgers* had competed many times before. (Rewrite the sentence using a singular personal pronoun to replace the italicized word.)

3. The crowd cheered Rodgers and *Shorter.* (Rewrite the sentence using a singular personal pronoun to replace the italicized word.)
4. The crowd knew that the marathon was a duel between Shorter and *Rodgers.* (Rewrite the sentence using a singular personal pronoun to replace the italicized word.)
5. In the newspaper it said that the runners were both in top form. (Rewrite the sentence to eliminate the incorrect use of a personal pronoun.)
6. Shorter was polite toward Rodgers when he won the Boston Marathon. (Rewrite the sentence to eliminate the confusion over who won. Rodgers had won.)
7. Shorter has run at higher altitudes than *Rodgers.* (Rewrite the sentence using a personal pronoun to replace the italicized word.)
8. Rodgers likes running in cold weather more than *Shorter.* (Rewrite the sentence using a personal pronoun to replace the italicized word.)
9. Some experts seemed to give Rodgers a better chance than *Shorter.* (Rewrite the sentence using a personal pronoun to replace the italicized word.)
10. Reporters, however, like Shorter as much as *Rodgers.* (Rewrite the sentence using a personal pronoun to replace the italicized word.)

1.d.2 Personal pronouns: possessive forms

As you can see on page 62, the possessive forms of personal pronouns are all familiar to you. For each personal pronoun there are actually two forms in the possessive because there are two uses. (For *he* and *it* the two possessive forms—*his* and *its*—are the same.)

First, you use possessive forms of personal pronouns before nouns, as determiners (see 1.e). Second, you use possessive forms alone, as you use nouns.

POSSESSIVE FORMS USED AS DETERMINERS

Jerry has **my** radio.

Jerry has **my** old radio.

Jerry has **my** much-played, battered, old radio.

POSSESSIVE FORMS USED ALONE

The radio in Jerry's hand is **mine**.

Mine is the radio in Jerry's left hand.

Jerry has a radio of **mine**.

Yours is better than **mine**.

AVOIDING ERRORS WITH POSSESSIVE PRONOUNS

1. Do not use an apostrophe with the possessive forms of personal pronouns.

   NOT She knew that the bicycle was ~~her's~~.
   BUT She knew that the bicycle was **hers**.

   NOT We believed that the prize could be ~~ours'~~.
   BUT We believed that the prize could be **ours**.

2. Do not confuse the possessive pronoun *its* with the contraction *it's (it is).* Use an apostrophe when you mean *it is.*

   NOT If ~~its~~ raining, the dog stays in ~~it's~~ kennel.
   BUT If **it's** raining, the dog stays in **its** kennel.

As a determiner, the possessive personal pronoun can also be used before a gerund, an *-ing* word that is a noun form; see 1.m.

EXAMPLES

I am pleased with **my** *radio.*
noun

I am pleased with **my** *bargaining* for the radio.
gerund

Will **my** *music* disturb you?
noun

Will **my** *practicing* the piano disturb you?
gerund

You may have to decide if an *-ing* word is a gerund or a participle before you can tell which pronoun to use before it. If it is a gerund, use a possessive form. If it is a participle, use an objective form. (See 1.k and 1.m.)

EXAMPLES

I like to read **his** writing. [*writing* as a gerund]

I like to watch **him** writing. [*writing* as a participle]

The possessive forms of personal pronouns may also be called **possessive adjectives**.

1.d.3 Personal pronouns: reflexive forms

Reflexive pronouns are used to refer back to another word *when the same person is involved.* Reflexive pronouns are also used to emphasize another word in the sentence. As you can see from page 62, the reflexive forms of personal pronouns do not have any case. Reflexive pronouns have only one form each with the exception of *yourself/yourselves.*

EXAMPLES

I almost killed **myself** working for her in the campaign. [object of verb]

He granted **himself** one privilege. [indirect object]

Today, for the first time in months, she is **herself**. [complement after linking verb]

As a team, they have no faith in **themselves**. [object of preposi-

You **yourself** told me to stop. [to emphasize a pronoun]

Rita **herself** met us. [to emphasize a noun]

EXERCISE 29. Supply the missing personal pronoun in each item below. The antecedent for each pronoun is italicized.

EXAMPLE You ride your horse, and *I* will ride ________ .

ANSWER *mine*

1. On August 5, 1978, eight *riders* and ________ horses completed a historic journey.
2. The *riders* had set out to retrace the Santa Fe Trail. ________ were successful.

AVOIDING ERRORS WITH REFLEXIVE PRONOUNS

1. Two reflexive pronouns require particular care: *himself* and *themselves.* Do not use *hisself* or *theirselves*; neither is correct.

   NOT He fixed the car ~~hisself~~.
   BUT He fixed the car **himself**.

   NOT They ~~theirselves~~ put out the fire.
   BUT They **themselves** put out the fire.

2. Be sure to use a reflexive pronoun when the pronoun refers to the same person as does the subject of the sentence.

   NOT I bought ~~me~~ a new book.
   BUT I bought **myself** a new book.

   NOT He found ~~him~~ a comfortable chair.
   BUT He found **himself** a comfortable chair.

3. Do not use a reflexive pronoun unnecessarily.

   NOT Lila and ~~myself~~ are going to the fair.
   BUT Lila and **I** are going to the fair. [*I* is the subject.]

3. *Allan Maybee* is from Riverton, Wyoming. Three of the riders were his wife, his son, and __________ .
4. *Allan Maybee* had once retraced the Oregon Trail. The idea for this trip was __________ .
5. *Susan Fawcett* is from Casper, Wyoming. Her stepson and __________ were two of the riders.
6. *Susan Fawcett* went because __________ great-great-grandfather had ridden the trail years ago.
7. Just before the trip, rider *Casey Meyers* had hurt __________ on the ranch where he works.
8. Meyers, who had broken his leg, said, "*I* had __________ share of troubles because of the cast."

9. *Patrick Bressler* was the seventh rider. __________ is Allan Maybee's brother.
10. The eighth rider was *Rhonda Ellwood.* __________ joined up when the group camped in her backyard.

Supply the missing personal pronoun in each item below. First, identify the antecedent to which the pronoun will refer.

11. Traveling on the Santa Fe Trail was not easy. __________ was nine hundred miles long.
12. The modern-day riders had a few luxuries. Travelers of old had a harder time than __________ .
13. Evelyn Vinogradov drove a truck ahead of the riders. __________ arranged for places for them to stay.
14. The truck carried food, and Vinogradov had filled __________ with jugs of water as well.
15. Evelyn Vinogradov was most helpful. The riders probably could not have done without __________ .
16. In days of old, travelers had to find food for __________ .
17. Travelers often had to find __________ meals along the trail.
18. Allan Maybee observed, "I looked down in the ruts. __________ saw wild strawberries growing."
19. Perhaps other strawberries grew there a century ago, and other riders ate __________ .
20. No doubt when they conquered the trail, travelers of old felt that the West was __________ .

1.d.4 Demonstrative pronouns

As the name suggests, a **demonstrative pronoun** is used to "demonstrate," "show," "point to" whatever it is that you are talking about, usually a noun. A demonstrative pronoun may be used as a determiner before a noun (1.e), or it may be used alone, in place of a noun. Demonstrative pronouns used as determiners are sometimes called **demonstrative adjectives**.

As you can see from the chart on page 63, there are only two demonstrative pronouns – *this* and *that* – each with a plural form – *these* and *those.*

EXAMPLES

This person is my friend.
These are the twins.
That trombone sounds good.
I like **those**.

AVOIDING ERRORS WITH DEMONSTRATIVE PRONOUNS

1. Do not use *this* in writing when you simply mean *a* or *an.*

   NOT There is ~~this~~ biography.
   BUT There is **a** biography.

2. When you mean *this,* do not use *this here* or *that there* or the plural forms.

   NOT ~~This here~~ biography is about Earhart.
   BUT **This** biography is about Earhart.

3. Do not use *them* when you mean *those.*

   NOT I have not read ~~them~~ books.
   BUT I have not read **those** books.

4. Do not use *this* or *that* alone unless it has a clear antecedent.

   NOT The prize-winning writer explained how difficult it was to write the book, and ~~this~~ made us feel better.
   BUT The prize-winning writer explained how difficult it was to write the book. **This explanation** made us feel better.
   OR The prize-winning writer made us feel better by **explaining** how difficult it was to write the book.

1.d.5 Interrogative pronouns

Interrogative pronouns are used to form questions, to *interrogate.* As you can see from the chart on page 63, there are three basic interrogative pronouns: *who, what, which.* The pronoun *who,* like some of the personal pronouns (see 1.d.1), has a form for the objective case: *whom.* It also has a form for showing possession: *whose.* In addition, there are the compound forms: *whoever, whomever,* and *whatever.* Many times a preposition must be used with an interrogative pronoun: ***for*** *which,* ***in*** *whose,* etc.

Interrogative pronouns may be used by themselves, as you would use a noun, a proper noun, or another kind of pronoun.

INTERROGATIVE PRONOUNS:
WHO?* OR *WHOM?

Many people no longer make the distinction between *who* and *whom* when asking or writing questions; they often tend to use only *who.* It is always a good idea to understand why there was, at least at one time, a distinction. Be aware that in most of *your* writing, you should distinguish correctly between *who* and *whom.*

1. The form *who* corresponds to the personal pronouns *he, she,* and *they.* Use *who* when you would use *he, she,* or *they.*

   Who is late? **He** is late. **She** is late. **They** are late.

2. The form *whom* corresponds to the personal pronouns *him, her,* and *them.* Use *whom* only when you would use *him, her,* or *them.*

   Whom did you call? Did you call **him**? Did you call **her**? Did you call **them**?

3. Make sure that you always use *whom* after a preposition:

   To **whom** are you speaking? Are you speaking *to* **him**?
   For **whom** is the gift? Is it *for* **her**?

INTERROGATIVE PRONOUNS USED ALONE

Who is there?
To **whom** do we give the ice cream?
Whoever could it be walking around alone this time of night?
Whose is that car?
What is that noise?
To **what** do you give credit?
Which is it?
Of **which** is it a part?
Whatever happened to you?

Some interrogative pronouns can be used as determiners before nouns or before nouns preceded by adjectives.

INTERROGATIVE PRONOUNS USED AS DETERMINERS

Which man have you decided to marry?

What cities will you visit?

Whose old book is that?

When you know the group that is in question, you usually use *which* instead of *what.* You cannot say *Which time is it?* but you can say *Which time of all those discussed suits you best?*

EXAMPLES

Which man — Harry, Strom, or Bill — have you decided to marry?
Which Italian cities will you visit?

AVOIDING ERRORS WITH INTERROGATIVE PRONOUNS

Do not confuse *whose* and *who's. Who's* is the contracted form for *who is* or *who has.*

NOT ~~Whose~~ in the house?
BUT **Who's** in the house? [*Who is* in the house?]

NOT ~~Who's~~ house is this?
BUT **Whose** house is this?

EXERCISE 30. Each numbered item below contains at least one error in the use of demonstrative or interrogative pronouns. Correct each error.

1. In South Dakota there is this famous landmark. This here landmark is called Mount Rushmore.
2. This here landmark is this great tourist attraction.
3. Who's been to the Black Hills? Whose seen Mount Rushmore?
4. Tourists saw them busts of famous Presidents.
5. Whose shown on Mount Rushmore? Who's faces are carved on it?
6. Them great leaders Washington, Jefferson, Lincoln, and Teddy Roosevelt are all carved in the granite.
7. Whose seen Stone Mountain? Who's been to Atlanta?
8. This here famous mountain is the world's largest granite rock in isolation.
9. To who is Stone Mountain dedicated? Whose carved on the northeastern face?
10. I saw the mountain on this visit to Georgia. Them heroic figures of the Confederacy are an amazing sight.

1.d.6 Relative pronouns

Relative pronouns are used at the head of subordinate clauses (see 2.p).

As you can see from the chart on page 62, there are three basic relative pronouns: *who, which,* and *that.* In addition, the relative pronoun *who* has the form *whom* for showing the objective case and the form *whose* for showing possession. If, after reading the following examples, you still have trouble deciding between *who* and *whom,* see 2.t.

■ who

Who (with its forms *whom* and *whose*) is used only for people.

SENTENCE 1: The pilot is my brother.
SENTENCE 2: The pilot landed the plane.
SENTENCE WITH RELATIVE PRONOUN: The pilot **who** landed the plane is my brother. [Pronoun refers to noun.]

■ whom

The objective form *whom* is a relative pronoun. It is used as the object of a verb or as the object of a preposition.

SENTENCE 1: The pilot landed the plane.
SENTENCE 2: We saw [whom?] the pilot.
SENTENCE WITH RELATIVE PRONOUN: The pilot **whom** we saw landed the plane. [Here, *whom* is the object of *saw*.]

SENTENCE 1: The pilot landed the plane.
SENTENCE 2: We gave the pilot the map.
SENTENCE WITH RELATIVE PRONOUN: The pilot to **whom** we gave the map landed the plane. [Here, *whom* is the object of *to*.]

Sometimes the relative pronoun *whom* is omitted.

EXAMPLES

She is the woman **whom** I admire.
She is the woman ^ I admire.

■ whose

The form *whose* is used when the subordinate clause is about something owned by, belonging to, or related to the main noun or pronoun.

EXAMPLES

The pilot **whose** map we borrowed landed the plane.
He **whose** name I forget will forget mine.

Whose is used at times when the main noun is not a person, but this usage is never very successful.

EXAMPLE

AWKWARD: That is the house **whose** roof caved in.
REPHRASED: The roof of that house caved in.

■ which

The relative pronoun *which* is used to relate to nouns, proper nouns, or pronouns that do not refer to people.

SENTENCE 1: The plane landed on time.
SENTENCE 2: The plane carried the equipment.
SENTENCE WITH RELATIVE PRONOUN: The plane **which** carried the equipment landed on time.

AVOIDING ERRORS WITH RELATIVE PRONOUNS

1. Do not use *that* when writing about people.

   NOT I am a student ~~that~~ reads a great deal.
   BUT I am a student **who** reads a great deal.

2. Do not use *which* unless there is a clear antecedent.

   NOT The writer described the South, ~~which~~ made us want to see it for ourselves. [What made us want to see it?]
   BUT The writer's description of the South made us want to see it for ourselves.

3. Do not repeat a preposition unnecessarily when using relative pronouns.

   NOT There are many women ~~for~~ whom I have admiration ~~for~~ now.
   BUT There are many women **for whom** I have admiration now.
   OR There are many women **whom** I have admiration **for** now.

   NOT That is the book ~~in~~ which I am interested ~~in~~ now.
   BUT That is the book **in which** I am interested now.
   OR That is the book **which** I am interested **in** now.

that

The relative pronoun *that* can be used as a substitute for *which* at times. In writing, *that* should not be used when referring to people; use *who.*

EXAMPLES

The plane **which** we saw landed on time.
The plane **that** we saw landed on time.

Most people prefer *that* to *which* when, as in the preceding case, the clause is essential, or restrictive. A clause is essential when it contains information necessary for identifying the noun. (Here, *that we saw* is essential; it identifies the noun *plane.*)

That cannot be used for *which* when a clause is extra (or nonessential or nonrestrictive). Such a clause contains extra information, not necessary for the identification of the noun. It is set off by commas.

EXAMPLE

The President's plane**, which** we happened to see on the way**,** landed on time. [The plane is already identified as the President's. The subordinate clause, therefore, contains extra information.]

With essential clauses only, the *that* or *which* can be omitted completely.

EXAMPLES

The plane **that** we saw landed on time.
The plane **which** we saw landed on time.
The plane ^ we saw landed on time.

EXERCISE 31. Identify each relative pronoun in each of the following sentences. More than one relative prounoun may appear in an item.

1. Golfer Nancy Lopez, who was Rookie and Player of the Year in the same year, became an overnight superstar.
2. The newcomer won five tournaments in a row; she amazed all those whom she played against.
3. The players whom she competes against speak highly of her.
4. She charms the audience of every television show that she appears on; everyone who attends her games becomes an instant fan.
5. More important is the stimulating effect that Lopez has had on her sport.
6. Women's golf, which had been relegated to small columns in sports sections, has become front-page news.
7. Lopez, whose first-year earnings were outstanding, often made the headlines.

8. The person who helped Lopez most in her career is her father.
9. Her father, Domingo, is the one to whom she gives credit.
10. It was he who gave her her first golf club; he is the person whose advice she most often quotes.

1.d.7 Indefinite pronouns

As you can see from the chart on page 63, **indefinite pronouns** are familiar words that you use all the time. You use them in the same way that you use nouns. Indefinite pronouns do not take the place of nouns, but sometimes you know the nouns to which they refer. Since, however, you often do not know exactly to what they refer, you call them indefinite.

EXAMPLES

They used to go everywhere together, and they seemed to know **everyone**. [You do not know the noun to which *everyone* refers.]

Both of the Espirito twins know how to play the clarinet. [You know here that the indefinite pronoun is referring to a certain pair of twins.]

Indefinite pronouns can be placed in the following four groups, depending on their meaning. This breakdown will help you remember them.

1. the universals—*all, everything*, etc.
2. the *some* group
3. the *any* group
4. the negatives—*nobody, nothing*, etc.

■ Subject-verb agreement

As you can see from the chart on page 63, indefinite pronouns can also be divided into the following three groups:

- those that are always singular
- those that are always plural
- those that can be either singular or plural, depending upon the nouns to which they refer

In some cases the action verb or linking verb that you use with an indefinite pronoun shows whether you consider the pronoun singular or plural (see 2.c.2).

EXAMPLES

ALWAYS SINGULAR: **Each** of the thirty players **has** a score card.

ALWAYS PLURAL: **Both** of the players **have** score cards.

SINGULAR OR PLURAL: We heard noises during the night, but the next morning **all was** as it should be. [singular]

All of the girls in my Spanish class **were** good Spanish students. [plural]

Pronoun-antecedent agreement

The indefinite pronoun determines whether the action verb or linking verb is singular or plural. In addition, the indefinite pronoun determines which personal pronoun is used. The personal pronoun must agree with the indefinite pronoun in the same way that it has to agree with a noun that is an antecedent (see 1.d.1). The pronoun and the antecedent must agree in number and in gender.

EXAMPLES

Each of the men wrote **his** novel.

Each of the women wrote **her** novel.

Each of the writers wrote **his** novel.

All of the writers wrote **their** novels.

When the indefinite pronoun may mean "man" *or* "woman," it is conventional to follow with *his* or *him*, as in the third example above. In speaking you may substitute two pronouns (to cover both males and females), but you should stay away from that usage in writing. Nevertheless, if you object to using a masculine pronoun when the indefinite pronoun may be referring to a female, consider rephrasing your statement in the plural.

EXAMPLES

CONVENTIONAL PHRASING IN WRITING: **Each** of the writers wrote **his** novel.

IN SPEAKING: **Each** of the writers wrote **his or her** novel.

PLURAL, IN WRITING: The **writers** wrote **their** novels.

EXERCISE 32. Supply the missing personal pronoun in each of the following sentences. The personal pronoun must agree with its indefinite pronoun antecedent.

1. Each of the Native American tribes had __________ own way of life.
2. Most of this cultural variety had __________ roots in the climate and the terrain.
3. Many of the people of the Plains obtained __________ food by hunting.
4. In the Southwest several of the tribes made __________ homes in *pueblos*, or villages.
5. Almost all of the pueblo groups built __________ stone homes on the mesas.
6. Among the Zuñi, houses were the property of women; each could sell or trade __________ home without hindrance.
7. A few of the Southwestern tribes earned __________ livelihood as shepherds.
8. The Navajo were known to wander, but all of the traveling had __________ limits.
9. In general, everyone had __________ three homes and journeyed within a fifty-mile radius.
10. Each of these homes, called *hogans*, had __________ earth covering and was below the ground.
11. No one could see these homes unless __________ knew what to look for.
12. The Crow men hunted buffalo; each might journey hundreds of miles in __________ search for buffalo.
13. Some of the warrior tribes, like the Comanche, ranged even farther in __________ travels.
14. Any of the tribes that gathered __________ food also journeyed with the seasons.
15. If most of an area received little rain, __________ residents had to travel to find food.

REVIEW EXERCISE E. Before you begin this exercise, you may want to review the following "Avoiding Error" boxes: "Avoiding Errors with Personal Pronouns" (page 64), "Avoiding Errors with Demonstrative Pronouns" (page 71), and "Avoiding Errors with Relative Pronouns" (page 76).

Revise each of the following sentences to eliminate its unclear or weak pronoun.

1. Many twentieth-century writers have come from the South, and this includes several women.
2. Eudora Welty was born in a house in Mississippi, and she set much of her fiction in it.
3. In Georgia they can boast of Carson McCullers, Flannery O'Connor, Alice Walker, and Margaret Mitchell.
4. McCullers wrote of loneliness and eccentricity, which in many ways resembles the works of Eudora Welty.
5. O'Connor's writings were often misunderstood; she speaks of this in her letters.
6. One anecdote relates how O'Connor tried to explain to her mother that she did not understand her work.
7. In Alice Walker's novel *Meridian*, it tells of a teen-ager changed by the civil rights movement.
8. Walker wrote about Flannery O'Connor, and it won the Front Page Award for Best Magazine Column.
9. Margaret Mitchell only wrote one novel, *Gone with the Wind*, but they read it everywhere.
10. Mitchell pictured the Old South, which takes the reader back to the nineteenth century.
11. The landmark film version was based on the novel; it is still popular.
12. Poet Nikki Giovanni wrote about the place where she was born; it is titled "Knoxville, Tennessee."
13. Giovanni explores her identity as a black poet, and this appears in many of her poems.
14. Texas-born Katherine Anne Porter is a descendant of Daniel Boone, which is not so well known.
15. Porter once met Flannery O'Connor, and she spoke with her and others in a panel discussion.

1.e DETERMINERS

A **determiner** is a word other than an adjective (or a participle used as an adjective) that can be used before a noun to identify the noun.

Five kinds of words can be considered determiners when used before nouns[1]:

1. articles *(the, a, an)*
2. indefinite pronouns (for example, *every, all, neither*)
3. possessive pronouns (for example, *his, her, its*)
4. demonstrative pronouns *(this, that, these, those)*
5. numbers and numerals

Determiners are different from adjectives in the following important ways[2]:

1. Adjectives are often used before a noun, but they may also be used in other positions in a sentence. Determiners can be used only before a noun—directly before a noun or before an adjective-and-noun combination (for example, ***the*** *car,* ***the*** *red car*).
2. Adjectives give you choices; determiners do not. That is, you almost always can choose from two or more words before deciding which adjective to use with a noun: You might decide to write about a *spongy* cake, a *moist* cake, or a *fresh* cake. You will see that you do not have such options with determiners. Furthermore, you never really *have* to use an adjective with a noun. On the other hand, a determiner is often required. For example, *I know* ***the*** *fear* is quite different from *I know fear.*

1.e.1 Articles

The words *a* (or *an*) and *the* are often called **articles**. *A* and *an* are called **indefinite articles**. *The* is called the **definite article**.

The definite article, *the*, helps to identify a noun. ***The*** *rickety train home* is different from ***a*** *rickety train home.* With the definite article you can identify a specific train—the rickety one. With the indefinite article you can imply that there might be several trains in this condition.

---

[1] Determiners can also be used before gerunds (see 1.m).

[2] Some grammarians and some teachers do prefer to consider pronouns and numbers before nouns *adjectives*. They are presented here as determiners because they do differ in important ways from "true" adjectives.

You can drop an article that begins the name of a book when you use the possessive (for example, instead of *The Good Earth*, you may write *Pearl Buck's* ***Good Earth***).

1.e.2 Indefinite pronouns as determiners

The same indefinite pronouns that can be used on their own (see 1.d.7) can also be used before a noun.

EXAMPLES

A **few** of the swimmers grew tired. [The indefinite pronoun *few* is the subject of the sentence.]
Few swimmers grew tired. [The indefinite pronoun *few* is here a determiner before the noun. The noun *swimmers* is the subject of the sentence.]
Some swimmers grew tired.
Many swimmers grew tired.

1.e.3 Possessive pronouns as determiners

The following possessive pronouns are used as determiners before a noun: *my, your, his, her, its, our, their.* In addition, some of the indefinite pronouns can have a possessive form and appear in front of a noun.

EXAMPLES

Their teammates grew tired.
Everyone's efforts failed.

1.e.4 Demonstrative pronouns as determiners

This and *that* are used as determiners before singular nouns. *These* and *those* are used before plural nouns.

EXAMPLES

This team lost.	**These** swimmers lost.
That water is cold.	**Those** swimmers won.

1.e.5 Numbers and numerals as determiners

Cardinal numbers and numerals (for example, *three* or *753*) and ordinal numbers and numerals (for example, *fifty-third* or *103rd*) can be considered determiners. Often, they are considered adjectives, but they do not always pass the test of true adjectives. A true adjective can always be used as a predicate adjective after *be*.

EXAMPLES

The child ate **three** desserts.
It was his **fifth** attempt at the pole vault.

EXERCISE 33. Identify each determiner in each of the following sentences. Remember that a determiner can be an article, a number, or a form of a pronoun. (The numeral in parentheses at the end of each item indicates the number of determiners in that sentence.)

1. Few facts are known about the behavior of dinosaurs. (2)
2. A recent find in Montana has given us some new clues. (2)
3. Near the town of Choteau a nest was found. (2)
4. The nest contained the skeletons of fifteen baby dinosaurs. (3)
5. Scientists have found nests with unhatched eggs, but this nest was the first one found with babies. (3)
6. The bowl-shaped nest was six feet across and three feet deep. (3)
7. The baby dinosaurs had mouths shaped like duck bills and seemed to have lived on a river bank. (2)
8. They were three feet long; their mother was thirty feet. (3)
9. The length is an estimate based on the size of an adult dinosaur skull found nearby. (4)
10. Many fossils, still encased in limestone, were moved from the site to Princeton University. (2)
11. Its Museum of Natural History employs geologist John Horner, who discovered the bones. (2)
12. His name for the species is *Maiasaura peeblesorum.* (2)
13. The Peebles family owned some land where the nest was found. (3)

14. The babies had bones sufficiently developed for walking, and their teeth were worn down. (2)
15. Those two facts, in addition to the duck bills, suggest ducklike behavior. (3)
16. Horner imagines that the mother took her young out to feed by day and returned them to the nest at night. (3)
17. Whatever the exact behavior, the nest suggests that these dinosaurs exercised some parental care. (4)
18. It appears that an unknown catastrophe killed the babies about seventy million years ago. (4)
19. Some volcanic ash was found in the nest, but this fact does not prove that an eruption caused the deaths. (5)
20. Horner plans more excavations at the Montana site because he thinks that it was once a dinosaur nesting ground. (3)

1.f ADVERBS

An **adverb** is a word that tells more about a verb, an adjective, or another adverb.

An adverb is a word that can tell *when, where, how,* or *to what degree.* It is generally used within a sentence to give information about a verb, an adjective, or another adverb—or, as you can say, to *modify* these other words. The following sentence illustrates the use of adverbs to tell *to what degree, when, where,* and *how*:

EXAMPLE
Extremely old eagles **now** fly **there happily**.

Each of the kinds of adverbs in the above sentence is discussed in 1.f.1.

1.f.1 Kinds of adverbs

As you will see on the following pages, there are five basic kinds of adverbs: adverbs of time, adverbs of place, adverbs of degree, adverbs of manner, and sentence adverbs.

Adverbs of time

Adverbs of time tell *when.* Some adverbs of time tell about a particular point in time *(now).* Some tell about duration *(briefly).* Some tell about frequency *(often).*

EXAMPLES

Old eagles **now** fly.
The baby cries **continually**.
The baby **never** cries.

The words in bold type in the following expressions are other common adverbs of time:

cry **afterward**
cry **again**
always cry
cry **before**
eventually arrive
finally arrive
speak **first**
speak **frequently**
just spoke
arrive **late**
never cry
speak **now**
often noisy
once happy
presently happy
rarely happy
spoke **recently**
seldom spoke
soon available
available **then**
usually available
published **weekly**

Certain words are sometimes used as nouns and sometimes used as adverbs of time. These words include *yesterday, today,* and *tomorrow.*

EXAMPLES

Tomorrow is another day.
noun

I'll leave **tomorrow**.
adverb of time

Adverbs of place

Adverbs of place tell *where.* Some adverbs of place tell about position *(here).* Some tell about direction *(eastward).*

EXAMPLES

Old eagles fly **there**.
The troops charged **forward**.

Certain words are sometimes used as nouns and sometimes used as adverbs of place. These words include *home, downtown,* and *upstairs.*

EXAMPLES

Home is where the heart is.
noun

I'll arrive **home** tomorrow.
adverb of place

Adverbs of degree

Adverbs of degree tell *to what degree.* When they are used with adjectives or other adverbs, they are sometimes called **intensifiers** because they indicate the level of intensity of the adjective or other adverb.

EXAMPLES

Very old eagles fly **quite** happily. [Adverbs tell the degree of oldness and of happiness.]

He **definitely** accepts their argument. [Adverb tells the degree of the acceptance.]

She was **completely** content. [Adverb tells the degree of contentment.]

Sometimes adverbs of degree are used to modify determiners or indefinite pronouns, as in *almost all* or *hardly anyone.* The words in bold type in the following expressions are other common adverbs of degree:

absolutely refused
almost always
certainly handsome
admired **greatly**
hardly often
however certain
indeed happy
only once
otherwise healthy
partly over
rather unhappy
really cried
scarcely spoke
simply exhausted
so far
cried **somewhat**
too far
very far

Adverbs of manner

Adverbs of manner can tell *how* an action is done (*fly **happily***) or *the means by which* an action is done (*treated **surgically***—that is, by "surgical means"). Adverbs of manner can also be used to give information about an adjective (***ridiculously*** *funny treatment).* Examples of adverbs of manner are noted in bold type below.

"HOW"	"BY WHAT MEANS"
carefully wired	**electrically** wired
argued **effectively**	argued **legalistically**
treated **kindly**	treated **radioactively**

Sometimes an adverb of manner is used to take the place of a longer expression.

EXAMPLES

That nation has much to learn **politically**. [instead of "in political terms"]

Socially, they are ill at ease. [instead of "in social situations"]

Most, but not all, adverbs of manner end in *-ly* (for example, *carefully, happily*). The *-ly* is added to an adjective to form an adverb of manner. Be aware of other common words that do not end in *-ly* but that are adverbs of manner (for example, *alone*, as in *walked* ***alone***).

Sentence adverbs

Sentence adverbs are adverbs of manner used to add information not about a specific word in the sentence but about the entire sentence. These adverbs allow the writer to comment on the whole or on part of what is being said.

EXAMPLES

Honestly, very old eagles fly there now.

Understandably, the workers were glad the strike ended.

Apparently, the house is empty.

The storm, **fortunately**, did little damage.

EXERCISE 34. Identify each of the italicized adverbs as (a) an adverb of time, (b) an adverb of place, (c) an adverb of degree, or (d) an adverb of manner.

1. *basically* solid
2. *overly* fond
3. scurried *rapidly*
4. zoomed *downstairs*
5. rocketed *upward*
6. celebrate *annually*

7. perform *flawlessly*
8. *carelessly* gossiping
9. *totally* foolish
10. answered *ambiguously*
11. *barely* audible
12. place *underneath*
13. rise *early*
14. *currently* open
15. *down* under
16. perched *above*
17. *partially* spoiled
18. encountered *lately*
19. visited *last*
20. live *happily* ever after

APPLICATION. Pick ten items from the preceding list. Write ten original sentences. Use one of the numbered items in each of your sentences.

EXERCISE 35. Each sentence below is followed by two choices. Indicate the adverb that is more appropriate for the sentence.

1. The period after the Civil War is __________ termed the Gilded Age. (a) frequently (b) frenetically
2. __________, the age was as materialistic as the term *gilded* implies. (a) Anxiously (b) Apparently
3. The "robber barons" made fortunes in business; many city bosses were __________ corrupt. (a) corruptly (b) certainly
4. The public __________ ignored the talented writers of the period. (a) sanely (b) shamefully
5. People of the time __________ considered Mark Twain a children's writer. (a) mistakenly (b) miserably
6. __________ Twain is thought of as our nation's greatest satirist. (a) Today (b) Then
7. Many people found the major works of Henry James __________ difficult to understand. (a) somewhat (b) stupidly
8. James went __________ and spent much of his life in England. (a) overly (b) overseas
9. Emily Dickinson, perhaps the best poet of the age, was __________ uninfluenced by other writers of the time. (a) relatively (b) royally
10. Dickinson's poems are __________ philosophical. (a) rapidly (b) deeply

APPLICATION. Look again at the adverb that you did *not* pick for each item above. Write one original sentence for each. (Use a dictionary if necessary.)

1.f.2 Negative words as adverbs

The word *not* and the contraction *n't* are considered adverbs. Other negative words can function as adverbs of time and place.

EXAMPLES

The cow is **not** in the barn.
I **never** saw a purple cow.
The cow is **nowhere** in sight.
The cow is **hardly** purple.
The cow **scarcely** chews her cud.
The cow is **only** chewing her cud.

1.f.3 Forms of adverbs: comparison

Most adverbs have three **degrees** – the regular form, the **comparative,** and the **superlative.** The comparative is used for a comparison of two things. The superlative is used for a comparison of more than two things.

Keep in mind that some adverbs of time, place, and degree have only one form each. You have a number of ways to express comparison with adverbs:

1. the use of *-er* and *-est*
2. the use of *more* and *most*
3. the use of *as*
4. the use of *less* and *least*

For adverbs ending in *-ly*, generally use *more* (or *less*) and *most* (or *least*). For other adverbs use *-er* and *-est*.

Notice the alternative wordings available for stating comparisons.

COMPARATIVE ADVERBS	SUPERLATIVE ADVERBS
John runs **more rapidly** than Tom.	John runs **the most rapidly**.
John runs **more rapidly**.	John runs **most rapidly**.
John runs **as rapidly** as Tom.	

1.f.4 Irregular adverbs: comparison

A small group of common adverbs has special forms for the comparative and superlative.

	COMPARATIVE ADVERB	SUPERLATIVE ADVERB
badly, ill	worse	(the) worst
well	better	(the) best
far	farther, further	(the) farthest, (the) furthest
little	less	(the) least

1.f.5 Adjective or adverb?

You may have noticed that some words are sometimes labeled adjectives and sometimes adverbs. To determine what part of speech a word is, you must see how the word is used in a sentence. (See 1.c for a review of adjectives.) A word that tells more about, or modifies, a noun is an adjective; a word that tells more about a verb, adjective, or adverb is an adverb.

EXAMPLES

The supersonic transport travels **fast**. [adverb: tells *how* the plane *travels*]

The SST is **fast**. [adjective: tells quality of SST]

The **fast** plane caused controversy. [adjective: tells quality of SST]

The jet leaves London **early**. [adverb: tells *when* the plane *leaves*]

The passengers are **early**. [adjective: tells quality of *passengers*]

Supporters of the SST worked **hard**. [adverb: tells *how* the supporters *worked*]

The fight for landing rights was **hard**. [adjective: tells quality of *fight*]

The first transatlantic flight took **long**. [adverb: tells about *took*]

The flight was **long**. [adjective: tells quality of *flight*]

Other words that can be either adverbs or adjectives are *straight, late, low.* When one of these words follows an action verb and tells more about the verb, it is an adverb; when it follows a linking verb, it is an adjective.

EXERCISE 36. In each of the following sentences, determine whether the italicized word is an adverb or an adjective.

1. a) In the late fifties Berry Gordy, Jr., worked *hard.*
   b) His daytime job in a Detroit factory was *hard.*
2. a) At night he struggled *tirelessly* as a songwriter.
   b) His *tireless* efforts paid off with "Lonely Teardrops."
3. a) Gordy *next* wrote "You Got What It Takes."
   b) The song became Gordy's *next* hit.
4. a) It is *rare* that songwriters make fortunes.
   b) Songwriters are *rarely* energetic enough.
5. a) Gordy was still not doing too well *financially.*
   b) He dreamed of *financial* success.
6. a) He saw that record companies made *substantial* profits.
   b) He decided that he could make *substantially* more money.
7. a) *Shortly* after, Gordy started a company named Tamla–Motown.
   b) Motown is *short* for "Motor Town," or Detroit.
8. a) With the start of Motown, the *final* chapter of Gordy's early career was written.
   b) Gordy was *finally* starting a new life.
9. a) Things looked *better* almost from the start.
   b) Motown worked out *better* than even Gordy expected.
10. a) For Motown, Detroit workers came *first.*
    b) Gordy developed his *first* groups locally.
11. a) One *early* group was the Marvelettes.
    b) The Miracles, with Smokey Robinson, did well *early.*
12. a) Motown meant a *straight* path to success for many.
    b) Mary Wells went *straight* to the top of the charts.
13. a) Motown was *fast* becoming the largest black corporation in America.
    b) The rocket to success is rarely so *fast.*
14. a) The Jackson 5 was a *hugely* successful group.
    b) Another *huge* hit was Gladys Knight & the Pips.
15. a) Marvin Gaye recorded *successfully* for Motown.
    b) In the mid-1960s the Supremes were most *successful.*

16. a) Rare Earth was among Motown's *later* stars.
    b) Diana Ross *later* recorded for Motown on her own.
17. a) Motown launched Ross's *highly* successful acting career.
    b) Ross received *high* acclaim for her acting.
18. a) The road to success can be *long* and difficult.
    b) Fame for Stevie Wonder did not take *long*.
19. a) Wonder was still *merely* twelve when Motown signed him.
    b) He was still a *mere* youth when he sang "Fingertips."
20. a) "Fingertips" brought Wonder *instant* attention.
    b) It *instantly* became number one on the charts.

1.f.6 *Good* vs. *well; bad* vs. *badly*

Good and *bad* are always adjectives. *Badly* should always be used as an adverb in writing. *Well* can be either an adverb or an adjective (meaning "in good health"). The following chart shows how each form should be used.

GOOD VS. WELL; BAD VS. BADLY

	good	***well***
adjective (after linking verb)	I feel **good**. [in good health; happy] I look **good** in that. [well dressed]	I feel **well**. [in good health; satisfactory]
adverb (after action verb)	DO NOT USE WITH ACTION VERB.	I play **well**. [how I play]

	bad	***badly***
adjective (after linking verb)	I feel **bad**. [in poor health; sad] I look **bad**. [in poor health]	DO NOT USE WITH LINKING VERB.
adverb (after action verb)	DO NOT USE WITH ACTION VERB.	It hurts **badly**. [how it hurts]

Two adverbs — *slowly* and *quickly* — have alternate, shorter forms that you will sometimes see on signs or hear in speech: *Drive* ***slow***, *Run* ***quick***. Both forms of these words are acceptable in command sentences, especially when spoken or on signs. In writing, you should use the longer forms *slowly* and *quickly*, especially when writing sentences that are not commands.

EXAMPLES

COMMANDS: Drive **slow**. *or* Drive **slowly**.
QUESTIONS: Was she driving **slowly**?
STATEMENTS: They drove there **slowly**.

EXERCISE 37. In each of the following sentences, decide if the italicized word is acceptable in writing for a wide audience. If it is unacceptable, give the correct form.

1. Mildred "Babe" Didrikson Zaharias was hailed *quickly* as the best all-around athlete of the century.
2. She performed *good* in more sports than any other athlete, male or female.
3. She won honors in track and field, golf, basketball, and skating; she even played lacrosse *well*.
4. She could throw a baseball as *good* as most outfielders.
5. She did not design dresses *bad* either; in fact, she won awards for her sportswear.
6. Naturally, she always looked *well* in her sports clothes.
7. Didrikson's schedule was *good* and rigorous.
8. Prominence in the sports world did not come *slow*.
9. From high school on, she rose *quick*.
10. Her performance in track and field was exceptionally *well* at the 1932 Olympics.
11. The track and field star looked very *good* on the golf course.
12. Wherever she played, crowds cheered *good*.
13. Between 1940 and 1950 Zaharias played as *good* as most male golf stars.
14. Unfortunately, her health was no longer *good*.
15. Learning of her illness, all Americans felt *badly*.
16. Her fans felt *well* about her comeback.
17. Despite a major operation, Zaharias' golf performances remained very *well*.

AVOIDING ERRORS WITH ADVERBS

1. Do not use two negative words (a **double negative**) in one main clause. One way to avoid a double negative is to remove the negative adverb.

   NOT Dr. Elizabeth Blackwell ~~never~~ went to ~~no~~ medical school in America.
   BUT Dr. Elizabeth Blackwell went to **no** medical school in America.
   OR Dr. Elizabeth Blackwell **never** went to an American medical school.

   NOT Some people do ~~not~~ want ~~no~~ change in the Constitution.
   BUT Some people want **no** change in the Constitution.
   OR Some people **do not** want any change in the Constitution.

   Notice that to create special emphasis two negative words may occasionally be placed together. The first negative word is, in effect, denying the second.

   I am **never not** on time.

2. Do not misplace an adverb. Make sure that your meaning is clear by placing an adverb of degree, for example, as close as possible to the word it refers to.

   NOT She has ~~almost~~ climbed all these mountains. [Did she never make it to the top of any?]
   BUT She has climbed **almost** all these mountains. [just a few to go]

18. Zaharias followed her schedules *good.*
19. Even though she did not feel *well,* she still won the 1953 Women's National Open.
20. Illness, however, *slowly* took over; Babe Didrikson Zaharias died in 1956.

REVIEW EXERCISE F. Before you begin this exercise, you may want to review these rules: 1.f.2, 1.f.3, 1.f.4, 1.f.5, 1.f.6, and "Avoiding Errors with Adverbs." Identify each adverb in each of the following sentences. There may be more than one adverb in each sentence. Remember that negative words can function as adverbs.

1. As a child, Pearl Primus came north to New York from Trinidad.
2. She later attended Hunter College.
3. She actually was planning to be a doctor.
4. Certainly, she did not expect to be a dancer.
5. Obviously gifted, Pearl Primus eventually won a scholarship to the New Dance Group.
6. She subsequently studied with Martha Graham, Doris Humphrey, and other masters of modern dance.
7. Afterward, she performed professionally and received rave reviews everywhere.
8. She certainly danced beautifully.
9. She was justifiably called the outstanding new dancer of 1943.
10. Remarkably, others who made their debut then included Maria Tallchief and Jose Greco.
11. Primus claims she auditioned nervously for her first long engagement.
12. She apparently performed well on opening night.
13. Her ten-day engagement soon was extended—for a ten month period.
14. Primus is widely credited with first introducing African dance steps here.
15. She always was greatly interested in African dance.
16. Her frequent Caribbean and African trips helped her substantially.
17. Primus was able to translate native dances meaningfully for all audiences.
18. At age sixty Primus hardly slowed down; she developed programs for the handicapped.
19. She never gave up work on her doctoral degree.
20. She finally received it in 1978, but she had taught in many universities earlier.

1.g PREPOSITIONS

A **preposition** is a word that shows the relationship of a noun or pronoun to some other word in the sentence.

Prepositions exist to help express space, time, and other relationships among words.

EXAMPLES

SPACE: The garage is **behind** the house. [*Behind* shows the spatial relationship of the house and the garage.]

TIME: The engine purred **after** the adjustment. [*After* tells the time relationship between the purring and the adjustment.]

OTHER: The car started **with** ease. [Here, *with* does not cover a spatial or time relationship, but it does relate *started* and *ease.*]

Unlike nouns, verbs, adjectives, adverbs, and pronouns, prepositions never undergo spelling or pronunciation changes. Each preposition has just one form.

COMMON PREPOSITIONS

about	by	over
above	concerning	past
across	despite	pending
after	down	regarding
against	during	respecting
along	except	since
amid	excepting	through
among	for	throughout
around	from	to
as	in	toward
at	inside	under
before	into	underneath
behind	like	until
below	of	unto
beneath	off	up
beside	on	upon
besides	onto	with
between	out	within
beyond	outside	without

Some prepositions, called **compound prepositions**, are made up of more than one word.

COMMON COMPOUND PREPOSITIONS

according to
apart from
aside from
as to
because of
in spite of
instead of
on account of
on top of
out of
owing to

EXERCISE 38. Identify each preposition in each of the following sentences. Remember that some prepositions are made up of more than one word. (The numeral in parentheses at the end of each item indicates the number of prepositions in that sentence.)

1. Willis O'Brien, a special-effects film creator, was born in Oakland, California, on March 2, 1886. (2)
2. At an early age he left home. (1)
3. After jobs as a rancher, a boxer, and a jockey, O'Brien worked for a stonecutting firm. (3)
4. One day, in boredom, he fashioned a boxer out of clay. (2)
5. When he was adjusting the clay model, an idea came to O'Brien. (1)
6. The principles of animated cartoons could be used with clay models. (2)
7. With the help of a friend who was a newsreel camera operator, O'Brien shot his first experimental film. (2)
8. High above San Francisco, on top of a bank building, he filmed the clay dinosaur on a miniature set. (3)
9. In spite of the jerkiness of this first attempt, a film exhibitor advanced O'Brien $5,000 for a remake of the film. (4)
10. For the second version, he made new dinosaurs from rubber and metal instead of clay and wood. (3)
11. The finished film was distributed by Thomas Edison throughout America in 1917. (3)
12. It was not until 1923, however, that O'Brien made his first full-length feature, *The Lost World.* (1)
13. The movie was based upon a book by Sir Arthur Conan Doyle, creator of Sherlock Holmes. (3)
14. The story is about the discovery of living dinosaurs deep within a jungle in South America. (4)

15. In one scene a brontosaurus is brought back to London, where it escapes and runs around the city. (3)
16. For certain special effects, O'Brien filmed the actors against rear-projection screens. (2)
17. He photographed the dinosaurs through panes of glass painted with foreground scenery. (3)
18. Because of O'Brien's experience as a rancher, a jockey, a boxer, and a stonecutter, the fighting monsters were believable. (2)
19. *The Lost World* took the public by storm. (1)
20. In spite of this success, however, there were still years of frustration in store for Willis O'Brien. (4)

1.g.1 Prepositional phrases; objects of prepositions

A **prepositional phrase** is a group of words that begins with a preposition and usually ends with a noun or pronoun.
The **object of a preposition** is usually a noun or pronoun that follows the preposition.

A preposition never stands alone; it is always part of a prepositional phrase. The object of a preposition is usually a noun or pronoun, but it can be any word or group of words that can be used the way a noun is used. In other words, the object of a preposition can be a noun, a proper noun, a pronoun, a gerund (see 1.m), another prepositional phrase, or a clause (see 2.n). There may, of course, be adjectives or determiners before the object. Furthermore, a preposition may have a **compound object** — two or more objects.[1]

EXAMPLES

The car is **in the garage**. [Object of the preposition *in* is *garage*.]

The car is **for shopping and sightseeing**. [Compound object of the preposition *for* is *shopping and sightseeing*.]

[1]Do not confuse the object of a preposition with the object of a verb, also called a direct object (see 2.j), or with an indirect object (see 2.k).

1.g.2 Personal pronouns after prepositions

A preposition generally takes a pronoun in the objective case.

Occasionally, a preposition takes a possessive pronoun, but you should never use a nominative pronoun as the object of a preposition. (For a review of the cases, see 1.d.1.)

EXAMPLES

The sports car belongs to **them**. [objective pronoun]

The station wagon is for his use; the compact is for **hers**. [possessive pronoun]

In writing, be careful to use *whom*, not *who*, as the object of a preposition.

EXAMPLES

Whom is the car for? **Whom** are you talking about?

1.g.3 Positions of prepositions

The word *preposition* means "placed before," but not every preposition always comes before its object. Sometimes the object comes before the preposition.

EXAMPLE

What are you looking **for**? [*What* is the object of *for.*]

1.g.4 Preposition or adverb?

Many of the words listed as prepositions on page 97 can, in some sentences, be abverbs. The way in which the word is used determines if you should label it an adverb or a preposition. If the word stands alone without an object, consider it an adverb. If the word has an object, consider it a preposition.

EXAMPLES

The players assembled **inside**. [adverb: By itself, the word tells *where.*]

The players assembled **inside** the auditorium. [preposition: The word has an object, *auditorium.*]

AVOIDING ERRORS WITH PREPOSITIONS

1. Be consistent in how you use prepositions when you have a series.

NOT That dealer sells cars in New York, Boston, and ~~in~~ Miami. [Two items have prepositions; one does not.]
BUT That dealer sells cars **in** New York, **in** Boston, and **in** Miami. [a preposition before each object]
OR That dealer sells cars **in** New York, Boston, and Miami. [only one preposition for the series]

2. Do not use too many prepositions.

NOT The show begins ~~in~~ an hour ~~from now~~.
BUT The show begins **in** an hour.
OR The show begins an hour **from** now.

NOT The cars fell ~~off of~~ the trailer.
BUT The cars fell **off** the trailer.

NOT ~~In~~ which car are you interested ~~in~~?
BUT **In** which car are you interested?
OR Which car are you interested **in**?

For a list of the preferred prepositions to use with particular adjectives, see 4.h. (For example, should you say *angry with* or *angry at*?)

1.g.5 Preposition or part of verb?

Many of the words listed as prepositions on page 97 are sometimes considered *not* prepositions, but part of a two-word verb (see 4.c).

EXAMPLES

The leaders ran **down** the track.
The secretary **ran down** the list of applicants and found no one with that name.

In the first example on the preceding page, *down* is a preposition with *track* as its object. In the second sentence *ran down* is a two-word verb with *list* as its object.

PREPOSITIONS	TWO-WORD VERBS
I looked **up** the mountain.	I **looked up** the phone number.
I turned **into** the parking lot.	The coach **turned into** a pumpkin.

1.g.6 Preposition or conjunction?

Some of the words listed as prepositions on page 97 can, at times, be subordinating conjunctions (see 1.h.4). If a whole statement—with a verb—follows the word, the word is a subordinating conjunction. If only a noun or noun equivalent follows, the word is a preposition.

PREPOSITIONS	SUBORDINATING CONJUNCTIONS
Turn left **before** the park.	Turn on the ignition **before** you *step* on the gas.
The car has been in the repair shop **since** yesterday.	The car has been in the repair shop **since** I *bought* it.

EXERCISE 39. Each of the following sentences has one prepositional phrase. For each sentence identify the preposition and the object of the preposition.

1. It was Merian C. Cooper who first had the idea for *King Kong.*
2. He planned an adventure movie about a giant ape.
3. *Kong* is an East Indian word for gorilla.
4. Cooper had wanted an actual gorilla in the film.
5. Because of the expense, the project seemed impossible.
6. Special-effects wizard Willis O'Brien had not made a film in six years.
7. When Cooper saw O'Brien's earlier work, he decided to use an animated ape instead of a real one.

8. King Kong was not an actor in a gorilla suit.
9. King Kong's skeleton was made from an aluminum alloy.
10. His muscles were made of rubber and cotton.
11. His hide was actually rabbit fur glued to his "skin."
12. A separate model was made for King Kong's head.
13. O'Brien apparently put himself into the ape's mind.
14. King Kong's gestures and facial expressions resemble those of O'Brien.
15. O'Brien worked with several assistants.
16. Yet O'Brien did all the animation himself on a large table.
17. One assistant stayed underneath the table and secured the models.
18. The film, released in 1933, was painstaking work.
19. King Kong is so lifelike that viewers forget he is only a model of a real gorilla.
20. The film was so popular that a new version was made in 1976.

1.h CONJUNCTIONS

A **conjunction** is a word that joins other words or groups of words.

Conjunctions are, in effect, connectives. They show the way in which words or groups of words are connected in meaning.

EXAMPLES

The tall ships sailed up the river, **and** the people on the shore cheered.

The people cheered **because** they had never before seen so many beautiful old-style sailing ships from so many different countries.

In the examples above, the conjunction *because* expresses a different kind of relationship from that expressed by the conjunction *and*. Almost every conjunction expresses a relationship that is somewhat different from that expressed by another.

There are four kinds of conjunctions:

1. coordinating conjunctions
2. correlative conjunctions
3. conjunctive adverbs
4. subordinating conjunctions

1.h.1 Coordinating conjunctions

The **coordinating conjunctions** are *and*, *but*, *or*, and *for*.

and: In general, use *and* to mean "also" *(She serves **and** volleys well)*, "plus" *(One **and** one make two)*, "as a result" *(Practice writing, **and** your style will improve)*.

but: Use *but* as a conjunction to express contrast *(He speaks only French, **but** she does not know a word of French)* or to mean "yet" *(She warmed up before running, **but** she pulled a muscle anyway)*.

or: Use *or* as a conjunction to introduce an alternative of two or more *(Do you want tea, coffee, **or** cocoa?)* or to mean "otherwise" *(Practice writing, **or** you will never improve)*.

nor: You will find *nor* used occasionally as a coordinating conjunction after an opening main clause that is clearly negative *(He had no homework to worry about, **nor** did he have work to do for the student council)*.

for: Use *for* as a conjunction to mean "seeing that," "inasmuch as," or "because" *(Let us eat and drink, **for** tomorrow we shall die)*.

NOTE: The words *yet* and *so* are conjunctive adverbs, not coordinating conjunctions (see 1.h.3).

COMMAS WITH COORDINATING CONJUNCTIONS

It is incorrect to use a comma with a coordinating conjunction that joins a compound verb.

NOT He reads French, but speaks only Spanish.
BUT He reads French **but** speaks only Spanish.

EXERCISE 40. Each of the following sentences has one or more coordinating conjunctions. Identify each one.

1. In the early nineteenth century, scientists in America, male and female, generally (but not always) worked in isolation from one another and from the community.
2. Women scientists had to rely on a male friend or a male relative to get scientific equipment and information.
3. Maria Mitchell's father taught her to make astronomical observations and calculations, but Maria and her father were at that time amateurs.
4. After 1847 Maria Mitchell was internationally known, for she had discovered a comet.
5. She was honored with memberships in the American Academy of Arts and Sciences and the American Association for the Advancement of Science, and she was hired to compute the position of Venus.

EXERCISE 41. Supply the coordinating conjunction that makes the most sense in each of the following sentences. Select from *and, but, for,* and *or.*

1. In colonial America there were no secondary schools __________ colleges open to women.
2. Women relied on private tutors __________ family members for their education.
3. Most women were not encouraged to study at all, __________ they were thought better suited to domestic concerns.
4. Women were believed to have three common traits—patience, perseverance, __________ neatness.
5. Women's schools first appeared in the 1820s, __________ Mount Holyoke, the first women's college, did not open until 1837.
6. The early women's colleges took science education very seriously, spending a great deal on scientific apparatus, books, __________ teachers.
7. Science was considered important to the development of the mind, __________ it was still not thought to be the basis of a career for a woman.
8. Most women were naturally incapable of serious scientific work—__________ so it was argued.

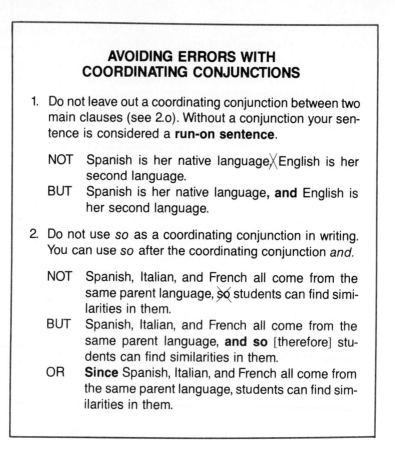

AVOIDING ERRORS WITH COORDINATING CONJUNCTIONS

1. Do not leave out a coordinating conjunction between two main clauses (see 2.o). Without a conjunction your sentence is considered a **run-on sentence**.

   NOT Spanish is her native language, English is her second language.
   BUT Spanish is her native language, **and** English is her second language.

2. Do not use *so* as a coordinating conjunction in writing. You can use *so* after the coordinating conjunction *and.*

   NOT Spanish, Italian, and French all come from the same parent language, so students can find similarities in them.
   BUT Spanish, Italian, and French all come from the same parent language, **and so** [therefore] students can find similarities in them.
   OR **Since** Spanish, Italian, and French all come from the same parent language, students can find similarities in them.

9. Clearly, this was not true of Ellen Swallow, ________ she became the first woman to attend a graduate school of science.
10. She was admitted as a special student in chemistry at M.I.T. in 1870 ________ later played an important role in the growth of ecology.

1.h.2 Correlative conjunctions

The **correlative conjunctions** are the following:

both . . . and	not only . . . but also
either . . . or	though . . . yet
just as . . . so	whether . . . or
neither . . . nor	

Like coordinating conjunctions (see 1.h.1), correlative conjunctions join words and groups of words of equal value in a sentence, but correlative conjunctions make the relationship between these words or groups of words a little clearer. You use the first part of the correlative conjunction before one word or group of words and the second part before the related word or group of words.

COORDINATING CONJUNCTIONS	CORRELATIVE CONJUNCTIONS
You **and** *I* must go.	**Both** *you* **and** *I* must go. [*You* and *I* are of equal value; they are related words. The correlative conjunction *both . . . and* makes the relationship clearer and stronger than the coordinating conjunction *and.*]
You **or** *I* must go.	**Either** *you* **or** *I* must go.
	Neither *you* **nor** *I* must go.
We saw *Paris* **and** *Rome.*	We saw **not only** *Paris* **but also** *Rome.*

EXERCISE 42. Each of the following sentences has one correlative conjunction. Identify both parts of each correlative conjunction.

1. The world's supply of both oil and coal is limited.
2. The cost not only of gasoline but also of electricity is rising.
3. Neither nuclear fusion nor nuclear fission is wholly safe and nonpolluting.
4. Either people must explore safe, clean energy sources, or they will seriously disrupt the ecology.
5. Whether people harness Niagara Falls or use the Pacific tides, clean energy can come from water.
6. Energy from the sun is neither polluting nor costly.
7. Whether a home is built on a bright mountaintop or placed in a shady valley, solar heat can cut down fuel use.
8. Home solar-heating systems can use either air or liquid to operate.
9. Both air and liquid systems use solar energy collectors.
10. Solar heating not only saves money but also conserves resources.

EXERCISE 43. The following paragraph has ten correlative conjunctions. Identify each pair.

[1]Neither the reporters nor the sightseers could at first decide whether the ship from Argentina or the one from Italy was their favorite. [2]Both the Argentinian and the Italian ships not only stood tall in the water but also had very elegant arrangements of sails. [3]Just as the Argentinians had been loudly applauded, so the Italians drew cheers. [4]Both the media and the public decided that the ship from Italy was the superior vessel. [5]Not only had the Italian ship looked magnificent, but also its crew had stood proudly on the rigging, neither faltering nor fidgeting. [6]Either the sailors were glued to the ropes, or they were very well trained. [7]Whether rain fell or the sun beat down, they remained at their posts.

1.h.3 Conjunctive adverbs

Conjunctive adverbs are used to clarify the relationship between main clauses (see 2.o). The two or more main clauses in a compound sentence are of equal importance. Conjunctive adverbs can take the place of coordinating conjunctions (see 1.h.1) in a sentence and are stronger and more precise. Conjunctive adverbs always require a semicolon as the mark of punctuation separating the main clauses.

Coordinating conjunction

The tall ships sailed away**, but** they had left us with a happy memory.

Conjunctive adverbs

The tall ships sailed away**; however,** they had left us with a happy memory.

The tall ships sailed away**;** they left us with a happy memory, **however**.

There are many conjunctive adverbs, and they have several uses, as follows:

1. to replace *and* or to reinforce: *also, besides, furthermore, moreover*
2. to replace *but: however, nevertheless, still, though, yet*
3. to state a result: *consequently, therefore, so, thus*
4. to state equality: *equally, likewise, similarly*

EXERCISE 44. Each of the following sentences has one conjunctive adverb. Identify each conjunctive adverb, and indicate how it is used: (a) to replace *and* or to reinforce; (b) to replace *but*; (c) to state a result or consequence; or (d) to state equality.

1. Solar-heating systems are costly; however, they eventually pay for themselves.
2. Solar-heating systems can cut fuel costs by 70 percent; moreover, they require little maintenance.
3. A solar heater for a swimming pool can pay for itself in reduced fuel costs in three years; similarly, a home solar heater can pay for itself in seven years.
4. Solar panels collect heat from the sun; therefore, some medium must be used to transfer the heat to the house.
5. Most solar-heating systems use liquid to store and transfer heat; nevertheless, in some cases a combination of air and stones is more effective.
6. Liquid solar-heating systems use water to collect heat; consequently, they must use antifreeze in cold weather.
7. Liquid systems require a maze of piping; thus, they should be installed as the house is being built.
8. Systems that use air are better suited to older buildings; furthermore, they operate at lower temperatures than liquid systems.
9. Liquid systems are more versatile; besides, they save more than air systems.
10. No solar-heating system can completely eliminate reliance on coal or gas; still, the system does save a considerable amount of fuel.

1.h.4 Subordinating conjunctions

Subordinating conjunctions are words or groups of words that are used to join subordinate clauses to main clauses in a sentence (see 2.p). They show the following relationships in meaning between a subordinate clause and a main clause:

a. reason — c. place
b. time — d. condition

SUBORDINATING CONJUNCTION	RELATIONSHIP
We cheered the tall ships **because** they were exciting.	reason
We cheered the tall ships **when** they arrived.	time
Wherever they may sail again, we will want to see them.	place
We will want to see them **if** they sail again.	condition

COMMON SUBORDINATING CONJUNCTIONS

Time	Place	Other
after	where	although
as	wherever	as
before		because
since		if
until		since
when		than
whenever		though
while		unless
		whereas
		while

Some of the above conjunctions appear in more than one column; they have more than one meaning. Some of the above conjunctions can also be used as other parts of speech. For example, *after, before, since,* and *until* can be prepositions; *when* and *where* can be question words. There are also compound subordinating conjuctions:

COMPOUND SUBORDINATING CONJUNCTIONS

Time	Place	Other
as long as	as far as	as though
as soon as		considering (that)
so long as		for fear that
		inasmuch as
		in order that
		in the hope that
		provided (that)
		seeing (that)
		so that
		supposing that
		to the end that

COMMAS WITH SUBORDINATING CONJUNCTIONS

1. If you begin a sentence with a subordinating conjunction (and a subordinate clause), use a comma after the subordinate clause.

   When they arrived**,** we cheered the tall ships.

2. In general, you do not need a comma before a subordinating conjunction that appears toward the end of the sentence.

   We cheered the tall ships **when** they arrived.

3. If the subordinating conjunction is *though* or *although,* do use a comma before it.

   We cheered the tall ships**,** although their sails were not up.

4. Do not use a comma before *as, while,* or *since* if you mean "when." Do use a comma before *as* or *since* if you mean "why" and before *while* if you mean "whereas."

   We cheered the tall ships **as** they came into the harbor.

   We cheered the tall ships**,** as they were a symbol of past greatness.

EXERCISE 45. Identify the subordinating conjunction in each of the following sentences. Remember that some subordinating conjunctions consist of more than one word.

1. Too often the proper fire precautions are not taken until a tragedy has occurred.
2. Many school buildings were redesigned after 175 lives were lost in Collinwood, Ohio.
3. The Lake View Elementary School in Collinwood had 325 pupils before disaster struck in March 1908.

4. Although the building was three stories tall, it had only three exits.
5. As soon as the students had settled down to work on the morning of March 4, the fire bell rang.
6. The pupils moved calmly, as though they were having a fire drill.
7. When they entered the corridor, they saw black smoke and flames near the front exit.
8. The children panicked for fear that they would be unable to escape through the front door.
9. Because the rear door was locked, many students crowded up against it to escape the flames.
10. Since the rear door opened inward, fire fighters could not use it to enter the building.

REVIEW EXERCISE G. Each of the following sentences has one conjunction. Identify the conjunction, and indicate whether it is a coordinating conjunction, a correlative conjunction, a conjunctive adverb, or a subordinating conjunction.

1. Many people are considered famous Americans, although they were not born in this country.
2. Irving Berlin was born in Russia; nevertheless, he wrote "God Bless America."
3. Anne Bradstreet was the first woman poet in America, but she was born in England.
4. Knute Rockne achieved his greatest recognition as an American football celebrity; however, he was born in Norway.
5. Both Andrew Carnegie and Alexander Graham Bell emigrated from Scotland.
6. After she had emigrated from Sweden, Greta Garbo won universal fame as a Hollywood star.
7. Rudolph Valentino was a farmer before he left Italy to become an American silent-film star.
8. Neither Ingrid Bergman nor Hedy Lamarr was born in this country.
9. Alfred Hitchcock made most of his sound films in Hollywood, but he directed several silent films in his native England.
10. Charlie Chaplin was born in London; yet he developed his talents as an actor in the United States.

1.i INTERJECTIONS

An **interjection** is a word or phrase that expresses emotion or exclamation. An interjection has no grammatical connection to any other words.

An interjection can be part of a sentence, or it can stand alone.

EXAMPLES

Oh, didn't you know?
Alas, it was too true!
"**Ah**, your father knows the recipe."
"**Why**, Harry!"

EXCLAMATION POINTS AND COMMAS WITH INTERJECTIONS

1. Use an exclamation point after an interjection that stands alone.

   Oh, no**!** Good for you**!** Oops**!**

2. Use a comma after an interjection at the beginning of a sentence.

   Whew**,** that was a close game!

1.j VERBALS

Verbals are formed from verbs and, therefore, carry the idea of action.

There are three kinds of verbals: **participles**, **gerunds**, and **infinitives**.

Verbals are not usually classified as parts of speech. When you see how they are used, however, you will see why it is helpful to think of them as such. You will see that verbals can be used in the same way that nouns, adjectives, and adverbs are used.

Here are sentences using the three kinds of verbals.

PARTICIPLES

I watched the **traveling** circus. [present participle]

I walked the **traveled** path. [past participle]

GERUNDS

Traveling is educational.

I love **traveling**.

INFINITIVES

To travel is educational.

I love **to travel**.

1.k PARTICIPLES AS ADJECTIVES

The present-participle form and the past-participle form of a verb can be used as adjectives.

EXAMPLE

Verb	Present participle	Past participle
travel	traveling	traveled[1]

Traveling gypsies reached our town.

They took a **traveled** road.

It is sometimes difficult (and often not necessary) to tell if a word is a participle used like an adjective—or if it is just a regular adjective. Nevertheless, it may help you to understand more about what a participle is if you do consider the difference between a participle and an adjective. On the following list, two of the words in bold type are participles and two are regular adjectives:

the **torn** dress	the **green** dress
the **flowing** dress	the **silken** dress

[1]The verb *travel* is a regular verb. Its present participle takes an *-ing* (as do all verbs in forming the present participle); because it is a regular verb, it takes an *-ed* to form the past participle. See 1.b.8 for past participles of irregular verbs.

Torn and *flowing* are the participles because they are formed from verbs—from *tear* and *flow*. *Green* and *silken* are pure adjectives. They do not come from verbs. Notice that to use a participle is to communicate some sense of action (for example, the action of tearing a dress or the action of a dress flowing). Pure adjectives cannot convey a sense of action. (See 4.e for advice on creating your own participles.)

EXERCISE 46. Nine of the following ten sentences have either a present participle or a past participle used as an adjective. Identify each such participle. Indicate which sentence does not have a participle used as an adjective.

1. Grandma Moses painted charming scenes from her early life.
2. This admired artist had much to remember, for she was 101 when she died in 1961.
3. Her recognized style is called primitive.
4. She painted carriages with whirling wheels.
5. Barn-raising parties were another subject of this truly American painter.
6. Trotting horses and tiny figures also filled her landscapes.
7. Grandma Moses lived most of her life on farms in northeastern America.
8. "I like to paint old-timey things," she said, and her affection produced works of sparkling detail.
9. Vanished bridges, mills, and farmhouses lived in her memory.
10. Near the end of her life she became a celebrated figure, but she was most herself when she was painting.

APPLICATION. Use each participle from Exercise 46 in an original sentence.

1.l PARTICIPIAL PHRASES

A **participial phrase** contains a participle and other words that describe, or modify, the participle.

EXAMPLES

I watched the **traveling** circus. [This sentence contains a participle.]

I watched the circus **traveling during the night**. [This sentence contains a participial phrase – a participle plus a prepositional phrase.]

The circus left town, **traveling quietly**. [This sentence contains a participial phrase—a participle plus an adverb of manner.]

The circus left town, **traveling quietly during the night**. [Here, the participial phrase is a participle plus an adverb of manner plus a prepositional phrase.]

They traveled on, **leaving the town**. [Here, the participial *leaving* and its object—*the town*—make up the participial phrase.]

The above examples show a present participle as the key word in a participial phrase. Past participles can also be used in participial phrases. Notice also that a participial phrase can be quite short or rather long, depending on the type of construction that you use to expand the participle. Furthermore, a participial phrase can be used in various positions.

EXAMPLES

Undefeated all season, our team looked forward to glory.

Surprisingly defeated, our team seemed glum.

Our team, **undefeated even by the former champion**, looked forward to the pennant.

We gave up on that team, **constantly defeated because its members never practiced enough**.

A past participle is often used with a form of the verb *be*.

EXAMPLES

Being undefeated, our team is smug.

Having been undefeated, our team became smug.

EXERCISE 47. Identify each participial phrase in each of the following sentences. Two of the ten sentences contain two participial phrases each.

1. Tito Gaona and his brother and sister were children experienced with the trampoline.
2. The young Gaonas, living in Mexico, had put together an act while their father, working as a circus clown, was in Florida.

AVOIDING ERRORS WITH PARTICIPLES AND PARTICIPIAL PHRASES

1. Do not misplace a participle or a participial phrase. If you do, you will create what is called a **"dangling" participial phrase.**

   NOT Running for the bus, ~~the heel~~ of my shoe broke.
   BUT Running for the bus, **I broke** the heel of my shoe.
   OR **I ran** for the bus, breaking the heel of my shoe.

   Who ran for the bus? Not the heel of the shoe. A sentence with a participial phrase should be able to be reworded as a sentence with two verbs. You cannot write *The heel of my shoe* ***broke*** *and* ***ran*** *for the bus.* Check, and rewrite if necessary, all sentences with participial phrases. Each participial phrase must be clearly related to the correct noun or pronoun in a sentence.

2. Do not use the participial expression *being that* or *being as* when you mean "because" or "since."

   NOT ~~Being that~~ it's raining, let's just stay in and do the crossword puzzle.
   BUT **Since** it's raining, let's just stay in and do the crossword puzzle.

3. Do not treat a participial phrase as if it were a sentence. A participial phrase is *not* a sentence. A sentence must have a real action verb or linking verb—not just a participle (see 2.a).

   NOT The bus coming around the corner, trying to make the light. [not a sentence]
   BUT I **saw** the bus coming around the corner, trying to make the light.
   OR The bus **came** around the corner, trying to make the light.

3. When Victor Gaona observed his children performing expertly, he realized that they were good enough to work in the circus.
4. Two years later an unusual event occurred, changing the family's course in life.
5. Watching the movie *Trapeze*, fourteen-year-old Tito decided to become an aerialist.
6. His family followed suit, learning to master the flying trapeze.
7. Undisturbed by a fall into the audience a year later, Tito returned to the trapeze.
8. Tito succeeded early with the triple somersault, attempting the difficult act when he was eighteen.
9. Extremely self-disciplined at a young age, Tito could soon perform the feat with a blindfold.
10. Never satisfied, Tito is one of those performers obsessed by increasingly difficult aerial exploits.

EXERCISE 48. Reword the following sentences to eliminate the misplaced or "dangling" participial phrases. After you have made the change, be sure to check your punctuation.

1. Born in California during the Gold Rush, people all over the world now wear blue jeans.
2. Guaranteed not to rip, gold prospectors liked jeans for their durability.
3. Designed originally for working men, women did not originally wear denim pants.
4. First gaining popularity in the West, cowboys wore jeans for work and for dress wear.
5. Worn by Marlon Brando in *The Wild Ones*, young people saw jeans as a symbol of rebellion.
6. Associated with roughnecks in the 1950s, schools around the country banned blue jeans.
7. Acquiring an anti-Establishment mystique in the 1960s, young people adopted jeans as a uniform.
8. Soon gaining fashion status, American and French designers styled blue jeans.
9. Available now in satin and velvet, people no longer assume their jeans will fade and shrink.
10. No longer associated with bucking broncos, men and women alike now consider jeans high fashion.

COMMAS WITH PARTICIPLES AND PARTICIPIAL PHRASES

1. A participle or participial phrase that adds *extra information* should be set off from the rest of the sentence with *extra commas.* (If the sentence makes sense without the participle or participial phrase, you can assume that you are dealing with "extra information.")

   The child**,** playing quietly**,** seemed pleased.
   I accepted the gift**, delighted that he had remembered.**

2. A participle or participial phrase that is essential to the meaning of the sentence should *not* be set off by commas. The following sentences would *not* make sense without the phrases that are in bold type; therefore, commas would be wrong.

   A child **playing with matches** is dangerous.
   I enjoy seeing someone **delighted by a gift**.

3. A participial phrase that begins a sentence is always followed by a comma.

   Playing quietly, the child seemed pleased.
   Delighted that he had remembered, I accepted the gift.
   Playing with matches, a child becomes a danger.
   Delighted by the gift, he was a joy to watch as he played with it.

1.m GERUNDS

A **gerund** is a verb form that ends in *-ing* and that is used in the same ways a noun is used.

Although used in the way a noun is used, a gerund communicates the idea of action or movement because it has its basis in a verb. Remember, a participle can be used as an adjective or an adverb is used; a gerund is used as a noun is used.

GERUNDS	NOUNS
Traveling is educational.	**Books** are educational.
We enjoy **traveling**.	We enjoy **books**.
We take pleasure in **traveling**.	We take pleasure in **books**.
Our greatest pleasure is **traveling**.	Our greatest pleasures are **books**.

EXERCISE 49. Each of the following sentences contains one gerund and one present participle. Both a gerund and a present participle, of course, end in *-ing*. Identify each *-ing* word below as either a gerund or as a present participle.

1. Flying can take many fascinating forms.
2. The adventurous scorn jet planes; they prefer less boring activities to sitting.
3. Ballooning has long attracted daring people.
4. Even riskier is hang gliding, a growing sport.
5. Pilots in engineless sailplanes take delight in soaring, enjoying the air about them.
6. Coasting among swirling currents can go on for hours if all conditions are right.
7. Parachuting provides a different but thrilling experience.
8. Falling is inspiring, especially after the parachute opens.
9. These flying devices require training for the sake of safety.
10. Travelers with a taste for exploring must also have an accompanying sense of survival.

1.n GERUND PHRASES

A **gerund phrase** contains a gerund and other words that describe, or modify, the gerund.

A gerund phrase can be quite short or rather long, depending on how the gerund is expanded.

EXAMPLES

Traveling is educational. [The sentence contains a gerund.]

Inexpensive traveling is still possible. [The sentence contains a gerund phrase – a gerund preceded by an adjective.]

Extended traveling may get expensive. [Here, the gerund phrase contains a gerund preceded by a past participle.]

Traveling on a freighter can be fun. [Here, the gerund phrase is made up of a gerund plus a prepositional phrase.]

The Eskimos' traveling by dog sled is efficient. [Here, you have not only a prepositional phrase after the gerund but a possessive noun before it.]

Traveling quickly overland was the goal of the Pony Express. [Here, the gerund is followed by two adverbs to form a gerund phrase.]

EXERCISE 50. Each of the following sentences contains two gerund phrases. Identify each.

1. Deep-sea diving makes the observing of marine life an adventure.
2. Looking at pictures or studying books cannot replace first-hand experiences under water.
3. Underwater breathing and rapid swimming are made possible by the use of scuba equipment and flippers.
4. Searching for treasure makes the diver's exploring potentially profitable.
5. Finding a school of fish and seeing a live sponge are rewarding in another sense.

1.o INFINITIVES

An **infinitive** is a verb form, usually preceded by the word *to,* that is used as a noun, an adjective, or an adverb.

The word *to* before a verb is *not* a preposition. An infinitive has a present form and a past form. This past form is sometimes called the perfect form. A past infinitive is made up of *to* + *have* + the past participle of an action verb or a linking verb.

PRESENT INFINITIVES	PAST (OR PERFECT) INFINITIVES
to travel	to have traveled
to do	to have done
to be	to have been
to seem	to have seemed

Infinitives can be used in sentences in the same ways that nouns, adjectives, and adverbs can be used.

EXAMPLES

Infinitives	Nouns
To travel is educational.	**Trips** are educational.
I plan **to travel**.	I plan **trips**.
To plan **to travel** is easy.	To plan **trips** is easy.
Planning **to travel** is fun.	Planning **vacations** is fun.
Our goal is **to travel**.	Our goal is **Europe**.
Infinitive	**Adjective**
We had the wisdom **to travel**.	We had **great** wisdom.
Infinitives	**Adverbs**
We were happy **to have traveled**.	We were **theoretically** happy.
We saved our money **to travel**.[1]	We saved our money **hopefully**.

Infinitives without "to"

Occasionally you will find an infinitive with the word *to* omitted before the form of the verb. The *to* is always understood, however.

EXAMPLES

Help me **do** my best. *or* Help me **to do** my best.
What she did was **travel** to Cuba. *or* What she did was **to travel** to Cuba.

[1] In this situation other forms of the infinitive might be *in order to travel* or *so as to travel.* The words *in order* and *so as* enforce the infinitive.

1.p INFINITIVE PHRASES

An **infinitive phrase** contains an infinitive and other words that describe, or modify, the infinitive.

EXAMPLES

We want **to travel**. [The sentence contains an infinitive.]

We want **to travel there quickly now**. [The sentence contains an infinitive phrase – an infinitive followed by three adverbs.]

We want **to travel through Transylvania in peace**. [Here, an infinitive phrase is made up of an infinitive plus two prepositional phrases.]

We want **to travel savoring each new sight**. [Here, the infinitive is followed by a participial phrase to form an infinitive phrase.]

To travel wherever we can is our goal. [The infinitive is followed by a clause; see 2.q.]

We want **to travel to gain experience**. [The first infinitive is expanded to an infinitive phrase by adding yet another infinitive.]

If you "split" an infinitive by placing an adverb between the *to* and the verb, be aware of what you are doing and why you are doing it. It is almost always advisable to place the adverb in front of the *to*, after the verb, or after the object.

EXAMPLES

SPLIT She likes ~~to now and then~~ climb a mountain.
NOT SPLIT She likes **now and then to climb** a mountain.

SPLIT She likes ~~to lazily walk~~ up a mountain.
NOT SPLIT She likes **to walk lazily** up a mountain.

SPLIT She likes ~~to quickly reach~~ the top of the mountain.
NOT SPLIT She likes **to reach** the top of the mountain **quickly**.

Professional writers sometimes intentionally split an infinitive for special emphasis—for example, *She likes to boldly attack the mountain.* The adverb *boldly* is emphasized more by being placed between *to* and the verb than it would be if it were placed anywhere else in the sentence.

EXERCISE 51. Identify the infinitive phrase in each of the following sentences. Remember that the word *to* is not always the first word of an infinitive; sometimes *to* is a preposition.

1. American financier Andrew W. Mellon provided the funds to build the National Gallery of Art in Washington, D.C.
2. He also had the foresight to acquire nine additional acres for expansion.
3. The museum hired I. M. Pei to design the new east wing for modern art.
4. The challenge was to work with "a wacky piece of land," according to the director of the gallery.
5. One day Pei was inspired to draw two triangles on the back of an envelope.
6. On the basis of that drawing, he designed a new wing consisting of two triangular buildings that join to form a trapezoid.
7. The building seems to move by itself as one walks by it.
8. From almost anywhere inside, a museum goer is able to view the outdoors or the courtyard.
9. Slats of aluminum reduce the light from the glass ceiling to protect the works of art from glare.
10. The glass ceiling and the light allowed Pei to add trees and plants to the furnishings of the lobby.

REVIEW EXERCISE H. Identify the verbal phrase in each of the following sentences as a participial phrase, a gerund phrase, or an infinitive phrase. Two of the sentences have two verbal phrases each.

1. The Pilgrims and the early missionaries were the first people to bring cats to America.
2. Wild cats had lived here for centuries, but cats domesticated by Europeans were a late arrival.
3. Imported to Pennsylvania in 1749, cats were needed to combat the rats.
4. So scarce were cats in the New World that paying a pound of gold for one was not uncommon.
5. As more settlers arrived, the number of cats appeared to increase gradually.

6. Then in the mid-nineteenth century longhair cats began to be seen in Maine.
7. Traveling here aboard Yankee clippers, these belonged to sailors coming from Turkey.
8. These cats tended to interbreed with local cats; the results were cats of the Angora type.
9. Because of their fur markings, these cats were thought to be part racoon and were called Maine Coon cats.
10. The importing of pedigreed cats from Britain began in earnest at the end of the nineteenth century.

SECTION REVIEW EXERCISE I. Identify the *verb* (or *verb phrase*) and the *adverb* in each of the following sentences. If you have trouble, review 1.b and 1.f.

1. Transportation facilities were extended westward in the United States in the early 1800s.
2. After years of debate, construction of the Erie Canal finally began on July 4, 1817.
3. Governor De Witt Clinton of New York opened the Erie Canal officially in 1825.
4. The canal boats were pulled slowly by horses from paths along the banks.
5. Sometimes canal boat passengers walked alongside the boat for a while.
6. The Erie Canal was widely hailed as an engineering triumph of the first degree.
7. Before the railroad era, land transportation could not compete successfully with the cheaper canal transportation.
8. Railroad companies first developed in the United States in the 1820s and 1830s.
9. Early railroads mainly supplemented water transportation.
10. Unfortunately, the first trains proved hazardous to travelers.
11. Sparks from the engine flew backward into the passengers' faces.
12. Railroads and canals soon became bitter rivals in the transportation battle.
13. Unlike canals, railroads could be built anywhere.

14. Eventually, railroads drove the canals out of business.
15. Today many early canals are used for recreational rather than commercial purposes.
16. Since 1900 railroads have been strongly challenged by automobiles and airplanes.
17. Many Americans have never ridden a train.
18. The railroads still carry a large share of the nation's freight.
19. Train travel rose again during the gasoline shortages of the 1970s.
20. Some people have always preferred the unique experience of train travel.

SECTION REVIEW EXERCISE II. Identify the *nouns*, *adjectives*, and *pronouns* in the following sentences. Some of the sentences contain more than one noun, adjective, or pronoun. If you have trouble, review 1.a, 1.c, and 1.d.

1. The cuisine of the United States reflects its broad ethnic diversity.
2. Our cuisine includes the tastiest dishes from a great number of countries.
3. Native American dishes, which include succotash and turkey, could be said to be the original American cuisine.
4. The early settlers who came from England left behind suppers of mutton, cabbage, and puddings.
5. Chicken, cowpeas, and grits is a favorite combination that originated in the South.
6. American cowboys were constantly on the move; they generally ate jerky (made from meat), which they could carry in the saddle with them.
7. Pioneers themselves were always traveling; they dried turkey, quail, and pheasant and ate those.
8. Early Americans picked and preserved plums and blackberries to carry on their journeys.
9. Mexican-American food, which includes burritos and tacos, is spicier than many other ethnic cuisines
10. No one walks away from the tasty gumbo and rice served by the Creoles in Louisiana.
11. German-American cuisine includes sauerkraut and many different kinds of sausage, which are called *wurst*.

12. Although you may consider hamburgers an American food, hamburgers originated in Germany.
13. The richest pastries and most delicate sauces are prepared by French-American chefs.
14. Whoever has eaten Italian-American food loves it.
15. Its combinations of pasta, sauce, and cheese are some of the most popular dishes.
16. The unusual tastes of Chinese-American cuisine interest everybody.
17. This cuisine involves the use of a large frypan called a *wok* to cook food for a short period of time.
18. You will taste ginger and very spicy mustard in Chinese-American dishes.
19. Middle Eastern cuisine is gaining popularity with its tasty mixture of chick peas in Syrian bread.
20. In New York City, famous for its restaurants, one can enjoy a different cuisine from time to time.

SECTION REVIEW EXERCISE III. Identify the *adjectives* and *participles used as adjectives* in the following sentences. Some of the sentences contain more than one adjective or participle. If you have trouble, review 1.c and 1.k.

1. Thousands of Irish immigrants, fleeing famine in their country, came to the United States in the 1840s.
2. Remaining in the Eastern cities, the Irish rapidly improved their economic status.
3. Germans disillusioned by political events immigrated here in large numbers after 1848.
4. Struggling Scandinavian farmers abandoned their rocky soil for the fertile Midwestern prairies.
5. Immigrants came from the Austrian and Russian empires.
6. European countries suffering from overpopulation sent their surplus labor to America.
7. Crowded into urban slums, immigrants often lived in miserable circumstances.
8. Their rented dwellings usually lacked adequate light, ventilation, and space.
9. The conditions seen and photographed by Jacob Riis shocked middle-class people.

10. Riis found some of the poorest immigrants living in filthy cellars.
11. Wooden buildings were common in cities, creating a constant danger of fire.
12. A fire traditionally blamed on a cow destroyed the young city of Chicago in 1871.
13. Unsanitary conditions helped to spread disease in overcrowded slums.
14. Water poisoned by sewage caused deadly epidemics of cholera.
15. Shocked by these conditions, reformers worked to improve the quality of urban life.
16. Reformers enacted laws requiring larger windows and better facilities in tenements.
17. A center called Hull House, established by Jane Addams, aided poor immigrants in Chicago.
18. Newly arrived immigrants, unprepared for cities, often found their new country bewildering.
19. A group of politicians, led by a boss, aided immigrants struggling with unfamiliar problems.
20. A famous poem by Emma Lazarus described the immigrants as "huddled masses yearning to breathe free."

SECTION REVIEW EXERCISE IV. Identify the *nouns* and the *gerunds* in the following sentences. Some of the sentences contain more than one noun or gerund. If you have trouble, review 1.a and 1.m.

1. One of the educational experiences of American settlers was learning the complex Native American languages.
2. Naming states after such tribes as the Delaware, the Illinois, and the Iowa was natural to settlers.
3. Studying Native American languages in the 1600s proved difficult because none had been written down.
4. Careful listening and memorizing were essential to mastering Native American languages.
5. Today, grammar books can help in teaching Dakotah, the language of the Teton Sioux.
6. Teton Sioux is the name of a particular branch of the Plains tribes.
7. Classifying the languages is complicated; there are more than two hundred Native American languages in North America.

8. Communicating by signs was not unusual among Plains tribes.
9. Signaling with smoke or drumbeats also bridged the communications gap between Plains tribes.
10. Translating the Dakotah word for hailstones to English produces "seeds of snow."
11. Naming the sky was simple for the Teton Sioux; *sky* is the same as *cloud.*
12. Identifying the color of the sky was difficult; there is no Dakotah word for blue.
13. Although red, black, yellow, and white are the only colors named in Dakotah, Sioux painting also uses blue and green.
14. The Dakotah believe that expressing the concept of self is a sacred act.
15. One's thinking cannot be expressed by another person; there is no Dakotah expression meaning "you think" – only "I think."
16. Doubting or assuming cannot be expressed in Dakotah; either you know, or you do not know.
17. The idea of freeing a person is unknown to the Dakotah; there is no Dakotah word meaning "free."
18. Feeling sorry or guilty is a concept that cannot be expressed in the language of the Sioux.
19. Traveling is measured not in miles but in the distance a person can walk or ride in a day.
20. Befriending animals is natural to Native Americans; a wolf is called a true dog and a rabbit is called tall ears.

SECTION REVIEW EXERCISE V. Identify the part of speech of each of the italicized words in the sentences below. Each of the italicized words is used in the sentence as an *adverb,* a *preposition,* or a *conjunction.* (Be alert for correlative conjunctions, which come in pairs.) If you have trouble, review 1.f, 1.g, and 1.h.

1. *Before* Europeans settled the New World, Native Americans inhabited *both* North *and* South America.
2. Native American tribes extend *from* Canada *through* Central America *down* to Argentina.
3. *When* European settlers came *over,* they discovered *extremely* talented Native American artists *and* crafts workers.

4. *Yet,* the purposes *of* Native American artwork stretched *beyond* mere artistic expression.
5. Native American arts *and* crafts express *not only* a love *for* color *and* symmetry *but also* a deep spirituality.
6. The Incas, the Aztecs, *and* the Mayas created *elaborately* carved stone sculptures *in* South *and* Central America.
7. *Furthermore,* the Incas, rulers *of* the largest empire *in* the Americas, wrote historical dramas *about* events occurring *before.*
8. The Montana tribe in North America made war bonnets *from* the feathers *of* eagles nesting *above.*
9. *Since* the feathers came *from* a brave *and* powerful bird, the Montanas used them to symbolize bravery.
10. *Either* the Apaches *or* the Navahos were the fiercest warriors *in* North America.
11. The Apaches lived *beside* the peaceful Pueblos, who made sand paintings *before* festival days.
12. *Over* a long period *of* time, the Apaches *periodically* raided the Pueblo tribe *and* fled *in* haste.
13. *Both* the Blackfoot *and* the Mohawk tribes decorated their buckskin clothing *with* colored quills.
14. *Sometimes,* Native Americans adapted dress styles *and* embroidery designs *from* the pioneers who rode *past.*
15. The Hidatsa tribe *of* North Dakota engaged in ritual dances *until* dawn.
16. The Tlingit tribe has been building totem poles *since* its migration *from* northern Russia.
17. Totem poles represent a spirit guarding *either* a family *or* an entire tribe.
18. *Though* wampum (strings *of* tiny shells) was not valuable *to* Europeans, *yet* the Lenape tribe *of* Pennsylvania presented William Penn *with* wampum.
19. Five great Native American tribes were combined *into* the Iroquois nation *under* the Mohawk chief Hiawatha.
20. Henry Wadsworth Longfellow later portrayed this event *in* a long poem.

PARTS OF A SENTENCE

2 Parts of a Sentence

Writing a good sentence is one of the fine accomplishments of being human. To do so takes thought and practice. First of all, you must understand all the essentials of a sentence, remembering that a sentence is more than just a group of words that starts with a capital letter and finishes with an end mark. A sentence is made up of distinct parts that you will have a chance to study in this section. When you better understand the parts of a sentence, you can improve the sentences that you write. In this section you will also see how the parts of speech (see Section 1) may be used in sentences.

We are all accustomed to reading sentences. In writing, remember that your reader expects to see sentences and, therefore, will more easily understand your material if it is presented in sentence form.

DIAGNOSTIC TEST 1

PART A: For each sentence below, write (a) the complete subject, (b) the simple subject, and (c) the complete predicate. Write the sentence parts on separate lines, and label each one correctly.

1. The National Parks system of the United States protects many wilderness areas.
2. Each park is quite different from the other parks.
3. Great Sand Dunes National Monument is one of the most unusual parks.
4. Strong winds have dropped sand in the parks.
5. The highest, longest, and widest sand dunes in the United States are visible in Great Sand Dunes National Monument.

6. Visitors to Yellowstone National Park see evidence of other natural processes.
7. Among the sights in Yellowstone Park are geysers of boiling water.
8. Mammoth Caves National Park offers visitors sights inside the earth.
9. Guides in the caves show hikers narrow passageways and huge stone caverns.
10. Hikers also find brightly colored stone "waterfalls" and lichens near the end of a walk through Mammoth Caves.

PART B: Refer to Sentences 1–10 above. For each sentence, first write the action verb or linking verb. Then write and correctly label any of the following parts of the predicate that the sentence may contain, abbreviating if you wish:

direct object, *d.o.*
indirect object, *i.o.*
predicate nominative, *p.n.*
predicate adjective, *p.a.*

If the sentence contains none of these predicate parts, write *none.*

DIAGNOSTIC TEST 2

For each of the numbered sentences in the paragraph below, write the subordinate clause or clauses. If there is no subordinate clause, write *none.* (You should find a total of ten subordinate clauses.) After each clause, tell what kind of clause it is: *noun clause, adjective clause,* or *adverb clause.*

(1) Most memorable fielding plays in baseball have been spectacular because the fielders caught the balls. (2) Many players have caught balls that seemed impossible to catch. (3) On some occasions hits that were high fly balls appeared at first to be certain home runs. (4) On other occasions what everyone thought would be safe hits were caught by a shortstop or baseplayer. (5) Not all memorable catches have been successful ones, however. (6) Sometimes a ground ball can take an unexpected hop, and the player who tries to catch it must twist and dive for it. (7) One ground ball did what neither the shortstop nor anyone else expected it to do. (8) The shortstop was Eddie Joost, and he was playing with the

Philadelphia Athletics team against the Boston Red Sox in 1948. (9) Billy Goodman hit a ground ball toward Eddie Joost, who got in front of it but could not quite catch it. (10) The ball hit Joost's glove, rolled up his arm, and disappeared into the sleeve of his shirt. (11) Joost looked everywhere for the ball before he realized that it was under his shirt. (12) He unbuttoned his shirt but still could not remove the baseball. (13) At last he simply pulled his shirttails out of his pants, and the stubborn baseball dropped out and rolled away from him. (14) Billy Goodman stood laughing on first base by this time, but Ted Williams, who was the runner on third and could have scored easily, was laughing too hard to run.

2.a THE SENTENCE

A **sentence** is a group of words that expresses a complete thought.

You may also be familiar with the definition that says that a sentence must contain a subject and a predicate. Here are examples of sentences. Each expresses a complete thought, and each contains both a subject and a predicate.

EXAMPLES

Eagles soar.
Our engineers constructed five new bridges last year.
New communities have developed in the Southwest.
Their ideas are quite original.

In the case of command sentences (see 2.c.3), the subject may be omitted but "understood."

EXAMPLES

Soar!
Build new bridges!
Be original.

Therefore, you can safely say that to be a sentence a group of words must have a subject and a predicate.

A group of words with a capital letter and an end mark but without both a subject and a predicate is known as a **sentence fragment**. Sentence fragments are occasionally used in dialogue to capture realistic speech patterns.

2.b SUBJECT AND PREDICATE

Every sentence can be divided into two parts: the **subject** and the **predicate**. The **subject** is the part about which you are speaking or writing. The **predicate** is the part that discusses the subject.

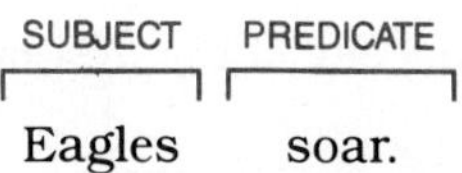

A word or a group of words is a predicate only if it includes an action verb or a linking verb. The action verb or linking verb tells what the subject does or is. The predicate can be a verb alone or a verb plus other words. The verb alone is called a **simple predicate**. The verb plus other words is called a **complete predicate**. The predicate must contain a *verb*—not just a participle or an infinitive.

SUBJECTS	PREDICATES
Eagles	**soar**.
Eagles	**soar gracefully**.
Eagles	**soared over the mountain yesterday**.
Eagles	**will soar**.
Eagles	**are falcons**.
Eagles	**are large.**
Eagles	**are on the mountain**.

The subject answers the question *who?* or *what?* about the predicate.[1]

SUBJECTS	PREDICATES
Eagles	soar.
Two bold eagles	soar.
Hungry-looking eagles	soar.
Eagles on the mountain	soar.

[1]For information about the simple subject, see 2.c.

EXERCISE 1. Indicate whether each of the following numbered items is a complete sentence or a sentence fragment.

1. One of the few truly American sporting events is the rodeo.
2. Professional cowboys and cowgirls who wrestle steers, lasso calves, and ride bucking broncos and bulls.
3. Rodeo competitors – loners and drifters – are symbolic of the pioneers of the Old West.
4. Deer Trail, Colorado, was apparently the site of the first organized rodeo.
5. Formerly one of the most glamorous superstars of the rodeo circuit, Casey Tibbs.
6. Steer wrestlers ride after the steer, leap from the saddle, and bring the animal to the ground – in less than five seconds.
7. One cowboy called broncobusting "just like dancing."
8. Staying seated on a wildly rearing and kicking bronco is no mean feat.
9. Two famous modern-day broncobusters, Sue Pirtle Hayes and Karen Christianson.
10. The rodeo contestants: ten-gallon hats, shiny boots, colorful skirts or chaps, glittering spurs, and bold neckerchiefs.

APPLICATION. Rewrite each item that you labeled *fragment* so that it is a complete sentence.

EXERCISE 2. Indicate where the subject ends and where the predicate begins in each of the following sentences.

1. Dr. Rosalyn Yalow has been head of nuclear medicine at a New York hospital since 1950.
2. She and a research partner developed an important scientific test in 1958.
3. The test detects organic substances, however small in quantity.
4. The medical journals thought this development too minor for publication.
5. The test has been used, however, in almost every branch of medical research.
6. Dr. Yalow received the Nobel Prize in 1977 for her work on this amazing test.
7. One could detect with the test the presence of a teaspoon of sugar in a lake.

8. The test is used most often for measuring the hormones, enzymes, vitamins, or viruses in a human body.
9. It has already provided valuable information about the virus responsible for leukemia.
10. The test may someday determine the chemical differences between a sick body and a healthy body.

2.b.1 The subject and the predicate in inverted sentences

The subject does not always precede the predicate in a sentence. At times a sentence is written in inverted order: predicate first, subject last.

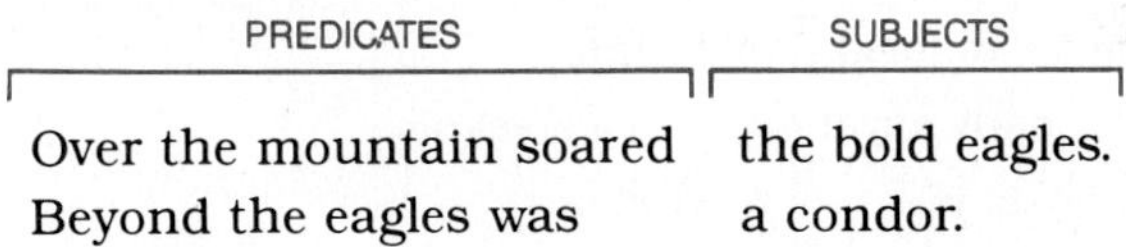

PREDICATES
SUBJECTS
Over the mountain soared
the bold eagles.
Beyond the eagles was
a condor.

In the above sentences the subjects follow the predicates. You can identify the subject by (1) finding the action verb or linking verb and (2) asking *who?* or *what?* before that verb. For example, in the above sentences, who or what *soared?* Who or what *was?*

2.b.2 The subject and the predicate with expletives

The words *there* and *it* are sometimes used as expletives. An **expletive** is a word used to introduce or to fill out a sentence. In sentences with expletives, the subject generally follows the predicate. Very often the expletive is followed by a form of *be.*

PREDICATES	SUBJECTS
There are	bold eagles.
It is necessary	to protect the bird.

Notice that the subject of a sentence is not necessarily a noun. The different kinds of subjects are discussed in detail in 2.c.

EXERCISE 3. Indicate the predicate in each of the following sentences. In some of these sentences, the predicate comes before the subject.

1. America has been the world leader in the production of farm machinery since the last century.
2. There had long been many small farms in the East.
3. It was unnecessary to use heavy machinery.
4. Only large-scale cultivation was profitable in the Midwest, however.
5. Large-scale agriculture demanded machines.
6. John Deere's invention of the steel plow was the first major development in farm implements.
7. There are many advantages to a steel plow.
8. Wet soil clings less to a steel plow.
9. After the steel plow came the invention of the mechanical reaper by McCormick in 1834.
10. There eventually were mechanical harvesters and combine harvesters.

AVOIDING ERRORS WITH PREDICATES

In order to avoid writing sentence fragments, do not use just a participle or an infinitive in your predicate (see 1.j). The predicate of a sentence must have a real verb—a real action verb or a real linking verb. A participle or an infinitive is not enough.

NOT Eagles ~~soaring~~.
BUT Eagles **are soaring**.

NOT Eagles ~~to soar~~.
BUT Eagles **know** how to soar.

2.c THE SIMPLE SUBJECT: AGREEMENT WITH VERB

The **simple subject** is the principal word or words in the subject.

The subject, which answers the question *who?* or *what?* about the predicate, is often made up of a *group* of words. In such a case, the group of words is called the **complete subject** and the most important word or words is called the **simple subject**.

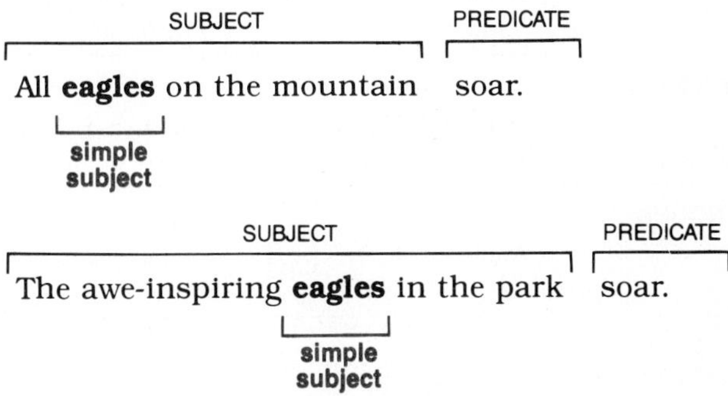

Notice that in both cases above, the complete subject contains a prepositional phrase—*on the mountain, in the park*. You must remember that the simple subject is *never* within the prepositional phrase. In both sentences the simple subject is *eagles*. (You can read more about prepositional phrases in 1.g.1 and in 2.h.)

The simple subject by itself can answer the question *who?* or *what?* before the action verb or the linking verb. The simple subject can be a noun (or a compound noun), a proper noun, a pronoun, a gerund, or an infinitive.

Here are additional examples of complete subjects and simple subjects. The complete subject is in italics. The simple subject is in bold type.

EXAMPLES

The ***East River*** *in New York City* was once home to eagles.

Benjamin Franklin *of Philadelphia* suggested the turkey for the national symbol.

You should be able to recognize simple subjects even when they have other words around them, as in the examples above. *The main reason for wanting to recognize the simple subject is so that you can make the action verb or linking verb agree in number with it. If the simple subject is singular, you must use one form of a present-tense verb; if the simple subject is plural, you must use another form.*

The following chart will help you review the various kinds of words that can be simple subjects.

KINDS OF SIMPLE SUBJECTS

	SUBJECT	***PREDICATE***
COMMON NOUNS		
Singular	The eagle	soar**s**.
Plural	The eagle**s**	soar.
PROPER NOUNS		
Singular	Wallenda	soar**s**.
Plural	The Wallenda**s**	soar.
COMPOUND NOUNS		
Singular	The jet plane	soar**s**.
Plural	Jet plane**s**	soar.
PERSONAL PRONOUNS		
Singular	I	scream.
	You	scream.
	He	scream**s**.
	She	scream**s**.
	It	scream**s**.
Plural	We	scream.
	You	scream.
	They	scream.
POSSESSIVE PRONOUNS		
Singular	My plane	soar**s**.
	Mine	soar**s**.
Plural	My plane**s**	soar.
	Mine	soar.
DEMONSTRATIVE PRONOUNS		
Singular	This	soar**s**.
	That	soar**s**.
Plural	These	soar.
	Those	soar.

KINDS OF SIMPLE SUBJECTS

	SUBJECT	PREDICATE
INDEFINITE PRONOUNS		
Singular	Another	work**s**.
	Anybody	work**s**.
	Anyone	work**s**.
	Anything	work**s**.
	Each	work**s**.
	Either	work**s**.
	Everybody	work**s**.
	Everyone	work**s**.
	Everything	work**s**.
	Neither	work**s**.
	Nobody	work**s**.
	No one	work**s**.
	Nothing	work**s**.
	One[1]	work**s**.
	Somebody	work**s**.
	Someone	work**s**.
	Something	work**s**.
Plural	Both	work.
	Few	work.
	Many	work.
	Several	work.

Singular or Plural

The indefinite pronouns below can be considered singular or plural, depending on what they refer to. The verb must *agree in number* with the subject.[1]

	SUBJECT	PREDICATE
all	S: All (of the water)	evaporate**s**.
	P: All (of the eagle**s**)	soar.
any	S: Any (of the trouble)	upset**s** me.
	P: Any (of the eagle**s**)	soar.
more	S: More (of the plant life)	grow**s** there.
	P: More (of the eagle**s**)	soar.
most	S: Most (of the plant life)	die**s** there.
	P: Most (of the glider**s**)	soar.
none	S: None (of the plant life)	grow**s** there.
	P: None (of the glider**s**)	soar.
some	S: Some (of the plant life)	die**s**.
	P: Some (of the glider**s**)	soar.

INFINITIVES AND GERUNDS		
Singular	To soar	is fun.
	Soaring	is fun.

[1]See 2.r.2 for more advice on subject-verb agreement in sentences such as ***One*** *of those eagles soar**s**.*

AVOIDING ERRORS WITH SUBJECTS AND PREPOSITIONAL PHRASES

Remember that the simple subject is never *within* a prepositional phrase. The action verb or linking verb must agree with the simple subject of the sentence, *not* with the object of the preposition.

NOT The **price** of the houses ~~amaze~~ us.
BUT The **price** of the houses amaze**s** us.

NOT The **designs** for the new house ~~is~~ attractive.
BUT The **designs** for the new house **are** attractive.

EXERCISE 4. In each of the following sentences, first identify the complete subject and then note the simple subject.

EXAMPLE The writer named Mark Twain used his own life as material for his writing.

ANSWER *The writer named Mark Twain; writer*

1. The characters in *The Adventures of Tom Sawyer* and *The Adventures of Huckleberry Finn* were based on real people.
2. Tom's Aunt Polly was modeled on Mark Twain's own mother.
3. The model for Huck Finn was Tom Blankenship, Mark Twain's best friend in Hannibal.
4. The town of Hannibal, Missouri, was Mark Twain's home.
5. This little town on the Mississippi has a Tom Sawyer festival every July.
6. The funniest event of the festival is the fence-painting contest.
7. Children between the ages of ten and thirteen may enter this contest.
8. Each contestant must have a costume, a frog, and a weed to chew.
9. The whitewashing of the fence is a frantic affair with paint splashing everywhere.
10. The contestants are judged on their costumes and on the speed and quality of their work.

2.c.1 Subject-verb agreement in "there sentences"

In a sentence that begins with *there* or *here*, you must clearly identify the simple subject before choosing the action verb or the linking verb for the sentence. The verb must agree in number with the simple subject.

EXAMPLES

There **is** an eagle on the mountain. [The simple subject, *eagle*, is singular; the linking verb agrees.]

There **are** eagles on the mountain. [The subject, *eagles*, is plural; the linking verb agrees.]

Here **goes** the last match. [The simple subject, *match*, is singular; the action verb agrees.]

Here **go** all the matches. [The simple subject, *matches*, is plural; the action verb agrees.]

EXERCISE 5. In each of the following sentences, first identify the complete subject and then note the simple subject. In some of the sentences, part of the predicate comes before the subject.

EXAMPLE Art in early America was in some ways unique.
ANSWER *Art in early America/Art*

1. There were many traveling artisans in colonial America in the seventeenth century.
2. These skilled crafts workers included candlemakers, blacksmiths, and painters.
3. Some of the painters decorated shop signs, coaches, and household items.
4. Painters of this kind would occasionally undertake a portrait.
5. There were not any painters of the traditional European school in the colonies.
6. All of the artisan-painters of the seventeenth and eighteenth centuries were self-taught.
7. These painters were called limners, or liners.
8. Most of them remain anonymous.
9. One painter by the name of Thomas Smith is an exception.
10. There was artistic balance in the limners' paintings.

11. Many of their subjects appear stiff and two-dimensional, however.
12. People of today do not consider the people on those canvases realistically portrayed.
13. There is nothing informal or even frolicsome about the worthy citizens.
14. Their bearing shows Puritan steadiness.
15. To act playful was, presumably, frivolous and sinful.
16. To appear frivolous was to be avoided at all costs.
17. There are some family portraits by limners.
18. All of the family members look sober and serious.
19. Everyone in these families stares out solemnly.
20. There are relatively few of these group portraits in public collections.

2.c.2 Subject-verb agreement with special subjects

Some subjects require additional attention when you select an action verb or a linking verb to go with them. The following chart will help you to see that most of these special subjects are third-person singular and, therefore, generally require a verb that ends in *s*.

SUBJECT-VERB AGREEMENT

collective nouns

When the noun refers to a group as a whole, its meaning is singular. When the noun refers to each member of a group individually, its meaning is plural. (See also 1.a.3.)

	SUBJECT	PREDICATE
singular	The squadron of planes	soar**s**.
	The crowd	cheer**s**.
	The New York Yankees	is a fine team.
plural	The squadron of planes	protect one another.
	The crowd	fight for seats.
	The New York Yankees	are in their uniforms.

special nouns

See 1.a.3 for further discussion.

	SUBJECT	PREDICATE
singular	Measles	is a disease.
plural	The scissors	were defective.
singular or plural	Politics	is boring. [singular]
	His politics	are unconscionable. [plural]

nouns of amount

When the noun refers to one unit, it is singular. When the noun refers to a number of individual units, it is plural.

	SUBJECT	PREDICATE
singular	Five dollars	is a fair price.
plural	Five dollars	are on the table.

titles

A title is always considered singular, even if a noun within the title is plural.

	SUBJECT	PREDICATE
singular	*The Adventures of Huckleberry Finn*	delight**s** readers of all ages.

the number, a number

	SUBJECT	PREDICATE
singular	The number of guests	is astounding.
plural	A number of guests	are late.

EXERCISE 6. Select the appropriate form of the action verb or the linking verb in parentheses in each of the following sentences.

1. Visiting amusement parks (is/are) a popular American pastime.
2. That (explains/explain) why, in 1976, over 13 million people went to Walt Disney World in Florida.

3. Three other famous parks (is/are) Coney Island in New York, Astroworld in Houston, and Hershey Park in Pennsylvania.
4. Each of these parks (has/have) a famous roller coaster.
5. Astroworld's roller coaster (bears/bear) the name Texas Cyclone.
6. One newspaper (calls/call) the Texas Cyclone the "ultimate roller coaster."
7. Pittsburgh's magnificent Thunderbolt (runs/run) through a real valley.
8. The roller coaster at Hershey Park (overlooks/overlook) the Hershey chocolate factory.
9. Everything in Hershey Park (has/have) the odor of chocolate.
10. Nothing (equals/equal) the curves and tunnels of Denver's Mister Twister.
11. There (is/are) many thrills on this kind of roller coaster.
12. Designing roller coasters (is/are) hard work.
13. For a view of the big drop ahead, cars (decreases/decrease) speed while climbing the first peak.
14. Everyone in these cars then (expects/expect) excitement and fear from the ride.
15. Each of the riders (dreads/dread) the inevitable descent.
16. Most of the fears (comes/come) not merely from the speed but from the rapid acceleration of the ride.
17. On roller coasters each car (accelerates/accelerate) from 5 mph to 60 mph within seconds.
18. To scream from sudden fear (is/are) almost involuntary.
19. There (is/are) reasons for people to avoid big roller coasters.
20. Thanks to each coaster's safety equipment, however, ours (is/are) mostly imagined dangers.

EXERCISE 7. Select the appropriate form of the action verb or the linking verb in parentheses in each of the following sentences.

1. Politics (is/are) defined as the science or the art of government.
2. Politics (is/are) also the political opinions or sympathies of a person.
3. The politics of America's founders (remains/remain) ingrained in our history.

4. The United States of America (has had/have had) two constitutions.
5. The original constitution (was/were) a document called the Articles of Confederation.
6. The Articles of Confederation (outlines/outline) the rights of the original thirteen colonies.
7. Ethics (is/are) a social science dealing with moral values.
8. A person's ethics (is/are) his or her moral standards.
9. Thomas Jefferson's writings (reveals/reveal) his ethical opposition to slavery.
10. His first draft of the Declaration of Independence (includes/include) a condemnation of slavery.
11. One of the virtues of the Declaration of Independence (is/are) its brevity.
12. The number of its faults (is/are) small.
13. A number of public documents (is/are) somewhat ambiguous, however.
14. Many varying points of view in America (is/are) accommodated in the Constitution.
15. According to the Constitution, each representative (serves/serve) a two-year term.
16. Six years (is/are) the term of office for each member of the Senate.
17. The Bill of Rights (contains/contain) the first ten amendments to the Constitution.
18. This group of amendments (guarantees/guarantee) the rights of the individual.
19. A number of later amendments (concerns/concern) voting.
20. The Twenty-sixth Amendment (lowers/lower) the minimum voting age to eighteen.

2.c.3 Subject-verb agreement in commands and questions

A **statement sentence** always has a subject and a verb. In general, the subject precedes the verb. With a third-person subject in the present tense, the subject and the verb must agree. (The term **declarative sentence** is also used.)

STATEMENT SENTENCE

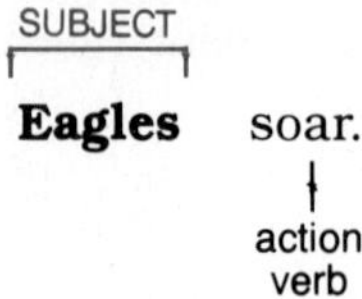

A **command sentence** (also called an **imperative sentence**) is one in which the subject is always "understood" to be *you*. You use the same form of the action verb or the linking verb whether you are talking to one or to more than one subject.

COMMAND SENTENCE

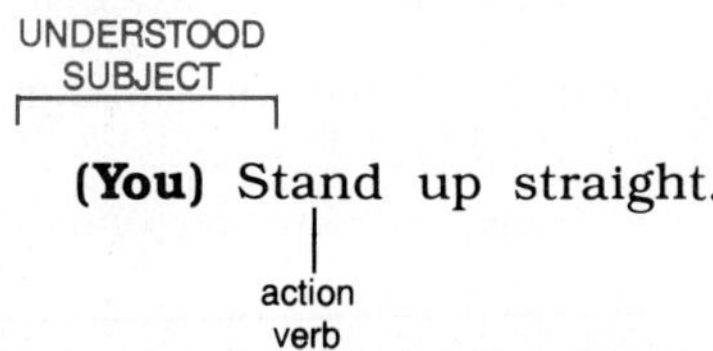

A **question sentence** (also known as an **interrogative sentence**) is one that asks a question. In a question sentence, the subject generally comes *after* a modal, a linking verb, or an auxiliary. The subject and the modal *do* (see 1.b.10), the linking verb, or the auxiliary *be* or *have* must always agree.

QUESTION SENTENCE

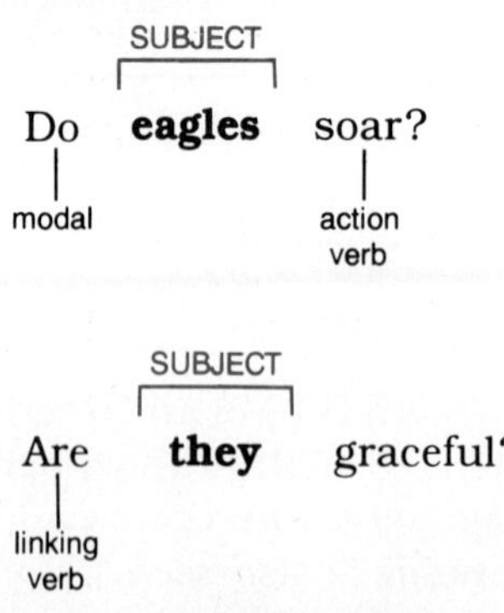

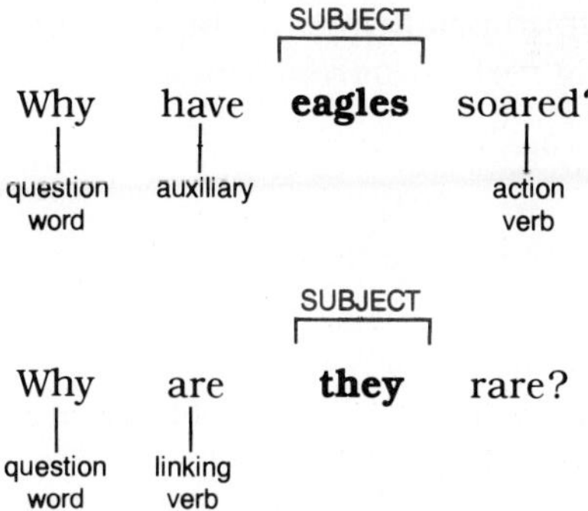

A **tag question** (also known as an **echo question**) can be added to a statement sentence to make the statement into a question. The subject and the modal in the tag question must agree. The tag question is preceded by a comma and is followed by a question mark.

TAG QUESTION

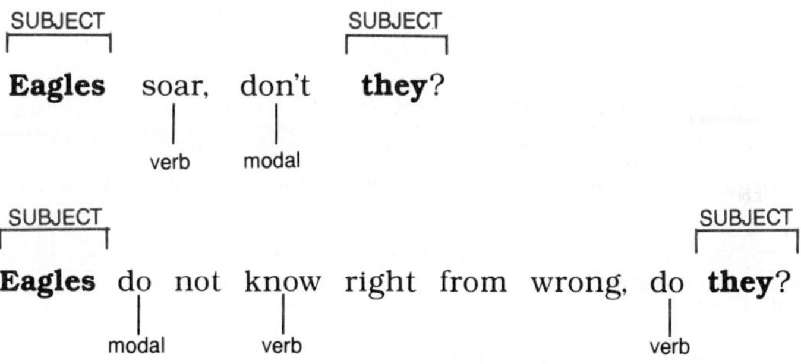

An **indirect question** is actually a statement sentence. An indirect question often has two separate subjects, each with its own verb, as the following example illustrates. Each verb must agree with its subject.

INDIRECT QUESTION

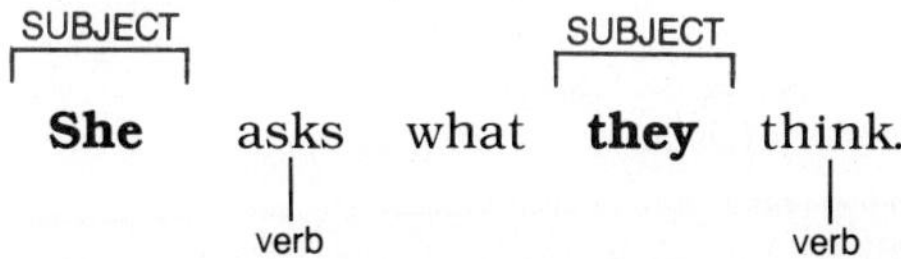

EXERCISE 8. Select the appropriate form of the auxiliary, modal, action verb, or linking verb in parentheses.

1. Tigers have antlers, (doesn't/don't) they?
2. A whale is a pink fish, (isn't/aren't) it?
3. (Doesn't/Don't) dogs chase police officers?
4. (Does/Do) cats eat fish?
5. Birds don't lay eggs, (does/do) they?
6. (Isn't/Aren't) lions cowardly?
7. Snakes have lovely fur, (does/do) they not?
8. The mouse is a crustacean, (isn't/aren't) it?
9. (Does/Do) wolves eat hay?
10. Elks don't grow horns, (does/do) they?
11. Pollen kills bees, (does/do) it not?
12. (Is/Are) honey the bear's favorite food?
13. The elephant has no memory, (does/do) it?
14. (Doesn't/Don't) robins catch worms?
15. (Is/Are) the unicorn found in Central Park?
16. The rhinoceros has two horns, (doesn't/don't) it?
17. Dolphins don't like to get wet, (does/do) they?
18. (Does/Do) the walrus like to sing?
19. (Doesn't/Don't) parrots fly south every winter?
20. Monkeys are allergic to bananas, (isn't/aren't) they?

APPLICATION. Rewrite each question, making singular subjects plural and making plural subjects singular.

2.d COMPOUND SUBJECTS

A **compound subject** is made up of two or more subjects that are joined by a conjunction and that have the same verb.

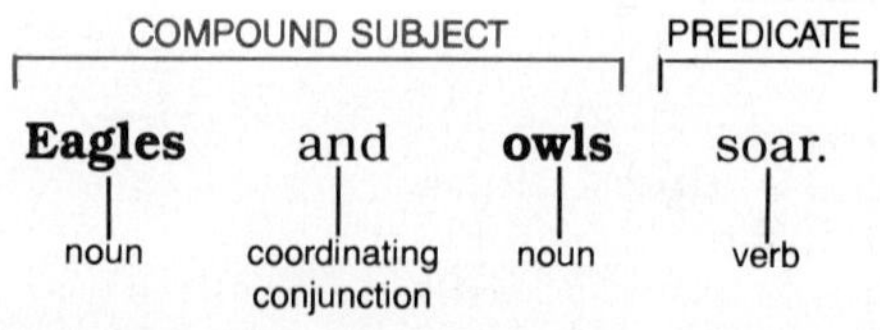

Usually, the parts of the compound subject are joined by a coordinating conjunction (*and* or *or*) or by a correlative conjunction (for example, *not only...but also, either...or, neither...nor*).

COMPOUND SUBJECTS

Common nouns

Eagles, **owls**, and **geese** are soaring.

Proper nouns

Smith and **Yang** are soaring in their jet.

Personal pronouns

He and **she** are soaring in their glider.

Possessive pronouns

Mine and **yours** are soaring in the wind.

Demonstrative pronouns

This and **that** are soaring.

Indefinite pronouns

All of the eagles and **all** of the owls are soaring.

Infinitives and Gerunds

To soar and **to glide** are fun.
Soaring and **gliding** are fun.

COMMAS WITH COMPOUND SUBJECTS

When a compound subject consists of three or more words, use a comma after each word in the series – except the last.

Eagles**,** owls**,** and geese soar.
Reading**,** writing**,** and studying take time.

Do not use commas if you use the word *and* or *or* between each part of the compound subject. (See also 7.g.6.)

Eagles and owls and geese soar.

EXERCISE 9. Identify the compound subject in each of the following sentences. The subject may be made up of nouns, pronouns, gerunds, or infinitives.

EXAMPLE Cars and musical instruments age differently.
ANSWER *cars (and) instruments*

1. Upon leaving the showroom, cars and motorcycles lose a third of their value.
2. Increasing years and mileage further reduce their resale price.
3. Your first car and your friends' first cars may be secondhand and, therefore, inexpensive.
4. Later, your job, your savings, or your credit may allow you to buy a new car.
5. Age and use do not reduce the market value of all articles.
6. Most of our art objects and many of our musical instruments increase in value with age.
7. The first violin or the first painting that you buy is likely to increase in value.
8. Not only this but also other factors make art a good investment.
9. Good paintings and sculpture become more valuable, but not actually better.
10. Most violins, violas, and cellos do actually improve with use and age.
11. Eventually, yours and mine will achieve a richer tone.
12. Not only many professionals but also some wealthy amateurs play very old instruments.
13. Many violins and other string instruments were made in Italy.
14. Stradivari and Guarneri were the world's most prestigious violin makers.
15. To play a Stradivarius and to own one are two dreams of many young violinists.
16. By the mid-nineteenth century Philadelphia and Boston had good violin makers.
17. Boston's Ira White and Asa White made many violins still in use today.
18. By 1900 the tone and the workmanship of American violins made them comparable to European violins.

19. Acquiring and refining skills in violin making are the goals of students at schools in Chicago and in Salt Lake City.
20. These students and even many musicians make very high quality instruments.

2.e SUBJECT-VERB AGREEMENT WITH COMPOUND SUBJECTS

With some compound subjects you must pay attention to the conjunction that joins the parts and to the meaning of the subject. Only then can you know which verb form to use with that subject.

The following chart shows examples of *agreement in number* between action verbs or linking verbs and compound subjects.

AGREEMENT OF VERBS AND COMPOUND SUBJECTS

and

Usually, compound subjects joined by *and* are considered plural. When the parts of the compound subject are actually parts of one unit or when they refer to the same person or thing, the subject is considered singular.

	SUBJECT	PREDICATE
plural	The eagle **and** the owl	soar.
	Sailing **and** swimming	are fun.
singular	Ham **and** eggs	cost**s** two dollars.
	Sitting **and** waiting	is boring.
	Her friend **and** teacher [One person is both the friend and the teacher.]	help**s**.

or, nor

With compound subjects joined by *or* or *nor*, always look at the subject nearer the verb. The verb must agree in number with that subject.

	SUBJECT	PREDICATE
plural	The eagle **or** the owls	soar.
	Neither the eagle **nor** the owls	soar.
singular	The eagle **or** the owl	soar**s**.
	Neither the eagle **nor** the owl	soar**s**.
	The eagles **or** the owl	soar**s**.

EXERCISE 10. Select the appropriate form of the action verb, linking verb, or auxiliary in parentheses in each of the following sentences.

1. October and Central Park (means/mean) the New York Marathon.
2. As the 1978 marathon approaches, 11,400 men and women (plans/plan) to run through New York City.
3. A police captain and three people with paint and paintbrushes (notices/notice) one another in the street.
4. Either marathon officials or three mischief-makers (is/are) painting an alternate route line and a new sign.
5. Neither the radio broadcast nor the television coverage (has/have) mentioned this detour.
6. Either a last-minute change or something illegal (is/are) taking place.
7. Neither the new sign nor the altered blue lines (points/point) the runners in the right direction.
8. Either the East River's bank or its muddy waters (is/are) at the end of the detour.
9. Neither these two men nor this woman (is/are) aware that the police officer is watching.
10. Criminal mischief and tampering with traffic control (is/are) their misdemeanors.
11. Over 11,000 runners and 2 million spectators (is/are) on the streets.
12. Neither the marathon organizers nor the city (has/have) expected such crowds.
13. Every state in the United States and many foreign countries (is/are) represented by runners.
14. New York with 5,467 entrants, New Jersey with 1,330, and Massachusetts with 855 (is/are) the most heavily represented.
15. Among foreign countries, Canada with 268 entrants and the United Kingdom with 77 entrants (is/are) foremost.
16. The men's title and the women's title (goes/go) to Bill Rodgers, a Bostonian who won twice before, and to Grete Waitz, a teacher from Norway.
17. The Boston runner and three-time New York winner also (holds/hold) other marathon titles.
18. Schoolteacher and champion Waitz (is/are) impressive.

19. At the finish line the first few men and every woman (receives/receive) tremendous cheers.
20. Either a winner or a runner-up (is/are) quoted as saying, "We ran through a tunncl of cheers."

2.f SUBJECT–VERB AGREEMENT WITH INTERVENING EXPRESSIONS

If a subject is linked with another word by an expression such as those listed below, the subject is still considered singular. These "intervening" expressions do not make compound subjects. They can be considered interrupters and do not affect the number of the subject.

EXPRESSIONS NOT AFFECTING NUMBER OF SUBJECT

accompanied by	in addition to	together with
as well as	plus	

The following are some examples of subjects with conjunctions and of subjects with intervening expressions. Notice the verb that follows each one.

EXAMPLES

Two **and** two *make* four. [conjunction]
Two **plus** two *makes* four. [interrupter]

The father **and** his daughter *are* arriving. [conjunction]
The father **as well as** his daughter *is* arriving. [interrupter]

If **many a** or **every** precedes a compound subject, the subject is considered singular.

EXAMPLES

Many a man, woman, and child *knows* hunger.
Every eagle, owl, and parrot *scares* me.

REVIEW EXERCISE A. Select the appropriate form of the action verb or linking verb in parentheses.

1. In the city many a worker and shopper (makes/make) use of public transportation.

2. Every city resident and every commuter (knows/know) about public transportation.
3. The bus as well as the subway (is/are) used frequently by many people.
4. Washington, San Francisco, and Philadelphia (has/have) subway systems.
5. Possibly, neither you nor anyone else (thinks/think) of elevators as public transportation.
6. Yet people and their belongings (rides/ride) elevators as often as trains and buses.
7. For some people horizontal transportation and vertical transportation (is/are) both essential.
8. To live or to work in a high-rise building without an elevator (is/are) unthinkable.
9. Energy plus endurance (helps/help) some people – but not most – to walk.
10. Huffing and puffing up a stairway to the twentieth floor (does/do) not appeal to most people.
11. A staircase as well as an elevator (is/are) always necessary, however.
12. The average passenger elevator or service lift (travels/travel) about 10,000 miles a year.
13. All passenger elevators and freight elevators (moves/move) by either hydraulic power or traction.
14. Compressed oil or water (pushes/push) the hydraulic elevator.
15. Its installation and mechanism (requires/require) a hole in the ground as deep as the building is high.
16. Pulleys and cables (hauls/haul) up traction elevators in these installations.
17. Their steel ropes and cables (has/have) to support eight times the elevator's weight.
18. Some warehouses and docks (has/have) elevators that transport loaded trucks.
19. Many a passenger and operator (is/are) somewhat afraid of elevators.
20. Actually, an elevator's "trip switch" in addition to its safety brake (makes/make) the elevator the safest form of public transportation.

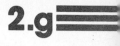

2.g COMPOUND VERBS

A **compound verb** is made up of two or more verbs that are joined by a conjunction and that have the same subject.

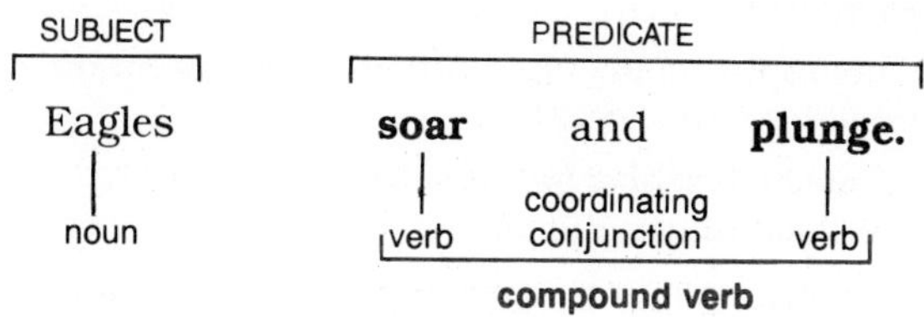

EXAMPLES

Sandy **will mail** the letter and **hurry** home.
Everyone **stood** and **sang**.
Our friends **arrived** depressed and **left** happy.
We have **lost**, or at least **misplaced**, the map.

More than two action verbs can be used to form a series.

EXAMPLES

Sandy **will buy** a stamp, **mail** the letter, and **hurry** home.
Everyone **applauded** loudly, **stood**, and **cheered**.
Our friends **arrived** depressed, **talked** endlessly, and **left** happy.

It is also possible to use two or more linking verbs in a predicate.

EXAMPLES

Harry **is** and **has been** a cheerleader for some time.
Our country **has been**, now **is**, and always **will be** free.
Linda either **is** here already or **will be** here momentarily.

EXERCISE 11. Identify the compound verb in each of the following sentences.

1. The following list of sports oddities will surprise athletes and perplex sports fans but amuse readers.
2. Land crabs sometimes grab golf balls and scamper to their holes.
3. Dogs often bury golf balls or swallow them.

4. During an extra-point kick in one football game, the ball exploded and split in half.
5. The ball hung in shreds but cleared the crossbar.
6. The fans neither believed their eyes nor accepted the score.
7. Notre Dame football players either practice ballet or shadowbox with each other.
8. According to Knute Rockne, both activities maintain strength and develop grace.
9. During one high school basketball game four of the five players fouled and sat on the bench.
10. The remaining player not only scored three points but also won the game.

APPLICATION. Reread each sentence that has a direct object. Rewrite each of those sentences, making the direct object the subject of the sentence. Your new sentences will be in the passive voice (see 1.b.20).

REVIEW EXERCISE B. Indicate whether the subject is compound and whether the verb is compound in each of the following sentences. Three sentences have no compounds.

1. Neither football nor tennis originated in the United States.
2. The ancestor of football, called "Dane's Head," was first played in the early Middle Ages in Europe.
3. The game of "Dane's Head" began halfway between two neighboring villages.
4. Each team maneuvered and kicked a ball toward the other team's village.
5. Soon towns and villages were neglecting archery practice and were playing football instead.
6. The government therefore issued a ban on football and maintained it until the seventeenth century.
7. By then, neither archery practice nor archery itself was necessary for the country's defense.
8. In football's early development, players could kick but could not throw the ball.
9. Throwing the ball and carrying it later became part of Rugby football.
10. This ancestor of American football was first played in 1823 in Rugby, England.

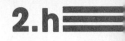

2.h PREPOSITIONAL PHRASES

A **prepositional phrase** is a group of words that begins with a preposition and usually ends with a noun or pronoun.

A prepositional phrase can occur in any part of a sentence. In general, a prepositional phrase tells more about a noun (as an adjective does), tells *where, when,* or *how* an action takes place (as an adverb does), or tells *where* or *when* a condition exists. A prepositional phrase may itself even be the subject of a sentence. The subject of a sentence, however, can never occur *within* a prepositional phrase. Notice that in the first example sentence below, the simple subject, *eagles,* is not within the prepositional phrase, *near the coast.* Rather, the prepositional phrase is actually part of the complete subject. (See also page 139.)

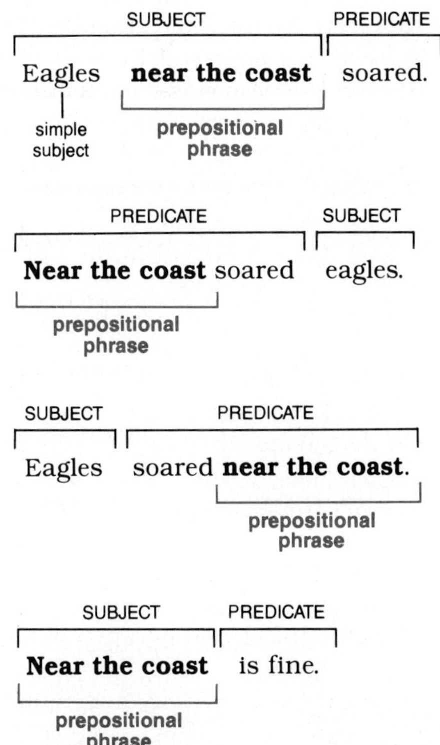

REVIEW EXERCISE C. Follow the directions or answer the question in parentheses at the end of each of the following items.

1. (Does/Do) ethnic music interest you? (Select the appropriate form of *do*.)
2. Every person (enjoys/enjoy) listening to a tuneful melody or a catchy rhythm. (Select the appropriate form of the verb.)
3. There are rich melodies and swaying rhythms in Latin American music. (What is the complete predicate of the sentence?)
4. Latin American music, an interesting blend of Spanish, Indian, and Caribbean tunes and rhythms. (How can you make the sentence fragment a complete sentence? Write the complete sentence.)
5. The exciting dance rhythms of the Caribbean are influenced by African music. (What is the complete subject of this sentence? What is the simple subject?)
6. Singing as well as dancing to Latin American music (is/are) an exciting experience. (Select the appropriate form of the linking verb.)
7. To preserve traditional Latin American music and to entertain modern audiences are the aims of Angel Sanabria and Pablo Vincente Morel. (What is the compound subject?)
8. Morel plays the harp and sings. (What is the compound verb of the sentence?)
9. Sanabria as well as Morel (belongs/belong) to the Chirigua tribe. (Select the appropriate form of the verb.)
10. Singing and playing the guitar, two of Sanabria's talents. (How can you make the sentence fragment a complete sentence? Write the complete sentence.)
11. Harmonics (is/are) essential to Latin American music. (Select the appropriate form of the linking verb.)
12. Either a traditional orchestra instrument or an exotic regional instrument (is/are) used in Latin American music. (Select the appropriate form of the linking verb.)
13. The regional instruments include *claves*, *timbales*, and the *marimba*. (What is the complete predicate of this sentence?)
14. Many a large drum (called a *timbale*) (provides/provide) a steady rhythm. (Select the appropriate form of the verb.)
15. *Claves*, or two wooden sticks, are struck together and used as a rhythmic accompaniment. (What is the compound verb?)

16. Playing the *marimba*, which is like playing a xylophone. (How can you make the sentence fragment a complete sentence? Write the complete sentence.)
17. A large guitar called a *guitarrón* is popular. (What is the complete subject of the sentence? What is the simple subject?)
18. There are many popular Latin American tunes. (What is the complete predicate of this sentence?)
19. "El Condor Pasa" (is/are) a traditional Latin American song sung by North American singer Paul Simon. (Select the appropriate form of the linking verb.)
20. One of the more recent Latin American singing groups (is/are) the rock group Santana. (Select the appropriate form of the linking verb.)

2.i OTHER PARTS OF THE PREDICATE

You know that a sentence must have a subject (sometimes "understood") and a predicate. You also know that a predicate must contain an action verb or a linking verb. By now you have probably noticed that many sentences have more than just a single or a compound verb in the predicate. The following items (2.j–2.m) will discuss the other elements that a predicate may contain.

2.j DIRECT OBJECTS

The **direct object** answers the question *what?* or *whom?* after a subject and an action verb.

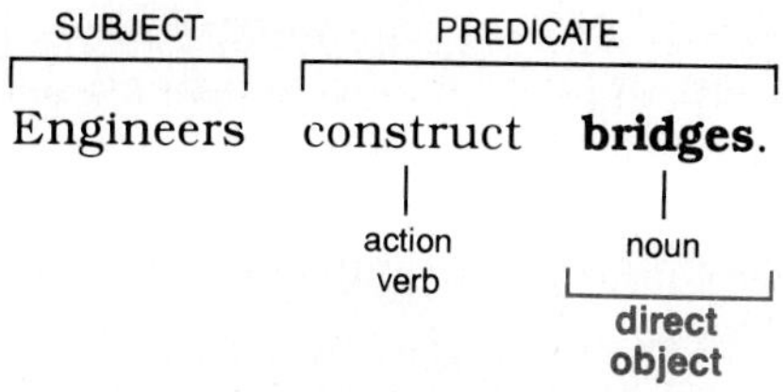

In the above sentence the noun *engineers* is the subject of the sentence. The noun *bridges* is the direct object of the verb *construct.* Direct objects, of course, can be modified by adjectives, determiners, and prepositional phrases, as the following examples show.

EXAMPLES

Engineers build safe **bridges**.
Engineers study many **plans**.
Engineers built a new **bridge** across the bay.

Various parts of speech can be used as direct objects just as various parts of speech can be used as subjects (see 2.c). A direct object can be a noun, a pronoun, a gerund, an infinitive, or a clause (see 2.n). A sentence can have more than one direct object.

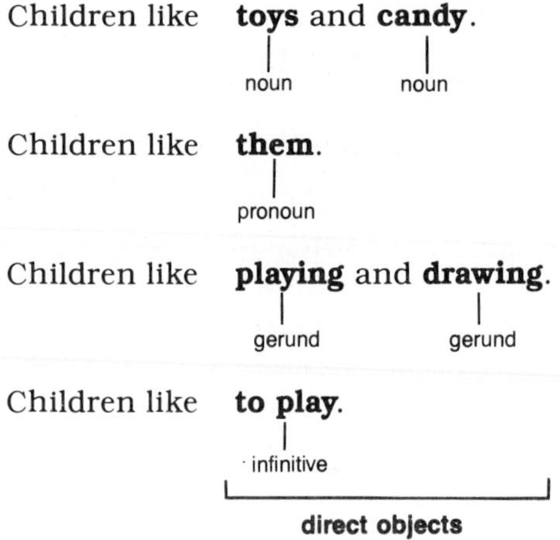

Notice the second sentence: A personal pronoun that is a direct object is in the objective case (see 1.d.1).[1]

Remember that to be a direct object a word or expression must answer the question *what?* or *whom?* after a subject and an action verb. If a word or expression answers instead the question *why?* or *how?* or *where?*, it is not a direct object. Look at the following four examples. Only the first sentence has a direct object.

[1] Notice the following exception: "They want **mine** (**hers**, **theirs**, **yours**)"; that is, "They want *my toy* (*her toy, their toy, your toy*)."

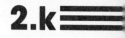

EXAMPLES

Engineers build **bridges**. [Engineers build *what?* Here, *bridges* is a direct object.]

Engineers build **to survive**. [Engineers build *why?* There is no direct object here.]

Engineers build **carefully**. [Engineers build *how?* There is no direct object here.]

Engineers build **everywhere**. [Engineers build *where?* There is no object here.]

EXERCISE 12. Indicate which of the following sentences contain a direct object. Identify each direct object.

1. English immigrants founded a little town in North Dakota in 1885.
2. They named it Rugby, after their home town in England.
3. The American town never managed to grow much.
4. Even today, fewer than three thousand people live there.
5. Nevertheless, Rugby, North Dakota, has a unique importance.
6. It lies in the exact center of the North American continent.
7. From Rugby, you can make a trip of 1,500 miles to the north, south, east, or west.
8. In Rugby, and elsewhere in North Dakota, most people enjoy working on farms.
9. You will find very little industry in North Dakota.
10. North Dakotans call their state the Sioux State.

2.k INDIRECT OBJECTS

An **indirect object** answers the question *to whom?* or *for whom?* or *to what?* or *for what?* after an action verb.

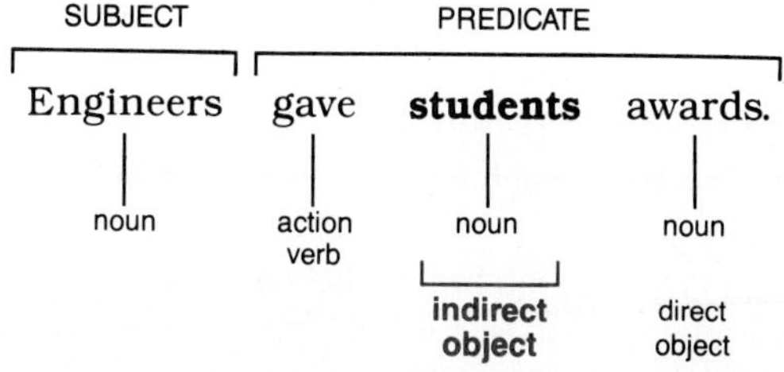

In the above sentence the noun *engineers* is the subject, and the noun *awards* is the direct object of the verb *gave*. The noun *students* is the indirect object. It tells *to whom* the engineers gave awards. An **indirect object** can be a noun, a pronoun, or a gerund. Remember that a sentence can have an indirect object only if it has a direct object and that the indirect object always goes before the direct object. A sentence may have more than one indirect object.

EXAMPLES

Engineers gave **students** awards.
Engineers gave **them** awards.
Students gave **engineering** consideration.

An indirect object *never* occurs within a prepositional phrase.

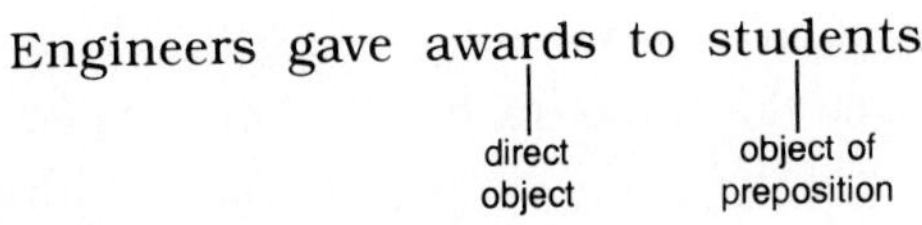

EXERCISE 13. Identify all the direct objects and indirect objects in the following sentences.

1. Winchester House guarantees San Jose, California, a mention in any guidebook.
2. Sarah Winchester never finished the costly monstrosity.
3. In 1881 her husband left her a bequest of 20 million dollars.
4. The source of the Winchester money caused Sarah great anxiety.
5. The famous Winchester rifle brought the family a fortune.
6. Sarah feared vengeance from victims of Winchester guns.
7. On the advice of a psychic medium, she built the family an enormous and wondrous house.
8. The house has 158 rooms, 10,000 windows, 2,000 doors, and 40 staircases.
9. According to the medium, such a house would attract friendly and protective ghosts.
10. In 1973 California granted this house the status of a historical landmark.

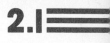

2.1 SUBJECT COMPLEMENTS

A **subject complement**, or completer, follows a subject and a linking verb and identifies or describes the subject.

A linking verb almost always needs one or more additional words after it in the predicate. After all, a linking verb *links* a subject to something else. The "something else" is the subject complement. There are three kinds of subject complements: predicate nominatives (2.1.1), predicate adjectives (2.1.2), and predicate adverbs (2.1.3).

2.1.1 Predicate nominatives

A **predicate nominative** is a noun or pronoun that follows a linking verb and that points back to the subject and further identifies it.

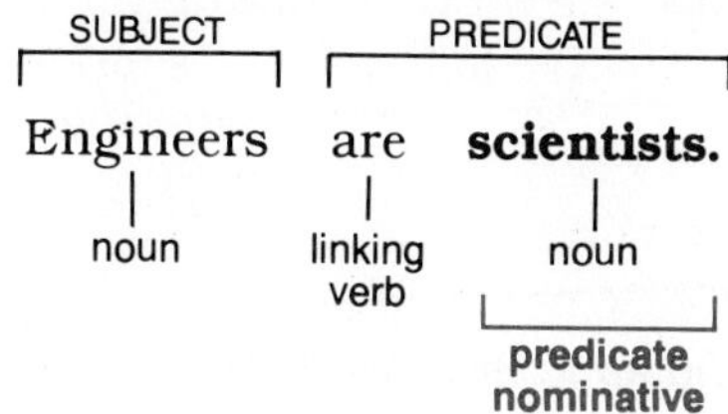

In the above sentence the noun *engineers* is the subject, and *are* is the linking verb. The noun *scientists* is the predicate nominative. Although a predicate nominative is usually a noun or a pronoun, it can be a gerund or an infinitive.

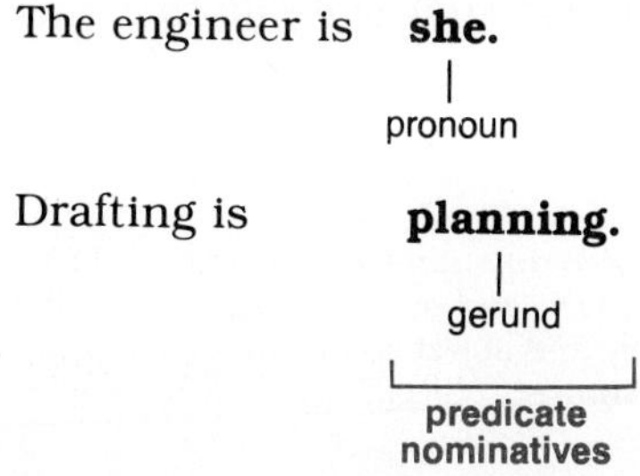

Notice in the second example above that the pronoun is in the nominative (or subjective) case. In general, personal pronouns following a linking verb are in the nominative rather than the objective case (see 1.d.1). A common exception is the use of *me* after a form of *be* in speech. According to traditional grammar rules, you should use *I*, but many people say *me*. In writing, however, *I* is still preferred.

EXAMPLES

WRITING: It is **I**.
SPEAKING: It is **me**.

WRITING: Do not act as if you are **I**.
SPEAKING: Don't act as if you are **me**.

WRITING: Is it **I** that you want?
SPEAKING: Is it **me** that you want?

Predicate nominatives are usually found in sentences that contain forms of the linking verb *be*. Often, these are sentences that classify things. A few other linking verbs (for example, *become, remain*) can be followed by a predicate nominative.

EXAMPLES

An eagle is a **bird**.
Nancy became a **singer** and an **actress** last year.
You are a **student** in my school.
Monday remains a **holiday** for us.
San Francisco is a **city**.
Jerry was a **friend** and **colleague** of mine.

The predicate nominative (as well as the other kinds of subject complements) always completes the meaning of the sentence. In fact, sometimes the term *subject completer* is used instead of the term *subject complement.*[1]

---

[1]Some grammarians use the term *complement* to include not only predicate adjectives, predicate nominatives, and predicate adverbs, as here, but also direct objects, indirect objects, and object complements. This book categorizes words as (1) direct and indirect objects, (2) subject complements, and (3) object complements.

AVOIDING ERRORS WITH PREDICATE NOMINATIVES

1. Do *not* make a linking verb agree with a predicate nominative. The linking verb must always agree with its *subject.*

   NOT The surprise ~~were~~ flowers and perfume.
   BUT The surprise **was** flowers and perfume.

2. Do *not* use the objective case for a pronoun that is a predicate nominative. A predicate pronoun should be in the nominative rather than the objective case. If a sentence sounds awkward you may want to rewrite it as in the third sentence below.

   NOT The culprit was ~~him~~.
   BUT The culprit was **he**.
   OR **He** was the culprit.

   The one exception is *me.* Remember, however, that although *me* and *I* are both acceptable after forms of *be* in speaking, *I* is still preferred in writing.

2.1.2 Predicate adjectives

A **predicate adjective** follows a linking verb and points back to the subject and further describes it.

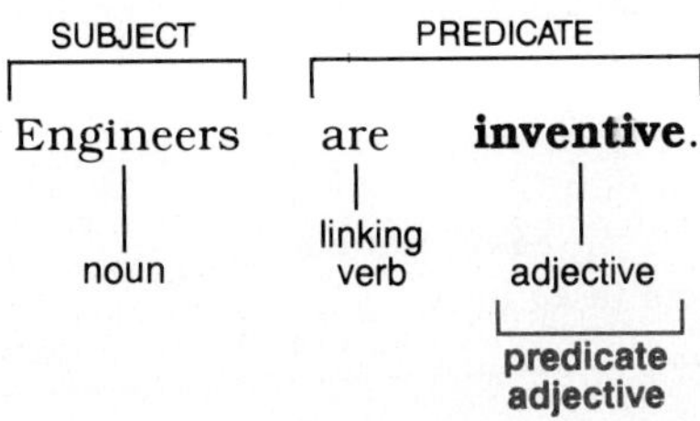

In the preceding sentence the noun *engineers* is the subject, and *are* is the linking verb. The adjective *inventive* is the predicate adjective. A predicate adjective can be an adjective or any expression that can function as an adjective—for example, a participle or a prepositional phrase.

Engineers are **inventive.**
adjective

Engineers are **educated.**
past participle

Engineers are **penetrating.**
present participle

Engineers are **on the increase.**
prepositional phrase

predicate adjectives

Predicate adjectives may follow any linking verb.

EXAMPLES

The hikers had become very **weary**.
Sheila seemed **eager** and **determined**.
The journey will be **tiring**.
The team looks **ready** for the game.
I feel **good**. [in spirit]
I feel **well**. [healthy]
The twins stayed **in good health** all year long.
The fire smells **smoky** tonight.
The plums tasted **sweet**.

The comparative and superlative forms of adjectives can also be used as predicate adjectives.

EXAMPLES

The nation grew **more hopeful**.
Of all my friends, Harry is the **most foolish**.
Of all the fruit, the plums taste **best**.

EXERCISE 14. Identify all predicate nominatives and predicate adjectives in the following sentences. Some sentences have more than one predicate nominative or predicate adjective.

1. The Bible is full of references to giants.
2. These giants were inspiring to George Hull.
3. Hull was the inventor of the Cardiff Giant.
4. The Cardiff Giant was funnier and more memorable than most other hoaxes.
5. The idea of this hoax was to manufacture a fake fossilized giant.
6. The year, 1869, was the time of the first great archaeological finds.
7. Fossils were in fashion.
8. Fake fossils might be profitable.
9. Hull, the originator of the hoax, was quite emaciated and very tall.
10. The model for the giant was he.
11. The raw material for the fake giant fossil was a block of gypsum.
12. After three months' work by two sculptors, the giant was ready.
13. The giant's surface looked too smooth and fresh for fossilized skin.
14. Hull's solution was to attack the surface with sulfuric acid and to jab it with a darning needle.
15. For the next year the giant's home was a garden grave in Cardiff, New York.
16. A year later, that very garden would be the site for a new well.
17. The well-diggers' discovery of a huge human fossil became popular with tourists.
18. Hull's intention was to make a great deal of money before the discovery of his hoax.
19. Even the truth was amusing to tourists.
20. Since 1948 the Cardiff Giant has been an exhibit at the Farmers' Museum in Cooperstown, New York.

2.1.3 Predicate adverbs: adverbs of place

A **predicate adverb** follows a linking verb and points back to the subject and states its condition.

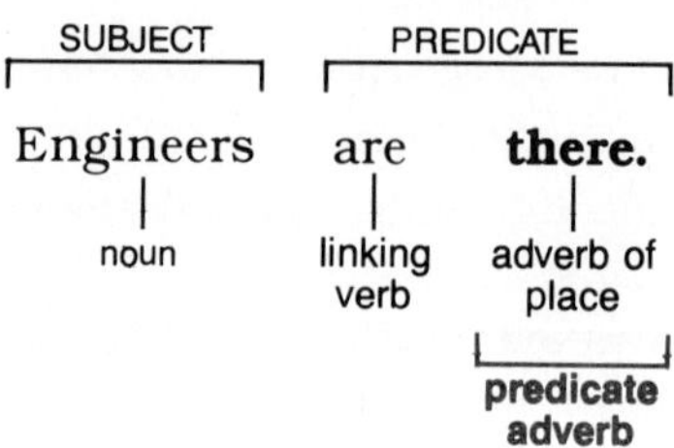

A predicate adverb may be one word or a prepositional phrase.

EXAMPLES

Engineers are **there**.
The engineers are **on the bridge**.
The bridges are **in our guidebooks**.

2.1.4 Prepositional phrases as subject complements

Predicate adjectives and predicate adverbs—two kinds of subject complements—can be either single words or prepositional phrases.

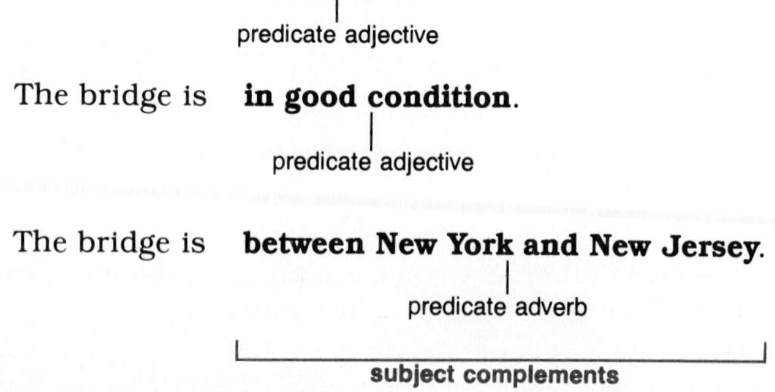

EXERCISE 15. Identify the subject complement in each of the following sentences. Indicate which subject complements are adverbs of place. One sentence has two complements.

1. James McNeill Whistler (1834–1903) was one of the first Impressionist painters.
2. A native of this country, he was a resident here until the age of twenty.
3. After Paris, London became Whistler's adopted home town.
4. He was in London until the end of his life.
5. Whistler's portraits, such as the famous one of his mother, were popular with the general public.
6. In his more revolutionary and controversial *Nocturnes*, the scenes of his shadowy blurs and bursts of color are outdoors.
7. To Ruskin, a somewhat pompous art critic, Whistler's *Nocturne in Black and Gold* appeared unfinished and overpriced.
8. Ruskin's vicious attack on it in print became the object of a humorous libel action.
9. As a result of Whistler's cross-examination during the trial, Ruskin appeared a complete fool.
10. Whistler's own witty account, entitled *The Gentle Art of Making Enemies*, was in many bookstores shortly after the trial.

REVIEW EXERCISE D. Identify the subject complement in each of the following sentences.

1. The life of the Impressionist painter Mary Cassatt (1845–1926) is remarkably similar to that of Whistler.
2. By the age of twenty, both were out of America.
3. Cassatt, like Whistler, was a resident in Europe for the rest of her life.
4. In Paris she was under the guidance of a teacher named Charles Chaplin.
5. After a short time, however, she grew weary of his formal, traditional style.
6. Her interest was in the bolder techniques of Degas, Manet, Renoir, and Whistler.
7. Degas's portrait of Cassatt is of a young artist.
8. Nearly all of Cassatt's paintings are vibrant and colorful portraits of women and children.

9. According to a young American in Paris in 1905, Cassatt was "a very vivid, determined personality."
10. In fact, this young man felt "scared to death" of Cassatt.

2.m OBJECT COMPLEMENTS[1]

An **object complement** answers the question *what?* after a direct object. That is, it *completes* the meaning of the direct object.

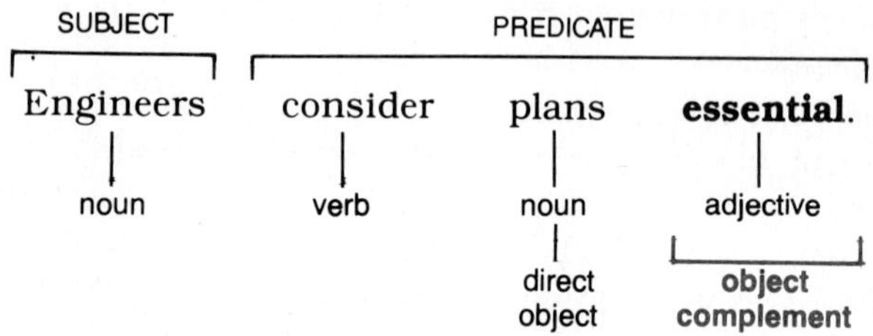

In the above sentence the noun *engineers* is the subject, and the noun *plans* is the direct object of the action verb *consider*. The adjective *essential* is the object complement. It tells *what* the engineers consider plans to be. An object complement occurs only in a sentence with a direct object and usually only in a sentence with one of the following action verbs meaning "make" or "consider":

appoint
call
choose
consider
elect
make
name
render

An object complement can be an adjective, a noun, or a pronoun.

[1]This book uses the term *object complement*; some grammarians prefer the term *objective complement.*

All engineers consider planning **essential**. (adjective)

Nations often make their bridges **symbols**. (noun)

The engineers consider that bridge **theirs**. (pronoun)

object complements

EXERCISE 16. Identify the object complement in each of the following sentences. One sentence has more than one object complement.

1. Do you consider money the root of all evil?
2. Does early to bed and early to rise make you healthy, wealthy, and wise?
3. Do you consider honesty the best policy?
4. Do you consider silence golden?
5. Do you consider the future yours?
6. Does absence really make the heart grow fonder?
7. Do you consider life a bowl of cherries?
8. Do you consider all history a lie?
9. Would you render something useless?
10. Do you make your conscience your guide?

2.n THE CLAUSE

A **clause** is a group of words that has a subject and a predicate and that is used as part of a sentence.

A clause, like a sentence, must have a subject and a predicate. When a sentence has more than one subject-and-predicate combination, each combination is called a clause. The following example sentence has two clauses.

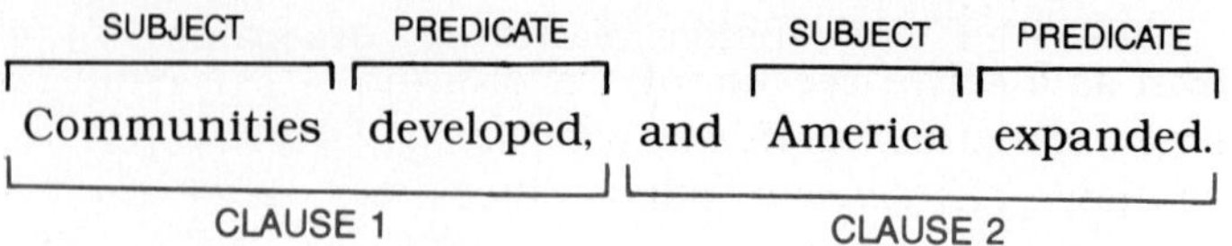

Remember that a **clause** has both a subject and a predicate. A **phrase** does not.

There are two kinds of clauses:

1. *main clauses,* also called independent clauses
2. *subordinate clauses,* also called dependent clauses

To tell the difference between a main clause and a subordinate clause, you must determine whether the clause can stand alone as a sentence. If the clause can stand alone as a sentence, it is a **main clause**. If the clause cannot stand alone as a sentence, it is a **subordinate clause**.

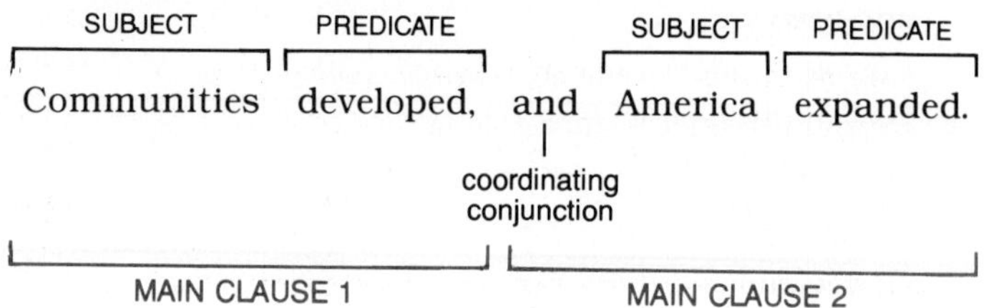

In the above example, both Clause 1 and Clause 2 can stand on their own as sentences: *Communities developed. And America expanded.* Both clauses are main clauses. When a coordinating conjunction such as *and* appears before a subject-and-predicate combination, you still have a main clause.

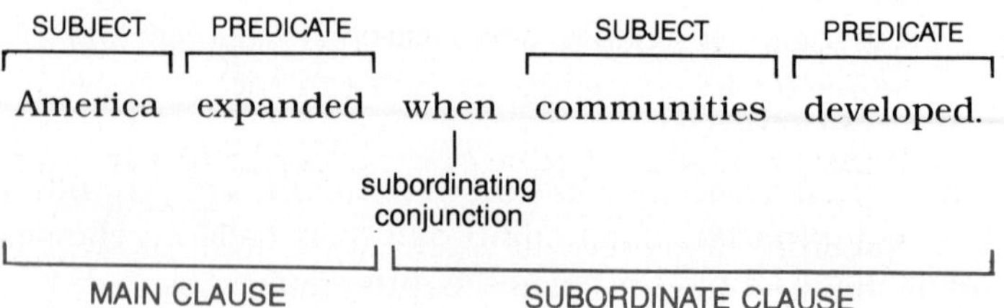

In the last example, the first clause can stand on its own as a sentence: *America expanded.* The second clause, *when communities developed,* cannot stand on its own as a sentence. The subordinating conjunction *when* converts the subject, *communities,* and the predicate, *developed,* into a subordinate clause.

2.o MAIN CLAUSES: SIMPLE SENTENCES, COMPOUND SENTENCES

A main clause has one subject and one predicate. The subject may be a compound subject; the predicate may have a compound verb. Both the subjects and the verbs may be expanded in any number of ways—for example, by adjectives, adverbs, infinitives, participles, and prepositional phrases. As long as a sentence has only one main clause, it is called a **simple sentence**.

EXAMPLES

Communities developed. [simple sentence]

Communities and businesses developed. [simple sentence with compound subject]

Communities developed and brought people together. [simple sentence with compound verb]

New communities in the Southwest have developed rapidly in recent years. [simple sentence expanded]

A sentence with two or more main clauses is called a **compound sentence**. The clauses in a compound sentence can be joined by coordinating conjuntions *(and, but, or, for)* or by a correlative conjunction (for example, *either. . .or, not only...but also*). See also 1.h.

EXAMPLES

Communities developed, **and** America expanded.

Communities developed, business prospered, **and** America expanded.

Either communities attract new people, **or** they become stagnant.

Not only will you see redeveloped inner cities, **but** you will **also** see new desert communities.

A sentence that has only one subject but two or more verbs is said to have a compound verb, but it is *not* a compound sentence. It is still considered a simple sentence because it has only one main clause.

SIMPLE SENTENCE

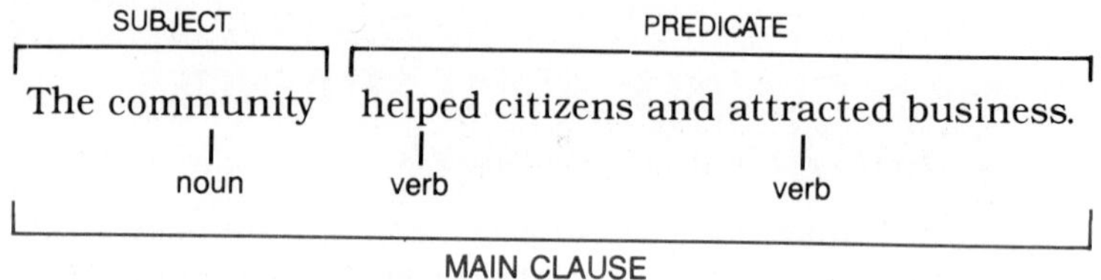

COMPOUND SENTENCE

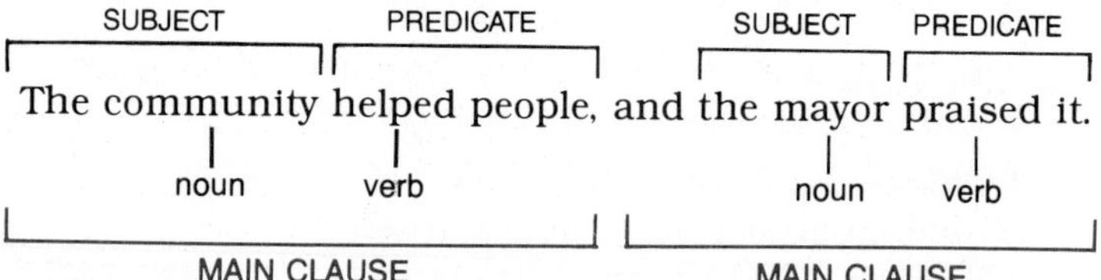

EXERCISE 17. Identify each main clause in the following compound sentences.

1. Some golfers wear out their golf balls, and other golfers lose them.
2. Golf balls usually disappear in long grass, but sometimes they meet with a more interesting fate.
3. One woman saw a squirrel carry her golf ball off, and she decided to follow the squirrel.
4. Eventually, they both arrived at the squirrel's nest, and there the woman found sixty-eight golf balls!
5. All birds are great collectors, but few can rival a certain thieving magpie.
6. Its home base was a Parisian golf course, and it had hidden thirty golf balls there.
7. Not only are crows famous as individual thieves, but they may also form robber gangs.
8. Ten crows once flew off together, and each of them had a golf ball in its beak.

9. You may consider cows law-abiding, but one cow swallowed twenty-nine golf balls.
10. Perhaps you should stick to football, baseball, or tennis, for even dogs steal golf balls.

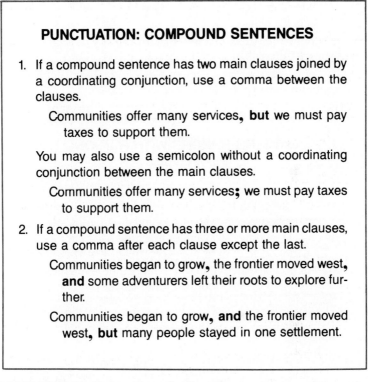

PUNCTUATION: COMPOUND SENTENCES

1. If a compound sentence has two main clauses joined by a coordinating conjunction, use a comma between the clauses.

   Communities offer many services**,** **but** we must pay taxes to support them.

   You may also use a semicolon without a coordinating conjunction between the main clauses.

   Communities offer many services**;** we must pay taxes to support them.

2. If a compound sentence has three or more main clauses, use a comma after each clause except the last.

   Communities began to grow**,** the frontier moved west**,** **and** some adventurers left their roots to explore further.

   Communities began to grow**,** **and** the frontier moved west**,** **but** many people stayed in one settlement.

EXERCISE 18. Determine whether there are one or two main clauses in each of the following sentences.

1. The image of the whitewashed colonial house is largely a myth and has little basis in historical fact.
2. The most expensive houses were painted all over, but the ordinary colonist's house had only a painted trim.
3. Most houses were trimmed in white, but houses in seventeenth-century New York often had a blue-gray trim.
4. Wooden shingles were usually left unpainted but were bleached white by sun.
5. The rooms inside most colonial houses stayed unpainted, for interior paint was not often used before 1700.

6. Public buildings were different, however, and often had gaudy color schemes such as orange and brown.
7. After 1700 interior house paint became popular but was potentially dangerous.
8. The finely ground pigments were mixed with arsenic, lead, or mercury, and these poisonous substances could be absorbed through the skin.
9. In some old houses the original paint can still be seen but now appears different in color.
10. The now green paint in many old New England homes was originally deep blue, but the pigment has faded.

AVOIDING ERRORS WITH RUN-ON SENTENCES

In a sentence with two main clauses, do not use *only* a comma to separate the clauses. You must use a coordinating conjunction along with the comma. Alternatively, you may use (1) a semicolon without a coordinating conjunction or (2) a period to create two sentences. If you use only commas, you will have a run-on sentence (one main clause simply running on into the next main clause).[1]

NOT Large communities have developed in the Southwest, more people have been moving there from the North.

BUT Large communities have developed in the Southwest**, and** more people have been moving there from the North.

OR Large communities have developed in the Southwest**.** More people have been moving there from the North.

OR Large communities have developed in the Southwest**;** more people have been moving there from the North.

[1]A notable exception is a series of extremely short main clauses that does not necessarily take coordinating conjunctions or semicolons: *I came, I saw, I conquered.*

2.p SUBORDINATE CLAUSES

Like a main clause, a subordinate clause contains a subject and predicate. A subordinate clause is different from a main clause because it begins with a word called a subordinator. A *subordinator* can also be referred to as an *introductory word*. A subordinator, or introductory word, reduces the subject-and-predicate combination to a nonsentence. Two kinds of subordinators are subordinating conjunctions (for example, *as* or *when*) and relative pronouns (for example, *who* or *that*). When you see a subordinator introducing a clause, you are dealing with a subordinate clause, a clause that cannot be a sentence in its own right.

Some subordinators *precede* the subject-and-predicate combination. Other subordinators, however, can actually be the subject of the subordinate clause.

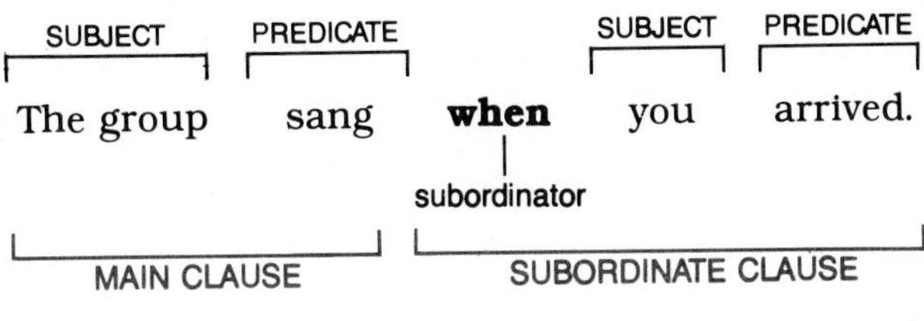

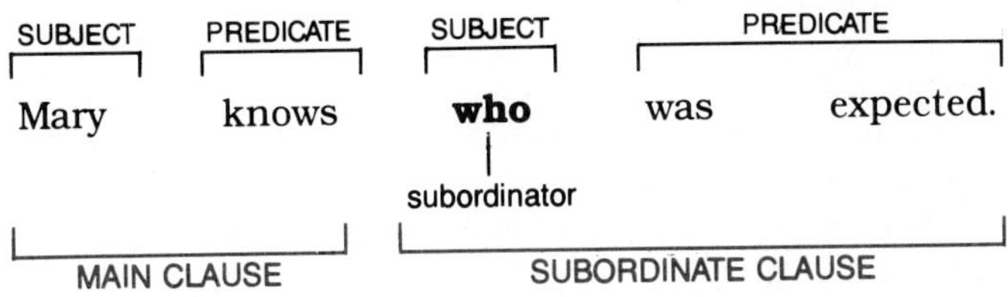

In each of the above examples, the second clause is a subordinate clause because it begins with a subordinator. In the second sentence the subordinator is also the subject of the subordinate clause.

A simple sentence with one or more subordinate clauses added becomes a **complex sentence**. A compound sentence with one or more subordinate clauses added becomes a **compound-complex sentence**.

COMPLEX SENTENCE

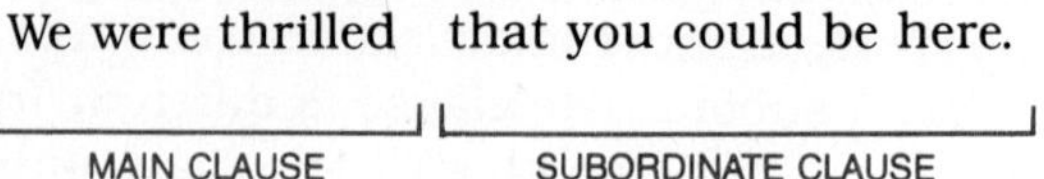
We were thrilled
that you could be here.
MAIN CLAUSE
SUBORDINATE CLAUSE

COMPOUND-COMPLEX SENTENCE

We sang | when you arrived, | and we cried | when you left.

MAIN CLAUSE | SUBORDINATE CLAUSE | MAIN CLAUSE | SUBORDINATE CLAUSE

The following list contains most of the common subordinators (see 2.q and 2.r).

COMMON SUBORDINATORS

Subordinating conjunctions

after	even though	unless
although	how	until
as	if	when
as if	in order that	whenever
as long as	provided (that)	where
as though	since	whereas
as soon as	so that	wherever
because	than	whether
before	though	while

Relative pronouns

that
what, whatever
which, whichever (in which, for which, of which, by which)
who, whoever
whom, whomever (in whom, for whom, of whom, by whom)
whose (in whose)

There are three kinds of subordinate clauses.

1. **Adverb clauses** perform the same role in a sentence as adverbs of time, adverbs of place, and adverbs of manner or degree.

EXAMPLES

When you arrive, I will go.
I will go **where you live**.
I will go **as quietly as you wish**.

2. **Adjective clauses** perform the same role as adjectives; they tell more about a noun.

EXAMPLES

I drove past the house **that you lived in**. [tells more about *house*]

She is the woman **who witnessed the accident**. [tells more about *woman*]

3. **Noun clauses** function the same way as a noun in a sentence.

EXAMPLES

I see **that you know**. [noun clause as object of verb]

What you don't know won't hurt you. [noun clause as subject]

AVOIDING ERRORS WITH SENTENCE FRAGMENTS

1. Do not confuse main clauses and subordinate clauses. A subordinate clause cannot stand on its own. It can never be a sentence unless you make it a main clause or add a main clause to it.

   NOT ~~When eagles soar.~~
   BUT **I watch** when eagles soar.

2. In your writing, avoid treating a subordinate clause as if it were a sentence. A subordinate clause treated as a sentence creates a **sentence fragment**. Remember that a subordinate clause is not a sentence, no matter how long and complicated it may be. Be sure that you can explain, therefore, why the first item below is not a sentence and why the second item is.

   NOT ~~Around 14th Street, when the car stopped, out of gas, headlights dim, holding up traffic – gosh, what a night!~~
   BUT Around 14th Street, **we got** nervous when the car stopped, out of gas, headlights dim, holding up traffic – gosh, what a night!

2.q ADVERB CLAUSES

An **adverb clause** is a subordinate clause that tells *when, where, how, why,* or *under what conditions.*

EXAMPLES

I was happy. [main clause]

Whenever you were around, I was happy. [Adverb clause tells *when.*]

Wherever I took a vacation, I was happy. [Adverb clause tells *where.*]

As though I did not have a care in the world, I was happy. [Adverb clause tells *how.*]

Because I won, I was happy. [Adverb clause tells *why.*]

Although you left, I was happy. [Adverb clause states conditions.]

I washed the car. [main clause]

After you left, I washed the car. [Adverb clause tells *when.*]

Wherever I spent the weekend, I washed the car. [Adverb clause tells *where.*]

As though my life depended on it, I washed the car. [Adverb clause tells *how.*]

Because I love to make a good impression, I washed the car. [Adverb clause tells *why.*]

Although the weather was bad, I washed the car. [Adverb clause states conditions.]

In general, the subordinators that introduce adverb clauses are subordinating conjunctions. They can be grouped according to meaning.

SUBORDINATORS FOR ADVERB CLAUSES

SUBORDINATORS THAT TELL WHEN: after, as, as long as, as soon as, before, since, until, when, whenever, while

SUBORDINATORS THAT TELL WHERE: where, wherever

SUBORDINATORS THAT TELL HOW: as if, as though, than

SUBORDINATORS THAT TELL WHY: as, because, in order that, since, so that

SUBORDINATORS THAT STATE CONDITIONS: although, as long as, even though, if, provided that, though, unless, whereas, whether, while

You will notice that some subordinators are listed in more than one category. These subordinators can have more than one meaning, depending on how they are used. For example, study the way *as* is used in the two sentences below.

EXAMPLES
As I left, he arrived. [*As* means "when."]
As I felt ill, I went home early. [*As* means "because."]

For a more complete list of subordinating conjunctions, see 1.h.4.

2.q.1 Placement of adverb clauses

An adverb clause can come either before or after a main clause.

EXAMPLES
After you left, I washed the car.
I washed the car **after you left**.

EXERCISE 19. Identify each adverb clause in the following sentences.

1. Until jet planes were invented, the North Pole was not on anyone's travel route.
2. No one had set foot on the North Pole, since no one had to pass that way.
3. When something has never been done before, adventuresome people long to try it.
4. If there was ever anyone with a taste for adventure, it was Matthew Henson.
5. Henson was born in Maryland after the Civil War ended.
6. Both his mother and father died before Henson was nine years old.
7. Since he did not get along with his stepmother, he ran away to Washington at the age of eleven.
8. After washing dishes for a year, he signed up as a cabin boy on the *Katie Hines*.
9. As that ship made its way to Hong Kong, the captain gave reading and writing lessons to his enterprising cabin boy.

COMMAS AND ADVERB CLAUSES

Use a comma after an adverb clause (even a very short one) that begins a sentence.

When she left**,** she felt relieved.

In general, you do not need a comma before an adverb clause that ends a sentence. Such a clause usually adds essential information and therefore should not be set off by a comma.

She felt relieved when she left.

If an adverb clause at the end of a sentence begins with *though* or *although,* use a comma before it.

She felt relieved**, although** she had left her friends.

If an adverb clause at the end of a sentence begins with *as, while,* or *since,* do not use a comma if you mean "when." Do use a comma before *as* or *since* if you mean "why" and before *while* if you mean "whereas."

She felt anxious as she began her journey.
She felt anxious**, as** she had never been away before.

10. Wherever he went during his five years on the *Katie Hines,* Henson learned something new.
11. While the ship lay aground in a Russian harbor one winter, Henson learned to speak Russian and to drive a sleigh.
12. Henson had a number of jobs in Washington before he met Robert Peary.
13. At that time Peary was only a civil engineer, though he later became a rear admiral.
14. When Peary asked Henson to go with him to Nicaragua, it was the beginning of a twenty-three-year friendship between the two men.
15. Whereas their first expedition took them southward, all their later expeditions took them due north.
16. They had to stay in the frozen Arctic for a year until a ship could pick them up.

17. Peary and Henson made several expeditions before they finally reached the North Pole.
18. The first seven expeditions fell short of the final destination because various mishaps occurred.
19. After they had driven a sleigh four hundred miles from base camp, Peary and Henson reached the North Pole on April 6, 1909.
20. At the pole Peary asked Henson to hoist the American flag so that the spot would be marked forever.

2.q.2 Elliptical adverb clauses

An **elliptical adverb clause** is an adverb clause from which some words have been omitted. The omitted words are understood, however, and can easily be supplied.

EXAMPLES

I swim better **than you** [swim].
It is colder today **than** [it was] **yesterday**.
Although [I was] **unhappy**, I put a smile on my face.

Sometimes you have to recognize an elliptical clause and be able to supply the omitted words in order to decide which form of a pronoun to use in the sentence. Use the form of the pronoun that you would use if the clause were complete.

EXAMPLES

I like Mark better than **he**. [The elliptical clause is *than **he*** because the complete clause would be *than **he** does.*]
I like Mark better than **him**. [The elliptical clause is *than **him*** because the complete clause would be *than I like **him**.*]

EXERCISE 20. Select the appropriate form of the pronoun in parentheses for the elliptical clause.

1. Eleanor Roosevelt, the wife of President Franklin D. Roosevelt, became almost as prominent a public figure as (he/him).
2. During the Roosevelts' lives the public did not know as much as (we/us) about their personal life.
3. Franklin's mother was much more dominating than Eleanor. After Eleanor married Franklin, his mother continued to dominate Franklin as well as (she/her).

4. Eleanor Roosevelt eventually proved to have no less energy than (he/him) for social reform.
5. No First Lady had ever been as active as (she/her).
6. The President's opponents often disliked Mrs. Roosevelt even more than (he/him).
7. Roosevelt trusted few of his advisers as much as (she/her).
8. Civil rights issues concerned Mrs. Roosevelt more than (he/him).
9. She was often more vehement than (he/him) in their political arguments.
10. In a speech Mrs. Roosevelt told male delegates that women can contribute as much as (they/them) to international peace.

2.r ADJECTIVE CLAUSES

An **adjective clause** is a subordinate clause that, like an adjective, gives more information about a noun, a pronoun, or a gerund in the main clause.

An adjective clause can appear in various positions within a sentence. In the examples below, the arrow relates the adjective clause to the word it describes.

EXAMPLES

The book is on the table. [main clause]

The book **that I borrowed** is on the table.

The book is on the table **that I borrowed**.

She **whom I admire most** has won the writing prize.

You should not avoid reading **that is difficult**.

The following subordinators are used to begin adjective clauses.

SUBORDINATORS FOR ADJECTIVE CLAUSES

who
whom (in whom, for whom, of whom, by whom)
whose (in whose)
which (in which, for which, of which, by which)
that
where
when

In adjective clauses, these are sometimes called relative pronouns (see 1.d.6).

Some of the preceding subordinators are used more often in adjective clauses that describe people, and some are used more often in adjective clauses that describe animals and things. The following table shows where and how the subordinators are generally used.(Pay attention to the note about *that.* You may hear someone use *that* to refer to people. In writing, however, you should use *who* whenever you are referring to a person.)

SUBORDINATORS IN ADJECTIVE CLAUSES

subordinator	***person***	***animal or thing***
who	I saw the man **who** jogs.	X
whom	I saw the man **whom** you admire.	X
whose	I saw the woman **whose** daughter won the contest.	[It is better not to use **whose** to refer to an animal or a thing.]
which	X	I saw the house **which** collapsed. I saw San Francisco, **which** is charming.
that	I saw the woman **that** you admire. [Remember that *who* is preferred in *writing* about people.]	I saw the dog **that** bit you. I saw the house **that** Jack built.

Below are additional examples of subordinators with adjective clauses. The arrow relates the adjective clause to the noun it describes.

EXAMPLES

I am surprised each time **that I win**.

I visited the house **where I lived as a child**.

I remember the summer **when we became friends**.

An adjective clause is sometimes called a **relative clause**.

2.r.1 Two kinds of adjective clauses

Sometimes an adjective clause is essential; without it, the reader would not be able to recognize the noun, or the sentence would become absurd.

EXAMPLE

Moby Dick is the only novel **that I read this year.**

Without the adjective clause, the above sentence becomes absurd; of course, *Moby Dick* is not the only novel. When an adjective clause is needed to clarify meaning or to avoid absurdity, it is called a **restrictive clause**, or an **essential clause**. Notice that in a restrictive, or essential, clause the subordinator can be omitted without losing sense. The caret indicates an omitted subordinator:

EXAMPLE

Moby Dick is the only novel ‸I read this year.

In some sentences the adjective clause is not essential; it simply adds *extra* information.

EXAMPLE

Moby Dick, **which I read this year**, is now one of my favorite novels.

The preceding sentence would be perfectly logical without the adjective clause. When an adjective clause is not absolutely needed, it is called a **nonrestrictive clause**, a **nonessential clause,** or an **extra clause**.

Both *that* and *which* can be used with essential clauses (although *that* is preferred). Only *which* can be used with extra clauses, however. Remember never to use *that* with an extra clause.

EXERCISE 21. Identify each adjective clause in the following sentences. Three sentences contain two adjective clauses each.

1. Tennessee Williams, who began life as Thomas Lanier Williams, was born in Mississippi in 1914.

2. The name *Tennessee*, which he adopted in the 1930s, was a nickname that he had been given in college.
3. Williams grew up in a family environment that was far from happy.
4. His father, who was unkind and stingy, never really understood his son.
5. Williams was a child who was crippled for years by diphtheria.
6. His favorite pastimes were reading and writing, which undoubtedly helped his career.
7. Many of the plays that Williams wrote have characters who were based on members of his family.
8. *The Glass Menagerie*, which brought Williams his first great success, had a character based on his own sister.
9. The play that Williams wrote next was *A Streetcar Named Desire.*
10. The successful plays that Williams wrote, which include *Suddenly Last Summer* and *Sweet Bird of Youth*, have firmly established his reputation as an outstanding dramatist.

ADJECTIVE CLAUSES AND COMMAS

1. With an extra (nonrestrictive) clause, use extra commas. If the clause comes at the end of the sentence, use just one comma before it; if the clause comes within a sentence, use a comma on either side of it.

   Chicago is known for its architecture**, which is indeed remarkable**.

   Chicago**, which is called the Windy City,** is just as famous for its architecture as it is for its weather.

2. With an essential (restrictive) clause, do not use commas.

   Chicago is the city **that** [or **which**] **I want to visit**.
   The city **that** [or **which**] **I want to visit** is Chicago.

EXERCISE 22. Select a relative pronoun *(who, that,* or *which)* for each blank in the sentences below. Then add any commas that are necessary so that extra (nonrestrictive) clauses are properly punctuated.

1. Vegetation __________ is too sparse for cattle can support goats __________ eat leaves as well as grass.
2. Those countries __________ do not control their goat populations have suffered from soil erosion __________ results from the goats' consumption of all vegetation.
3. This country's goat population __________ is estimated at three million consists of animals __________ produce either milk or mohair wool.
4. The milk __________ we get from cows is similar to goat's milk in composition.
5. The milk of water-living mammals __________ include seals and porpoises has a much higher fat content than does the milk of mammals __________ live on land.

2.r.2 Agreement in adjective clauses: *one of*

The action verb or linking verb in an adjective clause must agree with the antecedent to which the relative pronoun refers.

EXAMPLES

The eagle is one of the animals **that are becoming extinct**. [The adjective clause describes *animals*, a third-person plural noun requiring *are*.]

The eagle is the only one of the falcons **that is recognized by many people**. [The adjective clause refers to *the only one*, a third-person singular pronoun requiring *is*.]

Obviously, when the main clause contains the expression **one of**, it is necessary to exercise caution in choosing the verb form in any adjective clause that follows. You must decide if the verb refers specifically to *one* (as in the second example) or to the plural noun (as in the first example). Remember that the word *the* before the word *one* indicates that the verb must agree with *one*, not with the plural noun.

2.s NOUN CLAUSES

A **noun clause** is a subordinate clause used as a noun.

In effect, a noun clause can take the place of a noun, as illustrated in the examples below.

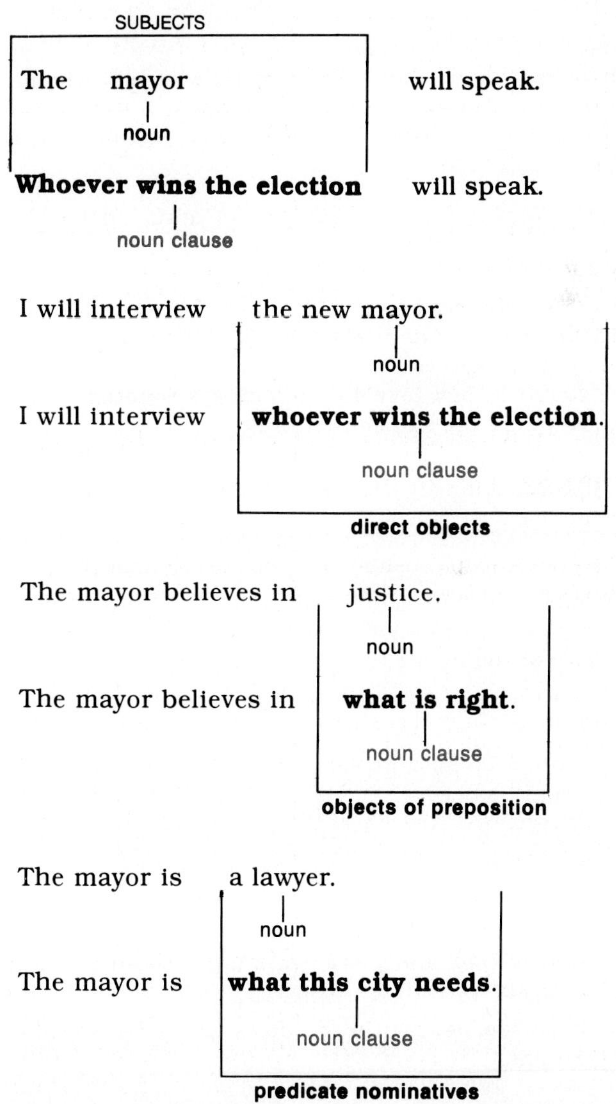

The following words are some of the subordinators that can be used to begin noun clauses. Some of these words are also called relative pronouns when they introduce adjective clauses (see 1.d.6).

SUBORDINATORS FOR NOUN CLAUSES

how	whichever
that	who
what	whoever
whatever	whom (in whom, for whom, by whom)
when	whose
where	why
which	

Below are some additional examples of noun clauses.

EXAMPLES

I know **for whom you voted.**
Whichever candidate is elected will face many problems.
You are **what you eat.**
The story tells **how love does not always conquer all.**
I know **where the sun shines**, Nellie.

EXERCISE 23. Identify the noun clause in each of the following sentences.

1. Whatever design a customer chooses determines the price of a tattoo, but the average customer pays between $25 and $50.
2. Where a customer wants the tattoo affects the price; tattoos on the arm or the leg are the least expensive.
3. One can choose whatever animal or geometric designs strike one's fancy.
4. That tattoos became fashionable in the 1970s was rather surprising.
5. Before then, whoever was tattooed was usually a sailor or a circus performer.
6. In the 1970s gossip columns reported that Janis Joplin had a heart tattoo and Peter Fonda had a dolphin tattoo.
7. Followers of rock and movie stars often buy whatever their idols suggest.
8. Later one can usually throw out or give away what one no longer wants.

9. Unfortunately, whoever follows the tattooing trend has a tattoo for life.
10. One should think twice before getting tattooed: Whatever has been advertised to remove tattoos has always failed.

REVIEW EXERCISE E. Identify each subordinate clause in the following sentences. Indicate whether the clause is an adverb clause, an adjective clause, or a noun clause, and tell why. Twelve of the sentences have two subordinate clauses each.

1. For many years scientists have been searching for what may be called our first humanlike ancestor.
2. This humanlike ancestor is believed by some to be a creature who existed for a long period of prehistory and then disappeared.
3. That the remains of such a creature were found was due in part to Charles Dawson, who discovered the remains near Piltdown, England, in 1912.
4. What Dawson found was a skull that had a braincase of human proportions but a jawbone of an ape.
5. The scientists of the day were thrilled with the so-called Piltdown Man, whose authenticity became an accepted fact.
6. After the Piltdown skull had occupied a place of honor for forty years, some tests in 1953 revealed that it had been fashioned from the artificially aged bones of a modern ape and a modern human.
7. Why this trick had been played remained a mystery until the British geologist J. A. Douglas voiced his suspicions in 1978.
8. When the Piltdown skull was first unearthed, Douglas had been working in the laboratory of William Johnson Sollas, who was a respected professor of paleontology.
9. At this laboratory Douglas once unpacked a shipment of potassium bichromate and wondered why Sollas had ordered this chemical.
10. Douglas remembered this incident in 1953, the year in which the tests proved that the Piltdown skull had been given its fossil appearance with potassium bichromate.
11. Another strange thing that Douglas remembered was that Sollas had borrowed the university's collection of apes' teeth about the same time.

12. These pieces of circumstantial evidence made Sollas a likely culprit, although he had a good reputation as a scholar.
13. Sollas' professional standing was then being challenged by Arthur Smith Woodward, who was a rising young anthropologist.
14. Douglas remembered how Woodward had ridiculed Sollas' views at professional gatherings and how furious Sollas had looked.
15. While Sollas had never counterattacked openly, he may well have been quietly planning revenge.
16. What Sollas may have planned was a fake fossil that Woodward would accept as genuine.
17. If this interpretation is true, Sollas was certainly successful because Woodward was convinced of the authenticity of the Piltdown Man.
18. What Sollas had not expected was that every one of his colleagues would also be deceived by his hoax.
19. If he now made Woodward look like a fool, Sollas would also make his other colleagues look foolish.
20. Douglas suspected that Sollas could never admit responsibility for the hoax because Sollas did not want to lose his reputation.

2.t WHO VS. WHOM IN SUBORDINATE CLAUSES

The case, or form, of the subordinator depends on how it is used within the subordinate clause.

When you have to decide between *who* and *whom*, decide how the word will be used in the subordinate clause. Do not be influenced by any other part of the sentence. Remember the following guidelines:

- If the subordinator is used as the subject or as the predicate nominative of the subordinate clause, use the nominative, or subjective, case (*who*).
- If the subordinator is used as the object of a verb or as the object of a preposition within the subordinate clause, use the objective case (*whom*).

Here are five examples worked out to show how to apply the preceding guidelines. Each subordinate clause is presented in italics. Following each problem sentence, you will find an explanation of how to choose the correct subordinator. You may be able to work the problems out on your own.

EXAMPLE 1

Subordinator as subject

The candidate, *(who/whom) announced her intention yesterday,* has the best chance.

The subordinator is the subject of the verb *announced* in the adjective clause. The subject of a clause must be in the nominative case. The subordinator should be *who.*

EXAMPLE 2

Subordinator as predicate nominative

She knows *(who/whom) her main rival is.*

The subordinator is the predicate nominative of the noun clause: *Her main rival is who.* A predicate nominative must be in the nominative case. The subordinator must be *who.* Notice that you must not pay attention to any other part of the sentence. If you do, you might think that you need the objective form (*whom*) after the action verb in the main clause (*knows*). Remember to concentrate on the subordinate clause.

EXAMPLE 3

Subordinator as object of a verb

The latest candidate, *(who/whom) you will support,* is the most experienced.

The subordinator is the object of the verb *support* in the adjective clause. The object of a verb must always be in the objective case. The subordinator must be *whom.*

EXAMPLE 4

Subordinator as object of preposition

She knows *(who/whom) you will campaign for this year.*

The subordinator is the object of the preposition *for.* The object of a preposition is always in the objective case. The subordinator must be *whom.*

EXAMPLE 5

The crowd gave support to *(whoever/whomever) promised the most.*

Look at the noun clause only: *(whoever/whomever) promised the most.* The subordinator is the subject of the verb *promised* and must be in the nominative case (*whoever*). Do not be tricked by the preposition *to,* which is outside the subordinate clause.

EXERCISE 24. Select the appropriate word from the parentheses in each item below. Remember that the case of the subordinator depends on its use within the subordinate clause.

1. The Nobel Prize for Literature goes to (whoever/whomever) the judges select.
2. The prize is awarded annually to (whoever/whomever) has contributed most to the field.
3. The award was established by Alfred Bernhard Nobel, the Swedish industrialist (who/whom) invented dynamite.
4. Ernest Hemingway, John Steinbeck, and Pearl Buck are American writers (who/whom) have received the Nobel Prize.
5. The writers (who/whom) the judges select are not the only talented writers of the day.
6. Often the prize simply reflects the tastes of those (who/whom) do the judging.
7. Leo Tolstoy was one writer (who/whom) the Nobel judges never honored.
8. Other nonwinners (who/whom) many critics admire were Thomas Hardy, Virginia Woolf, and Mark Twain.
9. Many people know (who/whom) the candidates are.
10. It is, however, always difficult to guess (who/whom) the winner will be.

2.u A REVIEW OF SENTENCES

There are four kinds of sentences:

1. **Simple sentence:** A simple sentence has one main clause and no subordinate clauses. A simple sentence,

therefore, has one subject (single or compound) and one predicate (a single or compound verb plus optional elements). The two example sentences that follow seem very different, but they are both simple sentences.

EXAMPLES

Eagles soar.

Our engineers constructed five new bridges and planned two others last year.

2. **Compound sentence:** A compound sentence has two or more main clauses and no subordinate clauses. Each of the main clauses in a compound sentence can function as a simple sentence, described above.

EXAMPLES

Eagles soar, and sparrows flit.

Our engineers constructed five new bridges last year, but yours managed to finish ten.

Our engineers constructed five new bridges last year, your engineers finished ten, but their engineers put up fifteen.

3. **Complex sentence:** A simple sentence to which at least one subordinate clause has been added becomes a complex sentence. A complex sentence, therefore, has one main clause and one or more subordinate clauses. Notice how different they can be in length.

EXAMPLES

I know that eagles soar.

Our engineers, who are among the best in the country, greatly improved traffic flow in the downtown areas.

After they built the bridge but before they tackled the tunnel, the engineers ran out of funding.

4. **Compound-complex sentence:** As you know, a compound sentence to which at least one subordinate clause has been added becomes a compound-complex sentence. A compound-complex sentence, therefore, has at least two main clauses and at least one subordinate clause.

EXAMPLE

Eagles, which are the national bird, are rare, but they are no longer in quite as much danger as they once were.

MODELS OF TRADITONAL DIAGRAMS

Diagraming is a method of showing the relationship of various words and parts of a sentence to the sentence as a whole. The following examples show the traditional method of diagraming various kinds of sentences.

You begin to diagram a sentence by finding the simple subject of the main clause, keeping in mind that many sentences have more than one clause, and that each clause has a subject, occasionally a compound subject. After you have found the subject of the main clause, find the action or linking verb that goes with it. Write the subject and the verb on a horizontal line, separating them with a short vertical line.

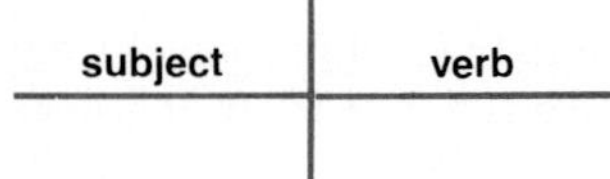

Additional clauses and additional sentence elements are added as indicated in the examples below.

Simple sentences

Each of the following examples of simple sentences contains a subject. The numbered items indicate the additional elements in each sentence.

1. Action verb
   Senators meet.

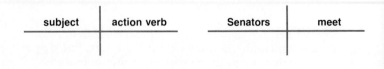

subject | action verb

Senators | meet

2. Action verb; determiner, adjective, and adverbs
The slightly older senators meet periodically.

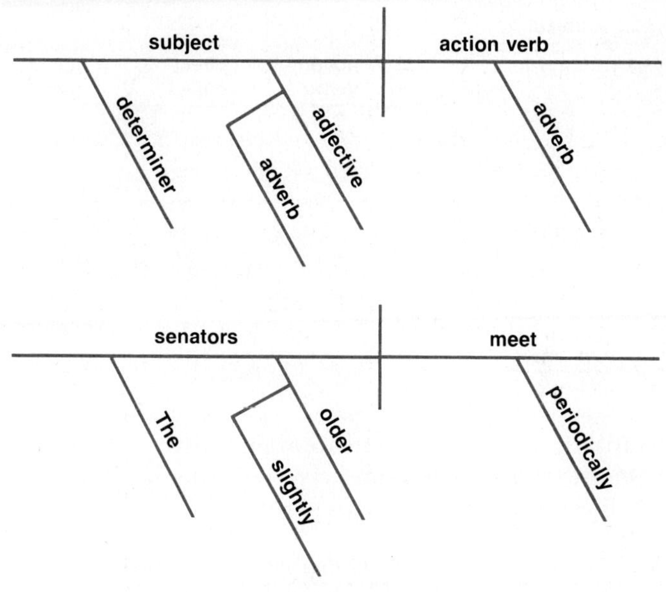

3. Action verb with direct object and indirect object
Experts give senators advice.

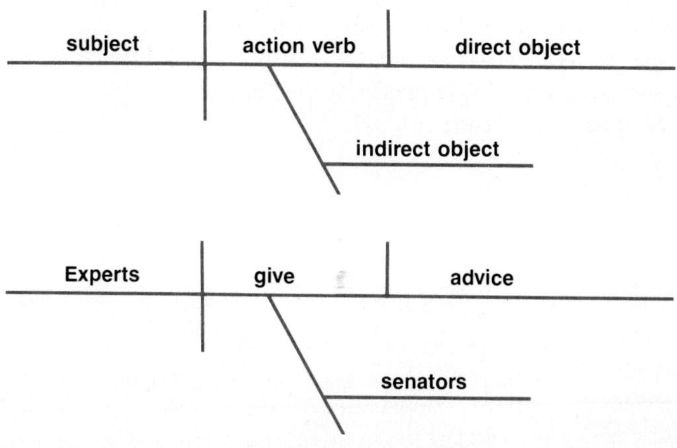

4. Action verb (for compound subject) with direct object and object complement
Staff and supporters considered him important.

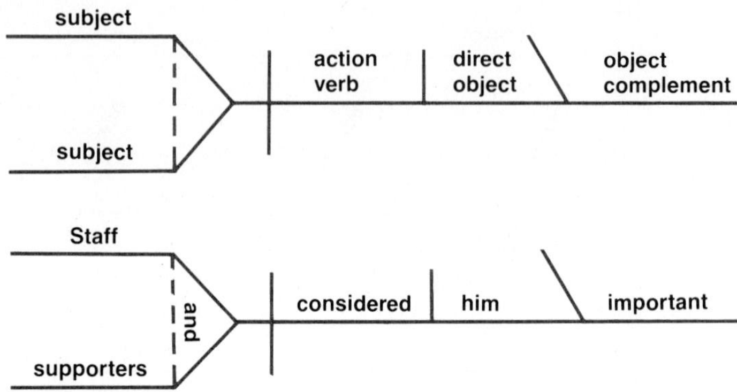

5. Linking verb with predicate nominative
Senators are legislators.

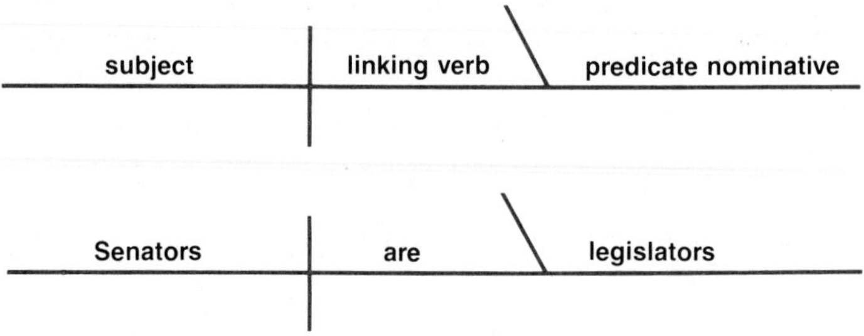

6. Linking verb with predicate adjective
Senators are helpful.

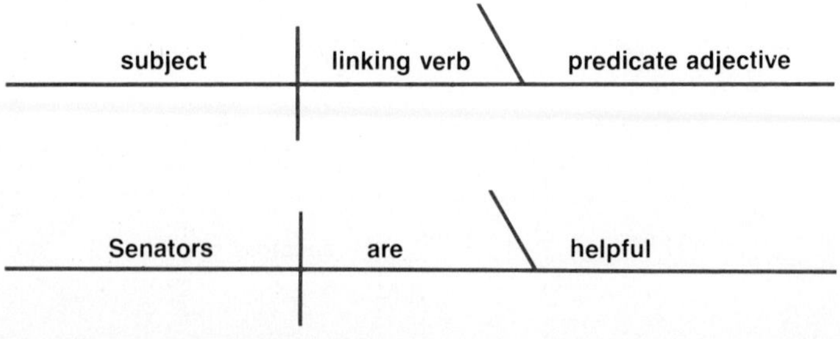

7. Two action verbs (compound verb); prepositional phrase
Senators in Washington consult and legislate.

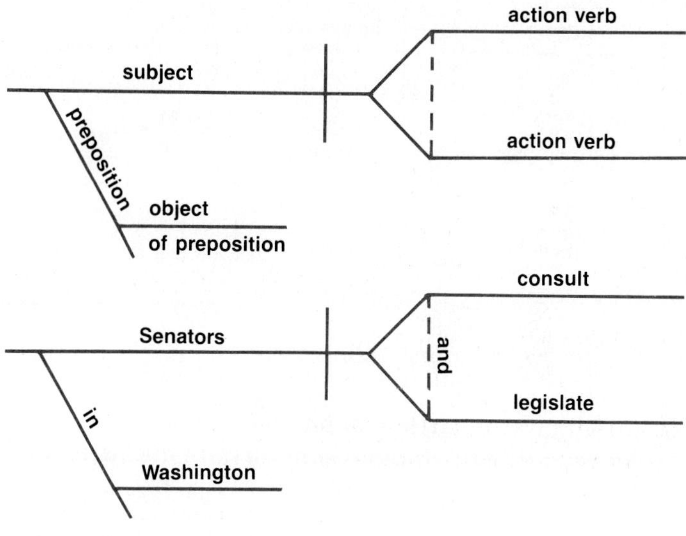

8. Action verb with infinitive phrase as object
Senators plan to work hard.

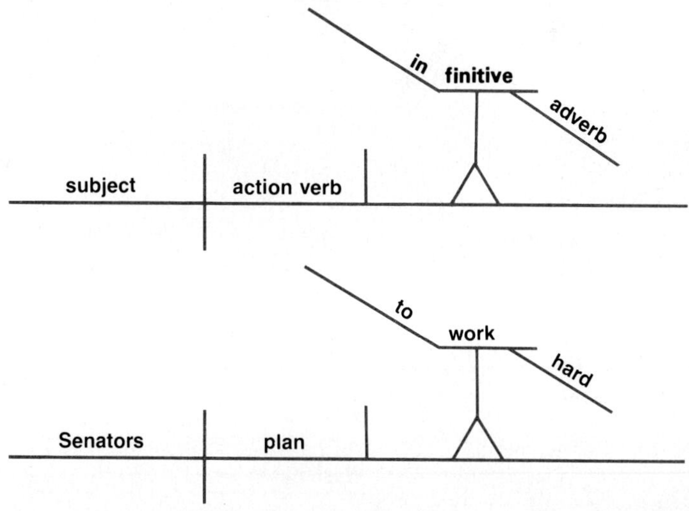

9. Action verb with gerund as object
Some senators enjoy debating.

gerund
subject
action verb
determiner

debating
senators
enjoy
Some

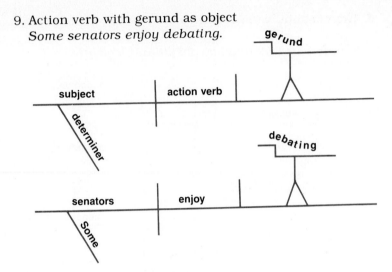

10. Linking verb; participial phrase
Arriving in Washington, senators are enthusiastic.

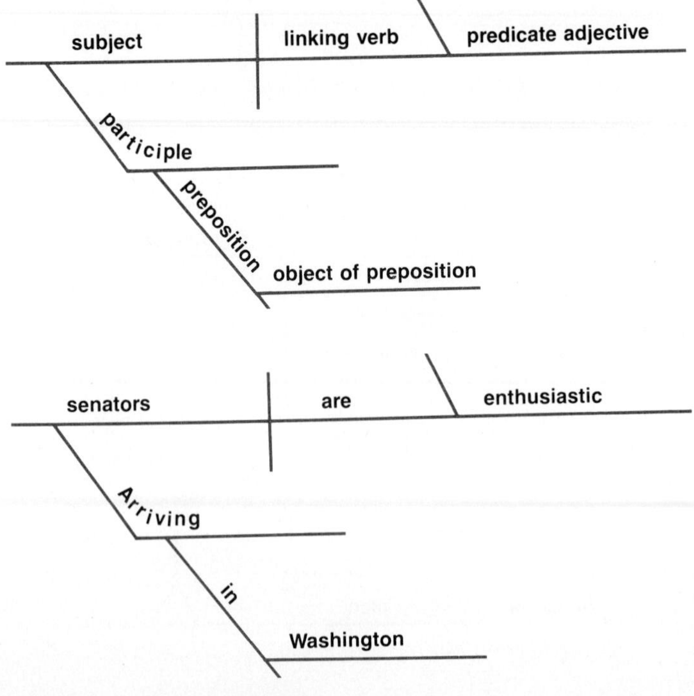

■ Compound sentence

11. *Older senators chair committees, and younger senators make speeches.*

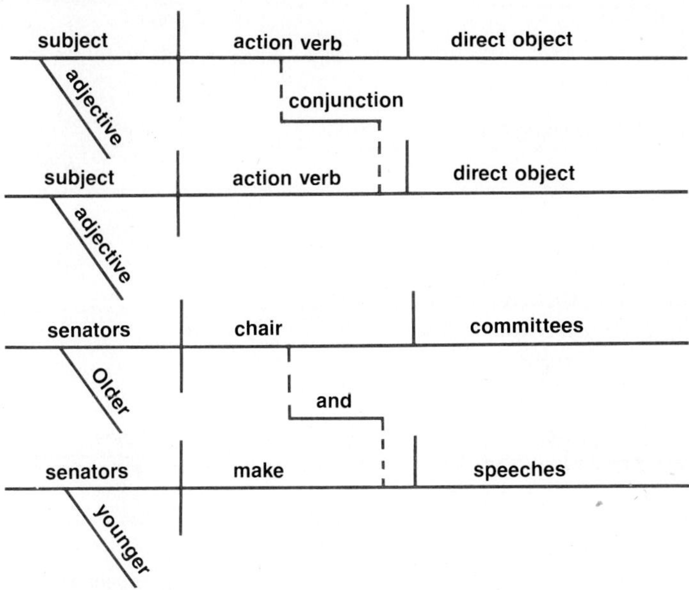

■ Complex sentences

12. Subordinate adjective clause
    A. *Senators who make speeches generally succeed.*

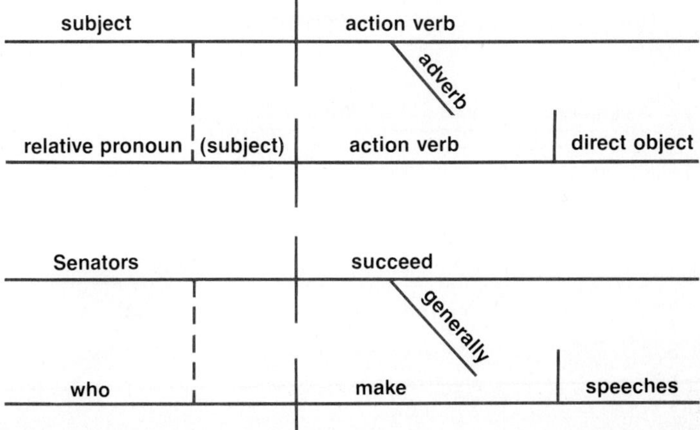

B. *Senators make speeches that newspapers print.*

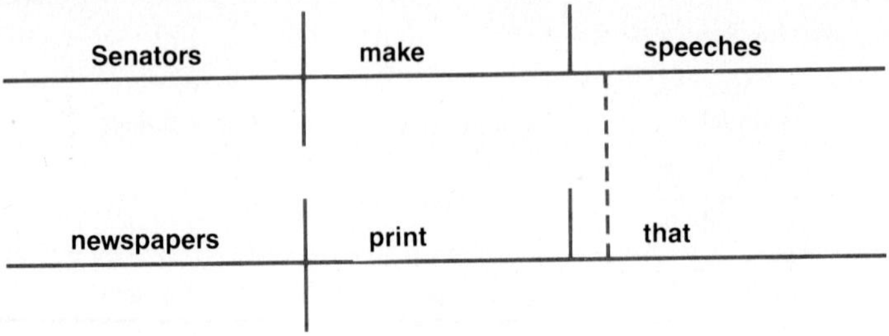

Senators
make
speeches
newspapers
print
that

13. Subordinate adverb clause
When senators make speeches, people take notes.

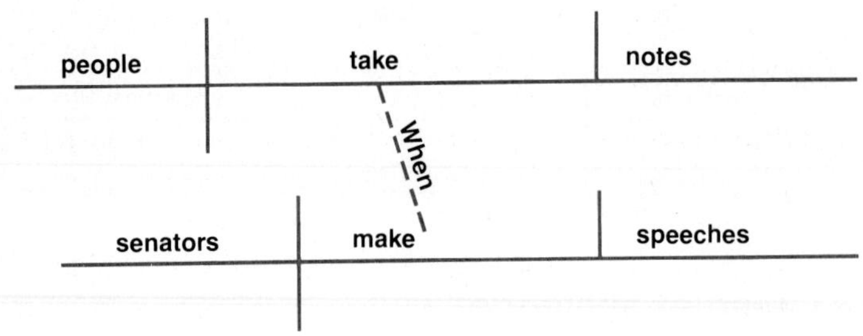

14. Noun clause (as subject)
What senators say is important news.

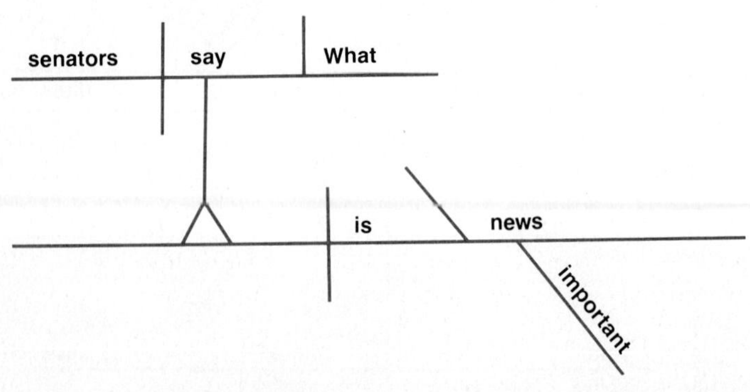

15. Noun clause (as direct object)
Senators remember what America means.

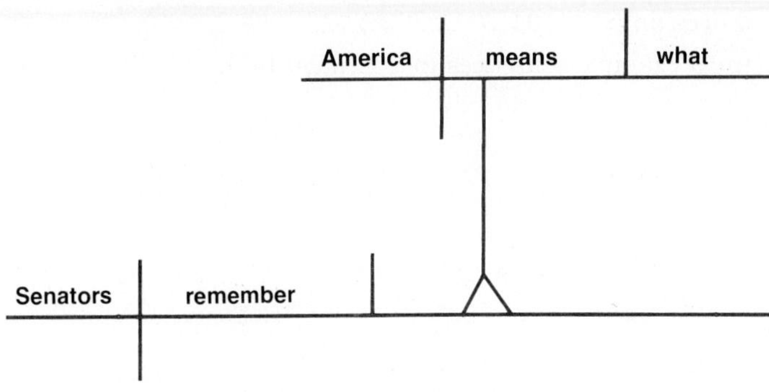

■ Compound-complex sentence

16. *Senators who make speeches succeed, but others fail.*

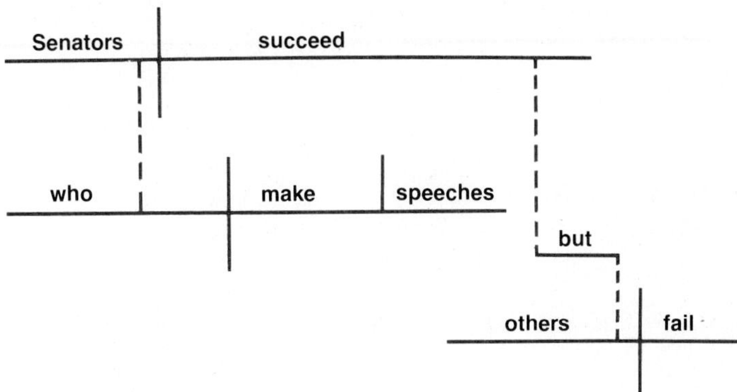

DIAGRAMING EXERCISE. Use models on pages 198–205 to diagram the following sentences that appear earlier:

1. the 2 example sentences at the bottom of page 139
2. the 3 example sentences at the top of page 162

3. the 3 example sentences on page 164
4. the first 4 example sentences on page 175
5. the 3 example sentences on page 180 and the 4 example sentences on page 181
6. the 9 example sentences in 2.u (page 197)

3

WRITING SENTENCES

Writing Sentences

All prose writing depends on sentences. In this section you will practice writing many varieties of sentences. Very simple sentences as well as more complicated sentences can add variety, interest, and maturity to your writing. You will see that most ideas can be expressed in a number of different ways. As you practice writing different kinds of sentences in this section, you will add to your ability as a writer.

WRITING SIMPLE SENTENCES

3.a SIMPLE SENTENCES

A **simple sentence** has only one subject (single or compound) and one predicate.

Good writers know how to use many different kinds of simple sentences. The twelve most common kinds will be referred to here as **basic simple sentences**. You do not need to memorize these twelve kinds of basic simple sentences, examples of which appear on the facing page, but it will help you as a writer to realize that one of these kinds of sentences is at the core of each simple sentence and of each clause that you write. That is, these basic simple sentences are the skeletons upon which most sentences are built. If you learn to recognize the skeleton within a sentence, you will be better able to edit and improve the sentences that you write.

Notice that what makes each kind of basic simple sentence different from the others is its predicate – the kind of action verb or linking verb it has and the kind of word or phrase that follows that verb.

Kinds of simple sentences

1. Frontiers **beckon**.
   subject + action verb

2. Frontiers **beckon adventurers**.
   subject + action verb + direct object

3. Frontiers **give people hope**.
   subject + action verb + indirect object + direct object

4. Frontiers **make people hopeful**.
   subject + action verb + direct object + object complement (adjective)

5. Frontiers **make people pioneers**.
   subject + action verb + direct object + object complement (noun)

6. Frontiers **are challenges**.
   subject + linking verb + predicate nominative

7. Frontiers **are lonely**.
   subject + linking verb + predicate adjective

8. Frontiers **were everywhere**.
   subject + linking verb + predicate adverb

9. Frontiers **seem to challenge us**.
   subject + linking verb + infinitive phrase

10. Frontiers **are for everyone**.
    subject + linking verb + prepositional phrase

11. Frontiers **were crossed by pioneers**.
    passive-voice sentence

12. **There are** frontiers.
    subject + linking verb (in inverted order)

3.a.1 Expanding simple sentences

You can add words or phrases to each of the twelve kinds of basic simple sentences above. Even with the addition of single words or phrases, the sentences remain simple sentences. If you expand any basic simple sentence, you will find that the words and phrases you add always tell more about (1) nouns or (2) verbs in the skeleton.

The chart on the facing page shows a number of ways of adding to, or expanding, a basic simple sentence. The sentence is *Frontiers beckon adventurers* (Sentence 2 on preceding page). The same kinds of expansions can also be applied to the other basic simple sentences.

EXERCISE 1. For each lettered category on the chart on the facing page, select one other word or phrase that may be used to expand the basic simple sentence.

EXERCISE 2: Expanding simple sentences with adjectives or participles used as adjectives. Rewrite each of the following simple sentences, adding to the italicized words the most appropriate choice from the Word Bank below. Use each Word Bank item only once.

1. Florida has *fruit.*
2. *Tourists* visit the *resorts.*
3. A *fountain* lured Ponce de Léon.
4. *People* sought youth.
5. Cape Canaveral launched *rockets.*

WORD BANK

a) suntanned	c) aging	e) seaside
b) citrus	d) legendary	f) jet-propelled

EXERCISE 3: Expanding simple sentences with adjectives or participles used as adjectives. Rewrite each of the following simple sentences, adding to the italicized words the most appropriate choice from the Word Bank below. Use each Word Bank item only once.

1. Utah is a *state* known for its copper, gold, and silver.
2. Navajos occupy *Utah.*
3. Utah citizens consider serious *problems.*
4. The Utah legislature fights *air pollution.*
5. Utah has *mountains* and *canyons.*

WORD BANK

a) environmental	c) increasing	e) mining
b) snow-topped	d) southwestern	f) deep

WAYS OF EXPANDING A BASIC SIMPLE SENTENCE

basic simple sentence	***expanded simple sentence***
Frontiers beckon adventurers.	
To tell more about nouns	
A. Add adjective	**New** frontiers beckon adventurers. Frontiers beckon **courageous** adventurers. **New** frontiers beckon **courageous** adventurers.
B. Add participle (or participial phrase) used as adjective	**Expanding into the unknown**, frontiers beckon **star-gazing**, **undaunted** adventurers.
C. Add possessive	**America's** frontiers beckon adventurers.
D. Add prepositional phrase as adjective	Frontiers **of America** beckon adventurers.
E. Add infinitive (or infinitive phrase) as adjective	Frontiers **to conquer** beckon adventurers. Frontiers **to conquer for glory** beckon adventurers.
To tell more about verbs (telling how)	
F. Add adverb of manner	Frontiers **silently** beckon adventurers.
G. Add prepositional phrase as adverb	**In silence**, frontiers beckon adventurers.
To tell more about verbs (telling where)	
H. Add adverb of place	Frontiers beckon adventurers **onward**.
I. Add prepositional phrase as adverb	Frontiers beckon adventurers **beyond the hills**.
To tell more about verbs (telling when)	
J. Add adverb of time	Frontiers **always** beckon adventurers.
K. Add prepositional phrase as adverb	**In this day and age**, frontiers beckon adventurers.
To tell more about verbs (telling why)	
L. Add infinitive (or infinitive phrase) as adverb	Frontiers beckon adventurers **to travel**. Frontiers beckon adventurers **to keep moving forward**.

EXERCISE 4: Expanding simple sentences with infinitives or prepositional phrases. Rewrite each of the following simple sentences, adding to the italicized words the most appropriate choice from the Word Bank below. Use each Word Bank item only once.

1. Hawaiian beaches are comfortable *places.*
2. Hawaii produces a large *crop.*
3. There are many Hawaiian *islands.*
4. Oregon traders brought *furs.*
5. There is increased *building.*

WORD BANK

a) to Hawaii
b) to sunbathe
c) of pineapples
d) to explore
e) of hotels

EXERCISE 5: Expanding simple sentences with infinitives or prepositional phrases. Rewrite each of the following simple sentences, adding to the italicized words the most appropriate choice from the Word Bank below. Use each Word Bank item only once.

1. Indiana is a Midwestern *state.*
2. *Sites* include the Indianapolis Speedway.
3. There are many Indianian *writers.*
4. The *beauty* makes Indiana a vacation spot.
5. Indiana has ideal *soil.*

WORD BANK

a) for growing corn
b) to learn about
c) with a large population
d) to visit
e) of the area

3.a.2 Choices in expanding simple sentences

When you write sentences with adverbs and prepositional phrases, you often have a choice of where to place these expressions. Many times adverbs and prepositional phrases can be placed in more than one position.

EXAMPLES

Eagerly, prospectors searched for gold.
Prospectors **eagerly** searched for gold.
Prospectors searched **eagerly** for gold.
Prospectors searched for gold **eagerly**.

In the late 1850s many settlers sought gold.
Many settlers **in the late 1850s** sought gold.
Many settlers sought gold **in the late 1850s**.

EXERCISE 6: Expanding simple sentences with prepositional phrases or adverbs. Rewrite each of the following simple sentences, adding to each the most appropriate choice from the Word Bank below. Use each Word Bank item only once.

1. Colorado's ski resorts draw visitors.
2. Many Coloradans raise wheat and potatoes.
3. People travel winding roads.
4. Many settlers sought gold.
5. Snow-capped mountains glisten.

WORD BANK

a) in the late 1850s
b) annually
c) on the plains
d) brightly
e) through the Rockies

EXERCISE 7: Expanding simple sentences with prepositional phrases or adverbs. Rewrite each of the following simple sentences, adding to each the most appropriate choice from the Word Bank below. Use each Word Bank item only once.

1. Colorful steamboats visited Louisiana.
2. Mardi Gras entertains tourists.
3. New Orleans jazz has been exported.
4. Many cultures and customs mix.
5. Hotels restaurants abound.

WORD BANK

a) throughout the world
b) in the French Quarter
c) during the 1800s
d) yearly
e) interestingly

EXERCISE 8. Review the sentences that you wrote in Exercises 6 and 7, and determine if the word or phrase that you added can be placed at a different point in the sentence. If so, rewrite the sentence showing the alternate position.

EXAMPLE Colorado's ski resorts draw visitors **annually**.
ANSWER *Colorado's ski resorts **annually** draw visitors.*

EXERCISE 9: Expanding simple sentences with infinitive phrases and participial phrases. Rewrite each of the following simple sentences, adding to each the most appropriate choice from the Word Bank below. Use each item once.

1. Horses are trained in Kentucky.
2. During the Civil War Kentuckians fought for both sides.
3. Gold is kept in Fort Knox.
4. Blue-hued grass grows in quantity.
5. Mammoth Cave's passageways are challenging.

WORD BANK

a) stored in safety
b) to race well
c) dividing their loyalties
d) to explore on your own
e) giving Kentucky the nickname "Bluegrass State"

EXERCISE 10: Expanding simple sentences with infinitive phrases and participial phrases. Rewrite each of the following simple sentences, adding to each the most appropriate choice from the Word Bank below. Use each item once.

1. North Carolina's coast is a dangerous place.
2. A group of early settlers vanished.
3. The Wright brothers made Kitty Hawk a famous place.
4. Much wood is used for North Carolina's furniture industry.
5. Fertile fields encourage agriculture.

WORD BANK

a) leaving no trace
b) to supply raw materials
c) to remember in aviation history
d) to flourish in North Carolina
e) to sail a boat

EXERCISE 11: Using all structures to expand sentences. Rewrite each of the following basic simple sentences in two different ways. First add Item *a* to the original sentence, creating one new sentence. Then add Item *b* to the original sentence, creating another new sentence. You have to decide at which point in the sentence to place Item *a* or Item *b*; sometimes you will have a choice.

1. People have enjoyed vacations.
   a) always
   b) to faraway places
2. American resorts grew.
   a) in the North and the South
   b) during the 1920s
3. Urban business people left the cities.
   a) for their vacations
   b) happily
4. Vacationers went to the beach or mountains.
   a) for relaxation
   b) every summer
5. Hotels were built for tourists.
   a) enormous
   b) primarily
6. Businesses opened each summer.
   a) booming
   b) before the tourist season
7. There were also cottages.
   a) expensive
   b) to rent
8. Some people stayed at spas.
   a) ailing
   b) to restore their health
9. Sufferers bathed in mineral springs.
   a) with muscle ailments
   b) flowing from the ground
10. Some vacationers brought tents.
    a) to sleep in
    b) with them
11. Camping pleased people.
    a) in tents
    b) nature-loving

12. Atlantic City's boardwalk was a site.
    a) famous
    b) to visit
13. In 1889 a storm destroyed one boardwalk.
    a) totally
    b) raging
14. A new boardwalk was built.
    a) in haste
    b) wooden
15. New Englanders stopped at Martha's Vineyard.
    a) frequently
    b) traveling
16. Nantucket Island turned to tourism.
    a) to survive
    b) following the death of whaling
17. Seafaring people visited Nantucket.
    a) to fish
    b) often
18. Block Island was a resort community.
    a) by 1890
    b) an exclusive
19. Photographers took pictures.
    a) at resorts
    b) souvenir
20. Resort towns emptied out.
    a) America's
    b) in winter

EXERCISE 12: Expanding simple sentences in a variety of ways. Rewrite each of the following simple sentences, adding to each the most appropriate choice from the Word Bank below. Use each Word Bank item only once.

1. The cotton gin was invented in Georgia.
2. Georgia is a grower of peanuts and peaches.
3. Ether was first used in Georgia.
4. Much income comes from textile mills.
5. Settlers came to Georgia.
6. Georgia gave eighteen-year-olds the vote.

7. General Sherman's troops marched across Georgia.
8. Pine trees grow exceptionally tall.
9. Georgia has much valuable marble.
10. Georgia's history and landscape have been immortalized.

WORD BANK

a) in songs and stories
b) to quarry
c) in Georgia's forests
d) famous
e) in Georgia
f) leading
g) from England
h) to kill pain
i) before the other states
j) destroying much property

EXERCISE 13. Review your revised sentences in Exercise 12, and determine if the word or phrase that you added could be placed at a different point in the sentence. If so, rewrite the sentence showing the alternate position. Indicate which version you prefer.

EXERCISE 14. Review the sentences that you wrote in Exercises 12 and 13. Identify the element that you added to each. That is, tell which part of speech or what kind of phrase you added.

EXERCISE 15: Expanding simple sentences in a variety of ways. Rewrite each of the simple sentences on the following page, adding to each a word or phrase from the Word Bank below the sentences. The letters at the end of each numbered sentence tell you from which lists in the Word Bank to choose the additions. Use each Word Bank item only once. (The ones used in the example have been crossed out.)

EXAMPLE Sleuths practice. *A, F*
ANSWER ***Amateur*** *sleuths practice* ***everywhere***.
A ***F***

1. People enjoy mysteries. *A, K*
2. Mystery stories have plots. *H, D*
3. Writers give readers clues. *D, E*
4. Clues are common tricks. *B, D*
5. Someone commits a crime. *H, I, G*
6. The detective questions suspects. *J*
7. The alibis are stories. *C, A*
8. The investigator tricks the culprit. *B, G*
9. Which one is lying? *F, G*
10. The motive is a mystery. *A, D*

WORD BANK

A. Adjectives

~~amateur~~
foolproof
complete
clever
allergic

B. Participles as adjectives

trained
misleading
ringing

C. Possessives

California's
suspect's

D. Prepositional phrases as adjectives

of mysteries
to everyone
in mystery stories
with a twist
for England

E. Infinitives as adjectives

to speak
to discover

F. Adverbs of place

~~everywhere~~
here
beyond

G. Prepositional phrases as adverbs

by yourself
to the police
by clever questioning
in the night

H. Adverbs of time

often
first
never

I. Adverbs of manner

devilishly
nationally

J. Participial phrases as adverbs

sharing the food
picking up clues

K. Infinitives as adverbs

to sew
to solve

■ Sentence stories

Exercise 16 below serves as a review of what you have learned in the preceding pages of this section about writing and expanding simple sentences. If you follow the instructions for Exercise 16 and the "Directions" beside each of the ten "Word Banks," you will end up with ten separate simple sentences. Each of these sentences might be thought of as a *very* short short story.

EXERCISE 16: Writing sentences from given data. Compose original simple sentences based on data given below and in the pages that follow. On the left you will find a column or two of words. On the right you will find a three-part direction for putting the words into one complete expanded simple sentence. Use every word in the Word Bank, but use each word only once.

1. WORD BANK

a, baby, crippled, dog, cried, later, like, night, that, the, under, their, window, brown

DIRECTIONS

a) Write a sentence in which the animal makes a noise.
b) Expand the sentence by telling when, where, and how the action took place.
c) Add two words to tell more about the animal. Write the complete sentence.

---

2. WORD BANK

striped
the
relentlessly
spotted
attacked
cat
on
the
pillow
chair
foam rubber
the

DIRECTIONS

a) Write a sentence telling what the animal did.
b) Expand the sentence by telling where and how the animal acted.
c) Add words that describe the animal and its target. Write the complete sentence.

---

3. WORD BANK

mentalist
from
the
San Diego
talented
mind
the
suavely
trembling
the
of
read
zookeeper

DIRECTIONS

a) Write a sentence naming the performer and a performance.
b) Expand the sentence by describing the performer, telling where he or she was from, and describing how he or she acted.
c) Add words to name and describe the participant. Write the complete sentence.

---

4. WORD BANK

around
pandas
in
ran
playful
circles
their
in
cage

DIRECTIONS

a) Describe what some animals did.
b) Add a word to describe the animals.
c) Expand the sentence to tell how and where they did the action. Write the complete sentence.

---

5. WORD BANK

blizzard
the
the
workers
after
tried
awe-struck
to
unsuccessfully
enormous
clear
drifts
the
main
roads
from

DIRECTIONS

a) Tell what some workers tried to do.
b) Expand the sentence to tell when and where and how they worked.
c) Add a word to describe the workers and a word to describe the snow. Write the complete sentence.

6. WORD BANK

disco
the
the
dancers
in
ease
danced
moving
on
with
skates

DIRECTIONS

a) Write a sentence telling what some people did.
b) Expand the sentence to tell where they did it.
c) Add words to tell how they did the action. Write the complete sentence.

---

7. WORD BANK

miser
methodically
a
coins
penny-pinching
in
saved
hidden
the
cellar
burlap
bags
in

DIRECTIONS

a) Write a sentence telling who saved what.
b) Tell how something was saved, what it was kept in, and where it was kept.
c) Add words to describe the person and the containers. Write the complete sentence.

---

8. WORD BANK

night
two
friends
one
winter
beach
imagined
and
tropical
palm trees
a
on
island

DIRECTIONS

a) Write a sentence describing what two people did.
b) Add words to tell when they did it.
c) Expand the sentence by adding words to describe what they envisioned. Write the complete sentence.

9. WORD BANK

darkened
in
audience
the
transported
the
movie
theater
to
Old West
the
magically
entranced
the

DIRECTIONS

a) Write a sentence telling what the movie did to whom.
b) Tell where the action happened.
c) Add words to describe the people and how the action took place. Write the complete sentence.

---

10. WORD BANK

final	the
game's	cheering
the	shooting
watched	player
at	basket
crowd	the
end	the

DIRECTIONS

a) Write a sentence telling what some people did.
b) Add words to describe what they saw, and when they saw it.
c) Add a word to describe the crowd. Write the complete sentence.

WRITING SENTENCES WITH TWO OR MORE MAIN CLAUSES

3.b JOINING MAIN CLAUSES

A **compound sentence** consists of two or more main clauses.

A main clause, as you know, can stand by itself as a sentence or can be joined with another main clause to form a longer sentence.

You write compound sentences every day, without thinking much about them. Your goal now is to think about them as you write them.

3.b.1 Using coordinating conjunctions to join main clauses

As a writer, you should learn how you can most effectively use the **coordinating conjunctions** *and, but, or,* and *for.* Look at the two simple sentences below, and then observe how they have been combined into compound sentences.

SIMPLE SENTENCES

1. He broke the glass vase.
2. I broke the china bowl.

COMPOUND SENTENCES

3. He broke the glass vase, **and** I broke the china bowl.
4. He broke the glass vase, **but** I broke the china bowl.

There is a slight difference in meaning between Sentence 3 and Sentence 4. Sentence 3 suggests that both accidents were equal in importance and that the blame should be equally shared. Sentence 4 suggests that breaking the bowl was more serious than breaking the vase. The differences between Sentence 3 and Sentence 4 are communicated through the choice of conjunction—*and* in Sentence 3, *but* in Sentence 4.

■ The coordinating conjunctions and their uses

The coordinating conjunctions are used between main clauses for different reasons, as the following examples show.

AND

1. The snow is falling, **and** the wind is blowing.
2. We wanted a big snow, **and** that is what we had.

In Sentence 1 the coordinating conjunction *and* balances the two main clauses; it shows that the clauses are both related to each other and equally important. In Sentence 2 the *and* connects two steps in a process: First this happened, and then that happened.

BUT

3. The snow was deep, **but** we arrived on time.

In Sentence 3 the coordinating conjunction *but* shows a contrast. The second clause is unexpected in view of what is said in the first clause.

OR

4. You can walk through the snowstorm, **or** you can wait until the roads are clear.

In Sentence 4 the coordinating conjunction *or* indicates that an alternative is given.

FOR

5. I am sorry that more snow is predicted, **for** I had hoped to leave tomorrow.

In Sentence 5 the coordinating conjunction *for* indicates that the second clause gives a reason for the statement in the first clause.

NOR

Nor is usually used with *neither* in the correlative conjunction *neither...nor* (see page 229).

EXERCISE 17. Rewrite the following sentences, adding the appropriate coordinating conjunction in each.

1. People often fear bats, _____ bats would rather feed on mosquitoes than on people.
2. There are millions of bats in the world, _____ their population is increasing.
3. Bats cannot get tangled in your hair, _____ they have no claws on their feet.
4. There are some vampire bats, _____ these bats do not live in the United States.
5. Were vampire bats the model for Dracula, _____ was it the other way around?
6. Bats tend to fly at night, _____ during the day they sleep.
7. Bats hang upside down to rest, _____ they seem to be comfortable.
8. Many infant bats die, _____ they fall from their roosts.
9. Bats are not blind, _____ they do use sound waves (not sight) to find their way.
10. Anyone bitten by a bat should see a doctor, _____ bats can carry rabies.

AVOIDING ERRORS WITH COORDINATING CONJUNCTIONS

1. In writing, do not use *so* as a coordinating conjunction.

   NOT The day was gloomy, ~~so~~ we stayed indoors.
   BUT The day was gloomy, **and so** we stayed indoors.

   The point to remember is that only *and, but, or,* and *for* are coordinating conjunctions. The word *so* is usually an adverb *(it is growing* **so** *late)* or a conjunctive adverb, like *nevertheless* and *therefore* (see 1.h.3).

   It was late; **therefore**, we went home.
   It was late; **so** we went home.

2. Do not use *yet* as a coordinating conjunction.

   NOT The day was gloomy, ~~yet~~ we enjoyed ourselves.
   BUT The day was gloomy, **and yet** we enjoyed ourselves.

   Like *so,* the word *yet* can be a conjunctive adverb used with a semicolon to join two main clauses.

   The day was gloomy; **nevertheless**, we enjoyed ourselves.
   The day was gloomy; **yet** we enjoyed ourselves.

COMMAS BETWEEN MAIN CLAUSES

Notice that a comma is used before the coordinating conjunction in compound sentences. The comma is used to avoid possible confusion, as in the first sentence below.

NOT I hugged the baby and the dog barked.
BUT I hugged the baby**,** and the dog barked.

Do you see how the comma in the second sentence prevents a misreading?

EXERCISE 18. Compose five compound sentences. For each main clause in Column I, find in Column II the main clause that logically follows it. Each clause from each column must be used.

Column I	Column II
1. We must apply for insurance,	a) and everyone had a good time.
2. We trudged through the snow to the polling place,	b) but we will win the war.
3. We planned the surprise for weeks,	c) or we may lose everything.
4. We all work in this family,	d) for every vote counts.
5. We may lose the battle,	e) for we must all learn the value of money.

EXERCISE 19. For the following sentence frames, write a second main clause that logically completes its meaning.

1. Today, photography is growing in popularity, and _______________.
2. It is not hard to take a picture, but _______________.
3. _______________, for much photographic equipment has become less expensive and easier to use.
4. Some people like to take pictures of people, but _______________.
5. Photographs are wonderful keepsakes, and _______________.
6. You can record a place or a moment with a camera, or _______________.
7. _______________, for everyone enjoys taking pictures.
8. Some pictures are in black and white, and _______________.
9. Moving pictures are fun, but _______________.
10. _______________, or you can become a photographer.

EXERCISE 20. For the following sentence frames, write a second main clause that logically completes its meaning.

1. The play has well-developed characters, but _______________.
2. _______________, and the scenery reinforces the eerie mood.
3. _______________, for the stage directions are vague.
4. _______________, or the show will close.
5. The critics generally praised the playwright's attempt, but _______________.

6. Trying to write plays after working all day in a store is exhausting, but ______________.
7. Many a novice playwright has learned the craft from bad reviews and failure, but ______________.
8. ______________, and they never write again.
9. ______________, or they learn to earn a living in some other way.
10. ______________, for they are aware that a single play can bring riches and lasting fame.

3.b.2 Joining more than two main clauses to form a sentence

Sometimes you may want to join more than two main clauses in the same sentence. For example, you may want to show the sequence of events in a series.

EXAMPLE

The man fell asleep, the candle fell over, **and** the room was soon ablaze.

You may want to set up a contrast involving more than two elements.

EXAMPLE

The roof collapsed, **and** the walls caved in, **but** everyone got out safely.

EXERCISE 21: Sentence Combining. Combine each of the following groups of sentences into a single compound sentence with three main clauses. The material that is in parentheses should be moved to the beginning of the sentence on that line, as the example shows.

EXAMPLE The house lights dimmed.
The conductor raised her baton. (,)
The usual hush fell over the audience. (, AND)

ANSWER *The house lights dimmed, the conductor raised her baton,* ***and*** *the usual hush fell over the audience.*

1. The overture ended.
   The curtains parted. (,)
   The audience gasped at the stage. (, **AND**)
2. The ballerina leapt across the stage.
   Her partner stepped too soon. (, **BUT**)
   She fell with a thud. (, **AND**)
3. The ballerina's toe shoes were too tight.
   Her feet hurt. (, **OR**)
   She tripped several times. (, **FOR**)
4. The music was beautiful.
   The performance was poor. (, **BUT**)
   The orchestra had not practiced long enough. (, **FOR**)
5. I was sitting too far away.
   The music was too soft. (, **OR**)
   I could not hear well. (, **FOR**)

For Sentences 6–10, provide your own punctuation and coordinating conjunctions.

6. The critics panned the ballet.
   People came in droves.
   Escapism and fantasy always have fans.
7. I took my sister to see the ballet.
   She enjoyed it greatly.
   Her tastes are similar to mine.
8. The ballet was made into a film.
   The same music was used.
   The story was changed.
9. The public did not enjoy the film.
   The critics' reviews were not flattering.
   I enjoyed the film.
10. Some films are appreciated by critics.
    They are not popular with the public.
    The public often has different standards than critics.

3.b.3 Using correlative conjunctions to join main clauses

As a writer, you may want to use a *pair* of conjunctions to join main clauses. Look at the first two sentences below, and then observe how they have been combined.

SIMPLE SENTENCES

1. My upstairs neighbors stomp around.
2. My downstairs neighbors play their stereo loudly.

COMPOUND SENTENCES

3. My upstairs neighbors stomp around, **and** my downstairs neighbors play their stereo loudly.
4. **Either** my upstairs neighbors stomp around, **or** my downstairs neighbors play their stereo loudly.

There is a difference in meaning between Sentence 3 and Sentence 4, even though both sentences are constructed from the same two main clauses. Sentence 3 suggests that the two disturbances occur at the same time. Sentence 4 suggests that they alternate. When *either* and *or* are used in the same sentence (as in Sentence 4), together they are called a **correlative conjunction**.

When writing compound sentences with main clauses joined by correlative conjunctions, be sure that there is a subject and a verb following each conjunction, as in the following examples.

EITHER ... OR

Either *Mr. Ozawa will conduct*, or *he will hire* a substitute.

JUST AS ... SO (TOO)

Just as a *conductor has* a right to expect attention from an orchestra, so (too) an *orchestra has* a right to expect courtesy from a conductor.

NEITHER ... NOR
NOT ONLY ... BUT ALSO

Neither did *Mr. Ozawa arrive*, nor did his *substitute conduct* well.

Not only *was* the *orchestra* annoyed, but *it* also *played* badly that night.

These negative correlative conjunctions usually sound awkward when they are used to join main clauses. (You can, of course, use *neither... nor* and *not only... but also* effectively to join individual words and phrases, as explained in 1.h.2.) Notice, in the example above, that *but also* will sometimes be split up in the sentence, with a subject, a verb, or an adverb (or a combination) between *but* and *also*.

EXERCISE 22. Complete the second main clause in each of the following sentence frames.

1. Either people will learn to stop killing whales, or soon ________________.
2. Just as the dodo bird became extinct, so the whale ________________.
3. Not only are hamsters gentle pets, but they also ________________.
4. Either efforts to save the whooping crane from extinction will succeed, or ________________.
5. Not only are some bears very large, but they also ________________.
6. Neither is Alaska the most populous state in the United States, nor is it ________________.
7. Just as people go to Vermont in the winter to ski, so they go to ________________.
8. Not only does California have deserts and mountains, but it also has ________________.
9. Neither is the Mississippi the longest river in the world, nor is it ________________.
10. Just as the Northeast has large urban centers, so the Midwest has ________________.

EXERCISE 23. Complete the second main clause in each of the following sentence frames.

1. Not only did the critics praise the play, but they also ________________.
2. Just as the actor stopped the show in the first act, so the actress ________________.
3. Either the playwright paid someone to write the show, or he ________________.
4. Neither did the audience expect such entertainment, nor did the producer ________________.
5. Not only did the show play on Broadway for five years, but it also ________________.

COMMAS WITH CORRELATIVE CONJUNCTIONS

Use a comma before the second part of the correlative conjunction when the conjunction joins main clauses.

Either my upstairs neighbors stomp around**,** or my downstairs neighbors play their stereo loudly.

EXERCISE 24: Sentence Combining. Combine each of the following groups of sentences into a single compound sentence. The material that is in parentheses should be moved to the beginning of the sentence on that line, as the example shows.

EXAMPLE The deadline must be extended. (**EITHER**)
I must stop all my other projects. (**, OR**)

ANSWER ***Either*** *the deadline must be extended****, or*** *I must stop all my other projects.*

1. Her first play brought her instant recognition. (**JUST AS**)
   Her second will secure her reputation. (**, SO**)
2. He just needs a rest. (**EITHER**)
   He has a permanent writing block. (**, OR**)
3. She is working harder. (**NOT ONLY**)
   She is playing harder. (**, BUT ALSO**)
4. The network will buy the rights. (**EITHER**)
   I will be very happy. (**, AND**)
   I will have to rewrite the teleplay. (**, OR**)
5. The novel was popular. (**JUST AS**)
   The film is breaking records now. (**, SO**)
   Neither will survive the test of time. (**, BUT**)

For Sentences 6–10, provide your own punctuation and correlative or coordinating conjunctions.

6. Poems are more dense and more concise than novels.
   Poetry depends more upon the sound and rhythm of words.
7. Novels are written in chapters.
   Songs are written in stanzas.
   Poetry is written in verses.

8. Her poetry is concise.
   Its rhythms are regular.
   It is appreciated by critics.
9. She must work faster.
   The deadlines must be extended.
   The book will not be finished in time.
10. Good poets are immediately popular.
    They are widely read and studied.
    They must wait many years for recognition.

3.b.4 Using a semicolon to join main clauses

In certain cases a writer may decide to use a semicolon between main clauses. If a semicolon is used in this way, no conjunction is needed.

A compound sentence formed by joining two main clauses with only a semicolon has a concise and formal sound and look. The clauses on either side of the semicolon must be brief and parallel, or the sentence will be confused and awkward. If, as a writer, you feel that you want to avoid the use of coordinating conjunctions, it is usually best to use semicolons to divide the sentence into separate clauses.

EXAMPLES

The needy are many**;** the rich are few.
Wed in haste**;** repent at leisure.
Some of the difficulty would exist in any company**;** some of it could exist only here.

3.b.5 Using conjunctive adverbs to join main clauses

A word such as *however* often functions as a **conjunctive adverb** (see 1.h.3). A conjunctive adverb can be used with a semicolon to join main clauses. Using a conjunctive adverb usually produces a stronger emphasis than using a semicolon alone or using a coordinating conjunction. For example, the conjunctive adverb *however* is generally considered stronger than the coordinating conjunction *but.*

EXAMPLE

Brad insisted he was not nervous; **however**, I could tell otherwise.

Although there are many conjunctive adverbs, they can be grouped according to meaning, as the following lists show. You will notice that some of the items included on these lists are made up of two or three words. These connecting phrases are similar to conjunctive adverbs in both meaning and function.

BASIC CONJUNCTIVE ADVERB	SIMILAR CONJUNCTIVE ADVERBS AND CONNECTING PHRASES
however	despite this, instead, nevertheless, nonetheless, on the other hand, still, yet
furthermore	also, besides, in addition, likewise, moreover, similarly
therefore	as a result, accordingly, consequently, hence
for example	for instance, to illustrate

EXERCISE 25. For each of the following sentences, substitute an appropriate conjunctive adverb to replace the blank.

1. As the earth goes through changes, fertile land can become arid; _____, the deserts of the Middle East were once lush and green.
2. People have mismanaged a great deal of the earth's land; _____, a large portion of the earth is becoming desert.
3. Overgrazing by livestock has destroyed land; _____, cutting down too many trees destroyed land.
4. In the past the land could recover from overuse; _____, now it is harder for depleted land to recover its nutrients.
5. Populations are growing; _____, more land is needed to support the people.
6. Developing nations face problems caused by spreading deserts; _____, arid land is spreading in the United States as well.
7. There are huge deserts in Africa and Asia; _____, there is much desert in the southwestern United States.
8. Many trees have been cut down in the United States; _____, the land is vulnerable to soil erosion.

9. Irrigation can even hurt the land; _____, too much irrigation can destroy the soil.
10. The increase of deserts is a worldwide problem; _____, human efforts and new technology can save the earth.

EXERCISE 26. For each of the following sentence frames, write a second main clause that logically completes its meaning. If you have trouble coming up with an idea to use in a main clause, check the Idea Bank below.

1. Today, many young people believe in higher education; therefore, ______________.
2. Today, many young people believe in higher education; however, ______________.
3. Jobs with prestige are not necessarily the best-paying jobs; for example, ______________.
4. Jobs with prestige are not necessarily the best-paying jobs; despite this, ______________.
5. Many women are now full-time members of the work force; accordingly, ______________.
6. Many women are now full-time members of the work force; in addition, ______________.
7. Reading and writing skills are essential in most occupations; thus, ______________.
8. Reading and writing skills are essential in most occupations; nonetheless, ______________.
9. Some people spend more than seven hours a day at work; as a result, ______________.
10. Some people spend more than seven hours a day at work; moreover, ______________.

IDEA BANK

higher enrollments
value of education
cost of education
competition for jobs
length of time in work force
employers' insistence on basic skills
lower test scores
effect on family life

PUNCTUATION WITH CONJUNCTIVE ADVERBS

Most conjunctive adverbs should be set off with punctuation marks. They should have some punctuation on either side of them unless they appear as the first word in a sentence.

> Some of the difficulty would exist in any company**;** **however,** some of it could exist only here.
> Some of the difficulty would exist in any company; some of it**, however,** could exist only here.
> Some of the difficulty would exist in any company; some of it could exist only here**, however**.

AVOIDING ERRORS WHEN JOINING MAIN CLAUSES

Do not put two main clauses together with just a comma, or you will have a **run-on sentence**. Use (1) a comma and a coordinating conjunction, (2) a semicolon, or (3) a semicolon and a conjunctive adverb. You may also begin a new sentence.

NOT We complained about the noise, our neighbor continued to ignore us.

BUT We complained about the noise**, but** our neighbor continued to ignore us.

OR We complained about the noise**;** our neighbor continued to ignore us.

OR We complained about the noise**;** **however**, our neighbor continued to ignore us.

OR We complained about the noise**.** Our neighbor continued to ignore us.

EXERCISE 27. For each of the following sentence frames, write a second main clause that logically completes it. If you have trouble coming up with an idea to use in a main clause, check the Idea Bank below.

1. Television advertisers reach millions of people; as a result, _______________.
2. Television advertisers reach millions of people; however, _______________.
3. Advertisers must make their products memorable to viewers; for example, _______________.
4. Advertisers must make their products memorable to viewers; on the other hand, _______________.
5. Television advertising time is limited and very expensive; therefore, _______________.
6. Television advertising time is limited and very expensive; still, _______________.
7. Television allows advertisers to show products well; moreover, _______________.
8. Television allows advertisers to show products well; nevertheless, _______________.
9. Some television commercials are entertaining; however, _______________.
10. Some television commercials are entertaining; in addition, _______________.

IDEA BANK

many advertisers on television
Everyone does not watch television.
to the point
show product clearly
Words should supplement.
Television ads are expensive.
show product too much
worth the money
demonstrate products
Ads sell products.

After you have completed this exercise, select five of your completed sentences and rewrite them using a coordinating conjunction between the two main clauses in place of the conjunctive adverb. Be sure to punctuate correctly.

WRITING SENTENCES WITH SUBORDINATE CLAUSES

Although compound sentences are informative and smooth, sentences with two main clauses have their limits. You talk in compound sentences much of the time. If you look for compound sentences in published writing, however, you will notice that they are not as common as you might expect. Professional writers find alternatives to compound sentences for two main reasons: (1) A long string of compound sentences becomes monotonous (one sentence sounds much the same as another), and (2) not all ideas can be accurately related to one another by means of coordinating main clauses. Sometimes a sentence with a subordinate clause creates a clearer relationship of ideas.

3.c WRITING COMPLEX SENTENCES

A **complex sentence** has one main clause and one or more subordinate clauses.

Remember that a subordinate clause must have a subject and a predicate but that it cannot stand alone as a complete sentence. A subordinate clause can be an adverb clause, an adjective clause, or a noun clause. Remember, too, that a subordinate clause begins with a subordinator, or an introductory word. Two kinds of subordinators are subordinating conjunctions and relative pronouns.

3.c.1 Writing adverb clauses that tell "when"

As a writer, you often need to tell when the action of the main clause takes place. You can do so by adding an adverb clause before or after the main clause.

EXAMPLES

The girl sang **before the guests arrived**.
The girl sang **until her throat was sore**.
After her father came home, the girl sang.
As soon as the audience became quiet, the girl began.

Subordinating conjunctions are among the subordinators that can be used to begin a clause that tells "when." (For a longer list of subordinating conjunctions see 1.h.4.)

SUBORDINATORS THAT TELL "WHEN"

after	as long as	before	until	whenever
as	as soon as	since	when	while

Tense sequence with clauses that tell "when"

Often you use the same tense for the verb in the main clause and the verb in the subordinate clause.

EXAMPLES

When she **sang**, the audience **listened**. [Both verbs are in the past tense.]

When she **speaks**, she **expects** attention. [Both verbs are in the present tense.]

At times, however, the action in one clause may take place before the action in the other. In such cases, different tenses are used in each clause.

EXAMPLE

When she **had sung** for an hour, she **asked** to take a break. [She stopped singing; then, she asked. One action preceded the other. The first verb is in the past perfect tense, the second in the past tense.]

EXERCISE 28. Compose five complex sentences. For each main clause in Column I, find in Column II a suitable "when" clause to follow it. Each clause from each column must be used. Begin each sentence with the main clause.

Column I

1. I go to the beach
2. She had not seen her brother
3. He watched television
4. We left the concert
5. You should not hand in a paper

Column II

a) as soon as Sarah had played her solo.
b) after he finished his homework.
c) whenever I can.
d) since he had grown a beard.
e) until you have checked it for errors.

EXERCISE 29. Add an adverb clause that tells "when" to each of the numbered items. In some cases a subordinating conjunction is given; in other cases you will have to choose one. Remember that an adverb clause must have a subject and a predicate.

1. Mary has been acting in amateur productions since ______________.
2. After ______________, the director suggested that she try out for a Broadway play.
3. She rehearsed the scene until ______________.
4. ______________, she suddenly became nervous for the first time in her career.
5. She felt relieved ______________.

EXERCISE 30: Sentence Combining. Combine each of the following pairs of sentences into a single complex sentence. Move the word or phrase that is in parentheses to the beginning of the sentence on that line. Place a comma after the subordinate clause. Use the example below as a model.

EXAMPLE John F. Kennedy was elected. (**UNTIL**)
No Roman Catholic had ever been President.

ANSWER ***Until*** *John F. Kennedy was elected, no Roman Catholic had ever been President.*

1. Franklin Roosevelt ran for Vice President. (**WHEN**)
   Warren Harding was running for President.
2. Franklin Roosevelt sought the Presidency. (**EVERY TIME**)
   He won the election.
3. Franklin Roosevelt was President. (**WHILE**)
   World War II broke out.
4. The final returns came in. (**UNTIL**)
   Harry Truman thought he had lost the 1948 election.
5. Dwight D. Eisenhower began his first term. (**WHEN**)
   American troops were fighting in Korea.
6. Lyndon Johnson was elected Vice President. (**BEFORE**)
   He was the Senate majority leader.
7. John F. Kennedy was assassinated. (**AFTER**)
   Lyndon Johnson was sworn in as President.
8. Gerald Ford was appointed Vice President. (**BEFORE**)
   He was the House minority leader.

9. Richard Nixon went to China. (**WHEN**)
   He dramatically changed American foreign policy.
10. Gerald Ford was President. (**WHILE**)
    The United States celebrated its 200th anniversary.

EXERCISE 31: Sentence Combining. Combine each of the following pairs of sentences into a single complex sentence. Move the material in parentheses to the beginning of the sentence on that line, as the example shows.

EXAMPLE The White House has been the President's home.
John and Abigail Adams occupied it. (**SINCE**)

ANSWER *The White House has been the home of the President* ***since*** *John and Abigail Adams occupied it.*

1. Martha Custis was a widow with four children.
   She married George Washington. (**WHEN**)
2. John and Abigail Adams moved into the White House.
   The building was completed. (**BEFORE**)
3. Thomas Jefferson never remarried.
   His wife died in 1782. (**AFTER**)
4. Dolley Madison often acted as White House hostess.
   The widowed Jefferson was President. (**WHILE**)
5. Dolley Madison's new drapes went up in flames.
   The British burned the White House in 1814. (**WHEN**)
6. Andrew Jackson's wife died.
   He was inaugurated as President. (**BEFORE**)
7. William Henry Harrison eloped with his bride.
   Her father refused his permission. (**WHEN**)
8. The White House was open to the public twice a week.
   Sarah Polk was First Lady. (**AS LONG AS**)
9. Millard Fillmore's wife died.
   She caught a cold at Franklin Pierce's inauguration. (**AFTER**)
10. James Buchanan was a confirmed bachelor.
    He became President in 1857. (**WHEN**)

EXERCISE 32: Sentence Combining. Combine each of the following pairs of sentences into a single complex sentence. Select a subordinator that tells "when," and put it at the beginning of the sentence on the top line. Use a comma after each introductory "when" clause, as in the example below. Try to use as many different *subordinators that tell "when"* as you can. (See the list on page 238 or 1.h.4.)

EXAMPLE The clock struck twelve.
Her coach turned into a pumpkin.

ANSWER ***When*** *the clock struck twelve,* *her coach turned into a pumpkin.*

1. Tom started to paint the fence.
Everyone else wanted to paint it, too.
2. The stock market went down.
I lost a million dollars.
3. The cooking was done by her brother.
Nobody felt like eating.
4. She saved enough to buy a $90 bicycle.
Its price went up to $100.
5. Somebody sang a lullaby.
His sister promptly went to sleep.
6. You tidy up your belongings.
You cannot find anything.
7. The doorbell rings.
Our dogs bark like maniacs.
8. Our dogs bark.
The neighbors get furious.
9. I knew the combination.
I could open the safe.
10. The musicians played Latin tunes.
Everyone danced.

EXERCISE 33: Sentence Combining. Combine each of the following pairs of sentences into a single complex sentence. Select a subordinator that tells "when," and put it at the beginning of the sentence on the second line. If you need help with commas, see page 250. Try to use as many different *subordinators that tell "when"* as you can. You may want to review the list at 1.h.4.

EXAMPLE Conversation flowed freely.
All the guests arrived.

ANSWER *Conversation flowed freely* ***as soon as*** *all the guests arrived.*
Conversation flowed freely ***when*** *all the guests arrived.*

EXAMPLE We headed home.
It became cold.

ANSWER ***When*** *it became cold, we headed home.*

1. The cars surge forward.
The traffic light changes.
2. My toothache disappears.
I go to the dentist.
3. We performed magic tricks.
We made many friends.
4. They insured their belongings.
Their apartment was robbed.
5. I fell off the horse quite often.
I took riding lessons.
6. She thought that he was a good writer.
She read his book.
7. They were extremely nervous.
They were on stage.
8. Her handwriting became legible.
She was fifteen years old.
9. My life became more interesting.
I bought myself a chimpanzee.
10. We understood every word.
They spoke Japanese.

3.c.2 Writing adverb clauses that tell "where"

To tell where the action of the main clause takes place, you can add an adverb clause beginning with the subordinating conjunction *where* or *wherever.*

EXAMPLE
The girl sang **where her voice could be heard**.
The girls sang **wherever they went**.

In addition, words or phrases that indicate place can be used as subordinators: *everywhere, everywhere that, every place, anywhere, anyplace.* An adverb clause that tells "where" almost always follows the main clause; occasionally, when *wherever* is used, the adverb clause may come before the main clause.

EXAMPLE

***Wherever* he went**, he found that Sandy had been there earlier.

AVOIDING ERRORS WITH ADVERB CLAUSES THAT TELL "WHEN"

1. Make sure that *both* the main clause and the adverb clause have a subject.

   NOT My son helps me cook and then clean up when ✕ visits on Sunday.
   BUT My son helps me cook and then clean up when **he** visits on Sunday.

2. Do not repeat the idea expressed in the "when" clause later in the sentence.

   NOT When my television breaks, I have to send it back to the manufacturer ~~every time something goes wrong with it.~~
   BUT When my television breaks, I have to send it back to the manufacturer.
   OR I have to send my television back to the manufacturer every time something goes wrong with it.

   Think of a clause that tells "when" as moving the sentence forward. Do not let the sentence circle back on itself.

3. Do not use a clause that tells "when" directly after a form of *be.* Sometimes you have to substitute another expression for the form of *be.*

   NOT A solar eclipse ~~is when~~ the moon comes between the sun and the earth.
   BUT A solar eclipse **takes place when** the moon comes between the sun and the earth.

EXERCISE 34. Compose five complex sentences. For each main clause in Column I, find in Column II a suitable "where" clause to follow it. Each clause in Column II must be used. Begin each sentence with the main clause.

Column I	Column II
1. The town was built	a) where no one would ever find it.
2. The ball flew into the air and landed	b) where there is little or no sun for long periods.
3. Nights and days look alike	c) where rainfall is insufficient.
4. He found the book	d) where the river empties into the sea.
5. Farmers use irrigation systems	e) where he had left it.

3.c.3 Writing adverb clauses that tell "how"

To tell how the action of the main clause takes place, you can add an adverb clause beginning with *as if, as though,* or simply *as.*

EXAMPLES

1. The girl sang **as though her heart would break**.
2. **As if this were her final performance**, the girl sang the song selected for the audition.
3. The girl sang **as she was taught to**.

The position of an adverb clause that tells "how" depends upon the sense and structure of the sentence.

Try rewriting the above sentences, putting the adverb clause in Sentence 1 first and putting the adverb clause in Sentence 2 after the main clause. You will discover that the new Sentence 1 is awkward, and the new Sentence 2 is confusing.

EXERCISE 35. Compose five complex sentences. For each main clause in Column I, find in Column II a suitable "how" clause to follow it. Each clause from each column must be used. Begin each sentence with the main clause.

Column I	**Column II**
1. She spent money	a) as if he had lived there forever.
2. He looked at ease,	b) as if he had lost his mind.
3. He slept	c) as if we had been friends since childhood.
4. We talked	d) as if he would never wake up.
5. They stared at him	e) as if her income were unlimited.

EXERCISE 36: Sentence Combining. Combine each of the following pairs of sentences into a single complex sentence with an adverb clause that tells "where" or "how." Move the material that is in parentheses to the beginning of the sentence on that line. If you need help with commas, see page 250. Use the example below as a model.

EXAMPLE People heard of gold in California. (**WHEREVER**)
They rushed to make their fortunes.

ANSWER ***Wherever*** *people heard of gold in California, they rushed to make their fortunes.*

1. Gold means instant wealth. (**AS IF**)
   The word itself has had a magical appeal.
2. Gold was mixed with sand or gravel. (**WHEREVER**)
   People used a panning method to extract it.
3. Everyone had a fortune. (**AS THOUGH**)
   Prices in California soared during the gold rush.
4. Miners had exhausted the gold supply. (**WHERE**)
   Only ghost towns were left.
5. In 1799 a young boy from North Carolina found a gold nugget.
   No one would expect such riches. (**WHERE**)
6. The child kept the nugget for a few years.
   It had no value. (**AS IF**)
7. Fortune hunters went in earnest.
   Gold might be found. (**EVERYWHERE THAT**)
8. People headed westward to seek gold.
   Bees swarm to honey. (**AS**)
9. Business people made money.
   They could sell supplies to prospectors. (**WHEREVER**)
10. Prospectors went to Pikes Peak.
    Its gold would make them rich. (**AS THOUGH**)

EXERCISE 37: Sentence Combining. Combine each of the following pairs of sentences into a single complex sentence by adding one of the following subordinating conjunctions: *as if, as though, where,* or *wherever.* Decide if you want the adverb clause first or last. If you need help with commas, see page 250.

EXAMPLE The snow fell heavily.
The clouds could no longer hold it.

ANSWER *The snow fell heavily,* ***as if*** *the clouds could no longer hold it.*

1. Snow covered the houses.
They were magical places.
2. Stardust had fallen.
Snow and ice clung to branches.
3. Streets are snowed under.
Buses and cars cannot move.
4. People travel by foot and on skis.
Noise and bustle disappear.
5. The roads were sheets of glass.
Cars skid dangerously at intersections.
6. Those people are dressed for summer.
They were going somewhere warm.
7. We always carry candles or a flashlight.
We travel in stormy weather.
8. The house was in shambles.
There had been an earthquake.
9. People talk about the weather.
They could do something to change it.
10. People seem more relaxed.
The weather is sunny and predictable.

3.c.4 Writing adverb clauses that tell "why"

To tell why the action of the main clause takes place, you can add an adverb clause beginning with one of the following subordinating conjunctions: *as, because, since, in order that, inasmuch as,* and *so that.*

EXAMPLES

They could not get him on the phone, **as he had an unlisted number.**

They could not get him on the phone **because he had an unlisted number.**

They could not get him on the phone, **since he had an unlisted number.**

They called him at home **in order that he would know their plans.**

They called him at home **so that he would know their plans.**

An adverb clause that tells "why" can precede or follow the main clause. It can work equally well in either position.

Revise each of the previous example sentences, putting the adverb clause ahead of the main clause.

EXERCISE 38. Compose five complex sentences. For each main clause in Column I, find in Column II a suitable "why" clause to follow it. Each clause from each column must be used. Begin each sentence with the main clause.

Column I	Column II
1. Fingerprints are a useful method of identification,	a) because the bank was closed.
2. I could not get any money	b) in order that people could vote after work.
3. Stores put old merchandise on sale	c) since she had studied for a week.
4. The test did not worry her,	d) as no two people have the same pattern.
5. The polls stayed open late	e) so that they can make room for new goods.

3.c.5 Writing adverb clauses that state conditions

To tell the conditions under which the action of the main clause takes place, you can add an adverb clause.

EXAMPLES

We left before the food was served, **although we were hungry.**

We left before the food was served, **even though we were hungry.**

We decided to stay **as long as the food lasted.**

We will see you tomorrow **if you go to the office.**

We will see you tomorrow **unless something goes wrong.**

We will see you tomorrow **whether or not it rains.**

The following subordinating conjunctions can be used to begin a clause that states conditions.

SUBORDINATING CONJUNCTIONS THAT STATE CONDITIONS

although	if	though
as long as	in case	unless
considering that	in that	whereas
even if	in the event that	whether (or not)
even though	provided that	while

Adverb clauses of condition can usually precede as well as follow the main clause of a sentence. Revise the sentences in the examples above, placing the adverb clause before the main clause.

EXERCISE 39. Compose five complex sentences. For each main clause in Column I, find in Column II a suitable adverb clause to follow it. Each clause from each column must be used.

Column I	**Column II**
1. Your violin recital was impressive,	a) provided that there is enough money.
2. Their final grades will be high	b) although it had rained all day.
3. The game was played,	c) though you are too modest to admit it.
4. He was a great mountaineer,	d) even though he claimed great fear.
5. They will build a new school	e) unless they have trouble with their essays.

EXERCISE 40: Sentence Combining. Combine each of the following pairs of sentences into a single complex sentence by adding a subordinating conjunction that tells "why" or expresses a condition (for example, *because, as, since, whereas, considering that*). Decide if the adverb clause should come first or last. Add a comma if necessary.

EXAMPLE The car would not start.
I walked five miles.

ANSWER ***Because*** *the car would not start, I walked five miles.*

1. It began to rain.
We took umbrellas with us.
2. There was a crippling snowstorm.
All the schools were closed.
3. There will be another power failure.
I always keep candles in the house.
4. You are allergic to cats.
You still have five of them.
5. You keep the cats outside.
They do not make you sneeze.
6. It is winter or summer.
I always eat ice cream.
7. They had a goat.
They would never have to mow their lawn.
8. Your dog likes crackers.
My cat likes spaghetti.
9. You have paid the rent.
You can live here all month.
10. The market is not open this evening.
I will do my shopping tomorrow.
11. Do not swim in the rough ocean.
You are a strong swimmer.
12. Everyone was amazed.
The parrot could speak French.
13. I must have walked slowly.
Everyone else arrived before I did.
14. The team will not win the pennant.
They have a secret strategy.
15. I bought a car.
I would not have to walk to work.
16. They wanted to see the film.
They had read the book.
17. You will not like the film.
You have read the book.
18. The corn is very tall.
There has been so little rain.

19. I buy most of my clothes.
    The stores have sales.

20. People in the audience waited quietly.
    The musicians tuned their instruments.

COMMAS AND ADVERB CLAUSES

1. Use a comma after an adverb clause (even a very short one) that comes *before* a main clause. This rule is designed to prevent misreading. Consider the following two sentences:

    When she tries to walk the dog gets in her way.
    When she tries to walk**,** the dog gets in her way.

    On first reading the first sentence, it seems as if she tries to walk the dog, not just walk. Do you see how the second sentence, with the comma, prevents this misreading?

2. In general, do not use a comma before an adverb clause that comes *after* a main clause.

    The dog gets in her way when she tries to walk.

    Some subordinating conjunctions, however, require the use of a comma when they follow a main clause. If an adverb clause following a main clause begins with *though, although,* or *even though,* use a comma before it.

    The baby began to cry**,** **although** I had not left.

    If an adverb clause following a main clause begins with *as, since,* or *while,* do not use a comma if the clause tells "when," but do use a comma if it tells "why" or states a condition.

    The baby began to cry as I was leaving.
    The baby began to cry**,** as it was hungry.

EXERCISE 41: Sentence Combining – review of all adverb clauses. Combine each of the following pairs of sentences into a single complex sentence. Move the material that is in parentheses to the beginning of the sentence on that line, as the example shows.

EXAMPLE Gasoline supplies were low that year. (**SINCE**)
People turned to railroads again.

ANSWER ***Since*** *gasoline supplies were low that year, people turned to railroads again.*

1. Many railroads were built in the late 1800s. (**BECAUSE**)
Settlement in the United States expanded.
2. Technical improvements were made. (**AS**)
Railroads became safer and more efficient.
3. Much money was needed to build railroads. (**SINCE**)
Wealthy individuals invested in them.
4. The Union Pacific Company built westward. (**WHEREAS**)
The Central Pacific Company built eastward.
5. The two lines met at Promontory, Utah, in 1869. (**WHEN**)
Builders hammered a golden spike.
6. The two lines competed to cover the most ground. (**BECAUSE**)
Railroad tracks were laid in record time.
7. There was no steam shovel. (**CONSIDERING THAT**)
The railroads were built fairly quickly.
8. The transcontinental line was completed. (**AFTER**)
People celebrated all over the country.
9. Most wheat was grown on the plains. (**EVEN IF**)
The railroads could carry it to the coasts.
10. Western products could not reach eastern markets.
The railroads stopped running. (**IN THE EVENT THAT**)
11. The railroads were running. (**AS LONG AS**)
Sections of the country were linked together.
12. Jim Hill built the Great Northern Line.
People would settle on the prairie. (**SO THAT**)
13. Farmers received equipment, money, and advice.
They settled along Jim Hill's railroad. (**IF**)
14. Some people built new rail lines.
Others combined existing lines. (**WHILE**)
15. The consolidation of railroads had some advantages.
Railroad service improved. (**IN THAT**)

16. Eventually, separate railroad lines could not prosper.
They became part of a larger system. (**UNLESS**)
17. A few powerful people fixed the price of railroad travel.
They made many improvements in railroads. (**ALTHOUGH**)
18. Railroad service improved in New York.
Grand Central Terminal was opened. (**WHEN**)
19. Railroad building progressed.
Problems resulted from the expansion. (**EVEN THOUGH**)
20. People are now sorry.
The building of railroads harmed many buffalo. (**BECAUSE**)

3.c.6 Writing adjective clauses

As a writer, you can use adjective clauses to give additional information about a noun, a pronoun, or a gerund. Adjective clauses used in this way are said to *modify* the noun, pronoun, or gerund.

EXAMPLES

SIMPLE SENTENCE: The book won a prize.
ADJECTIVE CLAUSE: that I love
COMPLEX SENTENCE: The book **that I love** won a prize.

SIMPLE SENTENCE: He traveled far.
ADJECTIVE CLAUSE: whom I love
COMPLEX SENTENCE: He **whom I love** traveled far.

SIMPLE SENTENCE: All is lost.
ADJECTIVE CLAUSE: that I love
COMPLEX SENTENCE: All **that I love** is lost.

SIMPLE SENTENCE: Jogging improved her health.
ADJECTIVE CLAUSE: which she loves
COMPLEX SENTENCE: Jogging, **which she loves**, improved her health.

The following subordinators may be used for adjective clauses:

For people	For animals, things, and ideas
who	which
whom	that
whose	

For places	For periods of time
where	when

Who, which, and *that* are relative pronouns. As such, they serve not only as subordinators but can also be the subject of their own subordinate clause.

Whom and *which* can also be the object of a preposition. A subordinate adjective clause, therefore, can begin with a preposition.

EXAMPLES

The driver **in whom we placed our trust** let us down.

The driver **in whose common sense we placed our trust** let us down.

The map **in which we placed our trust** let us down.

Where and *when* are not relative pronouns. They do not take the place of a noun; they themselves are not subjects of subordinate clauses. A subordinate clause beginning with *where* or *when* must have another word as its subject.

EXAMPLES

The place **where the pioneers met** is now a hardware store.

The day **when they met** has been long forgotten.

EXERCISE 42. Compose five complex sentences containing an adjective clause. For each main clause in Column I, find in Column II the subordinate clause that goes with it. Each clause from each column must be used.

Column I

1. A relatively unknown author has only now become famous.
2. Her brother remembers her fondly.
3. Recently the editor honored her in a brief article.
4. In an abrupt reversal of opinion, everyone now has a kind word for her.
5. Her children have become successful.

Column II

a) to whom one of her first books is dedicated
b) who was embarrassed by her books
c) who died in 1974
d) whose hard work she encouraged
e) with whom she was professionally associated for many years

EXERCISE 43. Compose five complex sentences containing an adjective clause. For each main clause in Column I, find in Column II the subordinate clause that goes with it.

Column I

1. Her settings were always far-off places in distant times.
2. Her plots were always intriguing.
3. Her characters always came to early and disastrous ends.
4. Publishers' schedules never seemed to suit her.
5. Film contracts never materialized.

Column II

a) who were drawn from her early life in New Mexico
b) under which she fretted and fumed
c) which she hoped for
d) with which she kept readers guessing
e) over which she cast an air of mystery

EXERCISE 44. Compose five complex sentences containing an adjective clause. For each main clause in Column I, find in Column II the subordinate clause that most logically completes it. Each clause from each column must be used.

Column I

1. Finally there arrived a sad day.
2. She moved back to her home town.
3. In the year 1970 she began to reap her just rewards.
4. She was able to travel to far-off places.
5. She spent her last years in famous resorts.

Column II

a) where her talents were unknown
b) when the book business was expanding
c) where she often made new friends
d) where people still knew her
e) when she could no longer write

EXERCISE 45: Sentence Combining. Combine each of the following pairs of simple sentences into a single complex sentence. Use the word in parentheses to replace the underlined words. The replacement word will become the first word in the new subordinate clause.

EXAMPLE We know a famous place.
The past comes to life there. (**WHERE**)

ANSWER *We know a famous place* ***where*** *the past comes to life.*

EXAMPLE There we can see a whole culture.
The culture is part of America's past. (**THAT**)

ANSWER *There we can see a whole culture* ***that*** *is a part of America's past.*

1. Native American culture survives in American towns.
Hopi and Navajo communities exist there. (**WHERE**)
2. The Hopis bar outsiders from a community.
The community is the longest populated U.S. settlement. (**THAT**)
3. The Navajos and Hopis use colors to decorate their pottery.
Colors dominate their landscape. (**THAT**)
4. Water is precious to people.
The people live on dry plains. (**WHO**)
5. The Hopis' religion centers on spirits.
Spirits bring rain. (**THAT**)
6. Certain buildings are traditional Navajo structures.
The buildings are called hogans. (**THAT**)
7. On the Hopis' territory there is one national park.
Ordinary citizens and park employees, live in the park. (**WHERE**)
8. In Hopi villages there are some men.
Men are the weavers. (**WHO**)
9. Follow a trail at the bottom of a canyon.
You can hike the trail. (**THAT**)
10. The Hopis have traditional ceremonies from another time.
There was no intrusion from the modern world then. (**WHEN**)

EXERCISE 46: Sentence Combining. Combine each of the following pairs of simple sentences into a single complex sentence. Use the phrase in parentheses to replace the underlined words. The replacement words will become the first words in the new subordinate clause. If the new subordinate clause is nonessential (if it adds extra, not essential, information to the sentence), be sure to set it off with extra commas.

EXAMPLE Our college president recently resigned.
We have great respect for him. (**FOR WHOM**)

ANSWER *Our college president*, ***for whom*** *we have great respect*, *recently resigned.*

1. The anthropologist Margaret Mead was tireless.
People found inspiration in her energy. (**IN WHOSE ENERGY**)

2. Mead studied with Franz Boas.
   She had great respect for him. (**FOR WHOM**)
3. Mead studied Polynesian cultures.
   She had great interest in these cultures. (**IN WHICH**)
4. She studied some societies.
   Anthropologists knew little of those societies. (**OF WHICH**)
5. We acknowledge Dr. Mead's contributions.
   Scientists have profited from her contributions. (**FROM WHICH**)
6. Some scientists challenged Mead.
   They took issue with her methods. (**WITH WHOSE METHODS**)
7. Students of anthropology turned to Mead.
   Important books were written by her. (**BY WHOM**)
8. Many young women admired Margaret Mead.
   They saw a model of a successful woman in her. (**IN WHOM**)
9. Illness did not curtail the activities of Dr. Mead.
   Work was of primary importance for her. (**FOR WHOM**)
10. Mead appreciated the South Seas people.
    She lived in their society. (**IN WHOSE SOCIETY**)

EXERCISE 47: Sentence Combining. Combine each of the following pairs of simple sentences into a single complex sentence. Use the word in parentheses to replace the underlined words. The replacement word will become the first words in the new subordinate clause. If the new subordinate clause is nonessential (if it adds extra, not essential, information to the sentence), be sure to set it off with extra commas.

EXAMPLE The French Quarter borders the Mississippi River.
Artists gather in the French Quarter. (**WHERE**)

ANSWER *The French Quarter, **where** artists gather, borders the Mississippi River.*

1. New Mexico is the home of Georgia O'Keeffe.
   Georgia O'Keeffe is a well-known American painter. (**WHO**)
2. The Betsy Ross House is in Philadelphia.
   The Betsy Ross House is a national monument. (**WHICH**)
3. Washington, D.C., is crowded in the spring.
   Tourists come to see cherry blossoms in the spring. (**WHEN**)
4. O'Hare is located in Chicago.
   O'Hare is the busiest airport in the United States. (**WHICH**)
5. There is a monument to Edison in Menlo Park, New Jersey.

He lived and worked in Menlo Park, New Jersey. (**WHERE**)

6. Saint Augustine, Florida, has beautiful old buildings.
Saint Augustine, Florida, is the oldest U.S. city. (**WHICH**)
7. Of major U.S. cities, Syracuse, New York, gets the most snow.
The snow averages 110.7 inches per year. (**WHICH**)
8. An Egyptian obelisk stands in New York City.
The obelisk was originally in ancient Alexandria. (**THAT**)
9. The Golden Gate Bridge is in San Francisco.
The Golden Gate Bridge is a popular attraction. (**WHICH**)
10. A giant arch dominates St. Louis.
The arch was designed by Eero Saarinan. (**WHICH**)

EXERCISE 48: Sentence Combining. Combine the three sentences in each numbered item to form one complex sentence with two subordinate clauses. Substitute the word in parentheses for the underlined word or phrase, and place the adjective clause in the appropriate spot. If the new subordinate clause is nonessential (if it adds additional, not essential, information to the sentence), be sure to set it off with commas.

EXAMPLE Local weeds can provide low-cost food.
Weeds are edible. (**THAT**)
Low-cost food helps a budget. (**WHICH**)

ANSWER *Local weeds that are edible can provide low-cost food, which helps a budget.*

1. Common weeds grow in parks.
Weeds can be eaten. (**THAT**)
Parks are open to the public. (**WHICH**)
2. Do not mistake milkweed for another plant.
Milkweed can be eaten. (**WHICH**)
Another plant is poisonous. (**THAT**)
3. People must envy naturalists.
People shop in supermarkets. (**WHO**)
Nature provides free food for naturalists. (**FOR WHOM**)
4. People should take a class.
People want to collect natural foods. (**WHO**)
A class teaches which foods can be eaten. (**THAT**)
5. Standardized rules for baseball were established by soldiers.
Baseball is the national sport. (**WHICH**)
Soldiers played it behind the lines during the Civil War. (**WHO**)

6. Settlers discovered lacrosse.
   Settlers came to America. (**WHO**)
   Lacrosse was popular among Native Americans. (**WHICH**)
7. The Native Americans played lacrosse with huge teams.
   The Native Americans' games were often dangerous. (**WHOSE**)
   The teams might number five hundred players. (**THAT**)
8. Basketball was invented in America.
   Basketball is a popular sport. (**WHICH**)
   It was first played in America in 1891. (**WHERE**)
9. Games are popular in winter.
   Games can be played indoors. (**THAT**)
   It is very cold outdoors in winter. (**WHEN**)
10. Football developed an enormous following because of TV.
   TV broadcasts the game to millions of people. (**WHICH**)
   Football might have been unknown to these people. (**TO WHOM**)

EXERCISE 49: Sentence Combining. Combine each of the following pairs of simple sentences into a single complex sentence. Use the word in parentheses to replace the underlined words. The replacement word will become the first word in the new subordinate clause.

If the clause is nonessential (if it adds additional, not essential, information to the sentence), be sure to set it off with commas.

EXAMPLE We will have a voice-changing invention.
The invention will make us opera singers. (**THAT**)

ANSWER *We will have a voice-changing invention* ***that*** *will make us opera singers.*

1. Scientists foresee new medicines.
   People will take medicines to raise their intelligence. (**THAT**)
2. We hope doctors will find a cure for cancer.
   Many people fear cancer. (**WHICH**)
3. We will no longer need some technicians.
   Robots will replace technicians. (**WHOM**)
4. Textile experts will produce fabrics.
   People can wear these fabrics in all kinds of weather. (**THAT**)
5. Soon you will be able to buy a miniature television.
   You can wear a miniature television on your wrist. (**THAT**)
6. People can skip boring chores.
   Computers will be able to do chores. (**WHICH**)

7. Scientists will develop tasty new plastics.
   We will be able to eat the plastics. (**THAT**)
8. Perhaps plastic gourmet meals will be prepared by new chefs.
   We will admire the chefs. (**WHOM**)
9. Meteorologists might unlock a secret system.
   We will use the system to control the weather. (**THAT**)
10. We may drive electric cars.
    We will operate cars without petroleum fuels. (**WHICH**)

3.c.7 Writing sentences with appositives

An **appositive** is a noun or pronoun (sometimes with modifiers) that is placed next to another noun or pronoun to identify it or to give additional information about it.

The purpose of an appositive is similar to that of an adjective clause. In an appositive, however, there is no verb, no subordinator, and no subject. Think of an appositive as an adjective clause that has been reduced to a word or phrase by the removal, or deletion, of unnecessary words. Notice that, generally, an appositive is set off by commas (see 7.g.15).

EXAMPLE

Sentence with adjective clause

The gift, **which was a gold watch**, made Harry very happy.

Sentence with appositive

The gift, ~~which was~~ a gold watch, made Harry very happy.
The gift, **a gold watch**, made Harry very happy.

EXERCISE 50: Sentence Combining. Combine the following pairs of sentences by forming an appositive phrase out of the second sentence in each pair. Delete all unnecessary or repeated words in the second sentence. Be sure to set off the appositive phrase with commas.

EXAMPLE Prairie architecture has features that give a building the appearance of being low and flat.
Prairie architecture is a style developed in the Midwest.

ANSWER *Prairie architecture, a style developed in the Midwest, has features that give a building the appearance of being low and flat.*

EXAMPLE Prairie architecture was successfully used in buildings designed by Frank Lloyd Wright.
Frank Lloyd Wright was an important modern American architect.

ANSWER *Prairie architecture was successfully used in buildings designed by Frank Lloyd Wright, an important modern American architect.*

1. In the nineteenth century architects introduced the skyscraper. The skyscraper is a tall, vertical building.
2. Chicago was rebuilt with many skyscrapers after a disaster. The disaster was the tremendous fire of 1871.
3. Some skyscrapers were built in the Gothic style. The Gothic style was the style of many medieval cathedrals.
4. Gothic buildings were decorated with gargoyles. Gargoyles are carvings of animallike creatures.
5. The Chrysler Building in New York City is art deco. Art deco is a decorative style based on geometric forms.
6. During the 1930s Rockefeller Center was built in New York. Rockefeller Center is a group of skyscrapers.
7. Some architects use the Chicago window. The Chicago window is one large pane and smaller panes.
8. New skyscrapers are sometimes covered in mirror glass. Mirror glass is a highly reflective surface.
9. The Transamerica Building stands in San Francisco. The Transamerica Building is a pyramid-shaped skyscraper.
10. Chicago has the innovative Marina Towers. The Marina Towers are circular buildings.

EXERCISE 51: Sentence Combining. Combine each of the following pairs of simple sentences in two ways.

a. Form a single complex sentence with an adjective clause.
b. Use the complex sentence to form a new sentence with an appositive in place of the adjective clause.

EXAMPLE News events are broadcast on cable television.
Cable television is a new method of transmission.

ANSWER A (sentence with adjective clause)
News events are broadcast on cable television, which is a new method of transmission.

ANSWER B (sentence with appositive)
News events are broadcast on cable television, a new method of transmission.

1. Each year television broadcasts the Super Bowl.
   The Super Bowl is the final football championship game of the season.
2. The game of football has been adjusted for television.
   Television is a medium with commercials.
3. Television news is not a substitute for newspapers.
   Newspapers are a format for reporting current events in depth.
4. *The $64,000 Question* was on television in the 1950s.
   The $64,000 Question was the first big-money quiz program.
5. Television broadcasts worldwide events via Telstar.
   Telstar is a communications satellite.

3.c.8 Writing sentences with noun clauses

As a writer, you may at times use a subordinate clause in the same way as you use a noun. A noun clause can function in a sentence in all the ways that a noun can—as the subject of a sentence, as the object of a verb or the object of a preposition, or as a predicate nominative after *be* and the other linking verbs.

EXAMPLE

AS SUBJECT: **That travel is educational** is a fact of life.
Whatever adds to our knowledge is educational.
AS OBJECT OF VERB: We will see **what you want us to see**.
AS OBJECT OF PREPOSITION: We make notes about **whatever we explore**.
AS PREDICATE NOMINATIVE: The fact is **that travel is educational**.

The words listed on the following page are some of the subordinators that can be used to begin noun clauses. Notice that the list includes words that in other cases can be used to begin adverb and adjective clauses.

COMMON SUBORDINATORS FOR NOUN CLAUSES

that
what (whatever)
who, whom, whose (whoever, whomever)
which (whichever)

where	I know *where* we are going.
when	I know *when* we are going.
how	I know *how* we are going.
why	I know *why* we are going.

Some of the above subordinators can be combined with prepositions – for example, *in whom, in which, around whose, along whatever.*

EXERCISE 52. Compose five complex sentences. For each incomplete sentence in Column I, find in Column II the noun clause that goes with it. One clause in Column II will be used twice.

Column I

1. I will welcome _____.
2. _____ becomes our treasure.
3. Sometimes one wonders _____.
4. It is difficult to believe _____.
5. Reveling in _____, we will spend our summers in the sand.

Column II

a) why settlers left the harbors and the sea
b) whatever toys the waves deliver
c) that this sea has held Magellan's ships
d) whatever the sea tosses on the shore

EXERCISE 53: Sentence Combining. Combine the following pairs of sentences to form a single sentence with a noun clause. Move the word in parentheses to the beginning of the sentence on that line. Remove any underlined word in that sentence. Then substitute your newly formed noun clause for the word SOMETHING, SOMEONE, or SOMEPLACE in the first sentence.

EXAMPLE SOMEPLACE can be an herb garden.
Someplace you find sunlight. (**ANYWHERE**)

ANSWER ***Anywhere*** *you find sunlight can be an herb garden.*

1. SOMETHING is a fact.
   Herbs are flavorful. (**THAT**)
2. SOMETHING is not totally understood.
   Herbs work as medicines. (**HOW**)
3. SOMEONE used to keep garlic nearby.
   Someone was superstitious. (**WHOEVER**)
4. SOMETHING was popularly believed.
   Garlic warded off evil spirits. (**THAT**)
5. SOMEONE can grow herbs.
   Someone likes to garden. (**WHOEVER**)
6. SOMETHING is debatable.
   Herbs taste best with chicken. (**WHICH**)
7. SOMETHING is not easy to learn.
   Herbs should be added in cooking. (**WHEN**)
8. SOMEPLACE smells fragrant.
   Dried herbs and flowers are kept somewhere. (**WHEREVER**)
9. SOMETHING tastes refreshing.
   Something is seasoned with mint. (**WHATEVER**)
10. SOMETHING is puzzling.
    People have superstitions about parsley. (**WHY**)

EXERCISE 54: Sentence Combining. Combine the following pairs of sentences to form a single sentence with a noun clause. Move the word in parentheses to the beginning of the sentence on that line. Remove any underlined words in that sentence. Substitute your newly formed noun clause for the SOMETHING or SOMEONE in the first sentence.

EXAMPLE Active people feel SOMETHING.
Hard work is rewarding. (**THAT**)

ANSWER *Active people feel* ***that*** *hard work is rewarding.*

1. All workers know SOMETHING.
   Everyone enjoys leisure time. (**THAT**)
2. American colonists considered SOMETHING.
   They could combine work and pleasure. (**HOW**)
3. Community chores formed SOMETHING.
   Chores really became contests. (**WHAT**)
4. Some Americans remember SOMETHING.
   Vacations were rare. (**WHEN**)
5. Holidays demand SOMETHING.
   People relax and celebrate. (**THAT**)

6. Americans applaud SOMEONE.
   Someone invents a new sport or game. (**WHOEVER**)
7. In the 1930s miniature golf caused SOMETHING.
   The game was to become a sensation. (**WHAT**)
8. Eventually employers ensured SOMETHING.
   Employees received paid vacations. (**THAT**)
9. Vacation time might influence SOMETHING.
   A person will work for someone. (**FOR WHOM**)
10. One's interests dictate SOMETHING.
    One spends leisure time somehow. (**HOW**)

EXERCISE 55. Use the word in parentheses as a subordinator to form a noun clause. Then use the noun clause to complete Sentences *a* and *b* in each numbered item.

EXAMPLE Life exists in the barren desert. (**HOW**)
a) Naturalists are amazed at ______________.
b) ______________ is a miracle of nature.

ANSWER a) *Naturalists are amazed at **how** life exists in the barren desert.*
b) ***How** life exists in the barren desert is a miracle of nature.*

1. The world's deserts are spreading. (**THAT**)
   a) We hear ______________.
   b) ______________ is alarming.
2. Rainfall is lessening. (**THAT**)
   a) Scientists realize ______________.
   b) ______________ is one factor in the expansion of deserts.
3. Some land has been overused. (**THAT**)
   a) People now regret ______________.
   b) ______________ was unavoidable.
4. New deserts will appear. (**WHERE**)
   a) Ecologists can predict ______________.
   b) ______________ is predictable.
5. Once-fertile land is now desert. (**WHY**)
   a) Experts are learning ______________.
   b) ______________ is becoming clear.
6. We can prevent more deserts from forming. (**HOW**)
   a) People are determining ______________.
   b) ______________ is an important issue.

7. People will work together. (**THAT**)
   a) Ecologists hope ______________.
   b) ______________ is encouraging.
8. Soil erosion must be prevented. (**THAT**)
   a) Experts know ______________.
   b) ______________ is unquestionable.
9. The land can recover. (**THAT**)
   a) Scientists hope ______________.
   b) ______________ is the hope of scientists.
10. The earth's land changes. (**HOW**)
    a) Scientists must study ______________.
    b) ______________ will affect everyone.

EXERCISE 56: Sentence Combining. Combine the following pairs of sentences to form a single sentence with a noun clause. Move the word in parentheses to the beginning of the sentence on that line. Remove any underlined words in that sentence. Substitute your newly formed noun clause for the SOMETHING, SOMEONE, or SOMEPLACE in the first sentence.

EXAMPLE In the 1950s drive-in movies were SOMETHING.
The public wanted something. (**WHAT**)

ANSWER *In the 1950s drive-in movies were **what** the public wanted.*

1. Drive-ins were SOMEPLACE.
   Many people went someplace for entertainment. (**WHERE**)
2. June 1933 was SOMETIME.
   People recall sometime as the birth of drive-ins. (**WHAT**)
3. Soaring land prices were SOMETHING.
   Many drive-in theaters later closed. (**WHY**)
4. New approaches are SOMETHING.
   Drive-ins need something. (**WHAT**)
5. A successful owner is usually SOMEONE.
   Someone is the most imaginative. (**WHO-EVER**)

EXERCISE 57: Sentence Combining. Combine the following pairs of sentences to form a single sentence with a noun clause. Move the word in parentheses to the beginning of the sentence on that line. Remove any underlined words in that sentence. Substitute your newly formed noun clause for the SOMETHING, SOMEONE, or SOMEPLACE in the first sentence.

EXAMPLE Exercise is important for SOMEONE.
Someone wants to be physically fit. (**WHOEVER**)

ANSWER *Exercise is important for* ***whoever*** *wants to be physically fit.*

1. Athletic people participate in SOMETHING.
Something is good exercise. (**WHATEVER**)
2. Americans have respect for SOMEONE.
Someone diligently exercises. (**WHOEVER**)
3. Adults should invest in SOMETHING.
Something builds up their hearts. (**WHATEVER**)
4. You should follow the exercise program of SOMEONE.
You choose someone. (**WHOMEVER**)
5. Some people travel an hour to SOMEPLACE.
Somewhere there is a jogging track. (**WHEREVER**)
6. Your mental state is affected by SOMETHING.
Your body feels somehow. (**HOW**)
7. Tennis is fun for SOMEONE.
Someone likes an active sport. (**WHOEVER**)
8. Tennis players run to SOMEPLACE.
The ball lands somewhere. (**WHERE**)
9. Surfers often wait for SOMETHING.
They consider the perfect wave. (**WHAT**)
10. Good health is the answer to SOMETHING.
People exercise for a reason. (**WHY**)

3.d WRITING INDIRECT QUESTIONS

A statement sentence that contains a noun clause and that *states* a question is called an indirect question.

EXAMPLE

DIRECT QUESTION: The mayor asked, **"Where are the fire fighters?"**

INDIRECT QUESTION: The mayor asked **where the fire fighters were.**

Notice the format and wording of an indirect question.

1. There are no quotation marks because the actual words of the speaker are not represented.
2. There is no question mark.

3. There is no comma before the noun clause.
4. The tense of the verb in the noun clause is sometimes different from what it would be in a direct question. For example, the present tense in a direct question usually becomes the past tense in an indirect question (as in the example above). The past tense usually changes to the past perfect. In an indirect question about a scientific fact or other general truth, however, the noun clause is always in the *present* tense.

   EXAMPLE

   DIRECT QUESTION: The student asked, "**Is** the sun a star?"
   INDIRECT QUESTION: The student asked if the sun **is** a star.

5. The entire verb or verb phrase *follows* the subject of the noun clause.

The following subordinators can be used to start a noun clause that is an indirect question:

WHO: He asked **who** was there.
WHOM: He asked **whom** we had seen.
WHOSE: He asked **whose** hat I had on.
WHICH: He asked **which** hat I had on.
WHAT: He asked **what** I wanted.
WHERE: He asked **where** we were going.
WHEN: He asked **when** we were going.
WHY: He asked **why** we were going.
HOW: He asked **how** we were going.
IF: He asked **if** we were going.
WHETHER (OR NOT): He asked **whether (or not)** we were going.

EXERCISE 58. After Bryant Allen had become the first person to fly the English Channel in a man-powered plane, reporters asked the young American pilot the questions on page 268. Use these direct questions to form sentences containing indirect questions by adding *if* or *whether* and beginning each sentence with the words *they asked*. You will also have to change the tense of the verb as you form indirect questions.

EXAMPLE "Was the plane built in America?"
ANSWER *They asked if the plane had been built in America.*

1. "Were you scared at any time?"
2. "Can the trip be duplicated?"
3. "Was the wind a problem?"
4. "Was the target area selected in advance?"
5. "Were the winds the biggest problem?"
6. "Did the engine overheat?"
7. "Was the training period a grind?"
8. "Did any design faults develop en route?"
9. "Was everyone convinced that the light was safe?"
10. "Was this the first plane of its kind that has been built?"

EXERCISE 59. Rewrite each of the following question sentences as a sentence containing an indirect question in the present tense.

EXAMPLE The class asked, "What is the composition of light?"

ANSWER *The class asked what the composition of light is.*

1. The teacher asked, "Is white light a mixture of all colors?"
2. The physics student asked, "Does blue light have a shorter wavelength than red light?"
3. The student asked, "How does the speed of light compare with the speed of sound?"
4. The traveler asked, "Why does the heat in the desert cause a mirage?"
5. The swimmer wondered, "Do sound waves travel through water?"
6. The teacher asked, "What are the colors of the spectrum?"
7. Scientists have wondered, "Is light made up of waves or of particles?"
8. The class asked, "Why does a rainbow occur?"
9. The teacher asked, "Do raindrops act like prisms to split sunlight into colors?"
10. Scientists debate, "Does gravity have any effect on light waves?"

What changes in punctuation did you have to make when you rewrote the sentences?

WRITING COMPOUND–COMPLEX SENTENCES

3.e ADDING SUBORDINATE CLAUSES TO COMPOUND SENTENCES

A **compound-complex sentence** consists of two or more main clauses and one or more subordinate clauses.

Subordinate clauses can be added to (or used with) compound sentences. A compound sentence with one or more subordinate clauses added to it becomes a compound-complex sentence. Because a subordinate clause often tells more about a noun or a verb in a main clause, a compound-complex sentence can carry more information than an ordinary compound sentence.

EXAMPLES

Compound sentence 1

The banana in the split was buried at the bottom of the dish, but it should have rested at the edge of the dish.

Compound-complex sentence 1

The banana in the split was buried at the bottom of the dish, **which was appropriately boat shaped**, but **as a true banana-split authority knows**, the banana should have rested at the edge of the dish.

Compound sentence 2

The shop's homemade ice cream is American-style, and the whipped cream is fresh, with a slight gloss.

Compound-complex sentence 2

The shop's homemade ice cream is American-style, and the whipped cream is fresh, with a slight gloss **that suggests the addition of sugar**.

You should keep in mind that too many compound-complex sentences strung together will affect your readers the same way that too many compound or too many simple sentences in a row will: Your readers will get bored. Practice writing compound-complex sentences, but do not overuse them.

EXERCISE 60. Rewrite each of the following compound sentences, making it a compound-complex sentence by adding, where the carets (‸) indicate, two of the three subordinate clauses that follow it. Be sure to punctuate correctly. Notice that two different sentences can be formed, depending on which clauses you choose to use.

EXAMPLE Greenwich Village‸ is in one of the oldest sections of Manhattan; Wall Street is near the harbor‸ .
a) which has narrow and crooked streets
b) which is a center for artists and bohemians
c) where New York City's businesses were first situated

ANSWER A *Greenwich Village,* ***which has narrow and crooked streets****, is in one of the oldest sections of Manhattan; Wall Street is near the harbor,* ***where New York City's businesses were first situated.***

ANSWER B *Greenwich Village,* ***which is a center for artists and bohemians****, is in one of the oldest sections of Manhattan; Wall Street is near the harbor,* ***where New York City's businesses were first situated.***

1. In colonial times New York City's Greenwich Village‸ was "in the country," and people visited it by traveling along Greenwich Avenue‸ .
   a) which was once a tiny village
   b) which is now a downtown section of the city
   c) which was originally a Native American trail
2. The country's first Executive Mansion was on Cherry Street in New York City‸ , but Washington lived mostly at Mount Vernon‸ .
   a) where he enjoyed country life
   b) which was the nation's capital
   c) which was his home in Virginia
3. It is hard to envision New York City covered with forests and meadows‸ , for the city is now a crowded metropolis‸ .
   a) that has millions of inhabitants
   b) which were filled with animals and flowers
   c) which means a major city
4. New York's Washington Square‸ does not seem a likely spot for public hangings; however, the square was indeed once a place for executions‸ .

a) which is in Greenwich Village
b) where New York University is now situated
c) which were once fairly frequent public events

5. One cannot envision Wall Street residents ^ defending themselves against the British, nor can one imagine Fifth Avenue ^ lined with farmhouses and barns.
a) who now inhabit the Stock Exchange
b) which is a very elegant street
c) which is now lined with shops and buildings

EXERCISE 61. Rewrite each of the following compound sentences, making it a compound-complex sentence by adding, where the carets (^) indicate, two of the three subordinate clauses that follow it. Be sure to punctuate correctly. Notice that two different sentences can be formed, depending on which clauses you choose to use. Use the example in Exercise 60 as a model.

1. Manhattan ^ is easy to travel around, but the city planners destroyed much of the area's natural charm ^ .
a) when hills were leveled and brooks were filled in
b) which has its streets organized on a grid
c) since it is relatively small

2. Manhattan's early settlers ^ were diverse, and the street names derive from different languages ^ .
a) who came from England, France, and the Netherlands
b) since they came from different countries
c) that reflect the city's ethnic variety

3. You must take a bridge or a tunnel to reach Manhattan ^ , for Manhattan is an island ^ .
a) which is between New York and New Jersey
b) which is bordered by the Hudson River and the East River
c) whenever you go there

4. ^ San Francisco is not easy to walk around, nor is it easy to park a car ^ .
a) since it is very hilly
b) because it could easily roll away
c) which must have its wheels turned against the curb

5. You must travel on freeways in Los Angeles ^ , for the city ^ is very spread out.
a) if you have a car
b) if you want to get places quickly
c) which lacks extensive public transportation

WRITING SENTENCES WITH PARTICIPIAL PHRASES

3.f SENTENCES WITH PARTICIPIAL PHRASES

A **participial phrase** is a group of words, the most important of which is a past or present participle. (See 1.1.)

EXAMPLES

Present participial phrases

Catching *the football*, Larry ducked.
Laughing *all the way*, Beth ran home.
No longer ***laughing*** *as happily*, Beth saw the smoke ahead.
Being *captain of the debating team*, Sandy accepted the award.

Past participial phrases

Unloved *by everyone*, Sheba slunk away.
Frightened *almost beyond their wits*, the shoppers panicked.
Lost *in one of the loneliest stretches of the island*, the children began to cry.

Participial phrases can be used in a sentence for many of the same purposes as clauses. A participial phrase, however, often allows you to reduce the number of words that you need.

EXAMPLES

He caught the football, and he smiled to himself. [two main clauses]
As he caught the football, he smiled to himself. [one adverb clause and one main clause]
Catching the football, he smiled to himself. [one main clause containing a participial phrase]
She finished the speech, and she knew it was good. [two main clauses]
She finished the speech, which she knew was good. [one main clause and one adjective clause]
She finished the speech, knowing it was good. [one main clause containing a participial phrase]

A participial phrase can come at the beginning, in the middle, or at the end of a sentence.

EXAMPLES

Laughing all the way, we went over the fields to grandmother's house.

We went over the fields, **laughing all the way**, to grandmother's house.

We went over the fields to grandmother's house, **laughing all the way**.

AVOIDING ERRORS WITH PARTICIPIAL PHRASES

Do not forget that a participial phrase identifies an action performed by a noun or pronoun. Be certain that the action is related to the correct noun or pronoun.

NOT Rattling down the street, my ~~brother~~ drove his old car.

BUT Rattling down the street, **my brother's old car** woke the neighbors.

An error of this kind is called a **dangling** or **misplaced modifier**. You can help to avoid errors of this kind by rereading your sentences and by diagraming sentences that have participial phrases (see page 202).

EXERCISE 62: Sentence Combining and Reducing. Combine each of the following pairs of sentences, making the first sentence into a participial phrase.

EXAMPLE We drove along.
We hummed a tune.

ANSWER ***Driving along***, *we hummed a tune.*

1. She rested her head in her hand.
   She pondered the problem.
2. Laura dashed for the phone.
   Laura knocked over the chair.
3. He bit into the apple.
   He broke a tooth.

4. The actor cleared his throat.
   The actor looked over the audience.
5. The dog barked loudly.
   The dog ran into the house.

EXERCISE 63. Rewrite each of the following compound sentences, turning one of the main clauses into a participial phrase. Some of the sentences, as the example shows, have two possibilities; you have to use only one.

EXAMPLE She looked at her watch, and she wondered where he could be.

ANSWER A *Looking at her watch, she wondered where he could be.*

ANSWER B *Wondering where he could be, she looked at her watch.*

1. He watched the snow fall, and he looked forward to his ski trip.
2. They practiced the new dance every night, for they hoped to win the contest.
3. She studied every map of the area that she could put her hands on, and she finally found the town on the postcard.
4. He turned a corner of the road, and he saw in front of him the old house.
5. They stopped the car, and they just sat there and waited for the parade to pass by.

EXERCISE 64. Compose five sentences. For each participial phrase in Column I, find in Column II the main clause that goes with it.

Column I	**Column II**
1. Having stayed up until 3 A.M.,	a) he resorted to pinching himself.
2. Trying desperately to keep awake,	b) Barbara could not help laughing.
3. Having fallen asleep at last,	c) the teacher continued her lecture.
4. Hearing the unexpected noise,	d) Jack was completely exhausted.
5. Not wanting to embarrass Jack,	e) Jack began snoring softly.

EXERCISE 65. Add a word or words after the present participle in each of the numbered items to make a participial phrase. The words you add can be adverbs, past participles, adjectives, nouns, pronouns, prepositional phrases, or noun clauses. The example shows two possibilities for each item.

EXAMPLE Leaving ________, the Pilgrims came to the New World.

ANSWER A *Leaving* ***their homes****, the Pilgrims came to the New World.*

ANSWER B *Leaving* ***what was familiar to them****, the Pilgrims came to the New World.*

EXAMPLE Moving ________, the combine harvested the corn.

ANSWER A *Moving* ***slowly****, the combine harvested the corn.*

ANSWER B *Moving* ***across the fields****, the combine harvested the corn.*

1. Seeing ________, a neighbor called the fire department.
2. Arriving ________, the fire fighters unrolled their hoses.
3. Leaning ________, a little boy screamed and waved his arms.
4. Being ________, the fire chief raced up the ladder.
5. Carrying ________, the chief reached the ground safely.

EXERCISE 66: Sentence Combining and Reducing. Combine each of the following pairs of sentences in two ways.

a. Form a single sentence with an adverb clause beginning with *as*.

b. Form a single sentence with a participial phrase.

EXAMPLE The old actress watched the ceremony.
The old actress felt proud.

ANSWER A *As she watched the ceremony, the old actress felt proud.*

ANSWER B *Watching the ceremony, the old actress felt proud.*

1. The old actor rose to speak.
   The old actor became emotional.
2. The children in the audience grew tired.
   The children in the audience started to whisper.

3. The band leader waited tensely for each cue.
   The band leader smiled steadily.
4. The winner of the best-film award held up the prize.
   The winner of the best-film award held back tears of joy.
5. All the other nominees headed for the nearest exit.
   All the other nominees felt disappointed and exhausted.

EXERCISE 67: Sentence Combining and Reducing. Combine each of the following pairs of sentences in two ways.

a. Form a single sentence beginning with an adverb clause as signaled.
b. Form a single sentence with a participial phrase.

EXAMPLE They draw the largest audience. (**BECAUSE**)
Popular shows charge the most for advertising.

ANSWER A *Because they draw the largest audiences, popular shows charge the most for advertising.*

ANSWER B *Drawing the largest audiences, popular shows charge the most for advertising.*

1. They indicate success. (**BECAUSE**)
   High ratings are the goal of every television programmer.
2. They win large audiences. (**SINCE**)
   Popular shows may run for several years.
3. They have thought up an idea for a series. (**WHEN**)
   Television writers try to interest the networks.
4. They have been shown in film theaters. (**AFTER**)
   Features films are often aired on television.
5. They have been purchased for television. (**AFTER**)
   Many films are edited, or cut.

EXERCISE 68: Sentence Combining and Reducing. Combine each of the following pairs of sentences in two ways.

a. Form a single sentence with an adjective clause as signaled.
b. Form a single sentence with a participial phrase.

EXAMPLE Daytime soap operas draw a large audience.
Daytime soap operas deal with sagas. (**WHICH**)

ANSWER A *Daytime soap operas, **which** deal with sagas, draw a large audience.*

ANSWER B *Daytime soap operas, dealing with sagas, draw a large audience.*

1. *Meet the Press* has been on for more than thirty years.
   Meet the Press features interviews with politicians. (**WHICH**)
2. Game shows give away money and prizes.
   Game shows attract millions. (**WHICH**)
3. Archie Bunker has become a household name.
   Archie Bunker is a character in a popular television series. (**WHO**)
4. Public television has introduced audiences to ballet.
   Public television broadcasts live performances. (**WHICH**)
5. Television viewers can see current feature films at home.
   Television viewers pay for a cable. (**WHO**)
6. Prime-time shows are meant for family viewing.
   Prime-time shows run between 8:00 and 10:00 P.M. (**WHICH**)
7. Commercials are often annoying.
   Commercials range from thirty seconds to a minute. (**WHICH**)
8. Television talk shows have popular guests.
   Television talk shows air during the morning hours. (**THAT**)
9. Some television stars become very well known.
   Some television stars also perform on stage. (**WHO**)
10. Television mini-series dramatize novels.
    Television mini-series take several nights. (**WHICH**)

3.g ABSOLUTE PHRASES

An **absolute phrase** usually consists of a noun followed by a participle.

Absolute phrases are different from regular participial phrases because the participle in an absolute phrase tells about, or modifies, its own noun or pronoun rather than a noun or pronoun elsewhere in the sentence.

EXAMPLES

Regular participial phrase

Checking her colleagues' equipment, the lead climber felt confident about their abilities. [Who did the checking? The *lead climber*—the subject of the entire sentence—did the checking.]

Absolute phrases

The equipment checked, the lead climber felt confident about their abilities. [Who or what was checked? The *equipment*, which is not the subject of the entire sentence, was checked. *Checked* does not refer to *lead climber*, which is the subject of the sentence.]

The journey begun, the travelers never looked back.

The weather being fair, the journey was easy.

Flags flying, **trumpets blowing**, the marchers swung up the avenue.

Absolute phrases can usually be placed (a) at the beginning of a sentence, (b) between the subject and the predicate, or (c) at the end of the sentence. Even a short absolute phrase should be set off from the rest of the sentence by commas.

EXAMPLES

a. **Flags flying**, the marchers swung up the avenue.

b. The marchers, **flags flying**, swung up the avenue.

c. The marchers swung up the avenue, **flags flying**.

EXERCISE 69: Sentence Combining. Combine each of the following pairs of sentences to form a new sentence containing an absolute phrase. Convert the second sentence in the pair into an absolute phrase by replacing the verb with a participle. Place the absolute phrase *first* in your new sentence. Make sure to place a comma after each absolute phrase.

EXAMPLE The umpire raised his mask.
His temper was beginning to flare.

ANSWER ***His temper beginning to flare***, *the umpire raised his mask.*

1. The basketball guard blocked the ball.
His arms were rising.
2. The hockey player skated swiftly.
Chips of ice were flying.
3. The tennis player served the second ball.
Her foot was carefully placed behind the line.
4. The batter bunted the ball.
His bat was held sideways.

5. The marathon swimmers glided through the water.
   Their bodies were coated with grease for protection.
6. The team ran back onto the court.
   Their captain was shouting.
7. The golfer assessed the tilt of the green.
   The crowd was watching in silence.
8. The runners were ready to race.
   Their toes were poised behind the starting line.
   Their bodies were tensed for action.
9. The player was ready to steal second base.
   His eyes were riveted on the pitcher.
10. The team formed a huddle.
    Their heads were bending forward.

EXERCISE 70. Rewrite each of your sentences from Exercise 69, moving the absolute to either a position at the end of the sentence or a position between the subject and the predicate, whichever position produces the clearest and smoothest sentence.

REVIEW EXERCISE. As you have learned in this section, you can add information to sentences by using many structures, some of which are listed here.

METHODS OF EXPANDING SENTENCES

1. adjectives or participles used as adjectives
2. adverbs
3. prepositional phrases
4. adverb clauses
5. adjective clauses
6. appositives
7. participial phrases
8. absolutes

Expand the numbered sentences on the following page, adding to each sentence the information given at its right. Rewrite each numbered sentence twice, using two different methods of expansion. Be sure that by the end of the exercise you have used each of the eight methods of expansion listed above at least once.

Review Exercise *(continued)*

Expand each of the sentences on the left by adding the information on its right. As you do, keep in mind the various methods of expanding sentences. They are listed on the preceding page.

Sentence	Additional Information
1. Rosemary resigned as captain of the women's track team at Washington High School.	Rosemary is a popular, hard-working student.
2. She handed her resignation to Dr. Francis.	Dr. Francis is the principal of the school.
3. Rosemary left the principal's office and headed for the nearest exit.	Her heart was pounding wildly.
4. Rosemary knew that she would be missed.	Rosemary has great power and endurance.
5. Rosemary was sorry, but she had done her best to combine studies, sports, and recreational interests.	She was in her last semester of school.
6. She could now look forward to reading books for her own pleasure.	Rosemary is an avid reader.
7. Rosemary even thought about taking in an occasional movie.	Rosemary is also a movie fan.
8. She wondered why Dr. Francis had not tried to persuade her to stay on as captain.	Dr. Francis is a kind and wise person.
9. "Perhaps I should at least continue to run in the quarter mile," she thought.	Rosemary remembered that she was the best middle-distance runner in the state.
10. She glanced at her wristwatch and headed for the nearest telephone booth.	The watch is gold and a gift from the Junior Chamber of Commerce honoring Rosemary for her work with children.

IMPROVING SENTENCES

The following suggestions are intended to help you improve individual sentences and the way you link sentences.

3.h STRONG SUBJECTS

Do not try to drag the abstract ideas of one sentence into the *subject* of the sentence that follows. Sentences should be clearly related to one another, but you should never sacrifice the power of the subject in any individual sentence.

EXAMPLE

Poor: Idea of previous sentence used as subject

[1]A very dry summer was followed by a rainless September and October. [2]**This fact** led to an outbreak of small brush fires in mid-October.

With the words *this fact,* the writer tries to connect Sentence 2 to Sentence 1 but succeeds only in spoiling the second sentence because *this fact* makes a dull and weak subject. Compare the example above with the improved sequence below.

Improved: Subject can stand on its own.

[1]A very dry summer was followed by a rainless September and October. [2]In mid-October, as a result of the drought, **small brush fires** broke out.

Here the writer has not forgotten Sentence 1 in Sentence 2; indeed, the sentences are clearly connected with *as a result of the drought.* This time, however, the writer has avoided the dull and weak expression *this fact.*

■ Advice

Try to get as strong and clear a subject as possible into every sentence. The subject should be able to stand on its own and not be designed solely as a reminder of the preceding sentence.

3.i CLEAR SUBJECTS

The *grammatical subject* of your sentence should also be the *logical subject* (the person, place, or thing that you are talking about).

EXAMPLE

You want to convey the idea that weather conditions in Maine in 1947 created forest fires. *Weather conditions* are the words that form your logical subject. They should, therefore, be the grammatical subject as well. Consider the following two sentences to make sure that you understand this point.

Poor: Logical subject is not grammatical subject.

The summer of 1947 in Maine with its weather conditions led to forest fires in the fall.

Improved: Logical subject is grammatical subject.

Weather conditions in Maine in the summer of 1947 led to forest fires in the fall.

■ Advice

Make sure that the logical subject of your sentence is also the grammatical subject. Ask yourself what you are really talking about, and check to see that your answer is the grammatical subject of the sentence.

3.j ACTION VERBS VERSUS FORMS OF BE

Try to use strong action verbs instead of linking verbs, especially instead of a form of *be.*

EXAMPLE

Poor: Weak linking verb

Forest fires **were** in all but the northern part of Maine, where heavy night frost kept the forests damp.

Improved: Strong verb

Forest fires **sprang up** in all but the northern part of Maine, where heavy night frosts kept the forests damp.

In the example above, replacing the form of *be (were)* with a strong verb *(sprang up)* makes the sentence stronger, clearer, and more interesting. In selecting an action verb, do not overlook verbs that are made up of two or more words (see 4.c).

■ Advice

Look over your sentences to see if they would benefit from the use of a strong verb in place of a form of the linking verb *be.*

3.k PARALLELISM

Parallelism means that all sentence elements that are alike in importance are expressed in the same way.

If you are writing a series, make sure that you use grammatically similar constructions. For example, two nouns should be followed by a third noun, not by an infinitive. Read the following example to see how the smoothness of a sentence can be destroyed by a *lack of* parallelism.

EXAMPLE

Poor: Clauses are not parallel.

Forestry departments lent technical advice, students served as volunteers, and we saw neighbor helping neighbor.

The first and second clauses above have as their subject the person or agency that performs the action. The third clause shifts the point of view by making the subject of the clause the personal pronoun *we.* Notice how the three clauses can be made parallel:

Improved: Clauses are parallel.

Forestry departments lent assistance, students volunteered, and neighbor aided neighbor.

Here is another example of a nonparallel sentence, followed by two suggested improvements. The revisions show that in this case you should use either two phrases or two clauses, not one phrase and one clause.

EXAMPLE

Poor: Sentence not parallel – one clause and one phrase.

A spring **that was excessively rainy** lent false hope, and a summer, **rainless as the Sahara**, set the stage for disaster.

Improved: Sentence contains parallel phrases.

A spring, **wet as a Caribbean rain forest**, lent false hope, and a summer, **rainless as the Sahara**, set the stage for disaster.

Improved: Sentence contains parallel clauses.

A spring **that was excessively rainy** lent false hope, and a summer **that was dangerously dry** set the stage for disaster.

The chart below will alert you to other parallel constructions.

PARALLEL CONSTRUCTIONS

nouns	*adjectives*	*verbs*	*infinitives*
We fear **fire**, **pestilence**, and **flood**.	Fires can be **friendly** or **destructive**.	The fire **smouldered**, **smoked**, and **subsided**.	They liked **to hunt**, **to fish**, and **to hike**.

participles

Shouting and **sweating**, the firefighters moved toward the lake.

prepositional phrases	*clauses*
A government established **by the people**, **for the people**.	He went **where he was told to**, **when he was told to**.

Advice

Make sure that sentence elements in pairs or in series have similar grammatical constructions.

3.I CONCISENESS

Be concise. Do not use unnecessary words. Reread your individual sentences and each sequence of sentences to check for wordiness or monotonous rhythms.

EXAMPLE

Poor: Too many words; unnecessary words

Instead of being defeated, all of the people in the area who had suffered from the forest fires looked toward a new future and were not discouraged. [27 words]

Improved: More concise

Undefeated, the victims of the forest fires looked hopefully toward the future. [12 words]

Often a single word (for example, *victim, hopefully*) can replace an entire group of words (here, *all of the people in the area who had suffered* and *and were not discouraged,* respectively).

Try also to remove all redundancies. A **redundancy** is a word or group of words that unnecessarily repeats the meaning of another word or group of words. Because there is no such thing as an *old* future, the word *new* in the first example sentence above is unnecessary and simply repeats the idea of *the future.* It is redundant.

There are two methods for being concise: (1) deletion and (2) compression. **Deletion** is the removal of a word or group of words without substitution. **Compression** is the substitution of a single word for a group of words. Compare the following examples.

EXAMPLES

Deletion

If this story were fiction, it would be a great yarn, but, as it is truth ~~rather than fiction,~~ it remains ~~an account that we can call~~ tragedy.

Compression

~~The forest was damaged beyond recognition with all its trees burned by fire.~~

The forest was destroyed by fire.

■ Advice

Try to be concise. Review your sentences to see if single words can clearly take the place of a number of words. Remove any words or phrases that unnecessarily repeat other words.

EXERCISE 71. In each passage, find at least six sentences that can be improved in one of the following ways. Rewrite them.

A. Eliminating the drag from one sentence to another
B. Improving the subject of the sentence
C. Substituting a strong verb for a linking verb
D. Keeping sentence elements parallel
E. Deleting or compressing

[1]*Wildfire Loose* by Joyce Butler is a true account of the disastrous series of forest fires that struck Maine in the fall of 1947. [2]By October 17, Governor Hildreth had to close the woods to hunters. [3]This action was a disaster in itself and, as many Mainers rely on hunters as a source of income, the disaster was an economic one. [4]Part of the fascination of the book is about the hardships of fighting the fires.

[5]One factor that made firefighting in Maine so difficult is that much of the sod is fire-retaining peat that will burn deeply below the ground level and come to the surface a long way off to start new fires. [6]Also, after a rainless summer, wells and streams were dry. [7]At such times, beavers have been known to fight firefighters. [8]The way in which a beaver would fight firefighters would be to build dams holding back the water. [9]Beavers would build a dam, and then it would be destroyed by firefighters. [10]Then the beavers would rebuild it again during the night. [11]The problem of firefighters fighting beavers as well as fire was thus a factor.

[1]There is no reason to let your running shoes go on vacation when you are away from home. [2]To prove this point, many people run at airports and along highways when on vacations or business trips. [3]One writer reports that he has followed out his jogging routine in twenty-six states and five foreign countries. [4]Running, a visitor sees more than he or she would from a car or sightseeing bus. [5]Jogging along the roadside gives one a feeling for the geography of a place. [6]Discoveries uncovered by joggers are not available to most people who do not run.

[7]Runners who travel and run while away from home on short business trips learn to rate cities on a basis of how close to a good hotel a pleasant running area can be found. [8]Chicago ranks high in this respect because it has an attractive park system through the lakefront parks and beaches easily available from downtown.

4

VOCABULARY

4 Vocabulary

A strong vocabulary helps you to score well on tests, to read without frequent trips to the dictionary, to understand daily conversations and formal speeches, and to speak fluently in any kind of situation. Perhaps most important of all, a strong vocabulary of the right kind is the foundation of good writing, actually of all writing. If you do not know the word for the thing or idea that you are thinking of, you will never get your sentence down on paper, or you will have to write around the missing word. If you do not know the word *assembly*, for example, you will have to write "a period when teachers and students gather together in the auditorium," taking eleven words instead of one and producing an awkward-sounding sentence.

You have four vocabularies: a reader's vocabulary, a listener's vocabulary, a speaker's vocabulary, and a writer's vocabulary. These four overlap, of course, but you go about building each of them in slightly different ways. In this section, you will learn various strategies for thinking about words and for increasing your writer's vocabulary.

EXPANDING YOUR VOCABULARY: PARTS OF SPEECH

Expanding your vocabulary is an important part of improving your ability as a writer. Thinking of your vocabulary in terms of nouns, verbs, adjectives, adverbs, and other parts of speech will make the process of expansion easier.

In this section, you will not be asked to memorize extensive vocabulary lists, but you will learn strategies for noticing, thinking about, and trying out words that are new to you.

4.a ADDING TO YOUR NOUN VOCABULARY

You can find a word—a noun—to name or identify almost every kind of thing or idea in the universe. New nouns are being added to the language constantly. There is a common noun to identify every kind of thing: kinds of people, kinds of jobs, kinds of natural objects, kinds of inventions, and parts of things. Common nouns are also used to identify kinds of ideas – for example, *subtraction, beauty, time, space,* and so on. Nouns that name objects are called **concrete nouns**; nouns that name ideas are called **abstract nouns**.

An interesting exercise is to take a group of concrete nouns and see what abstract noun they "add up to." For example, *gold medal, money,* and *laurel wreath* can add up to *success.* You can also do the reverse: Take an abstract noun (*beauty,* for example) and see what concrete nouns the abstract noun might be composed of—a rose, a sunset, a still-life painting, a violin concerto, and a poem, perhaps.

Concrete nouns and abstract nouns are interrelated so often that you should always try to think of one in terms of the other. For example, in writing about the abstract idea of *transportation,* you can help your reader visualize and understand the concept if you also use specific concrete nouns—such as *buses, subways, jets, camels,* and *sailing ships.* Similarly, you can help your reader form concepts out of concrete words by using an abstract word. In the following sentence the abstract noun *luxury* helps your reader summarize the preceding series of concrete nouns.

> After traveling in the snow for two days, we finally reached the miner's hut. Inside we discovered *cans of corned beef, coffee,* and *flour,* along with several *bunks* and a *fireplace.* We found pure *luxury.*

EXERCISE 1. Make a list of at least six concrete nouns that "add up to" each of the following abstract nouns.

1. happiness
2. climate
3. sadness

EXERCISE 2. Supply one or more abstract nouns for each of the following groups of concrete nouns.

1. cliff, hawk, wind, backpack, rope
2. ordinance, bench, attorney, gavel, plea

EXERCISE 3. Match the concrete nouns in the right-hand columns below with the abstract nouns in the left-hand column as shown in the example. Form three groups, each with one abstract noun supported by three concrete nouns.

EXAMPLE abstract noun: *danger*
concrete nouns: *street crossings, knives, matches*

Abstract nouns	Concrete nouns	
fun	maps	movies
research	balloons	aspirins
illness	test tubes	libraries
	thermometer	doctor
	cartoons	

4.b ADDING TO YOUR VERB VOCABULARY

As with nouns, the list of English verbs is vast and still growing. You will never be able to learn all of the verbs now in use. Even if you did, someone, somewhere, would invent a new way of doing something—perhaps a new way of deflecting light, for example—and then a new verb would have to be invented. You can, nevertheless, add to your vocabulary of verbs by listening closely for words that express specific actions and processes. When you hear or read a new verb, try to use it in your own writing.

4.c TWO-WORD VERBS

While collecting new verbs in general, you can also extend your stockpile of two-word verbs. **Two-word verbs** are usually made up of very simple, familiar verbs that somehow have become attached to words that are otherwise separate prepositions or adverbs.[1] For example, in such verbs as *take*

[1]Your teacher may want you to think of these expressions as verbs + adverbs rather than as two-word verbs. Follow your teacher's instructions.

up, call off, and *give out,* the words *up, off,* and *out* have actually become a part of the verb. Such words are sometimes called **particles** and combine with a verb to form a two-word verb. (Be careful not to treat every expression as a two-word verb: When you *turn down* a road, you have a verb and a preposition. When you *turn down* a job offer, you have a two-word verb.) Here are a few other two-word verbs.

EXAMPLES

take up	call up
bring up	turn up

Being aware of two-word verbs can help you increase your verb vocabulary in an important way: English is such a rich language that just about every two-word verb has a one-word verb equivalent. Two-word verbs are often more common and conversational than their one-word equivalents. For example, *turn down* is more conversational than *reject,* and *call off* is more conversational than *cancel.* Practice extending your verb vocabulary by trying to think of the one-word verb that means about the same thing as a two-word verb.

EXERCISE 4. Match each of the following two-word verbs on the left with a one-word verb on the right.

1. find out	a. explode
2. pick out	b. distribute; faint
3. point out	c. register
4. check in	d. depart
5. blow up	e. refuse
6. pass out	f. select
7. take off	g. discover
8. turn off	h. designate
9. look over	i. stop
10. pass up	j. examine

4.d ADDING TO YOUR ADJECTIVE VOCABULARY

There are fewer adjectives than nouns and verbs in our language but still thousands more than most writers take advantage of. You may have noticed that no matter how many new nouns you add to your language – and you add them almost daily—the adjectives that you assign to them are often the same old battle-scarred and "catchall" adjectives like *old, new, good, bad, big, little, beautiful, ugly, nice,* or *fine.* It is best in writing to be as precise and specific as you can in your descriptions and evaluations of everything: people, works of art, inventions, ideas, events, and performances. For example, it is more useful and more accurate to say that an actress' performance is *insensitive* rather than simply *bad.* A good way to add to your adjective vocabulary, therefore, is to seek out precise adjectives for given nouns, as in the examples below:

Noun	Adjectives
film	stark, eloquent, original
book	rich, anachronistic, illiterate
ball game	taut, suspenseful
opera	extravagant, flamboyant
actress	gaunt, elegant, believable

EXERCISE 5. Choose two adjectives – as specific and as descriptive as possible – to describe each of the following nouns. One adjective should have a positive connotation, or flavor; one adjective should have a negative connotation, or flavor.

EXAMPLE plan

ANSWER *an **ingenious** plan (positive)*
*a **destructive** plan (negative)*

1. aunt
2. play
3. painting
4. explanation
5. town
6. horse
7. mountain
8. poem
9. newspaper
10. typewriter

4.e USING PARTICIPLES AS ADJECTIVES

Present and past participles are formed from verbs. The verb *boil,* for example, can be made into the present participle *boiling* and into the past participle *boiled.* Participles—both past participles and present participles—can function in the same way that adjectives do. If you use participles instead of only adjectives before nouns, you can be even more expressive and descriptive. Instead of talking about the *hot* sun or a *hard* egg, you can talk about the *boiling* sun or a *boiled* egg.

Not every verb can be changed into a present or past participle to be used before a noun, but a large number of verbs can give you new ways to describe nouns. (Some participles are used so frequently as adjectives that they become classified as adjectives in dictionaries. The word *tired*—as in *the tired runner slipped*—is formed from the verb *tire*, "to grow weary." *Tired* may be classified as an adjective in your dictionary, however. Whether it is a participle or an adjective is not important to you as a writer. What should concern you is that many verbs can be turned into participles and used before nouns.)

You can practice expanding your vocabulary by trying to form participles from verbs. Look at a verb and try to use a participle form of it before a noun. Here is a sample list prepared by a student who went through a dictionary.

EXAMPLES

Verb	Present participle	Past participle
abandon (leave)	no	an *abandoned* boat
abash (embarrass)	no	an *abashed* student
abate (lessen)	the *abating* winds	no
abdicate (give up)	the *abdicating* queen	no
abduct (carry off)	no	an *abducted* official
abet (encourage)	the *abetting* criminal	no
abhor (detest)	no	the *abhorred* revolution
abide (remain)	an *abiding* hope	no
absorb (take in)	an *absorbing* sponge	an *absorbed* look

EXERCISE 6. Write three different present participles and three different past participles that could precede each of the following nouns.

EXAMPLE horse

ANSWER *present participles: galloping, neighing, sleeping*
past participles: exhausted, distracted, excited

1. face
2. winds
3. watch
4. weather
5. ideals
6. fire fighters
7. photographers
8. trees
9. waterfall
10. assignment

4.f USING COMPOUND ADJECTIVES AND PARTICIPLES

A good way of adding to your adjective vocabulary is to use both compound adjectives and compound participles before nouns. The lists below will give you an idea of the kinds of compounds you can use. Compound adjectives and participles can be unique. You as a writer can combine words in an original way to create unusual and powerful descriptions. Instead of saying that a room was lined with bookshelves and paneled with sheets of walnut, one high school student wrote of a *book-lined, walnut-paneled room.* Using compound adjectives and compound participles adds conciseness to your writing. Count the words that they save. Remember, however, that compounds are not appropriate to all kinds of writing and can be overused. (See 7.j for advice on the use of hyphens with compound words.)

Compound adjectives	Longer expressions
down-to-earth people	people who have their feet on the ground
bluish green dress	a dress that is mostly green with a touch of blue
all-purpose cleaner	a cleaner for all purposes
half-asleep baby	a baby who is halfway between sleep and wakefulness
once-in-a lifetime chance	a chance that occurs only once in a great while

Compound participles	Longer expressions
thirst-quenching drink	a drink that quenches the thirst
half-baked idea; **half-baked** cake	an idea that is badly thought out; a cake that is underdone
clay-colored dish	a dish that is the color of clay
back-breaking work	work that is exhausting

EXERCISE 7. Rewrite each of the following sentences using a compound adjective or compound participle formed from the words in the original sentence.

EXAMPLE The Transamerica Building, shaped like a pyramid, is a huge office building in San Francisco.

ANSWER *The pyramid-shaped Transamerica Building is a huge office building in San Francisco.*

1. Tourists admire David Smith's huge sculptures, which inspire them with awe.
2. A majority consisting of two thirds of the Senate is required to ratify a treaty.
3. The United States, Egypt, and Mexico are all countries that produce oil.
4. Submarines that are powered by nuclear energy are used by the United States Navy.
5. Georgia O'Keeffe's paintings of landscapes baked by the sun are imposing and stark.
6. Places that are out of the way are often the most interesting to visit.
7. Scientists have sighted a huge spot that is mainly orange with a touch of red on the planet Jupiter.
8. Cowpunchers who "bust" broncos can be found at any rodeo.
9. Legislators often make changes in bills at the last minute.
10. Tennessee's Smoky Mountains, covered with trees, take on a bluish tinge at twilight.

4.g ADDING TO YOUR VOCABULARY WITH ADVERBS OF MANNER

Adverbs of manner are essential to you as a writer because they help to describe actions more precisely. To describe an action, search for the most precise verb. Then, if you wish, describe the action even more precisely with an adverb of manner.

EXAMPLES

General verb	More precise verb	Adverb of manner
eat	gobble	frantically
drink	sip	daintily
run	gallop	thunderously

Before running for the plane, they **frantically** gobbled a pizza.
The child **daintily** sipped the rest of the milk.
I saw the horses as they galloped **thunderously** away.

Most adverbs of manner are derived from adjectives. The adverb *frantically* is derived from the adjective *frantic*; *daintily* is derived from *dainty*; *thunderously* is derived from *thunderous.* Therefore, an *affectionate* person smiles *affectionately*; an *amateurish* painter paints *amateurishly*; *automatic* doors open *automatically.* Notice, however, that not all adjectives can be transformed into adverbs of manner. For instance, a green giant does nothing *greenly.* Nor does an *old* person do anything *oldly*.

EXERCISE 8. Answer the following questions by giving the correct adverb of manner. Answer each question in complete sentences.

1. How might a skillful pianist play the piano?
2. How might a crafty lawyer develop an argument?
3. How might a malicious gossip write a newspaper column?
4. How might a nervous teenager walk in a procession?
5. How might a hungry child eat a sandwich?

What adverbs of manner might be used with each of the following verbs?

6. smile
7. think
8. survive
9. criticize
10. chat

4.h USING PREPOSITIONS

Prepositions may cause you doubt when there seems to be little or no distinction in meaning between two of them. Such may be the case when a prepositional phrase follows an adjective. In the following sentences, what is the difference in meaning between the prepositions *with* and *at* after the adjective *angry*?

We were angry *at* the firings.
We were angry *with* management.

The difference in meaning is slight, but most good writers prefer to say *angry at things* but *angry with people.* There is no logical reason for this choice; it has simply become conventional usage. Here are other examples of traditional uses of adjectives and prepositions.

EXAMPLES

adequate *to*
adjacent *to*
candid *about*
capable *of*
contemporary *with*
deficient *in*
identical *with*
independent *of*
inseparable *from*
mistrustful *of*
obedient *to*
observant *of*
sensitive *to*
similar *to*
superior *to*
thoughtful *of*

EXERCISE 9. Write ten sentences, each of which uses one of the above combinations of adjective and preposition.

EXPANDING YOUR VOCABULARY: WORD BUILDING

You are probably used to looking at word *parts* as a word-attack skill when you read. You know that if you break down a word (for example, *nonprofitable*) into its various parts, or elements, you may stand a better chance of understanding what it and the rest of the sentence mean. For example, when you break down *nonprofitable,* you find *non-* ("not") + *profit* ("gain") + *-able* (marking the word as an adjective) so that you can understand the word as "an adjective having to do with not making gains."

What you may not realize is that you can use the reverse method to build your *writer's* vocabulary. Instead of analyzing the parts of the words you read, you can put word parts together yourself to form useful longer words for your own writing. You can put roots and base words (4.i), prefixes (4.j), combining forms (4.k), and suffixes (4.l) together to help you save time, to increase your precision with language, and to vary your wording. Examine the following pages, and do the exercises.

4.i WORD ROOTS AND BASE WORDS

A **word root** is the main part of a word, but it is not a complete word in itself.

A word root (or, simply root) must have another element added to it at its beginning or at its end. For example, the root *-junct-* means "join," but there is no English word *junct.* The root needs another element before it or after it (or before *and* after it) for it to become a complete English word, as in ***con****junct*, *junct****ion***, or ***con****junct****ion***. Similarly, the root *-scrib-* means "write," but it is not a free-standing English word: It needs a word element before it or after it for it to become a complete English word, as in ***pre****scribe* or *scrib****al***.

Many English words are obviously made up of a root plus another word element. Many other English words, however, have only one element and can comfortably stand alone as such: *walk, read, table, run, sky, write, join.* These words are called base words. A **base word** often takes another element but does not *need* to have any other element added to it, as a root must.

	EXAMPLES	*ENGLISH WORD?*	*WITH OTHER ELEMENTS*
ROOT	**-junct-**	no	conjunct, junction
	-scrib-	no	prescribe, scribal
BASE WORD	join	yes	rejoin, joinable
	write	yes	rewrite, writer

The elements that are added to roots and to base words are **prefixes** and **suffixes**. In the following pages you will see how prefixes and suffixes are important to you as a writer who is interested in expanding a writing vocabulary. You will also see that there are really two kinds of prefixes—separable prefixes and inseparable prefixes.

LATIN WORD ROOTS

Root	Meaning	Examples
-ag-, -act-	do, drive	agent, agriculture, enact, transact
-am-	love	amiable, amorous
-audi-	hear	audience, inaudible
-ben-	good; well	beneficial, benefit
-brev-	short	abbreviate, brevity, brief
-cand-	shine	candle, incandescent
-cap-	head	captain, decapitate
-cid-	kill; cut	suicide, incision
-cli-	slope	decline, inclination, incline
-cogn-	know	cognizant, recognize
-cred-	believe	credible, incredulous
-culp-	blame	culpable, culprit
-domin-	a lord	dominate, dominion
-duc-	lead	abduct, conductor, introduce
-equ-	equal	equal, equation
-err-	stray	aberration, error
-fac-, -fec-	do; make	affect, effect, fact, manufacture
-fer-	bear	circumference, proffer, transfer
-fid-	belief; faith	confide, faith, infidel
-fin-	end	confine, finality
-frag-, -frac-	break	fracture, fragment
-fus-	pour	effusive, transfusion
-gen-	kind; origin	congenital, generic, progenitor

Root	Meaning	Examples
-jac-, -ject-	throw	eject, interjection
-jud-	a judge	judge, prejudice
-jung-, -jug-, -junct-	join	conjugal, join, subjunctive
-jur-	swear	jury, perjury
-leg-, -lect-	collect; read	intellect, legible, recollect
-loc-	a place	dislocate, local, locate
-loqu-	speak	eloquent, loquacious, soliloquy
-magn-	great	magnificent, magnify
-mal-	bad	malady, malice
-man-	hand	manual, manuscript
-mitt-, -miss-	send	emissary, mission, transmit
-mor-	die	morbid, mortal, mortuary
-ped-	foot	biped, pedal, quadruped
-pend-, -pens-	weigh; hang	depend, impending, pendant
-pon-, -posit-	place	opponent, opposite, position
-port-	carry	export, portable, transport
-pos-, -pot-	be able	possible, potent
-prim-	first	premier, prime, primitive
-pugn-	fight	impugn, pugnacious, repugnant
-pung-, -punct-	point	punctual, punctuation
-reg-, -rect-	rule	correct, rectify, regular
-rump-, -rupt-	break	abrupt, interruption, rupture
-sang-	blood	consanguinity, sanguine
-sci-	know	conscious, science
-scrib-	write	inscribe, manuscript, scribble

Root	Meaning	Examples
-sent-, -sens-	feel	presentiment, sensual
-sequ-, -secut-	follow	consecutive, sequel
-sol-	alone	desolate, solitude, solo
-son-	a sound	consonant, sonata, unison
-spir-	breath	inspire, spirit
-string-, -strict-	pull tight	astringent, strict
-trah-, -tract-	draw	distract, traction
-ut-, -us-	use	abuse, utensil, utilize
-ven-, -vent-	come	adventure, prevent
-verb-	word	adverb, verbal
-vert-, -vers-	turn	divert, reverse
-via-	a way	deviate, viaduct
-vid-, -vis-	see	evident, visual
-vit-	life	vitality, vitamin

GREEK WORD ROOTS

Root	Meaning	Examples
-anthrop-	man; human being	anthropology, misanthropic
-bibli-	book	bibliography
-chrom-	color	chromatic, chromosome
-cosm-	world	cosmos, macrocosm
-crat-	rule; power	aristocracy, democracy
-cycl-	circle; cycle	circle, tricycle
-dem-	people	democracy, epidemic
-gen-	race	genealogy, genesis
-hom-	same	homogenous
-morph-	form	amorphous, metamorphosis
-neo-	new	neolithic, neophyte

Root	Meaning	Examples
-path-	suffering; feeling	apathy, pathos, sympathy
-phob-	fear	phobia
-polis-	city	metropolis, Minneapolis
-psych-	soul; mind	psyche, psychology
-soph-	wise	philosopher, sophomore
-zo-	animal; life	protozoa, zoology

4.j PREFIXES: ADDING TO YOUR WRITING VOCABULARY

Prefixes are word elements that are attached to the beginning of roots and base words.

Actually, there are two kinds of prefixes: (1) *inseparable prefixes,* which are permanently joined with *roots* in whole words, and (2) *separable prefixes,* which you can add to or subtract from *base words* to produce (derive) a new word with a related but different meaning. The second kind—the separable prefixes that can be added or subtracted – are more important to you as a writer. Here are some examples.

SEPARABLE PREFIXES

Prefix		Base word	New word
un-	add to	happy	**un**happy
a-	add to	social	**a**social

Word		Prefix	Base word
unable	detach	**un**-	able
preschool	detach	**pre**-	school

Prefixes can help your writing in two ways.

1. Once you have learned how to use prefixes, you can automatically expand your writing vocabulary. For example, the word *unfriendly* is one that you would think of easily, but the word *asocial* may be a new addition to your writing vocabulary, acquired as you learn the prefix *a-*.

2. When you use a prefixed word in your writing, you tighten your sentence, usually reducing the number of words that you would otherwise need to express your ideas. Consider the following pairs of sentences. Notice that the second sentence in each pair contains fewer words and is more direct.

EXAMPLES

They went on a voyage **across the Atlantic**.
They went on a **transatlantic** voyage.

Lindbergh made a solo flight **that was not believable** across the Atlantic.
Lindbergh made an **unbelievable** solo flight across the Atlantic.

Parents should use only paint **that is not poisonous** in a child's room.
Parents should use only **nonpoisonous** paint in a child's room.

Most prefixes have only one written form. Some prefixes, however, have slightly changed, or variant, forms when they are attached to base words beginning with vowel sounds or with specific consonants.

EXAMPLES

anti- becomes *ant-* before base words beginning with some vowel sounds: *ant*acid, *ant*arctic
in- changes before base words beginning with *b, l, m, p,* and *r*: *im*balance, *il*legal, *im*mobile, *im*possible, *ir*regular

Most prefixes have only one or two meanings. You can usually add these meanings directly onto the meaning of the base word.

EXAMPLES

The prefix *a-* can mean "not"; therefore, *asocial* means "not social," and *atypical* means "not typical."
The prefix *in-* can mean "not"; therefore, *ineffective* means "not effective," and *inaccurate* means "not accurate."

Occasionally you will find two or more prefixes with similar meanings. For example, both *un-* and *in-* mean "not," and both *de-* and *dis-* can mean "do the opposite of," as in *defrost* and *disjoin*. There are no clear rules for deciding which prefix to use with a particular base word. Sometimes a base word can even take two similar prefixes: ***in**experienced*, ***un**experienced.* When in doubt about which prefix to attach to a specific base word, check a dictionary.

The following lists will introduce you to six groups of prefixes and their meanings. You may use many prefixed words naturally in your own writing. The exercises will show you appropriate ways to use prefixed words to revise your writing so that it will be smoother and more concise.

PREFIXES WITH NEGATIVE MEANINGS

Prefix	Meaning	Useful base words
a-	without; not; lacking in	moral, typical, septic, tonal
dis-	not; opposite of	please, agreeable, respect, obey, tasteful
in-	not; without; lacking	decent, credible, conclusive, coherent, complete
il-	variant of *in-*	legal, literate, logical, legitimate
im-	variant of *in-*	passable, mortal, mature, pertinent
ir-	variant of *in-*	revocable, responsible, rational, regular
mal-	bad; wrongful; ill	form, function, nourish, treat, nutrition
mis-	wrongly; astray	behave, calculate, construe, judge, understand
non-	not	profit, taxable, partisan, absorbant
un-	not; opposite of	disturbed, familiar, grateful, predictable

Sometimes a prefixed word can replace a whole clause. You will have to place the newly formed prefixed word *before* the noun that the clause told about in order to make your revision read correctly.

EXAMPLE

Oxygen deficiency can cause brain damage *that is not reversible.* (variant of *in-*)

Oxygen deficiency can cause *irreversible* brain damage.

EXERCISE 10. Revise each of the following sentences by combining the negative prefix (given in parentheses) with a base word in the underlined section. Make sure the prefixed word is placed so that your revision reads smoothly.

1. A needle that is not septic must be used to extract a splinter, or the chance of infection will increase. (a-)
2. Mr. Spock criticized Captain Kirk's response because of the captain's emotions that were not logical. (variant of in-)
3. Scrooge was not agreeable about spending money. (dis-)
4. In Massachusetts, groceries, food, and clothing are items that are not taxable. (non-)
5. Many foresee a future that is not predictable; however, others claim that those who ignore history are doomed to repeat it. (un-)
6. To avoid paragraphs that are not coherent, good writers organize their thoughts before writing their first drafts. (in-)
7. Evidence of bad nutrition can be found in advanced as well as in developing countries. (mal-)
8. The Declaration of Independence states that every human being is born with certain rights that are not revocable. (variant of in-)
9. The characters of many people may be judged wrongly if these people are seen with those who have doubtful reputations. (mis-)
10. A student who wants attention will often raise a question that is not pertinent. (variant of in-)

PREFIXES THAT REVERSE ACTIONS

Prefix	Meaning	Useful base words
de-	to reverse an action; to deprive of; to remove	frost, centralize, emphasize, sensitize, humidify, segregate
dis-	to reverse an action; to take away; to remove	arm, color, integrate, assemble, qualify, continue, connect
un-	to reverse an action; to deprive of	tie, pack, lock, saddle, horse

EXERCISE 11. Revise and shorten the underlined portion of each sentence by using a verb with the prefix in parentheses.

EXAMPLE It is necessary to remove the frost from some refrigerators regularly. (de-)

ANSWER *It is necessary to* ***defrost*** *some refrigerators regularly.*

1. If you reverse the centralization of power at the federal level, you will have more power at state and local levels. (de-)
2. Geneva, Switzerland, is the site of many conferences on ways to remove arms from world powers. (dis-)
3. To remove the sensitivity of a nerve, a dentist uses Novacain. (de-)
4. Many stables require their customers to take the saddle off the horse they rode. (un-)
5. Officials will invalidate the qualifications of athletes who use medication to improve their performance. (dis-)
6. Many colleges have attempted to reverse the emphasis on interscholastic athletic competition in favor of more intramural sports. (de-)
7. Raccoons have been known to open the lock on campers' food supplies. (un-)
8. Machines have been built to remove the humidity in the air. (de-)
9. One of Harry Truman's accomplishments as President was to eliminate the segregation of military units. (de-)
10. Damage from water and fire will often change the color of clothes and furnishings. (dis-)

PREFIXES INDICATING TIME OR ORDER

Prefix	Meaning	Useful base words
ante-	before	date, chamber
ex-[1]	previous; former	president, mayor, officer, actress
fore-	before; in front of	father, feet, finger, knowledge, thought, tell, shadow

[1]Always hyphenate *ex-* before the base word.

Prefix	Meaning	Useful base words
neo-	new; recent	natal, classical, liberal, conservative
post-	after	graduate, war, test, inaugural, revolutionary
pre-	before	historic, determined, school, game
re-	again; back	echo, emphasize, marry, finance, open

Sometimes a prefixed word can replace an entire clause or prepositional phrase. You will have to place the newly formed prefixed word *before* the noun that the clause or phrase modified in order to make your revision read correctly. Notice that your new sentence will be more concise.

EXAMPLE

The harsh reality of reconstruction *after a war* can be as grueling as the war itself. (post-)

The harsh reality of *postwar* reconstruction can be as grueling as the war itself.

EXERCISE 12. Revise each of the following sentences by combining the prefix given in parentheses with a base word in the underlined part. Be sure the prefixed word is placed so that your revision reads smoothly.

1. Traditionally, stores show their spring fashions during sales <u>that occur before Easter</u>. (pre-)
2. An elected candidate who runs for <u>election again</u> is called an incumbent. (re-)
3. Bob Lemon, the <u>former pitcher</u>, became the manager of the Yankees. (ex-)
4. Sports commentators must be adept at giving concise wrap-ups <u>after a game</u>. (post-)
5. Holidays offer families the opportunity to <u>unite repeatedly</u> on a regular basis. (re-)
6. Potential jury members are questioned about the degree to which they have <u>judged beforehand</u> the defendant's innocence or guilt. (pre-)
7. If a pretest is given to a class in September, <u>a test given afterward</u> in June can be used to indicate improvement or the lack of it. (post-)

8. Most baking recipes suggest that the oven be heated before use. (pre-)
9. Some liberals of the early 1960s became the new conservatives of the 1970s. (neo-)
10. Most permanently pressed materials that are shrunk before sale are guaranteed not to shrink more than 3 percent. (pre-)

PREFIXES INDICATING LOCATION

Prefix	Meaning	Useful base words
circum-	around	solar, navigate, lunar, polar
extra-	outside; beyond	terrestrial, judicial, curricular, legal
inter-	between; among	connected, continental, national, state
intra-	within	city, company, state, muscular, departmental, nasal, tissue
mid-	in the middle of	century, flight, November, summer
sub-	under; beneath	surface, soil, cellar, structure, basement, conscious, continent
super-	above; over	structure, imposed
trans-	across	polar, Pacific, Atlantic, continental, oceanic, Siberian

Notice how a prefixed word replaces a prepositional phrase in each of the following sentences. Each prefix refers to location.

EXAMPLE

We took a trip *across the Pacific.*
We took a transpacific trip.

We took a train *across Siberia.*
We took a trans-Siberian train. [Notice here that the noun *Siberia* becomes the adjective *Siberian.*]

We went on an expedition *around the moon.*
We went on a *circumlunar* expedition. [Notice here that the noun *moon* is replaced with a related adjective, *lunar.*]

EXERCISE 13. From the Word Bank below, select a prefixed word that can replace the prepositional phrase in each of the following sentences. (The preposition may serve as a clue.) Then revise the sentence, placing the prefixed word *before* the noun preceding the prepositional phrase.

1. Rain in the middle of November may cause flooding if the ground is frozen.
2. At a pretrial hearing, a court may dismiss a case if it involves issues outside the law.
3. Many settlers in California made a journey across the entire continent by wagon train.
4. Radiation may cause mutations within a cell that are irreversible.
5. The devastating effects of war among many nations can be felt for decades.
6. Many scientists believe that life beyond the earth is a reality.
7. Explosions under the earth's surface can hinder the rescue of trapped miners.
8. At one time a nonstop flight around the South Pole was pure fantasy.
9. Ships on voyages across the Atlantic are often forced to proceed through the infamous Bermuda Triangle.
10. Bus service between cities in some states is controlled by one or two major companies.

WORD BANK

circumpolar	intracellular
extralegal	mid-November
extraterrestrial	subsurface
international	transatlantic
interurban	transcontinental

PREFIXES INDICATING DEGREE, QUALITY, OR SIZE

Prefix	Meaning	Useful base words
arch-	first; foremost	rival, bishop, diocese, fiend, enemy, villain
extra-	beyond; more than	ordinary, musical, thick, active

Prefix	Meaning	Useful base words
out-	going beyond; surpassing	draw, live, sell, distance, match
over-	excessive; too much	achieve, growth, confidence, burden, developed, simplify
sub-	lower in status than; less than	group, committee, freezing, normal, system, routine, lease
super-	greater than; more than; beyond	man, tanker, natural, sensitive, abundant, star, market
ultra-	extremely; beyond	efficient, modern, violet
under-	insufficient; too little	pay, nourished, estimate

EXERCISE 14. Revise each of the following sentences by combining the prefix given in parentheses with a word in the underlined section. Make sure the prefixed word is placed so that your revision reads smoothly.

1. Most oil is shipped throughout the world in <u>larger-than-average tankers</u>. (super-)
2. Mozart's <u>foremost rival</u> was a musician named Nunzio Clementi. (arch-)
3. In a duel, the man who could <u>draw faster than</u> the other usually won. (out-)
4. If one <u>indulges to excess</u> a liking for candy, one must consequently resort to dieting. (over-)
5. The Supersonic Transport is an <u>extremely modern</u> variation of the Wright brothers' first airplane. (ultra-)
6. A <u>bishop of the highest rank</u> presides over an archdiocese. (arch-)
7. February often has temperatures <u>below the freezing point</u>. (sub-)
8. Errors on tests occur as frequently from <u>excessive confidence</u> as from the lack of confidence. (over-)
9. Babies born in developed countries generally <u>live longer than</u> those born in underdeveloped countries. (out-)
10. An <u>insufficiently developed</u> nation needs both financial and technical aid. (under-)

PREFIXES INDICATING SUPPORT OR OPPOSITION

Prefix	Meaning	Useful base words
anti-	against; opposite	slavery, freeze, acid
co-	together with; joint	existence, signers, author, captain
contra-	against; opposite	distinction, indicate
counter-	returning an action against someone or something; opposite	charge, measure, part, balance, act, clockwise, flow
pro-	on the side of; in favor of	Western, democratic, slavery, business

EXERCISE 15. Revise each of the following sentences by combining the prefix given in parentheses with a word in the underlined section. Be sure the prefixed word is placed so that your revision reads smoothly.

1. Most ecologists feel that humans must learn how to exist together with nature. (co-)
2. In the 1950s a controversial Senatorial committee investigated activities that were against democratic principles. (anti-)
3. The Republican party has been traditionally associated with a platform that is on the side of business. (pro-)
4. On the other hand, the Democratic party has usually been associated with a platform that is in favor of labor. (pro-)
5. Abraham Lincoln served the cause of justice and equality by signing the proclamation that made slavery illegal. (anti-)
6. South of the equator water spins down the drain in a clockwise direction; north of the equator water spins in a direction opposite to clockwise. (counter-)
7. William F. Buckley, Jr., generally expresses ideas that are in favor of conservative action. (pro-)
8. A plot directed against another plot is often present in a literary work. (counter-)
9. International treaties in the late 1970s were concerned with devices that would provide a defense against a guided missile. (anti-)
10. In the late 1960s many private men's colleges became combined male and female educational institutions. (co-)

MORE ON INSEPARABLE PREFIXES

There are many words that begin with letters that seem, at first glance, to form one of the prefixes listed in the preceding pages (302–311). These letters, however, form elements that are *not* separable as are the listed prefixes. Take the word *predict*, for example. If you remove what seems to be the ordinary prefix *pre-* from the word, the part that remains *(-dict-)* is unable to stand on its own as an English word. It is a word *root* (see 4.i). Words with elements that cannot be separated have to be learned as *whole words*. Other examples are ***re**vert*, ***in**spect*, ***ex**pire*, ***de**cide*. Compare these with words that have regular, separable prefixes: ***re**test*, ***in**complete*, ***ex**-mayor*, ***de**frost*.

4.k FORMATIVES (combining forms)

Formatives are word elements that combine with full English words and with one another. Formatives are regularly used to create new technical terms.

Formatives are sometimes called **combining forms**. Formatives can be used in many ways that are important to you as a writer. A formative can function in one word as a beginning part, in another word as a root, and in another word as a final element.

EXAMPLES

In *graphology*, *graph-* is a beginning element.
In *graphics*, *-graph-* is the root; it contains the essential meaning of the word.
In *telegraph*, *-graph* is a final element.

Regardless of how or where a formative is used, it generally has only one meaning. The formative *graph*, for example, means "writing or recording" in each of its uses above. Notice the meaning of the formatives in the following charts. Few have more than one meaning. If you learn the meanings of only a small number of the formatives, you will be able to understand—and to create or write—many hundreds of English words.

FREQUENT FORMATIVES INDICATING QUANTITY

Formative	Meaning	Examples
uni-	one	unicycle, unilateral
mono-	one	monorail, monograph
bi-	two	biannual, bilateral
tri-	three	triangle, tricolor
quadr-	four	quadruplets, quadrangle
deca-	ten	decagram, decagon
cent-	hundred	centigrade, centipede
milli-	thousand	milligram, millipede
multi-	many	multilingual, multipurpose
poly-	many	polygon, polytonal
omni-	all	omnipotent, omnipresent
pan-	all	panorama, pan-American

FORMATIVES INDICATING QUALITY, SUBSTANCE, OR RELATIONSHIP

Formative	Meaning	Examples
aero-	air	aeronautics, aerodynamics
aqua-	water	aquamarine, aquaplane, aquanaut
auto-	self	automobile, automotive
astro-	star	astronaut, astrology
bio-	life	biography, biology
chrono-	time	chronograph, chronology
crypto-	secret	cryptograph, cryptogram, cryptic
geo-	earth	geometry, geophysics, geology
hydro-	water	hydrology, hydroelectric
hyper-	over; above	hypercritical, hypertension, hyperactive
hypo-	under; less	hypodermic, hypothesis
macro-	large	macroscopic, macrocosmic
micro-	small	microcosmic, microscopic
mega-	great	megaton, megawatt
meta-	along with; indicating change	metamorphosis, metabolism

Formative	Meaning	Examples
para-	beside	parathyroid, paragraph
peri-	around	periscope, perimeter
philo-	love	philosophy, philanthropy
phono-	sound	phonograph, phonology
photo-	light	photograph, photoelectric
proto-	first	prototype, protozoa
pseudo-	false	pseudonym, pseudo-glamorous
syn- (sym-)	together	synonym, sympathy
tele-	far off	television, teletype
thermo-	heat	thermostat, thermodynamics

FORMATIVES IN FINAL POSITION

Formative	Meaning	Examples
-graph (y)	writing; recording	photograph, telegraph
-logy	science; study of	biology, phonology
-meter	instrument	thermometer, micrometer
-onym	name	pseudonym, cryptonym
-scope	instrument for observing	thermoscope, microscope

EXERCISE 16. The following phrases define real words that were coined by scientists using the formatives discussed above. For each definition, find the corresponding word in the Word Bank on the next page.

1. an instrument for observing changes in heat ___________
2. the science of very small plant and animal life ___________
3. the story of a person's life written by that person ___________
4. a system of secret writing ___________
5. an instrument for measuring the amount of light ___________
6. the science dealing with water on the land ___________
7. a way of recording the images of far-off objects by the use of light ___________

8. an instrument for measuring the amount of heat in the air or in a body ________
9. an instrument used to measure very small lengths ________
10. a false or assumed name ________
11. an instrument for keeping exact measurement of time ________
12. too small to be visible to the naked eye ________
13. large enough to be visible to the naked eye ________
14. the science dealing with earth and the rocks of which it is composed ________
15. a sound-reproducing machine using records ________
16. a unit of length equal to one thousandth of a meter ________
17. a unit of length equal to one hundredth of a meter ________
18. an instrument for recording the exact time of occurrences ________
19. an instrument for testing the quality of strings for musical instruments ________
20. an instrument for performing extremely small writing ________

WORD BANK

autobiography	macroscopic	phonometer
centimeter	microbiology	photometer
chronograph	micrograph	pseudonym
chronometer	micrometer	telephotography
cryptography	microscopic	thermometer
geology	millimeter	thermoscope
hydrology	phonograph	

4.1 DERIVATIONAL SUFFIXES

A **derivational suffix** is a meaningful group of letters that can be added at the end of a base word or word root to form (*to derive*) a new word with a different but related meaning.

The term **derivational suffix** is just a more accurate way of referring to the kind of suffix that you often use.

A derivational suffix very often changes the part of speech of the original word.

EXAMPLES

Word	Part of speech	Derivational suffix	New word	Part of speech
child	noun	-**hood**	child**hood**	noun
child	noun	-**ish**	child**ish**	adjective
childish	adjective	-**ly**	childish**ly**	adverb
short	adjective	-**en**	short**en**	verb
short	adjective	-**ly**	short**ly**	adverb
short	adjective	-**ness**	short**ness**	noun

In the following pages you will find suffixes grouped according to the part of speech that they can create (or derive).

With a good grasp of derivational suffixes, you will have alternative ways of expressing yourself. Notice the two different ways of stating the same idea, below. The boldface words in each sentence are almost the same—but not quite.

EXAMPLE

A country whose **economy relies** on the urge to **compete** may **continue** to **prosper**.

A country's **reliance** on **economic competition** may result in **continued prosperity**.

You cannot really say which of the above sentences is "better" unless you know where the sentence is supposed to appear and the kinds of words used in the sentences that precede and follow it. You should be aware, however, that the two sentences illustrate options that become available when you work with derivational suffixes.

SPELLING: ADDING DERIVATIONAL SUFFIXES

Remember to apply the basic spelling rules when you add derivational suffixes to words (see 5.c.3).

NOUN-FORMING SUFFIXES

Suffix	Meaning	Base word or word with root	New noun
-acy	state, quality	candidate confederate	candidacy confederacy
-age	result of action	drain stop	drainage stoppage
-al	action	rent arrive	rental arrival
-ance, -ence	state, quality	guide resist exist confer	guidance resistance existence conference
-ant; -ent	agent	consult inhabit reside	consultant inhabitant resident
-ate	office	consul protector	consulate protectorate
-ation	action, state, result	condemn realize	condemnation realization
-dom	domain, condition	free wise	freedom wisdom
-ee	one receiving action	trust interview	trustee interviewee
-eer	one in an activity	engine mutiny	engineer mutineer
-er, -or	agent, instrument	teach bake act narrate	teacher baker actor narrator
-ful	amount	spoon hand	spoonful handful
-hood	state, condition	state child	statehood childhood
-ion	action, result, state	act fuse	action fusion
-ism	system	social feudal	socialism feudalism
-ist	follower, doer	violin art	violinist artist

Suffix	Meaning	Base word or word with root	New noun
-ition	action, result, state	nutrient repeat	nutrition repetition
-ity	state, quality	placid fatal	placidity fatality
-let	small	book drop	booklet droplet
-ling	small, young	prince duck	princeling duckling
-ment	action or its result	amaze refresh	amazement refreshment
-ness	quality, state	dark vivid	darkness vividness
-(e)ry	people, things as a whole	rob jewel	robbery jewelry
-ship	state, condition	member scholar	membership scholarship
-tude	quality, state	fortify multiply	fortitude multitude
-ure	act, result, means	depart press	departure pressure
-y	result, action	jealous	jealousy
-y	state, condition, study of	geographer philosopher	geography philosophy

ADJECTIVE-FORMING SUFFIXES

-able, -ible	able to be acted upon	reason palate creed vision	reasonable palatable credible visible
-al	characteristic of	season law music	seasonal legal musical
-ary	tending to	fragment element	fragmentary elementary
-ate	full of	affection animal	affectionate animate
-en	made of, like	gold earth	golden earthen

Suffix	Meaning	Base word or word with root	New adjective
-esque	having the style of	picture statue	picturesque statuesque
-ful	full of, having	help thanks	helpful thankful
-ic	belonging to, showing	German atom	Germanic atomic
-ish	like, characteristic of	wolf child	wolfish childish
-ive	characterized by	attract permit	attractive permissive
-less	without, lacking	life hope	lifeless hopeless
-like	similar	child ape	childlike apelike
-ly	like, characteristic of	world mother	worldly motherly
-ory	pertaining to, tending to	contradict contribute	contradictory contributory
-ous	full of, of the nature of	venom thunder	venomous thunderous
-some	apt to	bother frolic	bothersome frolicsome
-ward	in the direction of	west earth	westward earthward
-y	like, showing	shade dust	shady dusty

NOUN- AND ADJECTIVE-FORMING SUFFIXES

Suffix	Meaning	Base word or word with root	New adjective
-an, -ian	belonging to	republic Ghana	republican Ghanaian
-ese	of a style or place	journal Burma	journalese Burmese
-ine	characteristic of	female crystal Alps	feminine crystalline Alpine
-ite	characteristic of, belonging to	social Israel	socialite Israelite
-ile	characteristic of	servant merchant	servile mercantile

VERB-FORMING SUFFIXES

Suffix	Meaning	Base word or word with root	New verb
-ate	become, form	vaccine hyphen	vaccinate hyphenate
-fy, *-ify*	cause, make	solid terror	solidify terrify
-ize	make, cause to become	emphasis central	emphasize centralize
-en	make, cause to become	wide length	widen lengthen

You can use the preceding lists to predict which suffix goes with what kind of base word to form a new word. For example, you will learn to predict that an adjective ending in *-ious* can often be changed to a noun ending in *-ity*; that an adjective ending in *-id, -al,* or *-ar* can usually be changed to a noun ending in *-ity*; and that an adjective or noun ending in *-ate* can often be changed to a noun ending in *-acy*. Here are additional examples.

-ious	***-ity***
feroc*ious*	feroc*ity*
loquac*ious*	loquac*ity*
perspicac*ious*	perspicac*ity*
precoc*ious*	precoc*ity*
pugnac*ious*	pugnac*ity*

-id* or *-al* or *-ar	***-ity***
stup*id*	stupid*ity*
rig*id*	rigid*ity*
form*al*	formal*ity*
leg*al*	legal*ity*
singul*ar*	singular*ity*
famili*ar*	familiar*ity*

-ate	***-acy***
accur*ate*	accur*acy*
delic*ate*	delic*acy*
immedi*ate*	immedi*acy*
intric*ate*	intric*acy*
legitim*ate*	legitim*acy*

The following exercises will give you practice in adding suffixes to words that you already know so that you can form new, related words.

EXERCISE 17. The base word given in parentheses at the end of each item below can take the suffix *-ity*. Use the base word and the new word to complete each item.

EXAMPLE The ____ of a foundation will be assured if the builder uses ____ cement. (solid)

ANSWER *The **solidity** of a foundation will be assured if the builder uses **solid** cement.*

1. It is not difficult to give a ____ explanation of a complex concept. Organizing your information and giving examples contribute to ____. (lucid)
2. The ____ land of the Middle East is difficult to farm; however, irrigation solves some of the problems of ____. (arid)
3. ____ air will warp musical instruments; consequently, musicians often attach gauges that measure ____ to their instrument cases. (humid)
4. The Beatles gained ____ in the early 1960s and have remained ____ for two decades. (popular)
5. Before the nineteenth century, the Japanese people were considered ____ in their attitudes; their ____ was reduced somewhat by Matthew Perry, who turned them toward trading with American merchants. (insular)
6. The narrator in Edgar Allen Poe's "The Tell-Tale Heart" encounters the police with a ____ nervousness. Poe does not reveal whether or not the police notice this ____ of behavior. (peculiar)
7. A ____ motif in a piece of literature or a painting is one that most people can understand. Authors and painters often find it difficult to achieve ____. (universal)
8. The hero of Jack London's "To Build a Fire" became a ____ of the Yukon icefields. His ____ error was in not listening to the advice of an experienced traveler. (fatal)
9. ____ writing is shallow and insensitive; ____ may be avoided by thinking deeply and writing thoroughly about a subject. (superficial)
10. It is not difficult to detect when a reporter is ____ to a subject; extreme ____ can lead to biased or slanted writing. (partial)

EXERCISE 18. The word given in parentheses at the end of each item below can have an *-ity* form. Use the given word and the new word to complete each item.

EXAMPLE A double-decker bus is a _____ vehicle; it has a _____ for holding over one hundred people. (capacious)

ANSWER *A double-decker bus is a* ***capacious*** *vehicle; it has a* ***capacity*** *for holding over one hundred people.*

1. Etta Place was the _____ sweetheart of the Sundance Kid; she, Butch Cassidy, and the Sundance Kid had the _____ to pose for pictures while the law was on their trail. (audacious)
2. Susan B. Anthony was a _____ advocate for women's rights; her _____ inspired many other women to petition for suffrage. (tenacious)
3. The _____ of the butterfly larva is phenomenal; its _____ appetite forces it to consume its own shell the first day it is born. (voracious)
4. Liza Minelli is a _____ singer; her _____ is a quality that her mother, Judy Garland, also had. (vivacious)
5. The oldest members of many Native American tribes were considered the most _____; they were expected to apply their _____ in settling disputes and in giving advice. (sagacious)

EXERCISE 19. The word given in parentheses at the end of each item below can have an *-acy* form. Use the given word and the new word to complete each item.

EXAMPLE The _____ of Grandma Moses' paintings is phenomenal; in her paintings of the seasons she handles the most _____ details of dress and foliage. (intricate)

ANSWER *The* ***intricacy*** *of Grandma Moses' paintings is phenomenal; in her paintings of the seasons she handles the most* ***intricate*** *details of dress and foliage.*

1. Ralph Nader is a consumer _____ whose _____ has in some instances resulted in federal legislation. (advocate)
2. Jane Austen's *Pride and Prejudice* is, in part, about an _____ woman. The heroine's _____ almost causes her to lose the man whom she loves. (obstinate)

3. _____ is not related to intelligence; many talented, creative, and intelligent people belong to non_____ societies. (literate)

4. A fielder's _____ can harm a good baseball team; an _____ throw can result in runs for the opposing team. (inaccurate)

5. Early Egyptians were faced with the problem of _____ rainfall. The use of irrigation methods corrected this _____. (inadequate)

EXERCISE 20. The word given in parentheses at the end of each item below can have an *-ance* or *-ancy* or an *-ence* or *-ency* form. Use the given word and the new word to complete each item.

EXAMPLE To measure the _____ of a machine, compare the amount of energy put in with the amount of work that the machine produces; most machines are less than 50 percent _____. (efficient)

ANSWER *To measure the* ***efficiency*** *of a machine, compare the amount of energy put in with the amount of work that the machine produces; most machines are less than 50 percent* ***efficient****.*

1. Many plants are _____ during the winter months. During _____, which is like suspended animation, no growth occurs. (dormant)

2. Greenland is not as _____ as its name implies; in fact, it is barren in comparison with the _____ of some tropical countries. (verdant)

3. If a doctor can diagnose the _____ of a tumor early, and if the _____ tumor can be removed completely, chances of recovery are great. (malignant)

4. Although most Americans eat sufficient quantities of food, their meals are often _____ in vitamins. Supplements are often taken to overcome a vitamin _____. (deficient)

5. An active youth center with many facilities and activities can help reduce juvenile _____, since _____ behavior often arises from boredom. (delinquent)

6. During a trial, lawyers are allowed to ask only _____ questions; they must, therefore, plan the _____ of their examination. (relevant)

7. A _____ paragraph supplies a topic sentence, develops this statement with support, and then concludes. _____ is a necessity for a good paragraph. (coherent)

8. _____ in a musical sense is a quality of Schoenberg's music; however, not all of this German composer's music is defined as _____. (dissonant)
9. Do not be _____ in using footnotes to cite the sources of borrowed words or ideas; your _____ can lead to plagiarism. (negligent)
10. During the 1920s stockbrokers were very _____ about the state of the market; their _____ was shattered by the stock market crash in 1929. (complacent)

4.m DERIVATIONAL PATTERNS

The many derivational suffixes listed above (4.1) can be of greatest help to you as a writer if you study them in subgroups, according to useful patterns. By observing patterns—the way certain words take certain suffixes—you will begin to sense certain qualities about words.

1. An important point that you will notice is that one "family" of verbs may change to nouns in one way and that another "family" of verbs may change to nouns another way. For example, verbs like *accept* take *-ance*, whereas verbs like *protect* take *-ion*.
2. You will also notice that two words that are alike in one way may be alike in another way, too. Let's say that you know that *select* can become *select**ion*** and *select**ive***. You may be able to conclude that since *elect* (like *select*) can become *elect**ion*** (to match *select**ion***), then *elect* can also become *elect**ive*** to match *select**ive***. You may never have used the word *elective* before, but now you will have it in your personal word stock.

You will find eleven patterns on the following pages. Within each pattern you will find a group of words, all of which can take the same two derivational suffixes to form two related words.

NOTE: The verbs in Patterns 1–5 can be transformed into two different kinds of nouns.

PATTERN 1

Verb	Noun	Noun
advertise	advertisement	advertiser
arrange	arrangement	arranger
bewitch	bewitchment	bewitcher
discern	discernment	discerner
embellish	embellishment	embellisher
endorse	endorsement	endorser
enforce	enforcement	enforcer
enlarge	enlargement	enlarger
manage	management	manager

PATTERN 2

Verb	Noun	Noun
amplify	amplification	amplifier
glorify	glorification	glorifier
identify	identification	identifier
pacify	pacification	pacifier
sanctify	sanctification	sanctifier

NOTE: *Satisfy* becomes *satisfaction.*

PATTERN 3

Verb	Noun	Noun
authorize	authorization	authorizer
memorize	memorization	memorizer
organize	organization	organizer
popularize	popularization	popularizer
stabilize	stabilization	stabilizer
sterilize	sterilization	sterilizer

PATTERN 4

Verb	Noun	Noun[1]
animate	animation	animator
communicate	communication	communicator
decorate	decoration	decorator
demonstrate	demonstration	demonstrator
indicate	indication	indicator
isolate	isolation	isolator
legislate	legislation	legislator

---

[1]Notice that both *-er* and *-or* have the same meaning: "one who does." The suffix *-or* is used to form a noun from verbs that end in *-ate.*

PATTERN 5

Verb	Noun	Noun
adapt	adaptation	adapter
condemn	condemnation	condemner
inform	information	informer
reform	reformation	reformer
relax	relaxation	relaxer
tempt	temptation	tempter
transform	transformation	transformer

The verbs in Patterns 6–9 can be transformed into nouns *and* adjectives.

PATTERN 6

Verb	Noun	Adjective
assert	assertion	assertive
correct	correction	corrective
corrupt	corruption	corruptive
create	creation	creative
direct	direction	directive
digest	digestion	digestive
elect	election	elective
inflect	inflection	inflective
legislate	legislation	legislative
predict	prediction	predictive
project	projection	projective

PATTERN 7

The verbs in Pattern 7 undergo almost the same kinds of changes as the words in Pattern 6; however, notice the spelling changes as the word moves from verb to noun.

Verb	Noun	Adjective
apprehend	apprehension	apprehensive
compel	compulsion	compulsive
comprehend	comprehension	comprehensive
corrode	corrosion	corrosive
deceive	deception	deceptive
exclude	exclusion	exclusive
erode	erosion	erosive
expel	expulsion	expulsive
perceive	perception	perceptive
protrude	protrusion	protrusive

PATTERN 8

Verb	Noun	Adjective
accept	acceptance	acceptable
avoid	avoidance	avoidable
comply	compliance	compliable
contrive	contrivance	contrivable
inherit	inheritance	inheritable
govern	governance	governable
perform	performance	performable
pursue	pursuance	pursuable
rely	reliance	reliable
suffer	sufferance	sufferable
utter	utterance	utterable

PATTERN 9

Verb	Noun	Adjective
abhor	abhorrence	abhorrent
adhere	adherence	adherent
cohere	coherence	coherent
converge	convergence	convergent
defer	deference	deferent
emerge	emergence	emergent
excel	excellence	excellent
refer	reference	referent

The nouns in Patterns 10 and 11 can be transformed into adjectives and verbs.

PATTERN 10

Noun	Adjective	Verb
drama	dramatic	dramatize
economy	economic	economize
emphasis	emphatic	emphasize
harmony	harmonic	harmonize
philosophy	philosophic	philosophize
rhapsody	rhapsodic	rhapsodize
schema	schematic	schematize
symbol	symbolic	symbolize
synthesis	synthetic	synthesize
trauma	traumatic	traumatize

The adjectives or nouns in Pattern 11 can be transformed into nouns and other adjectives.

PATTERN 11

Adjective or Noun	Noun	Adjective
federal	federalism, federalist	federalistic
ideal	idealism, idealist	idealistic
imperial	imperialism, imperialist	imperialistic
material	materialism, materialist	materialistic
opportune	opportunism, opportunist	opportunistic
natural	naturalism, naturalist	naturalistic
real	realism, realist	realistic
social	socialism, socialist	socialistic
symbol	symbolism, symbolist	symbolistic

The following exercises will give you a chance to use the various forms of the preceding words. You will see how the nouns, verbs, and adjectives do indeed interrelate. Keep in mind that in your own writing you usually will not use two or three related forms in the same sentence. These exercises were constructed to give you controlled practice in moving quickly from one form to another.

EXERCISE 21. Substitute the word given in parentheses or one of its derived forms for each blank in each of the numbered items below. (The derived forms will end in *-er* or *-ment.*)

1. The _____ rate usually increases when an _____ hires more people for a holiday rush. (employ)
2. A police officer is a law _____; one of the officer's duties is to _____ speed limits. Many a driver has felt the impact of speed _____. (enforce)
3. Some people consult Jeanne Dixon for _____ about their future. Dixon tries to _____ them about events and people in their future. (enlighten)
4. Clients who are dissatisfied with the _____ of their investments should discuss their complaints with a _____ of the company. (manage)
5. The program _____ said, "I would like to _____ that the winner of the violin competition is Myrna Thompson." Myrna was overjoyed with the _____. (announce)
6. A conscience is often a severe _____. Mental anguish may provide greater torment than any physical _____. (punish)

7. During the Middle Ages, monks were trained to _____ pages of the Bible with gold leaf. An _____ could take the form of a painted letter or an intricate border design. (embellish)
8. A celebrity often serves as an _____ of a product. The famous person's _____ is likely to make the product more appealing to the public. (endorse)
9. A machine called an _____ can make a 5″ x 7″ photograph into an 8″ x 10″ _____. (enlarge)
10. High school baseball players dream that their favorite professional baseball team will _____ them; however, a _____ will often tell them that _____ is confined to college students. (recruit)

EXERCISE 22. Substitute the word given in parentheses or one of its derived forms for each blank in each of the numbered items below. (The derived forms will end in *-ification* or *-ifier.*)

1. The Red Cross will _____ Senior Lifesavers who meet the age requirement and who pass the difficult tests for _____. Many swimmers choose the Red Cross as their _____ because of its high standards. (certify)
2. Most rock music sounds best at high _____. To _____ the music most effectively, the potential of the _____ should correspond to the potential of the speakers. (amplify)
3. Vitamins are often added to food products to _____ their food value; for example, vitamin D is a milk _____. _____ is not uncommon in processed foods. (fortify)
4. In order that a municipality may build a new _____ plant to _____ its water supply, funds for the new _____ must be obtained. (purify)
5. One way to _____ an infant is with a _____; however, _____ is virtually impossible once teething begins. (pacify)

EXERCISE 23. Substitute the word given in parentheses or one of its derived forms for each blank in each of the numbered items below. (The derived forms will end in *-ization* or *-izer.*)

1. Hospitals have a _____ to _____ the instruments used in an operating room. The _____ of all instruments considerably reduces the spread of infection. (sterilize)

2. The _____ of voices can be achieved in a barbershop quartet if the _____ uses a small pitch pipe to determine the first note. (harmonize)
3. In chemistry, a _____ added to an explosive or a plastic causes the other substance to _____. Such _____ prevents an unwanted change in state. (stabilize)
4. Hannibal, the Carthaginian general who lived from approximately 247 to 183 B.C., was an accomplished _____. He had to _____ his troops and march them across the Alps in order to invade Italy. The historic _____ involved transporting an army of elephants. (mobilize)
5. _____ can be aided by mnemonic, or memory, devices. An easy way to _____ the difference between *horizontal* and *vertical* is to remember that the word *horizon* occurs in *horizontal*. (memorize)

EXERCISE 24. Substitute the word given in parentheses or one of its derived forms for each blank in each of the numbered items below. (The derived forms will end in *-ation* or *-or*.)

1. Walt Disney was a renowned _____, whose _____ has been appreciated by millions of people. Many other artists have unsuccessfully tried to _____ characters as well as Disney did. (animate)
2. Thomas Robert Malthus is best known for his economic theory of _____, which states that the world tends to _____ itself faster than the available food supply increases. (populate)
3. A _____ uses a sextant to _____ the ship. _____ with a sextant involves measuring the angles of heavenly bodies with reference to a point on earth. (navigate)
4. John Dewey was an American philosopher and _____ whose theories on _____ continue to be influential. (educate)
5. In medieval times an infected person was placed in _____ to prevent the spreading of disease. To _____ the sick one, an authority would place the patient in a house that had its windows and doors boarded up. (isolate)

EXERCISE 25. Substitute the word given in parentheses or one of its derived forms for each blank in the following numbered items. (The derived forms will end in *-ation* or *-er.*)

1. Many Greek myths deal with the _____ of human beings into animals and natural objects; the _____ in most cases was the ruling god, Zeus. (transform)
2. Foreign travelers should carry an _____ to _____ their electrical appliances to alternating or to direct current. Damaged equipment can result without the _____ of current. (adapt)
3. The greatest of Biblical _____ was the Devil, who disguised himself as a snake to _____ Eve with an apple. The _____ to taste the forbidden fruit was great. (tempt)
4. Often when the police need _____ about a crime, they offer a reward to anyone who can _____ them of facts that will lead to an arrest. The identity of the _____ is kept confidential. (inform)
5. In Arthur Miller's *The Crucible*, a teen-age girl was the most vocal _____ of witches. Her testimony against those she disliked often led to their _____. (condemn)

EXERCISE 26. Substitute the word given in parentheses or one of its derived forms for each blank in each of the numbered items below. (The derived forms will end in *-ion* or *-ive.*)

1. _____ offices are the basis of the United States government; a Presidential _____ is held every four years. (elect)
2. Poet Kenneth Koch takes a _____ approach in his poetry; he often gives humorous _____s on how to write, how to make friends, and how to impress people. (direct)
3. Jacques Dalcroze, a Swiss composer, devised a _____ approach to developing a sense of rhythm in children. His method, called eurythmics, encouraged the _____ of interpretive dance. (create)
4. A _____ essay provokes thought on controversial issues. The concluding paragraphs often give a _____ for further consideration. (suggest)
5. Insects often have the _____ of coloration. The gypsy moth, for example, has a _____ color that matches the foliage it feeds upon. (protect)
6. A good detective does not always need _____ evidence to solve a crime; quite often circumstantial evidence can lead to the right _____. (conclude)
7. The _____ of United States territory in those years led to the development of an _____ transportation system. (extend)

8. At a diplomatic ____ for foreign ambassadors, the President must be gracious and ____ to representatives of all countries. (receive)
9. Skunks ____ their enemies by emitting a ____ odor that lingers for hours. (repel)
10. The ____ force of an atom bomb can cause considerable damage miles away from the immediate area of the ____. (explode)

EXERCISE 27. Substitute the word given in parentheses or one of its derived forms for each blank in each of the numbered items below. (The derived forms will end in *-ize* or *-ic*.)

1. An ____ statement is often followed by an exclamation point; however, you should use underlining, or italics, to ____ an individual word. (emphasis)
2. A ____, or severe shock, can result from a ____ experience. The sight of a violent accident can sometimes ____ a person for a short time. (trauma)
3. One of George Gershwin's most famous musical compositions is the "____ in Blue." The piece's unconventional form and intense mood make it particularly ____. (rhapsody)
4. A ____ is something that stands for something else. The Stars and Stripes is a ____ object that can ____ the American people or their way of life. (symbol)
5. A ____ is an outline or diagram. It often helps to ____ a mechanical process before describing it. (schema)
6. ____ is quite different from melody; a melody can be sung by one voice, whereas harmony involves two or more voices singing at different ____ intervals. (harmony)
7. ____ writer Lillian Hellman wrote plays that were later ____ on the screen. (drama)
8. Despite his ____ condition, Franklin D. Roosevelt was one of the most active American presidents. When his ____ interfered with his duties, his wife, Eleanor, assumed his responsibilities. (paralysis)
9. The ____ of a country can move from an ____ depression to a sudden boom. Whatever the stock market does, however, it pays to ____. (economy)
10. Philosopher and writer Ayn Rand ____ about the condition of modern people. Her ____ outlook is based upon a purely capitalistic ____. (philosophy)

EXERCISE 28. Substitute the word given in parentheses or one of its derived forms for each blank in each of the items. (The derived forms will end in *-ism*, *-ist*, *-istic.*)

1. George Bernard Shaw wrote a book entitled *The Unsocial* _____, which is about a wealthy young man with unusual ideas about _____ and marriage. (social)
2. Utopian literature is concerned with _____ societies. The _____ of society is expressed by the main character, an _____ as well. (ideal)
3. Scrooge was a _____. He was greedy and _____ in the way he ran his business and treated his friends and relatives. One Christmas Eve three ghosts showed Scrooge the cold and lonely future he would have if he did not renounce his _____. (material)
4. As coal and oil supplies are depleted, many public officials feel that America must be _____ and face its responsibility to develop other sources of energy; also, _____ should guide our consumption. (real)
5. Someone who is a _____ tries to be as accurate and as fair as possible; _____ writing is characterized by precision and objectivity. (journal)
6. The government of the United States is based upon _____, a system by which individual states give certain powers to a central _____ government. (federal)
7. _____ is a device whereby the writer has something to stand for, or represent, something else. Nathanial Hawthorne and Edgar Allan Poe are _____ writers. (symbol)
8. An _____ person is someone who takes advantage of a situation with little regard for consequences or ethical principles; thus, an _____ is often criticized. (opportune)
9. An _____ nation seeks to establish colonies. Ancient Rome expanded through its policy of _____. (imperial)
10. A _____ is one who studies animals and plants; the _____ environment is a laboratory for this study. (natural)

WORD LIST FOR WRITERS

The following list contains words that you will find useful in your writing. For most of the words on the list, you will find several related forms. Related forms of a word are given so that you, the writer, can see all the possibilities that you have.

The words on this list come from an examination of the words used by people who write for American magazines with highly rated nonfiction and by people who write for television news programs. The words, therefore, have already proved useful to professional writers.

Keep the following points in mind as you examine the list:

1. As many as six forms of a single word can be found on the list: noun, verb, adjective, present participle used as adjective, past participle used as adjective, and adverb of manner. Only those adverbs of manner that are most commonly used in writing are listed, although other forms may exist. If more than one noun or adjective exists for a word, both are given (see *acuity*).
2. Adjectives, participles, and adverbs of manner are listed in the last column on the right.
3. In order to show how participles can be used as adjectives before nouns, each participle is followed by a noun in parentheses.
4. The most familiar form of the word is the form that is defined on the list (in italics).
5. Words that have complicated meanings are followed by a sentence that demonstrates their use.

As these words are words that will be useful to you in writing—not just in reading—you must do more than just recognize them and know what they mean. You should feel confident about using them in sentences and about spelling them correctly (check a dictionary whenever necessary). Do not try to digest this list all at once. Try getting to know a few words at a time, and try to begin always with the most familiar form of the word (the one that has been defined). Write a sentence using this form of the word. Then write other sentences using other forms of the word as they appear on the list.

VERB	NOUN	▲ ADJECTIVE ● PARTICIPLE	■ ADVERB OF MANNER
abase *degrade*	abasement	▲ --- ● abased (feeling)	■ ---

My *abased* feeling increased with her criticisms.

VERB	NOUN	▲ ADJECTIVE ● PARTICIPLE	■ ADVERB OF MANNER
abhor *hate*	abhorrence	▲ abhorrent ● abhorred (revolution)	■ ---
---	abjectness	▲ abject *wretched* ● ---	■ abjectly
abound	abundance	▲ abundant *plentiful* ● ---	■ abundantly

There was an *abundance* of oranges that year.

VERB	NOUN	▲ ADJECTIVE ● PARTICIPLE	■ ADVERB OF MANNER
---	acuity; acuteness	▲ acute *sharp* ● ---	■ acutely
---	aesthete; aesthetics	▲ aesthetic *artistic; sensitive to art* ● ---	■ aesthetically

Colorful forms appealed to her *aesthetic* sense.

VERB	NOUN	▲ ADJECTIVE ● PARTICIPLE	■ ADVERB OF MANNER
agitate *shake up*	agitation	▲ --- ● agitated (behavior)	■ agitatedly

The heckler *agitated* the speaker with her remark.

VERB	NOUN	▲ ADJECTIVE ● PARTICIPLE	■ ADVERB OF MANNER
---	ambiguity	▲ ambiguous *unclear* ● ---	■ ambiguously

It was *ambiguous* whether she was pleased or not.

VERB	NOUN	▲ ADJECTIVE • PARTICIPLE	■ ADVERB OF MANNER
analyze *separate into parts*	analysis	▲ analytic; analytical • ---	■ analytically
She *analyzed* the evidence and presented her case.			
antagonize	antagonism *hostility*	▲ antagonistic • antagonizing (remark)	■ antagonistically
---	apathy *indifference*	▲ apathetic • ---	■ apathetically
They did not vote because of sheer *apathy*.			
assert *declare*	assertion	▲ assertive • ---	■ assertively
avert *turn away; prevent*	aversion	▲ --- • averted (eyes)	■ ---
He *averted* his eyes from the scene of the accident.			
bias *prejudice*	bias	▲ bias *diagonal* • biased (opinion) *prejudiced*	■ biasedly
A judge should not make a *biased* judgment against a defendant.			
---	blandness	▲ bland *dull* • ---	■ blandly
---	caprice *passing fancy* capriciousness	▲ capricious • ---	■ capriciously

VERB	NOUN	▲ ADJECTIVE ● PARTICIPLE	■ ADVERB OF MANNER
---	chaos *disorder*	▲ chaotic ● ---	■ chaotically
---	compatibility	▲ compatible *in agreement* ● ---	■ compatibly
---	complacency	▲ complacent *self-satisfied* ● ---	■ complacently
comply	compliance	▲ compliant *submissive* ● ---	■ compliantly
Her ready *compliance* cheered her father.			
contemplate *meditate; consider*	contemplation	▲ contemplative ● ---	■ contemplatively
---	contempt	▲ contemptuous *scornful* ● ---	■ contemptuously
defer *yield*	deference *respect*	▲ deferential ● deferred (judgment)	■ deferentially
deliberate *consider carefully*	deliberation; deliberateness	▲ deliberate deliberative ● deliberating (committee)	■ deliberately; deliberatively
This problem required some *deliberation.*			

VERB	NOUN	▲ ADJECTIVE ● PARTICIPLE	■ ADVERB OF MANNER
discern *perceive distinctions*	discernment	▲ discernible ● discerning (person)	■ discernibly
I could not *discern* the difference between the original and the copy.			
disdain *scorn*	disdain	▲ disdainful ● ---	■ disdainfully
elaborate *give additional information*	elaboration; elaborateness	▲ elaborate *complicated* ● ---	■ elaborately
---	euphemism *inoffensive substitute word*	▲ euphemistic ● ---	■ euphemistically
Correctional institution is a *euphemism* for the word *prison.*			
---	fallacy	▲ fallacious *erroneous* ● ---	■ fallaciously
---	flamboyance	▲ flamboyant *showy* ● ---	■ flamboyantly
---	fluency	fluent *freeflowing; smooth* ● ---	■ fluently
---	futility	▲ futile *useless; vain* ● ---	■ futilely

VERB	NOUN	▲ ADJECTIVE ● PARTICIPLE	■ ADVERB OF MANNER
---	hyperbole *an exaggeration*	▲ hyperbolic ● ---	■ hyperbolically

Her excuse for being late was lengthy and *hyperbolic.*

VERB	NOUN	▲ ADJECTIVE ● PARTICIPLE	■ ADVERB OF MANNER
---	idyll *a kind of literary form*	▲ idyllic *pleasing; simple* ● ---	■ idyllically

He wanted to paint the *idyllic* countryside of his homeland.

VERB	NOUN	▲ ADJECTIVE ● PARTICIPLE	■ ADVERB OF MANNER
imply *suggest*	implicitness	▲ implicit ● implied (criticism)	■ implicitly *unquestion-ingly*
---	inanity	▲ inane *silly* ● ---	■ inanely

The *inanity* of his remarks embarrassed us all.

VERB	NOUN	▲ ADJECTIVE ● PARTICIPLE	■ ADVERB OF MANNER
---	incoherence	▲ incoherent *disjointed; rambling* ● ---	■ incoherently

His speech was *incoherent.*

VERB	NOUN	▲ ADJECTIVE ● PARTICIPLE	■ ADVERB OF MANNER
---	inexplicability	▲ inexplicable *not easily explained* ● ---	■ inexplicably
---	infamy	▲ infamous *having a bad reputation* ● ---	■ infamously

We saw a film about the *infamous* Jesse James.

VERB	NOUN	▲ ADJECTIVE ● PARTICIPLE	■ ADVERB OF MANNER
infer *draw a conclusion*	inference	▲ inferential ● ---	■ ---
Her *inference* proved to be incorrect.			
---	inordinateness	▲ inordinate *excessive* ● ---	■ inordinately
He was paid an *inordinate* sum for his services.			
---	inscrutability	▲ inscrutable *mysterious; difficult to understand* ● ---	■ inscrutably
We could not read the *inscrutable* expression on the child's face.			
---	intricacy *complexity*	▲ intricate ● ---	■ intricately
intrude *to force in*	intrusion	▲ intrusive ● intruding (salesperson)	■ intrusively
lament *mourn*	lamentation	▲ lamentable ● ---	■ lamentably
It was a *lamentable* accident.			
---	nostalgia *longing for the past*	▲ nostalgic ● ---	■ nostalgically
I felt very *nostalgic* at my high school reunion.			

VERB	NOUN	▲ ADJECTIVE ● PARTICIPLE	■ ADVERB OF MANNER
obscure	obscurity	▲ obscure *dark; not famous* ● ---	■ obscurely
---	omniscience	▲ omniscient *all-knowing* ● ---	■ omnisciently
---	opulence	▲ opulent *rich* ● ---	■ opulently

The fashion model wore an *opulent*, silk dress.

VERB	NOUN	▲ ADJECTIVE ● PARTICIPLE	■ ADVERB OF MANNER
---	paradox *an apparently false statement that is actually true*	▲ paradoxical ● ---	■ paradoxically

It is a paradox that so many poor people lived in such a rich country.

VERB	NOUN	▲ ADJECTIVE ● PARTICIPLE	■ ADVERB OF MANNER
---	pastoral	▲ pastoral *of the country* ● ---	■ pastorally

The *pastoral scene* included cows, haystacks, and a barn.

VERB	NOUN	▲ ADJECTIVE ● PARTICIPLE	■ ADVERB OF MANNER
---	pedant *narrow-minded scholar*	▲ pedantic ● ---	■ pedantically

The long, *pedantic* lecture pleased no one.

VERB	NOUN	▲ ADJECTIVE ● PARTICIPLE	■ ADVERB OF MANNER
perceive *observe*	perception	▲ perceptive ● ---	■ perceptively

VERB	NOUN	▲ ADJECTIVE • PARTICIPLE	■ ADVERB OF MANNER
perplex *puzzle*	perplexity	▲ --- • perplexing (behavior) perplexed (expression)	■ perplexingly
The sudden stillness of the noisy gym *perplexed* Tim.			
personify *represent as human*	personification	▲ --- • personified (object)	■ ---
In some Renaissance paintings, the wind is *personified* by angels blowing with puffed cheeks.			
persuade *convince*	persuasion	▲ persuasive • ---	■ persuasively
---	poignancy	▲ poignant *piercing; evoking emotion* • ---	■ poignantly
The *poignant* scene in the tragedy made me cry.			
---	pragmatism	▲ pragmatic *practical* • ---	■ pragmatically
My adviser told me to be more *pragmatic* in my career plans.			
predominate *be dominant in influence, amount, number, etc.*	predominance	▲ predominant • ---	■ predominantly
The power of the queen *predominated* at last.			
---	prodigy *a genius*	▲ prodigious *huge; powerful* • ---	■ prodigiously
Mozart was a child *prodigy*.			

VERB	NOUN	▲ ADJECTIVE ● PARTICIPLE	■ ADVERB OF MANNER
---	proficiency	▲ proficient *highly skilled* ● ---	■ proficiently
---	profusion	▲ profuse *giving forth freely* ● ---	■ profusely
prophesy	prophecy *prediction* prophet	▲ prophetic ● ---	■ prophetically
---	provincial	▲ provincial *unfashionable; narrow-minded* ● ---	■ provincially
---	prudence	▲ prudent *cautious* ● ---	■ prudently
---	repugnance	▲ repugnant *offensive* ● ---	■ ---
reveal *make known*	revelation	▲ revelatory ● revealing (behavior)	■ revealingly
revere *worship*	reverence	▲ reverent ● revered (leader)	■ reverently

VERB	NOUN	▲ ADJECTIVE ● PARTICIPLE	■ ADVERB OF MANNER
---	rigor	▲ rigorous *strict* ● ---	■ rigorously
scandalize *shock*	scandal	▲ scandalous ● scandalizing (behavior) ● scandalized (community)	■ scandalously
scrutinize *inspect closely* The doctor *scrutinized* her wound.	scrutiny	▲ --- ● scrutinizing (glance)	■ ---
---	sophistication	▲ --- ● sophisticated (woman) *worldly-wise*	■ ---
speculate *think about*	speculation	▲ speculative ● ---	■ speculatively
---	spontaneity	▲ spontaneous *unrehearsed* ● ---	■ spontaneously
stabilize	stability	▲ stable *steady* ● stabilizing (effect) stabilized (environment)	■ ---

VERB	NOUN	▲ ADJECTIVE ● PARTICIPLE	■ ADVERB OF MANNER
stigmatize	stigma *mark of disgrace*	▲ --- ● ---	■ ---
Her petty shoplifting was a *stigma* on an otherwise good record.			
---	succinctness	▲ succinct *concise* ● ---	■ succinctly
surmise	surmise *guess*	▲ --- ● ---	■ ---
I *surmised* the real reason that she had called.			
---	susceptibility	▲ susceptible *easily affected* ● ---	■ susceptibly
Palm trees are highly *susceptible* to disease.			
---	tangibility	▲ tangible *touchable; definite* ● ---	■ tangibly
We could find no *tangible* evidence that he had been there.			
---	tedium	▲ tedious *tiresome* ● ---	■ tediously
transcend *surpass*	transcendence	▲ transcendent ● ---	■ ---

VERB	NOUN	▲ ADJECTIVE • PARTICIPLE	■ ADVERB OF MANNER
transform *change in form*	transformation	▲ transformable • transforming (effect) • transformed (person)	■ ---
I wrote about the *transformation* of carbon dioxide into oxygen.			
---	turbulence	▲ turbulent *agitated* • ---	■ turbulently
She felt sick as she watched the *turbulent* waves.			
---	ultimate	▲ ultimate *final* • ---	■ ultimately
validate *declare legally binding*	validity	▲ valid *well-grounded* • validated (passport)	■ validly
Her logic was not *valid.*			
verbalize	verbalization	▲ verbal *pertaining to words* • ---	■ verbally
---	versatility	▲ versatile *adaptable* • ---	■ versatilely
John McEnroe is a very *versatile* tennis player.			
vibrate *quiver*	vibrancy	▲ vibrant *lively* • vibrating (machinery)	■ vibrantly
The heroine of *Sister Carrie* is a beautiful and *vibrant* woman.			

OTHER WORDS USEFUL TO WRITERS

Try using each one of these words in a sentence. If, you have trouble at first, look up the meaning of the unfamiliar word in a dictionary.

VERBS

abandon
absolve
accumulate
acquiesce
advocate
alienate
allege

bewilder

collaborate

detect
deter
disquiet
divide

embody
endow
exalt
exhort

foster

impair
implicate
impose
induce
inhibit
initiate

orient
overshadow
overstate

penalize
permeate
perpetuate
peruse
proliferate
provoke

query

requisition

saturate

taunt
thwart

venerate
vex

waive

NOUNS

anomaly
atrocity

banter

caricature
cataclysm

demeanor
devastation

essence

facade
fragment

ideology
illusion
infirmity

jeopardy

luxury

menace

obligation

pallor
periphery
ploy
predisposition
preponderance
prestige
prototype

retrospect
rite
ritual

serenity
stagnation

tranquility
transition

vengeance
virtuoso

whim

zeal

ADJECTIVES

affluent
anachronistic
arbitrary
astute

banal
blatant
boisterous

candid
copious

deft
despondent
dolorous

eccentric
eloquent
elusive
eminent
episodic
erratic
eventual
explicit
exquisite

facile
frugal

haughty
heedless

immaculate
immobile
impartial
impenetrable
imperative
imperturbable
impervious
impulsive
inarticulate
incorrigible
individualistic
indomitable
inflexible
inherent
innocuous
insidious
irrational

lavish

monotonous
mundane

naive
notorious

objective
oblique
ominous
opaque

passive
pathetic
perverse
phenomenal
pompous
precarious
premature
profound

reticent

sardonic
simultaneous
sinister
skeptical
solemn
solicitous
stark
strenuous
stringent
suave
supercilious
superficial

tenacious
topical
trivial
tumultuous

uncanny

vapid
vehement
veritable
vigilant
vital
volatile
vulgar

SPELLING

5 Spelling

Spelling is a vital element in writing. Good spelling—faultless spelling—is never noticed. On the other hand, even one spelling error jars a reader and spoils a sentence. Different people have different spelling problems and, therefore, need different kinds of help. A particular strategy may be helpful to one speller but not to another. Following are eight strategies for reducing spelling errors.

1. Try to *visualize* words. Make an effort to form mental pictures of common spelling patterns so that you know when words "look right."
2. Be aware of *pronunciation clues.* Sound out words carefully, syllable by syllable. Make sure not to add or subtract any sounds.
3. Keep *lists* of your own particular spelling demons. Write the problem words over and over until you can spell them almost without thinking.
4. Make up *memory aids* for words that are especially troublesome. Good spelling is more than memorization, but sometimes these devices help.
5. Learn the *spelling rules* that are most useful to you.
6. Never hesitate to consult a *dictionary.* Doubt is sometimes a speller's best friend. (For advice on using the dictionary, see Section 6.)
7. Be aware of the *grammatical patterns* that affect the spelling of word endings.
8. *Proofread.* Check over your writing carefully, first looking at the words as words, and then looking at them in their context.

5.a PRONUNCIATION AS A SPELLING AID

No language is spoken as exactly and precisely as it must be written. In speech we run some words together and draw others apart, often quite arbitrarily stressing some words while gliding over others. For example, *could have* may be pronounced (but never spelled) *could of*. Some words have more than one common pronunciation. The *au* in *aunt*, for example, may be pronounced as the *a* in *car* or as the *a* in *fat;* the *oo* in *roof* may be pronounced as the *oo* in *tool* or as the *oo* in *look.* There are regional differences in pronunciation. The same word may be pronounced one way in the South and another way in the Midwest.

No matter how many ways there are to pronounce a word, there is usually only one way to spell it. Pronunciation can be a guide to spelling if you learn to recognize certain clues. You can hear the difference in pronunciation between *hope* and *hop;* the long *o* sound in *hope* is your signal to add a final *e.* Learn to pronounce words slowly, syllable by syllable, before writing them. Take special notice of word endings, which often blur or even drop off in everyday speech. For example, you might say *tole*, but be careful to write *told.* Also, make sure that in spelling words you neither add nor subtract any syllables: Write *literature*, not *litrature.* When sounding words out for spelling, it might help to exaggerate your pronunciation to make sure that you hear all the sounds. Train your ears so that they help rather than hinder your spelling.

5.a.1 Mispronunciation as a cause of misspelling

Mispronunciation can hinder good spelling. For instance, if you say *athalete* instead of *athlete*, chances are that you will have difficulty spelling this noun. Being aware of the common problems caused by English pronunciation will help you with your spelling. Study the following five categories of common pronunciation pitfalls that can cause misspellings. Once aware of these pronunciation pitfalls, you should be able to avoid the spelling mistakes that they often cause.

PRONUNCIATION PITFALLS THAT CAUSE MISSPELLINGS

1. *adding extra vowel sounds*

correct spelling	*incorrect spelling*
athletics	athaletics
disastrous	disasterous
grievous	grievious
hindrance	hinderance
laundry	laundery
umbrella	umberella

2. *dropping vowel sounds*

correct spelling	*incorrect spelling*
accidentally	accidently
conscientious	conscientous
convenient	convenent
grammatically[1]	grammaticly
laboratory[1]	labratory
temperament[1]	temperment

3. *dropping consonant sounds*

correct spelling	*incorrect spelling*
consumption	consumtion
government	goverment
identical	idenical
landlord	lanlord
probably	probaly
pumpkin	pumkin

4. *slurring or eliminating final consonant sounds*

correct spelling	*incorrect spelling*
and	an
attract	attrac
contact	contac
excerpt	excerp
least	leas
past	pas

5. *reversing the order of sounds and confusing sounds*

REVERSING SOUNDS

correct spelling	*incorrect spelling*
ask	aks
children	childern
hundred	hunderd

CONFUSING *D* AND *T*

correct spelling	*incorrect spelling*
bandit	bandid
battle	badle
metal	medal[2]

CONFUSING *F* AND *V*

correct spelling	*incorrect spelling*
safely	savely
strive	strife[2]
wives	wifes

[1] In rapid speech you may pronounce these words as /grə • mat • i • klē/, /lab • rə • tôr • ē/, and /tem • per • ment/, but in writing you must remember to include each syllable.

[2] *Medal* and *strife* are correct spellings of other words. Be careful not to confuse *medal* with *metal* or *strife* with *strive*.

EXERCISE 1. Write the following phrases, correcting any misspelled words. Identify the spelling pitfall by number from the chart on page 352.

1. accidently dropped the dish
2. an experiment in the labratory
3. famous work of litrature
4. became a star athalete
5. a valuable contac to have
6. carried an umberella
7. heard a familar song
8. three men and their wifes
9. washed the week's laundery
10. a grammaticly correct sentence
11. made of medal
12. bought the idenical dress
13. threw out the emty can
14. a hunderd pennies
15. a pumkin pie
16. an excerp from the article
17. overthrew the goverment
18. paid rent to the lanlord
19. a conscientous worker
20. a disasterous earthquake

5.a.2 Variant spellings of some sounds

Many sounds in English have more than one spelling, but there are several simple patterns that will help you to figure out which spelling to use. The /f/ sound, for example, can be spelled *f*, *ff*, *gh*, and *ph*, as in *first*, *staff*, *tough*, and *photo*. There are patterns, however, that can help you figure out when to use *f*, *ff*, *gh*, or *ph*. Study the spelling patterns for the /f/ sound and for other sounds on the following pages. Learning these patterns will help you to spell correctly a vast number of words. At the very least, be aware that these sounds may cause you spelling problems. Think twice about them as you write.

1. *oi* or *oy*?

In general, use *oi* in the middle of a word before a consonant.	b**oi**l b**oi**sterous	h**oi**st n**oi**se
In general, use *oy* at the end of a syllable or of a word.	en·**joy** em·pl**oy**·er	j**oy** r**oy**·al

2. *tch* or *ch*?

In general, use *tch* at the end of a one-syllable word with a short vowel sound. Also use *tch* in a similar compound word and in a derived word.	ca**tch** ca**tch**er	wi**tch** wi**tch**craft
	Common exceptions:	
	mu**ch** su**ch**	tou**ch** whi**ch**
Use *ch* in all other cases.	approa**ch** bea**ch**	bea**ch**ball sandwi**ch**

3. The /k/ sound: *c, k,* or *ck*?

Initial /k/ sound:		
Use *k* before *i* or *e*.	**k**ite	**k**ettle
Use *c* before *a, o,* or *u*.	**c**ape **c**oach	**c**urrency
Final /k/ sound:		
Use *ck* at the end of a one-syllable word with a short vowel sound and at the end of a stressed syllable.	la**ck** at·ta**ck**′ ba**ck**′ward	fli**ck** be·de**ck**′ [*not* zinc]
Use *c* at the end of a final syllable without primary stress.	a·rith′me·ti**c** clas′si**c**	ge·o·graph′**ic** mu′si**c**
Before suffixes beginning in e, i, *or* y: When a word ending in *c* is connected to a suffix beginning with *e, i,* or *y*, insert a *k* after the *c*.	froli**c** + ed = froli**ck**ed shella**c** + ing = shella**ck**ing pani**c** + y = pani**ck**y	

4. *f, ff, gh,* or *ph*?

In general, use *ff* at the end of a one-syllable word or at the end of a syllable with a short vowel sound.	cli**ff** co**f**·**f**in	mu**f**·**f**ler su**f**·**f**er
Use *gh* after *au* or *ou* at the end of a word or a syllable.	cou**gh** e·nou**gh**	lau**gh** rou**gh**·neck
Use *ph* in a few words that came to English from Greek.	epita**ph** gra**ph**	**ph**ysical ty**ph**oid
Use *f* in all other instances.	aw**f**ul de**f**er	**f**riend **f**ul**f**ill

5. The /j/ sound: *j, g, ge,* or *dge*?

Initial /j/ sound: In general, use *j* at the beginning of a word or a syllable.	en·**j**oy **j**eans	**j**ilt **j**ob
Use *g* for the initial /j/ sound only before *e* and *i*.	**g**em **g**eology	**g**inger **g**ist
Final /j/ sound: Use *dge* after a short vowel sound.	ba**dge** dre**dge**	fu**dge** knowle**dge**
Use *ge* most often after a long vowel sound or after a schwa (unstressed vowel) sound.	a**ge** *Common exceptions:* bin**ge** hin**ge**	sie**ge** sin**ge** tin**ge**
When *-ment* is added to a word ending in *dge*, drop the *e*.	acknowle**dge** + ment = acknowle**dg**ment ju**dge** + ment = ju**dg**ment abri**dge** + ment = abri**dg**ment	

6. *-sion* or *-tion*?

Use *-sion* when the final syllable is pronounced "zhən" (as in *explosion*) and after *l* or *s* (as in *compulsion)*.	emis**sion** expul**sion**	persua**sion** pas**sion**
Use *-tion* in all other cases.	ambi**tion** fric**tion**	mo**tion** pronuncia**tion**

7. *-sede, -ceed,* or *-cede*?

Use *-sede* in only one word.	super**sede**	
Use *-ceed* in only three words and their related forms.	ex**ceed** pro**ceed**	suc**ceed** pro**ceed**ing
Use *-cede* in all other cases.	con**cede** inter**cede** ante**cede**	pre**cede** re**cede** con**cede**

8. *-er* or *-re*?

-Er is most common in American English; *-re* is more typical of British English.	*American* cent**er** theat**er**	*British* cent**re** theat**re**
Learn the common American words that end in *-re*.	ac**re** medioc**re** og**re**	

9. *-able* or *-ible*?

-Able is used much more often than *-ible*. In general, use *-able* if the word is complete or missing only a final *e*.	accept**able** mov**able** comfort**able** us**able** *Accept* and *comfort* are complete base words; *mov* and *us* are missing only a final *e*. *Common exception:* contemptible
If the base word ends in *y*, change the *y* to *i* and add *-able*.	duty + able = dut**iable** envy + able = env**iable** rely + able = rel**iable**
If the base word ends in *-ate*, drop the *-ate* and add *-able*.	demonstrate + able = demonstr**able** separate + able = separ**able** tolerate + able = toler**able**
In general, if the preceding sound is a hard /c/ or /g/ sound, use *-able*.	amic**able** despic**able** irrevoc**able**
Ordinarily, use *-ible* if the root is not a complete word.	cred**ible** horr**ible** feas**ible** terr**ible** *Cred, feas, horr,* and *terr* are not complete English words.
If a double *s* precedes the ending, generally use *-ible*.	access**ible** permiss**ible** admiss**ible** poss**ible**
If a word has an *-ion* form, use *-ible*.	corrupt, corruption, corrupt**ible** suggest, suggestion, suggest**ible**
If the preceding sound is a soft /c/ or /g/, use *-ible*.	conduc**ible** illeg**ible** elig**ible** neglig**ible**

EXERCISE 2. Write the following phrases, filling in the blanks with *oi* or *oy*.

1. a l____al friend
2. sweat and t____l
3. pleasure and enj____ment
4. the r____al family
5. a m____st cake
6. a b____sterous party
7. br____led chicken
8. a difficult ch____ce
9. a silver all____
10. empl____ment office

EXERCISE 3. Write the following phrases, filling in the blanks with *ch* or *tch*.

1. tou____ football
2. a total misma____
3. a deep di____
4. a dog that will fe____ the newspaper
5. irrigation di____
6. whi____ one?
7. the wicked wi____
8. voodoo and wi____craft
9. a scree____ owl
10. ea____ other

EXERCISE 4. Write the following phrases, filling in the blanks with *c* or *ck*.

1. musi____ box
2. plasti____ surgery
3. an asthma atta____
4. li____ the bowl
5. nip and tu____
6. arithmeti____ problem
7. pi____ and choose
8. metri____ system

9. a picni____ in the park
10. a basi____ disagreement

EXERCISE 5. Write the following phrases, filling in the blanks with *c* or *k*.

1. ____onquer the enemy
2. ____itchen curtains
3. ____alm and ____ollected
4. fly a ____ite
5. tea ____ettle
6. ____etchup and mustard
7. ____ampaign promises
8. a ____oherent argument
9. the lunch ____ ounter
10. dog ____ennel

EXERCISE 6. Write the following phrases and sentences, filling in the blanks with *f, ff, ph,* or *gh.*

1. blind man's blu____
2. Lau____ it up!
3. rou____ and ready
4. paragra____ indentation
5. de____er payment
6. a job o____er
7. al____abet soup
8. to ____ul____ill an obligation
9. laws of ____ysics
10. a ty____oid shot

EXERCISE 7. Write the following phrases, filling in the blanks with *g, j, ge, dg,* or *dge.*

1. ____inger cookies
2. hot fu____ sundae
3. ____ob security
4. universal suffra____
5. a peace ____esture

6. blue ____ eans
7. police ba____
8. turn the pa____
9. a door hin____
10. ju____ ment day

EXERCISE 8. Write the following phrases, filling in the blanks with *-sion* or *-tion.*

1. an awkward posi____
2. a terrible tempta____
3. a slang expres____
4. a loud explo____
5. total immer____
6. jet propul____
7. multiplication and divi____
8. a wide selec____
9. suntan lo____
10. a dangerous expedi____

EXERCISE 9. Write the following phrases and sentences, filling in the blanks with *-sede, -ceed,* or *-cede.*

1. If at first you don't suc____. . . .
2. legal pro____ings
3. ex____ all expectations
4. The waves re____d.
5. to super____ the boss
6. pro____ with caution
7. to con____ defeat
8. ac____ to the throne
9. se____ from the Union
10. inter____ in the dispute

EXERCISE 10. Write the following phrases and sentences, filling in the blanks with *able* or *ible.*

1. easily access____
2. a predict____ conclusion

3. accept____ but not outstanding
4. a dirig____ in the sky
5. a terr____ idea
6. insepar____ friends
7. comfort____ shoes
8. a memor____ event
9. His contribution was neglig____
10. mov____ parts
11. reli____ sources
12. a deduct____ contribution
13. an amic____ settlement
14. a practic____ plan
15. The proposal was feas____ .
16. illeg____ handwriting
17. an envi____ situation
18. a most cred____ witness
19. a sens____ solution
20. a vis____ difference

5.b SPELLING GRAMMATICALLY

Sometimes spelling problems are caused by grammar problems. There are three main areas of grammar that may cause you problems in spelling: spelling noun plurals, spelling possessives, and spelling the tense of verbs.

5.b.1 Spelling noun plurals

As a writer and speller, remember that if you want to indicate that there is more than one of the same noun, you must show this in the noun itself. Even if the word *two*, or another number word, precedes the noun (*car*, for example), you must change the noun itself (from *car* to *cars*). You cannot let the number word do all the work.

All but a few special nouns (see 7 and 8 on page 362) form their plurals by changing their spelling in some way. The following chart shows the most common rules and patterns.

5.b

SPELLING NOUN PLURALS

Rule	Examples	
1. To form the plural of most singular nouns and proper nouns, add *s*.	day, day**s** Smith, Smith**s** table, table**s**	
2. To form the plural of nouns and proper nouns ending in *s*, *ss*, *sh*, *ch*, *x*, *z*, and *zz*, add *es*.	box, box**es** bus, bus**es** or buss**es** dress, dress**es** lunch, lunch**es** waltz, waltz**es**	
3. To form the plural of nouns ending in a consonant + *y*, change the *y* to *i* and add *es*. With proper names, add *s*.	baby, bab**ies** county, count**ies** Kennedy, Kennedy**s** *exception:* standby, standby**s**	
To form the plural of nouns ending in a vowel + *y*, add *s*.	boy, boy**s** tray, tray**s**	valley, valley**s** way, way**s**
4. To form the plural of most nouns ending in a vowel + *o*, add *s*.	cameo, cameo**s** folio, folio**s** radio, radio**s**	
To form the plural of nouns ending in a consonant + *o*, generally add *es*, but sometimes add only *s*.[1]	echo, echo**es** hero, hero**es** potato, potato**es** banjo, banjo**s** photo, photo**s**	
Add only *s* to many words of Italian origin.	alto, alto**s** ghetto, ghetto**s** piano, piano**s** solo, solo**s**	

[1]Some nouns ending in *o* have two acceptable plural spellings; the plural of *cargo*, for example, can be *cargos* or *cargoes*.

5. To form the plural of most nouns ending in *f* and all nouns ending in *ff*, add *s*.	chief, chief**s**; roof, roof**s** muff, muff**s**; staff, staff**s**
To form the plural of some nouns ending in *f* or *fe* and many nouns ending in *lf*, change the *f* to *v* and add *es*.	leaf, lea**ves**; life, li**ves**; thief, thie**ves** calf, cal**ves**; self, sel**ves**; wolf, wol**ves**
Notice that some nouns ending in *arf* have alternativepluralforms. Both are acceptable.	dwarf, dwarf**s** or dwar**ves** scarf, scarf**s** or scar**ves** wharf, wharf**s** or whar**ves**
6. Some nouns have irregular plural forms; that is, they do not follow any one spelling rule. Learn the most common irregular plurals.	child, child**ren**; ox, ox**en** foot, f**ee**t; tooth, t**ee**th louse, l**ice**; mouse, m**ice** man, m**e**n; woman, wom**e**n
7. Some nouns ending in *s* have the same form in both the singular and the plural.	corps headquarters means series
8. The names of some fish and mammals have the same forms in both the singular and the plural.	deer fish[2] moose salmon sheep

[2]The plural form *fish* denotes more than one individual fish. *Fishes* denotes more than one kind, or species, of fish.

9. Some nouns that came to English from other languages form the plural by adding *s*.	aquarium, aquarium**s** gymnasium, gymnasium**s** stadium, stadium**s**
Many nouns from foreign languages, however, form the plural according to patterns in their original languages. Learn the most common of these words.	alumnus, alumn**i**/alumna, alumn**ae** basis, bas**es**; crisis, cris**es** datum, dat**a**; medium, medi**a** radius, radi**i**; stimulus, stimul**i**
Some words from foreign languages have alternative plural forms — the original and a newer English form. In these cases, the English plural is preferred.	appendix, append**ices** or appendix**es** concerto, concert**i** or concert**os** memorandum, memorand**a** or memorandum**s** bureau, bureau**s** (rather than bureaux) cactus, cactus**es** (rather than cacti) formula, formula**s** (rather than formulae)
10. To form the plural of numerals, letters, signs, and words used as words, add *'s*.	*8*'**s** *t*'**s** &'**s** no *if*'**s,** *and*'**s,** or *but*'**s**
11. To form the plural of units of weight and measure, add *s*.	three mile**s** two pair**s** 150 ton**s**
Do not pluralize units of weight and measure in compound adjectives before a noun.	two-quart saucepan six-foot person fifty-mile hike

12. To form the plural of compound nouns written as one word, add *s* or *es*.	cupful**s** notebook**s** playground**s** spoonful**s**
To form the plural of compound nouns that consist of a noun followed by a modifier, make the noun plural.	attorney**s**-general runner**s**-up sister**s**-in-law
There is no consistent pattern for forming the plural of compound nouns that consist of a noun or a verb plus an adverb. Check your dictionary.	going**s**-on hanger**s**-on sit-in**s** take-off**s**

EXERCISE 11. Write the plural forms of the following nouns and proper names.

1. mouse
2. mother-in-law
3. hoax
4. city
5. self
6. cupful
7. book
8. potato
9. radius
10. deer
11. rodeo
12. Nelson
13. foodstuff
14. child
15. composition
16. key
17. going-on
18. basis
19. alumnus
20. ghetto

5.b.2 Spelling possessives

Remember that in writing possessives you must know when and how to use the apostrophe. You must pay particular attention to pronouns: A possessive personal pronoun does not take an apostrophe (*hers*, for example); a possessive indefinite pronoun does take an apostrophe (*someone's*).

Learn the following rules. See 7.k.1 for additional information.

Add **'s** to form the possessive of singular and plural nouns not ending in *s*.

EXAMPLES

Zoe**'s** research project
Wayne**'s** patients
the men**'s** store
the children**'s** dog

Add an apostrophe alone to form the possessive of singular nouns of more than one syllable that end in *s* and of all plural nouns that end in *s*.

EXAMPLES

Doris**'** horse
William Carlos Williams**'** poetry
the teachers**'** cafeteria
a girl**s**' club

Add **'s** to form the possessive of singular nouns of one syllable ending in *s*.

EXAMPLES

the boss**'s** decision
Willie Mays**'s** batting average
the gas**'s** fumes
the bus**'s** brakes

Add **'s** to form the possessive of indefinite pronouns, such as *someone* or *anybody*.

EXAMPLES

somebody**'s** purse
everyone**'s** best friend
anybody**'s** guess

Write personal pronouns without any apostrophes.

EXAMPLES

It is his apartment. The apartment is his.
They are her shoes. The shoes are hers.

EXERCISE 12. Write each of the following numbered items making the italicized words possessive.

1. *Phyllis* dictionaries
2. *Yosemite* spectacular valleys.
3. *Tom* sailboat
4. the *plumbers* union
5. *San Francisco* famous fog
6. The decision is *yours*.
7. *anyone* guess
8. *John Updike* latest story
9. *his* neckties
10. two *weeks* notice
11. *Beverly Sills* recent recital
12. the *man* umbrella
13. the *cats* favorite toys
14. *Peggy* fur coat
15. *Edith Wharton* New York
16. *St. Louis* famous arch
17. the *Rockefellers* estate
18. *Boston* traditional baked beans
19. the *writers* conference
20. *Jimmy Connors* serve

5.b.3 Spelling the present tense of verbs

As a speller, keep in mind that a verb must agree in number with its subject. In the present tense most verbs have two forms—with a final *s* (for example, *skates*), and without a final *s* (for example, *skate*). The key to spelling the present tense of verbs is to know when to add the final *s*. Add the *s* when the subject is any one of the following:

1. a singular noun: *Joe sing**s** well.* [not a plural noun: *Birds sing.*]
2. a single gerund: *Learning take**s** time.* [not two or more gerunds: *Studying and learning take effort.*]

3. a third-person singular pronoun: *She live**s** here.* [not *you, I, we,* or *they: You live.*]

When the subject is a singular noun or a third-person singular pronoun, you may have to make some spelling adjustments in the verb. The following chart summarizes the spelling of singular present-tense verbs.

SPELLING PRESENT-TENSE VERBS

	seem	rush	hurry
noun [*the dog*]	seem**s**	rush**es**	hurr**ies**
personal pronoun [*he, she, it*]	seem**s**	rush**es**	hurr**ies**
indefinite pronoun [*anyone*]	seem**s**	rush**es**	hurr**ies**
gerund [*pushing*]	seem**s**	rush**es**	hurr**ies**

5.b.4 Spelling present and past participles

You must understand the difference between present and past participles in order to spell certain verb forms correctly. The present participles of irregular verbs (for example, *taking*) are sometimes pronounced in such a way that they sound much like the past participle of the same verb (for example, *taken*). If you understand how the present and the past participles differ in meaning and in use, you will be able to eliminate misspellings in your written work.

Study the differences between present and past participles in the following examples.

PRESENT PARTICIPLE	PAST PARTICIPLE
She is **taking** her time	She is **taken** with the kitten.
Falling leaves drift down.	**Fallen** leaves lie underfoot.
Drawing quietly, she seems content.	**Drawn** well, the picture will win a prize.

EXERCISE 13. Write the following sentences, supplying the appropriate participial forms of the verb given in parentheses.

1. John is ______ her now; they have not ______ each other for two years. (see)

2. That team was soundly ______ in the recent bridge tournament. (beat)

3. ______ the circumstances, I am surprised that he is ______ you anything at all! (give)

4. We are ______ now. Would you like some pie, or have you already ______ ? (eat)

5. ______ leaves may be lovely to watch, but ______ ones have to be raked. (fall)

6. Jane has ______ many difficult courses, but never any as difficult as the Latin class she is ______ this semester. (take)

7. It is ______ difficult to find just the right painting for our living room wall. (prove)

8. Her ______ look told me that she had ______ my secret for a long time. (know)

9. The taxi driver was terribly ______ by the collision; hours later his hand was still ______ . (shake)

10. That dress is so expertly ______ that it is certain to win a prize in the upcoming ______ contest. (sew)

5.c SPELLING RULES

Many spelling patterns can be learned with the help of specific spelling rules. This is especially true in words that contain *ie* or *ei* spellings, in words that contain prefixes, and in words that contain suffixes. These spelling patterns are quite predictable and can be mastered with the help of the following rules. Learn these rules. Like all rules, they have exceptions, which also must be learned. The rules do apply most of the time, however, and are well worth the effort it takes to memorize them.

5.c.1 *IE* or *EI*?

Write *i* before *e*
except after *c*
or when sounded like *a*
as in *neighbor* and *weigh.*

The long *e sound* may be spelled in a number of ways, including *ie* or *ei*. The *ei spelling* can be pronounced several ways — for example, as a long *e* or as a long *a*. The preceding rule and its exceptions will help you to decide when to write *ie* and when to write *ei*.

EXAMPLES

i before e	except after c	or when sounded like *a* as in *neighbor* and *weigh*
bel**ie**	c**ei**ling	b**ei**ge
f**ie**ld	dec**ei**ve	fr**ei**ght
gr**ie**f	perc**ei**ve	n**ei**ghbor
n**ie**ce	rec**ei**pt	r**ei**gn
s**ie**ge	*Exception:* sc**ie**nce	v**ei**n

EXCEPTIONS

_ei_ for a long e when there is no c

either	prot**ei**n
l**ei**sure	s**ei**ze
n**ei**ther	w**ei**rd

Notice that the above examples illustrate words in which the problematic vowel sound is a long *e* or a long *a* (except for *science*). Sometimes you must decide between the *ie* and *ei* spellings in a word with another vowel sound. Let the following lists be your guide.

OTHER *EI* WORDS	OTHER *IE* WORDS
forf**ei**t	financ**ie**r
for**ei**gn	fr**ie**nd
h**ei**ght	misch**ie**f

EXERCISE 14. Write the following phrases, filling in the blanks with *ie* or *ei*. Check any spellings you are unsure of in the dictionary.

1. my fr____ndly n____ghbor
2. a loaded fr____ght train
3. two dollars ap____ce
4. full of misch____f
5. a blood-curdling shr____k
6. a br____f visit

7. the conc____ted actor
8. to conc____ve an idea
9. n____ce and nephew
10. a sales rec____pt

EXERCISE 15. Write the following words, filling in the blanks with *ie* or *ei.* Check any spellings you are unsure of in the dictionary.

1. f____nd
2. perc____ve
3. ____ght
4. w____ner
5. conc____t
6. n____gh
7. ach____ve
8. n____ther
9. rec____pt
10. c____ling
11. surv____llance
12. s____ge
13. s____ze
14. w____rd
15. f____ld
16. y____ld
17. v____l
18. l____sure
19. fr____nd
20. h____ght

5.c.2 Adding prefixes

The spelling of a word remains the same when a prefix is added to it.

EXAMPLES
in- + exact = inexact
re- + pay = repay
dis- + satisfied = dissatisfied
mis- + spell = misspell

Do not subtract any letters from the original word. Many writers mistakenly eliminate one of two consecutive identical letters in a word such as *dissatisfied.*

■ Common changes in prefixes

Some prefixes change slightly when they are added to certain English words. For example, you must change *in-* to *il-* when you add it to *legal;* you say and write *illegal.* This change makes pronunciation easier and explains why many prefixed words have double consonants. There are, of course, many other English words with doubled consonants. Some of these are words that have come into English from Latin complete with a prefix that had already been changed for the same reason—ease in pronunciation. For example, *in-* was changed to *im-* when it was attached to the Latin word *maculatus* ("soiled") to produce *immaculatus*, which became the English word *immaculate*.

Study the following prefixes and their alternate forms. You will find examples of prefixes added to English words and to words derived from Latin. (For a more detailed discussion of prefixes, see 4.j.)

IN- becomes il-, im-, and ir-

il- + l (illiterate, illustrate)
im- + m (immoderate, immaculate)
im- + b (imbalance, imbibe)
im- + p (impossible, improvise)
ir- + r (irregular, irrigate, irrelevant)

COM- becomes col-, con-, and cor-

col- + l (collect, collide)
con- + n (connect, connote)
cor- + r (correspond, correct, corrode)

AD- becomes ac-, af-, ag-, al-, an-, ap-, ar-, as-, at-, and a-

ac- + c (accustom, accommodate)
af- + f (affix)
ag- + g (aggression)
al- + l (allege, allow)
an- + n (annul, announce)
ap- + p (appoint, appear, appeal)
ar- + r (arrive, arrange)
as- + s (assure, assistant)
at- + t (attend, attach, attempt)
a- + sc (ascribe, ascend)
a- + sp (aspect, aspire)
a- + st (astringent)

EXERCISE 16. Write the following phrases, combining the prefix in parentheses with the italicized word.

1. two *related* events (inter-)
2. was *elected* to the Presidency (re-)

3. *spelled* the word (mis-)
4. added a *necessary* comment (un-)
5. met the *movable* force (im-)
6. a *satisfied* customer (dis-)
7. a valuable *commendation* (re-)
8. acted *responsibly* in the situation (ir-)
9. a highly *rated* film (over-)
10. suddenly *appeared* (dis-)

EXERCISE 17. Add the prefix *in-* to the following words, changing it to *il-*, *im-*, or *ir-*, as appropriate. Write the new words.

1. movable
2. legible
3. precise
4. balance
5. partial
6. logical
7. relevant
8. passive
9. legitimate
10. modest

EXERCISE 18. Add the appropriate forms of the prefixes *in-*, *com-*, or *ad-* to the following items to form words that have the same meaning as those words in parentheses. Write the new words.

1. ____peal (beg)
2. ____rode (wear away)
3. ____possible (not possible)
4. ____tempt (try)
5. ____range (prepare)
6. ____note (suggest)
7. ____low (permit)
8. ____pire (seek after)
9. ____mature (childish)
10. ____lide (clash)

5.c.3 Adding suffixes

Sometimes words change slightly when suffixes are added. For example, when you add *-ness* to *happy*, the *y* changes to *i*. When you add *-ed* to *omit*, the *t* is doubled. As a speller, you must know these patterns and the guiding principles behind them. This subsection contains some simple rules that will help you to spell suffixed words ending in *y*, those ending in silent *e*, and those ending in a single consonant. (For a more detailed discussion of suffixes, see 4.1.)

Words ending in *y*

When adding a suffix to a word that ends in a consonant + *y*, change the *y* to *i*.

EXAMPLES

BEAUTY: beaut**i**ful
CARRY: carr**i**es, carr**i**ed, carr**i**er
HAPPY: happ**i**est, happ**i**ness

EXCEPTIONS

The above rule works in general, but remember that the *y* is retained in the following circumstances.

With suffixes beginning in i	With the suffixes -hood, -like, or -ship	With words formed from certain one-syllable words
bab**y**ish	bab**y**hood	dr**y**ly, dr**y**ness[1]
carr**y**ing	cit**y**like	fr**y**er[2]
	lad**y**ship	sh**y**ly, sh**y**ness[3]

When adding a suffix to a word that ends in a vowel + *y*, generally keep the *y*.

EXAMPLES

COY: co**y**ly, co**y**ness
DESTROY: destro**y**ed, destro**y**ing, destro**y**er
DELAY: dela**y**s, dela**y**ed, dela**y**ing

EXCEPTIONS

DAY: da**i**ly
LAY: la**i**d
PAY: pa**i**d
SAY: sa**i**d

[1]Notice, however, the comparative forms *drier* and *driest*. *Drily* is also acceptable.
[2]Notice, however, the forms *fries* and *fried*. *Frier* is also acceptable.
[3]*Shyer/shier* and *shyest/shiest* are all acceptable. *Shyer* and *shyest* are preferred. The past participle is *shied*.

EXERCISE 19. From each pair of phrases below, select the one phrase that is spelled correctly, and write it. Review the preceding rules for suffixes if necessary.

1. a) such sillyness
   b) such silliness
2. a) an enjoyable evening
   b) an enjoiable evening
3. a) our dayly bread
   b) our daily bread
4. a) my employer
   b) my emploier
5. a) just as I sayed
   b) just as I said
6. a) the sorryest sight ever seen
   b) the sorriest sight ever seen
7. a) her ladyship
   b) her ladiship
8. a) smiled coyly
   b) smiled coily
9. a) employment agency
   b) emploiment agency
10. a) drying the dishes
    b) driing the dishes

EXERCISE 20. Combine the following words and suffixes. Write the new words. Review the preceding rules for suffixes if necessary.

1. carry + -ing
2. happy + -ness
3. annoy + -ance
4. gray + -ish
5. duty + -ful
6. buy + -er
7. mercy + -ful
8. fry + -er
9. play + -ful
10. dry + -ness
11. busy + -ly
12. enjoy + -able
13. day + -ly
14. cry + -ing
15. portray + -al
16. say + -ed
17. lady + -ship
18. bury + -ed
19. clumsy + -ly
20. boy + -ish

Words ending in silent e

When adding a suffix that begins with a consonant to a word that ends in a silent *e*, generally keep the *e*. If the word ends in *dge* or *ble*, however, drop the *e*.

EXAMPLES

care + -less = car**e**less
excite + -ment = excit**e**ment
hate + -ful = hat**e**ful
manage + -ment = manag**e**ment
sure + -ly = sur**e**ly

Words ending in *dge* or *ble*

acknowledge + -ment = acknowledgment[1]
judge + -ment = judgment[1]
double + -ly = doubly
incredible + -ly = incredibly

There are important reasons for keeping the *e* before each suffix in the first group above: to retain the vowel sound in the original word and to prevent confusion with another word. Look at the word *careless*, for example. If the final *e* in *care* were dropped, the new word would be *carless*, a word with an entirely different sound and meaning.

EXCEPTIONS

argue + -ment = argument
awe + -ful = awful
due + -ly = duly
loathe + -some = loathsome
nine + -th = ninth
true + -ly = truly
wise + -dom = wisdom

When adding *y* or a suffix that begins with a vowel to a word that ends in a silent *e*, generally drop the *e*. If the word ends in *ce* or *ge*, and the suffix starts with *a* or *o*, keep the *e*.

---

[1] Notice that *acknowledgement* and *judgement* are acceptable British spellings.

EXAMPLES

noise + -y = noisy
bite + -ing = biting
desire + -able = desirable
flake + -ed = flaked
move + -able = movable[1]

Words ending in *ce* or *ge*

notice + -able = notic**e**able
advantage + -ous = advantag**e**ous
manage + -able = manag**e**able

In the above two groups, the guiding principle is *sound.* You can drop the silent *e* from *bite,* for example, because the vowel sound (a long *i*) stays the same without it when the vowel suffix is added. (Compare what happens when you add a suffix beginning with a consonant to *spite:* You must retain the silent *e* or the word becomes *spitful* instead of *spiteful.*) On the other hand, in words ending in *ce* or *ge,* you must keep the final *e* before a vowel suffix in order to maintain the soft sound of the *c* or *g.*

EXCEPTIONS

One-syllable words ending in *ie* + *-ing*

die + -ing = d**y**ing   lie + -ing = l**y**ing

Other words

mileage	hoeing	cagey
	shoeing	dopey
	toeing	gluey
		homey

EXERCISE 21. Combine the following words and suffixes, and write the new words. Be careful to use American spellings.

1. use +-ful
2. nature + -al
3. rare + -ity
4. acknowledge + -ment
5. die + -ing
6. hope + -less
7. change + -able
8. lie + -ing

[1]Notice that *moveable* is an acceptable British spelling. Similarly, *likable/likeable* and *lovable/loveable* are all acceptable.

9. awe + -ful
10. awe + -some
11. bare + -ly
12. incredible + -ly
13. desire + -able
14. judge + -ment
15. truc + -ly
16. dope + -y
17. divine + -ity
18. notice + -able
19. nine + -th
20. noise + -y

EXERCISE 22. Write the following phrases, correcting any misspelled words. Be careful to use American, not British, spellings.

1. the dieing swan
2. a noticeable mistake
3. a difficult judgement
4. hoping all is well
5. a hopless situation
6. simply unbelievable
7. duely noted
8. the ninth arguement this week
9. an incredibly easy exam
10. singing her dress with the hot iron

Doubling the final consonant

When adding a suffix that begins with a vowel to a one-syllable word that ends in a single vowel + a single consonant, double the final consonant.

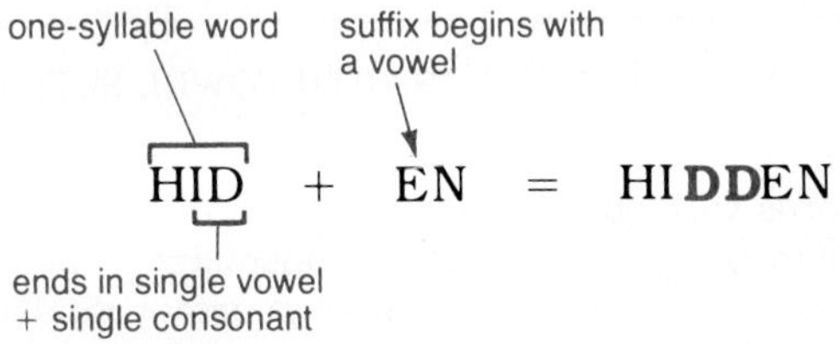

one-syllable word — suffix begins with a vowel

HID + EN = HI**DD**EN

ends in single vowel + single consonant

EXAMPLES

PLAN: pla**nn**er, pla**nn**ing
RIP: ri**pp**er, ri**pp**ing
RUN: ru**nn**er, ru**nn**ing
TAP: ta**pp**ed, ta**pp**ing

NOTE: Do not double a final consonant that is preceded by two vowels: *braid, braided, braiding.*

The consonant is doubled to keep the preceding vowel sound short. *Tap,* for example, becomes *tapped* to retain the short *a* sound. If the *p* is not doubled, the word becomes *taped,* which has an entirely different sound and meaning.

EXAMPLES

hop + -ing = ho**pp**ing BUT hope + -ing = ho**p**ing
strip + -ed = stri**pp**ed BUT stripe + -ed = stri**p**ed

Prefixed and compound words related to one-syllable words follow the above rule for doubling consonants.

EXAMPLES

recap + -ing = reca**pp**ing
outfit + -ed = outfi**tt**ed

When adding a suffix that begins with a vowel to a multisyllable word ending in a single vowel + a single consonant, double the final consonant only if the stress is on the last syllable or if it is a prefixed or a compound word.

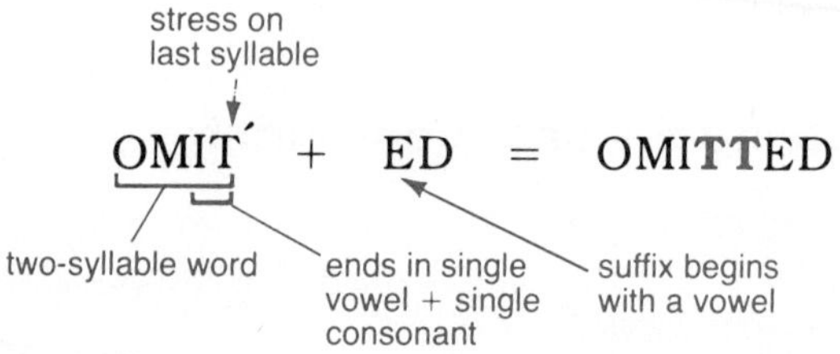

ALTERNATE SPELLINGS WITH VOWEL SUFFIXES

You should be aware that there are alternate spellings for some words with vowel suffixes. Americans generally follow the principle of not doubling the consonant if the accent is not on the last syllable; the British generally do double the consonant. Hence, we have *traveled* [American] and *travelled* [British]; *canceled* [American] and *cancelled* [British]; *benefited* [American] and *benefitted* [British]. Furthermore, there are two words that have two acceptable suffixed forms even in America: *kidnaped/kidnapped* and *worshiped/worshipped.*

EXAMPLES

BE·GIN′: begi**nn**er, begi**nn**ing

E·QUIP′: equi**pp**ed, equi**pp**ing [The *u* goes with the *q*, not with the *i*.]

PRE·FIT: prefi**tt**ed

RE·GRET′: regre**tt**ed, regre**tt**able

NOTE: If the stress is on the first syllable, do not double the final consonant: *of′fer, of′fered, of′fer•ing.*

Sometimes the addition of a suffix shifts the stress in a word and affects the decision of whether or not to double the consonant. Words ending in *fer* are good examples of this principle.

re•fer′ + -ed, -er, -ing: re•fe**rr**ed′, re•fe**r′r**er, re•fe**r′r**ing

re•fer′ + -ence, -ent, -ential, -ee: ref′er•ence, ref′er•ent, ref•er•en′tial, ref•er•ee′

NOTE: Never double a final *x* or *w* before a suffix: *guffa**w**ing, mi**x**ing, sa**w**ing, transfi**x**ed.*

Never double a final consonant before a suffix beginning with a consonant.

EXAMPLES

commit + -ment = commi**t**ment BUT commi**tt**ed, commi**tt**ing, commi**tt**ee

sin + -ful = si**n**ful BUT si**nn**ed, si**nn**ing, si**nn**er

EXERCISE 23. Combine the following words and suffixes and write the new words. Be careful to use American spellings.

1. hop + -ed
2. begin + -er
3. outfit + -ing
4. rob + -er
5. rob + -ery
6. tap + -ing
7. sin + -ing
8. unwrap + -ed
9. commit + -ed
10. mop + -ed
11. transfix + -ing
12. trim + -ness
13. recap + -ed
14. refer + -ed
15. refer + -ence
16. forget + -ful
17. forget + -ing
18. mix + -ing
19. soul + -ful
20. prefer + -ing

EXERCISE 24. Write the following sentences, correcting any misspelled words.

1. The prizefighter had strong preferences when it came to referrees.
2. The Girl Scouts came equiped with all the latest in camping equippment.
3. She was hopping against hope that she had passed her Russian test.
4. Being a member of that committee required a tremendous personal committment.
5. Laura and Leo are city planners; they studied planing at the university.
6. The Sunbelt is an area of the United States that is characterized by a warm, suny climate.
7. When asked which color I prefered, I had to admit that I had no preferrences.
8. I was transfixxed from start to finish by Ambrose Bierce's story, "An Occurence at Owl Creek Bridge."
9. Linda and Steve could not decide between the stripped wallpaper and the doted wallpaper.
10. After checking Ms. Kelly's referrences, the recruiter referred her to three departments for further interviews.

5.d SPELLING HOMOPHONES

Homophones are words that sound alike and may cause spelling problems.

The difficulty is that two or three different words may sound alike, but they are usually not spelled alike. You do not, for example, want to write *there* if you mean *their.* Moreover, it is difficult to see your mistake once you have written the wrong word. After all, it does not *look* misspelled. Homophone errors are therefore very often skipped over in proofreading.

Study the following common homophones and their most common meanings. It may help to consider the grammatical differences between the words. For example, remember that *there* is an adverb and *their* is a pronoun. Learn the mnemonic (memory) devices suggested in some of the groups, or create your own. For example, remember that *their* contains the word *heir*, another word relating to possession, whereas *there* contains the word *here*, another word that pertains to place. Learn to proofread with an eye for homophones. Because they are often difficult to pick out, you must be on the lookout for them.

As you study the following list of homophones, test yourself by supplying the correct word in parentheses in each sentence.

altar a table or platform where religious ceremonies are performed
alter to change

Because the dress was too large, I had to (altar/alter) it.
The bride and groom exchanged vows at the (altar/alter).

aural relating to listening and the ear
oral spoken; relating to the mouth

The old woman was interviewed for an (aural/oral) history of the region.
Listening to tapes in the language lab is good (aural/oral) practice.

base a main element; a bottom supporting part; dishonorable
bass the lowest range in music

In most operas the (base/bass) singer never wins the heroine.
Shall we meet at the (base/bass) of the monument?

berth a bed on a ship or train
birth the act of being born

Every (berth/birth) was reserved for the winter cruise.
The whole family awaited the (berth/birth) of the first grandchild.

born brought into life
borne the past participle of *bear*; supported; endured

My sister was (born/borne) on the Fourth of July.
The old woman has (born/borne) much pain over the years.

capital a city that is the seat of government
capitol a building in which a legislature meets

Sacramento is the (capital/capitol) of California.
Each house of the state legislature met in its own room of the (capital/capitol).

coarse rough; crude
course a path or direction; an academic subject; a part of a meal

The (coarse/course) cloth of the shirt irritated her skin.
The President's advisers urged a conservative (coarse/course) of action.

complement to complete or balance; something that completes [hence, the *e* after the *l*]
compliment to praise; an expression of praise

The rhythm of the drums (complements/compliments) the harmony of the strings.
The Mayor paid the speaker a gracious (complement/compliment).

core the central or innermost part
corps a military unit; a group of people acting or working together

Dr. Lee served in the medical (core/corps).
Jane quickly ate the apple right down to the (core/corps).

council a group of advisers
counsel advice; to give advice

Every member of the town (council/counsel) was present.
We decided to follow our lawyer's (council/counsel).

dew light moisture in small drops
do to act or perform
due owed; payable; expected to arrive

The front lawn sparkled with (dew/do/due) drops.
(Dew/Do/Due) unto others as you would have them (dew/do/due) unto you.
Erica is (dew/do/due) on the noon flight from San Diego.

discreet tactful; prudent
discrete distinct; separate [Notice that the *e*'s are separate in *discrete*, a word that means "separate."]

The detective was (discreet/discrete) when discussing the case.
The word *civil* has several (discreet/discrete) meanings.

foul very unpleasant; bad
fowl chickens, turkeys, ducks, and other domestic birds

The sailboat pitched and tossed in the (foul/fowl) weather.
I buy all my (foul/fowl) at the corner market.

guerrilla a fighter engaged in irregular defensive warfare, usually including ambushes and sudden raids; relating to such a fighter
gorilla the largest ape

Children always love feeding bananas to the (guerrilla/gorilla).
The decisive battles of the war were fought in the mountains by (guerrilla/gorilla) bands.

hole a hollow place in something solid; an opening [Notice that the adjective is *holey*.]
whole complete [Notice that the adverb is *wholly*.]

He wore a sweater to cover the (hole/whole) in his shirt.
Peggy has the (hole/whole) set of Jane Austen novels.

idle not working or operating
idol an image of a god or goddess; a person who is greatly admired

My grandfather has been and always will be my (idle/idol).
The shutdown of the auto plant left workers (idle/idol).

its belonging to it
it's contraction of *it is* or *it has*

The alligator opened (its/it's) enormous jaws.
(Its/It's) only a five-minute walk to the train station.

liable legally responsible for; apt or likely
libel false or malicious written information that damages a person's reputation

The owner of the car was (liable/libel) for damages.
The actor successfully sued the newspaper publisher for (liable/libel).

peace a period of no war; tranquility
piece a portion or fragment of a whole

The Treaty of Paris brought (peace/piece) to the weary combatants.
May I bring you a (peace/piece) of apple pie?

pedal the foot-operated part of a machine; to work the pedals of
peddle to sell goods

It is no easy job to (pedal/peddle) vegetables at a produce fair.
My sewing machine is operated by stepping on and off a (pedal/peddle).

plain simple, not fancy; a flat expanse of ground
plane a flat surface; a carpenter's tool; an airplane

The (plain/plane) truth is that the experiment did not succeed.
I love to travel by (plain/plane).

principal the head of a school; greatest or first; main
principle a basic truth; a rule of conduct; integrity

Mrs. Schwartz was always known as a woman of (principal/principle).

Mr. Alvarez was the most popular (principal/principle) in the school system.

stationary fixed; unmoving
stationery writing paper and envelopes
[Notice the *a* in stationary as in *stay.*]

The train remained (stationary/stationery) for twenty minutes.
We get a discount on all paper goods at the local (stationary/stationery) store.

straight not curved; erect
strait a narrow waterway connecting two large bodies of water

The windjammer sailed a (straight/strait) course for the island.
The sailboat was becalmed in the (straight/strait) off the Florida Keys.

their belonging to them
there in that place
they're contraction of *they are*
[Notice the *heir* in *their*, both words relating to possession. Notice also the *here* in *there*, two words about location.]

(Their/There/They're) are only five houses on Ridge Road.
(Their/There/They're) owners commute to the city by train every day.
(Their/There/They're) all members of the PTA.

threw the past tense of *throw*
through in one side and out the other; from beginning to end; finished

The chairperson kept her composure (threw/through) many hours of heated debate.
The speaker's ill-tempered remarks (threw/through) the meeting into confusion.

vain conceited; ineffectual
vane a wind indicator; weather vane
vein a blood vessel carrying blood to the heart

The rooster you see on the roof is actually a weather (vain/vane/vein).
The lifeguard made a (vain/vane/vein) effort.
The medicine must be injected right into the (vain/vane/vein).

weather atmospheric conditions
whether if

According to the (weather/whether) report, it may snow.
I do not care (weather/whether) or not it snows all week!

who's contraction of *who is* or *who has*
whose possessive case of *who*

(Who's/Whose) bathing suit is on the line?
(Who's/Whose) the owner of that red pickup truck?

your belonging to you
you're contraction of *you are*

Please take (your/you're) place in line!
I believe that (your/you're) next.

EXERCISE 25. Write the following sentences, correcting any homophone errors.

1. The little-known movie *The Berth of the Blues* will be shown tonight on the late show.
2. Castroville, California, is the artichoke capital of the world.
3. Because of some unexpected changes in the course of Hurricane David, officials had to altar evacuation plans.
4. Several name brands of foul now compete in the supermarkets.
5. Do you swear to tell the truth, the hole truth, and nothing but the truth?
6. The architect I. M. Pei was borne in China.
7. Mikhail Baryshnikov is one of the principle dancers in American ballet today.
8. Its a bird; its a plane; its Superman!
9. *Plane Speaking* is the title of a popular biography of Harry Truman.
10. The police officer tried in vein to get any information out of Sam Spade.

5.e SPELLING COMMONLY CONFUSED WORDS

The words in each of the following sets are commonly confused, even though they are not pronounced exactly alike. For example, some people confuse the words *affect* and *effect.* In proofreading your writing, check the spelling of these words just as you check for homophones.

accept to agree to take; to assume
except but

Will you (accept/except) our invitation?
I would, (accept/except) that I have to work.

affect to influence
effect a result of some action

A serious earthquake can (affect/effect) an entire country.
Its (affects/effects) can be devastating.

choose to select
chose the past tense of *choose*

Which courses will you (choose/chose)?
Last year he (choose/chose) German, American literature, and physics.

clothes [klōthz] garments
cloths [klôthz, klôths] fabrics

Put on your (clothes/cloths) before you eat breakfast.
You can find dust (clothes/cloths) in the rag bag.

desert [di · zurt′] to abandon
desert [dez′ · ərt] a dry, barren region
dessert [di · zurt′] the last course of a meal

The (desert/dessert) has been the home of nomads.
Jane ordered a hot-fudge sundae for (desert/dessert).
I could never (desert/dessert) a friend in need.

formally politely; according to custom or rule
formerly previously

[Notice the *formal* in *formally* and the *former* in *formerly*.]

The new state constitution will be (formally/formerly) adopted tomorrow.
That ballplayer (formally/formerly) played in the minor leagues.

later the comparative form of *late*; after some time
latter the second of two mentioned

Given a choice between rooting for the Boston Red Sox or the New York Yankees, I chose the (later/latter).
I will study now and go for a walk (later/latter).

loose free; not confined; not snug
lose to have a loss

I cannot find my umbrella anywhere; I hope I did not (loose/lose) it.
Each night John puts all his (loose/lose) change on his dresser.

moral [mor′ · əl] virtuous; ethical; the lesson of a fable or event
morale [mə · ral′] spirit; mental condition

The Abolitionists were opposed to slavery on (moral/morale) grounds.
After three days of final examinations (moral/morale) at the university was extremely low.

personal [pur′s′n · əl] individual; private
personnel [pur · sə nel′] the people employed at any place of work

Most of us keep our (personal/personnel) problems to ourselves.
Applications for employment may be obtained from the (personal/personnel) department.

quiet making little or no noise
quite completely; very; rather

Joanne enjoys the peace and (quiet/quite) of country life.
Cities have always made her (quiet/quite) nervous.

than in comparison with
then at that time; next

Cans were much cheaper (than/then).
They seemed much more content (than/then) their parents.

EXERCISE 26. From each pair of phrases or sentences below, select the one that is spelled correctly, and write it.

1. a) the morale of the story
   b) the moral of the story
2. a) see you later
   b) see you latter

3. a) We drove past the house, and then turned around.
   b) We drove past the house, and than turned around.
4. a) a matter of personnel taste
   b) a matter of personal taste
5. a) Is that quiet clear?
   b) Is that quite clear?
6. a) clothes conscious
   b) cloths conscious
7. a) What is for desert?
   b) What is for dessert?
8. a) We accept the invitation with pleasure.
   b) We except the invitation with pleasure.
9. a) pick and choose
   b) pick and chose
10. a) at loose ends
    b) at lose ends

5.f FREQUENTLY MISSPELLED WORDS

Certain English words are misspelled so frequently that they are now referred to as spelling demons. The following list contains four-hundred such words. Some of them can be learned using the preceding strategies—pronunciation clues, spelling rules, grammatical patterns, etc.—but others seem to defy any logic or rule. If all else fails, such words must be memorized.

Study the following words, ten or twenty at a time, to see which ones are difficult for you. If possible, have someone dictate them to you to spell. Keep a list of these words that give you trouble. Study them individually to fix them in your mind and your eye. Single out the part of the word that gives you trouble. Say each word syllable by syllable. Make up a memory device to help you remember the words that are problems for you. For example, if you sometimes forget the second *h* in *shepherd*, remember that it contains the word *herd*. Make yourself aware of which words cause you problems, try to learn them, and — most important — know when to turn to the dictionary. (See Section 6.)

If you master these words, you are well on your way to being a good speller.

FOUR HUNDRED SPELLING WORDS

accept
accessible
accommodation
accumulate
accurate
ache
achievement
acknowledgment
acquaint
acquire
acquitted
across
address
admittance
adolescent
advantageous
advertisement
aerial
afraid
aggravate
aggressive
aisle
allotment
all right
almost
alphabet
already
altogether
aluminum
analysis
analyze
annihilate
anonymous
answer
antecedent
antidote
anxiety
apologetic
apparatus
appearance
appreciate
appropriate
arctic

argument
arrangement
ascend
assassinate
assistance
athletics
attitude
autumn
auxiliary
awkward

bachelor
balloon
bankruptcy
basis
battalion
beggar
beginning
behavior
beneficial
benefited
biscuit
bookkeeper
bouillon
boulevard
bruise
budget
bureaucrat

calendar
campaign
canister
caricature
catastrophe
cellophane
cemetery
centennial
changeable
chauffeur
coincidence
colonel
colossal

comfortably
commission
committee
comparatively
compatible
compel
competent
competition
complexion
concede
conceive
condemn
conscience
conscious
consensus
consistency
controlled
corps
correspondence
counterfeit
coupon
courtesy
criticize
curriculum
cylinder

deceitful
decibel
defendant
defense
deference
deficient
definitely
dependent
descendant
desirable
despair
desperate
detriment
diarrhea
dictionary
difference

dilemma
dilettante
diphtheria
disappear
disappointment
disastrous
discernible
disciple
discipline
discuss
disease
dissatisfied
dissipate

ecstasy
eighth
eligible
embarrassment
emphasize
endeavor
environment
epistle
equipped
equivalent
essential
exaggerate
exceed
excess
exercise
exhibit
exhilarate
exhort
existence
extravagant

fallacy
familiarize
fascinating
fascism
fatigue
feasible
February
fictitious
fiery
financier
forehead
foreign
forfeit
forty
fourteen
fulfill

gaiety
gauge
gorgeous
government
grammatically
grievous
guarantee
guidance
guttural
gymnasium
gypsy

handicapped
handkerchief
harassment
height
hemorrhage
heroes
hindrance
humorous
hygiene
hypocrisy

immediately
impossible
inconsistent
incredible
indelible
indictment
indispensable
ingenious
innocuous
inoculate
insistence
installation
intellectual
intelligent
interpretation
interruption
iridescent
irrelevant
irresistible

jewelry

kerosene

laboratory
leisure
liaison
library
license
lieutenant
lightning
liquefy
literature
livelihood
loneliness
lovable
luxurious

magnanimous
magnificent
maintenance
malicious
maneuver
marriage
mathematics
medieval
millennium
millionaire
miniature
minuscule
miscellaneous
mischievous
missile

misspell
modern
mortgage
mosquitoes
muscle

necessary
neighbor
neither
nickel
niece
ninth
noticeable
noticing
nuclear
nuisance

occasion
occur
occurred
occurrence
often
omission
omitted
opponent
opportunity

pamphlet
pandemonium
pantomime
paraffin
paralleled
paralyze
paraphernalia
parliament
pastime
penicillin
perceive
permanent
permissible
perseverance
persistent
persuade
phenomenon
Philippines
phlegm
picnicking
plaintiff
plausible
playwright
pneumonia
pollution
Portuguese
possess
practice
precedent
preference
prevalence
privilege
process
pronunciation
propaganda
prophecy [noun]
prophesy [verb]
propeller
psalm
psychology

questionnaire
quietly

receive
recognize
recommendation
reference
referred
regrettable
reign
relevant
remembrance
reminisce
repentance
repetition
representative
resistance
responsibility
restaurant
resurrect
rheumatism
rhubarb
rhyme
rhythm
righteous
roommate

saccharine
satellite
schedule
scheme
scintillate
scissors
secretary
seize
separation
sergeant
several
shepherd
sheriff
shriek
siege
significance
silhouette
similar
skillful
sovereignty
specimen
strenuous
stubbornness
substantiate
subtle
suddenness
supersede
superstitious
suppress
susceptible
syllable
syllabus
symmetrical
synonymous

tangible
tariff
technique
though
through
tomorrow
tonight
tortoise
tournament
traffic
transferred
trespass
twelfth

tyranny

unanimous
uncontrollable
unnecessary
unscrupulous
usage

vacuum
various
vehement
vehicle
vengeance

veteran
vicinity
villain

waive
Wednesday
weird
wholly

yacht

zealot
zinc

THE DICTIONARY

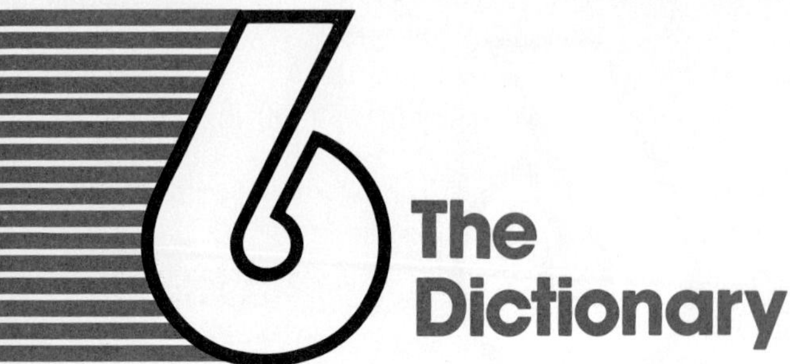

6 The Dictionary

The following word entry from a standard college dictionary shows the kinds of information that can be found in any good dictionary.

entry word — pronunciation — inflected forms — example in context — one of many definitions — usage label — part-of-speech label — etymology — regional label (Americanism) — specialized plural — subject label — two-word verb (See 4.c.) — synonyms — synonym study — antonyms

tie (tī) ***vt.* tied, ty'ing** [ME. *tien* < OE. *tigan, tegan* < base of *teag*, a rope: for IE. base see TOW[1]] **1.** to fasten, attach, or bind together or to something else, as with string, cord, or rope made secure by knotting, etc. [to *tie* someone's hands, to *tie* a boat to a pier] **2.** *a*) to draw together or join the parts, ends, or sides of by tightening and knotting laces, strings, etc. [to *tie* one's shoes] *b*) to make by fastening together parts [to *tie* fishing flies] **3.** *a*) to make (a knot or bow) *b*) to make a knot or bow in [to *tie* one's necktie] **4.** to fasten, connect, join, or bind in any way [*tied* by common interests] **5.** to confine; restrain; restrict **6.** *a*) to equal the score or achievement of, as in a contest *b*) to equal (a score, record, etc.) **7.** [Colloq.] to join in marriage **8.** *Music* to connect with a tie —***vi.*** **1.** to be capable of being tied; make a tie **2.** to make an equal score or achievement, as in a contest —***n.*** [ME. *tege, teige* < OE. *teag, teah*, a rope] **1.** a string, lace, cord, etc. used to tie things **2.** something that connects, binds, or joins; bond; link [a business *tie*, *ties* of affection] **3.** something that confines, limits, or restricts [legal *ties*] **4.** *short for* NECKTIE **5.** a beam, rod, etc. that holds together parts of a building and strengthens against stress ☆**6.** any of the parallel crossbeams to which the rails of a railroad are fastened; sleeper **7.** *a*) an equality of scores, votes, achievement, etc. in a contest *b*) a contest or match in which there is such an equality; draw; stalemate **8.** [*pl.*] low shoes fastened with laces, as oxfords **9.** *Music* a curved line above or below two notes of the same pitch, indicating that the tone is to be held unbroken for the duration of their combined values —***adj.*** that has been tied, or made equal [a *tie* score] —**tie down** to confine; restrain; restrict —☆**tie in** **1.** to bring into or have a connection **2.** to make or be consistent, harmonious, etc. —☆**tie into** [Colloq.] to attack vigorously —**tie off** to close off passage through by tying with something —☆**tie one on** [Slang] to get drunk —**tie up** **1.** to tie firmly or securely **2.** to wrap up and tie with string, cord, etc. **3.** to moor (a ship or boat) to a dock ☆**4.** to obstruct; hinder; stop **5.** to cause to be already in use, retained, committed, etc.

SYN.—**tie** and **bind** are often interchangeable, but in discriminative use, **tie** specif. implies the connection of one thing with another by means of a rope, string, etc. which can be knotted [to *tie* a horse to a hitching post], and **bind** suggests the use of an encircling band which holds two or more things firmly together [to *bind* someone's legs]; **fasten,** a somewhat more general word, implies a joining of one thing to another, as by tying, binding, gluing, nailing, pinning, etc.; **attach** emphasizes the joining of two or more things in order to keep them together as a unit [to *attach* one's references to an application] —***ANT.*** **separate, part**

From *Webster's New World Dictionary*

College dictionaries have approximately 150,000 entries. **Unabridged** dictionaries have more than twice as many entries. *Webster's Third New International Dictionary of the English Language, Unabridged*, has 450,000 words. The definitions are more detailed than those in a college dictionary, and often include illustrative literary quotations.

The labels on the entry for *tie* will be explained in the following pages.

6.a INFORMATION FOR READERS: MEANINGS AND ORIGINS

As a reader, you will consult a dictionary most often to find a word's meaning. Some words have only one meaning, but most words have more than one. Since the dictionary lists the various meanings of a word, it is wise to read through *all* the definitions to determine which meaning best fits a specific context.

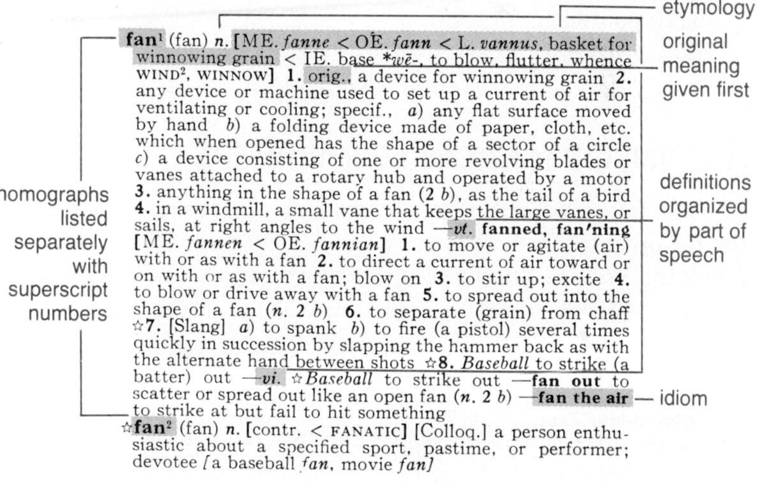

fan[1] (fan) *n.* [ME. *fanne* < OE. *fann* < L. *vannus*, basket for winnowing grain < IE. base **wē-*, to blow, flutter, whence WIND[2], WINNOW] **1.** orig., a device for winnowing grain **2.** any device or machine used to set up a current of air for ventilating or cooling; specif., *a)* any flat surface moved by hand *b)* a folding device made of paper, cloth, etc. which when opened has the shape of a sector of a circle *c)* a device consisting of one or more revolving blades or vanes attached to a rotary hub and operated by a motor **3.** anything in the shape of a fan (2 *b*), as the tail of a bird **4.** in a windmill, a small vane that keeps the large vanes, or sails, at right angles to the wind —*vt.* **fanned, fan'ning** [ME. *fannen* < OE. *fannian*] **1.** to move or agitate (air) with or as with a fan **2.** to direct a current of air toward or on with or as with a fan; blow on **3.** to stir up; excite **4.** to blow or drive away with a fan **5.** to spread out into the shape of a fan (*n.* 2 *b*) **6.** to separate (grain) from chaff ☆**7.** [Slang] *a)* to spank *b)* to fire (a pistol) several times quickly in succession by slapping the hammer back as with the alternate hand between shots ☆**8.** *Baseball* to strike (a batter) out —*vi.* ☆*Baseball* to strike out —**fan out** to scatter or spread out like an open fan (*n.* 2 *b*) —**fan the air** to strike at but fail to hit something

☆**fan**[2] (fan) *n.* [contr. < FANATIC] [Colloq.] a person enthusiastic about a specified sport, pastime, or performer; devotee [a baseball *fan*, movie *fan*]

From *Webster's New World Dictionary*

You also check a dictionary to find the **etymology**, or origin, of a word.

Words that are spelled the same but have different origins and meanings are called **homographs** and are listed as separate entries with superscript numbers.

6.b INFORMATION FOR SPEAKERS: PRONUNCIATION

The dictionary lists the pronunciation of an entry word in parentheses or between slanted lines directly following the word. Dictionaries use special symbols to represent the forty-five sounds in the English language; each symbol stands for only one sound. Different dictionaries have different sets of symbols. One dictionary may phonetically represent the word *youth* as /yo͞oth/, while another shows it as /yüth/. The sounds are the same, of course. The symbols are explained in a key in the front of the dictionary and also in a shortened key at the foot of each page spread.

Stressed syllables are indicated by accent marks. Primary stress is shown by a heavy mark; secondary stress is represented by a lighter mark. The actual accent mark can be above or below the line and before, after, or right above the syllable. For example, here are two representations of the word *cauliflower*:

kôl ′i flou′ ər
ˈkȯl-li-ˌflau(-ə)r

6.c INFORMATION FOR WRITERS

For writers the dictionary is an essential tool. The entry for *tie* on page 394, the entry for *fan* on page 395, and the following entries illustrate what types of information a dictionary can give writers.

variant spelling

coun·se·lor (koun′sə lər, -slər) *also, British,* **coun·sel·lor.** *n.* **1.** one who gives counsel or advice; adviser: *a guidance counselor in a high school.* **2.** lawyer, esp. one who conducts cases in court. Also, **counselor-at-law. 3.** person employed to supervise activities and care for children at a camp. **—coun′se·lor·ship′,** *n.* —**Syn. 2.** see **lawyer.**

derived word

From *Macmillan Dictionary*

syllabification

cap·i·tol \ˈkap-ət-ᵊl, ˈkap-tᵊl\ *n* [L *Capitolium,* temple of Jupiter at Rome on the Capitoline hill] **1 a** : a building in which a state legislative body meets **b** : a group of buildings in which the functions of state government are carried out **2** *cap* : the building in which the U.S. Congress meets at Washington

capitalized form

From *Webster's New Collegiate Dictionary*

6.c.1 Spelling

The spelling given in the entry word is the preferred spelling. Any alternative spellings, or variants, follow. If the variants have any restrictions, they are so labeled: *Counsellor*, for example, is usually labeled as a British spelling.

Any inflected forms that are either unique or likely to cause spelling difficulties are listed in the dictionary – for example, irregular noun plurals, verb forms, and comparative and superlative forms of adjectives. Thus, *tying* is given in the entry on page 394 because the writer must make a change before adding the *-ing*. Whenever you are uncertain about doubling a final consonant, changing a *y* to an *i*, or dropping a final *e*, check the dictionary.

Note that the entry word is broken into syllables. Syllable breaks are indicated by a dot, a dash, or a space.

6.c.2 Capitalization

Dictionaries indicate when nouns and adjectives should be capitalized. Usually, the words are shown capitalized; sometimes, they are merely labeled *cap*, as in the preceding sample entry for *capitol*. A dictionary will indicate when a word may be capitalized for some senses but not for others.

6.c.3 Derived forms

Derived forms are words formed by adding a prefix or a suffix to an existing word. Some derived forms are listed as main entries, but others are listed at the end of the entry for the original word. In the *Macmillan Dictionary*, for example, *counselorship* is a derived form listed at the end of the entry for *counselor*.

6.c.4 Usage labels

Usage labels indicate that a word or definition is restricted to a certain geographic or subject area or to a certain level of language use. For example, the entry on page 394 for the word *tie* has a label indicating a specialized meaning in music. Sometimes dictionaries use special symbols to indicate usage restrictions. *Webster's New World Dictionary* marks Americanisms with a ☆, for example (see the sixth sense of the word *tie).*

6.c.5 Synonyms and antonyms

Dictionaries often give synonyms and antonyms at the end of an entry. Some dictionaries even include short discussions pointing out subtle distinctions among words that are very close in meaning, such as the comparison of *tie, bind,* and *fasten* on page 394.

EXERCISE 1. Use the following dictionary entries to answer the ten questions below.

1. Trace the word *pipe* back to its Latin meaning.
2. What are the proper syllable divisions for *pioneer*?
3. What is the archaic meaning of *pious*?
4. List meanings in music of the word *pipe.*
5. What is the meaning and level of usage of the idiom *to pipe down*?
6. What is the plural of *pipeful*?
7. What are the subtle distinctions in meaning among the synonyms *pious, devout,* and *religious*?
8. How is the English word *pioneer* related to the Latin word *pēs* (foot)?
9. What does the verb *pipe* mean in sewing?
10. What noun form of the word *pious* is given in the entry below?

pi·o·neer (pī′ə nēr′) *n.* **1.** one who is first or among the first to explore or settle a region. **2.** one who is first or among the first to open up or develop an area of thought, inquiry, or endeavor: *He was a pioneer in modern medical practice.* —*v.t.* **1.** to explore or settle: *They pioneered the Northwest Territory.* **2.** to open up or develop. —*v.i.* to be a pioneer. [French *pionnier* settler of previously unsettled land, soldier who goes ahead to clear the way for an army, from Old French *peon* foot soldier, from Medieval Latin *pedo,* from Latin *pēs* foot.]

pi·ous (pī′əs) *adj.* **1.** having reverence for God; devoutly religious: *a pious woman.* **2.** of, relating to, or proceeding from religious devotion: *pious writings.* **3.** characterized by a false or hypocritical religious devoutness. **4.** *Archaic.* respectful or dutiful to one's parents. [Latin *pius* devout, dutiful.] —**pi′ous·ly,** *adv.* —**pi′ous·ness,** *n.*

Syn. 1. Pious, devout, religious mean showing fervor in the practice of religion. **Pious** emphasizes the zealous performance of one's religious duties and obligations, esp. those involving outward acts or worship not necessarily reflecting a genuine reverence for God: *The pious man attended Mass every day.* **Devout** stresses a state of mind deeply imbued with an inward love of God and a sincere attachment to the tenets of one's faith: *I was often devout, my eyes filling with tears at the thought of God* (Yeats, 1923). **Religious** implies a formal faith in a particular religion and a constant adherence to a way of life sanctioned by that religion: *The old woman led a religious life.*

pipe (pīp) *n.* **1.** hollow cylinder for the conveyance of a gas or liquid; tube. **2.a.** implement for smoking tobacco, consisting of a tube with a bowl at one end, that is usually made of briar or clay. **b.** amount of tobacco that fills the bowl of a pipe. **3.a.** wind instrument, as a flute. **b.** one of the tubes in an organ in which tones are produced. **4. pipes. a.** instrument consisting of a series of tubes bound together; panpipe. **b.** bagpipe. **5.a.** *also,* **pipes.** sound of the voice, esp. when singing. **b.** song or note of a bird. **6.** any natural formation resembling a tube, as a cylindrical passage opening into the crater of a volcano. **7.** boatswain's whistle. **8.a.** cask for wine holding 126 gallons. **b.** unit of measure equivalent to this. —*v.t.* **1.** to convey by means of a pipe or pipes: *to pipe water.* **2.** to supply with pipes: *to pipe a new house for gas.* **3.** to play (music) on a pipe. **4.** to utter in a loud, shrill voice: *The child piped his objections.* **5.** to summon by sounding a boatswain's whistle: *The boatswain piped all hands on deck.* **6.** to finish or trim (fabric) with piping. —*v.i.* **1.** to make a loud, shrill sound. **2.** to play on a pipe. **3.** to summon the crew or give orders by sounding a boatswain's whistle. **4. to pipe down.** *Slang.* to be quiet. **5. to pipe up.** to begin to play, sing, or speak, esp. in a loud, shrill voice. [Old English *pīpe* tube, musical wind instrument, going back to Latin *pīpāre* to chirp.]

pipe cleaner, tufted wire used esp. to clean the stem of a tobacco pipe.

pipe dream, fanciful notion or wish.

pipe·ful (pīp′fool′) *pl.,* **-fuls.** *n.* amount of tobacco sufficient to fill the bowl of a pipe.

From *Macmillan Dictionary*

EXERCISE 2. Find the answers to the following questions in your dictionary.

1. What is the origin of the word *silhouette*?
2. What is the meaning of *cf*?
3. Who was Chaliapin?
4. What are the possessive forms of the word *thou*?
5. What is the population of Irkutsk?
6. Where does the word *hocus-pocus* come from?
7. What are the subtle distinctions in meaning among the synonyms *trip, voyage, tour,* and *journey*?
8. What is *bossa nova*? Trace the word's etymology.
9. What does the abbreviation *IPA* stand for?
10. Who was Arachne?

THE OXFORD ENGLISH DICTIONARY

The *Oxford English Dictionary* (OED) is the historical dictionary of the English language. Its thirteen volumes contain over 500,000 separate definitions and almost 2 million example quotations. The OED lists all words that have come into the English language since 1150.

The *Shorter Oxford English Dictionary* is an abridged version of the OED. It contains approximately 40 percent of the words and citations that are in the complete dictionary. The following entry for *nice* is from the abridged version.

Nice (nəis), *a.* ME. [a. OF. *nice* :—L. *nescius* ignorant, f. *nescire*, f. *ne-* not (see NE) and *scire* to know.] **†1.** Foolish, stupid -1560. **†2.** Wanton, lascivious -1606. **†3.** Strange, rare -1555. **†4.** Tender, delicate, over-refined -1720. **†5.** Coy, (affectedly) modest; shy, reluctant -1676. **6.** Difficult to please or satisfy; fastidiously careful, precise, or punctilious; 'particular'. Now *rare* or *arch.* 1551. **7.** Requiring or involving great precision, accuracy, or minuteness 1513. **8.** Not readily apprehended, difficult to decide, determine, or distinguish; minutely or delicately precise 1513. **†9.** Slender, thin; unimportant, trivial -1604. **10. †a.** Critical, doubtful -1710. **b.** Delicate, needing tactful handling 1617. **11.** Able to discriminate in a high degree, finely discriminative 1586. **b.** Delicate in manipulation 1711. **12.** Minutely or carefully accurate; finely poised or adjusted 1599. **13.** Of food: Dainty, appetizing 1712. **14.** *colloq.* Agreeable; delightful 1769. **b.** *To look n.*, to have an agreeable, attractive, or pretty appearance 1793. **c.** Kind, considerate, or pleasant (to others) 1830. **d.** In ironical use. Also *n. and* 1846. **e.** In negative contexts: Refined, in good taste *c* 1860.

2. *L. L. L.* III. i. 24. *Ant. & Cl.* III. xiii. 180. **4.** He ..was of so n. and tender a composition, that a little rain or wind would disorder him CLARENDON. **5.** Ere ..The n. Morn on th' Indian steep From her cabin'd loop hole peep MILT. †Phr. *To make it n.*, to display reluctance, make a scruple -1677. *John* III. iv. 138. **6.** The Parliament is alwayes very n. and curious on this point 1661. Some people are more n. than wise COWPER. I should..not be too n. about the means 1887. **7.** N. philosophical experiments 1822. **8.** One of the nicest problems for a man to solve 1847. The nicer shades of meaning 1870. **9.** *Oth.* III. iii. 15. *Jul. C.* IV. iii. 8. **10.** 1 *Hen. IV*, IV. i. 48. **b.** The nicest political negociations 1777. **11.** A n. observer of mens actions and manners 1617. A n. pallate in good liquor had made my landlord a favourite companion 1755. A n. sense of elegance and form 1845. **12.** Despight his n. fence, and his actiue practise SHAKS. Weigh arguments in the nicest intellectual scales 1875. **13.** You must give us something very nice, for we are used to live well JANE AUSTEN. **14.** The n. long letter which I have..received from you JANE AUSTEN. How n. it must be to be able to get about in cars, omnibuses and railway trains again! 1897. **c.** 'Not n. of Master Enoch', said Dick T. HARDY. **d.** You'll be n. and ill in the morning D. JERROLD. Hence **Ni·cely** *adv.* **Ni·ceness.**

7

CAPITALIZATION AND PUNCTUATION

7 Capitalization and Punctuation

Capitalization and punctuation are often referred to as the mechanics of writing. The word *mechanics* implies that the uses of punctuation and such things as capital letters and abbreviations are purely "mechanical" — that is, that they arise from habit or convention. It is true that some rules of mechanics are merely conventional: for example, placing quotation marks around short works, using italics for long works, or using commas in dates and place names. Many elements of mechanics also perform the very important function of conveying meaning, however. For example, you will express your thoughts more precisely and also help your reader understand your writing if you end a complete thought with a period, signal a question with a question mark, place a colon before an example or list, or surround a nonessential clause with commas.

After you finish a piece of writing, remember to check very carefully the punctuation, capitalization, and other mechanics of your paper. This checking process is called *proofreading.*

7.a CAPITALIZATION

Capital letters identify and distinguish important words and abbreviations. They identify words beginning a sentence or a direct quotation as well as important words in titles. They distinguish proper nouns from common nouns and proper adjectives from common adjectives (see 1.a and 1.c). The opposite of a capital letter is a small, or lowercase, letter.

You will find that not everyone follows the advice on the

following pages to the letter. Publishers, writers, advertisers, and sign makers may use various manuals of style when deciding what to capitalize. The advice on the following pages, however, represents sensible and current trends. Your first goal should be to understand why you capitalize certain words and lowercase others. Your second goal should be to try to be *consistent*—to treat similar words and expressions in the same way. The more careful you are in writing, the more interested your audience will be in reading.

7.a.1 Capitalization of the pronoun I and the interjection O

Capitalize the pronoun *I* and the interjection *O*.

As **I** arrived at the auditorium, she had just begun to recite her poem.

"Your scent, **O** rose," she began dramatically, "is as sweet as a child's."

Do not capitalize the interjection *oh* unless it is the first word of a sentence.

"But, Carol—**o**h, it doesn't matter anyway," she hastened to say.

7.a.2 Capitalization of sentences

Capitalize the first word of every sentence, including the first word of a complete sentence that follows a colon.

Traditionally, a comedy ends with a marriage between the principal characters.
The rumor that came from the dugout was this: **T**wo outfielders were to be traded for a star pitcher.
Resolved: **N**o person shall be elected to the office of President more than twice.

Do not capitalize a sentence within parentheses that is contained within another sentence. Do capitalize a sentence in parentheses that stands by itself.

A major cotton-producing state in the antebellum South (**a***ntebellum* means "before the war") was Georgia. [No capital letter (or period) is needed.]

Webster's first dictionary encouraged a distinctive American spelling of English words. (**F**or instance, the English *honour* was replaced by the American *honor.*) [A capital letter and a period are needed.]

EXERCISE 1. Rewrite the following passage, correcting all errors in capitalization. (Try to find twenty errors.)

[1]today i discovered a new heroine—Oh, i had heard the name Amelia Earhart before, but i never knew very much about this great American's accomplishments. [2]earhart, who was born in 1898, accomplished many "firsts" in the history of flying: she was the first woman to make a solo flight across the Atlantic, the first woman to pilot a plane across the United States (In both directions), and the first woman to fly from Hawaii to the mainland. [3]she was also the first woman to receive the Distinguished Flying Cross. [4](this she received for her fifteen-hour solo Atlantic crossing.) [5]amelia Earhart (Or perhaps i should call her "Lady Lindy," the nickname associating her with record-breaking pilot Charles Lindbergh) was always ready to accept a challenge: she tested new aircraft and was a "barnstormer" in California. [6](during the early days of flying, "barnstorming," or stunt flying, was a popular entertainment at fairs and exhibitions throughout rural America.) [7]sadly, Earhart's last challenge ended in tragedy: in 1937, in an attempt to fly around the world, she and her copilot were lost near Howland Island in the Pacific Ocean. [8]no trace of them or their airplane was ever found. [9]Your inspiring example, o Amelia, i hope someday to follow. [10]i hope to be the first woman to make a dangerous and challenging flight to the moon or beyond.

7.a.3 Capitalization of direct quotations

Capitalize the first word of a direct quotation that is a complete sentence.

Do not capitalize a direct quotation that is a partial sentence.

Robert E. Lee once wrote, "**D**uty is the sublimest word in our language."

The ecologist reminded the audience to save "**t**he air, the water, the animals, and the trees."

Do not capitalize an indirect quotation. (An indirect quotation does not quote the person's exact words. It is often introduced by the word *that.*)

Article VI of the U.S. Constitution states that **a**ccused persons have the right to a speedy trial.

EXERCISE 2. Rewrite correctly each of the following sentences that has errors in capitalization. Some sentences contain no errors. (You may assume that all quotation marks are used properly.)

1. One line of Langston Hughes's poem "Harlem" asks, "what happens to a dream deferred?"
2. Thomas Jefferson wrote that all people have the right to "Life, liberty, and the pursuit of happiness."
3. Helen Keller said that One can never consent to creep when one feels an impulse to soar.
4. Ralph Waldo Emerson argued, "Nothing is at last sacred but the integrity of your own mind."
5. Anne Frank wrote, "laziness may appear attractive, but work gives satisfaction."
6. Abraham Lincoln said that Frederick Douglass was "the most meritorious man of the nineteenth century."
7. It was Golda Meir who said, "to deny oneself various comforts is also easier in talk than in deed."
8. Marian Anderson once said that where there is money, there is fighting.
9. The complete line from Edna St. Vincent Millay's poem is "My candle burns at both its ends."
10. Anaïs Nin wrote, "one handles truths like dynamite."

7.a.4 Capitalization of proper nouns

Capitalize a proper noun.

Do not capitalize a common noun unless it is the first word of a sentence.

Proper nouns	**Common nouns**
England	**c**ountry
Emily **D**ickinson	**p**oet
***M**oby **D**ick*	**n**ovel
Mississippi **R**iver	a mighty **r**iver

In reviewing the following sections, remember to capitalize only the important words (excluding articles, conjunctions, and prepositions of under five letters) in proper nouns of several words.

1. names of individuals

John **F.** **K**ennedy	**B**abe **R**uth
Katherine **H**epburn	**U**ncle **S**am
Grandma **M**oses	**A**thena

2. titles of individuals

Capitalize titles used before a proper name.

President **L**incoln	**C**ongresswoman **R**ankin
Queen **E**lizabeth II	**C**ardinal **C**ooke
Chief **T**ecumseh	**G**eneral **M**acArthur

Do not capitalize titles used alone or following a proper name unless you wish to show respect or to indicate a high official. For example, when referring to the President of the United States, always capitalize the title. Do not capitalize titles used as common nouns to refer to a general class or type.

The Republican **S**enator from Wyoming	*but*	the life of a **s**enator
Tecumseh, **C**hief of the Shawnees	*but*	The **c**hiefs bargained with each other.

In general, capitalize the title of a family relationship used with or in place of a proper name. Do not capitalize the title if a possessive is used before it (unless the title is considered part of the name).

Dear **C**ousin Jenny,	*but*	My **c**ousin Jenny arrived late.
Did you ask **M**other?	*but*	my husband's **m**other
Won't you write, **U**ncle?	*and*	My **U**ncle Carlos visited.[1]

---

[1] Here *Uncle* is considered part of the name and is therefore capitalized even though it is preceded by the possessive *my*.

3. names of ethnic groups, national groups, and languages

Americans
Chinese
Afro-**A**mericans
Apache
Latin
Russian

4. organizations, institutions, political parties and their members, firms

Knights of **C**olumbus
Ohio **S**tate **U**niversity
Senate
Supreme **C**ourt
Republican party
a **D**emocrat
General **M**otors
United **A**irlines

Do not capitalize common nouns such as *court* or *university* unless they are part of a proper noun. The word *party* is not capitalized.

She visited two members of the **S**upreme **C**ourt.
Lawyers spend a great deal of time in **c**ourt.

5. monuments, bridges, buildings

Tomb of the **U**nknown **S**oldier
Golden **G**ate **B**ridge
Empire **S**tate **B**uilding
Sears **T**ower

6. trade names

Coke
Wheaties
Comet
Sanka

Do not capitalize the common noun that follows the trade name.

Crest **t**oothpaste
Lipton **t**ea

7. documents, awards, laws

Declaration of **I**ndependence
Treaty of **V**ersailles
Nobel **P**rize
Oscar
Sherman **A**ntitrust **A**ct
Boyle's **L**aw

8. geographical terms

Capitalize the important words in the names of continents, countries, states, counties, cities, bodies of water, topographical features, regions, and streets.

Asia
United **S**tates
Kentucky
Essex **C**ounty
Denver
Pacific **O**cean
Snake **R**iver
Lake **E**rie
Rocky **M**ountains
Grand **C**anyon
Mojave **D**esert
Long **I**sland
Tropic of **C**ancer
Southeast **A**sia
Pennsylvania **A**venue
Main **S**treet

Do not capitalize such terms as *river* and *street* when these words are used in the plural following more than one name.

the Ohio and Mississippi **r**ivers
First and Main **s**treets

9. planets and other heavenly bodies

Jupiter
Venus
Milky **W**ay
Big **D**ipper

Do not capitalize *sun* and *moon*. *Earth* is capitalized only when it is used in conjunction with the names of the other planets. *Earth* is never capitalized when it is used with the definite article, *the*.

The **s**un was shining today, and the **m**oon is full tonight.
Mercury, Venus, and **E**arth are the planets closest to the sun.
We looked from the sky above to the **e**arth below.

10. compass points

Capitalize *north*, *east*, *south*, and *west* when they refer to a specific area of the country or of the world or when they are part of a proper name. Do not capitalize them when they merely indicate direction.

the **S**outh *but* **s**outh Florida
the **E**ast **C**oast *but* the **e**ast coast of Maine
North **D**akota *but* **n**orth Texas

NOTE: You may sometimes see compass points capitalized when they are used as adjectives, but that is not preferred usage.

southern cooking
western rodeo
eastern cities
northern winters

11. ships, planes, trains, spacecraft

U.S.S. ***C****onstitution* — ***A****ir* ***F****orce* ***O****ne*
P*hiladelphia* ***F****lyer* — ***A****pollo I*

12. historical events, eras, calendar items

Boston **T**ea **P**arty	**T**uesday
Korean **W**ar	**J**anuary
Renaissance	**T**hanksgiving **D**ay

Do not capitalize a historical period when it refers to a general span of time.

Columbus discovered America in the **f**ifteenth **c**entury.
The Beatles became popular in the **s**ixties.

Do not capitalize the names of the seasons (*spring, summer, autumn, fall, winter*).

13. literary, artistic, and philosophical movements and their followers

Impressionism	**S**ymbolist
Existentialists	**S**toicism

Do not capitalize these words if they are used in a general sense rather than a specific historical sense.

The philosopher Zeno founded the school of **S**toicism.
She faced her problems with great **s**toicism.

14. religious terms

Capitalize names of religions, denominations, and their adherents; words referring to the Deity; and religious books and events.

Judaism	the **H**oly **S**pirit
Protestantism	**K**oran
the **C**atholic **C**hurch	**B**ible
Church of England	**E**aster
the **L**ord	**Y**om **K**ippur

Do not capitalize such words as *god* or *rabbi* when they are used as common nouns to refer to a general class or type.

Greek mythology includes fascinating tales of **g**ods and **g**oddesses.
The **r**abbi wanted to build a new synagogue.

15. school courses

Capitalize only those school courses that are languages or that are titles of specific courses rather than general names of subjects.

English	*but*	**m**ath
The **T**wentieth **C**entury	*but*	**h**istory
Economics 101	*but*	**e**conomics

EXERCISE 3. From each pair of phrases below, select the one phrase that is correctly capitalized.

1. a) the Golden Gate bridge
   b) the Golden Gate Bridge
2. a) the Democratic Party
   b) the Democratic party
3. a) Good friday
   b) Good Friday
4. a) the Hawaiian Islands
   b) the Hawaiian islands
5. a) the battle of Wounded Knee
   b) the Battle of Wounded Knee
6. a) the Lincoln Memorial
   b) the Lincoln memorial
7. a) the Daughters of the American Revolution
   b) the daughters of the American revolution
8. a) I agree with you, Mother, about Father's present.
   b) I agree with you, mother, about father's present.
9. a) the Volstead act
   b) the Volstead Act
10. a) The spacecraft returned from Mars to Earth.
    b) The spacecraft returned from Mars to earth.
11. a) Zeus and the other Gods of mount Olympus
    b) Zeus and the other gods of Mount Olympus
12. a) Tuskegee Institute, a College in Alabama
    b) Tuskegee Institute, a college in Alabama
13. a) Super Bright toothpaste
    b) Super Bright Toothpaste
14. a) the rock 'n' roll of the fifties
    b) the rock 'n' roll of the Fifties
15. a) Martin Van Buren, the eighth President
    b) Martin Van Buren, the eighth president

16. a) the Dodgers and other baseball teams on the West Coast
    b) the Dodgers and other baseball teams on the west coast
17. a) the President's Mother
    b) the President's mother
18. a) the Ten Commandments, given in the Bible
    b) the ten commandments, given in the bible
19. a) *apollo XI*, the first spacecraft to land people on the Moon
    b) *Apollo XI*, the first spacecraft to land people on the moon
20. a) the corner of Hollywood and Vine Streets
    b) the corner of Hollywood and Vine streets

EXERCISE 4. Rewrite the following sentences correctly, adding or eliminating capital letters as necessary.

1. The puritans were protestants in England.
2. They felt that the church of england followed practices that were not approved by god or the bible.
3. Those puritans who wanted to leave the church of england were called Separatists.
4. Under elizabeth I, queen of england, two Separatists were executed, and many were imprisoned.
5. A Group from a Village named scrooby immigrated to holland.
6. Unhappy there, they decided to travel to north America and to settle in virginia.
7. They received permission from the london company to settle in that Company's territory in virginia.
8. Their Ship, the *mayflower*, was blown North and landed on cape cod.
9. The puritans named their Settlement plymouth; the Site of their landing is now called plymouth rock.
10. These Settlers, now called pilgrims, drew up the Document known as the mayflower compact.
11. Only half of the group survived the first new england Winter.
12. The pilgrims were aided by the Native inhabitants (who had mistakenly been called "indians" by the European explorers).
13. In the Fall of 1621 the pilgrims held a celebration (now a National Holiday, thanksgiving) to give thanks to god.
14. They feasted on north American turkey, maize, and succotash.
15. Other puritans in england sailed West across the atlantic and settled at massachusetts bay colony.

16. One was roger williams, who believed that king charles should not grant Charters without first buying the land from the native inhabitants.
17. Fearful that williams would anger king charles, the puritans banished him.
18. Soon after, the puritans banished anne hutchinson, Sister-In-Law of reverend John Wheelwright.
19. Hutchinson openly criticized many Ministers and claimed to have spoken with god.
20. She joined williams in rhode island, a refuge for those who "separated" from the puritans.

EXERCISE 5. Rewrite each of the following sentences correctly, adding capital letters that are needed and eliminating those that are incorrect.

1. At the end of the Eighteenth Century, spain controlled the Mouth of the Mississippi river and the vast territory stretching West.
2. The Area, once owned by france, was called louisiana after Louis XIV, king of france.
3. With the treaty of san ildefonso in 1800, emperor napoleon bonaparte regained the land for france.
4. The French government monopolized The Mississippi river and the Port of new orleans.
5. Although the U.S. Constitution did not explicitly authorize land purchase, president jefferson planned to acquire the land owned by the french.
6. The president instructed robert r. livingston to buy new orleans.
7. Livingston was startled when he was offered the entire Territory.
8. Apparently, napoleon was in need of money for his military exploits in europe.
9. New england residents, most of whom belonged to the federalists (a political party), criticized the proposed Purchase.
10. In the senate the debate between federalists and republicans was fierce.
11. The Purchase was finally approved, and the house of representatives appropriated the money.
12. The united states paid for the louisiana purchase with a check

for $15 million and a promise to grant citizenship to louisiana's roman catholics.

13. The president then sent meriwether lewis and william clark to explore the new Territory.
14. The explorers traveled up the missouri river and crossed the rocky mountains.
15. Sacajawea, nicknamed "the bird woman," acted as their Guide and Interpreter.
16. A member of the shoshone tribe, sacajawea had been captured and sold into slavery at an Early Age.
17. During the Expedition she was reunited with her Tribe, who lived by the salmon river in idaho.
18. The expedition continued West down the snake and columbia rivers to the pacific ocean.
19. This Territory was also explored by captain robert gray.
20. The pacific fur company's settlements in this area of Western north America later became the State of oregon.

7.a.5 Capitalization of proper adjectives

Capitalize proper adjectives; do not capitalize common adjectives.

Proper adjectives are adjectives formed from proper nouns (see 1.c.6). Common adjectives refer to a general class of things.

Capitalize the following categories of proper adjectives:

1. formed from names of people

Shakespearean
Newtonian
Lutheran
Jeffersonian
Hitchcockian
Calvinist
Machiavellian

2. formed from place names and names of national and ethnic groups

Roman
European
Asian
Canadian
Swedish
Afro-American
Chicano

3. **formed from political and religious terms**

Democratic[1]	**I**slamic
Congressional	**J**ewish
Communist	**P**rotestant

4. **formed from names of literary, artistic, and philosophical movements**

Symbolist	**E**xistentialist
Classical[2]	**R**omantic

Do not capitalize words that are normally proper adjectives when they are considered part of a compound noun. If you are unsure about whether to capitalize a particular adjective, check your dictionary.

french fries	**v**enetian blinds
manila envelope	**i**ndian summer

Do not capitalize hyphenated prefixes or suffixes such as *anti-*, *-elect*, *-born*, *ex-*, or *un-* attached to proper nouns and proper adjectives.

ex-**P**resident	**a**nti-**C**ommunist
President-**e**lect	**p**ost-**C**lassical
un-**A**merican	**A**tlanta-**b**orn

EXERCISE 6. Correct all errors in capitalization of nouns and adjectives in the following sentences. Rewrite each sentence, adding capital letters that are needed and eliminating those that are incorrect.

1. John Calvin (1509–1564), a french protestant, founded the religious movement called Calvinism.
2. In New England the Intellectual revolt against calvinist beliefs produced the unitarian Religion.
3. The famous unitarian minister William Ellery Channing preached the value of "christian" kindness and mercy.
4. The unitarian Church attracted affluent and intellectual ex-puritans in America.
5. The introduction of Romanticism, a european Artistic and

[1]Terms such as *Democratic* and *Communist* are capitalized only when they refer to a party rather than to a political philosophy.

[2] Terms such as *Classical* and *Romantic* are capitalized only when they refer to a specific movement.

Philosophic movement, also had a strong effect on american intellectuals.

6. The ideas of german philosophers and english poets spread throughout the New England states.
7. Ralph Waldo Emerson, an Ex-Unitarian, was a romanticist.
8. He and other residents of Concord, Massachusetts, formed the transcendental Club.
9. Both unitarian and romantic philosophies formed the basis of Transcendentalism.
10. Transcendentalism also owed much to the quaker religion and to oriental ideas.
11. The Transcendentalists, like the Unitarians, rejected the calvinists' conception of God.
12. Margaret Fuller edited *The Dial*, a transcendentalist publication.
13. It was salem-born Elizabeth Peabody, a relative of Nathaniel Hawthorne, who published *The Dial*.
14. Henry David Thoreau moved to a cabin on Walden Pond to prove the emersonian concept of self-reliance.
15. Thoreau wrote *Walden* as Indian Summer turned to crisp autumn, to icy winter, and to mild spring.
16. The name jacksonian democracy was given to the political movement associated with President Andrew Jackson.
17. Jackson, a congressional leader from Tennessee, stressed simplicity in government.
18. The poet Walt Whitman used transcendentalist ideas in his major work, *Leaves of Grass*.
19. The pre–civil war edition of *Leaves of Grass* went unnoticed in north America but was well received in latin american nations.
20. Later editions of *Leaves of Grass* brought the Brooklyn poet to the transcendentalists' attention.

7.a.6 Capitalization of titles of works

Capitalize the first and last words and all important words in titles of works.

Capitalize prepositions if they are five or more letters. Also capitalize words that are part of a verb (as in *call* **up** or *sit* **down**). In general, do not capitalize articles or conjunctions unless they are first or last words. (For a discussion of quotation marks and italics in titles of works, see 7.l.2 and 7.m.1).

To *the* **Lighthouse**	the **Washington Post**
"**Bartleby** the **Scrivener**"	**Bill** of **Rights**
Gone *with the* **Wind**	"**America** the **Beautiful**"

Capitalize articles (*a, an, the*) at the beginning of a title only when they are part of the title itself. It is preferred usage not to capitalize (nor to italicize) articles preceding the title of a newspaper or a periodical. In general, do not capitalize (or italicize) the word *magazine* following the title of a periodical.

"**The** Open Boat"	*but*	**the** *New York Times*
"**A** Dirge"	*but*	She has **a** *Time* magazine.

7.a.7 Capitalization of abbreviations

Capitalize abbreviations of proper nouns and proper adjectives.

Also capitalize the abbreviations A.M., P.M., A.D., and B.C. (See 7.b for a complete discussion of abbreviations.)

A.M.	**UNESCO**	**J**r.	**U.S.A.**
P.M.	**NAACP**	**M**rs.	**W. V**a.
A.D.	**P**h.**D.**	**S**t.	**M**ar.
B.C.	**D**r.	**C**orp.	**M**on.

EXERCISE 7. Correct all errors in capitalization of titles of works in the following sentences. Rewrite each sentence, adding capital letters that are needed and eliminating those that are incorrect.

1. Pearl S. Buck, who wrote *the good earth*, won the Nobel Prize for Literature in 1938.
2. Ernest Hemingway, the Nobel Prize-winning novelist, wrote "a clean, well-lighted place" and other short stories.
3. N. Scott Momaday won the Pulitzer Prize in fiction in 1969 for *house made of dawn.*
4. In 1945 Karl Shapiro won the Pulitzer Prize for his collection *v-letter and other poems*.
5. Gwendolyn Brooks, who won the Pulitzer Prize in 1950, wrote the poem "the bean eaters."

6. Among the Pulitzer Prize-winning works on a historical subject is *the american revolution*, written by Charles Howard McIlwain.
7. The Pulitzer Prize was won by the *washington post* in 1973 for meritorious public service.
8. This prize has been won by the *new york times* on three occasions.
9. In 1977 the *ladies' home journal* presented its Woman of the Year Award to opera singer Marian Anderson.
10. Anwar Sadat was named Man of the Year by *Time* Magazine in 1978.
11. Aaron Copland won the Pulitzer Prize in music in 1945 for *appalachian spring.*
12. In 1976 Stevie Wonder won a Grammy for his album *songs in the key of life.*
13. Among the songs that have won Oscars are "the way we were" and "you light up my life."
14. Films that have won the Academy Award include *one flew over the cuckoo's nest* and *from here to eternity.*
15. Ellen Burstyn won a Tony for her performance in the play *same time, next year.*
16. Opera singer Clamma Dale received a Tony nomination for her role in the revival of *porgy and bess.*
17. Rita Moreno won an Oscar for *west side story*, a Tony for *the ritz*, and an Emmy for her contributions to *the muppet show.*
18. Among the Emmy winners for the 1976–1977 television season were *roots* and *eleanor and franklin.*
19. Andrew Wyeth, the painter of *christina's world*, received honorary doctorates from many universities.
20. Mary Cassatt (1845–1926), whose paintings include *a cup of tea* and *at the opera*, was honored at the Salon of Paris.

Before you start Review Exercises A and B, you may want to review the rules in the chart on the following page.

REVIEW EXERCISE A. From each pair of phrases and sentences below, select the one item that is correctly capitalized.

1. a) the President and i discussed the issues.
   b) The President and I discussed the issues.
2. a) hanuka
   b) Hanuka

SUMMARY OF CAPITALIZATION RULES

capitalize	*do not capitalize*	*for further instruction, see*
Your color, **O** Spring, is green.	"But—**oh**, it doesn't matter anyway."	7.a.1
He told us to turn to page 506 for the rules of capitalization. (**There** was no page 506!)	He told us to turn to page 506 (**there** was no page 506) for the rules of capitalization.	7.a.2
She said, "**He** liked it very much."	She said that **he** liked it very much.	7.a.3
Grandma Moses	My **g**randmother is eighty-five years old.	7.a.4
Surgeon General	My **s**urgeon advised me.	7.a.4
Afro-Americans; **J**apanese; **I**talian		7.a.4
Ohio State **U**niversity	a **u**niversity in Ohio	7.a.4
Joslyn **A**rt **M**useum	the **a**rt **m**useum on the corner	7.a.4
Dial soap; **C**rest toothpaste		7.a.4
the U.S. **C**onstitution	Our club drew up a **c**onstitution.	7.a.4
Atlantic **O**cean; **T**imes **S**quare; **E**ighth **S**treet	the **s**quare at the end of the **s**treet.	7.a.4
Jupiter; **V**enus; **M**ars	**s**un; **e**arth; **m**oon	7.a.4
the **M**idwest; the **S**outh; **N**orth **A**merica	**s**outh of the city	7.a.4
*Air **F**orce **O**ne; **S**putnik IV*		7.a.4
Civil **W**ar	The two countries were engaged in **w**ar.	7.a.4
Koran; **E**aster Sunday; **H**anuka		7.a.4
German; **A**rt **H**istory II	**m**ath; **e**conomics; **h**istory	7.a.4
the **F**rench language	**f**rench fries	7.a.5
***S**omething **H**appened;* "**P**aul's **C**ase"		7.a.6
Leslie Schmidt, **P**h.**D**.	She received her **d**octorate in English.	7.a.7

3. a) Mark Twain said that One of the striking differences between a cat and a lie is that a cat has only nine lives.
   b) Mark Twain said that one of the striking differences between a cat and a lie is that a cat has only nine lives.

4. a) the Salvation Army
   b) the Salvation army
5. a) America, o America
   b) America, O America
6. a) Yale university
   b) Yale University
7. a) the Conservative party
   b) the Conservative Party
8. a) a college in the Midwest
   b) a College in the midwest
9. a) the Transamerica Building
   b) the Transamerica building
10. a) Countee Cullen said, "good poetry is a lofty thought beautifully expressed."
    b) Countee Cullen said, "Good poetry is a lofty thought beautifully expressed."
11. a) Maxwell House coffee
    b) Maxwell House Coffee
12. a) General Douglas MacArthur
    b) general Douglas MacArthur
13. a) Abigail Adams was the wife of President John Adams. (She was also the mother of President John Quincy Adams.)
    b) Abigail Adams was the wife of President John Adams. (She was also the Mother of President John Quincy Adams.)
14. a) De Kooning is an Abstract Expressionist painter.
    b) De Kooning is an abstract expressionist painter.
15. a) The Mexican War had many causes: the annexation of Texas and the dispute over Texas' boundaries were among them.
    b) The Mexican War had many causes: The annexation of Texas and the dispute over Texas' boundaries were among them.
16. a) Flavia Rivera, president of our club
    b) Flavia Rivera, President of our club
17. a) why, oh why
    b) why, Oh why
18. a) The Marines promise to defend our country from "the halls of Montezuma to the shores of Tripoli."
    b) The Marines promise to defend our country from "the halls of montezuma to the shores of tripoli."
19. a) *Death of a Salesman*
    b) *Death Of A Salesman*
20. a) *Succotash* is an Algonquian word (to be precise, it is Narra-

gansett) referring to a dish of lima beans and corn.

b) *Succotash* is an Algonquian word (To be precise, it is Narragansett) referring to a dish of lima beans and corn.

REVIEW EXERCISE B. From each pair of phrases and sentences below, select the one item that is correctly capitalized.

1. a) Maria Rios, ph.d.
   b) Maria Rios, Ph.D.
2. a) the *Christian Science Monitor*
   b) The *Christian Science Monitor*
3. a) *To Kill A Mockingbird*
   b) *To Kill a Mockingbird*
4. a) the Sun, the Moon, and the nine planets
   b) the sun, the moon, and the nine planets
5. a) the *Niña*, the *Pinta*, and the *Santa María*
   b) the *niña*, the *pinta*, and the *santa maría*
6. a) the San Diego and San Bernadino freeways
   b) the San Diego and San Bernadino Freeways
7. a) mardi gras
   b) Mardi Gras
8. a) freudian ideas
   b) Freudian ideas
9. a) Bryce Canyon National Park
   b) Bryce Canyon national park
10. a) the planet Mars, named for the Roman God
    b) the planet Mars, named for the Roman god
11. a) southern hospitality
    b) Southern hospitality
12. a) Pre-Revolutionary period
    b) pre-Revolutionary period
13. a) Rockaway Peninsula in Queens County
    b) Rockaway peninsula in Queens county
14. a) Houston, a city in the Southwest
    b) Houston, a city in the southwest
15. a) American History II and math
    b) American History II and Math
16. a) a Buddhist temple
    b) a buddhist temple
17. a) If spring is here, can summer be far behind?
    b) If Spring is here, can Summer be far behind?

18. a) the Presidential elections of the sixties
    b) the Presidential elections of the Sixties
19. a) East of the Hudson River
    b) east of the Hudson River
20. a) "Where I Lived, and What I lived for" by Henry D. Thoreau
    b) "Where I Lived, and What I Lived For" by Henry D. Thoreau

7.b ABBREVIATIONS

Abbreviations are shortened forms of words. Abbreviations are often more familiar than the words that they represent. They save space and time and prevent unnecessary wordiness. For instance, "800 B.C." is more concise and easier to write than "800 years before the birth of Christ."

Capitalize all abbreviations of words that are themselves capitalized. Place a period after most abbreviations (see 7.d). Use only one period if an abbreviation occurs at the end of a sentence that would ordinarily take a period of its own. If an abbreviation occurs at the end of a sentence that ends with a question mark or an exclamation point, you must use both the period and the second mark of punctuation.

She arrived at 7 P**.**M**.**
Did she arrive at 7 P**.**M**.?**
She arrived at 7 P**.**M**.!**

7.b.1 Abbreviations of titles of people

Use abbreviations for some personal titles.

Titles such as *Mrs.*, *Mr.*, *Sr.*, and *Jr.* and those indicating professions and academic degrees (*Dr.*, *M.D.*, *B.A.*) are almost always abbreviated. *Ms.* and *Miss* are not abbreviations, although *Ms.* is followed by a period. Titles of government and military officials and members of the clergy are frequently abbreviated when used before a name.

Mrs. Robert Kennedy
Mr. Fred Astaire
Ms. Gloria Steinem
Gov. Ella Grasso
Sen. Everett M. Dirksen
Dr. Margaret Mead

Sammy Davis, **Jr.**
Simone Yang, **B. S.**
Consuela Melo, **M.D.**
Col. June E. Williams
Rev. Billy Graham
Fr. John Reilly

7.b.2 Abbreviations of businesses, organizations, agencies

Use abbreviations for names of business firms, organizations, and government agencies.

IBM	**UN**	**FBI**
RCA	**NCAA**	**ACTION**
NOW	**Y.W.C.A.**	**FCC**

Usually, you should spell out such names the first time they appear in a piece of writing, giving the abbreviation in parentheses after the name. You can then use the abbreviation alone in subsequent references.

The European Economic Community (EEC) was founded in 1957 by six countries. Three more countries joined the EEC in 1973.

NOTE: Although most abbreviations require periods, most abbreviations of businesses, organizations, and government agencies do not take periods. Acronyms — abbreviations that are pronounced as a word — and certain other abbreviations in common use also do not take periods. If you are unsure whether to use periods with a particular abbreviation, check your dictionary.

7.b.3 Abbreviations of places

Spell out the names of countries, states, and streets in regular prose writing.

When writing addresses, you may abbreviate these names, although it is better not to do so in business letters.

U.S.A.	Butte, **Mont.**	1763 Monument **Ave.**
U.K.	Raleigh, **N.C.**	484 **W.** Main **St.**

The names of most states of the United States may be abbreviated in two forms, as shown in the following list. The second form, consisting of two capital letters with no periods, should be used only when the ZIP code is also used.

Alabama Ala. AL
Alaska Alas. AK
Arizona Ariz. AZ
Arkansas Ark. AR
California Calif. CA
Colorado Colo. CO
Connecticut Conn. CT
Delaware Del. DE
Florida Fla. FL
Georgia Ga. GA
Hawaii HI
Idaho ID
Illinois Ill. IL
Indiana Ind. IN
Iowa IA
Kansas Kans. KS
Kentucky Ky. KY
Louisiana La. LA
Maine ME
Maryland Md. MD
Massachusetts Mass. MA
Michigan Mich. MI
Minnesota Minn. MN
Mississippi Miss. MS
Missouri Mo. MO
Montana Mont. MT
Nebraska Nebr. NB
Nevada Nev. NV
New Hampshire N.H. NH
New Jersey N.J. NJ
New Mexico N. Mex. NM
New York N.Y. NY
North Carolina N.C. NC
North Dakota N.Dak. ND
Ohio O. OH
Oklahoma Okla. OK
Oregon Oreg. OR
Pennsylvania Pa. PA
Rhode Island R.I. RI
South Carolina S.C. SC
South Dakota S.Dak. SD
Tennessee Tenn. TN
Texas Tex. TX
Utah UT
Vermont Vt. VT
Virginia Va. VA
Washington Wash. WA
West Virginia W.Va. WV
Wisconsin Wis. WI
Wyoming Wyo. WY

7.b.4 Abbreviations of dates and times

Do not abbreviate the names of months and days of the week in regular prose writing.

Certain abbreviations related to dates and times are always acceptable, however. These abbreviations are listed below.

A.D. *(anno Domini)*, "in the year of the Lord"; placed before the date—*A.D. 66*

B.C. (before Christ); placed after the date—*336 B.C.*

A.M. *(ante meridiem)*, "before noon"
P.M. *(post meridiem)*, "after noon"

7.b.5 Abbreviations of units of measure

You may abbreviate units of measure in scientific and statistical writing.

Do not abbreviate units of measure in prose writing.

English system		Metric system	
ft.	foot	cg	centigram
gal.	gallon	cl	centiliter
in.	inch	cm	centimeter
lb.	pound	g	gram
mi.	mile	kg	kilogram
oz.	ounce	km	kilometer
pt.	pint	l	liter
qt.	quart	m	meter
tbsp.	tablespoon	mg	milligram
tsp.	teaspoon	ml	milliliter
yd.	yard	mm	millimeter

AVOIDING ERRORS WITH ABBREVIATIONS

Do not misuse or overuse abbreviations in formal prose.

NOT Amy Lowell was b. in Brookline, Mass., in 1874. She was the leader of a no. of Am. and Brit. poets who called themselves the Imagists. Two of the most impt. beliefs of the Imagists were that poets must use the lang. of common speech and be free to choose even the most ordinary subj. matter.

BUT Amy Lowell was **born** in Brookline, **Massachusetts**, in 1874. She was the leader of a **number** of **American** and **British** poets who called themselves the Imagists. Two of the most **important** beliefs of the Imagists were that poets must use the **language** of common speech and be free to choose even the most ordinary **subject** matter.

7.b.6 Latin abbreviations

Use the correct abbreviations for common Latin expressions.

Most Latin abbreviations are italicized (underlined), but a few, such as the three below, are so commonly used that they need no italics.

etc. *(et cetera)*, "and the rest"
We learned the marks of punctuation—commas, periods, exclamation points, parentheses, **etc.**

i.e. (*id est*), "that is"
It has not been proved that speech is a natural function—**i.e.**, that our vocal chords were designed for speech as our legs were designed for walking.

e.g. (*exempli gratia*),"for example"
Some abbreviations (**e.g.**, *gym* as an abbreviation for *gymnasium*) need no period at the end.

EXERCISE 8. Rewrite the following paragraph, eliminating all abbreviations—except for the O. in O. Henry. (You should find ten errors.)

[1]Although best known for his Xmas story "The Gift of the Magi," O. Henry also wrote many stories based upon his personal experience of the criminal underworld. [2]One of Am.'s most prolific writers of short stories, O. Henry was sentenced to five yrs. in a fed. prison for embezzling funds from the First Nat. Bank in Austin, TX. [3]A no. of O. Henry's most popular stories were written during his imprisonment in Columbus, O. [4]After serving three yrs. and three mo. he was released. [5]O. Henry died in 1910.

EXERCISE 9. Match the abbreviations in the left column with the words they stand for in the right column.

1. Rd.	a. Sweden
2. ITT	b. square
3. Swed.	c. association
4. co.	d. Road
5. lat.	e. dialect
6. sq.	f. obsolete
7. assoc.	g. International Telephone and Telegraph
8. dial.	h. New Testament
9. NT	i. latitude
10. obs.	j. company

7.c NUMBERS AND NUMERALS

Some numbers are spelled out in writing, and some are expressed in figures. Numbers expressed in words are called numbers; numbers expressed in figures are called numerals.

7.c.1 Numbers (spelled out)

In general, in prose spell out cardinal and ordinal numbers that can be written in one or two words and numbers that occur at the beginning of a sentence.

The Senate consists of **one hundred** members – **two** senators from each of the **fifty** states.
Five thousand people were at the concert.
The building is **sixty-eight** feet tall.

Wisconsin was the **thirtieth** state to be admitted to the Union.
John Adams was the **second** President; John Quincy Adams, the **sixth.**

7.c.2 Numerals (figures)

Use figures to express numbers of more than two words.

Use the comma in numerals that have more than three digits (except in dates, addresses, and references [see 7.g.5]).

The Homestead Act allowed farmers to claim **160** acres of land.
The present area of the United States is **3,615,122** square miles.
The present area of the United States is roughly **3,600,000** square miles.
The Civil War ended in **1865.**
The address of the White House is **1600** Pennsylvania Avenue.

NOTE: Large numbers in the millions and billions are often written as a numeral followed by the word *million* or *billion.* Do not place a hyphen between the numeral and the word.

The present area of the United States is roughly **3.6 million** square miles.

Do not mix numbers and numerals in the same sentence. Use all numerals, even though you might spell one out if it appeared alone.

The House of Representatives consists of **435** members; these **435** are reapportioned every **10** years. [In a sentence where it was the only number, *10* would appear as *ten.*]

I placed **116th** in the competition; my sister placed **43rd.** [In a sentence where it was the only number, *43rd* would appear as *forty-third.*]

7.c.3 Numerals for money, decimals, and percentages

In general, use figures to express amounts of money, decimals, and percentages.

Also use figures to express measurements in statistical writing. There is more than one correct way to express an amount of money, a fraction, or a percentage. If you decide to spell out dollars and cents or to use fractions instead of decimal points, use the *same* notation throughout your sentence, paragraph, or paper. Be consistent.

$398,000,000 *or* **398** million dollars
$19.50
$.86 *or* **86¢** *or* **86** cents
2.5 kilograms *or* **2$^{1}/_{2}$** kilograms
57% *or* **57** percent *or* **.57**
Use **3.14159** for *pi*.

EXERCISE 10. Rewrite the following sentences correcting all errors in the use of numbers and numerals.

1. Higher player salaries and ticket prices have not hurt professional sports 1 bit.
2. The average salary in the National Football League has more than doubled in the last 14 years.
3. Some athletes earn over two hundred thousand dollars a year.
4. In 1929 baseball salaries accounted for thirty-five point two percent of the costs of running a team.
5. Today, baseball salaries account for twenty-six percent of the costs of running a team.

6. In 1976 (the 92nd anniversary of the World Series games), only eight out of 24 baseball teams made a profit.
7. 700,000 admission tickets were sold to the San Francisco Giants' baseball fans during a losing year.
8. In a winning year, one point seven million fans came to see the San Francisco Giants play ball.
9. Television advertisers for the World Series games pay an average of $30,000 for 1 second of commercial time.
10. As many as 72-million people may watch a single World Series game on television.

7.c.4 Numerals for dates and times

Use figures to express years, days of the month, and references to time using A.M. or P.M.

The First Continental Congress met on September **5, 1774.**
The President was scheduled to meet the ambassador at **3:15 P.M.**
The President was scheduled to meet the ambassador at approximately **three o'clock.**

NOTE: Spell out the names of historical periods.

the Gay **Nineties**
the **seventeenth century**
the **twenties**

7.c.5 Numerals for addresses

In general, use figures to express numbered streets and avenues over ten; spell them out if they are ten or under.

111th Street
12th Avenue

Third Avenue
Ninth Street

Use figures to express house, apartment, and room numbers.

526 West 111th Street, **6**-D
18 East 12th Avenue

866 Third Avenue
52 South Ninth Street, Room **8**

7.c.6 Numerals for references

Use figures for page, line, act, and scene numbers.

Numbers and numerals are also used in footnotes and bibliographies (see 16.k).

Look on pages **9** and **24** for references to André Watts.
Read lines **360–414** in Book Four of the poem.
We performed Act **5,** Scenes **1** and **2,** of the school play.

EXERCISE 11. Rewrite the following sentences, correcting all errors in the use of numbers and numerals.

1. According to the U.S. Department of Labor, in nineteen hundred and seventy-two 3 percent of America's dentists were women.
2. These data were first published in nineteen hundred and seventy-three.
3. 96 percent of all American dental hygienists are women.
4. Out of every 150 physicians, eighteen are women.
5. 1 in every 20 veterinarians is a woman.

EXERCISE 12. Rewrite the following sentences, correcting all errors in the use of numbers and numerals.

1. In 1960 there were ninety-seven point one males for every hundred females.
2. The number of males for every hundred females dropped by 2 during the 60s.
3. The population of Native Americans increased over fifty percent in the 1960s.
4. In 1973 there were six thousand, five hundred and sixty-seven Native Americans on the Hopi reservation in Arizona.
5. One out of every 10 Americans is over 65.

7.d PERIODS

Use a period at the end of a sentence, in initials and abbreviations, and as a decimal point in writing numerals.

Place a period at the end of a declarative sentence, or statement, a polite command, or a statement including an indirect question. (See 2.u for a discussion of the different kinds of sentences.)

> At first Bartleby did an extraordinary quantity of writing. [declarative sentence] —Herman Melville
>
> "Go to the next room and tell Nippers to come to me." [polite command] —Herman Melville
>
> She asked him if he had ever read Melville. [indirect question]

Place a period at the end of a sentence in parentheses if it stands by itself. Do not place a period at the end of a sentence in parentheses if it is contained within another sentence. (See 7.n.)

> Pennsylvania is one of four states officially called commonwealths. (The other three are Kentucky, Massachusetts, and Virginia.)
>
> The Amish are a group of the Pennsylvania Dutch (the Pennsylvania Dutch are actually of German descent, not Dutch) who are known as the Plain People. [no period needed within parentheses]

PERIODS USED WITH OTHER MARKS OF PUNCTUATION

1. Always place the period *inside* quotation marks.

   NOT Bartleby said, "I would prefer not to".
   BUT Bartleby said, "I would prefer not to."

   NOT Cleopatra was called "Queen of the Nile".
   BUT Cleopatra was called "Queen of the Nile."

2. Use only one period if an abbreviation occurs at the end of a sentence that would ordinarily take a period of its own. If an abbreviation occurs at the end of a sentence that ends with a question mark or an exclamation point, you must use both the period and the second mark of punctuation. (See 7.b.)

EXERCISE 13. Rewrite the following sentences, correcting all errors in the use of periods. (Some sentences require that you substitute a period for another mark of punctuation that has been used incorrectly.)

1. Baseball fans are forever arguing about who the greatest baseball player is?
2. The list of baseball greats is a long one—Babe Ruth, Ted Williams, Joe DiMaggio, Jackie Robinson, Roberto Clemente, Sandy Koufax, etc..
3. Ask yourself who you think the greatest American baseball player is?
4. Many people think it is Willie Mays
5. Born in Alabama, William H Mays started out playing stickball in the streets of New York
6. In 1951 Willie Mays joined professional baseball as a center fielder for the New York Giants (He ended his career with the New York Mets).
7. Mays electrified crowds with his exceptional fielding, explosive hitting, and fearless base running
8. Fans of all ages loved his enthusiasm and friendliness and soon nicknamed him the "Say-Hey Kid".
9. Children greeted him with a rousing "Say hey, Willie!" and never thought to address him as Mr Mays.
10. Willie Mays was the hero of every schoolchild in New York (although there was a spirited rivalry between Mays, the Yankees' Mickey Mantle, and the Dodgers' Duke Snider.)
11. When the Giants moved to San Francisco, Mays became a favorite on both coasts
12. He was named the National League's Most Valuable Player in 1954. and in 1965.
13. Mays will always be remembered as a thrilling center fielder (and is known especially for a phenomenal catch in the 1954 World Series.)
14. That catch was undoubtedly one of the most spectacular plays in baseball history
15. Mays's hitting statistics (he had a career batting average of .302.) were also impressive.
16. He hit 660 home runs (Only Babe Ruth and Henry Aaron hit more).
17. In 1979 Willie Mays was elected to the National Baseball Hall of Fame

18. The election was almost unanimous, but sportswriters are still asking who voted for someone other than Willie Mays?
19. When reporters asked Mays who *he* thought was the greatest player, Mays smiled broadly and said, "I think I was the best baseball player I ever saw".
20. Many people, especially in New York and San Francisco, would agree

7.e QUESTION MARKS

Use question marks to indicate a direct question and to express uncertainty about a name, date, or word.

Was Benjamin Franklin born in 1706 or 1707**?**
My friend whispered, "Why did she ask you that**?**"

Ambrose Bierce (1842–1914**?**) was a contemporary of Mark Twain's.
She told me that the color (**?**) of the water was crystal clear.

Do not place a question mark after an indirect question. (An indirect question does not quote the person's exact words.)

My teacher asked me whether Benjamin Franklin was born in 1706 or 1707**.**
I wondered if I should ask my history teacher**.**

In general, do not place a question mark after a polite request.

Will the assembly please be seated**.**

7.f EXCLAMATION POINTS

Use exclamation points to show strong feeling and to indicate a forceful command.

That woman looks exactly like me**!**
We cannot print a stolen document**!**
What a colorful garden**!**
Don't you ever say that again**!**

QUESTION MARKS USED WITH OTHER MARKS OF PUNCTUATION

1. Place the question mark *inside* quotation marks if the question mark is part of the quotation.

   After the show was over, he leaned over and asked, "Who wrote the lyrics**?"**

   Place the question mark *outside* quotation marks if the question mark is part of the entire sentence.

   Why did she say, "That's all I wanted to hear**"?**

   If both the sentence and the quotation at the end of the sentence need a question mark, use only *one* question mark placed *inside* the quotation marks.

   Did he ask, "Do you love me**?"**

2. Place the question mark *inside* the parentheses if the question mark is part of the parenthetical expression.

   He proudly informed me that he had bought an original Wyeth painting (did he mean Andrew or Jamie Wyeth**?)** for his living room.

   Place the question mark *outside* the parentheses if the question mark is part of the entire sentence.

   How many of Dickinson's poems were published posthumously (after 1886**)?**

3. Do not place a comma or a period after a question mark at the end of a quotation.

   NOT "Why did she ask me?~~,~~" I thought to myself.
   BUT "Why did she ask me**?"** I thought to myself.

   NOT I thought to myself, "Why did she ask me?"~~.~~
   BUT I thought to myself, "Why did she ask me**?"**

EXCLAMATION POINTS USED WITH OTHER MARKS OF PUNCTUATION

1. Place the exclamation point *inside* quotation marks if the exclamation point is part of the quotation.

   My aunt exclaimed, "How tall you've grown**!"**

   Place the exclamation point *outside* quotation marks if the exclamation point is part of the entire sentence.

   How relieved I felt when he said, "Good night to you all**"!**

   If both the sentence and the quotation at the end of the sentence need an exclamation point, use only *one* exclamation point *inside* the quotation marks.

   What a panic he caused by yelling "Fire**!"**

2. Place the exclamation point *inside* the parentheses if the exclamation point is part of the parenthetical expression.

   My mother believed Susan's explanation (what a fantastic story**!)** of how the window was broken.

   Place the exclamation point *outside* the parentheses if the exclamation point is part of the entire sentence.

   How odd that a fourth-story window should be broken by a falling branch (I think it was a flying baseball**)!**

3. Do not place a comma or a period after an exclamation point at the end of a quotation.

   NOT "Turn the music down!X" he shouted.
   BUT "Turn the music down**!"** he shouted.

   NOT He shouted, "Turn the music down!"X
   BUT He shouted, "Turn the music down**!"**

EXERCISE 14. The sentences below use periods, question marks, and exclamation points correctly. For each sentence cite the rule that is illustrated.

1. If the people be governors, who shall be governed**?**
   —John Cotton
2. Give me liberty, or give me death**!** —Patrick Henry
3. How surprised I was to hear that Daniel Webster was the one who asked for "liberty and union, now and forever, one and inseparable"**!**
4. Was it really Queen Victoria of England who said, "We are not amused"**?**
5. "Doesn't anybody stay in one place anymore**?**" Carole King asked in her 1971 song "So Far Away."
6. President Woodrow Wilson called for force (and this was after he had been elected on an antiwar platform**!**) in a famous speech.
7. What a difference it makes to come home to a child**!**
   —Margaret Fuller
8. Mavis Gallant asked herself if it was really important if even one-tenth of a lie is true.
9. Do you remember whether it was Rachel Carson who said that the ocean is a place of paradoxes**?**
10. The man who first said "Remember the Alamo" (Colonel Sydney Sherman**?**) did not foresee the slogan's popularity.

7.g COMMAS

As you study the rules for comma usage, keep in mind that to set off an element with commas means to put commas *before* and *after* it. Of course, if the set-off element occurs at the beginning or at the end of a sentence, only one comma is needed—either after it (for a beginning element) or before it (for a final element).

Many writers have actually expressed fear of commas and feel quite insecure about using them. Perhaps if these writers understood that there really is a method—not madness—to the use of commas, they would realize that commas are not mysterious or threatening at all: They are wonderfully helpful and—once understood—quite simple to use.

CONVENTIONAL USES

7.g.1 Commas in titles of people

Use commas to set off titles when they follow a person's name.

When titles (such as *Ph.D., Jr., Sr.,* and *Queen of England*) appear in a complete sentence, it is preferred usage to place commas both *before* and *after* the titles.

Maria Lopez, Ph.D.
Dale Bumpers, Governor of Arkansas
Henry James, Sr.[1]
My cousin Alberta Picconi, D.D.S., has been a dentist for five years.

7.g.2 Commas in addresses

Use commas to set off the various parts of an address or of a geographical term.

In a complete sentence it is preferred usage to place commas *before* and *after* all the parts of an address or of a geographical term, except before the first part.

Black Hills, South Dakota
Lancaster County, Pennsylvania
Montpelier, Vermont
Macmillan Publishing Company has offices at 866 Third Avenue, New York, New York, and in other cities.
Until last year 51 South Spring Lane, Valley Forge, Pennsylvania 19460, was my home address.

7.g.3 Commas in dates

Use commas to set off the parts of a date.

Specifically, use commas to set off the day from the month and numeral and to set off the month and numeral

---

[1] You may omit the comma before *Jr.* or *Sr.*, but it is preferred usage to include it.

from the year. In a complete sentence it is preferred usage to place commas *before* and *after* all the parts of a date, except before the first part.

June 28, 1906
Tuesday, August 21, 1980
Physicist Marie Goeppert-Mayer was born on June 28, 1906, in Germany.
Tuesday, August 21, 1980, was my sixteenth birthday.

Do not use the comma in dates in military form (with the numeral before the month). Do not use the comma if only the month and the numeral or if only the month and the year are given.

28 June 1906	July 4
16 April 1954	July 1776

7.g.4 Commas in letter writing

Place a comma after the salutation of an informal letter and after the closing of all letters.

Dear Juan,	Dear Aunt Miriam,
Sincerely,	Love,

7.g.5 Commas in references

Use commas to set off the parts of a reference that direct the reader to your exact source.

In a complete sentence place commas *before* and *after* all the parts of a reference, except before the first part. Commas are also used in footnotes and bibliographies (see 16.k).

Volume II, second edition
"Birches," line 8
The End of the Road, pages 114–118
Macbeth, Act III, scene i
We performed Act III, scene i, of Shakespeare's *Macbeth*.

EXERCISE 15. Rewrite the following letter, inserting the ten commas that are missing.

714 Williams Road
Winchester Virginia
September 12, 1963

Dear Greta

I'm enclosing a clipping from a recent speech in case you didn't hear or read it. The article is from the September 9 1963 edition of *Newsweek* magazine page 21. Maybe you can use it for your English assignment.

On August 23 1963 there was an important civil rights march in Washington, D.C. The march was led by Dr. Martin Luther King, Jr., who is a church leader.

Dr. King believes in nonviolent protest. He organized a boycott of the segregated bus system of Montgomery Alabama in December 1955.

I hope the speech and this background information will help you.

Best
Eileen

ITEMS IN SERIES

7.g.6 Commas and words in series

Use commas with nouns, adjectives, verbs, and adverbs in a series.

There are three basic forms in which a series can appear:

A**,** B**,** and C [This is the most common form.]
A**,** B**,** C
A and B and C [Notice that commas are not used here.]

It is preferred usage to place a comma before the *and* in the first form (A, B, and C) because the comma helps to avoid ambiguity. For instance, in the sentence "I ate eggs, broccoli, macaroni and cheese" it is not clear whether the writer had macaroni and cheese combined as a single dish or some macaroni as one dish and some cheese as another. In the latter case, a comma after the word *macaroni* would help make that clear.

1. nouns in series

Place a comma after every noun (except the last) used in a series. (Always place a comma after the abbreviation *etc.* occurring in the middle of a sentence.)

> Alaska, Texas, and California are the three largest states in the United States.
>
> We bought mittens, earmuffs, boots, scarves, etc., for the ski trip.

NOTE: Nouns used in pairs (*pen and ink, ham and eggs, bread and butter*) are considered single units and should not be divided by commas. The pairs themselves must be set off from other nouns or groups of nouns in a series.

> The short-order cook prepared ham and eggs, bacon and eggs, and French toast.

2. adjectives in series

Place a comma between adjectives in a series if it would sound right to reverse their order or to put the word *and* between them. In punctuating, you can think of such adjectives as *coordinate adjectives.*

> It was a long, dull, humorless movie.

Do not use a comma between adjectives in a series if they sound unnatural with their order reversed or with *and* between them. Adjectives that do not need commas between them usually describe different aspects of the word they refer to—for example, size and age.

> The big old oak desk stood in one corner of the room.

Sometimes commas are used between some adjectives in a series but not between others.

> A noisy, dilapidated green pickup truck roared down the street.

In this sentence a comma is used between *noisy* and *dilapidated* because *and* would sound natural between them. It would not sound natural to use *and* between *dilapidated* and *green* or between *green* and *pickup.* In addition, it would not sound natural to use *dilapidated, green,* and *pickup* in any other order.

7.g.7 Commas and main clauses in series

Place a comma after every main clause (except the last) used in a series.

Preheat the oven, beat the eggs, sift the flour, and measure the almond extract.

AVOIDING ERRORS WITH COMMAS AND ITEMS IN A SERIES

1. In general, do not place a comma before the first item or after the last item in a series.

   NOT For lunch he had, soda, tuna fish salad, and an apple.
   BUT For lunch he had soda, tuna fish salad, and an apple.

   NOT California, New York, and Pennsylvania, are the three most populous states in the United States.
   BUT California, New York, and Pennsylvania are the three most populous states in the United States.

2. Do not place a comma after the conjunction before the last item in a series.

   NOT His answers were imprecise, illogical, and, ungrammatical.
   BUT His answers were imprecise, illogical, and ungrammatical.

3. Do not use commas if all items are joined by *and, or,* or *nor.*

   NOT She lectured on the animal life, and the plant life, and the rock strata of the Middle East.
   BUT She lectured on the animal life and the plant life and the rock strata of the Middle East.

EXERCISE 16. Each of the following sentences contains items in a series. Rewrite each sentence correctly, adding commas that are needed and eliminating those that are incorrect.

1. The American Film Institute is continually trying to popularize old films to discover new talent and to encourage innovative filmmaking.
2. Actors actresses and filmmakers, greatly value the institute's Life Achievement Award.
3. The institute's annual, award ceremony is publicized in newspapers in trade publications and on television.
4. Jane Fonda Cicely Tyson Olivia De Havilland and others presented the 1977 Life Achievement Award to Bette Davis.
5. This famous, screen actress was the first woman to receive the Life Achievement Award.
6. Many celebrities, retraced evaluated and praised Davis' career.
7. Davis was one of the first actresses to play hard, and abrasive, and aggressive women.
8. In *Mr. Skeffington* Davis played a selfish vain and, childish character.
9. She was convincing she was powerful and she was vibrant in more than eighty film roles.
10. In these films, Davis was a flamboyant star fond of flashing her eyes waving her hands and striding proudly.

INTRODUCTORY ELEMENTS

7.g.8 Commas for introductory adverb clauses

Use commas to set off introductory adverb clauses.

Although the crossword puzzle was difficult**,** I was able to complete it.
Because it was a beautiful day**,** we decided to eat outdoors.
When you see someone in trouble**,** try to help.

Adverb clauses in an internal position that interrupt the flow of the sentence are also set off with commas.

Elizabeth**,** because she knew the way**,** acted as our guide.

In general, do not set off an adverb clause at the end of a sentence unless the clause is parenthetical or unless the sentence would be misread without the comma. Use a comma if the clause begins with *although*, *though*, or *while* meaning "whereas." Also use a comma before *as* or *since* if the clause tells "why." Do not use a comma before *as*, *while*, or *since* if the clause tells "when."

We decided to eat outdoors because it was a beautiful day. [no comma]

He stayed until ten o'clock, although he had previously decided to leave early in the evening. [comma because clause begins with *although*]

I bought chocolate candy and crossword puzzles, since we had to wait another hour. [comma because *since* clause tells "why"]

I have disliked him since I first met him. [no comma because *since* clause tells "when"]

7.g.9 Commas for introductory prepositional phrases

Use a comma to set off a single short introductory prepositional phrase only if the sentence would be misread without the comma.

Always use a comma after the final element in a *succession* of connected introductory prepositional phrases unless the verb immediately follows the final element. Do not use commas *between* introductory prepositional phrases unless the phrases are a series.

Among those voting, women were well represented. [comma needed to avoid misreading]

Beside the soldiers stood an unarmed man. [comma not needed]

Beside the ocean in the pouring rain in the dead of winter, she caught a bad cold. [comma needed after a succession of connected prepositional phrases]

Under the tree at the edge of the lawn were two robins collecting twigs to build a nest. [comma not needed after a succession of connected prepositional phrases immediately followed by a verb]

7.g.10 Commas for introductory participles and participial phrases

Use commas to set off introductory participles and participial phrases.

Running after my sister, I sprained my ankle badly.
Galloping, the horses headed for the barn.

NOTE: Do not confuse an introductory participle or participial phrase with a gerund or gerund phrase (see 1.1). A gerund or gerund phrase may serve as the subject of the sentence. If the sentence contains a gerund or gerund phrase, do not set it off with commas.

Practicing the piano night and day, I was tired but more confident of winning the competition. [An introductory participial phrase needs a comma.]

Practicing the piano night and day was tedious but necessary preparation. [An introductory gerund phrase does not take a comma.]

EXERCISE 17. Rewrite each of the following sentences correctly, adding commas that are needed and eliminating those that are incorrect.

1. Throughout art history, only a few modern artists can be said to have changed the course of painting.
2. Many art critics point to Jasper Johns as he is considered to be one of the more influential modern artists.
3. Because Jasper Johns and Robert Rauschenberg have influenced each other critics consider both artists equally significant.
4. Putting aside their traditional training both artists preferred to work in the abstract.
5. Their finished works of art although they were carefully planned out and executed look haphazard.
6. In the middle of a splash of oil paint beside a scrap of newspaper on a huge canvas Rauschenberg hung a light bulb.
7. Art critics have faced a tremendous challenge, ever since they attempted to interpret Rauschenberg's confusing collages.
8. Astounded the critics panned the early exhibits of Johns and Rauschenberg.

9. The critics' puzzled eyes pondered everyday objects until the objects took on new meanings.
10. Giving new meaning to ordinary objects, had been the artists' message all along.

EXTRA ELEMENTS

An extra element is a word, phrase, or clause that gives extra information—interesting information, perhaps, but not information that is essential to the meaning of the sentence. An extra element requires extra commas to set it off.

7.g.11 Commas for interjections and parenthetical expressions

Use commas to set off interjections and parenthetical expressions such as *yes, no, well, on the contrary, on the other hand, in fact, by the way, to be exact,* and *after all.*

After all**,** I did my best. [introductory position]
The game**,** alas**,** was lost in the first quarter. [internal position]
Philadelphia**,** on the other hand**,** is more than two hundred years old. [internal position]
I can't make it for lunch today**,** by the way. [final position]

7.g.12 Commas for conjunctive adverbs

Use commas to set off conjunctive adverbs (such as *however, moreover, besides, nevertheless, therefore, furthermore,* and *consequently*).

Note that a conjunctive adverb often has a *semicolon* before it and a comma after it.

Therefore**,** I hope to build my own home one day. [introductory position]
We did not**,** incidentally**,** have enough ginger ale left to make the punch today. [internal position within a clause]
We drank two bottles of ginger ale last night**;** consequently**,** we did not have enough left to make the punch today. [internal position at the beginning of a clause]

She had intended to use the money to buy a new stereo, however. [final position]

7.g.13 Commas for nonessential participles and infinitives

Use commas to set off participles, infinitives, and their phrases if they are not essential to the meaning of the sentence.

Remember that a nonessential element is an *extra* element that requires *extra* commas.

She sat there by the window, watching silently. [participial phrase]
My brothers, having eaten, ran out to play. [participle]
We must, to understand his actions, put ourselves in his place. [infinitive phrase]
I have not received the money, to be perfectly honest. [infinitive phrase]

Do not set off participles, infinitives, and their phrases with commas if they are essential to the meaning.

The girl sitting by the window is my sister. [participial phrase; tells *which* girl]
Persons bitten by a dog should see a doctor. [participial phrase; tells *which* persons]
To study my notes would not help you much. [infinitive phrase used as subject]
We intend to go. [infinitive used as object]
Now is the time to act. [infinitive used as adjective]
She said it to sound intelligent. [infinitive used as adverb]

EXERCISE 18. Rewrite the following sentences, adding commas where needed and eliminating those that are incorrect.

1. Bette Davis could not afford drama-school tuition; nonetheless she dreamed of studying to be an actress.
2. She came to New York and in fact was able to enroll in the Murray Anderson School of the Theatre.
3. She auditioned well and moreover won a scholarship to pay for her tuition.
4. In dance class she fulfilled her desire, to study, under Martha Graham.

5. Davis studied modern dance learning the proper physical movements for stage acting.
6. She left school, to make progress, in her career.
7. Davis finally had her New York premiere in 1928 performing in *The Earth Between.*
8. The playhouse that produced this play had also launched the career of Paul Robeson by the way.
9. It was as a screen actress to be exact that Bette Davis achieved lasting fame.
10. Therefore some people do not know that she was also famous for her roles in many stage plays.

7.g.14 Commas for nonessential adjective clauses

Use commas to set off a nonessential adjective clause.

A nonessential (nonrestrictive) clause can also be considered an *extra* clause; it gives additional information about a noun or a noun equivalent. An *extra* clause does not change, but adds to, the basic meaning of the sentence. Remember that an *extra* clause calls for *extra* commas.

The basic meaning of the following sentence is unchanged if the nonessential clause is deleted. Therefore, use commas to set off the extra adjective clause.

> Jackson Pollock**,** who was an American painter**,** was greatly influenced by his study of Zen Buddhism. [nonessential clause: *who was an American painter*]

Do not set off an essential adjective clause with commas. An essential (restrictive) clause gives necessary information about a noun or noun equivalent. It is needed to convey the exact meaning of the sentence.

The basic meaning of the following sentence would be changed if the essential clause were deleted. Therefore, do not use commas.

> The only American writer whom she read was Ernest Hemingway. [essential clause: *whom she read*]

EXERCISE 19. Rewrite each of the following sentences correctly, adding commas that are needed and eliminating those that are incorrect. Three of the sentences contain no errors.

1. Many American artists, who have written, directed, and acted in films, are world-renowned.
2. The silent film which was invented by Thomas Edison replaced the nickelodeon in America.
3. Charles Chaplin, who was formerly a vaudeville comedian, was an extremely popular silent film star.
4. The role, that Chaplin made famous, was a dignified tramp.
5. Buster Keaton who was also a successful silent film star was an acrobat as a child.
6. Keaton's death-defying stunts and expressionless features are characteristics, that make him unique.
7. Keaton's *The General* and *Battling Butler* which were filmed in 1926 are filled with breathtaking acrobatics.
8. Greta Garbo who began as a silent film star is most famous for her speaking roles.
9. Garbo's face is one of the few, that has been called masklike, striking, and timeless.
10. F. Scott Fitzgerald who is best known for his novels and short stories wrote for the screen during his career.
11. Some of the plays, that Lillian Hellman has written, have been adapted for the screen.
12. A famous screenwriter is Joan Tewkesberry who wrote the screenplay for *Nashville*.
13. *Nashville*, which deals with the lives of country singers in Tennessee, was directed by Robert Altman.
14. Mike Nichols and Elaine May who began as comedians have written many screenplays.
15. Nichols and May who were partners at one time are now independent filmmakers.
16. Jeanne Moreau is one of the French actresses, who later became directors.
17. The modern comedian, actor, and director, who is most similar to Charlie Chaplin, is Woody Allen.
18. Pauline Kael and Judith Crist, who write film reviews, love American comedies.

19. The directors, that film critic Andrew Sarris likes the most, are Howard Hawks and John Ford.
20. Many of the films, that John Ford directed, are westerns starring John Wayne.

7.g.15 Commas for nonessential appositives

Use commas to set off an appositive unless it is essential to the meaning of the sentence.

An **appositive** is a noun or pronoun (sometimes with modifiers) that is placed next to another noun or pronoun to identify it or to give additional information about it. An appositive is similar to an adjective clause in purpose, but an appositive has no verb, no subordinator, and no subject. It might help you to think of an appositive as an adjective clause that has been reduced to a phrase by the removal of certain words.

A nonessential appositive can be considered an *extra* appositive that calls for *extra* commas.

Nonessential (nonrestrictive) appositives

Lionel Trilling**,** a famous writer and teacher**,** was an expert on Romantic literature.
Many American cities**,** especially Boston and New York City**,** are major cultural centers.
Two people**,** Susan and I**,** had to do all the work.
Even he**,** the original sponsor of the bill**,** voted against it.

A nonessential appositive is sometimes placed before the word to which it refers.

A historic city**,** New Orleans was originally settled by French colonists.

Essential (restrictive) appositives

Robert Altman's film *The Long Goodbye* is an homage to Hollywood detective films. [If commas were placed around the essential appositive *The Long Goodbye*, the sentence would imply that this was Altman's *only* film.]

The *Iliad* and the *Odyssey* are traditionally attributed to the poet Homer. [The sentence does not make sense without the appositive *Homer.*]

The term *function* has a special meaning in mathematics. [The appositive *function* is essential to the meaning of the sentence.]

7.g.16 Commas and direct address

Use commas to set off words or names used in direct address.

Carlos, are you sure that you can get tickets for the baseball game?

Remain in your seats, students, until the introductory lecture is over.

Please don't forget to call me tomorrow, Cindy.

7.g.17 Commas for antithetical expressions

Use commas to set off an antithetical expression.

An antithetical expression uses such words as *not* or *unlike* to qualify what precedes it.

Alaska, not Texas, is the largest state in the United States of America.

Australia, unlike New Zealand, is considered to be a continent.

7.g.18 Commas for tag questions

Use commas to set off a tag question.

A tag, or echo, question, such as *shouldn't I?* or *haven't you?* emphasizes, or echoes, the implied question of the sentence.

You handed in your paper, didn't you?

You'll clean up the kitchen, won't you, before you go to the movies?

You have read that book, haven't you?

EXERCISE 20. Rewrite the following sentences correctly, adding or eliminating commas as necessary.

1. You appreciate pop art don't you?
2. Pop art lovers do you know about Jasper Johns the father of pop art?
3. The term, *pop*, is short for the word, *popular.*
4. It was the Dadaists not the pop artists who first introduced everyday objects like light bulbs and brooms into their work.
5. You see don't you how light bulbs and brooms might be called "popular" subjects?
6. Dadaism a post–World War I art movement attempted to portray the absurdity of modern life.
7. Many art critics have compared the artist, Jasper Johns, to Marcel Duchamp the French Dadaist.
8. Johns's works can be both positive and negative; the Dadaist, Duchamp's are only negative.
9. Johns's use of everyday objects especially brooms and light bulbs is meant to be symbolic not merely absurd.
10. The everyday items become beautiful and mysterious objects unlike ordinary light bulbs and brooms.

BETWEEN MAIN CLAUSES

7.g.19 Commas for compound sentences

Use commas between the main clauses in a compound sentence.

Place the comma before the coordinating conjunction (*and*, *but*, *or*, and *for*).

I carefully picked up the vase, but it crashed to the floor.
I told my sister what he said to me, and she advised me to forget all about it.

You may omit the comma between very short main clauses that are connected by a coordinating conjunction, but it is always a good idea to use the comma.

I opened the door and Fritz ran in.
I opened the door, and Fritz ran in.

Long main clauses may be separated by a semicolon instead of a comma and a coordinating conjunction. Always use a semicolon when conjunctive adverbs (see 3.b.5) are used.

> Austria and Switzerland are inland countries**;** however, most European countries are bounded by at least one large body of water.

AVOIDING ERRORS WITH COMMAS BETWEEN MAIN CLAUSES

1. Do not confuse a sentence that has a compound verb (see 2.g) with a sentence that has two or more main clauses. A compound verb with only two parts needs no comma before the conjunction. A sentence with two or more main clauses needs commas before each coordinating conjunction.

   NOT The quarterback threw the ball, and then stopped running. [compound verb]
   BUT The quarterback threw the ball and then stopped running.

   NOT The quarterback threw the ball and then he stopped running. [main clauses]
   BUT The quarterback threw the ball**,** and then he stopped running.

2. Remember to use coordinating conjunctions or semicolons between main clauses. If you use only a comma between main clauses, you will end up with a **run-on sentence** (also called a comma splice or comma fault).

   NOT The Pennsylvania state flag is blue and gold, the state flower is the mountain laurel. [run-on sentence]
   BUT The Pennsylvania state flag is blue and gold**, and** the state flower is the mountain laurel.
   OR The Pennsylvania state flag is blue and gold**;** the state flower is the mountain laurel.

AVOIDING ERRORS WITH COMMAS (GENERAL)

1. Do not use a comma between a subject and its action verb or linking verb.

   NOT What she thought fit to do, was beyond my comprehension.
   BUT What she thought fit to do was beyond my comprehension.

2. Do not use a comma between an action verb and its object or between a linking verb and its complement.

   NOT After dinner we rehearsed, the play.
   BUT After dinner we rehearsed the play.

   NOT The ingredients for the turkey stuffing are, bread crumbs, eggs, ham, sausage, and spices.
   BUT The ingredients for the turkey stuffing are bread crumbs, eggs, ham, sausage, and spices.

3. Do not place a comma between the parts of a compound subject or a compound object if all the parts are separated by *and* or *or* (see 2.d and 2.j).

   NOT The clean clothes that we needed, and the dirty clothes that we did not want were packed together in the suitcase. [compound subject]
   BUT The clean clothes that we needed and the dirty clothes that we did not want were packed together in the suitcase.

   NOT We finished the pie from last week, and the coffee from this morning. [compound object]
   BUT We finished the pie from last week and the coffee from this morning.

Continued

4. Do not place a comma between an indirect object and a direct object.

   NOT Martin Luther King showed us, Gandhi's methods of nonviolent resistance.
   BUT Martin Luther King showed us Gandhi's methods of nonviolent resistance.

5. Do not place a comma between the parts of a compound subordinating conjunction (*so . . . that, such . . . that, so . . . as, such . . . as*).

   NOT Such was the skill and determination of the Revolutionary troops, that the British redcoats could not gain the upper hand.
   BUT Such was the skill and determination of the Revolutionary troops that the British redcoats could not gain the upper hand.

   NOT This generator is so well designed and efficient, that its output of energy is nearly equal to its input.
   BUT This generator is so well designed and efficient that its output of energy is nearly equal to its input.

6. Do not place a comma before an indirect quotation or an indirect question.

   NOT He claimed, that he was involved in two lawsuits at the same time.
   BUT He claimed that he was involved in two lawsuits at the same time.

   NOT She asked, if she could take a break at this point.
   BUT She asked if she could take a break at this point.

EXERCISE 21. Rewrite each of the following sentences correctly, adding commas that are needed and eliminating those that are incorrect.

1. Frances Steloff never finished sixth grade but she became a leading figure in the literary world.
2. Steloff grew up in the exclusive summer spa of Saratoga Springs; however she was far from wealthy.
3. Her family, was always hungry and books were far from everyone's minds.
4. Frances was needed at home, and was forced to leave school at an early age.
5. She never had time to read at home; therefore books became almost sacred to her.
6. Steloff came to New York City, and took a job selling corsets in a department store.
7. She was transferred to the book department during the holiday rush and the ambitious woman remained there.
8. She loved selling books and she opened her own bookshop thirteen years later.
9. Frances as a youngster sold flowers to strangers but Steloff as an adult sold rare editions to famous friends.
10. She called her shop the Gotham Book Mart and it has been a New York literary center for over fifty years.

REVIEW EXERCISE C. Rewrite each of the following items correctly, adding commas that are needed and eliminating those that are incorrect.

1. Humphrey Bogart has played both the sympathetic, villain and the cynical disillusioned hero.
2. In *Our Town* Act I, the Stage Manager describes Grover's Corners New Hampshire.
3. Woody Allen wrote, and directed, and starred in *Love and Death*, *Sleeper* and, *Annie Hall*.
4. Emily Dickinson is credited with originating, "identical," "vowel," and "imperfect" rhymes.
5. Sammy Davis, Jr. sings acts and dances in films, on television and in nightclubs.
6. In April, 1939 75000 people attended Marian Anderson's concert at the Lincoln Memorial.

7. Joan Baez's songs protested social problems defined her generation and revealed her soul.
8. Art lovers do you think Andy Warhol paints seriously humorously, or meaninglessly?
9. Film star Ethel Waters, died on September 1, 1977 in Chatsworth, California.
10. Cordially
    May Lin Chang Arts Editor

REVIEW EXERCISE D. Rewrite each of the following sentences correctly, adding commas that are needed and eliminating those that are incorrect.

1. Fred Astaire's career virtually spanned, the twentieth century and his musicals are film classics.
2. Moreover Astaire was still talented and graceful in his later years dancing on television at the age of sixty.
3. It is understandable to be sure why his films enjoyed such amazing success in the thirties.
4. The films immersed audiences in a glamorous fairy tale, and made them forget the Depression.
5. In fact Astaire's films are popular today and they do not appear dated at all.
6. To some people watching Fred Astaire dance is a treasured memory.
7. Fred Astaire "the Pied Piper of dance", was enrolled in ballet school, when he was four.
8. Astaire's mother had decided, to move to New York as her husband's business had failed.
9. When Fred was six he and his sister who was eighteen months older than he entered the world of show business.
10. Touring the country Fred and Adele became vaudeville stars.
11. They performed in a Broadway revue, that was a flop; however Fred and Adele were an immense success.
12. After the revue, came three Broadway hits.
13. Fred and Adele were the toast of New York, and caused quite a stir in London.
14. Adele met Charles Cavendish whom she married in 1932 and she retired from show business.
15. Fred could not make it on his own could he?

16. On the contrary he proceeded, to set out for Hollywood obtain a film contract and, get married.
17. After a role as a dancer in *Dancing Lady* he won a supporting part in the film, *Flying Down to Rio.*
18. He was paired with Ginger Rogers (a last-minute choice) and his film career took flight.
19. Such was the success of the dancing duo, that they costarred in nine more films.
20. Their smash hits included *Roberta*, *Top Hat* and *The Barkleys of Broadway.*
21. "Ginger was a great personality" Astaire once remarked admiringly.
22. Filming the dance sequences, was grueling work to be sure.
23. Astaire and Rogers determined to achieve perfection went through forty takes for a routine in *Follow the Fleet.*
24. Astaire danced with other talented performers—for example Rita Hayworth and Cyd Charisse.
25. Astaire once commented, that Hayworth and Charisse were a little too tall for him however.
26. What made Astaire a success, was his ability not his appearance.
27. He was not devastatingly handsome—does that matter by the way?—except when he began to dance.
28. To improve his dance numbers Astaire took the greatest care with the technical aspects of each film.
29. In fact Astaire's contributions were so significant, that he greatly advanced the development of film techniques.
30. Fred Astaire's grace and beauty as a dancer however is what fans remember.

7.h SEMICOLONS

Semicolons are used in two ways to mark sentence breaks that are too strong for a comma but not strong enough for a period. Semicolons can be used to separate main clauses within the same sentence. Semicolons can also be used to separate clauses or items in a series that themselves contain commas. The rules that follow will help you learn when to use or avoid using semicolons in your writing.

7.h.1 Semicolons to separate main clauses

Use a semicolon to separate main clauses that are not joined by the coordinating conjunctions *and, but,* and *for.*

The acting and directing ability of Orson Welles is considered phenomenal, **and** his film *Citizen Kane* is still studied and appreciated.

The acting and directing ability of Orson Welles is considered phenomenal; his film *Citizen Kane* is still studied and appreciated.

Use a semicolon to separate main clauses joined by conjunctive adverbs, such as *however, therefore, nevertheless, moreover, furthermore,* and *consequently,* or by such expressions as *for example* or *that is.*

In general, a conjunctive adverb or an expression like *for example* is followed by a comma.

In her youth Mary Cassatt was strongly discouraged from any artistic endeavors; nevertheless, she later became one of America's foremost painters.

It is sometimes difficult to decide whether to use a semicolon to separate main clauses or whether to make the clauses into separate sentences. If the clauses are not very closely related, make them into separate sentences by adding periods and capital letters.

North Carolina was once the gold-mining capital of the country; however, many of its mines were abandoned during the California Gold Rush of 1849. [The clauses are closely related; use a semicolon.]

Miami's name is a Seminole word meaning "sweet water." This subtropical American city is bordered by the Atlantic Ocean, Biscayne Bay, and the Everglades. [The clauses are both about Miami, but they deal with different aspects of the city. Therefore, use a period and a capital letter for each statement.]

Remember that semicolons, like all the other marks of punctuation, should help your reader understand your meaning. Do not use semicolons unless they truly help.

7.h.2 Semicolons to separate expressions containing commas

Use a semicolon to separate clauses or items in a series that themselves contain commas.

Notable members of the Transcendental Club were Ralph Waldo Emerson, who wrote *Nature*; Henry David Thoreau, who wrote *Walden*; and Margaret Fuller, who edited *The Dial*.

SEMICOLONS AND QUOTATION MARKS

Always place the semicolon *outside* quotation marks.

On our vacation we visited New York, "the Empire State"; Virginia, "the Old Dominion"; and Georgia, "the Empire State of the South."

EXERCISE 22. Rewrite each of the following sentences correctly, adding semicolons that are needed. Three of the sentences require two semicolons; the others require one.

1. Persons attempting to find a motive in this narrative will be prosecuted persons attempting to find a moral in it will be banished persons attempting to find a plot in it will be shot. —Mark Twain
2. Mark Twain attached the above notice to *Huckleberry Finn* he felt that too much analysis of art made it less enjoyable.
3. The trouble with music appreciation in general is that people are taught to have too much respect for music they should be taught to love it instead. —Igor Stravinsky
4. Stravinsky and Twain both appealed for an informal approach to art however, art in America has too often been neglected or misunderstood.
5. Stravinsky lived and worked in Leningrad, Russia Paris, France and the United States.
6. Oscar Wilde said, "All art is quite useless" he felt that art should not instruct but rather give pleasure.
7. Art does not reproduce the visible rather, it makes visible. —Paul Klee

8. Art and politics rarely go together nevertheless, on occasion art gets support from the state.
9. Art takes many forms: Painting, film, and photography please the eye music pleases the ear.
10. We must never forget that art is not a form of propaganda it is a form of truth. —John F. Kennedy

7.i COLONS

Colons are used to introduce lists, quotations, and illustrations or examples. Colons also have certain conventional uses in writing the time, in citing sections of the Bible, and in writing business letters. Capitalize the first word of a complete sentence after a colon.

7.i.1 Colons before a list

Use a colon to introduce a list, especially after such expressions as *the following* or *as follows.*

To make a real Italian spaghetti sauce, you will need the following ingredients**:** celery, onions, ground beef, tomato sauce, olive oil, and seasonings.

Perform the following operations to start a stick-shift car**:** 1) Step on the clutch, 2) put the car into first gear, 3) turn the ignition key, and 4) slowly press down the accelerator as you take your foot off the clutch.

Do not use a colon if the list is immediately preceded by an action verb, a linking verb, or a preposition.

Actor and director Woody Allen has written plays, screenplays, monologues, and comedy sketches. [The list is preceded by the verb phrase *has written*.]

7.i.2 Colons before a quotation

In general, use a colon to introduce an indented quotation.

Indent quotations of more than three lines of poetry and of more than two lines of prose. Do not place quotation marks around indented material (see 7.1.1).

Stephen Crane admits the following in his poem "Truth":

For truth was to me
A breath, a wind,
A shadow, a phantom,
And never had I touched
The hem of its garment.

7.i.3 Colons before an illustration or example

Use a colon to introduce material that illustrates or provides an example of what precedes.

Do not forget to capitalize the first word of the material if it is a complete sentence.

The winters in Wainwright, Alaska, are bitterly cold**:** On a windy morning you can see your breath freeze into ice crystals in front of your face.

7.i.4 Colons in notations of time

Use a colon between the hour and the minute in writing the time.

5**:**45 P.M. 8**:**30 A.M. 12**:**15 A.M. 6**:**05 P.M.

7.i.5 Colons in Biblical references

Use a colon between the chapter and the verse in writing Biblical references.

Proverbs 31**:**19–12 I Kings 11**:**1–13

7.i.6 Colons in business letters

In general, use a colon after the salutation of a business letter.

Madam**:** Dear Sir**:** Members of the Board**:**

COLONS USED WITH OTHER MARKS OF PUNCTUATION

1. Always place the colon *after* closing quotation marks.

   William Faulkner uses these words to describe the heroine in his short story "A Rose for Emily"**:** "Miss Emily had been a tradition, a duty, and a care."

2. Always place the colon *after* closing parentheses.

   T. S. Eliot wrote the following in an article in the *New York Times* (March 30, 1959**):** "A young writer needs the society of other writers, both his contemporaries and benevolent older writers whom he can respect."

EXERCISE 23. Rewrite each of the following sentences correctly, adding colons that are needed.

1. There are two times in a man's life when he should not speculate when he can't afford it and when he can. —Mark Twain
2. Among the natural rights of the colonists are these firstly, a right to *life;* secondly, a right to *liberty;* thirdly, to *property.* —Samuel Adams
3. There are three faithful friends an old wife, an old dog, and ready money. —Benjamin Franklin
4. I hoped that the trip would be the best of all journeys a journey into ourselves. —Shirley MacLaine
5. Dorothy Parker asked to have this epitaph engraved on her tombstone "Excuse my dust."
6. A famous haiku poem by Ezra Pound follows

   The petals fall in the fountain,
   the orange-colored rose-leaves,
   Their ochre clings to the stone.
7. This line, engraved on the Statue of Liberty, is from Emma Lazarus' poem "The New Colossus" "Give me your tired, your poor."
8. The following quotation appeared in Eleanor Roosevelt's autobiography, *This Is My Story* (1937) "No one can make you feel inferior without your consent."

9. In "The Still Voice of Harlem" Conrad Kent Rivers writes "I am the hope of your unborn."
10. In reading over Genesis 21 1–21, keep in mind that *Sarah* means "princess," and *Isaac* means "laughter."

7.j HYPHENS

Hyphens are used in certain compound nouns and compound adjectives and with numbers and numerals. Hyphens are also used to divide words at the end of a line.

7.j.1 Hyphens for prefixes and suffixes

Most words with prefixes and suffixes do not take hyphens.

There is a current tendency toward closing up most words rather than using hyphens. There are, however, certain instances, discussed below, where hyphens are required. It is best to check your dictionary for the hyphenation of any word you are unsure of.

Prefixes

Words with the prefixes *all-*, *ex-* (meaning "former"), and *self-* need a hyphen after the prefix. A hyphen is required with any prefix before a proper noun or a proper adjective. The prefix *anti-* takes a hyphen before a word beginning with *i*. The prefix *vice-* usually takes a hyphen; however, *Vice President* (of the United States) is usually written as two words.

self-admiration	ex-governor
all-inclusive	un-American
anti-inflation	pro-French

A hyphen is often required when the prefix *re-* meaning "to do again" is joined to a verb. The hyphen helps to avoid confusion between words such as those below:

re-count the ballots	*but*	recount a story
re-lay the tiles		relay the message
re-mark the papers		remark about her condition

Suffixes

Place a hyphen before the suffix *-like* only if the preceding word is a proper noun or a word ending in *-ll*.

a bell-like sound	*but*	tissuelike cloth
Astaire-like grace		ghostlike apparition
Miami-like weather		pearllike shine

Some words have a hyphen before the suffix *-elect*.

mayor-elect   President-elect

7.j.2 Hyphens in compound adjectives

A compound adjective that precedes the noun is generally hyphenated.

If a compound adjective follows the noun, it is usually not hyphenated.

up-to-date references	*but*	The references are up to date.
eye-catching scarf		The scarf was eye catching.
sixteen-year-old boy		He was sixteen years old.

Hyphenate compound adjectives beginning with *well-*, *ill-*, or *little-* when they precede a noun.

Do not hyphenate these compound adjectives when they are preceded by an adverb.

ill-natured child	*but*	extremely ill natured child
well-educated girl		very well educated girl

NOTE: An expression made up of an adverb that ends in *-ly* and an adjective or past participle is not hyphenated.

a happily married couple   a mainly green interior

7.j.3 Hyphens in numbers and numerals

Use a hyphen in ordinal and cardinal compound numbers, in fractions used as adjectives, in adjectives made up of numbers and units of measure, and between connected numerals.

1. compound numbers

Hyphenate ordinal and cardinal compound numbers between twenty-one and ninety-nine.

forty•five eighty•eighth
thirty•one sixty•fourth

2. fractions used as adjectives

Hyphenate fractions used as adjectives (but not as nouns).

two•thirds majority	*but*	two thirds of the members
a one•eighth portion		one eighth of the pie
a four•fifths increase		four fifths of my salary

3. connected numerals

Hyphenate numerals that show a span.

pages 354•392 1884•1903
lines 4•18 1978•79

If you use the word *from*, you must use the word *to*, not a hyphen. If you use the word *between*, you must use the word *and*, not a hyphen.

from 1884 **to** 1903 **between** 1884 **and** 1903

EXERCISE 24. Rewrite correctly each of the following items that has errors in hyphenation. Some items contain no errors.

1. self reliant child
2. pro American countries
3. pre Columbian pottery
4. father in-law
5. one-half of the lettuce
6. balllike flower
7. all American player
8. a totally silly notion
9. a very well-behaved wolf
10. forty-eighth
11. yellow bellied sapsucker
12. exmayor

13. well planned vacation
14. war-like behavior
15. selfmade
16. a three fifths reduction
17. The vacation was well planned.
18. between 1911-1923
19. no-where
20. a one horse town

7.j.4 Hyphens to divide words at the end of a line

In order to keep the right-hand margins of your paper fairly even, you may want to use a hyphen to divide a word at the end of a line.

Words are generally divided between syllables or between pronounceable parts. Because it is frequently difficult to determine where a word should be divided, check your dictionary to be sure.

Do not let a single letter from a divided word stand alone at the end of a line. Do not let fewer than three letters from a divided word stand at the beginning of a line. Try not to divide words at the end of a page or at the end of a paragraph. Following are some general rules on dividing words at the end of a line:

1. one-syllable words

Do not divide one-syllable words or a single syllable within a word.

NOT	str-ing	clim-bed	slip-ped	voraci-ous	courage-ous
BUT	string	climbed	slipped	vora-cious	coura-geous

2. double consonants

In general, divide a word with double consonants between the two consonants.

ar-rested	skip-per	big-gest
sil-liest	trap-per	ruf-fled

If a suffix such as *-ing* or *-est* has been added to a complete word ending with two consonants, divide the word after the two consonants.

roll-ing	full-est
canvass-ing	track-ing
kiss-ing	black-est

If a word contains two consonants standing between two vowels, you should ordinarily divide the word between the consonants.

rep-resentative
impor-tant
insig-nificant

3. proper nouns, proper adjectives, abbreviations

Do not divide proper nouns, proper adjectives, or abbreviations.

NOT Mar✗garet Mead
BUT Margaret Mead

NOT ap✗prox.
BUT approx.

NOT Presiden✗tial
BUT Presidential

NOT NA✗ACP
BUT NAACP

EXERCISE 25. Correct all errors in word division in the items below. Some items are correct as written.

1. Rachel Car-son
2. baff-led
3. sur-fing
4. mort-al
5. ras-cal
6. th-rough
7. sel-ling
8. mallea-ble
9. chan-ged
10. Leonard Bern-stein

7.k APOSTROPHES

Apostrophes are used to form the possessive of nouns and of indefinite pronouns; to indicate letters omitted in contractions; and to form the plural of letters, numbers, signs, and words used to represent themselves.

7.k.1 Apostrophes for the possessive

1. nouns not ending in *s*

Use the apostrophe and *s* to form the possessive of singular and plural nouns not ending in *s*. This rule applies to both common and proper nouns.

Dickinson's poetry	women's rights
Colorado's mountains	children's activities

NOTE: Do not italicize the 's in the possessive of italicized words such as the titles of works.

Saturday Review'**s** cartoons
Macbeth'**s** plot and structure
Newsweek'**s** editorial

2. plural nouns ending in *s*

Use the apostrophe alone to form the possessive of plural nouns ending in *s*. This rule applies to both common and proper nouns.

the Hawaiian Islands' exports	purple mountains' majesty
the *Ladies' Home Journal*	the citizens' demands

3. singular nouns ending in *s*

When forming the possessive of a singular noun ending in *s* (or an *s* sound), look at the number of syllables in the word. If the noun has only one syllable, use the apostrophe and an *s* to form the possessive. If the noun has more than one syllable, you can usually add the apostrophe alone.

my boss's instructions	Socrates' teachings
Sandy Glass's party	the countess' horse
Groucho Marx's humor	Ulysses' ship
the fox's fur	Confucius' sayings

NOTE: The above rule is not absolute, and some books do not conform to it. Thus, although the rule states preferred usage, it is not incorrect to use both an apostrophe and an *s* after a singular noun of more than one syllable ending in *s*.

4. indefinite pronouns

Use the apostrophe and an *s* to form the possessive of indefinite pronouns such as *someone, one, anybody, everybody, somebody else,* and *each other.*

one**'**s duty
no one**'**s fault
everyone**'**s rights
somebody**'**s clothes

5. compound words

Use the apostrophe and an *s* (or the apostrophe alone) after the last part of a hyphenated or nonhyphenated compound.

my father-in-law**'**s camera
the sergeant-at-arms**'** order
the heir apparent**'**s throne
the Surgeon General**'**s warning

6. joint possession

If two or more persons possess something jointly, put only the name of the last person mentioned in the possessive form. The names of businesses and organizations should also be treated in this way.

Bill and Kristen**'**s home
Gilbert and Sullivan**'**s operettas
Strawbridge and Clothier**'**s prices

NOTE: If the second word in an expression of joint possession is a possessive pronoun, make the first word a possessive also: "Gilbert**'s** and his operettas." If the expression sounds too awkward, you can reword it: "operettas of Gilbert and Sullivan."

7. individual possession by more than one person

If two or more persons (or things) each possess something individually, put each name in the possessive form.

My father**'**s and mother**'**s parents
Newman**'**s and Streisand**'**s screen roles
Ford**'**s and General Motors**'** cars

AVOIDING ERRORS WITH APOSTROPHES

1. Use the apostrophe to form the possessive.

    NOT That is Marilyn suitcase.
    NOT That is Marilyns suitcase.
    BUT That is Marilyn's suitcase.

2. Do not misplace the apostrophe in the possessive of a proper noun that ends in *s*.

    NOT We read Wallace Steven's poetry. [The poet's name is Wallace Stevens with an *s* at the end.]
    BUT We read Wallace Stevens' poetry.
    OR: We read Wallace Stevens's poetry.

3. Do not use an apostrophe with the possessive personal pronouns (*mine, his, hers, its, ours, yours, theirs*). These pronouns are already possessive in form.

    NOT Did you tell them that it was your's?
    NOT Did you tell them that it was yours'?
    BUT Did you tell them that it was yours?

8. double possessives

If something belongs to a *specific person*, you can show possession by using *of* before the noun referring to the person and the apostrophe and an *s* (or the apostrophe alone) after it. Use this construction, called the double possessive, only if the owner could possess more than one thing of the kind.

that red suitcase of Marilyn's
a poem of Wallace Stevens'
some friends of my parents'

Do not use the double possessive if the owner could possess only one thing of the kind, or if the thing possessed is preceded by *the*.

the sister of the President — the mother of my friend
the poems of Wallace Stevens — the identity of the victim

9. units of time and money

Use the apostrophe and an *s* (or the apostrophe alone) to form the possessive of units of time (*second, minute, hour, day, week, month, year*) and money (*cent, nickel, dime, dollar*). Use a hyphen if the unit is not in the possessive form.

one minute's time	*but*	a one-minute break
five cents' worth		a five-cent candy
six days' rest		a six-day rest

EXERCISE 26. Write the possessive form of each of the following nouns.

1. Faulkner
2. Wisconsin
3. mice
4. cactus
5. *The Scarlet Letter*
6. Dallas
7. marble
8. wives
9. Charles Dickens
10. thyme
11. *Newsweek*
12. press
13. leaves
14. Santa Fe
15. Langston Hughes
16. geese
17. ticks
18. Troilus
19. Angelou
20. moss

EXERCISE 27. From each pair of phrases below select the one phrase that correctly expresses the possessive.

1. a) someone record
   b) someone's record
2. a) no one's responsibility
   b) no one responsibility
3. a) Rodgers and Hammerstein's *Oklahoma!*
   b) Rodgers' and Hammerstein's *Oklahoma!*
4. a) anyone guess
   b) anyone's guess
5. a) the district attorney case
   b) the district attorney's case
6. a) his sister-in-law's friend
   b) his sister's-in-law friend
7. a) Bob and Deborah's feet
   b) Bob's and Deborah's feet

8. a) five hours' sleep
   b) five hours sleep
9. a) a million dollar's worth of advertising
   b) a million dollars' worth of advertising
10. a) one day's notice
    b) one days notice
11. a) a friend of my mother
    b) a friend of my mother's
12. a) an essay of John Simon's
    b) an essay of John Simon
13. a) the minute hand of the clock
    b) the minute hand of the clock's
14. a) a poem of Gwendolyn Brooks's
    b) a poem of Gwendolyn Brooks
15. a) the United States responsibilities
    b) the United States' responsibilities
16. a) the victory was her's
    b) the victory was hers
17. a) David and Jonathan's fight with each other
    b) David's and Jonathan's fight with each other
18. a) the wit of Samuel Clemens's
    b) the wit of Samuel Clemens
19. a) the present participle's function
    b) the present participle function
20. a) the duck's and the sparrow's nests
    b) the duck and the sparrow's nests

7.k.2 Apostrophes in contractions

Use the apostrophe in place of letters omitted in contractions.

A contraction is a single word made up of two words that have been combined by omitting letters.

I'm	*formed from*	I am
you're		you are
it's		it is, it has
there's		there is, there has
who's		who is, who has
won't		will not
doesn't, don't		does not, do not

Use the apostrophe in place of omitted numerals in such expressions as "the class of '82" and "the '76 election results."

EXERCISE 28. For each contraction below, write the two words from which it is formed.

1. weren't
2. it's
3. couldn't
4. wasn't
5. I'm
6. he's
7. won't
8. they're
9. you're
10. can't

AVOIDING ERRORS WITH CONTRACTIONS

1. Do not confuse the contraction *it's* (*it is*) with the possessive pronoun *its*. Only use the apostrophe when you mean *it is*.

   NOT Its going to be a sturdy desk as soon as I reinforce it's legs.
   BUT **It's** going to be a sturdy desk as soon as I reinforce **its** legs.

2. Do not misplace the apostrophe when writing contractions.

   NOT I told you that I could'nt go.
   BUT I told you that I couldn't go.

   NOT He does'nt remember the story.
   BUT He doesn't remember the story.

3. Do not write *should of* in place of the contraction *should've*. *Should of* is always incorrect. Use *should've* or, preferably, *should have* instead. (This rule also applies to *could've* and *would've*.)

   NOT She should of told me sooner.
   BUT She should've told me sooner.
   OR She should **have** told me sooner.

7.k.3 Apostrophes for special plurals

Use the apostrophe and an **s** to form the plural of letters, numbers, signs, and words used as words.

Italicize (underline) the letter, number, sign, or word, but do not italicize the 's.

Your *a*'s are indistinguishable from your *o*'s.
All of the *8*'s had been typed as *3*'s.
Please replace your *&*'s with *and*'s.
While editing my paper, I changed all the *til*'s to *until*'s.

NOTE: Use an *s* or an *es* without the apostrophe to form the plural of a proper name.

The Jones**es**, the Brown**s**, and the Smith**s** dominate the telephone book.

EXERCISE 29. Write the plural form of each of the following.

1. *e* and *y*
2. 5 and 7
3. # and &
4. Montez and Picconi
5. *u* and *v*
6. *2* and *4*
7. *my* and *mine*
8. the Davis and the Wilson
9. % and ¢
10. *if*, *and*, and *but*

REVIEW EXERCISE E. Rewrite the following sentences, correcting all errors in the formation of the possessive as well as in other uses of the apostrophe.

1. The moons surface is better known than the ocean floor.
2. On the bottom of the ocean theres enough copper to supply the world for six thousand years.
3. Compared to the seven seas riches, the forty years reserve of copper on land seems puny.
4. There is 150,000 years worth of nickel under the ocean but only 100 years worth on land.
5. The federal governments annual bill for importing metals is $2 billion.
6. A company called Deepsea Ventures undertakes millions of dollars worth of investments in ocean mining.
7. In hunts for sunken treasure, what are such companies rights?
8. Whos to control the ocean floor, and whose rights supersede everyone elses rights?

9. Time-lapse photography over a six-month period revealed much activity miles below the Pacifics surface.
10. Everyones estimates of the activity proved inaccurate; the ocean floors activity level was quite high.
11. A rocklike things sudden movement surprised scientists.
12. The animals and sea plants interaction has yet to be studied.
13. Big business chief interest isnt with animals and plants, however, but with manganese nodules.
14. These nodules components may also include copper, aluminum, nickel, iron, and cobalt.
15. Coppers uses include electrical wiring, tubing, roofing, and coloring for paints.
16. Irons uses are numerous.
17. A plant fertilizers list of ingredients includes manganese.
18. There are about 1.5 trillion tons of manganese nodules on the worlds ocean floors.
19. Nodules sometimes form around a sharks tooth or a whales earbone.
20. No ones theory on these nodules formation is universally accepted.
21. Manganese nodules are growing faster than humankinds ability to use them.
22. The Pacifics nodules differ from the Atlantics; the formers are softer.
23. Back in 59 John Mero wrote one of the first articles in favor of deep-sea mining.
24. Theres no need to drill or blast to find these mineral riches.
25. Scattered across the ocean floor, theyre easy to photograph through the cameras lens.
26. The line bucket of John Mero is the simplest system of mining; Deepsea Ventures suspended derrick is more complicated.
27. The derrick is suspended so that its pipe wont break when the mining ship rocks.
28. The effects of deep-sea mining on underwater animals and plants lives have caused concern.
29. The law of the sea, as stated in the Geneva Convention of 58, has not been fully defined.
30. The third-world countries belief is that these resources are everyones.

7.l QUOTATION MARKS

Quotation marks are used to emphasize and to distinguish other people's words, special elements, and definitions used in a sentence. Use double quotation marks to enclose direct quotations, titles of short works, borrowed expressions, words and expressions you wish to call to the reader's attention, and English translations of foreign words. Make sure that you place quotation marks at the beginning and at the end of the material you wish to enclose.

7.l.1 Quotation marks for direct quotations

Use quotation marks to enclose a direct quotation.

Place quotation marks around *only* the quoted material, not around any part of your own sentence. Always quote exactly what was spoken or written if you are using quotation marks. Do not add your own words or punctuation to the quotation; do not delete any of the author's words or punctuation unless you use ellipses (see 7.q).

Quotations of more than three lines of poetry or more than two lines of prose should be set off and indented. Indented quotations do not need quotation marks. Quotations of less than three lines should be run into the text of your paper and enclosed by quotation marks. In general, use a comma to set off a quotation run into the text of your paper. You may, however, use a colon to set off somewhat longer quotations within the text of your paper (see 7.i.2). Use footnotes to cite the source of a significant quotation.

> Socrates wisely said, "As for me, all I know is that I know nothing."
>
> "Learn how to cook!" advises culinary artist Julia Child.
>
> "I celebrate myself, and sing myself," wrote the poet Walt Whitman.

1. capitalization of the first word of a quotation

Capitalize the first word of a quotation that is a complete sentence. Do not capitalize a quotation that is only a partial sentence.

Dorothy Parker wrote, "**P**oets alone should kiss and tell."

Oscar Wilde admitted that he could resist "**a**nything but temptation."

2. commas before or after quotations

Set off a quotation with a comma (or a colon) only if the quotation is a complete sentence. Do not set off a quotation that is a partial sentence.

Henry Clay stubbornly maintained**,** **"**Sir, I would rather be right than be President.**"**

Elizabeth Barrett Browning begins her most famous sonnet with these words**:** **"**How do I love thee? Let me count the ways. **"**

"There is no new thing under the sun**,"** writes the unknown author of Ecclesiastes.

Daniel Webster declared that liberty and union were **"**one and inseparable.**"**

3. split quotations

When a quotation is interrupted with such words as *she wrote* or *he said*, enclose both parts of the separated quotation in quotation marks. Set off each part with some kind of punctuation. If the second part of the quotation is a complete sentence, be sure to begin it with a capital letter.

"Those who deny freedom to others**,"** said Abraham Lincoln**,** **"** deserve it not for themselves.**"**

"I am always busy**,"** wrote Elizabeth Cady Stanton**,** **"**which is perhaps the chief reason why I am always well.**"**

"I never think of the future**,"** wrote Albert Einstein**.** **"**It comes soon enough.**"**

4. indirect quotations

Do not use quotation marks in an indirect quotation (or an indirect question). An indirect quotation does not quote the person's exact words.

ORIGINAL: **"**I never intended to become a run-of-the-mill person.**"**

—Barbara Jordan

INDIRECTLY QUOTED: In fact, Barbara Jordan said that it was never her intention to become a run-of-the-mill person.

5. single quotation marks

Use single quotation marks to enclose a quotation within a quotation.

> My instructor smiled and replied, "It was Sarah Bernhardt who said, 'An *artiste* with short arms can never, never make a fine gesture.' "

6. dialogue

In writing dialogue, begin a new paragraph and use a new set of quotation marks every time the speaker changes.

> Mr. Blakely smiled pleasantly. "I was looking out of the window a minute ago," he said, "and I saw a dog run across the street and turn the corner."
>
> "What kind of a lookin' dog was it?" Penrod inquired, with languor.
>
> "Well," said Mr. Blakely, "it was a — it was a nice-looking dog."
>
> "What color was he?"
>
> "He was — ah — white. That is, I think —"
>
> —Booth Tarkington

7.1.2 Quotation marks for titles of short works

Use quotation marks to enclose titles of short works such as stories, poems, essays, newspaper and periodical articles, chapters, songs, and television episodes.

"The Gold Bug"
"To Build a Fire"
"The Road Not Taken"
"Birches"
"Self-Reliance"
"Peace Treaty Signed"
"America the Beautiful"
"Yesterday"

NOTE: Italicize (underline) titles of long works such as books, films, and plays, and names of periodicals and newspapers, television series, and paintings (see 7.m.1).

7.1.3 Quotation marks for borrowed expressions

Use quotation marks to enclose unfamiliar slang, technical terms, and other unusual expressions.

A once-popular slang expression was “zounds.”
At the top of each page is the book’s “folio,” or page number.
My roommate used to call the clumps of dust under the bed “dust bunnies.”

7.1.4 Quotation marks for translations

Use quotation marks to enclose an English translation of a foreign word or expression.

The foreign word is usually italicized (underlined). If the foreign word or expression has more than one English equivalent, make sure to enclose each English translation separately.

Zeitgeist is a German word meaning “spirit of the time.”
Le mot juste is a French expression meaning “the right word” or “the exact word.”

AVOIDING ERRORS WITH QUOTATION MARKS

Do not forget to place quotation marks (single or double) both *before* and *after* the quoted material. The omission of closing quotation marks is a frequent error.

NOT He yelled, “Help! Help!✗
BUT He yelled, “Help! Help!”

NOT We read “A Worn Path✗in class today.
BUT We read “A Worn Path” in class today.

NOT *Ex libris Caroli* is a Latin phrase meaning “from the library of Charles✗
BUT *Ex libris Caroli* is a Latin phrase meaning “from the library of Charles.”

QUOTATION MARKS WITH OTHER MARKS OF PUNCTUATION

1. Always place a comma or a period *inside* closing quotation marks.

   "Everything had its wonders, even darkness and silence," wrote Helen Keller, who was blind and deaf from birth.

   Billie Jean King responded, "Women can be great athletes."

2. Always place a semicolon or a colon *outside* closing quotation marks.

   A male swan is a "cob"; a female swan is a "pen"; a baby swan is a "cygnet."

   There are two Spanish verbs that mean "to be": *ser* and *estar.*

3. Place the question mark or exclamation point *inside* the closing quotation marks when it is part of the quotation.

   My friend asked, "How did you manage to persuade your mother to let you go to the concert?"

   My father kept saying, "That's incredible!"

   Place the question mark or exclamation point *outside* the quotation marks when it is part of the entire sentence.

   Why did he say, "This is only the beginning"?

   How wonderful that she intends to print your short story "Winter"!

   NOTE: If both your sentence and the quotation at the end of your sentence need a question mark (or an exclamation point), use only *one* question mark (or exclamation point) placed *inside* the quotation marks.

   When did he say, "Will the car be fixed in time for the concert?"

   Don't you dare say to me, "That's enough out of you!"

EXERCISE 30. Rewrite each of the following sentences correctly, adding quotation marks and other punctuation that are needed. Three of the sentences are correct as written.

1. Albert Einstein's uncle taught him algebra. It is a merry science he told the boy; when the animal that we are hunting cannot be caught, we call it *x*.
2. You will never amount to anything, Einstein said the great physicist's elementary school teacher.
3. In later years Einstein said that the teachers in elementary school appeared to him like sergeants.
4. A teacher of his once said, Your presence in this class destroys the respect of the students.
5. The German-born Einstein had trouble getting a job in Switzerland, where he was ridiculed as a paper Swiss.
6. I am a horse for a single harness Einstein later said not cut out for tandem or teamwork.
7. Einstein once joked, In my relativity theory I set up a clock at every point in space, but in reality I find it difficult to provide even one clock in my room.
8. In 1911 Einstein published a short paper entitled The Influence of Gravity on the Propagation of Light.
9. If Einstein's theory should prove correct, said Max Planck, he will be considered the Copernicus of the twentieth century.
10. The most incomprehensible thing about the world, said Einstein, is that it is comprehensible.
11. The concepts known as force, acceleration, and absolute space have no place in Einstein's theory of gravitation.
12. Einstein was looked upon as an *enfant terrible*, a French expression meaning a person who causes embarrassment.
13. The year 1915 was Einstein's *annus mirabilis*, or wonderful year: He published his short paper General Theory of Relativity.
14. One of Einstein's great contributions was the all motion is relative" idea.
15. An American reporter asked Einstein if he would explain his theory of relativity in a few sentences.
16. It was formerly believed that if all material things disappeared out of the universe, time and space would be left, replied Einstein.
17. According to the relativity theory, however, he continued, time and space disappear together with the things.

18. It is not so very important for a person to learn facts, said Einstein. The value of an education is . . . the training of the mind to think something that cannot be learned from textbooks, he continued.
19. According to Philipp Frank's book *Einstein: His Life and Times*, the scientist "always steered clear of actual politics.
20. After coming to America, Einstein gave many lectures; one of them was entitled On Physical Reality.

7.m ITALICS (UNDERLINING)

Italic type is a special slanted type that is used in printing. (*This is printed in italics.*) Indicate italics on the typewriter or in handwriting by underlining. (This is underlined.)

7.m.1 Italics for titles of long works

Italicize (underline) titles of long literary and artistic works, including books, films, plays, long poems, long musical compositions, and paintings. Also italicize (underline) the names of newspapers, periodicals, television series, and court cases.

Wuthering Heights	*Newsweek*
On the Waterfront	*Mona Lisa*
Macbeth	*Appalachian Spring*
The People, Yes	*Nova*
the *Baltimore Sun*	*Furman* v. *Georgia*[1]

Italicize (underline) and capitalize articles (*a*, *an*, *the*) written at the beginning of a title only when they are part of the title itself. It is preferred usage not to italicize (underline) or capitalize articles preceding the title of a newspaper or periodical. In general, do not italicize (or capitalize) the word *magazine* following the title of a periodical.

The Red Desert	*but*	the *Boston Globe*
A Farewell to Arms		He placed a *Reader's Digest* on the counter.
An American in Paris		an *Atlantic Monthly* magazine

[1]Do not italicize the *v.* in court cases.

EXERCISE 31. Rewrite each of the following sentences correctly, underlining those elements that should be italicized.

1. Zora Neale Hurston was born in Eatonville, Florida, which she later described in her novel Their Eyes Were Watching God.
2. At an early age she found a copy of Paradise Lost in a heap of rubbish and became entranced with it.
3. Her short story "Drenched in Light" was published in Opportunity, a magazine edited by Charles S. Johnson.
4. The New Yorker magazine called Zora Neale Hurston "one of our few genuine, Grade A folk writers."
5. Hurston felt that the play Emperor Jones by Eugene O'Neill was not representative of true black folklore.
6. Composer Scott Joplin, whose ragtime music was used in the 1973 film The Sting, used black folklore in his opera Treemonisha.
7. The first black newspaper, Freedom's Journal, was started in 1827 in New York City.
8. Black theater was quite vital in the twenties; Jacob Lawrence's painting Vaudeville is based upon his memories of the Apollo Theater in those days.
9. Cicely Tyson, who appeared in the television series Roots, learned her craft in the New York theater.
10. In the famous Dred Scott v. Sanford case a Missouri slave sued his owner for freedom.

7.m.2 Italics for names of spacecraft, airplanes, ships, trains

Italicize (underline) names of spacecraft, airplanes, ships, and trains.

Sputnik I
Air Force One
Queen Elizabeth 2
Nautilus

U.S.S. *Constitution*[1]
Congressional Limited
Titanic

[1]Do not italicize *U.S.S.* in the name of a ship.

7.m.3 Italics for foreign words

Italicize (underline) foreign words and expressions that are not used frequently in English.

Do not italicize a foreign word or expression that is commonly used in English. For example, the word *siesta* (italicized here because it is referred to as a word) is usually not italicized, although it is a Spanish word. The French expression *enfant terrible*, however, is normally italicized because it is less frequently used. Enclose in quotation marks the English translation of a foreign word or expression (see 7.1.4).

7.m.4 Italics for words and letters used to represent themselves

Italicize (underline) words, letters, numbers and signs used to represent themselves.

Why does the author use the word *essence* instead of *life*?
The *i* and the *t* were reversed in the title.
I used the *%* instead of the word *percent* in my analysis.

NOTE: Use an 's to indicate the plural of words, letters, numbers, and signs used to represent themselves. This 's is not italicized.

There are two *m*'s, two *t*'s, and two *e*'s in the word *committee.*
I deleted all of the *well*'s, *so*'s, and *indeed*'s from my paper.

EXERCISE 32. Rewrite each of the following sentences correctly, underlining those elements that should be italicized.

1. In Jules Verne's 1865 science fiction novel, From the Earth to the Moon, the space travelers were launched from southern Florida.
2. Just over a century later the Apollo XI astronauts were launched from the John F. Kennedy Space Center in southern Florida.
3. Apollo is the name of the classical god of the sun and comes from the Greek word Apollōn.
4. The launching was observed by Charles Lindbergh, who in 1927 had made the first nonstop transatlantic flight in The Spirit of St. Louis.

5. Unlike the characters in Verne's sequel, Round the Moon, the American astronauts actually stepped on the moon.
6. The flat areas on the moon are often called maria, which is a Latin word meaning "seas."
7. The ia in maria is the plural ending; in Latin a single sea is mare.
8. The term sea, however, is not exactly le mot juste ("the right word") for these areas of the moon.
9. The word sea is not accurate because there is no water on the moon.
10. The returning astronauts were hoisted onto the deck of the carrier U.S.S. Hornet after their splashdown.

7.n PARENTHESES

Use parentheses to set off extra material.

Commas and dashes are also used for this purpose, the difference between the three marks being one of degree. Set off with commas extra material that is fairly closely related to the rest of the sentence. Use parentheses for material that is not intended to be part of the main statement but is nevertheless important enough to include. Use dashes for material that more abruptly interrupts the sentence and that you wish to emphasize.

> Cody, Wyoming, was named after William Frederick Cody **(** "Buffalo Bill," 1846 – 1917**)**, an American scout and sharpshooter.
>
> Minnesota **(**from the Dakota Sioux word meaning "cloudy water"**)** was first explored by French scouts.

A sentence (or phrase) within parentheses is not capitalized (nor does it need a period) if it is contained within another sentence. A capital letter and a period are needed if a complete sentence in parentheses stands by itself.

> Nebraska contains two of the widest and flattest rivers in the country: the Missouri River and the Platte River. **(**The name *Nebraska* comes from the Indian word *Nibrathka*, meaning "flat water."**)**
>
> As gold and silver mining waned **(**mining declined in the 1870s**)**, cattle ranching became Nevada's principal business.

PARENTHESES USED WITH OTHER MARKS OF PUNCTUATION

1. Always place a comma, semicolon, or colon *after* closing parentheses.

   Although Death Valley may appear barren (it is called a desert by most people), you will find cactuses, wildflowers, snakes, and fourteen varieties of birds.

   One of the problems of pioneer towns was the lack of women (more than half the population of Seattle were bachelors); however, in 1864 a settler brought a group of widows and orphans to Seattle.

   Washington State is the site of these fur-trapping posts (all built before 1833): Spokane, Walla Walla, and Nisqually.

2. Place a question mark or exclamation point *inside* parentheses if it is part of the parenthetical expression.

   There is a city named Clinton (named after American statesman De Witt Clinton?) in almost every state in the United States.

   Many names have been suggested for the Black Hills of South Dakota (they were almost named the Purple Mountains!).

   Place a question mark or exclamation point *outside* parentheses if it is part of the entire sentence.

   Did you visit the famous "cowpoke capitals" of the Old West (Dodge City, Cimarron, Wichita, and Abilene)?

   How surprised I was to find out that a Franciscan mission was the site of the battle at the Alamo (Antonio de Valero Mission)!

3. Use brackets to enclose a parenthetical expression within parentheses.

   Mississippi comes from two Chippewa words that describe the waterway (*mici* ["large"] and *zibi* ["river"]).

7.o DASHES

Indicate the dash by writing or typing two hyphens (- -). Do not place a comma, semicolon, colon, or period before or after a dash.

7.o.1 Dashes to emphasize supplemental material

Use dashes to emphasize supplemental material.

If it is not necessary to emphasize the material, set it off with commas.

Strong man Louis Cyr once lifted 588 pounds off the floor—using one finger. [The dashes emphasize the last part of the sentence.]

Gertrude Ederle, a remarkable American Olympic swimmer, swam the English Channel in fourteen hours and thirty-one minutes. [It is not necessary to emphasize the supplemental material; use commas.]

7.o.2 Dashes to set off interrupting or additional material

Use dashes to set off interrupting or additional material that is not grammatically connected to the rest of the sentence.

Parentheses can also be used; see 7.n.

Billie Jean King — or should it be Queen? — is a champion for women's rights as well as a crack tennis player.

7.o.3 Dashes to signal an abrupt change in thought

Use dashes to signal an abrupt change in thought within the sentence.

What was it — I paused to think — what was it that so unnerved me in the contemplation of the House of Usher?

—Edgar Allan Poe

7.o.4 Dashes to indicate hesitation in speech

In writing dialogue, use dashes to indicate hesitating or faltering speech.

"You're — you're not taking me to the police station?" she stammered.

—Katherine Mansfield

EXERCISE 33. In the items below, other punctuation is used incorrectly with the dashes and parentheses. Rewrite each sentence correctly.

1. . . . nobody sees a flower — really; — it is so small . . . .

   —Georgia O'Keeffe

2. Those hills! They go on and on; — it was like looking at two miles of gray elephants.

   —Georgia O'Keeffe

3. The painter Georgia O'Keeffe (is that her real name)? lived most of her life in the American Southwest.
4. O'Keeffe was married to the famous photographer Alfred Stieglitz. (Both Stieglitz and Edward Steichen [1879–1973] were responsible for transforming photography into an art form).
5. Because she knows too much about paintings, O'Keeffe once remarked (in a newspaper article,) she does not really enjoy looking at them.

7.p BRACKETS

Use brackets ([ ]) to enclose information that you insert into a quotation from someone else's work.

Such an insertion is called an authorial addition.

This is the only place that I really belonged [the Texas Panhandle], that I really felt at home. —Georgia O'Keeffe

She [Margaret Mead] was, and still is, the symbol of the woman thinker in America. —Betty Friedan

He [George III, King of Great Britain] has plundered our seas, ravaged our coasts, burnt our towns, and destroyed the lives of our people. —Declaration of Independence

7.q ELLIPSES

Use a series of spaced periods called ellipsis points or ellipses (. . .) to indicate the omission of material in a quotation.

Use three spaced periods if the omission is at the beginning or in the middle of a sentence. Use four spaced periods (no space before the first period) if the omission is at the end of a sentence. The first period (or question mark or exclamation point) serves as the end mark for the sentence. The sentence that precedes or follows four ellipsis points must be grammatically complete.

> For example, Katherine Mansfield's story "The Garden Party" begins with a discussion of the weather that states, in part, ". . . They could not have had a more perfect day for a garden-party if they had ordered it. . . . The gardener had been up since dawn, mowing the lawn . . . until the grass . . . seemed to shine. . . ."

EXERCISE 34. Following is an excerpt from *Anne Frank: The Diary of a Young Girl.* Delete the material in brackets and insert the proper form of ellipses. Add the following "authorial addition" where there is an asterisk: [her family's secret apartment].

> Anyone who claims that the older ones have a more difficult time here *certainly doesn't realize to what extent our problems weigh down on us [problems for which we are probably much too young, but which thrust themselves upon us continually, until, after a long time, we think we've found a solution, but the solution doesn't seem able to resist the facts which reduce it to nothing again. That's the difficulty in these times:] Ideals, dreams, and cherished hope rise within us, only to meet the horrible truth and be shattered.
>
> It's really a wonder that I haven't dropped all my ideals [because they seem so absurd and impossible to carry out.] Yet [I keep them, because] in spite of everything I still believe that people are really good at heart. [I simply can't build up my hopes on a foundation consisting of confusion, misery, and death. I see the world gradually being turned into a wilderness. I hear the ever approaching thunder, which will destroy us too, I can feel the sufferings of millions and yet, if I look up into the heavens,] I think that it will all come right, that this cruelty too will end, and that peace and tranquility will return again.

GLOSSARY OF USAGE PROBLEMS

8 Glossary of Usage Problems

Language is always changing. Words come and go. Traditionally, there have been several ways of classifying language. Many people divide language into standard language and nonstandard language; some further draw the line between formal and informal.

Standard English is the language of writing found in education, business, government, and similar fields. It is the language you read in general newspapers and magazines. **Nonstandard English** includes the language of a particular region and words considered *slang.* Standard and nonstandard have many varieties, or *dialects.*

It is possible to divide standard English into two distinct levels: formal and informal. **Formal English** is found in most writing that is intended for a general audience—business correspondence, newspaper articles, some schoolwork such as research papers. Formal English is serious in tone and mostly impersonal in viewpoint. **Informal English,** on the other hand, is used in casual conversation and casual writing. It is more appropriate for a personal type of audience—friends or close colleagues. Informal English is more chatty in tone and more personal in viewpoint. That is, it is more relaxed than formal English.

Of course, no distinctions are hard and fast. Some situations in which you might expect to find formal English at times lend themselves to informal English—a business memo to a trusted colleague, for example. Language is, after all, subject to a constant drift, which tends to break down any such distinctions. All levels, or kinds, of language are now recognized as being appropriate in their own time and place. Moreover, the "appropriateness" itself is constantly being

A SAMPLE LIST OF APPROPRIATE LANGUAGE

situation	***research papers*** ***business letters*** ***most books, magazines, newspapers***	***conversation*** ***personal letters*** ***casual (or informal) discussion***
structures	*whom* as object *It is he.* *if he were older...* no contractions no split infinitives more subordinating conjunctions complete sentences only	*who* as object *It is him.* *if he was older...* contractions split infinitives more coordinating conjunctions some fragments and run-ons
words and expressions	*fairly good* *very good* *She is certainly bright.* *drive slowly*	*pretty good* *real good* *She's sure bright.* *drive slow*

redefined. What was slang twenty years ago may have become quite respectable today. The words *hairdo, handout,* and *shabby,* for example, all began as slang and have since taken their place in the vocabulary of standard English. On the other hand, some slang disappears over time.

Perhaps the most useful distinction to be made is between **spoken language** and **written language.** In general, you should be more formal in writing than you are in speaking. You tend to speak in spurts, but you are usually careful to measure your written words. In speaking, you aim mainly to communicate a message, and if you do not at first make yourself clear, you usually have the opportunity to stop and explain yourself. Your written words, however, are intended to last, at least for a while, and it is important to compose sentences that have variety, rhythm, and coherence. Written words must speak for themselves; they are either clear or not. Written language, then, generally requires more precision and care than spoken language.

As a writer and speaker of English, you should try to develop a sense of language appropriateness. Be aware of the differences between the English that is appropriate in a job interview and that which is acceptable in a casual telephone conversation. The above chart will give you an idea of these two levels of English. The chart classifies some of the words, expressions, and structures by situation. It is only a sampling, but it can help you to begin to develop a sense of when certain language is appropriate or inappropriate.

Some points of vocabulary and grammar cause everyone problems. These include words and structures that are both misused and confused. The following glossary lists many such usage problems with explanations and examples. Study the glossary, and do the exercises that follow.

a, an Use *a* before a word beginning with a sounded consonant, including a sounded *h: a rocket, a helicopter, a history.* Use *an* before a word beginning with a vowel or an unsounded *h: an endowment, an heir.* Use *a* before a word beginning with the "yew" sound: *a European, a union.*

affect, effect See page 386.

ain't There is no reason to use *ain't* in standard English; use *I'm not, you're not, she's not,* etc. Use *ain't* mainly when showing dialect.

> No, you **ain't.** You **ain't** the only person that's ben shaked down wrongfully out'n a high place.
>
> —Mark Twain, *The Adventures of Huckleberry Finn*

all right This is always two words (never ~~*alright*~~).

all the farther, all the faster These are very informal ways of saying *as far as* and *as fast as*. In writing, it is best to use *as far as* or *as fast as*.

Just work **as fast as** you can!

and etc. *Etc.* is an abbreviation of *et cetera*, a Latin expression that means "and the rest." *Etc.* must not be preceded by *and* because *et* means "and."

anywheres, everywheres Write these words and others like them without an *s: anywhere, everywhere, somewhere.*

bad, badly See 1.f.6.

being as, being that Many people use these expressions informally to mean *because* or *since*. In writing always use *because* or *since.*

Because I could not stop for Death—
He kindly stopped for me—

—Emily Dickinson

beside, besides These are two different words. *Beside* means "at the side of"; *besides* means either "in addition to" or "moreover."

Who is that little girl sitting **beside** Jeremy?
Besides Sergio, I'm inviting James, Karl, and Luiz.
Sonia is too busy to attend the play; **besides,** she is feeling ill.

between, among Use *between* with two elements and *among* with more than two elements. Notice, however, that *between* may be used with more than two elements if they are actually considered two at a time.

Merced is a small town **between** San Francisco and Los Angeles.
Most people feel relaxed and comfortable **among** friends.
I cut out snacks **between** breakfast, lunch, and dinner.

bring, take Note the direction indicated by each of these words. Use *bring* to mean movement toward the speaker or writer and *take* to mean movement away from the speaker or writer. *Bring* is related to *come* as *take* is to *go*.

When you **come** back from Maui, will you **bring** me a pineapple?
Should I **take** the dog when I **go** to the park?

cannot help but The problem with this expression is that it is a double negative (*but* has a negative sense here). Say *cannot help.* (See page 95.)

Alberta **cannot help** liking sourdough bread.

continual, continuous *Continual* describes action that is repeated, but with pauses; *continuous* describes action that has no interruptions.

The **continual** banging of the door made it difficult to concentrate, and the blare from the TV was **continuous.**

convince, persuade Both words mean "cause another person to believe or to do something." *Convince* implies an appeal to reason or logic; *persuade* implies an appeal to feeling. *Persuade* can often imply action; you *convince* someone *of* something, but you *persuade* him or her *to do* something.

I **convinced** Tim of my sincerity.
Unfortunately, I could not **persuade** him to stay.

could of, might of These expressions are incorrect. Some people carelessly write *could of* and *might of* instead of *could have* and *might have* because these phrases are often pronounced alike in informal conversation. Be sure to write *could have, might have, must have,* etc.

He thought of the theaters she **must have** been to, the pictures she **must have** looked at, the sober and splendid old houses she **must have** frequented, the people she **must have** talked with . . . .

—Edith Wharton, *The Age of Innocence*

criteria This word is plural and always takes a plural verb. The singular form is *criterion.* The same is true of *data, media,* and *strata;* their singular forms are *datum, medium,* and *stratum.*

Two **criteria** for judging a long-distance runner are speed and endurance.

different from, different than Always write *different from* before a noun or pronoun. Before clauses or some phrases it is acceptable to use *different than.*

Nebraska is **different from** Vermont.
Life in Nebraska is **different from** life in Vermont.
Driving in Nebraska was **different than** it was in Vermont.

disinterested, uninterested *Disinterested* implies impartiality; *uninterested,* apathy. It is therefore possible to be *disinterested* without being *uninterested.*

Umpires must be **distinterested** in a game, but they cannot be **uninterested.**

done The word *done* must always be accompanied by a form of *have* or *be—was done, had done, will be done,* etc. *Done* is not the past tense of *do*; it is the past participle.

. . . and there may be two or three
Apples I didn't pick upon some bough.
But I **am done** with apple-picking now.
—Robert Frost, "After Apple-Picking"

doesn't, don't *Don't* is a contraction of *do not*. Use it with *I, you, we, they,* or plural nouns. *Doesn't* is a contraction of *does not*. Use it with *he, she, it,* or singular nouns.

I don't know the answer, and **she doesn't** either.

due to, because of Use *due to* only when it relates to a particular noun or pronoun. Otherwise, use *because of.*

The delay was **due to** bad weather.
The train was delayed **because of** bad weather.
Because of bad weather, the train was delayed.

enthuse This verb grew out of the noun *enthusiasm*, but is not yet accepted in formal English. Use *be enthusiastic* or *become enthusiastic* instead. (A similar verb to avoid is *burgle*, which came from the noun *burglar*; use *burglarize* instead.)

The critics could not have **been** more **enthusiastic** about the film.

famous, notorious *Famous means "widely and favorably known"; notorious,* "widely and unfavorably known."

Roberto Clemente was a **famous** right fielder for the Pittsburgh Pirates.
Charles Dickens' Scrooge is **notorious** for hoarding money.

farther, further *Farther* refers to physical distance; *further* is usually used to refer to time or degree.

. . . **farther** down the corridor . . .
—Willa Cather

. . . people can have no **further** illusions about it. . . .
—Franklin D. Roosevelt

fewer, less Use *fewer* with nouns that you can count; use *less* with nouns that you cannot count. Notice, however, that *less* is normally used with figures that are seen in terms of a single quantity or amount.

fewer dog biscuits
less dog food
The job took **less** than eight hours. (Eight hours is seen as a single period of time.)
It paid **less** than $1,000. (The money is seen as a single sum, not as individual dollars.)

frightened Use *frightened by* or *frightened at*, not *frightened of*. Say *frightened by* lightning or *afraid of* lightning.

Aunt Bessie, who had already been **frightened,** twice, **by** a clock-work mouse, whimpered at the sideboard and had some elderberry wine.

—Dylan Thomas, "A Child's Christmas in Wales"

good, well See 1.f.6.

had of See **could of, might of**

had ought Do not use *had* with *ought*.

He is just what a young man **ought to** be . . . sensible, good-humored, lively; and I never saw such happy manners!

—Jane Austen, *Pride and Prejudice*

healthful, healthy Use *healthful* to mean "promoting health" and *healthy* to mean "having good health." Carrots and apples may be *healthful*; people may be *healthy*.

imply, infer These words are not interchangeable. *Imply* means "suggest" or "hint." *Infer* means "draw a conclusion from."

The article **implied** that no one was to blame.
From the article, I **inferred** that no one was to blame.

in, into, in to *In* indicates location. *Into* indicates direction to a place. *In to* indicates direction to something other than a place.

Mr. and Mrs. Ng were **in** the dining room.
Mr. and Mrs. Ng went **into** the dining room.
Mr. and Mrs. Ng went **in to** supper.

incredible, incredulous An *incredible* person or thing is unbelievable; an *incredulous* person is unbelieving or skeptical.

The view from the Sears Tower in Chicago is truly **incredible.**
When the discovery was made, most scientists were **incredulous.**

ingenious, ingenuous Someone who is *ingenious* is clever or inventive. Someone who is *ingenuous* is naive or unsophisticated.

Tomio came up with an **ingenious** solution to the chess problem.
No one but an **ingenuous** person will believe this witness' story.

in regard to Never use ~~*in regards to*~~ (though *as regards* is correct).

In regard to your proposal, I have the following comment.

irregardless, regardless ~~*Irregardless*~~ is not an accepted word because it expresses a double negative—*ir-* and *-less* both have negative meanings. Use *regardless.*

this kind, these kinds *This, that, these,* and *those* should agree in number with *kind, kinds; sort, sorts;* or *type, types.*

that kind of problem
those sorts of solutions

kind of a The *a* is unnecessary after expressions such as *kind of, sort of,* or *type of.*

What **kind of** flower is that?

lay, lie *Lay* means "put" or "place." *Lie* means "recline" or "be situated." *Lie* never takes an object.

Lay the book on the table.
That cat loves to **lie** in the sun.

Be careful not to confuse the other forms of these verbs. Pay particular attention to the past tense: The past tense of *lay* is *laid,* and the past tense of *lie* is *lay.*

BASIC VERB	**lay**	**lie**
PRESENT PARTICIPLE	**laying**	**lying**
PAST TENSE	**laid**	**lay**
PAST PARTICIPLE	**laid**	**lain**

learn, teach These words are not synonyms. *Learn* means "acquire knowledge," and *teach* means "impart knowledge." Instructors *teach;* students *learn.*

leave, let *Leave* means "go away," and *let* means "allow." Although the expressions *leave alone* and *let alone* are used interchangeably, there is a subtle difference between them: *Leave alone* means "go away from," and *let alone* means "allow to be alone."

The plane to Phoenix **leaves** in two hours.
Please, **let** us help with the dishes!
Because Armando was very shy, we were careful not to **leave** him **alone** at the picnic.
If those children do not **let** Aunt Rose **alone,** she is never going to visit again!

like, as *Like* is a preposition and introduces a prepositional phrase; *as* introduces a subordinate clause.

Myra talks **like** a Texan.
She talks **as** a Texan talks.
A breeze blew through the room, blew curtains in at one end and out the other **like** pale flags, twisting them toward the frosted wedding-cake of the ceiling, and then rippled over the wine-colored rug, making a shadow on it, **as** wind does on the sea.
—F. Scott Fitzgerald, *The Great Gatsby*

Do not use *like* to mean *as if.*

NOT It looks ~~like~~ it was new.
BUT It looks **like** new.
OR It looks **as if** it were new.

off of Use *off* only; the *of* is unnecessary.

Take the atlas **off** the shelf.

or, nor Use *or* after *either;* use *nor* after *neither.*

We can go to the beach **either** today **or** tomorrow.
Neither Celia **nor** Jess will be able to go with us.

oral, verbal Both of these terms mean "pertaining to words" or "in words." *Oral* refers to spoken words only; *verbal* refers to spoken or written words.

An **oral** history of California is on tape at the Bancroft Library at the University of California.
A **verbal** agreement may be spoken or written.

raise, rise Both words mean "move to a higher position"; however, *raise* always takes an object (*raise* a hand), and *rise* never takes an object (heat *rises*).

Most people **raise** their voices in anger.
Antonio **rises** every morning at six and runs two miles before going to work.

reason is because *Because* means "for the reason that." Therefore, the expression *the reason is because* is repetitive and incorrect. Use either *the reason is that* or *because.*

The **reason** Jane cannot come to the party **is that** she will be out of town.
Jane cannot come to the party **because** she will be out of town.

respectfully, respectively *Respectfully* means "with respect." *Respectively* means "in the order named."

Some of Grandpa's stories go on for hours, but we always listen **respectfully.**
Peggy and Michael are, **respectively**, author and editor of the book.

says, said Be careful not to use the present tense *says* when you mean the past tense *said.*

Yesterday he **said** that he would meet us outside the theater.

sit, set *Sit* usually means "be or place oneself in a sitting position" and rarely takes an object (*he* **sits**). *Set* means "place" or "put" and usually takes an object (*he* **sets** *the* *clock*). Notice, however, the following common use of *set* without an object: *The sun* **sets.**

As soon as Tom **sets** the table, we can all **sit** down.

try and, try to *Try and* is an informal way of saying *try to* but is illogical and incorrect. Consider the sentence *I will* **try and** *finish soon.* The sentence suggests that the speaker will do two things: (1) make an effort and (2) finish soon. It is more precise to say *I will* **try to** *finish soon.*

Try to be cheerful now; the traveling is at an end, and you have nothing to do but rest and amuse yourself as you please.
—Emily Brontë, *Wuthering Heights*

way, ways Some people use *ways* to mean *way*—for example, a long *ways* off. This usage is incorrect and should be avoided in writing.

The election is still a long **way** off, but both candidates have begun to campaign.

where at Never use *at* after *where.*

NOT *Where* is she ~~at~~?
BUT **Where** is she?

who, whom See 1.d.5, 1.d.6, 2.t, and corresponding "Avoiding Errors" boxes.

EXERCISE 1. In each of the sentences below, select from the choices in parentheses the word or phrase that represents preferred usage. (This exercise covers items *a, an* through *bring, take* in the Glossary of Usage Problems.)

1. Today, Americans (everywhere/everywheres) are discovering patchwork quilts.
2. There (ain't/isn't) any other craft more typically American than quilting.
3. The original colonists did not (bring/take) patchwork quilts with them when they came from Europe.
4. Patchwork was originally invented in America as (a/an) necessity rather than as (a/an) art.

5. People discovered that the colorful coverlets were not only (all right/alright) but quite extraordinary as bed covers.
6. Most patchwork patterns have quaint names—log cabin, sunburst, nine patch, grandma's flower garden, (and etc./etc.).
7. (Because/Being as) it is difficult to quilt a coverlet, many people sew only the patchwork top, which they give to a church group to be quilted.
8. Members of the Holy Ghost Lutheran Church Quilting Club in Fredericksburg, Texas, work (all the faster/as fast as) they can.
9. (Beside/Besides) wanting to raise money for the church, the members of a quilting club want to see each other.
10. The object of a quilting bee is not to work (all the faster/as fast as) you can, but to socialize (between/among) friends.

EXERCISE 2. In each of the sentences below, select from the choices in parentheses the word or phrase that represents preferred usage. (This exercise covers items *cannot help but* through *doesn't, don't* in the Glossary of Usage Problems.)

1. At a pot-luck supper people eat and chat for hours; the event is one of (continual/continuous) fun.
2. Anyone who likes variety (cannot help but like/cannot help liking) a meal for which each guest has brought a different dish.
3. The food at a pot-luck supper is quite (different from/different than) ordinary hamburgers and hot dogs.
4. Pot-luck meals have something for everyone; for those who are (disinterested/uninterested) in baked ham, there is always fried chicken.
5. Americans always (done/have done) imaginative meal planning.
6. The most important criteria for a successful pot-luck supper (is/are) good food and lots of friends.
7. Years ago the ice cream (might have/might of) been hand cranked.
8. Today's pot-luck suppers (doesn't/don't) have homemade ice cream, but they usually have three or four desserts.
9. (Because of/Due to) popular demand, someone usually brings an apple pie.
10. With enough flattery, the cooks can sometimes be (convinced/persuaded) to give out their recipes.

EXERCISE 3. In each of the sentences below, select from the choices in parentheses the word or phrase that represents preferred usage. (This exercise covers items *done* through *had ought* in the Glossary of Usage Problems.)

1. Everyone (had ought/ought) to experience the fun, music, and dancing at a hoedown.
2. After a hard day's work, people are relaxed and (enthused/enthusiastic).
3. The excitement increases as the musicians get (farther/further) involved in the lively tunes.
4. There is no reason for the dancers to be (frightened by/frightened of) the steps; one does not have to be an expert.
5. A square dancer (had ought/ought) to worry about nothing other than having a good time.
6. As newcomers make (fewer/less) errors, they attempt more complicated square dances.
7. People travel far to hear banjos and perhaps (farther/further) to hear combs, spoons, and washboards making music.
8. Some American country music, called bluegrass music, is now (famous/notorious) around the world.
9. (Fewer/Less) Americans were intrigued by country music a decade ago.
10. Ballad lyrics tell familiar tales of heroes and heroines and of villains (famous/notorious) for their exploits.

EXERCISE 4. In each of the sentences below, select from the choices in parentheses the word or phrase that represents preferred usage. (This exercise covers items *hanged, hung* through *kind of a* in the Glossary of Usage Problems.)

1. Homeowners who do their own home repairs can get (healthful/healthy) exercise.
2. Recent reports (imply/infer) that many Americans could use the exercise.
3. From the reports homeowners can also (imply/infer) that being handy saves money.
4. It does not take an (ingenious/ingenuous) mechanic to follow home-repair manuals.
5. Many homeowners have (incredible/incredulous) success in repairing things on their own.

6. It is always wise to consider the cost before calling a plumber or a carpenter (in/into/in to) your home.
7. Many people are quick to call for a specialist (irregardless/regardless) of the problem.
8. A broken drawer or a clogged drain is not the (kind of/kind of a) problem that requires expert assistance.
9. (In regard to/In regards to) something like a leaky roof, it is probably best to call an expert.
10. (Those sort/Those sorts) of repairs, which take more time or expertise, require professional assistance.

EXERCISE 5. In each of the sentences below, select from the choices in parentheses the word or phrase that represents preferred usage. (This exercise covers items *lay, lie* through *oral, verbal* in the Glossary of Usage Problems.)

1. A family reunion is (like/as) a page out of the past.
2. The moment family members step out of their cars or (off/off of) the train, memories arise; it is almost (as if/like) they are in the past.
3. In the afternoon, parents (leave/let) the young children play games—tug-of-war, hide-and-seek, and so on.
4. The adults (lay/lie) their problems aside and talk about the old days.
5. Everyone likes to (lay/lie) down on the grass and look over old photographs.
6. Some relatives no longer look (as/like) they used to look.
7. An old group photograph is often (laid/lain) out for viewing.
8. Dinner is usually either a barbecue (or/nor) a picnic.
9. After dinner, the cooks (learn/teach) one another old family recipes.
10. (Oral/Verbal) storytelling is also traditional—anecdotes and jokes are exchanged between mouthfuls.

EXERCISE 6. In each of the sentences below, select from the choices in parentheses the word or phrase that represents preferred usage. (This exercise covers items *raise, rise* through *where at* in the Glossary of Usage Problems.)

1. At one Halloween party, the host (says/said) his home was haunted, calling attention to a strange knocking.

2. When the guests tried to find (where the ghost was/where the ghost was at), they found a noisy radiator.
3. Imaginative costumes go a long (way/ways) toward creating a successful Halloween party.
4. The (reason is because/reason is that) costumes make well-known people mysterious, and mystery is an important part of Halloween.
5. Most guests try (and/to) choose an unusual costume.
6. Cleopatra asks, "Shall we dance?" and a Cowardly Lion nods (respectfully/respectively).
7. Guests often go bobbing for apples, trying to (raise/rise) apples floating in a bucket of water.
8. It is traditional to turn off all the lights and to (sit/set) a jack-o-lantern in the window.
9. At midnight everyone (sits/sets) around a table in the dark.
10. The guests wait for the table to (raise/rise).

REVIEW EXERCISE A. In each of the sentences below, select from the choices in parentheses the word or phrase that represents preferred usage.

1. Field lacrosse is a sport in America that has become popular (between/among) both men and women.
2. Three attackers on each team are positioned near the opponent's goal and try (and/to) score.
3. The attackers are supposed to get the ball (in/into/in to) the net.
4. Three midfielders (bring/take) the ball toward the attackers.
5. The midfielders move the ball (all the farther/as far as they can) to the three attackers.
6. A goalie defends the goal, and three defenders try (and/to) get the ball away from the attacking team.
7. The goalie and the defenders of the attacking team can relax briefly, but (continual/continuous) activity is required in case the ball is taken away from their team.
8. Except for the goalies, the players (doesn't/don't) use their hands.
9. Each player carries (a/an) lacrosse stick with a net at the end for catching and throwing the ball.
10. (Beside/Besides) needing speed and agility, lacrosse players must be able to judge distance.

11. (Disinterested/Uninterested) referees make sure that no player hurts another with the stick.
12. Referees are careful not to (leave/let) all the players bunch up at one end of the field.
13. Lacrosse is (a/an) French name for a game that originated with Native Americans.
14. *La crosse* means "the cross" and (could of/could have) described the sticks used by the players.
15. Native American tribes must (have/of) used the game to (learn/teach) warriors courage and coordination.
16. Today, lacrosse is quite different (from/than) the game played by the Iroquois and Hurons.
17. It is still fast paced, however, and players are not allowed to (sit/set) the ball down on the ground.
18. Modern lacrosse may not train warriors for battle, but it does keep its players (healthful/healthy).
19. Speed and endurance (is/are) two criteria for being a good lacrosse player.
20. Many football players play lacrosse; in fact, Jim Brown was once (a/an) all-American lacrosse player.

REVIEW EXERCISE B. In each of the sentences below, select from the choices in parentheses the word or phrase that represents preferred usage.

1. Many people who (ain't/aren't) particularly interested in history become more (enthused/enthusiastic) when they visit restored villages.
2. History books (verbally/orally) describe how people in the past might (have/of) lived.
3. Restored villages actually show people living (like/as) they did many years ago.
4. There are restored villages (everywhere/everywheres) in the United States.
5. They can be found in New England, the South, the West, (and etc./etc.)
6. In Old Town San Diego and Historic St. Augustine one can, (respectfully/respectively), sample traditional Mexican dishes and old Spanish recipes.
7. St. Augustine, Florida, is the oldest (continual/continuous) European settlement in the United States.

8. (Beside/Besides) the James River in Virginia are restored buildings from the Jamestown settlement.
9. Visitors to the restoration of Williamsburg, Virginia, cannot help (being/but be) impressed.
10. The Pennsylvania Farm Museum of Landis Valley is especially important (being that/because) the Pennsylvania Dutch way of life is slowly changing.
11. Naturally, the Pennsylvania Dutch (doesn't/don't) want their old customs to be lost.
12. The Ancient Cherokee Village at Tsa-La-Gi, Oklahoma, tries (and/to) preserve (a/an) heritage that may be disappearing.
13. In an effort to preserve their (oral/verbal) language, artisans at Tsa-La-Gi speak only Cherokee.
14. (Beside/Besides), they do not think it proper to speak in a language different (from/than) that of their ancestors.
15. At Plimoth Plantation, Massachusetts, restorers (respectfully/respectively) use the original spelling of the town's name.

REVIEW EXERCISE C. In each of the sentences below, select from the choices in parentheses the word or phrase that represents preferred usage.

1. Reading *The Adventures of Tom Sawyer* (convinces/persuades) some people to take up the hobby of exploring caves.
2. People grow interested when they (learn/teach) of the treasures supposedly hidden in caves.
3. Legends say that some pirates (laid/lay) their booty in caves hundreds of years ago.
4. Many spelunkers—cave explorers—take these (incredible/incredulous) stories seriously.
5. All caves contain one special (kind of/kind of a) treasure—the treasure of scientific miracle.
6. Caves are the homes of unusual animals (like/as) blindfish, bats, and transparent crayfish.
7. Caves also hold clues about life (like/as) it was thousands of years ago.
8. Much archaeological research (done/is done) in caves.
9. Limestone caves are (famous/notorious) for their beautiful rock formations.
10. (These kind/These kinds) of cave are the largest known in the world.

CATCHING, CLASSIFYING, AND CORRECTING ERRORS

9 Catching, Classifying, and Correcting Errors

In any area of life—friendships, sports, business—there are large-scale errors that you can make and smaller-scale errors. In writing, also, there are large-scale errors and smaller-scale ones. If you have written a composition or a letter and your readers cannot at all understand your message, you have made a large-scale error. Something major has gone wrong: Probably you have not organized your thoughts clearly. If you have made an error on the grand scale, no matter how fine your individual sentences are, you have not succeeded as a writer. After all, your first and foremost goal as a writer is to communicate, to be understood. You will find much practice in developing paragraphs and compositions with clear messages in Sections 10, 11, 12, 13, 14, 16, and 17.

In this section you will be paying more attention to the smaller-scale errors that can plague you both as a writer and as a reader. These are the errors that usually involve no more than a sentence here and a sentence there within a composition, but they are errors that annoy readers and spoil your writing even though the basic message of the composition is clear.

Everybody who writes makes sentence-level errors, but if you are to write for school or college or on a job, you must learn to find your errors, correct them, and not repeat them. Finding an error—of any sort, in any activity of life—can be an important and happy event. One reason for studying English in this book is to learn to spot errors, your own and others'. In earlier sections of the book, you have noticed "Avoiding Errors" boxes that will help you in this respect.

Always discuss errors freely. Do not be ashamed of making them, only of repeating them. Avoiding them is a matter of being on the lookout for them. There is no excuse for having errors in a final draft—of any kind of writing.

Examine the Editing Chart that begins on page 510. The chart has three columns: The center column shows corrected errors; the left column indicates the signals that you can use to identify errors; the right column refers you to the section of this book that explains the basis of each error. Become familiar with the categories on the chart. Use the chart as a reference tool for (1) spotting errors when reading your own and someone else's writing and (2) tracking down errors noted by your teacher on your written work. As you become familiar with the categories and the signals on the chart and combine them with your awareness of errors from Sections 4, 5, 7, and 8, you will find that editing your writing and the writing of others becomes a constructive and important step in the writing process. Here is a summary of sentence-level errors and the signals that can be used to mark them.

ERRORS	SIGNALS
Vocabulary: effective word choice (Section 4)	*vocab*
Spelling (Section 5)	*sp*
Capitalization (Section 7)	*cap*
Punctuation: unnecessary or missing (Section 7)	*p*
Usage: commonly confused words and commonly misused forms (Section 8)	*use*
Subject-verb agreement	*agree*
Case of pronouns	*case*
Pronoun reference	*ref*
Negative expressions	*neg*
Parts of speech	*pl poss tense adj pro adv prep*

ERRORS	SIGNALS
Joining clauses	run-on frag conj shift voice
Clarity and style	dangling misplaced sag not parallel split wordy

Here are a few other signals that you will find useful in editing.

Problem in paragraphing (See Section 11.)	¶
Missing word or punctuation	^
Unclear or awkward	unclear

Many of the example sentences on the following chart come directly out of the writing of high school students.

EDITING CHART

ERRORS IN SUBJECT–VERB AGREEMENT

agree 1. A verb must agree in number with its subject.

The President always seem to put the United States before anything else.

Johnny Carson get to meet many new and unusual people.

In other words, he like all people.

We was hoping to get tickets for the Super Bowl.

She don't know the answer to the problem.

Each of us need friends.

The coach is the one of all the teachers who have the most influence on my life.

The President is only one person among many who seeks justice.

My mother and my father makes my good life possible. 2.d

Such determination, courage, drive, and ability makes him the person I admire most.

Optimism or courage are essential for someone like Helen Keller.

The longterm goal have always been peace and prosperity. 2.l.1

ERRORS IN CASE

case 2. Pronouns that are objects of action verbs, objects of prepositions, or appositive objects must be in the *objective* case. 1.d.1; 2.t

Who do you want?

The project brought Jeremy and I together.

We sent greetings to Charles and she.

I will go along with whoever you want.

Give it to we kids.

case 3. Pronouns that are subjects and predicate nominatives must be in the *nominative*, or *subjective*, case. 1.d.1; 2.t

Us children have never had much responsibility.

Mary and him have tickets for the ballet.

Her and Tom had lunch together last week.

It was them who began the argument.

Could it be her on the phone right now?

The reward is for whomever helps the police.

case 4. Pronouns must be in the appropriate case after *than* or *as*. 2.g.2

Jane knows Wilma better than he. [The writer means to say that Jane knows Wilma and knows *him*.]

case — Jane knows Wilma better than ~~him~~ he. [The writer means to say that Jane and *he* know Wilma.]

REFERENCE ERRORS WITH PRONOUNS

Incorrect Reference

ref — 5. A personal pronoun must agree with its antecedent in number. .d.1; .d.7

A person can look all over, and ~~they~~ he will never find a greater quarterback than Joe Namath.

One can always dream, can't ~~they~~ he?

ref — 6. In writing, *that* or *which* should not be used to refer to people. .d.6

The person ~~that~~ who taught Helen Keller was Annie Sullivan.

Weak Reference

ref — 7. A pronoun must always have a clear antecedent and should not refer to an unstated idea. .d.1; p.61

In the memorandum ~~it~~ the director stated that Monday would be a holiday.

He is a very well-read man, and ~~it~~ his education shows in his life.

She worked hard, ~~which~~ and her hard work made her rich.

ref — 8. A pronoun must not have two possible antecedents. .d.1

The director ~~told~~ knew that the actor ~~that he~~ was going to be very busy and told him so.

ref — 9. A pronoun should not refer to an entire preceding sentence. p.71

Daniel Webster's speech ruined his future in politics. ~~This did not bother him~~ Webster never had any regrets, however, because he had done what he thought was right.

ERRORS WITH THE NEGATIVE

neg 10. In general, two negatives should not be used in the same clause. 1.f.2

There is not no better place to live than Los Angeles.

Most people will not scarcely know the difference between the two cars.

King was a man who didn't like no kind of violence.

ERRORS WITH PARTS OF SPEECH

Nouns

pl 11. The plural form of the noun must be used to show the plural even if a number word makes the meaning clear. 1.a.3; 5.b.1

He had many hardship.

The house had four broken window.

poss 12. The possessive form of a noun must include an apostrophe. 1.a.6; 5.b.2

We can now foresee the series end.

Are those Johns red socks?

Do you remember Ted Williams number?

Verbs

tense 13. Past-time verbs must have the appropriate word endings. 1.b.14–1.b.18

He like all people whether they were rich or poor.

It has work for me before.

Michelle use to live in Pennsylvania, but now she lives in New York.

Have you ever study another language?

She did tried her best!

tense 14. The present tense should not be used if another tense is more logical. 1. b. 12

She ~~is~~ was said to be very pretty as a young girl.

tense 15. The past perfect must be used to describe the earlier of two past actions. 1. b. 18

By the time I told him, he had already heard.

tense 16. *Would have* should never be used in an *if*-clause. 1. b. 18

If the spaceship ~~would have~~ had come in too steep, it would have burned up.

tense 17. A sentence should not shift verb tenses unnecessarily between clauses. 1. b. 11

He ~~is~~ was faithful to his team and stood by them.

Adjectives

adj 18. A comparative adjective must be used when comparing two items, and a superlative adjective must be used when comparing more than two. 1. C.3; 1. C.4

Between Maui and Kauai, Kauai is the ~~most~~ more beautiful.

Of Maui, Kauai, and Hawaii, Kauai is ~~more~~ the most beautiful.

adj 19. A double comparison must be avoided. p. 53

I admire Winston Churchill because I think he was one of the ~~most~~ fittest men during World War II.

adj 20. An incomplete comparison must be avoided by adding *other* or *else*. p. 53

Henry Kissinger spent more time overseas than any other ~~S~~secretary of State.

adj 21. It is necessary to include the second *as* in making a comparison. p. 53

Lou Brock is as fast as if not faster than, any other baseball player.

adj 22. Some adjectives do not logically have comparative or superlative forms — for example, *perfect, unique, round.* p. 53

Some would say that the Beatles' music is more perfect than the Rolling Stones'.

interesting

Pronouns

pro 23. *Hisself* and *theirselves* are not words: *himself* and *themselves* should be used instead. 1.d.3

He did the problem hisself.

himself

pro 24. A reflexive form should be used for a pronoun that refers to the subject. 1.d.3

I got me a present.

myself

pro 25. A reflexive pronoun should not be the subject of a sentence or a clause. 1.d.3

My best friend and myself hope to visit Chicago this summer.

I

pro 26. A subject should not be followed by a pronoun that repeats it.

Aunt Alberta she loves tennis.

Pronouns used as determiners

pro 27. In writing, *this* should not be used to mean simply *a* or *an*. 1.d.4

There is this building in San Francisco that is shaped like a pyramid.

a

pro 28. *This here* should not be used to mean *this*. 1.d.4

Is this here book yours?

pro 29. *Them* should not be used to mean *those*. 1.d.4

For three hours we studied them verbs.

those

Adverbs

adv 30. The *-ly* ending must not be omitted from adverbs of manner. 1.f.1

The Panovs seem to dance effortless.

ly

Prepositions

prep 31. A sentence should contain no extra, unnecessary, or repeated prepositions. p.101

Regina could not get her problems off ~~of~~ her mind.

The lecture should last for ~~from~~ two to three hours.

Martin Luther King went to jail because of the things in which he believed ~~in~~.

ERRORS IN COMPLETING AND JOINING CLAUSES

Joining Main Clauses

run-on 32. A comma alone should not be used to join main clauses. (The error results in a run-on sentence.) 2.0

I admired John F. Kennedy. He was an honest man.

frag 33. A sentence must have both a subject and a linking verb or action verb; without both elements a group of words is a sentence fragment. 2.b

Martin Luther King was a man who liked to help others.

The two girls were jogging through Tilden Park.

conj 34. Main clauses should not be joined with *so* or *yet*, but rather with *and so* or *and yet*. 1.h.1

Robert Kennedy knew that going out into big crowds was like playing Russian roulette, and yet he continued to go out.

Katherine Anne Porter grew up in the South, and so she often writes about life in her southern home.

Joining Subordinate Clauses

shift 35. A sentence should not shift subordinators.

I see a street that looks familiar and a house that looks like home.

shift 36. A sentence should not shift subjects unnecessarily between clauses.

Ever since we saw Pelé, ~~it has been fun to play~~ *we have enjoyed playing* soccer.

voice 37. A sentence should not shift unnecessarily from the 1.b.20
active to the passive voice, or vice versa, between clauses.

Although she had a lot of talent, the poet was ~~known to be~~ undisciplined.

ERRORS IN CLARITY AND STYLE

Dangling or Misplaced Words, Phrases, and Clauses

dangling 38. A phrase or clause should clearly modify one word 1.k
in the sentence; if it does not, the phrase or clause is said to be *dangling.*

~~Stepping~~ *When I stepped* on the brake, the car stopped.

misplaced 39. A phrase or clause should be placed as close as possible to the word it is modifying.

Adlai Stevenson discussed peace and prosperity at the Democratic Convention.

~~At an early age~~ *When I was young,* my parents taught me the difference between right and wrong.

misplaced 40. An adverb of degree should be placed as close as 1.f.1
possible to the word it refers to.

We had only completed four of the six games.

Sagging Sentences

sag 41. If a subject and a verb are not clearly connected 3.h;
—both logically and grammatically—the sentence 3.i
sags. The performer that is logically the most important performer in that particular sentence should be the subject of the main clause.

A sagging sentence can be improved in one of the ways listed on the next page. Some rewriting is usually required.

sag

(1) Make the word or words that are most important the subject of the main clause.

(2) Select a new, and more logical, word or words as the subject of the main clause.

(3) Substitute a logical word or words for a weak pronoun as the subject of the main clause.

~~The camera can fool the human eye, and in conjunction with makeup and costuming makes for an enjoyable film.~~

[This sentence sags because the most important performer is not the subject of the main clause. What makes a film enjoyable? The camera? No. More likely, *clever photography* makes for the enjoyable film. These words should be the subject.]

Clever photography in conjunction with makeup and costumes makes for an enjoyable film.

[Now the subject *clever photography* has the main role.]

~~Plays don't have the advantages of camera angles and editing techniques that film directors have.~~

[This sentence sags because the subject *plays* does not serve as the logical subject of *don't have the advantages.*]

Stage directors don't have the advantages of camera angles and editing techniques that film directors have.

[The logical subject, *stage directors,* is now stated clearly.]

~~In the job that I really want, I need to know Spanish.~~

[This sentence sags because it places the most important word or words—the job—in an introductory prepositional phrase. *The job* should be the subject.]

The job that I really want requires Spanish.

People who know only Russian or Japanese, there are not many jobs in America.

People who know only Russian or Japanese do not have many job opportunities in America.

42. The subject should not be lost in a prepositional phrase.

As to the energy crisis and the recent gasoline shortage, it is upsetting for all Americans.

By limiting gasoline sales may not completely solve the problem.

The use of gasohol was made to ease the fuel shortage.

43. The subject should not be lost in a subordinate clause.

Although soccer has for many years been popular in South America is still fairly new in North America.

If Brazilians were asked to choose between the San Francisco Giants and the Los Angeles Dodgers would first have to find out what baseball is.

Lack of Parallelism

44. Parallel ideas should be expressed in the same grammatical form.

I look up to any person who is honest in his actions and what he says.

Her favorite courses were art, science, and historical.

He is not only a talented writer but is famous as a biologist.

45. In parallel constructions an article, preposition, or pronoun must be repeated when necessary for clarity.

Football is more important to me than you.

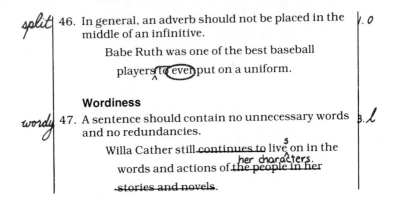

split 46. In general, an adverb should not be placed in the middle of an infinitive. 1.0

Babe Ruth was one of the best baseball players ^to ever put on a uniform.

Wordiness

wordy 47. A sentence should contain no unnecessary words and no redundancies. 3.l

Willa Cather still ~~continues to~~ lives on in the words and actions of ~~the people in her stories and novels~~ her characters.

USING EDITING SIGNALS

From time to time you may be asked to read another student's paper and to act as a critic. You may have to look for large-scale problems such as weak topic sentences, lack of unity, lack of coherence, lack of logic, and so on. These are the matters that you will study in detail in Sections 10–14 of this book. You may also be asked to pay particular attention to individual sentences and to call sentence-level errors to the student's attention. When you find problems with individual sentences, you should point them out clearly. Unless your teacher gives you special instructions, you can mark editing signals in the margins of the paper, as shown on the following page. These are the signals that are listed on the Editing Chart, pages 510–520. Notice that the signals are written in the margins but that circles, brackets, and carets are marked on the compositions themselves. Seeing these signals, a writer can check back to the Editing Chart, where there are cross references to the rules governing each kind of error.

The following sample compositions are based on compositions written by high school students who were asked to identify a person whom they admired and to tell why. So that these two sample compositions could show you how to mark many different kinds of sentence-level errors, additional errors were introduced into the original compositions. (Detailed discussions of writing *beyond* the sentence — writing paragraphs and compositions — begin in Section 10.)

Composition 1

The person I am writing about is one of the most

pl famous person I know. Her name is Helen Keller. She [has

tense been] born blind. Due to this physical handicap, she had use

to create her own world. [Without seeing or being able to dangling

talk,] her world was still a world of light. [A world in frag

which determination, hard work, and showing

understanding to one another were worth more than a

life of "wrongseeing."] Her committment to others and sp

her spirit was great. agree

She worked hard learning hand language and

trying to convert it into conversation. She [didn't neg

never] give up because she knew this task could help

other blind people. By helping someone else meant more sag

to her than sight itself.

Composition 2

I admire Florence Nightingale because long ago

cap in the crimean war she became one of the first Army

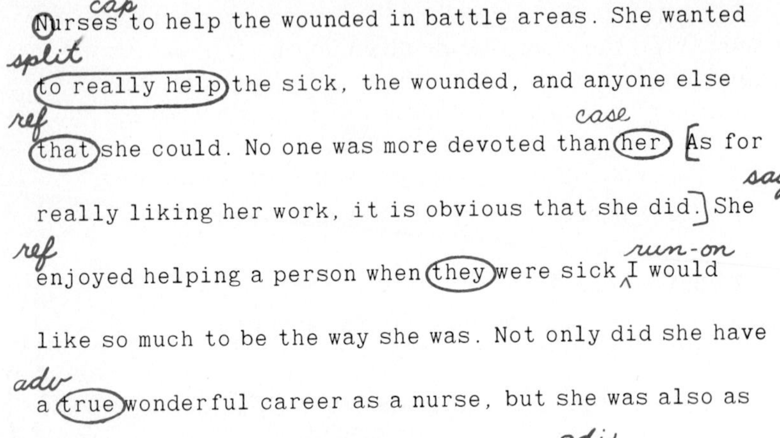
Nurses to help the wounded in battle areas. She wanted to really help the sick, the wounded, and anyone else that she could. No one was more devoted than her. As for really liking her work, it is obvious that she did. She enjoyed helping a person when they were sick I would like so much to be the way she was. Not only did she have a true wonderful career as a nurse, but she was also as a young girl more prettier than others.

EXERCISE 1. Each of the following sentences contains one error. Find the error, decide how to correct it, and write the complete corrected sentence. In the first five sentences the error is identified by an editing signal from the preceding chart. In the last five you must identify the error and supply the appropriate editing signal before you rewrite the sentence.

1. Whenever Leontyne Price come to town, the opera always has a standing-room-only crowd. *agree*
2. Price is perhaps the more famous sopranos of our time. *adj*
3. Her voice has a range of from low A to high D. *prep*
4. Born in Laurel, Mississippi, critics first noticed Price when she sang Bess in Gershwin's *Porgy and Bess*. *dangling*
5. In 1955 she electrified the nation with her televised performance of Puccinis *Tosca*. *poss*
6. By the time Leontyne Price opened at the Metropolitan Opera in 1961, most people already heard her.
7. She made her a star.
8. In 1967 it was her who was asked to open the new Metropolitan Opera House in New York City.
9. Price is special known for her portrayals of the great Verdi heroines.
10. Few sopranos sing *Aida* better than her.

EXERCISE 2. Each of the following sentences contains one error. Find the error, decide how to correct it, and write the complete corrected sentence. In the first five sentences the error is identified by an editing signal from the preceding chart. In the last five you must identify the error and supply the appropriate editing signal before you rewrite the sentence.

1. A journalist can look far and wide, but they might never spot Greta Garbo. *ref*
2. Garbo is one of many artists who wishes to be left alone. *agree*
3. Under wide-brimmed hats and behind sunglasses, she avoid all publicity. *agree*
4. Garbo is one of the most famous actresses to ever perform in American cinema. *split*
5. She was born in Sweden, her real name is Greta Lovisa Gustafsson. *run-on*
6. Known for her portrayals of mysterious and tragic heroines.
7. Among her best-known films is *Anna Karenina, Camille,* and *Ninotchka.*
8. Them old Garbo films are shown over and over in theaters around the world.
9. One of the few stars to be equally successful in both silent and sound films.
10. When *Anna Christie,* her first sound film, opened in 1930, headlines around the world announce GARBO SPEAKS.

EXERCISE 3. Each of the following sentences contains one error. Find the error, decide how to correct it, and write the complete corrected sentence. In the first five sentences the error is identified by an editing signal from the preceding chart. In the last five you must identify the error and supply the appropriate editing signal before you rewrite the sentence.

1. In the thirties Clark Gable was named "The King" in a newspaper popularity poll, and it stayed with him for the rest of his life. *ref*
2. Filmgoers were charm by Gable's grin and his robust manner. *tense*
3. He is born to a German-American family and grew up in Ohio. *tense*

4. *Gable* is actually a name that come from *Goebel.* agree
5. At an early age, Gable's parents encouraged him to study medicine. misplaced
6. He chose to be an actor, however, and brought an entire new kind of masculine image to the screen.
7. Jean Harlow, Carole Lombard, and Marilyn Monroe were among the actresses with who he starred.
8. A young Judy Garland recorded this song, "Dear Mr. Gable, You Made Me Love You."
9. He was nominated for an Oscar three time and won for his performance in *It Happened One Night.*
10. Gable is most remember, however, as Rhett Butler in *Gone with the Wind.*

EXERCISE 4. Each of the following sentences contains one error. Find the error, decide how to correct it, and write the complete corrected sentence. In the first five sentences the error is identified by an editing signal from the preceding chart. In the last five you must identify the error and supply the appropriate editing signal before you rewrite the sentence.

1. Frank Lloyd Wright once said that there were not no better dwellings in the world than the seashell. neg
2. A snail's home, Wright said, are both beautiful and functional. agree
3. In his view, "Nature only knows circular forms." misplaced
4. In Wright's later buildings he considered the spiral the most perfect shape of all. adj
5. One of his most famous structures, New Yorks Guggenheim Museum, is shaped like a spiral. poss
6. Many modern architects consider theirselves heirs of Frank Lloyd Wright.
7. Wright hisself never had such a high opinion of most other architects and called their high-rise buildings "glassified filing cabinets."
8. Wright would have been more popular with the architectural establishment if he would not have had such a sharp wit.
9. Even so, Frank Lloyd Wright has been more influential than any twentieth-century architect.
10. The beauty of his buildings are timeless: Each was built for its site, its purpose, and its inhabitants.

EXERCISE 5. Each of the following sentences contains one error. Find the error, decide how to correct it, and write the complete corrected sentence. In the first five sentences the error is identified by an editing signal from the preceding chart. In the last five you must identify the error and supply the appropriate editing signal before you rewrite the sentence.

1. Twentieth-century American architecture owe a great deal to the theories of Frank Lloyd Wright. *agree*
2. Before Wright, American buildings included houses that looked like Swiss chalets and banks which looked like Greek temples. *shift*
3. Wright would not accept no such fakery or pretentiousness. *neg*
4. He set out to design a dwelling that would be both sensible and real American. *adv*
5. Wright he believed that the shape of a building should be determined by its function. *pro*
6. Moreover, he refused to ever deface or dominate the landscape.
7. Wright's own home was built just off of a hilltop—"not *on* the hill, but *of* the hill."
8. Because he thought it important for a building to be in harmony with its setting, it was common for Wright's buildings to be of local stone.
9. In a typical Wright house, the use of porches, terraces, and gardens is made to blur the line between the inside and the outside.
10. Wright insisted that the point of a building were not the walls, ceilings, and floors, but the living space that they enclose.

EXERCISE 6. Each of the following sentences contains one error. Find the error, decide how to correct it, and write the complete corrected sentence. In the first five sentences the error is identified by an editing signal from the preceding chart. In the last five you must identify the error and supply the appropriate editing signal before you rewrite the sentence.

1. In the dictionary it says that the word *be-bop* is an imitation of the sound made on a trumpet. *ref*
2. Be-bop music are characterized by complex rhythms and experimental harmonies. *agree*
3. A jazz movement that is associated with the great trumpet player Dizzy Gillespie. *frag*

4. Born John Birks Gillespie, many people consider him the ambassador of jazz. *dangling*
5. Actually, Charlie Parker and him invented be-bop music in the 1940s. *case*
6. Gillespie's musical improvisations are noted for their energy and how witty they are.
7. Many Gillespie composition, including "Salt Peanuts" and "Billie's Bounce," are now considered jazz standards.
8. Gillespie has been called the world's greatest trumpet virtuoso, most jazz trumpet players are indebted to him.
9. Some even consider him the world's most unique jazz soloist.
10. Indeed, Dizzy Gillespie's bulging cheeks and upturned trumpet has almost come to symbolize jazz.

EXERCISE 7. Each of the following sentences contains one error. Find the error, decide how to correct it, and write the complete corrected sentence. In the first five sentences the error is identified by an editing signal from the preceding chart. In the last five you must identify the error and supply the appropriate editing signal before you rewrite the sentence.

1. Albert Einstein was the most famous scientist that ever lived in the United States. *ref*
2. He is as well known, if not more well known than, any other American scientist. *adj*
3. It was him who gave the world $E=mc^2$. *case*
4. This here equation altered the world's concepts of space and time. *pro*
5. Einstein was awarded the Nobel Prize in 1921, but he is remembered by many as this absent-minded professor. *pro*
6. He was a scientist whose genius seem to leave no room for the trivia of everyday life.
7. Einstein once helped a young girl with her arithmetic and had got the wrong answers.
8. Another time he used an uncashed check as a bookmark and then the book was lost.
9. His was probably the most greatest scientific mind of our century.
10. When he died, scientists studied Einsteins brain.

EXERCISE 8. Each of the following sentences contains one error. Find the error, decide how to correct it, and write the complete corrected sentence. In the first five sentences the error is identified by an editing signal from the preceding chart. In the last five you must identify the error and supply the appropriate editing signal before you rewrite the sentence.

1. Edith Wharton grew up in New York in the late 1800s, which enabled her to write about its social codes and moral values. *ref*
2. Not many could have described the habits and rituals of Victorian New York as well as her. *case*
3. That part of New York having good homes, good English, and good manners. *frag*
4. Of all Wharton's novels, *The Age of Innocence* is the more well known. *adj*
5. Like many of her novels, *The Age of Innocence* is set in New York, in Newport, and Paris. *not parallel*
6. Wharton treated this here world of gardenias and archery contests with both satire and sentiment.
7. A society in which people worried about such things as the proper time to pay an after-dinner call.
8. Wharton is often compare with Henry James, who wrote about a similar world.
9. James and herself both grew up in New York and later moved to Europe.
10. Each of them are associated with New York at the turn of the century.

EXERCISE 9. The selection on the next page has been planted with sentence errors. The instructions that follow the selection ask you to spot specific kinds of errors and to use signals from the preceding Editing Chart. You may duplicate the selection, making several copies so that you can edit it several times in the ways called for in the instructions (A–F).

First read the entire Editing Practice Selection, all twenty-five sentences. Then follow the instructions (A–F). The final step will be to correct the errors by rewriting the sentences in which they occur.

EDITING PRACTICE SELECTION

[1]Known as a famous traveler, the trip that I felt essential was to the one place that I had not been to. [2]Between you and I, the trip was among my most unique experiences. [3]Pan American, they offered a package to the cities that I wanted to visit. [4]I did not stay with a tour group, I just booked the Pan Am plane.

[5]At the airport in Nishi, the crowds greet me as a famous traveler. [6]A chauffeur-driven limousine took me to the Narita Hotel in Tokyo. [7]The hotel is beautiful. [8]It is one of a number of Tokyo hotels that has an international reputation.

[9]At the hotel I was met by a smiling person that would be my personal guide. [10]She reminded me of a guide with whom I had had a pleasant time with in Mexico. [11] At times like this I cannot forget that us Americans need more help abroad than do other travelers. [12]We are weak in languages. [13]I admire people from other parts of the world, especially from Europe, who speak several languages. [14]Perhaps young people in other countries work hard to learn languages. [15]My guide was one of these people, she was able to conduct tours all over the world. [16]She is a woman whom impresses me.

[17]At translating she was as fast as, if not more faster, than any other translator I had ever met. [18]By translating during visits with Japanese families helped me enjoy myself.

[19]During my visit we ate in many exquisite restaurants. [20]The specialty of most Japanese restaurants are raw fish. [21]In regard to the raw fish, it is tasty and refreshing.

[22]Everybody I know likes to travel. [23]Everybody thinks differently in choosing vacation spots, however. [24]I for one can recommend visiting Japan because of the high quality of its hotels, its friendly people, and how you can see ancient sites.

[25]I have now complete my world travels.

A. Reread the Editing Practice Selection, and spot all errors involving *dangling or misplaced phrases or clauses.* If you are working on a copy of the selection, circle the errors, and in the margin place the appropriate signal from the Editing Chart. If you are working from the book, write down the number of the sentence, and then write the appropriate editing signal.
B. Following the procedure described in *A*, spot all errors involving parts of speech.
C. Now spot all *run-on sentences.*
D. Now spot all errors in *subject-verb agreement.*
E. Now spot all errors involving *sagging sentences.*
F. Now spot the *lack of parallelism.*

10

GENERATING IDEAS

10 Generating Ideas

Ideas for writing can come from anywhere. You really never have to worry about having something to write about if you approach the world with a curious, active mind. Whenever your thoughts touch on the world around you, you create an idea. The idea can then be further developed and written about, especially once you have learned to generalize and to classify.

10.a GENERATING IDEAS BY ASKING QUESTIONS

You as a writer bring something unique to the objects, facts, designs, impressions, scraps of prose—to all the data[1]—that you come across. You bring your experience and your imagination. Consider the items—the data—on the next page, one at a time. In what way or ways can each one touch on your own experience? Think about each item for a while. Then ask yourself the following questions. They should help to jog your thoughts in relation to the item so that you can get the beginnings of some writing ideas.

1. What story, real or imagined, does it suggest?
   a) What may have immediately preceded it?
   b) What may follow it?
   c) What may have caused it?
   d) What may it cause?
   e) What might it become?

[1]*Data* is a useful term to cover everything that might be used as a source of ideas for writing, everything from sunsets to statistics.

2. What is it similar to?
   a) What does it remind me of from my personal experience?
   b) What does it remind me of from what I have read or observed in others' lives?
   c) What general events can I associate with it?
3. What is it different from?
   a) How does it differ from others like it that I have come across before?
   b) How does it differ from what I expected?

A

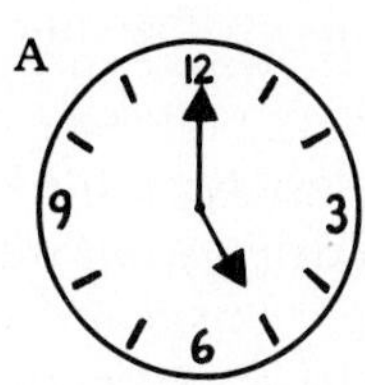

B

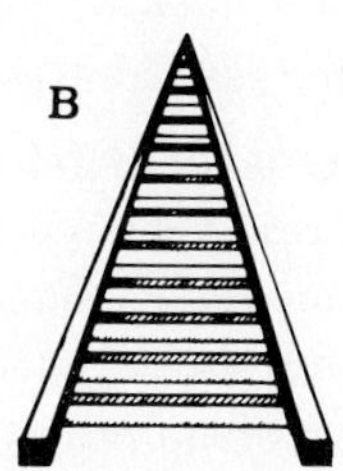

C

(Footnotes in the novel *Watership Down*): Rabbits can count up to four. Any number above four is hrair—"a lot" or "a thousand." Thus, they say U hair—"The thousand" to mean, collectively, all the enemies (all elil, as they call them) of rabbits—fox, stout, weasel, cat, owl, man, etc. Nearly all warrens have an owsla, a group of strong or clever rabbits—second year or older—surrounding the chief rabbit and his doe, and exercising authority.

D

LINEAGE
My grandmothers were strong.
They followed plows and bent to toil.
They moved through fields sowing seed.
They touched earth and grain grew.
They were full of sturdiness and singing.
My grandmothers were strong.

My grandmothers are full of memories.
Smelling of soap and onions and wet clay
With veins rolling roughly over quick hands
They have many clean words to say.
My grandmothers were strong.
Why am I not as they?

—Margaret Walker

Here you will find responses to the preceding items. These responses are, in effect, ideas for writing that occurred to various people.

Ideas for Item A (clock face)

- a short story with a plot that hinges on a clock that shows incorrect time
- a comparison of people's reactions to the sounds of clocks
- an imaginative essay on clocks of the future
- a report on the time needed by different people to complete the same task
- an essay contrasting the notions of time in different cultures

Ideas for Item B (railroad tracks)

- a research report on history of railroads in the United States
- an essay comparing and contrasting rail travel, air travel, ship travel
- a biographical sketch of a veteran engineer
- a summary of a journey taken as a child
- an explanation of the concept of perspective (in art and in life)

Ideas for Item C (footnote)

- a research paper on communication among animals
- a fantasy story involving special language by animals
- an explanation of power struggles in the animal kingdom
- a narrative report about a rabbit hunt
- a description of a secret language you once used with friends

Ideas for Item D (poem)

- a biographical sketch of a grandparent
- an essay contrasting the experiences of three generations in a family
- an essay about memories shared by grandparents
- a poem entitled "Lineage" about my family
- a letter to a grandparent

The preceding material was designed to make the point that anything and everything can be the source of ideas—and, therefore, the source of a writing experience. In school and business situations, however, your assignment most often is to write about not just anything but about particular data: a particular novel for an English class, a particular person or event for a history class, a particular phenomenon for a science class, a particular product for an advertising agency, and so on. You may not always be told just what aspect to write on; you will have to come up with an angle—an idea—on your own.

As before, though, you can help yourself to get ideas by *asking questions* of the material, be it a piece of literature, a historical event, or a scientific experiment. For example, assume that you have read a short story and you have been asked to write *something* about one of the characters. In order to help yourself to figure out just which aspect of the character you can profitably write about, ask yourself the following questions. You will find one or several that you either have plenty of answers to or that you are curious enough about to look into more seriously.

- What may have made the character act the way he or she does?
- Does the character remind me of someone else? In what ways?
- Would I like to meet the character? Why or why not?
- How is the character different from someone else in the story? In real life?
- What would I talk to this character about?
- What kinds of interests, other than those mentioned in the story, does this character probably have?
- Do the other characters like this character? Why or why not?
- Is the character human? In what ways?
- Is the character an idealized figure? In what ways?

10.b GENERATING IDEAS BY INTERPRETING DATA: NARRATIVES

A **narrative** is a form of writing that tells a story, real or imagined.

Sometimes your task as a writer is to take data that have been put into one order and to select or to rearrange the items for yourself. When you write a narrative, or tell a story, you highlight only certain elements rather than repeat *all* the information.

A good way to practice getting ideas for narratives is to look at the data about a baseball game, usually given in the form of a box score. A professional sportswriter, Robert Creamer, senior editor for *Sports Illustrated* magazine, was asked if he could take the information in a box score and use it as the basis for writing a brief narrative account of the game. Remember that a narrative is a story—in this case, the true story of a real game. In a narrative people perform actions.

The writer's job here is to make this box score come to life. The players listed in the box score come up to bat. They hit, run, and score runs at times. To a writer a box score is full of verbs. The players' names form subjects for these verbs, and sentences are born. These sentences tell what happened in the game. In a short account Creamer could report only the highlight events, but these events tell a story. Let's see how Creamer might have gone about his assignment.

First, study the box score on the facing page.

Looking at the box score, Creamer can see at the bottom of the "runs" (r) column and at the end of the "inning-by-inning" record that Oakland beat Texas, 2–1. He can see, under "hits" (h), which players on both teams got hits. He can use the inning-by-inning record to see in which innings hits added up to runs. He can also see that one of Oakland catcher Newman's hits was a home run (HR), his fourth of the season.[1] The pitchers' record at the bottom of the box score shows how each of the pitchers fared during the game.

Playing the role of a Texas sportswriter, Creamer now asks himself questions, such as the following. (Remember that questioning is the key to generating ideas.)

1. How did Oakland win?
2. What was the pitching like on each side?
3. From the Texas point of view, what was the trouble?
4. How can I tell the story in a few sentences and make it as interesting as possible?

---

[1] Baseball fans may be interested in figuring out how the writer could tell that Newman's home-run hit came in the eighth inning, not in the first inning (the only other inning in which Oakland scored a run).

BOX SCORE

OAKLAND (A.)	ab	r	h	bi	TEXAS (A.)	ab	r	h	bi
Wallis cf	2	1	1	0	Hargrv 1b	3	0	1	1
Dilone rf	2	0	0	0	Cmonrs ss	4	0	0	0
Alston lf	3	0	1	0	Wills 2b	4	0	0	0
Guerrer ss	4	0	1	0	Zisk lf	3	0	0	0
TDuncn 3b	4	0	1	1	Alomar pr	0	0	0	0
Page dh	4	0	0	0	Bonds rf	4	0	2	0
Armas cf	4	0	0	0	Putnm dh	4	0	0	0
Revrng 1b	3	0	0	0	Sundbrg c	2	0	0	0
Gross 1b	0	0	0	0	Harrah 3b	2	1	0	0
Newman c	3	1	2	1	BThmps cf	2	0	0	0
Piciolo 2b	3	0	0	0					
Edwrds 2b	0	0	0	0					
Total	32.	2.	6.	2	Total	28.	1.	3.	1

inning by inning					
	Oakland...	100	000	010—2
	Texas	000	010	000—1

E—Edwards. DP—Oakland, 2. LOB—Oakland 4, Texas 7.
HR—Newman (4). SB—Harrah, Alston. S—Alston, B Thompson.

pitchers' records		IP.......	H	R	ER	BB	SO
	Renko, W,2–2	7	2	1	1	4	3
	Lacey	1	0	0	0	1	0
	Sosa	1	1	0	0	1	0
	Matlack L, 5–8	9	6	2	2	0	5

Save—Sosa (10). T—2:18 A—17,029.

Meaning of Abbreviations

(A.) American League
ab at bat
r runs
h hits
bi runs batted in
E errors
DP double play
LOB left on base
HR home run
SB stolen base
S sacrifice
W winner
L loser
T time
A attendance

For pitchers
IP innings pitched
H hits given up
R runs given up
ER earned runs
BB bases on balls
SO strikeouts

Appearing after names
1b first base
2b second base
3b third base
ss shortstop
rf right field
cf center field
lf left field
c catcher
p pitcher
dh designated hitter

Here are his answers:

1. Oakland won on a home run; they also limited the Texas Rangers to three hits.
2. Matlack, the Rangers' pitcher, scattered six hits and then gave up a home run. Renko, the winning pitcher, pitched seven strong innings; then the Oakland relief staff, especially Sosa, took over and "saved" the game.
3. Not enough hits; Matlack continues to lose ball games.
4. Taking it in time sequence (narrative organization), inning by inning, I can tell about a tight pitcher's battle and a climactic home run. No storyteller could ask for more!

Most writers make notes of some kind before writing. It is a good idea for you to consider. Sportswriter Creamer's notes may have looked something like the following. Some he got from the data—the facts in the box score—but others came from his own knowledge and experience as a sportswriter. (The two sources are separated here for your convenience.)

NOTES

From data in box score

At end of 7 innings, Renko and Matlack locked in 1–1 tie
Newman's homer in 8th
Lacey lifted after base on balls in 8th
Oakland to Sosa in 9th

From experience

Matlack one of best left-handers
He must have felt bad at loss.
Oakland nervous about Lacey
Sosa is star reliever.

Here is the narrative report that Creamer wrote.

BASEBALL BRIEFS: OAKLAND 2, TEXAS 1

Oakland's Steve Renko went seven strong innings against one of the best left-handers in baseball, Jon Matlack, and was locked in a 1–1 tie going to the top of the eighth. Then in the eighth Oakland scored, on Catcher Newman's fourth homer of the season, to go ahead 2–1, and they brought in Lacey to hold the lead. After Lacey walked a man, making the A's nervous, they moved to Sosa, their star reliever, in the ninth, and, although Sosa gave up a hit and a walk, he got the "save," and

Renko and the A's got the victory. It was another tough loss for Matlack, whose record sagged to five wins, eight defeats.

EXERCISE 1. From your own examination of the data in the box score and from your own experience, add to Creamer's report, or start again and write your own report of the same game.

EXERCISE 2. The following travel information from Japan Air Lines shows prospective customers what they can look forward to on a two-week tour of Japan. It shows the cities they will visit, how long and where they will stay in each city, and the special dinners and other entertainment available.

Pretend that you have taken this tour. Use your imagination. Perhaps you will want to consult an atlas and a menu. Write an account of the trip, giving one or two sentences to each city.

Like Creamer, you may first want to jot down notes based both on the given data and on your experience.

TWO-WEEK TOUR OF JAPAN

	cities in order of visit	*hotels*	*highlight/ meals*	*other features*
one day	Tokyo	Narita Area	Traditional Dinner	
three days	Taipei	Grand	Chinese Dinner/Show Mongolian Barbecue	City Tour
three days	Manila	Philippine Plaza	Philippine Dinner/Show	City Tour
six days	Hong Kong	Excelsior	Dinner at Floating Restaurant	Island Tour Tour of Kowloon & New Territories Restaurant/ Cooking Tour Sunset Cruise

10.c CLASSIFYING DATA

Classifying is the grouping of items or data according to some kind of order.

One way to develop a writing idea is to begin by reorganizing the data that you are given. When you are dealing with many facts, you usually have to find a way to analyze the material, a way to divide the facts into easier-to-handle categories. When you take a list or a group of data and (1) figure out categories for the data and (2) place each item in its appropriate category, you are classifying the data.

You usually have to classify the data regardless of what kind of writing you set out to do—whether, for example, you decide to write about how two people *compare* with each other, about the possible *causes* of a particular event, or about the *reasons* behind an opinion that you have and want people to share.

The travelers' forecast that appears below provides you with weather data that are arranged in a straightforward, easy-to-use way.

TRAVELERS' FORECAST

Atlanta:
Showers likely. 54–43.
Boston:
Continued showers. 59–50.
Chicago:
Snow likely. 36–24.
Cleveland:
Rain likely. 53–34.
Dallas:
Partly cloudy. 67–39.
Denver:
Partly cloudy. 55–29.
Houston:
Partly cloudy. 71–38.
Kansas City:
Partly cloudy. 38–18.
Las Vegas:
Mostly fair. 72–46.
Los Angeles:
Mostly fair. 71–48.
Miami:
Partly cloudy. 79–60.
Minneapolis:
Partly cloudy. 29–15.
New Orleans:
Mostly fair. 67–44.
Philadelphia:
Showers likely. 65–40.
St. Louis:
Partly cloudy. 38–20.
San Francisco:
Mostly fair. 68–52.
Seattle:
Mostly fair. 59–40.
Washington:
Showers likely. 67–45.

The forecast, as it is printed, arranges the data in a way that will indeed help travelers find the information they may need. The data are listed alphabetically by city. Instead of stopping with just one long list, however, you may wish to look further and to see whether there is, indeed, anything interesting to note about the weather that day. To do so, you will have to *classify* the data. You can classify these particular data in at least two ways.

First, you can see how many *kinds* of weather there are and group together those cities that have that kind of weather. Here is the beginning of that classification.

CLASSIFICATION BY KIND OF WEATHER

Showers or rain likely

Atlanta
Cleveland
Philadelphia
Washington

Continued showers

Boston

Snow likely

Chicago

Second, you can classify by *region* of the country. Here is the beginning of such a classification.

CLASSIFICATION BY REGION

Northeast and mid-Atlantic

Boston: continued showers
Philadelphia: showers likely
Washington: showers likely

Southeast

Atlanta: showers likely
Miami: partly cloudy
New Orleans: mostly fair

Midwest to the Rockies

Chicago: snow likely
Cleveland: rain likely
Denver: partly cloudy
Kansas City: partly cloudy
Minneapolis: partly cloudy
St. Louis: partly cloudy

Most data, as the above analysis shows, can be classified in more than one way. The following exercises have been designed to help you practice classifying data and to write statements that involve classification. Once you classify data, you are a step closer to being able to write because you have begun to sort out your ideas.

EXERCISE 3. There are at least two ways that the following items can be classified. They can be divided according to

1. manual skills required ("a lot" vs. "not many") or
2. type of education required ("at least liberal arts college" vs. "possibly trade school or apprenticeship")

Select one method of classification, and group the items appropriately.

electrician	chemist
lawyer	doctor
bricklayer	X-ray technician
plumber	high school teacher

EXERCISE 4. The list below contains names of types of vehicles. Decide on a method of classification, and divide the items above as necessary. [*Suggested ways to classify:* (1) by power; (2) by wheels; (3) by use.]

sailboat	jeep	bicycle
sports car	canoe	ocean liner
motorcycle	station wagon	tugboat
rowboat	cabin cruiser	barge

EXERCISE 5. The following list can be divided into several groups. Identify the kind of classification you choose, and explain your choice. Then look at the list again, and name another classification system that you can use.

manual lawn mower	dishwasher	feather duster
vacuum cleaner	plunger	washing machine
electric blender	hoe	hedge clipper
shovel	broom	rake

EXERCISE 6. Complete each of the numbered sentences by choosing an appropriate word or phrase. Each of the numbered sentences is a statement of classification.

categorized
types
kind
divided
groups
style
most important
literary style
personal attributes
records
basic
classification
regions
classified

1. Coaches can be _____ according to their _____.
2. Three _____ of movies appeal to me.
3. Your _____ of handwriting reveals many _____.
4. Candy bars are one _____ of junk food.
5. Can you name the _____ cities in the world?
6. What are the four _____ food groups?
7. Many writers can be divided according to their _____.
8. In general, people fall into one of two _____: readers and nonreaders.
9. The Northeast, the Southeast, the Midwest, the Southwest, and the West form the five _____ of the United States.
10. Weather can be _____ as fair, cloudy, or rainy, to name one method of _____.

10.d GENERALIZING

A **generalization** is a statement that gives an overview about items or data.

After you have classified data (see 10.c), you may want to communicate an insight that you arrived at during the classification process. The statement that provides an overview is called a generalization. You will realize, soon enough, that not every generalization grows out of the classification process, but it is rare that you classify data without then making a generalization. For example, assume that you have come up with the following list of home-entertainment items.

video recorder
television
dart board
piano
stereo set
books
home computer
crossword puzzles

You now decide to classify these items. Your classification may be along the following lines:

Items requiring electricity	**Items not requiring electricity**
video recorder	dart board
television	piano
stereo set	books
home computer	crossword puzzles

Once you have classified the data, you may have moved on to a generalization, such as one of the following:

Some people seem to divide their time equally between energy-consuming entertainment and energy-saving entertainment.
The most modern home-entertainment items compete with the most time-honored ones in some homes.

As you write, you will find that there is an alternating rhythm between generalizations and specific details. When you have written one, you will want to consider the other. For example, you may first write a *generalization* such as the following:

Life in cold climates is difficult.

You may then want to support this statement with *specifics*, such as the following:

Machinery fails.
People struggle to keep warm.
Snow snarls transportation.
Electricity fails.

On the other hand, you may find yourself writing with *specifics*, first.

The days were balmy, nights gentle. Flowers seemed to leap out of the ground. Birds were busy buildng nests.

You may then want to generalize about what you have written by adding a *generalization*.

It was a typical spring.

The specifics, of course, must be *relevant* to the generalization. That is, the specifics must truly have some connection with the generalization.

The exercises below will give you practice with specifics and generalizations.

EXERCISE 7. Match each of the following sets of specifics with one or more of the generalizations listed below the sets.

Set A

a quickly served, precooked dinner
short supply of paper drinking cups
spilled milk

Set B

a hot dog from a vendor
a cool drink turning warm in the eighth inning
popcorn

Set C

a piece of dried meat that made me retch
a trickle of water left in the canteen
a handful of grain for the camels

Set D

a speckled trout rising to the bait
breakfast under a rain-drenched tent
the smell of cooking fish

Generalizations

1. A camping trip can be a mixed pleasure.
2. One of the joys of summer is an afternoon ball game.
3. The air trip was fast, rocky, and unpleasant.
4. Food of some sort is essential.

EXERCISE 8. Complete each of the following statements. Some will be generalizations; some will be statements of specifics.

1. Television, today, is often too _____.
2. Many animals are _____.
3. Generally speaking, _____ is a good place for a vacation.
4. For example, tourists can _____ and _____ there.
5. Department stores are usually _____.
6. On holidays, for instance, department stores _____.
7. My jobs (chores) have generally been _____.

8. As proof of the above statement, I will tell you about the time _____.
9. Books are _____.
10. For example, _____ and _____ are _____ which _____.

Examine the sentences that you have written. Which are generalizations? Which are statements of specifics?

EXERCISE 9. Read the following information about early art.

1. Thirty thousand years ago people covered the walls of their caves with paintings.
2. Early painters made brushes from split wood or fur.
3. Drawing and painting predated architecture and farming.
4. Artists of the Stone Age studied with a master.

On the basis of the information above, make a generalization about the human need for art.

THE PARAGRAPH

11 The Paragraph

A **paragraph** is a group of sentences that relate to one main idea or incident.

You see a paragraph before you read it. Take a quick look at the article "The Airport World," that begins on the next page. Almost the first thing that you see is a series of paragraphs. By using paragraphs, the writer divides a piece of writing so that readers can more easily deal with the whole. Notice that a paragraph creates a visual break at which readers may pause for a moment. A paragraph is, however, more than a visual aid. As this section will show, a paragraph is also a writing and a thinking aid.

A paragraph forms a logical, self-contained link in the chain of a story or an article. Although you will read and write many different kinds of paragraphs and paragraphs of various lengths, you should always be able to see how the sentences within a given paragraph are connected in meaning to one topic and to one another.

The paragraph itself is also usually a link in a chain of paragraphs that form the whole composition. For you as a writer, it is important to recognize that each paragraph is generally constructed with another paragraph in mind. When, for example, you write the first paragraph of a story or of exposition, you think of it as a beginning. You write it with the thought that other paragraphs will follow. Similarly, when you write the final paragraph of any piece of writing, you write it with the thought that it has been preceded by other paragraphs.

How do you know when to stop one paragraph and begin another? Your study of the main characteristics of paragraphs in this section will help you answer that question.

■ Paragraphs for study

THE AIRPORT WORLD

[1]No longer is an airport a place just outside of town to which travelers run to catch a flight. We are in the era of the Airport World—an eerily quiet, climate-controlled series of concrete caverns. Molded plastic chairs stare at coin-operated television sets; doors careen open by themselves; escalators never stop and conversations never start.

topic sentence (11.a)

specifics: concrete details (11.b.1)

[2]Here at "Everywhere International," the human cargo numbly waits in line, looks for answers on too-high screens, watches luggage disappear behind rubber-toothed curtains, gets electronically frisked, is moving-sidewalked to buses or subways, is directed by tape recordings to a telescoping sleeve, and finally is wedged into a seat in a wide room which purports to be an airplane.

more specifics

[3]But that is only part of the experience of life at Everywhere International. Thanks to computer-planned disconnecting flights, and to sales agents who demand the passenger's presence at the airport long in advance of flight time, the person inserting himself into the travel cocoon is encouraged to spend enough time in the Airport World to browse in the gift shops . . . peruse the paperback racks, and enjoy an invigorating sauna and shoe shine in the men's room.

more specifics

[4]What's going on here? A bureaucrat's idea of the future is going on, I submit, and submission is the name of the game. Most modern airports are built by "authorities," quasi-governmental entities removed from voter accountability. The guiding mission of the faceless authority is supposed to be efficiency, but its passion is the expression of a social manipulator's dream.

topic sentence: question-and-answer generalization

more specifics: facts (11.b.3)

[5]This is no plea for the rinky-dink aerodrome, with pilots in leather caps and goggles,

without needed radar, meteorological devices, and quick-opening air-sick bags. But I suggest that some urban planners' idea of modernity is at least a generation behind the times. Massive scale is now out; regimentation is out; while our dehumanizing airport-builders have zigged, American society has zagged.

topic sentence

specifics

[6]Look at the new airport in Portland, Oregon: cushions on the seats, individual stores open early and late. Granted, Portland is not a metropolis, but it has resisted the urge of other mid-sized cities—from Pocatello to Huntsville, Alabama—to build their own versions of Everywhere International.

specifics

generalization

[7]Airport "authorities" concerned with the character of their communities should make an effort to bring in local private enterprise: a friendly *bodega* or a kosher deli would be worth attracting to the spaces now allocated to the multinational concessionaires of Sameness, Inc.

topic sentence with treatment (11.a)

specifics: examples (11.b.2)

[8]The planners of the next generation of airports should stop trying to add to the distance between airport entrance and airport gate. They should strive to combat that proliferation of hotels, office buildings, and shops that turns a way station into an end in itself. Hapless flight attendants and passengers should not be forced to drag their luggage on litter "schleppers" for miles just to satisfy some civic booster's idea of grandeur or some tax-exempt authority's lust for nonprofit.

topic sentence with treatment

specifics

—William Safire

11.a TOPIC SENTENCES

The **topic sentence** of the paragraph states the main idea of the paragraph.

A topic sentence can be a great help in developing a paragraph. Although each individual sentence in a paragraph should be related to the main idea, or topic, of the paragraph, the topic sentence serves the special purpose of announcing that topic. That is to say, a topic sentence can help the reader to identify more easily the central point that the writer is making. Basically, a topic sentence is a generalization. It sums up and sometimes comments upon the specifics or the other generalizations in the paragraph.

You should know from the outset that not every paragraph needs a topic sentence for the reader to follow the writer's thoughts. Narrative paragraphs usually do not have topic sentences. Rather, a writer of narrative tells the events as they occur without necessarily stopping at the beginning of each paragraph to announce those events. Not all expository paragraphs have topic sentences either. Look again, for example, at Paragraphs 2 and 6 on pages 547 and 548. Those paragraphs do not have stated topic sentences, although they are made up of specifics and generalizations and the reader can easily recognize the topic of each paragraph. Even though professional writers may not include topic sentences all the time, you should be aware of how helpful they are for readers and, wherever possible, make an effort to include one.

A topic sentence has one essential function and one nonessential but helpful function. The essential function of a topic sentence is to tell readers what topic is being discussed in the paragraph. Very often, the topic sentence is the first sentence in the paragraph, as illustrated in the following example.

EXAMPLE

Some automobiles are now unsafe. Cutting corners on materials while providing sleep-inducing ease of driving and maximum speed capability is dangerous. It is like arming all Americans with deadly weapons. We must protest this recent trend of some automobile manufacturers.

Is there any doubt which sentence in the above paragraph is the topic sentence? Is there any doubt that it tells the reader what the paragraph is about?

The helpful but optional function of a topic sentence is to tell the reader what the writer *thinks* about the topic or how the writer will *treat* the topic. Notice how the following topic sentence is different from the one above.

EXAMPLE

There is no excuse for the lack of safety in some automobiles today. Cutting corners on materials....

Is the topic still clear with this topic sentence? Do you now have a better idea of the writer's attitude from the outset?

11.a.1 Judging topic sentences

Some topics lend themselves to a topic sentence that simply states the topic; other topics lend themselves to a topic sentence that includes the topic *and* the treatment or attitude of the writer (see the two example topic sentences in 11.a above). Whichever kind of topic sentence you have, it can be evaluated, as usual, by asking a few questions.

1. Does the topic sentence present one—and only one—topic?
2. Is the topic sentence an overgeneralization? (See 14.c.)
3. Does the sentence give strong direction to the whole paragraph?

Actually, it is difficult to say that a topic sentence is "good" or "bad." It is possible, however, to say that one topic sentence is better than another. For example, look again at the preceding paragraph about cars, and consider the two topic sentences below.

TOPIC SENTENCE *A*: Some automobiles are now unsafe. [Original topic sentence.]

TOPIC SENTENCE *B*: Automobiles are made differently now. [Possible new topic sentence.]

Why is Sentence *B* not as good as Sentence *A* for the given paragraph? Consider the following questions and answers.

1. Does Sentence *B* present one clear topic? In a way, it does, but the details that follow are only about safety features, not about any other differences; maybe this topic sentence is not clear enough after all.
2. Is Sentence *B* an overgeneralization? Unfortunately, yes. Sentence *B* seems broader than necessary, given what is actually discussed in the rest of the paragraph.

3. Does Sentence *B* give strong direction to the whole paragraph? No, it does focus a discussion of safety.

EXERCISE 1. After each of the following paragraphs, you will find a choice of two possible topic sentences with which to begin that paragraph. Indicate which topic sentence is better for that particular paragraph, and explain why. Use the questions in 11.a.1 to help you to reach your decision.

PARAGRAPH *A*

...Some people openly welcome the challenge of competition no matter what its form. Their faces light up, their movements quicken, and their concentration intensifies. Other people deny they are competitive, plotting all the while how to win. These are people who never seem to lose. Are there any people who are not competitive? They probably stopped competing for oxygen long ago.

Topic sentences

1. Competition is important to the American way of life.
2. There are two types of people in the world when it comes to competition.

PARAGRAPH *B*

...For the daring among us, there are the thrills of mountain climbing and skydiving. Less adventurous but still active people might opt for tennis or skiing. Golfing and backpacking, on the other hand, seem to require less exertion for their enjoyment.

Topic sentences

1. Each of us has to find the combination of exercise and fun that is right for us.
2. Some sports are more popular and more demanding than others in terms of money, equipment, time, and patience.

PARAGRAPH *C*

...The Caribbean and Gulf Stream waters offer ideal conditions for exotic marine life—coral reefs to shelter vibrant fish, shells, and anemones, and a constant water temperature. The water is as transparent as crystal; the visibility often exceeds 100 feet; the color and variety of marine life are breathtaking. To make underwater exploration even more exciting, there are hundreds of ships that have foundered on the rocks and reefs over the centuries, adding to the dreamlike nature of an undersea visit and raising the possibility—however unlikely—of sunken treasure.

Topic sentences

1. Underwater exploration is growing in popularity.
2. Some of today's most popular underwater exploration is happening in the Caribbean.

PARAGRAPH *D*

... Obviously, commercials employ many people. Researchers, producers, technicians all find employment in the great world of television ads. It is also important to note that ads create needed breaks in viewing. When else would people do chores, talk on the phone, or eat meals? And, as if anything further needed to be said, it should be mentioned that commercials offer the slickest, most professional, highest-quality, carefully researched bit of programing on the air. Remember this the next time you are tempted to say a rude "So what?" to a thirty-second spot for razor blades.

Topic sentences

1. So much has been said in criticism of television commercials that it is time to enumerate their good points.
2. Commercials are an important part of the television industry.

EXERCISE 2. Practice writing sentences that can be used as topic sentences. These topic sentences should be the kind that both state a topic and tell how you, the writer, are going to treat the topic. Write two distinct topic sentences—and choose two distinct treatments—for each of the following topics.

Topics: commercials, clothing, computers, college, country music

Attitudes or treatments: express fear, express excitement, express anger, express pleasure, urge acceptance, view with caution, express surprise, display humor

EXAMPLES

topic: clothing
treatment #1: view with caution

topic sentence #1: As unpleasant as the fact is, the garment industry may be threatened by competition from low-cost imports.

topic: clothing
treatment #2: express anger
topic sentence #2: The tendency to overhaul the "in" look every year can be nerve-racking and expensive.

11.a.2 Position of the topic sentence

A topic sentence may appear any place in an expository paragraph, even though it usually appears as the first sentence. There is an obvious advantage to having it first or near the beginning of the paragraph: It alerts your reader to what is to come. When it is in the middle of a paragraph, a topic sentence can serve to unite the specific sentences on either side of it. It can create a welcome change of pace, perhaps. When placed at the end of a paragraph, a topic sentence can serve to summarize the specifics in the paragraph.

The topic sentence at the end may serve as a **clincher sentence**—that is, a sentence that helps "clinch" the idea. Sometimes, a paragraph has both a topic sentence at the beginning and a clincher sentence at the end.

Notice that the topic sentence *Some automobiles are now unsafe*, slightly reworded, appears in the paragraphs below in two other positions—middle and end. What advantages do you see to each?

MIDDLE

Cutting corners on material while providing sleep-inducing ease of driving and maximum speed capacity is dangerous. It is like arming all Americans with deadly weapons. *Obviously, some automobiles are now unsafe.* We must protest the recent trend of some automobile manufacturers.

END

Cutting corners on materials while providing sleep-inducing ease of driving and maximum speed capability is dangerous. It is like arming all Americans with deadly weapons. We must protest this recent trend of some automobile manufacturers. *Some automobiles, we must admit, are now unsafe.*

11.a.3 Kinds of topic sentences

A topic sentence can make a generalization, ask a question, or give a command.

EXAMPLES

GENERALIZATION: Some automobiles are now unsafe.

QUESTION: Are some automobiles now unsafe? Have you considered how unsafe some automobiles have become?

COMMAND: Make it known that you will not buy unsafe automobiles.

If you select a question as your topic sentence, make sure that it manages to give clear direction to your paragraph.

Be aware, also, that sometimes a topic sentence is actually two sentences long, depending on what your particular style and purpose are in a piece of writing. Notice, for example, how the one-sentence topic sentence used earlier can be reworded to become a two-sentence topic sentence.

EXAMPLE

There is no excuse for the lack of safety in some automobiles today.

Some of today's automobiles are not as safe as drivers might expect. There is no excuse for this state of affairs.

In the two-sentence version the topic is announced in the first sentence ("lack of safety"), but the real treatment, or focus, of the topic is held out until the second sentence ("no excuse").

Notice that both Pair *A* and Pair *B* below have the same first sentence; they are about the same topic, television. The second sentence in Pair *A* sets the topic in one direction; the second sentence in Pair *B* sets the topic in another direction. You could, therefore, have two paragraphs beginning with the same sentence but developing in two different ways. In effect, then, you could say that both Pair *A* and Pair *B* are two-sentence topic sentences.

PAIR A: Television holds up a mirror to nature. As America has become a nation of city-dwellers, so television programs have come to center on city life.

PAIR B: Television holds up a mirror to nature. Television programing proves that everyone tries to copy success.

How would a paragraph beginning with Pair *A*'s two sentences be different from a paragraph beginning with Pair *B*'s two sentences?

EXERCISE 3. Given the following pairs of sentences, write two different paragraphs of your own.

PAIR A: Baseball has long been considered America's national pastime. It is easy to see why baseball became so popular.

PAIR B: Baseball has long been considered America's national pastime. It is no longer as important as it used to be, however.

11.b DEVELOPING THE TOPIC SENTENCE: THE SPECIFICS

There are at least three ways to develop a topic sentence into a complete paragraph: Use (1) concrete details, (2) examples or incidents, or (3) facts or statistics.

The topic sentence, as has been explained, can be thought of as a generalization, and a generalization almost always must be supported by specifics: by (1) concrete details, (2) examples or incidents, or (3) facts or statistics.

The process of writing a paragraph can begin at just the opposite end: You can gather a number of specific points first, and then you can produce a topic sentence that grows out of the specifics. Either way – generalization first, specifics next, or vice versa – you should be aware of the three basic forms that specifics can take.

11.b.1 Concrete details

You can use distinct words to communicate sensory impressions that support your topic sentence. The words will describe the appearance, sound, smell, taste, and feel of the object, place, or event under discussion in your paragraph and, in so doing, will produce a concrete – a real – picture. Notice the underlined topic sentence and the underlined concrete details in the following paragraph:

The beach at Amagansett that summer was very special. The sand was finer than usual, or so it seemed, but was crisply punctuated more than ever by tire tracks from the haul seiners (net-fishing locals). The tracks were series of small mounds that would crumble underfoot but squish delightfully as they fell between the toes. The fineness of the sand may have caused the surprising squeakiness that greeted each footstep and made each baby gurgle in delight. Even the surf itself seemed different — more friendly, more playful, and curiously more salty. | topic sentence

EXERCISE 4. Write a paragraph that uses concrete details based on your senses to develop the following topic sentence:

> The city that winter was a mixture of fantasy and cold, hard reality.

Here are concrete details, arranged according to sense, that you can use, or make up your own:

SIGHT: snow always falling (air full of "feathers"); snow mounds turning black from traffic

SOUND: traffic sounds generally muffled; ambulances blaring through the night

FEEL: fun of sliding down icy sidewalks; blasts of cold air outside and feeling of being overheated on buses

SMELLS: "chestnuts roasting on an open fire"; garbage uncollected because trucks removing snow

11.b.2 Examples or incidents

You can cite examples or incidents that illustrate the generalization stated in the topic sentence. A number of brief examples or an incident — sometimes called an anecdote — can often help your readers to see clearly the meaning of the topic sentence. Here is the same topic sentence used in 11.b.1. Notice how different specifics — this time two incidents — produce a paragraph with an entirely different meaning and character.

The beach at Amagansett that summer was very special. First, there was the offshore July 4th bonfire, visible for miles by sun worshipers who needed the excitement to lift their spirits, sagging from a truly overcast day. What made this bonfire unusual was that its fuel was a fifty-five-foot pleasure craft named *Vicki*. Smoke had been noticed in the electrical wiring system, and eventually fire and spectacular explosions awed those on the beach until the Coast Guard sank *Vicki* with its firehoses. Later that month — on Bastille Day — vacationers witnessed one more special event, the private fireworks at a celebrity's beach house. The fireworks were misdirected and came down on the house instead of in the dunes. Again, public servants came to the rescue. This time the fire department hosed down the area, preventing a possible disaster.

topic sentence

one incident

another incident

EXERCISE 5. Write a paragraph that uses a couple of examples or incidents to develop the following topic sentence:

The city that winter was a mixture of fantasy and cold, hard reality.

Suggested examples of "fantasy" element: all schools and businesses closed; people of all ages having carefree snowball fights on city streets

Suggested example of cold, hard reality: no fuel or food deliveries

11.b.3 Facts and statistics

You can use a variety of different kinds of facts to support, or fill out, your topic sentence. A fact can be a statement that has been proven by experience, observation, or study. One form that facts can take is statistics. Here is the same topic sentence used in 11.b.1 and 11.b.2 but this time developed basically with facts and statistics, which are underlined.

The beach at Amagansett that summer was very special. Because gasoline prices had soared to the dollar range, the summer community decreased a good 10 percent, making the usually uncrowded beach almost a private retreat. Furthermore, the fog that most vacationers expect to battle every summer never materialized, being replaced instead by one glorious weekend after the next, the sun always there even if at times hazy, the temperature, generally a comfortable 80 degrees.

topic sentence

EXERCISE 6. Write a paragraph that uses facts or statistics to develop the following topic sentence:

The city that winter was a mixture of fantasy and cold, hard reality.

Suggested facts and statistics for "fantasy" element: snow drifts six feet high; reservoir frozen six inches deep; no cars visible because all buried under snow; crime down by 10 percent

Suggested facts and statistics for cold, hard reality: one out of every four people struck by flu; 10 percent increase in home fires

REVIEW EXERCISE A. Use the kind of specifics suggested in parentheses to develop each of the following topic sentences into a paragraph.

1. Jogging has found followers in all age groups. (facts or statistics)
2. The common cold makes you "senseless." (concrete details)
3. Daylight Savings Time has definite advantages. (examples or incidents)
4. Every American and every tourist should experience autumn in New England (or the Rockies). (concrete details)

11.c UNITY IN A PARAGRAPH

A good paragraph has **unity**: All the sentences have a relationship to one another and to the main idea.

The first two paragraphs below have unity. The third does not; its italicized sentences destroy the unity. (The three paragraphs, incidentally, are each one-paragraph summaries of long film reviews.)

PARAGRAPH *A*

In *The Revenge of the Pink Panther*, Peter Sellers stars once again as the expert in *gaffes*, Inspector Clouseau, whose armored ineptitude periodically drives Herbert Lom, as his boss, into mental institutions. The story is by Blake Edwards. He also directed the picture. The result is familiar and amusing.

—*The New Yorker*

PARAGRAPH *B*

Days of Heaven is an eloquent and important film about Americanness and the pangs of exile. Terence Matlick wrote and directed the picture, set in Texas in 1916. There is little or no sense of our being in a land about to enter a world war; we are in an entirely cut-off land of wheat fields that are more brightly lit than the characters' lives. The film reports, accurately and wonderfully, on a new society trying to cohere yet wishing to dissent.

—*The New Yorker*

PARAGRAPH *C*

A farce-parody of Hollywood's mad-scientist movies. You have to let Mel Brooks's comedy, *Young Frankenstein*, do everything for you, because that's the only way it works. *Mary Shelley, who wrote the original story about Frankenstein, was married to the famous poet, Percy Bysshe.* If you accept the silly, zizzy obviousness of the movie, it can make you laugh helplessly. Gene Wilder is the old Baron's scientist-grandson. Peter Boyle is the new Monster, and Madeline Kahn is the scientist's fiancée, who becomes the Monster's bride. The picture is in black-and-white, which holds it visually close to the film it takes off from. *Black and white has generally not been used effectively since color was introduced in the earlier part of the century.* It's Brooks's most sustained piece of moviemaking—the laughs never let up.

— *The New Yorker (with italicized sentences added)*

Paragraph C, above, does not have unity because the two italicized sentences do not relate directly enough to the main idea of the paragraph. The paragraph is supposed to be about one director's achievement with a particular movie—Mel Brooks and *Young Frankenstein.* The information about (1) Mary Shelley's marriage and (2) black-and-white film, in general, has nothing to do with that main idea as expressed in other sentences. The italicized sentences simply pick up from a key word in a preceding sentence and show that the writer was, in effect, free-associating. The sentences may be interesting, but they certainly are also side-tracking. The writer should have been paying closer attention to the main idea under discussion.

EXERCISE 7. Point out the sentences that spoil the unity in each of the following paragraphs.

PARAGRAPH *A*

For such spectacular beauty, Namibia must be one of the least spoiled places in an overpopulated world. Namibia—South West Africa on most maps—has only about one million people in an area larger than France, and a population density of less than one person per square kilometer. And most of these people live far to the north in Ovamboland. Europeans first reached this area in 1851.

PARAGRAPH *B*

The sand is cream-colored, so unmarred that it reflects clouds passing overhead as if it were water. Mysterious and silent, the dunes—to anyone who ventures even a few hundred yards into them—offer a solitude as vast as the sea, and as elemental. Air travel is sporadic, however. The best method of travel is by car. Gulls pass overhead in wheeling flights, the winds ceaselessly altering the landscape, like an artist unwilling to abandon his work.

—*A* and *B* from "An Unknown Beauty"
by Tom Wicker

PARAGRAPH *C*

For many of us the summer is a time for forming new friendships. Today millions of Americans vacation abroad, and they go not only to see new sights but also—in those places where they do not feel too strange—with the hope of meeting new people. No one really expects a vacation trip to produce a close friend. Few Americans stay put for a lifetime. But surely the beginning of a friendship is possible? Surely in every country people value friendship?

—From *A Way of Seeing*
by Margaret Mead and Rhoda Metraux

EXERCISE 8. Each set below contains data that can be put into sentences. The sentences can then be placed together to form a paragraph. Each set, however, contains one piece of data that might make the paragraph lose its unity. Identify that item in each set below.

DATA SET A: For a paragraph that gives advice on going for a job interview, discuss:

1. importance of dressing appropriately
2. speaking clearly
3. being on time for appointment
4. working conditions in other countries

DATA SET B: For a paragraph on the variety of extracurricular activities, discuss:

1. writing for the school newspaper
2. acting in the school production of *Romeo and Juliet*
3. current theories about teaching Shakespeare in twelfth-grade English classes
4. swimming on the varsity team

DATA SET C: For a paragraph on varieties of late-night television programs, discuss:

1. talk shows
2. reruns of Hollywood movies
3. reruns of old television programs
4. the popularity of midday soap operas

DATA SET D: For a paragraph on why people like ocean beaches, discuss:

1. ice cream cones
2. riding waves
3. fresh salt air
4. jogging on the sand

DATA SET E: For a paragraph on choosing a college, discuss:

1. costs of tuition, room, etc.
2. the rise in tuition costs between 1950 and 1970
3. distance from home
4. course offerings in field of interest

EXERCISE 9. Review the following sentences and divide them into two groups so that you can present two separate paragraphs, each with unity. (The sentences were written by Barbara Lang Stern for *Vogue* magazine.)

1. When you meet people who are different from you, chances are you sometimes find the dissimilarities attractive.
2. Each is infuriated by the "impossible" way the other is behaving.
3. Or you may respond warmly to someone who brings out a side of you that you approve of, or who satisfies a need you may have—for warmth, reassurance, approval, etc.
4. For example, maybe you've been in a meeting or even a family discussion where one person angrily demands that a decision be made, while another shakes her head adamantly, protesting that there's just not enough information available.
5. "She's very open about her feelings. I'd like to be more like that," you might think.
6. But you may also react to "differences" with negative feelings of hostility or anxiety.

11.d COHERENCE IN A PARAGRAPH

A good paragraph has **coherence:** The sentences are sequenced according to a clear, logical plan of development.

If readers say to themselves, "What are these sentences doing together in this order in this paragraph?", then that paragraph probably lacks coherence.

Coherence in a paragraph depends chiefly on ordering the sentences according to a logic that is easy to follow. One sentence should logically, sensibly, grow out of the preceding sentence, as if the writer's thoughts are flowing on and on. Often the plan of development is so easy that readers may be unaware of it. Read the two following paragraphs and decide which is the more coherent:

PARAGRAPH *A*

Poets are usually quite able to do rough work and to earn their living in ordinary ways. Masefield was an able seaman. Davies was a cattleman and tramp. Hodgson was a dog fancier and boxing authority. Frost worked in mills and did farming for years.

PARAGRAPH *B*

Farmers and millworkers are not always famous poets or literary lights. Robert Frost was all three at one time or another, however. Masefield, Davies, and Hodgson were not farmers or millworkers necessarily, but, at one time or another, they also did rough work or were interested in the sporting scene.

Why is Paragraph *A* easier to follow—more coherent—than Paragraph *B*? The sentences in Paragraph *B* wind back and forth so many times that they simply do not work together (cohere) well. The writer does not seem sure if the paragraph is about farmers or about millworkers or about poets.

Coherence comes from order. There are several ways to order data, depending on what *kind* of data you have. Here are four of the more popular ways of ordering information:

1. If your data are the steps or events that add up to a story, use *chronological order.*
2. If your data are objects in a given space or objects that you have seen as you have moved around, use *spatial order.*
3. If your data are various points that you want your reader to remember, use *order of importance.*
4. If your data are all equally important specifics, present them as equally important, working in generalizations.

You can make the order that you choose very clear to your readers by the words that you use to connect one sentence to the next. These words are, logically enough, often referred to as **logical connectives**[1] because they make clear not only the order but also the meaning of the writing. Each order has its own logical connectives, as the following pages will show.

11.d.1 Chronological order

The following paragraph is coherent. The data are presented in a clear order—in **chronological,** or time, order. The chronological order is made even clearer by the use of connectives and other expressions of time. Chronological order is especially useful when writing narratives.

[1] Logical connectives are one kind of *transitional device.* For other kinds of transitional devices, see 13.f.

After a time he was aware of the first faraway signals of sensation in his beaten fingers. The faint tingling grew stronger till it evolved into a stinging ache that was excruciating but which the man hailed with satisfaction. He stripped the mitten from his right hand and fetched forth the birch bark. The exposed fingers were quickly going numb again. Next he brought out his bunch of sulphur matches. But the tremendous cold had already driven the life out of his fingers. In his effort to separate one match from the other, the whole bunch fell in the snow. He tried to pick it out of the snow, but failed. The dead fingers could neither touch nor clutch. He was very careful. He drove the thought of his freezing feet and nose and cheeks out of his mind, devoting his whole soul to the matches. He watched, using the sense of vision in place of that of touch, and when he saw his fingers on each side of the bunch, he closed them, for the wires were down, and the fingers did not obey. He pulled the mitten on the right hand and beat it fiercely against his knee. Then, with both mittened hands, he scooped the bunch of matches, along with much snow, into his lap. Yet he was no better off.

—Jack London, "To Build a Fire"

EXERCISE 10. The data in the following paragraph are arranged in chronological order. To make the paragraph even more coherent, indicate where each logical connective suggested on the next page will help the most. (The connectives were in the original paragraph.)

(a)_____, Vanne and I felt ill at the same time. It was undoubtedly some sort of malaria, but since we had been told by no lesser person than the doctor in Kigoma that there was no malaria in the area we had no drugs with us. How he came to believe such a strange fallacy I cannot imagine. We were too naive to question him at that time. (b)_____ we lay side by side on our low camp beds in our hot, stuffy tent sweating out the fever. (c)_____ we mustered the strength to take our temperatures: Neither of us felt like reading so there was nothing else to do to pass the time. Vanne had a temperature of 105 degrees almost constantly for five days, and it dropped slightly only during the coolness of the nights. (d)_____ we were told that she had been lucky to pull through at all. To make everything worse, the whole camp was pervaded, (e)_____, by the most terrible smell—rather like bad cabbage water. It was the flower of some tree—I forget its name now—I always think of as the "fever flower tree."

—Jane van Lawick-Goodall

Logical connectives
Occasionally
About three months after our arrival
throughout our illness
Afterward
For nearly two weeks

11.d.2 Spatial order

The following paragraph explains certain details about the incredibly jeweled Easter eggs that were designed in the nineteenth century by a man named Fabergé. The paragraph is coherent. The bulk of the data is presented in a clear order—in **spatial** order. The spatial order is made even clearer by the use of the underlined logical connectives. Spatial order is particularly useful when writing descriptions.

> The first [Fabergé Easter egg] was made for Alexander III as an Easter gift for his wife, Maria Feodorovna, probably in 1886. It was a relatively simple white-enameled gold shell which opened to reveal a matte gold yolk <u>containing</u> a nest of gold straw. <u>On the straw</u> sat an enameled gold hen. When the beak of the hen is lifted, the body opens. Originally, hidden <u>inside</u> was a tiny replica of the Imperial crown which, itself, contained a ruby pendant. The crown and pendant have since disappeared. That magnificent gift began a fashion and tradition among the wealthy which lasted until the Russian revolution.
>
> —Erica Brown

where nest is in relation to yolk

where hen is in relation to straw

where replica is in relation to hen

In order to explain how intricate the Easter egg was, the writer moved from the outside ("gold shell") inside to gold yolk to gold straw to gold hen to replica to ruby—a very clear and a very coherent explanation.

The next paragraph, about the layout of the city of Pompeii, also has its details arranged spatially, but here the viewer is moving through space. The viewer's **vantage point** is changing as the description progresses. (In the description of the Easter egg, the viewer stood in one place, in a stationary vantage point.) Notice the underlined spatial connectives.

> One logical way that visitors can explore Pompeii is to start with main streets and public monuments. They can enter Pompeii through the Marine Gate at the city's southern corner, which leads to the Forum and the Via dell'Abbondanza. At the gate itself, to the right is the Antiquarium, a small modern museum worth a visit if only for such early fragments as the sixth-century B.C. terra cotta decorations of the Greek temple. A step farther, on the right, is the platform of the Temple of the Pompeian Venus, patron goddess of the city, but there is little to see because the postearthquake rebuilding had not even begun. A little farther along, on the left, is the Temple of Apollo, set in a rectangular precinct with columned portico, partly restored in modern times, with copies of a bronze statue of Apollo and a bust of Artemis placed to right and left, where the originals were found.
>
> —Blanche R. Brown, "How the City Grew"

Many other spatial connectives are listed in 12.b.

EXERCISE 11. The data in the following paragraph are arranged spatially. To make the paragraph even more coherent, indicate where each logical connective suggested below the paragraph will help the most. (The connectives were in the original paragraph.) Use the diagram to help you place the connectives correctly.

> The hills seem to recede as the traveler speeds down the eastern half of the bridge: He sees a flat rectangular strip of land on which most of the industrial and business sections of the East Bay rest, as on a stage to which the residential hills are the backdrop. Ahead (a)_____ are the tall buildings of downtown Oakland, key city of the area, where the industrial district crowds down to the Outer Harbor in the foreground. (b)_____ to the far right a ferryboat dock—reminiscent of a vanishing era in Bay transportation—affords the only glimpse of Alameda, the island city. Far to the southeast, (c)_____, are San Leandro and Hayward. Although the vast panorama of homes and business buildings shows no visible gaps, it is a jigsaw puzzle of independent communities closely fitted together—Piedmont, a residential community in the hills (d)_____; Emeryville, an industrial town crowding to the shore (e)_____; Berkeley (f)_____, best identified by the white campanile and stadium on the university campus,

(g)____; El Cerrito, and Richmond, residential and industrial towns (h)_____. With a combined population of over a half-million, these municipalities form a continuous urban unit, yet maintain their political independence.

—"San Francisco," *American Guide Series*

Logical connectives

far to the left	almost directly ahead
spreading up the slopes beyond	beyond the traveler's range of vision
to the left	across the water
in the left foreground	and to the right

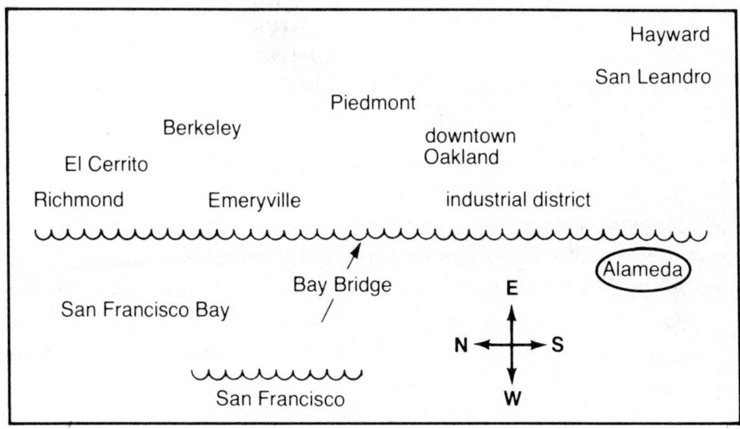

11.d.3 Order of importance

The information in the following paragraph is arranged according to **order of increasing importance.** The data are thus made clear and understandable. The most important point is saved for last. Notice how the underlined logical connectives make the order even clearer.

The Egyptians were splendid portraitists. Egyptian art shows us many faces and types—fat and flabby noblemen, humpbacked dwarfs, dark-eyed and full-lipped women—which must have been telling likenesses of their models. And yet, when we look at the statues of the

an important point

kings, they appear suspiciously alike. Moreover, this similarity seems to have been deliberate. Kings are known to have usurped the statues of earlier rulers simply by changing the name on the base. In fact, many Egyptian statues, especially those of rulers, are "idealized." By this we mean that they resembled not the individual they were meant to represent, but an ideal type of what a king should look like.

a more important point

final point—to stress the fact

—Ariane Ruskin, *History in Art*

Here are other expressions that can be used to emphasize order of importance.

the least important
more importantly
most importantly
another important point

EXERCISE 12. Write a coherent paragraph for each set of data below. Use the kind of order suggested for each set. Use logical connectives.

DATA SET A: Use chronological order.

pitched tent
dug fire pit
gathered wood
Late sun broke through the clouds.
One rainbow appeared.
Another rainbow appeared.
We watched.
I took a walk to take a photograph.

DATA SET B: Use spatial order.

Use the same data as in Data Set A, above, but this time organize the details to stress *spatial* rather than *time* order.

DATA SET C: Use order of importance in putting the following data into a paragraph that tells someone what to pack for a two-week vacation at the shore. Put the most important items first—or last.

tennis racket and balls
sandals, jogging shoes, tennis shoes
books, writing paper, pen, address book

portable barbecue
beach blanket and towels
T-shirts, jeans, sweaters for evening
sunburn protection
bathing suits

DATA SET D: Use order of importance in putting the following data into a paragraph that tells someone what to look for in buying a used car.

mileage
condition of paint job
condition of transmission and engine
spare tire? snow tires?
records of maintenance

REVIEW EXERCISE B. Reorder the sentences in the following paragraphs to give them coherence.

[1]When it hit 126 knots, the plane unexpectedly nosed up before the pilot had pulled on the control column for takeoff. [2]It was nearly midnight at the San Diego airport as a Delta Air Lines jet accelerated down the runway, bound for Los Angeles. [3]The amazed pilot desperately slammed the control column forward as far as possible to try to force the nose back down. [4]Speeding into the heavy clouds over the ocean, the nose pitched even higher.

[5]It was also the beginning of one of the most harrowing 55 minutes in recent aviation history. [6]After a series of potentially disastrous maneuvers, the plane landed safely at Los Angeles International Airport. [7]This incident was the beginning of Delta Flight 1080 on April 12, last year. [8]Indeed, at least one of them was furious about being delayed. [9]Although the passengers had been told of a control problem, they never learned how close they had come to tragedy.

11.e PARAGRAPHING NARRATIVE WRITING

When you write most compositions for school, you will be able to determine when to start a new paragraph based on what you now know are the elements of most good paragraphs: (1) a clearly stated topic sentence, (2) related specifics that develop the topic sentence, (3) unity, (4) coherence.

When you write a narrative or a story—fiction or nonfiction—it is even easier to decide when to start a new paragraph. You begin a new paragraph at the following points:

a. when you introduce conversation

b. when the speaker changes

c. when the narrative picks up again after dialogue

d. when the scene shifts for any length of time

e. when you move from one character to another for any length of time

Read the following narrative. Be ready to explain why the writer began each new paragraph where he did.

. . . and in this way we finally reached the top. I could not have gone a step further," Gil said. *a*

"Does that include going down the mountain?" I asked, trying to make a joke out of the situation. *b*

Night was indeed threatening behind the dark clouds in the west. It was time for us to give serious thought to our next move. *c*

At about the same time that Gil and I were wondering what action to take, three miles below the cloud cover, the main party was beginning to worry. *c, d*

Laura told me later that she did not really feel concerned until she heard the scarpa guide talk about sending out a search party. *d*

EXERCISE 13. Rewrite and paragraph the following passage. Be prepared to explain your decisions.

He got out at the corner, stuck a bill at the cabbie, took off along the shrub-bordered walk. The red brick buildings were inked in darkness, the myriad windows bright squares of yellow. The walks were empty of bicycles and roller skates, and no children were in sight. Philip looked for Callie, for Fip and Mary Frances, but there was only the evening parade of husbands and fathers. He ran up the flagstone walk of Number 10. Mrs. Yates was at the elevator. He held the door for her. On the ride up, she kept casting speculative glances at him. "I spoke with your charming wife this morning. That darling boy of yours!" "Thank you." "Seems to be feeling better—Mrs. Hallard, I mean." Why did Callie have to worry him like this? Why did she have to ruin their night out together? He blamed her for everything . . . . why? Just let her be home, just let him find her safe with the children. A tiny birdlike woman with red hair gestured at him from the door of the apartment. A fur piece was skewered round her neck from which the rest of her appeared to be suspended. She blinked agitated eyes and said, "Mr. Hallard? I am Miss Watkins. Is Mrs. Hallard with you? I returned promptly at five, as we agreed. I had to go home to feed Tommy—" At the opposite end of the hall, Mrs. Yates was taking unconscionably long with her door key. "I've been here since five," Miss Watkins went on. "I looked downstairs, came back up . . ." Philip unlocked the door and went in. "Callie," he called. Fip's wooden train curved out from the table in the alcove, where it had been when he'd left for work that morning. Hurrying past, he kicked over the Lego blocks. "Callie?" He went through the apartment, calling his wife's name.

—Arthur Cavanaugh, *The Children Are Gone*

11.f WRITING A SUMMARY PARAGRAPH

From time to time, for a variety of reasons, you will be asked to summarize material that you have heard or read. If you can do so in a single paragraph, the summary will have the added benefit of being brief. (You might look again at the summaries of movie reviews in 11.c.)

For example, suppose that you were asked to summarize the article appearing on pages 547-548 ("The Airport World"). Your summary would be acceptable if written as follows:

SUMMARY

In the article, "The Airport World," the author expresses his dissatisfaction with large airports that have become worlds of their own. The authorities responsible for developing airports do not pay attention to public opinion. They have sought efficiency and profit at the expense of passenger comfort and local color. Airports have become so similar, so inhuman, and so devoid of regional differences that a traveler cannot tell one from another. Regardless of locale, most airports have been housing only the same nationally franchised stores selling an array of nondescript products. The new airport in Portland, Oregon, however, signals a change of attitude toward passengers and local communities. Other airports would do well to imitate Portland, and add a touch of humanity while providing local interest. They could do so by opening the airport to local merchants, who would operate stores, profit from airport business, and let a traveler know what part of the country he or she is in. The writer would like to see mass scale and regimentation replaced by smaller scale and individuality.

Suggestions for writing a summary paragraph

1. Before you can summarize an article, you must be sure that you understand it. You will have to read it at least twice.
2. Make notes of the main ideas in the article: Look for the generalizations including those that are topic sentences. These generalizations will be the basis of your summary. Set aside the specifics. If you include specifics, you will not be summarizing but rewriting the original.

Here is a list of the generalizations that might be listed for the article "The Airport World."

1. Airports are no longer a place to catch a plane; they are a world of their own. [Paragraph 1]
2. All major airports seem alike. [Paragraph 2]
3. No generalizations in Paragraph 3.
4. Airports are run by authorities that are not checked on by voters. [Paragraph 4]
5. Airport authorities like to manipulate travelers. [Paragraph 5]
6. Portland is trying to break the pattern. [Paragraph 6]
7. Airport authorities should let local private enterprise try marketing their products in airports. [Paragraph 7]

Are all the above generalizations treated in the summary paragraph?

EXERCISE 14. Write your own version of a summary paragraph of "The Airport World." Begin by making your own notes, or use the ones above.

11.g WRITING A PRÉCIS

A **précis** is a brief summary.

A précis (prā sē') provides a summary of written material, but it differs from a regular summary paragraph in a few important respects. Basically, a précis is a more formal statement of the generalizations in a longer piece. In forming a précis a writer must concentrate on general points and on communicating the *tone* and *essence* of the original. Here is an example of one less-than-perfect précis of the article "The Airport World" from pages 547-548.

PRÉCIS: DRAFT 1

Major airports, no longer only places where one goes to catch a plane, have become worlds of their own. All similar to one another, these airports never reflect the characteristics of the community or region. They are a product of the faceless "authorities" who run them and who are not responsible to the voters. These authorities have as their aim the manipulation of travelers, forcing them to spend long periods of time waiting at airports, buying the goods and services available at airport stores, all national franchises. These authorities should change their aims and, as a start, permit local merchants to participate in the commerce of airports. A store or two, local in character, could be added. Local merchants would profit, and, at the same time, they would add variety and regional flavor for the traveler. The author shrewdly suggests that authorities should also scale down the airports to focus on passenger needs, rather than strictly on profits or grandeur. (160 words)

The above précis is a first draft, requiring revisions. Study the following aims for a précis in order to evaluate the first draft above.

Aims in writing a précis

1. To reduce the material to not more than one third
2. To omit specifics and to include only the main points
3. To use your own words, not the words of the author
4. To omit your opinions or comments
5. To omit reference to the author or to the article; for example, omit "The author says . . . ."

EXERCISE 15. What weaknesses do you find in the first-draft précis? Check it against the aims listed on page 573. Then read a compressed version of the pécis (Draft 2, below). Point out ways in which the number of words was reduced.

PRÉCIS: DRAFT 2

No longer just places where one can catch a plane, large airports are now worlds of their own. Standardized and totally disconnected from local communities or regions, major airports reflect the aims of the unresponsive authorities who direct them. These authorities seek to manipulate people, forcing them to wait and tempting them to patronize the franchised stores. To give airports a local character and interest, these authorities should open airports to local merchants. Authorities should further scale down airports to conform to modern American needs. (83 words)

EXERCISE 16. Make additional reductions in the précis above before reading Draft 3.

PRÉCIS: DRAFT 3

Major airports have become so sleek and sterile that they give a traveler no sense of place. Nationally franchised stores in airports cheat passengers of regional color and deprive local businesses of the chance to share airport profits. Authorities who run the airports have abused their power for the sake of profits. A generation behind the times, airport authorities still provide regimentation and grand scale when Americans are now looking for intimacy and local color. (75 words)

CHARACTERISTICS OF A SUMMARY	CHARACTERISTICS OF A PRÉCIS
1. contains generalizations	1. contains generalizations *and* style of original
2. is in your own words	2. is in your own words
3. condenses basic ideas	3. condenses basic ideas
4. makes reference to original	4. makes *no* reference to original
5. may contain your opinion or comment	5. *no* opinion or comment
6. length optional	6. one-third the original

11.h REVISING YOUR PARAGRAPHS

You should not consider a paragraph or any piece of writing finished until you have read it over and revised it. Even professional writers find it extremely difficult to write a polished paragraph the first time around. The last sentence that they have written may make them want to go back and change the first sentence, for example. Writers know that revising is a very important step in the writing process.

It is at the revision stage that you can clarify ideas, add details, and improve the flow of your sentences. As you read over your paragraph, ask yourself the questions on the following checklist.

Checklist for revising a paragraph

1. Does the topic sentence clearly state one main idea and give strong direction to the paragraph? (See 11.a.)
2. Does each sentence relate to the main topic of the paragraph but add more rather than just repeat? (See 11.b and 11.c.)
3. Is there a logical order to the arrangement of the sentences in the paragraph? (See 11.d.)
4. Are logical connectives and other transitional devices used effectively to connect sentences and ideas? (See 11.d.)

11.i EDITING AND PROOFREADING PARAGRAPHS

Once you have revised your paragraph, you should carefully edit and proofread it for matters of grammar and usage, capitalization and punctuation, and spelling. Use the questions on the following Editing and Proofreading Checklist as a guide. The cross references in parentheses indicate other sections of this book to check for review if necessary.

As you edit and proofread your own or someone else's paragraph, you may use Editing Signals, such as those below, from Section 9.

Editing and proofreading checklist

1. Are all sentences complete? (See 2.a.) *frag*
2. Are varied sentence structures used? (See Section 3.)
3. Have you used the voice (active or passive) that is most effective in each sentence? (See 1.b.20.) *voice*
4. Are verb tenses consistent? (See 1.b.11.) *tense*
5. Do subjects and verbs agree? (See 2.c, 2.e, and 2.f.) *agree*
6. Do pronouns agree with antecedents? (See 1.d.1 and 1.d.7.) *ref*
7. Is parallel construction used where appropriate? (See 3.k.) *not parallel*
8. Is vocabulary precise but varied? (See Section 4.) *vocab*
9. Are words spelled correctly? (See Section 5.) *sp*
10. Is punctuation correct? (See Section 7.) *cap , p*

PATTERNS OF THINKING AND WRITING

12 Patterns of Thinking and Writing

The work of writing is chiefly a matter of combining thinking and language. You must think about each sentence that you write and about making one sentence lead sensibly to another. Every sentence is, in its way, a unit of thought. Then as you move from sentence to sentence and from paragraph to paragraph, you begin to shape a *pattern.* Sometimes you will use several patterns within the same piece of writing, some similar, some different from one another. In this section, however, you will concentrate on one pattern at a time.

Each pattern of thinking and writing is actually a process. If you think of writing itself as a process, you will not be overwhelmed by all the *kinds* of writing that you may be asked to do. There are many kinds of writing—history, sports, science, letters, stories, to mention a few—but you will see that the *kinds* of writing involve only a limited number of processes, or patterns.

The patterns of thinking and writing that you will work with in the following pages are listed here[1]:

a. "This is what happened."
b. "This is what it looks, sounds, smells, feels, acts like."
c. "This is like (or unlike) that."
d. "This is what it is."
e. "This is how to do something."
f. "This caused that."

You are already familiar with these patterns but under different names. They are traditionally labeled *narration, description, comparison/contrast, definition, explanation of process* and *cause-effect.*

[1]Adapted from Mina P. Shaugnessy, *Errors and Expectations* (New York, Oxford University Press, 1977).

For each pattern you will find in the following pages

1. an introduction
2. models by professional writers
3. a list of steps to follow and suggestions for improving coherence
4. Warm-ups — exercises taking one step at a time
5. Pattern Practices — assignments giving you data to convert into different kinds of writing that follow the pattern under discussion

As you examine the steps necessary for getting each pattern onto paper, you will find yourself in a dialogue with yourself and an imaginary reader. Good writers do talk to themselves. They are actively engaged in thinking about generalizations and about details to support them. They think, experiment, reject, and think again with the reader in mind.

12.a NARRATION: "This is what happened."

Narration is the kind of writing that tells a story, real or imagined.

Perhaps the most common pattern of thinking and writing is the one that tells "this is what happened." It is the key to all reporting and to all storytelling — to the kind of writing that is called narration. Relating "what happened" is one of the oldest and most useful forms of communication. Human beings could not have survived without daily reports from those who ventured out beyond the cave and the campfire. Not long ago people listened for the first time to reports from astronauts who walked on the moon. The welfare of thousands of people may depend on reports of what happened in a test tube in a laboratory. Anyone who can use the "what-happened" pattern effectively in writing is a valuable asset to society.

Few patterns of thinking and writing are more natural or more interesting to human beings than "this is what happened." You may have enjoyed reporting your amusing or frightening experiences to others, committing your experiences to journals or diaries, or reading or hearing accounts of the experiences of others. You bring all this experience and enjoyment with you when you write something that will tell readers "what happened."

The following model about a woman watching a frog is an example of the pattern of thinking and writing that tells "this is what happened."

Model: "This is what happened."

A couple of summers ago I was walking along the edge of the island to see what I could see in the water, and mainly to scare frogs. Frogs have an inelegant way of taking off from invisible positions on the bank just ahead of your feet, in dire panic, emitting a froggy "Yike!" and splashing into the water. Incredibly, this amused me, and, incredibly, it amuses me still. As I walked along the grassy edge of the island, I got better and better at seeing frogs both in and out of the water. I learned to recognize, slowing down, the difference in texture of the light reflected from mudbank, water, grass, or frog. Frogs were flying all around me. At the end of the island I noticed a small green frog. He was exactly half in and half out of the water, looking like a schematic diagram of an amphibian, and he didn't jump.

Notice the underlined words, which help to tell the sequence of events. (See page 582.)

He didn't jump; I crept closer. At last I knelt on the island's winterkilled grass, lost, dumbstruck, staring at the frog in the creek just four feet away. He was a very small frog with wide, dull eyes. And just as I looked at him, he slowly crumpled and began to sag. The spirit vanished from his eyes as if snuffed. His skin emptied and drooped; his very skull seemed to collapse and settle like a kicked tent. He was shrinking before my eyes like a deflating football. I watched the taut, glistening skin on his shoulders ruck and rumple and fall. Soon, part of his skin, formless as a pricked balloon, lay in floating folds like bright scum on top of the water: it was a monstrous and terrifying thing. I gaped bewildered, appalled. An oval shadow hung in the water behind the drained frog; then the shadow glided away. The frog skin bag started to sink.

—Annie Dillard, *Pilgrim at Tinker Creek*

Skills for telling "this is what happened"

When you set out to tell "this is what happened," you will find it helpful to follow certain *steps* to make your writing more coherent.

1. **List events; eliminate unnecessary or unrelated events; do not forget necessary events.**

   (Assume that you want to tell about skiing down a slope. You may use phrases rather than full sentences at this point.)
   I face the steep incline with a beginner's dread
   Skiing slightly out of control, I brush some of the pine trees bordering the slope.
   As I try to skirt a dangerously icy spot, I lose one ski.
   I take off the other ski and hike down the rest of the slope.
   ~~I go into the lounge, buy a cup of coffee, and sit by the fire.~~
   Without pushing off with my poles, I begin to move down the icy slope.
   Another skier races by; we narrowly avoid a collision.
   The chair lift takes me to the top of the intermediate slope.
   ~~I watch kids fearlessly race down the slope.~~
   ~~I sit in the chair lift and shut my eyes.~~

2. **Sequence the events in chronological (time) order, using a time line, perhaps. Watch your tenses in telling time.**

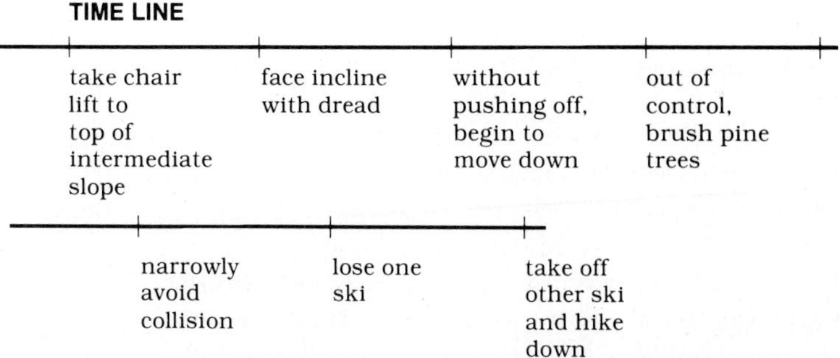
TIME LINE
take chair lift to top of intermediate slope
face incline with dread
without pushing off, begin to move down
out of control, brush pine trees
narrowly avoid collision
lose one ski
take off other ski and hike down

The following list contains some of the logical connectives that you will find helpful in telling "what happened." You will certainly not use all of this vocabulary in any one piece of writing, but it is a helpful list to have.

LOGICAL CONNECTIVES AND VOCABULARY FOR TELLING "THIS IS WHAT HAPPENED"

after
as soon as
at the same time as
before
between _____ and _____
during
earlier
every second (minute, hour, day, week, month, year)
for a few seconds (minutes, hours, days, weeks, months, years)
former
formerly
in _____
just as
just before
later
latter
next
now
nowadays
previously
prior to
simultaneously
since _____
soon
subsequently
then
till
until
when
while

as an adult
at birth
at death
in adolescence
in childhood
in infancy
in old age

at last
finally
first, second, *etc.*
in conclusion
in the first place
in the next place
to begin with

Warm-ups: "This is what happened."

WARM-UP 1: Use the data in the sample time line (page 581) to write a short piece that tells "this is what happened." Use the logical connectives and other vocabulary where possible.

WARM-UP 2: Eliminating unnecessary events. Study the following list of events. Decide which events do not belong on the list.

1. British colonists settle in New England, which later becomes part of the American colonies.
2. Peter the Great becomes czar of Russia.
3. Great Britain imposes heavy taxes on its American colonies.
4. The American colonies protest taxes imposed by Great Britain.
5. The Revolutionary War between Great Britain and the American colonies begins.
6. The Treaty of Paris ends the Revolutionary War.
7. The American colonies, now free from British rule, name their new nation the United States.
8. Mozart writes the opera *Don Giovanni.*
9. George Washington is elected President of the United States.
10. The French leader Napoleon conquers Italy.

WARM-UP 3: Sequencing events. The following sentences are adapted from a published paragraph. They are out of order. List them in the correct chronological (time) order. The logical connectives in bold type are clues. (The original paragraph appears in Monica Sone's *Nisei Daughter.*)

1. **Then** a man burst out of the door.
2. **Early in the morning** Henry and I were dumped into a taxicab, screaming and kicking against the injustice of it all.
3. We kept up our horrendous shrieking and wailing **until we reached the entrance.**
4. The inevitable, dreaded first day at Nihon Gakko [the school] arrived.
5. Mother **then** half carried us up the hill to the entrance.
6. **When** the cab stopped **a while later** in front of a large, square gray-frame building, Mother pried us loose, though we clung to the cab door like barnacles.
7. His face seemed to have been carved out of granite, and his black marble eyes crushed us into a quivering silence.

WARM-UP 4: Making a time line. Study the items on the following list. List the events in correct chronological (time) order, so that they tell a story, by placing the events on a time line. (You can use phrases or simply the letters on your time line.) Notice the logical connectives, which will give you clues to the correct order.

1. **Soon** Athena's jealousy led her to challenge Arachne to a weaving contest.
2. **Once upon a time,** during the mythological age in Greece, the girl Arachne was born.
3. **When** the goddess Athena heard stories of Arachne's skill, she became jealous.
4. **Before** the contest could be fairly judged, Athena declared herself to be the winner and turned Arachne into a spider.
5. **Today,** spiders are known as "arachnids," after Arachne.
6. **Ever since Arachne became a spider,** spiders have woven webs to remind us of the girl's talents.
7. **In her adolescent years** Arachne grew to be a skillful weaver.
8. **At the start of the contest,** both goddess and mortal strung their looms.

WARM–UP 5: Using logical connectives. Each of the following numbered items forms the second half of a sentence. Match each with one of the expressions containing a logical connective provided on the next page. When you have matched the items correctly, you will have composed a baseball story that clearly tells "this is what happened." The numbered data are already in the correct order. The first sentence of the story is completed for you.

EXAMPLE *Throughout the baseball game the Mudville Nine have been trailing by two runs.*

1. ~~the Mudville Nine have been trailing by two runs.~~
2. the Mudville Nine get up to bat—their last chance.
3. the disappointed crowd begins to thin out.
4. two batters—the tying runs—get on base.
5. a cheer goes up from the crowd.
6. Casey is the team's last hope.
7. the umpire yells, "Strike one!"
8. the crowd grows anxious.
9. Casey unleashes his powerful swing, blowing dust into the fans' faces.
10. the fans realize that mighty Casey has struck out.

Logical connectives

After Casey ignores the first pitch,
~~Throughout the baseball game~~
Suddenly
After the first two batters strike out,
When a second strike is called against Casey,
Now, in the bottom of the ninth inning,
After two outs,
At the third pitch
As soon as mighty Casey, the last batter, steps up to the plate,
When the air finally clears, however,

■ Pattern Practices: "This is what happened."

The following Pattern Practices will give you experience in using some of the narrative skills taken up individually on pages 581–582. Remember to proceed chronologically — in time sequence — telling what happened.

PATTERN PRACTICE 1: Fiction. Use the following story elements to write a story in which you tell "this is what happened." Begin a new paragraph where necessary (see 11.e). The verbs given below only suggest the action that may take place. You may want to use more vivid verbs once you decide on your story. Decide also if you want the verbs to convey past time, present time, or future time. Revise and edit your work. See the checklists in 11.h and 11.i.

time	*place*	*characters*	*verbs*	
sunset	lonely stretch of railroad track	engineer of train	brake	see
			walk	sit
night	surrounded by forest	two-year-old girl with flashlight	fall	stop
			hear	amaze
			reach	

PATTERN PRACTICE 2: Sportswriting. As the model on the next page illustrates, a sports story usually tells "this is what happened" and requires the same writing skills outlined on page 581. The model is excerpted from a longer article about how Hank Aaron broke Babe Ruth's record. Read it, and then read the assignment following it.

Downing pitched ball one inside, and Aaron watched impassively. Then came the second pitch, and this time Henry took his first cut of the night. The ball rose high toward left-center as the crowd came to its feet shouting, and as it dropped over the inside fence separating the outfield from the bullpen area, the skyrockets were fired and the scoreboard lights flashed in six-foot numerals: "715."

The underlined words help to emphasize the time sequence.

Aaron, head slightly bowed and elbows turned out, slowly circled the bases as the uproar grew. At second base he received a handshake from Dave Lopes of the Dodgers, and between second and third from Russell.

By now two young men from the seats had joined Aaron but did not interfere with his 360-foot trip around the bases into the record books.

As he neared home plate, the rest of the Atlanta team had already massed beyond it as a welcoming delegation. Aaron's 65-year-old father, Herbert Aaron, Sr., had jumped out of the family's special field-level box and outraced everybody to the man who had broken Babe Ruth's record.

By then the entire Atlanta bullpen corps had started to race in to join the fun with House leading them, the ball gripped tightly in his hand. He delivered it to Aaron, who was besieged on the grass about 20 feet in front of the field boxes near the Braves' dugout.

Besides the ball, Henry received a plaque from the owner of the team, Bill Bartholomay; congratulations from Monte Irvin, the emissary from Commissioner Kuhn; and a howling, standing ovation from the crowd.

The game was interrupted for eleven minutes during all the commotion, after which the Braves got back to work and went on to win their second straight, this time by 7–4.

—Joseph Durso

The following chart gives the details of the 1979 Boston Marathon. Bill Rodgers, a Bostonian, won the race that year for the third time. Your assignment is to report the race in chronological order, making sure to tell how Rodgers moved from seventh position early in the race to be the first across the finish line in a record time of 2 hours, 9 minutes, 27 seconds. Use the information on the chart and any other details that you have available or that you can invent.

The race started in Hopkinton, Massachusetts, and ended in Boston, 26.2 miles away.

Revise and edit your report. See the checklists in 11.h and 11.i.

TRACKING THE MARATHON

checkpoint	*Framingham 6.75 miles*	*Natick 10.5 miles*	*Wellesley 13.75 miles*	*Woodland 17.75 miles*	*Lake Street 21.5 miles*	*Coolidge Corner 24.12 miles*	*Boston 26.2 miles*
time	***31.54***	***50.08***	***1:05.01***	***1:25.28***	***1:46.20***	***1:58.41***	***2:09.27***
1st	Fleming	Fleming	Fleming	Bjorklund	Rodgers	Rodgers	Rodgers
2nd	Ryan	Ryan	Rodgers	Rodgers	Seko	Seko	Seko
3rd	Takami	Kardong	Bjorklund	Seko	Bjorklund	Bjorklund	Hodge
4th	Thomas	Mahoney	Mahoney	Fleming	Fleming	Hodge	Fleming
5th	Shorter	Rodgers	Seko	Hodge	Hodge	Fleming	Bjorklund
6th	Stewart	Stewart	Kardong	Mahoney	Mahoney	Ryan	Ryan
7th	Rodgers	Hodge	Ryan	Ryan	Ryan	Mahoney	Doyle

PATTERN PRACTICE 3: Historical writing. History textbooks and nonfiction best sellers about history have at least one thing in common: They both set out to tell "this is what happened."

Use the following calendar as the basis of a brief historical account entitled "Gold Fever." Select the events you want to use. Use some of the logical connectives from page 582 to help make the sequence of this account as clear as possible.

Revise and edit your account. See the checklists in 11.h and 11.i.

Major Events	Dates	Other notable happenings
Gold strikes in Montana and Colorado spawn Gold Creek and Pikes Peak booms; first wagon road blazed over northern Rockies from Fort Benton to Walla Walla, Washington; Minnesota becomes 32nd state as Leech Lake Indian uprising suppressed.	1858-1859	Weekly mail service begins from Independence to Salt Lake City. Butterfield stage starts twice-monthly runs from Tipton, Missouri, to San Francisco; postage twenty cents an ounce.
Fabulously rich Comstock Lode silver mine established in Nevada; boom gives birth to Virginia City with overnight population of 25,000 — and only 100 saloons.	1859	
Russell, Majors, and Waddel open Pony Express mail service, starting riders out simultaneously from St. Joseph, Missouri, and San Francisco, California.	1860	Idaho added to gold boom region with strikes at Pierce and Boise City; American Fur Company's *Chippewa* first steamboat to reach head of Missouri River navigation at Fort Benton in Montana; gold finds at Leadville cause another Colorado stampede.
Transcontinental telegraph joined at Salt Lake City.	1861	Civil War begins; Sam Houston deposed as Texas Governor for refusing allegiance to Confederacy; Dakota Territory created and settlement spurts.
James Fisk pioneers Minnesota-Montana route to Bannack gold camps; building of Central Pacific and Union Pacific	1862	

Major Events	Dates	Other notable happenings
railroads begins at Sacramento and Omaha, respectively; Overland Trail starts with establishment of Fort Halleck in Wyoming.	1862	
Alder Gulch gold strikes create Virginia City as Montana's roughest mining camp; Bozeman Trail opened to gold fields; Utah experiences first settlement boom with silver discoveries in Bingham Canyon.	1863	Idaho Territory created to include Montana, and Territory of New Mexico reduced by creation of Arizona Territory; Sam Houston dies in Texas.
Montana Territory created as gold boom switches to Last Chance Gulch, where Helena is established.	1864	

—Eugene Fodor, *Fodor's Old West*

12.b DESCRIPTION: "This is what it looks, sounds, smells, feels, acts like."

Description is the kind of writing that creates an impression of a person, place, or thing.

Another common pattern of thinking and writing tells what something is like—what it looks like, sounds like, smells like, feels like, acts like. Telling "what it looks, sounds, smells, feels, acts like" is a pattern that you use every day as you talk to your family and friends about, for example, a new stereo, a person you recently met, a new bicycle you bought, or the memory of a particular vacation spot. When you use this pattern and tell about the appearance or other sensory aspects of something, you are describing.

You have to observe closely and record accurately when you set out to tell "this is what it looks, sounds, smells, feels, acts like." For example, Louis Agassiz, a nineteenth-century zoologist, once had a student who had received the highest diplomas and honors. The student went to Agassiz for his final approval. Agassiz showed the student a small fish. Then the following dialogue took place.

> Postgraduate Student: "That's only a sunfish."
>
> Agassiz: "I know that. Write a description of it."
>
> After a few minutes the student returned with the description *Ichthus Heliodiplodokus*, or whatever term is used to conceal the common sunfish from vulgar knowledge, family of *Heliichterinkus*, etc., as found in textbooks of the subject.
>
> Agassiz again told the student to describe the fish.
>
> The student produced a four-page essay. Agassiz told him to look at the fish. At the end of three weeks, the fish was in an advanced state of decomposition, but the student knew something about it.
>
> —Ezra Pound, *ABC of Reading*

The student learned what makes a good description:

1. noticing details with as many senses as possible
2. carefully ordering the details

When you want to tell what something looks, sounds, smells, or feels like, you must search out details with all your senses, get a focus on the details, and organize the details clearly so that your final product—a piece of descriptive writing—holds your reader's attention. Sometimes you will concentrate on one sense; sometimes, on many.

Model: "This is what it looks, sounds, smells, feels, acts like."

I would take the subway to work every morning—the Seventh Avenue IRT from the Upper West Side. I bought the *New York Times* at the newsstand on Broadway and 94th and headed downstairs to get the express to Penn Station. As soon as I got to the platform in the stale, airless place, I folded the *Times* to the news-index section; then I started my preliminary jousts for position near the track in order to be closer to the door of the train when it

Notice the underlined sensory details. What senses does the writer use in his observations?

arrived. In three years of waiting on this platform I had yet to hear one "Good morning" exchanged among any of my fellow passengers, for human communication was normally restricted to atavistic grumbles.... Far down the track, in an eerie dark, the light of the express glared and winked, and then in a terrible roar and screech of brakes it was upon us. The crowds at the platform waited for the people to emerge from the car; then there would be one solid mass of flesh pushing forward through the doors.... There was a loudspeaker in the station, and the voice would say: "Step lively, folks, step lively." And after a pause, "Get that arm out of the door, buddy!" or "Pull in that leg, sister!" Once this mass was crammed into the subway car, two or three hardy souls, holding back the doors when they were closing, would literally squeeze themselves in, which served to push the mass even closer upon itself.

Notice how the writer's feelings of alienation emerge from his sensory bombardment during the morning rush hour.

At this moment, if I had three or four inches of elbow room and a reasonably secure position, I would bring out the paper and read the news-index section three or four times during the fifteen-minute trip south. If this elbow room was not available, however, I read the advertisements on the wall of the train, about quick cash loans, employment agencies, Miss Subway contests.... Then I would stare sullenly at the other passengers, who sullenly stared back, seeking diversion as much as I. Once I spent the full fifteen minutes examining a peculiar wart under the nose of a neighbor three or four inches away—a strange yellow wart.... There was a certain identifiable expression on the faces of New Yorkers in these moments. It was "subway glaze": their eyes might be open but they were not looking.... The train rocked and moaned, sometimes knocking a few passengers against one another....

—Willie Morris

■ Skills for telling "this is what it looks, sounds, smells, feels, acts like"

When you decide to tell "this is what it looks, sounds, smells, feels, acts like," you should follow certain *steps*.

1. **Determine the dominant impression you want to convey.**
   The school halls are chaotic between periods.

2. **Observe with all your senses, list observations, and select the specific details that you want to include.**
   light from windows
   ~~music from marching band outside~~
   cafeteria smell coming upstairs
   shuffling feet
   lockers clanging open and shut
   smell of gymnasium
   announcements on P.A. system
   posters falling off bulletin boards
   teachers and students rushing by
   groups of people pressed together
   heat
   ~~exhaustion from lack of sleep~~
   fresh air blowing from windows
   talking

3. **Classify the details, using an observation table, perhaps.**

OBSERVATION TABLE

look	*sound*	*smell*	*feel: touch, movements*
light from windows	shuffling feet	cafeteria	people moving
posters falling off	clanging lockers	gymnasium	heat
people rushing by	P.A. announcements	industrial arts shop	fresh air—windows
	talking	science classroom	

4. **Compare and contrast the object or experience with other objects or experiences. Highlight the similarities and differences.**
   chaos between acts of play as stage set is changed
   chaos whenever a major change occurs in a person's life—college, marriage, childbearing, career change, death of a friend or relative

5. **List the details that you have observed in the order in which you want to discuss them.** (You may want to order them by individual senses. If you are dealing *only* with visual details, you may want to put them in *spatial* order.)
   a. touch
   b. sound
   c. smell
   d. look

The following list contains some of the logical connectives (and other key words) that you will find helpful in telling "this is what it looks (sounds, smells, feels) like." You will not use all of this vocabulary in any one piece of writing. In fact, most of the connectives are more useful for telling what something *looks* like than what something sounds, smells, or feels like.

LOGICAL CONNECTIVES AND VOCABULARY FOR TELLING "WHAT IT LOOKS . . . LIKE"

To help you classify the details

aspects
attributes
categories
characteristics
classes
divisions
factors
kinds
qualities
types

To help you establish directions

north
northern
to the north
south
right
to the right
left
ahead
under
over
on top of
above
below
beneath
exterior
on the exterior
inside
in which
into which

opposite (to)
parallel (to)
perpendicular (to)
overlapping with
at the intersection of
vertically
horizontally
diagonally

To help you describe shapes

rectangular
circular
semicircular
square

To help you compare

as	like
have in common	resemble
in the same way	similar to
just as	

■ Warm-ups: "This is what it looks, sounds, smells, feels, acts like."

WARM–UP 6: Use the data in the example observation table (page 592) to write a short piece that tells "this is what the school halls look, sound, smell, and feel like" between periods on an average day.

WARM–UP 7: Observing details. You may not realize how important it is to notice and include sensory details in your writing until you read a piece of writing without them. First read the following sentences by Flannery O'Connor. They have adjectives, participles, and adverbs. Then read the second version without the details:

> The sky was a **dying violet** and the houses stood out **darkly** against it, **bulbous liver-colored** monstrosities of a **uniform** ugliness.... Each house had a **narrow** collar of dirt around it in which sat, **usually**, a **grubby** child.

> The houses stood out against the sky. They were ugly monstrosities. Near each house sat a child.

Here is another sentence by Flannery O'Connor, but the sensory details have already been removed, as the ellipses show. Add details from your imagination. Then read Flannery O'Connor's own version on the next page (below the observation table).

> He would stand on the ... porch, listening to the ... leaves, then wander through the ... hall into the parlor that opened onto it and gaze at the ... rugs and ... draperies.

WARM–UP 8: Classifying sensory details—an observation table. Look again at the article by Willie Morris (page 590–591). Copy the observation table on the next page, and fill it in with the sensory details from the article. By so doing, you will gain practice in organizing your own observations.

OBSERVATION TABLE			
look	***sound***	***smell***	***feel: touch, movements***

Flannery O'Connor's own version:
He would stand on the *wide* porch, listening to the *rustle of oak* leaves, then wander through the *high-ceilinged* hall into the parlor that opened onto it and gaze at the *worn* rugs and *faded* draperies.

WARM–UP 9: Ordering spatial details. The details below and on the next page describe a room. The details are difficult to follow because they jump all over the room. Copy the diagram, and complete it based on the description.

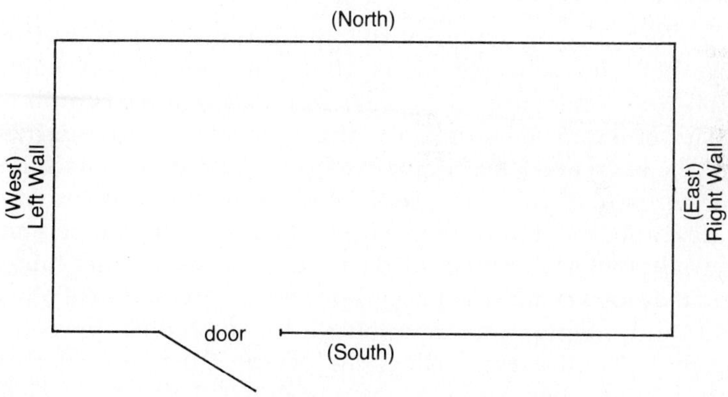

a. There is an easy chair to the right of the door.
b. The room is rectangular.
c. The door is near the southwest corner of the room.
d. There is a large window on the left wall.
e. To the left of the door is an easy chair.
f. The easy chair to the right of the door has a TV to its right.
g. Opposite the door is a sofa.
h. A chest of drawers stands on the right-hand wall.
i. There is a rose-and-blue rug in front of the chest of drawers.

j. In front of the sofa is a coffee table.

k. The rug under the coffee table is rose.

l. There is a desk in the corner to the right of the sofa.

m. To the right of the sofa is a lamp.

n. A straight-backed chair sits in front of the desk.

The room would be much easier for someone without the diagram to visualize if the details were arranged more sensibly. Try the following plan to rearrange the sentences. First, assume that you are standing in the doorway of the room. From that vantage point, describe what is on either side of the door. Second, describe what is on the left wall. Third, describe what is in front of you on the opposite wall. Fourth, describe what is on the right wall. Fifth, describe the floor.

■ Pattern Practices: "This is what it looks, sounds, smells, feels, acts like."

The following activities will give you practice in putting together the separate skills that you refined on pages 594–595. There are many ways to organize a paragraph or series of paragraphs that tell "this is what it looks, sounds, smells, feels, acts like." If, for example, you want to tell what a person is like, you may group physical features in the first paragraph, mental traits in a second paragraph, and personality characteristics in a third paragraph. On the other hand, you may focus your first paragraph on the interaction of physical and mental characteristics—for instance, how her bright, attentive eyes reflect the person's bright, attentive mind. In another example, if you wish to tell about a place or thing, you may proceed from the top to the bottom or from the right to the left, or you may group together related objects, such as furnishings or decorations.

PATTERN PRACTICE 4: Character sketch. The following selection is an unusual character sketch—it centers on a man's nose. Usually a character sketch focuses on the whole person. In any case, a character sketch is a kind of description. What do Al Weber's words and actions tell you about him besides the fact that he is an expert fish-sniffer? What *overall impression* of Al Weber has the writer given you?

Caruso's tonsils, Namath's arm, Heifitz' hands, Einstein's brain.

And. . . .

Weber's Nose.

There it is, sitting in the Food and Drug Administration labs in Brooklyn, a large, 70-year-old nose, attached to the bespectacled face of Al Weber.

Al Weber is an organoleptic analyst for the FDA.

A fish-sniffer.

An artist. . . .

The FDA is responsible for keeping decomposed or spoiled food from being sold to the consumer.

When it comes to seafood, the most effective test has proven to be nature's own tester, the nose. And Albert L. Weber has proven the best nose in the East.

When he started, he was just another food chemist. One day, they needed a fish-sniffer. All the sniffers were out of the lab.

They didn't know if Weber had what it took, just that he was available. . . .

Al Weber went out and smelled fish. A star was born.

He'll never forget what happened at the end of that day. First people started moving away from him on the subway. Then he got home to his wife. "She gives one sniff and says, . . . 'You stink! Get your clothes off and take a shower.' "

He did but lived to sniff again. From then on, resistance or no, Weber's destiny was clear. He devoted more and more time to fish-sniffing. Today, he is the acknowledged expert hereabouts. His nose has produced government evidence in regulatory cases. He has trained others to sniff, and he has been sent to Japan for a tuna examiners' training program.

The Weber Technique: "We have some people who stick their nose into it. I don't believe in that." He cuts open a piece of rock lobster to illustrate and holds it close to The Nose, not quite touching.

"Short sniffs," he says, short-sniffing.

The technique takes its toll. "You're not breathing properly all day," he says. "It makes you tired." . . .

The odor of badly spoiled shrimp, he admits, what used to be known as "Class 4: Advanced Putrid," can make him lose his breakfast.

Fortunately, none of this has affected his taste for seafood, which he likes. "I don't eat shellfish because it's not kosher," he said. "But I had a tuna salad sandwich for lunch today, and last night we had baked sea trout." The main problem, he says, is finding a good fresh fish store.

Weber has been somewhat inventive in his work and helped work out what is now the standard technique for sniffing large frozen fish.

What he does is take an electric drill and put a small hole in the frozen fish, wobbling it a little. The heat of the drill thaws enough fish matter for Weber's nose to go into action. . . .

He expects to work another year or so, finishing some programs he's started and training some replacements to carry on the task. And then a great fish-sniffer will sniff no more.

Will he miss it?

Are you kidding?

"It's one thing I'll never miss."

—Lewis Grossberger, "The Nose That Weighs Scales"

Write a character sketch that focuses on someone's eyes, ears, or hands. You should be able to relate them to the whole person. Revise and edit your work. See the checklists in 11.h and 11.i.

PATTERN PRACTICE 5: Description of place (stationary vantage point). The following selection tells "what it looks like" from a *stationary vantage point*. That is, the writer stands in one spot and tells where everything is in relation to that spot. As you read the selection, make a list of the logical connectives and other spatial words in the selection. Then use these same words and phrases in a description of your own house, apartment, or room.

Revise and edit your description. See the checklists in 11.h and 11.i.

The outside of Solomon's house looked nice. It was not painted, but across the porch was an even balance. On each side there was one easy chair with high springs, looking out, and a fern basket hanging over it from the ceiling, and a dishpan of zinnia seedlings growing at its foot on the floor. By the door was a plow-wheel, just a pretty iron circle, nailed up on one wall and a square mirror on the other, a turquoise-blue comb stuck up in the frame, with the wash stand beneath it. On the door was a wooden knob with a pearl in the end, and Solomon's black hat hung on that, if he was in the house.

Out front was a clean dirt yard with every vestige of grass patiently uprooted and the ground scarred in deep whorls from the strike of Livvie's broom. Rose bushes with tiny blood-red roses blooming every month grew in threes on either side of the steps. On one side was a peach tree, on the other a pomegranate. Then coming around up the path from the deep cut of the Natchez Trace below was a line of bare crape-myrtle trees with every branch of them ending in a colored bottle, green or blue.

—Eudora Welty

PATTERN PRACTICE 6: Travel writing (moving vantage point). The following selection tells "what it looks like" from a *moving vantage point*. The writer, Paul Theroux, is traveling on a train, and he describes what he sees as the train moves along. After reading the selection, write your own description of an area from a moving vantage point. You may tell "what it looks like" as you travel by foot, car, bus, train, or plane.

Revise and edit your description. See the checklists in 11.h and 11.i

The Belgrade outskirts were leafy and pleasant, and as it was noon by the time we had left the station, the laborers we passed had downed their tools and were sitting cross-legged in shady spots by the railway line having lunch. The train was going so slowly one could see the plates of sodden cabbage and could count the black olives in the chipped bowls. . . .

The underlined words and phrases reinforce the movement of the train and tell where things are in relation to the observer.

The landscape was low and uneven, barely supporting in its dust a few farm animals, five motionless cows, and a herdsman leaning on a stick watching them starve in the same way the scarecrow, two plastic bags on a bony cross-piece, watched the unharvested fields of cabbages and peppers. And beyond the rows of blue cabbage, a pink pig butted the splintery fence of his small pen, and a cow lay under a goal of saplings in a disused football field. . . .

A woman paused to tip a water bottle to her mouth; she swallowed and bent from the waist to continue tying up cornstalks. I saw large ochre squashes sitting plumply in fields of withering vines; people priming pumps and swinging buckets out of wells on long poles; tall, narrow haystacks; and pepper fields in so many stages of ripeness I first took them for flower gardens. It was a feeling of utter quietness, deep rural isolation which the train briefly penetrated. It went on without a change for hours, this afternoon in Yugoslavia, and then all people disappeared, and the effect was eerie: roads without cars or bicycles, cottages with empty windows at the fringes of empty fields; trees heavy with apples and no one picking them. Perhaps it was the wrong time—3:30; perhaps it was too hot. But where were the people who stacked that hay and set those peppers so carefully to dry? The train passed on—that's the beauty of a train, that heedless movement— but it passed on to more of the same: six neat beehives; a derelict steam engine with wildflowers garlanding its smokestack; a stalled ox at a level crossing. . . . Then I saw a man, bent over in a field, camouflaged by cornstalks which were taller than he; I wondered if I had missed all the others because they were made so tiny by their crops.

—Paul Theroux

12.c COMPARISON/CONTRAST: "This is like (or unlike) that."

Comparison is the kind of writing that tells about similarities. **Contrast** is the kind of writing that tells about differences.

You probably seldom tell "what happened" or tell what something "looks like" without also thinking "this is like (or unlike) that." When you do so, you are engaging in the process known as comparison. Technically, when you are telling how two things are alike, you are *comparing*, and when you are telling how two things are different, you are *contrasting*.

Telling how "this is like (or unlike) that" involves observing both the similarities and the differences among things or people. It is natural to compare our mood of today with our mood of yesterday, this year's win-loss record with last year's, or two pairs of shoes in a store. People, books, states of mind, or even foods can be grouped together as "like" or "unlike" depending upon how you think of them. For example, an orange, a lemon, and a grapefruit can be classified as "like" because they are all citrus fruits or "unlike" because they have different sizes, colors, and tastes.

When you examine two people or objects, you may be misled into searching for similarities without paying attention to the importance of the differences you observe. Be sure to observe carefully, noting both similarities and differences.

The following model is an example of the pattern of thinking and writing that tells "this is like (or unlike) that." The writer is comparing two American institutions that are not usually thought of as alike.

Model: "This is like (or unlike) that."

During my three-year odyssey through the world of American prisons, an elusive, half-formulated thought kept nagging at the back of my mind. Are there not disturbing similarities between the prison business and an earlier preoccupation of mine, the American funeral industry? What do prison administrators and undertakers have in common? A friend to whom I posed this question answered somewhat flippantly, "That's easy, they're both in the business of shutting people up in boxes."

Underlined words signal similarities.

True, yet having now had a chance to mull it all over, it seems to me the parallel by no means ends there. To illustrate:

Costs: American funerals are the most expensive in the world. A burial in the style decreed by undertakers will cost you as much as a new car or down payment on a house, unless you keep your eyes open. American prisons do not lag behind in this respect. I was told by a researcher for the California State Assembly that it costs as much to keep a man in San Quentin as it would to send him to Harvard (which suggests an interesting possibility of exchange scholarships between these two institutions). Needless to say, this money benefits neither corpse nor convict, but it finds its way straight into the pockets of their respective keepers.

Beautifications: Coffins and hearses, formerly cast in funeral black, now come in delightful shades of peach pink, cerulean blue, apple green. Likewise, prison gray is out of style. For example, the spanking new Southern Ohio Correctional Facility, built at the cost of $60 million, features cells in pastel blues, pinks, yellows. (The *Cleveland Plain Dealer* of August 10, 1973, reports that the occupants of these gilded cages "have been abused, stripped naked for as long as seven days, deprived of all possessions, including toothbrushes and eyeglasses, locked in solitary twenty-four hours a day for conducting a work stoppage in protest against intolerable conditions.")

Underlined words signal similarities.

In and Out Language: Thanks to the perseverance of undertakers, coffins have long since become "caskets"; hearses, "professional cars"; corpses, "Beautiful Memory Pictures" to be displayed in a "slumber room"; undertakers, "funeral directors," and so on. In the world of prisons notable advances have also been made recently in prettying-up the nomenclature. Guards are now "correctional officers"; solitary confinement punishment cells, "adjustment centers"; prisons, "therapeutic correctional communities"; convicts, "clients of the Department of Corrections." In both cases the idea is to package the product under a more agreeable name and incidentally to upgrade the occupations of embalmer and prison guard alike to the coveted status of "profession."

. . . .

I could go on and on. Embalmer and prison warden alike jealously guard their operations from public scrutiny. In most states the funeral lobby has succeeded in passing laws excluding reporters from the embalming room, and I soon discovered that wardens, despotic rulers in their own domain, use prison walls not only to keep the convicts in but to keep the would-be investigator out. Both lines of endeavor have borrowed freely from the language of psychiatry to justify their practices; thus lavish and expensive funerals are "grief therapy" for the survivors, just as beatings, macings, solitary confinement are, in the lingo of the up-to-date prison man, "aversion therapy." Prisons and funerals offer lucrative markets for ancillary industries; hardware companies flock to conventions of the American Funeral Directors Association with exhibits of the latest in casket handles and to the annual Congress of the American Correctional Association to display the newest in chains and handcuff design.

Underlined words signal similarities.

In short, both prison business and funeral industry are vast, immensely profitable financial empires built on the suffering of others, nourished by hypocrisy, greed, and public gullibility.

—Jessica Mitford, "Prisons and Funerals"

Skills for telling "this is like (or unlike) that"

Preparing to tell how "this is like (or unlike) that" is a bit more complicated than getting organized to write the two previous patterns discussed in this book. Still, the method is straightforward and logical. You will, as usual, have to go through several steps.

1. **Select the points of comparison or contrast on which you want to concentrate.**

   Comparing and contrasting records and cassette tapes

   quality of sound
   durability
   cost
   cost of accompanying hardware
   portability

2. **Group the points of similarity together and give examples. Group the points of difference together and give examples. Use a comparison frame.**

COMPARISON FRAME

points of comparison (+) and contrast (−)	*records*	*cassettes*
cost (+)	A record sometimes costs less than a tape.	A tape sometimes holds more, however.
sound quality (+)	Good	Good
cost of hardware (+)	$149 for turntable I like	$139 for cassette deck
durability (−)	Can get scratched	Difficult to damage
portability (−)	Stereo is relatively fixed.	Tapes can be used in car.

3. **List the points of similarity and difference in the order in which you will discuss them.**

(order of importance to me)

sound (+) portability (−) cost of hardware (+)
durability (−) cost (+)

The following list contains some of the logical connectives and other expressions that you will need to tell how "this is like (or unlike) that." You will not necessarily use all of this vocabulary in any one piece of writing, but it is a helpful list to have.

LOGICAL CONNECTIVES AND VOCABULARY FOR "THIS IS LIKE (OR UNLIKE) THAT"

To help you point out similarities

as
common characteristics
correspond to
correspondingly
have in common
just as
like
likewise
resemble
similar to
similarly

To help you point out differences

although	a smaller percentage than
but	better than
even so	differ from
however	different from
in spite of the fact that	faster than
on the contrary	in contrast to
on the other hand	in opposition to
otherwise	less than
whereas	more than
	unlike

Warm-ups: "This is like (or unlike) that."

WARM–UP 10: Use the data in the sample comparison frame (page 604) to write a short piece that tells how "records are like (or unlike) tapes." Pay attention to the suggested order for the presentation of your statements (see number 3, page 604).

WARM–UP 11: Finding similarities. Read the piece by Jessica Mitford again, looking especially for the specific kinds of similarities she says exist between prisons and the funeral industry. Then copy the comparison frame below, and finish filling it in.

COMPARISON FRAME

points of comparison (+)	*prisons*	*funeral industry*
cost (+)	expensive	expensive
beautifications (+)		
"in" and "out" language (+)		
hiding operations (+)		
language of psychiatry (+)	Use such terms as "aversion therapy"	
markets for other industries (+)		

WARM–UP 12: Writing short comparisons. Complete each of the comparisons below using logical connectives and other vocabulary to make comparisons. (suggestions: *remind, resemble, like, just as, as, similar to*)

EXAMPLE An octopus is

ANSWER An octopus is *like a well-organized committee: enough helpers but only one authority.*

1. A bird's song is
2. The cat was not as soft
3. The inside of the rabbit's ears are as pink
4. The tone of her voice does not
5. The child's black hair
6. His freckles are
7. Her fingers are not shaped
8. Her whisper is
9. A piece of chalk
10. The inside of my drawer is

WARM–UP 13: Writing short statements of contrast. Write five statements of contrast about differences between you and

1. someone older than you
2. someone younger than you
3. someone your own age
4. your pets or other animals
5. the way you would like to be

Begin each statement of difference with one of the expressions below. Use each expression once.

I am different from _____.
I am unlike _____.
I am _____, in contrast to _____.
As opposed to _____, I am _____.
I am less _____ than _____.

EXAMPLE I am unlike *my younger sister because I think before I act and she acts before she thinks.*

WARM-UP 14: Finding similarities and differences. Look at the following assortment of figures. Sort the figures according to their similarities in *shape* so that you get at least four groups. As you sort the shapes, think "_____ is like _____."

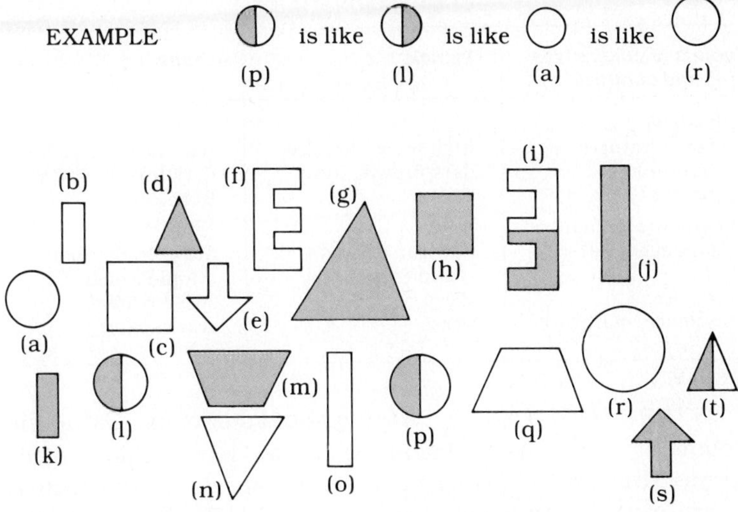

Look again at each of your sorted groups. The figures in each group are *similar in shape.* Now write a sentence stating how the figures in each group *differ* from one another in *shading* or *direction.*

Pattern Practices: "This is like (or unlike) that."

The following Pattern Practices will give you experience in using the "like/unlike" skills in realistic situations.

There are many ways of organizing a piece of writing that tells how "this is like (or unlike) that." Much of the organization depends on whether you are going to discuss *only* similarities or *only* differences or *both* similarities and differences. Let us assume that you have found a number of similarities and a number of differences between two teen-age twins, Patricia and Letitia. You can first organize your information in a comparison frame, as on the next page.

When you plan your actual writing, you may decide to group all similarities in one paragraph and all differences in another. You may, on the other hand, want to discuss physical similarities and differences in one paragraph and then go on to discuss academic similarities and differences in a second paragraph.

COMPARISON FRAME		
points of comparison (+) and contrast (−)	***Patricia***	***Letitia***
physical		
facial features (+)	high brow, dimples	high brow, dimples
hair (+)	dark brown, shiny	dark brown, shiny
height (−)	5′ 8″	5′ 3″
academic strengths		
languages (+)	fluent in Spanish and French	fluent in Spanish and French
reading (+)	speed reader	speed reader
science, math (−)	weak	very capable

PATTERN PRACTICE 7: Writing about statistics. Using the following table as a basis, write a "like/unlike" piece comparing and contrasting various aspects of the United States population in the years 1900 and 1975. Do not merely summarize the data; try to supply reasons for changes.

Revise and edit your work. See 11.h and 11.i.

	1900	1975
Population estimate	76,094,000	213,540,000
Population per square mile	25.6 people	60.2 people
Median age of population[1]	22.9 years	28.8 years
Number of households	15,964,000	71,120,000
Average household size	4.76 people	2.94 people

[1]*Median* refers to the number standing in the middle of a series of numbers. In the series *1, 3, 5, 7, 9,* the median is *5*.

PATTERN PRACTICE 8: Political science writing. The following data tell you about the extent of communications systems in various countries in the mid-1970s. The data include the numbers of telephones, newspapers, radios, and televisions that were available for every one hundred people. Use this data to write several paragraphs that compare and contrast *communications systems* in capitalist countries with those in communist countries in the mid-1970s.

Revise and edit your work. See the checklists in 11.h and 11.i.

COMMUNICATIONS SYSTEMS IN LEADING CAPITALIST AND COMMUNIST COUNTRIES (Mid-1970s)

leading CAPITALIST countries	*telephones per 100 people*	*newspapers per 100 people*	*radios per 100 people*	*televisions per 100 people*
U.S.A.	69.5	29.3	197.6	59.5
Canada	57.2	23.5	86.3	35.0
Japan	40.5	52.6	61.6	22.2
West Germany	31.7	28.9	34.1	30.8
France	26.2	22.0	31.9	23.1
leading COMMUNIST countries	*telephones per 100 people*	*newspapers per 100 people*	*radios per 100 people*	*televisions per 100 people*
U.S.S.R	6.6	38.8	44.5	20.1
China	n.a.[1]	n.a.[1]	.1	.05
Poland	7.5	23.7	22.7	17.4
East Germany	15.2	45.2	36.8	30.7
Yugoslavia	6.1	8.7	18.6	12.7

[1]Data not available

PATTERN PRACTICE 9: Consumer affairs writing. Write a composition in which you compare and contrast two products on the market. You may choose related products (for example, tea versus coffee) or different brands of the same product. Think about this question: "In what ways are products X and Y alike? Unlike?" List your points on a comparison frame. Examine the following model, which compares and contrasts tea and coffee, and note the logical connectives.

> Are those continued high prices weaning you from coffee? Tea is a thrifty alternative. Though more expensive by the pound than coffee, tea goes a lot further. A pound of well-made ground coffee will yield about 40 cups, at a cost, as this issue went to press, of nearly 9 cents a cup. A pound of tea provides 200 cups, at a cost that can run as low as 0.8 cents a cup. Next to water, tea is the cheapest drink there is.
>
> Nor do you give up much of coffee's stimulating effect by switching to tea. Like coffee, tea contains caffeine—about two thirds as much as coffee does. If you now depend on coffee for a boost in the morning, you may find that tea serves nicely. Of course, you give up coffee's taste, but the switch may prove easier than you think. After all, the English—those quintessential tea drinkers—were once a nation of coffee drinkers.
>
> —*Consumer Reports*

Remember that the following vocabulary can help you to express judgments about the products.

is better than
is worse than
is superior to
is inferior to
is faster than
is slower than

12.d DEFINITION: "This is what it is."

Definition is the kind of writing that identifies an object or an idea.

If, as you write, you are thinking primarily, "How can I explain what X is?" you are using the process called definition. Telling "this is what it is" arises from the need to give a name to experiences and to answer the question "what's that?"

Some definitions, such as dictionary entries and scientific definitions, are short. They may, in fact, be simply synonyms. They indicate features that we can see. The following piece that tells "what it is" reveals what the student (Bitzer) can see:

> "Bitzer," said Thomas Gradgrind. "Your definition of a horse."
>
> "Quadruped, Graminivorous. Forty teeth, namely twenty-four grinders, four eye-teeth, and twelve incisive. Sheds coat in the spring; in marshy countries, sheds hoofs, too. Hoofs hard, but requiring to be shod with iron. Age known by marks in mouth." Thus (and much more) Bitzer.
>
> "Now girl number twenty," said Mr. Gradgrind. "You know what a horse is."
>
> —Charles Dickens, *Hard Times*

The kind of definition given by Bitzer is not very different from a description (see 12.b).

Other pieces that tell "this is what it is"—such as attempts to define friendship, religion, or anger—are more complicated and cannot be based solely upon visual details.

The following two passages define the word *community*. They tell "this is what it is" in rather different ways, however.

Model 1: Scientific definition of *community*

All ecosystems are made up of living organisms and their nonliving environment. Very few of these organisms live alone. The survival of each depends on the other organisms in the area. All the plants and animals living in a certain area make up a community. All the animals and plants living in a forest are called a forest *community*.

term being defined

Many communities are made up of smaller communities. As you walk through the forest, you may come upon a stream. The organisms living here make up a stream community. Farther along, the stream may enter a pond. This would be a pond community. A seashore may have a sandy beach, a rock breakwater, a salt marsh, or a tidepool. Each is a community. A nearby park may contain pond, open field, and flowerbed communities. A single tree can be a community. It may be home to many insects, birds, and squirrels. . . .

examples to help define

Humans live in communities, too. When we study human communities, we really study two different communities. First, there is the natural community. This includes humans and the other organisms around them. It includes the food webs of which humans are a part. . . .

The other type of community is a social community. In general, there are three types: urban, suburban, and rural. . . .

varieties of the term being defined

—*Life Science*

Model 2: Personal definition of *community*

A community is not merely a condition of physical proximity, no matter how admirable the layout of the shopping center and the streets, no matter if we demolish the horizontal slums and replace them with vertical ones. A

a statement of negation: what a community is not

listing of features

community is the mental and spiritual condi-tin of knowing that the place is shared, and that the people who share the place define and limit the possibilities of each other's lives. It is the knowledge that people have of each other, their concern for each other, their trust in each other, the freedom with which they come and go among themselves.

underlined words signal a definition coming

Now it has become urgent that the sense of community should include the world, that it should come to be a realization that all men ultimately share the same place, the same nature, and the same destiny. But this most necessary feeling that the world is a neighbor-hood cannot, I think, be expected to grow among the crowds of strangers that fill the cit-ies. If it is to be hoped for at all, it is to be hoped for among the people who have had the experi-ence of being involved responsibly and know-ingly, and at some expense of their feelings and means, in the lives of their neighbors.

Against a longstanding fashion of antip-athy, I will venture to suggest that the best model we have of a community is still the small country town of our agricultural past. I do not mean that this was ever a perfect community, or that it did not have serious faults, or that it can be realistically thought of as a possibility that is still before us. But with its balance of va-riety and coherence, it is still more suggestive of the possibility of community, of neigh-borhood, than anything else we have exper-ienced. . . . Different sorts of people, different kinds of experience and levels of education were in constant touch with each other and were taught and disciplined by each other. Knowl-edge of neighbors was encouraged and culti-vated, by the natural curiosity that produced either gossip or understanding, and also by the caution and interest of business dealings. . . .

example of community

—Wendell Berry, *The Long-Legged House*

■ Skills for telling "this is what it is"

To explain clearly what something is, you can try various techniques: classifying the term, narrowing the term, extending the term, giving examples, relating an incident.

1. **Name the term being defined.**
   greed
2. **Classify the term as either concrete or abstract.**
   greed – abstract
3. **Identify the term's category, class, or type.**
   historically, one of the famous "deadly sins," which also include pride, anger, and envy; also, a personal quality, a feeling
4. **Tell what the term is *not*, or otherwise limit it.**
   not the same as *envy*
   not ordinary desire or ambition
   not quite avarice either, though
5. **Give the distinguishing features of the term, give examples, or relate an incident (that is, tell "this is what happened").**
   originally meant an intense desire for wealth (the King Midas story)
   can now refer to an intense desire for food, power, experience: a greedy child, greedy for power, a greed for experience
   derived from Anglo-Saxon word meaning "hungry"
6. **List the distinguishing features in their order of importance to you.**
   Anglo-Saxon definition
   original meaning
   expanded meaning

The following list contains some of the logical connectives and other key expressions that you will need to tell "this is what it is." You will not necessarily use all of this vocabulary in any one piece of writing, but it is a helpful list to have.

LOGICAL CONNECTIVES AND VOCABULARY FOR TELLING "THIS IS WHAT IT IS"

to clarify	by _____ is meant
to define	by _____ I mean
to explain	by _____ I do not mean
in other words	a _____ is
to paraphrase	

In defining, you will also use words such as the following, which are important to any kind of *classification*:

aspects	forms
attributes	kinds
categories	methods
characteristics	properties
classes	species
conditions	types

Warm-ups: "This is what it is."

WARM–UP 15: Write a paragraph telling "this is what *greed* is." Use the skills information given on pages 613–614.

WARM–UP 16: Defining concrete objects. When you are defining something concrete, you can use the following form:

_______ is a kind of _______ that _____________ .
(concrete object) (class) (distinguishing feature)

EXAMPLES A *dictionary* is a kind of *book* that *gives definitions.*
An *apple* is a kind of *fruit* that *is hard, generally red or green, and stemmed.*
A *mule* is a kind of *animal* that *looks similar to a horse*.

Complete the following one-sentence definitions of concrete objects.

1. A chair is a piece of _____ that _____ .
2. A ballpoint pen is _____ that _____ .
3. A refrigerator is _____ that _____ .
4. Eyeglasses are _____ that _____ .
5. A window is _____ that _____ .
6. Contact lenses are _____ that _____ .
7. A typewriter is _____ that _____ .
8. Mud is a kind of _____ that _____ .
9. A computer is a kind of _____ that _____ .
10. A football is _____ that _____ .

WARM–UP 17. Giving examples: What is "common sense"? Have you ever met anyone who seemed to have a great deal of common sense? List several actions that such a person might take in a given situation. Then list several actions that a person with no common sense might take in the same situation. (Possible situations: approaching final exams; getting lost in a big city; backpacking)

WARM–UP 18. Telling what the term is not: Look at the following diagramed definition of the word *bachelor*.

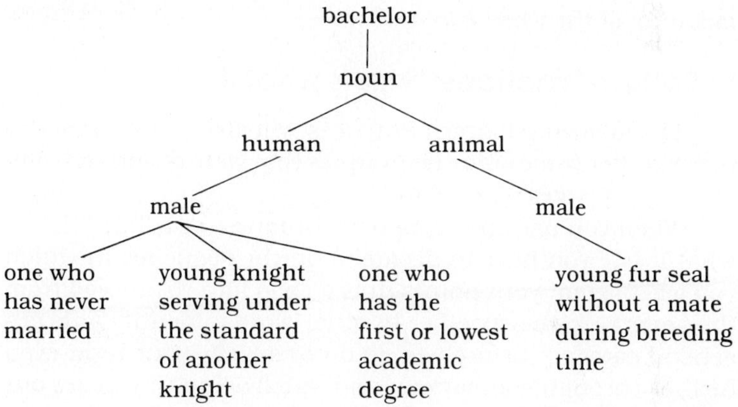

Notice how the features of the word are listed in an inverted tree diagram in the order of least specific (top) to most specific (bottom). Write a paragraph about one of the specific meanings of *bachelor*. Begin your paragraph with the following sentence:

By *bachelor*, I do not mean ______.

WARM–UP 19. Limiting the definitions. A word can have more than one definition, as you know from looking at a dictionary and from reading the two definitions for the word *community*, above. Obviously, the context of a word is important. A word can often be defined only in reference to a particular framework.

Read the passage on the next page. It gives a famous psychoanalytic definition of the term *ego*. Then read the questions that follow the passage.

> The principal characteristics of the ego are these: . . . the ego is in control of voluntary movement. It has the task of self-preservation. As regards *external* events, it performs that task by becoming aware of the stimuli from without, by storing up experiences of them (in the memory), by avoiding excessive stimuli (through flight), by dealing with moderate stimuli (through adaptation), and, finally, by learning to bring about appropriate modifications in the external world to its own advantage (through activity).
>
> —Sigmund Freud, *An Outline of Psychoanalysis*

What does *ego* mean to you? How else is the word *ego* often used? List a few examples that will help define this other meaning of the word *ego*.

■ Pattern Practices: "This is what it is."

The following Pattern Practices will give you a chance to put together some of the techniques that were discussed individually on pages 613 – 614.

When you use one or more techniques for telling "this is what it is," you have to decide upon the sequence in which you will present your points. It is a good idea to proceed from the general to the specific. In other words, identify a term's general category before you go on to specify your term even further through comparison and subdivision. If you set out to define the concrete term *film*, for instance, you might devote your first paragraph to discussing how film fits into the general class of creative arts. Your following paragraphs might go on to define different kinds of film, such as the western, the musical comedy, the art film, and the detective film.

PATTERN PRACTICE 10: Personalized definition. Read through the list of abstract words below:

action	ideal
authentic	individual
companionship	joy
ethical	life
family	living
fidelity	pride
fresh	purpose
genuine	trust
honest	world

Now read the poem "Checklist" by Eve Merriam. The poem is written about the above list of abstract words. How has Merriam defined these words?

ACTION: Used principally to describe carbonated beverages, toothpaste, aspirin. For specific usage, see "the bubbling-action soda," "the foaming-action toothpaste," the "quick-action headache reliever."

AUTHENTIC: A reproduction, as in "an authentic reproduction of early American."

COMPANIONSHIP: Quality denoting the relationship between an animate object and an inanimate one, such as "the companionship of an outdoor motor," power tool, pop-up toaster, electric blanket.

ETHICAL: Drug requiring a prescription.

FAMILY: A series of cars or food products, such as The Family of General Motors or The Family of General Mills.

FIDELITY: (a) see **TRUST;** (b) hyphenated with **HI-**

FRESH: Associated with **FACTORY** or **FROZEN;** cf. "factory-fresh cigars," "frozen-fresh orange juice."

GENUINE: See **AUTHENTIC.**

HONEST: An unmentholated cigarette.

INDIVIDUAL: A single portion.

LIVING: Suffix of **BETTER,** surrounded by a kitchen.

PURPOSE: Compound with **ALL,** as in "all-purpose cleaner."

TRUST: A bank.

WORLD: Of pleasure, of satisfaction, as in chewing gum.

IDEAL, JOY, LIFE, PRIDE: These are all copyright brand names and the use or pursuit thereof is restricted to the properly identified product, viz.: Ideal is a dog food, Joy is a detergent, with Life there is a choice of three— magazine, cereal, or filter-tip cigarette—and Pride is a floor wax.

—Eve Merriam

Merriam has defined the words in terms of what they mean to advertisers. Choose one of the words from "Checklist," and write a definition that explains what the word means to *you.* Use the following sentence to begin your definition:

> One of the best ways to explain what I mean by _____ is to exclude certain meanings from my definition and to give examples.

Revise and edit your work. See the checklists in 11.h and 11.i.

PATTERN PRACTICE 11: Scientific definition. Telling "what it is" often involves classifying elements. For example, you can make a definition of *food additives* clearer by classifying them into three groups. Use the following chart to write a definition of food additives that begins with the following sentence:

Food additives can be divided into three classes: ____, ____, and ____.

Give at least two examples of each class of food additive. In that way, you will help your reader understand the distinctions you are making between classes.

Revise and edit your work. See the checklists in 11.h and 11.i.

SAFETY OF COMMON FOOD ADDITIVES[1]

I: AVOID

Artificial Colorings: Most are synthetic chemicals not found in nature. Some are safer than others, but names of colorings are not listed on label. Used mostly in foods of low nutritional value, usually indicating that fruit or other natural ingredients have been omitted.

additive	***use***	***comment***
Blue No. 1	In beverages, candy, baked goods	Very poorly tested
Butylated Hydroxytoluene (BHT)	Antioxidant; cereals, chewing gum, potato chips, oils, etc.	Stored in body fat; can cause allergic reaction; safer alternatives
Caffeine	Stimulant; naturally in coffee, tea, cocoa; added to soft drinks	Causes sleeplessness

II: CAUTION

additive	***use***	***comment***
Artificial Coloring: Yellow No. 6	Beverages, sausages, baked goods, candy, gelatin	Appears safe, but can cause allergic reactions
Artificial Flavoring	Soda, candy, breakfast cereals, gelatin, desserts	May cause hyperactivity in some children
Monosodium Glutamate (MSG)	Flavor enhancer; soup, seafood, poultry, cheese, sauces, stews, etc.	Damages brain cells in infant mice; causes tightness in temples

[1]Adapted from Center for Science in the Public Interest

III: SAFE

additive	*use*	*comment*
Beta Carotene	Coloring, nutrient; margarine, shortening, nondairy creamers, butter	Body converts it to Vitamin A.
Calcium (or Sodium) Propionate	Preservative; bread, rolls, pies, cakes	Prevents mold growth
Lactose	Sweetener; whipped topping mix, breakfast pastry	Slightly sweet carbohydrate from milk
Lecithin	Emulsifier, antioxidant; baked goods, margarine, chocolate, ice cream	Common in animals and plants

PATTERN PRACTICE 12: Giving word histories. Below are words that have come into English from the names of mythological characters. You may not know the character, but you may be quite familiar with the English word.

Mythological character	Word
Tantalus	tantalize
Odysseus	Odyssey
Narcissus	narcissistic
Echo	echo
Arachne	arachnid

Choose one English word and read the myth from which it comes. (You might check a collection of myths, such as Edith Hamilton's *Mythology.*) Use the myth as an aid in telling what the English word means. You might begin your brief account with the following sentence or with a similar sentence.

> One way to illustrate what _____ means is by retelling the following story.

Revise and edit your account. See the checklists in 11.h and 11.i.

PATTERN PRACTICE 13: Personal definition (autobiography). One of the major ways in which some people "define themselves" is by telling about their job. To do so is one way to answer the question, "Who are you?" Unless you have a full-time job while you are in school, however, it makes more sense to define yourself as a "student." Give your definition of being a student. Give examples of what makes you a student.

Revise and edit your work. See the checklists in 11.h and 11.i.

12.e EXPLANATION OF PROCESS: "This is how to do something."

An **explanation of process** is the kind of writing that tells how to reach a goal or how something works.

You engage in thinking "this is how to do something" whenever you try to explain a step-by-step process to someone, be it a mechanical, psychological, social, or political process. Often, as you write a proposal for action—calling for a change of some kind—you must also organize your thoughts along "how to" lines. For example, you must tell your readers not only that a new law is necessary but what must be done to get it enacted.

The most effective way to tell someone how to bake cookies, how to overcome shyness, or how to control pollution is to enumerate steps in a clear and simple sequence, keeping in mind the capabilities and limitations of the audience. For instance, the words and details you use to explain the process of nuclear fission will differ depending upon whether you are talking to a teen-ager or to a physics professor.

At times you may want to express your own feelings in your explanation of a process. Notice how the writer of the following excerpt communicates his feelings toward the process that he is explaining.

> I haven't cooked anything since I whipped up a mud pie when I was eight years old. The recipe was: mix well some good backyard dirt with a half cup of water from the garden hose and a good hawking of spittle. Shape into a patty and sprinkle well with sand from an anthill, dotting with a dead cricket. Put out in the sun for half the day and then feed it to your father when he

comes home tired from work. If he won't eat it, look disappointed, as if you plan to rob banks when you grow up because of his neglect.

—Paul Zimmer, *John Keats's Porridge*

The recipe comes alive because Paul Zimmer's mischievous pleasure is part of the explanation.

The following model about how to find and prepare clams is another pattern of thinking and writing that tells "this is how to do something."

Model: "This is how to do something."

The cost of sea clams—the big ones whose shells, back in the days when people smoked, were often used for ashtrays—has not gone up in 30 years. They are still free for the taking, provided you have gone to the Truro Town Hall and bought your annual shellfish license, for $2. The only inflationary aspect of sea-clamming, as far as I am concerned, resulted from somebody's swiping my wire clam basket one winter, obliging me to buy a new one the next spring. I forget what it cost.

Step 1: Buy a license.

I generally go out sea-clamming once a month, when the moon is full and the tides are at their lowest. There are two low tides, of course, in every 24-hour span, but sea-clam hunters who take the sport seriously regard the afternoon low tide as, so to speak, infra dig.[1] The best time to go sea-clamming is before breakfast—indeed, if tide and time are neatly juxtaposed, just at sunrise.

Step 2: Decide when to go clamming.

The best place is at North Truro, in Cape Cod Bay, a couple of hundred yards offshore. The clams are to be found either lurking just under the strands of sand that are exposed for an hour or so as the water ebbs (they can be spotted by a little trail of spit marks they leave when they spout water to the surface) or in the water itself.

Step 3: Decide where to go.

[1] Below one's dignity

Sea clams live in colonies, and if you are lucky you can wade out on top of a colony and feel the edges of their shells—they live upright—with your bare feet. Then it is simply a question of reaching down and hauling them in. When you come upon such a cluster, you can fill your basket in a couple of minutes.

Step 4: Find and collect the clams. Note the underlined logical connectives.

It is not unlike, farther out in the bay, encountering a school of striped bass while fishing. If your boat stumbles upon them, as once and only once a boat I was in did, the foolish fish will grab at a bare hook and practically beg to be gaffed.

Once I even found a not discreditably sized pearl inside a sea clam.

Deer hunters sometimes come home empty-handed. So do clam stalkers. If, though, one does happen upon a colony and fills his basket fast, he is faced with a profound moral dilemma. Should he tell anybody else where they are?

I went out the other day with my son Tony, a Cape Cod year-rounder nowadays, and as we were strutting back to shore, our baskets heavy with our catch, we met some old friends heading out to search. I directed them to the spot where we knew clams lay in abundance. Tony at first was aghast at my blabbing, but later he grudgingly acknowledged that in this instance it was probably all right to share the secret, inasmuch as our acquaintances were on an errand of mercy—fetching clams for still another old friend, now in his 80's, who has had, regrettably, to stop sea-clamming because of failing eyesight.

The toughest part of sea-clamming is cleaning the critters. It is not for the squeamish. You have to squeeze their stomachs out while they are still alive and fighting back. Strangely, no one in my household ever offers to relieve me of this sadistic chore. It takes me

Step 5: Clean the clams.

about two minutes to clean each clam, and if there are five or six dozen to wrestle with, the rest of that summer morning is apt to be shot.

I find myself slowed down, too, because of the irresistible temptation, every so often, to stop and nibble at one of the big clam's raw muscles. These are about the size of small scallops, and they taste, to me at least, like candy.

The next step is to divide up the clam meat, by now no longer wriggling, into manageable pieces. There are two schools of thought about this. One school favors using an old-fashioned, hand-cranked meat grinder. The other school advocates using a food processor. Oddly, the people I know who do not have a processor tend to be partial to the meat grinder. Then one chops up a mess of onions (here a processor makes the task both less tedious and less careful), sautés them, and then cooks up the minced clams with them, adding—in my case more or less at random—butter, Worcestershire sauce, salt, pepper, whatever herbs may be within reach, lemon juice, garlic. . . .

Step 6: Divide up the clam meat.

Step 7: Add other ingredients to make clam pie.

There are some nuts who add potatoes to clam pie. They should be hanged, or deported, or whatever will cause them the greatest suffering.

What is the attitude of the author toward sea-clamming?

—E. J. Kahn, Jr.

Skills for telling "this is how to do something"

When you decide to tell someone what steps to follow in a process, you should go through the steps yourself, at least in your mind, so that your explanation is totally clear.

1. **Make sure you know the audience to whom you will be explaining the process.**

   telling a young adult how to start to drive a stick-shift car

2. **List the essential steps of the process in the correct (usually, chronological) order. Exclude steps that are irrelevant to your audience.**

a. Make sure that the emergency brake is on.

b. If the car is not in neutral gear, shift into neutral by pressing down on the clutch (the foot pedal on the left) and by moving the gear into the central position, where it can move freely.

c. Insert the key into the ignition switch, and start the engine by turning the switch clockwise.

d. When you are ready to move, press down on the footbrake to keep the car stationary, and then release the emergency brake.

e. Then press down on the clutch, and move the gear shift into first gear.

f. Release the footbrake.

g. Slowly release the clutch, and press down lightly on the accelerator (the foot pedal on the far right). The car will then move forward.

Steps excluded

If you assume that your audience is familiar with automobiles in general, you do not have to include steps such as the following:

Fasten seat belt.
Adjust rear-view mirror.

3. **Consider putting the steps into a different order—perhaps into distinct phases, stages, or actions. Decide whether these changes make the process clearer.**

Braking actions
Emergency brake on
Foot brake down; release emergency brake
Release foot brake

Clutching actions
Press down on clutch, and shift into neutral.
Press down on clutch, and shift into first.
Release clutch, and press down lightly on accelerator

The following list contains some of the logical connectives and other special vocabulary that you may find useful in telling "this is how to do something." You will not use all of this vocabulary in any one piece of writing, but it is a helpful list to have. Notice that the list has a separate grouping of expressions to use in a proposal for action. Such a proposal tells how to do something but stresses personal involvement.

LOGICAL CONNECTIVES AND VOCABULARY FOR TELLING "HOW TO DO SOMETHING"

first, second, third, etc.
firstly, secondly, etc.
in the first place, in the second place, etc.
next, then, subsequently, at last, in conclusion, finally.
the most important, the least important, the most complex, the least complex

Special vocabulary for writing a proposal for action[1]

I propose that	I would forbid
It seems feasible	I would exclude
I would suggest that	I would bar
I would urge that	I would prevent
I would demand that	I would prohibit
I would advocate that	

Warm-ups: "This is how to do something."

WARM–UP 20: Use the data within the list of skills on pages 623 –624 to write a short piece that tells "this is how to drive a stick-shift car." Remember that you are explaining the process to a teen-ager.

WARM–UP 21: **Being aware of the audience.** One of the most common situations in which you must tell "how to do something" involves giving instructions to a child. Choose one of the actions below, and write a paragraph using simple language and instructions that could be read to a four-year-old child.

1. how to snap your fingers
2. how to tie a shoelace
3. how to brush your teeth
4. how to jump rope
5. how to do a plié

Now write a second paragraph, explaining the same process to a teen-ager.

[1] Adapted from Mary S. Lawrence, *Writing as a Thinking Process* (Ann Arbor: The University of Michigan Press, 1976), page 184.

WARM–UP 22: Sequencing steps. The Heimlich Maneuver is used to clear the breathing passages of a person who is choking on a piece of food. A choking victim cannot speak or breathe, turns blue, and will die within four minutes if not helped. The steps of the Heimlich Maneuver are listed below—but not in the proper order. Put the steps in the correct order.

1. Make a fist with one hand, and place your fist against the victim's abdomen, above the navel and below the rib cage.
2. Repeat several times if necessary.
3. Stand behind the victim.
4. With the second hand, press your fist into the victim's abdomen with a quick upward thrust.
5. Call a physician as soon as the victim is breathing normally once again.
6. Wrap your arms around the victim's waist.
7. Grasp your fist with your other hand.

WARM–UP 23: Presenting the steps in a clear order. The following newspaper editorial is a call for action. The writer wants to see an end to the sale of college term papers. Read the editorial, and tell where the writer moves from giving background to suggesting steps to be taken. Identify the steps. In what order are the steps presented? Which is the most important step?

> Commercial trading in term papers, though by no means a new phenomenon, has become more brazen and apparently more profitable. Shady merchants of such papers advertise in student newspapers and, in their public statements, try to give the impression that they are engaged in a legitimate business.
>
> Their sole purpose is to profit from providing means for successful deception. Theirs is a racket through which students, who are foolish enough to be the customers, are as cruelly deceived as the society which takes it for granted that a certificate or degree attesting to certain attainments stands for real achievement.
>
> Recent attacks on the term paper peddlers by [New York] State Attorney General Louis Lefkowitz have helped to call attention to this problem. But effective legal action rather than mere expressions of disapproval is needed to stop the abuse. Colleges can help by spelling out the penalties to be invoked

against students caught engaging in such fraud. Student newspapers moreover should have a high enough regard for academic integrity to reject thesis-for-sale advertisements.

—*New York Times*

Pattern Practices: "This is how to do something."

The following Pattern Practices will give you opportunities for explaining "this is how to do" various activities. Remember to use an order of presentation that is appropriate to the process you wish to explain. For simple mechanical processes, such as giving a recipe or telling how to throw pottery, a chronological order is best. Giving instructions for a more complicated process, such as "how to take a good photograph," may require grouping the steps in order of importance. For instance, in the first paragraph you might discuss how to find the right subjects, in the second paragraph you might explain how to develop a good eye for balance and composition, and in the third paragraph you might give simple mechanical instructions on how to operate a camera.

PATTERN PRACTICE 14: Explaining a chemical process. The following diagram shows the steps involved in converting fuel (such as coal or oil) to energy for operating stoves, radios, lights, etc. Assume that you cannot show such a diagram to an audience of high school students. Explain the process in words. Revise and edit your explanation. See the checklists in 11.h and 11.i.

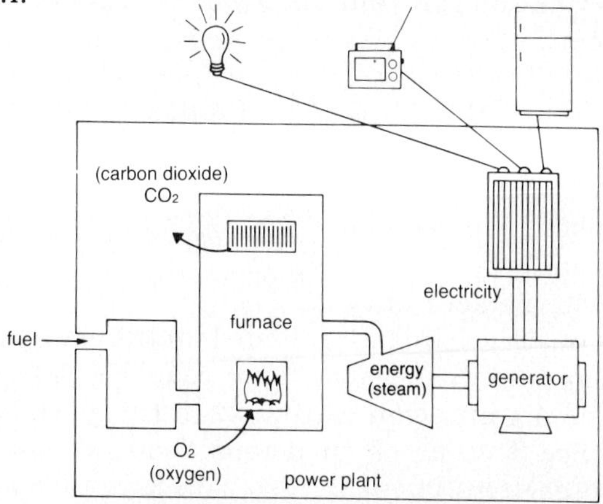

PATTERN PRACTICE 15: Proposal for action (problem solving). Read the following passage about dishonesty.

> There was one course in college which was known to be very difficult. It was an elective (not required) course in which the professor assigned five papers during the semester.
>
> A senior in college took this course and wrote the first four papers. When the time came to hand in the fifth paper, he had many other things to do in order to graduate. One of his friends had taken the course two years previously and still had his papers. He asked this friend for one of the papers. He rewrote some parts of it and handed it in, believing that the teacher would never remember a paper that had been written that long ago, especially since many people take the course. However, the professor recognized the paper and the name of the student who had originally written it.
>
> —Moshe Blatt *et al.*

Put yourself in the position of someone giving advice to the professor. What steps would you suggest the professor take and why? Would you suggest taking steps against the student or against the student's friend? Would you suggest that the professor direct his actions toward preventing such events from occurring in the future?

Use one or more of the following expressions in your proposal for action:

I would urge . . .
I would prevent . . .
I would prohibit . . .

Revise and edit your proposal. See the checklists in 11.h and 11.i.

PATTERN PRACTICE 16: Proposal for action (letter writing). Instead of just complaining about a situation, a creative citizen can suggest action. A citizen can tell the responsible parties how they might improve or change the situation.

Write a letter from your position as a high school student to one of the organizations listed on the next page about the problem cited there. Make sure that your letter clearly tells how the organization can improve the situation — step by step. (See Section 17 for details about format and style in business letters.)

Organization	Problem
a. a television network	too much violence on prime-time shows
b. assistant superintendent for instruction or curriculum director	elimination of extra-curricular school activities
c. a corporate headquarters	the pollution of local waterways by a manufacturing plant
d. a sanitation department	slow garbage collection or slow snow removal
e. a transit company	delays in bus or train service

12.f CAUSE-EFFECT: "This caused that."

Cause-effect writing shows the connection between events.

Sometimes you only suspect that a certain action caused another action. At other times you are relatively sure that one action caused another. In both cases, however, you are engaged in the kind of thinking and writing generally called cause-effect. Telling how "this caused that" can involve answering questions as simple as "What is causing that rattle in the car's engine?" and as complicated as "What makes cancer cells grow?"

During your early years you probably saw movements in nature as having simple causes. For instance, you may have thought that the wind is pushed by someone or that it moves itself, as did the child of seven quoted here by Jean Piaget:

> What makes the wind blow? Is someone pushing it? I thought it would have to stop when it went against a house or a big tree. Does it know that it is making our pages blow over?

As you grew older, you realized that different conditions depend on one another and cause certain events: The wind is a condition caused by the change in current, moisture, pressure, speed, and temperature of air passing over water and land. Both as a child and as a young adult—in fact, all your life—you think in terms of causes and effects, effects and causes.

The search for causes is fundamental to people of all cultures and all times. Greek myths tried to explain how the world, human beings, the seasons, and even the berries on the mulberry tree were created.

In general, you will find more complex relationships between causes and effects than those discussed in myths. Some causes can also be considered effects, and vice versa. Here is a picture of what a cause-effect network might look like:

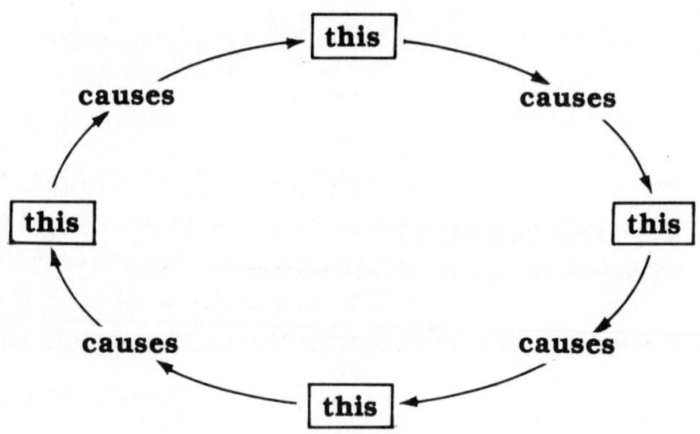

Model: "This caused that."

There is a great variety of butterfly color patterns whose survival value is not so obvious. There are some species, for instance, which are brilliantly colored and seemingly very conspicuous indeed. Such color patterns would appear to advertise the butterflies and place them at risk from predators rather than offering them protection, but such coloration may have its purpose in fulfilling some role other than a protective one. In particular, brilliant colors and striking patterns may play their part in recognition between individual butterflies for the purpose of territorial behavior and courtship, just as they do in many birds. Certainly it is possible to attract the blue male *Morpho* butterflies by waving a piece of bright blue card in the sunlight in the localities which they inhabit.

signals cause-effect discussion

In these particular insects, the brilliant iridescent blue color probably also serves another function. They inhabit tropical rain forests and are usually found near water, especially waterfalls. The butterflies follow stream courses with a fast erratic flight dashing through the dappled light and shade. As they pass through a sunny patch the wings flash electric blue, but in the shadows they appear only as dark silhouettes, making it difficult for predators to follow them in flight because one moment a brilliant blue object is being chased but the next instant it has disappeared, to be replaced by a dark shape. This in turn suddenly erupts into brilliant blue on reaching a sunny patch. The momentary confusion and indecision induced in a potential predator may be sufficient to help the butterfly escape unharmed.

signals cause-effect discussion

Note that the cause is a complex issue.

—*The Illustrated Encyclopedia of the Butterfly World*

Skills for telling "this caused that"

You have to work with many details when you write a cause-effect piece. The following steps are suggested to help you organize your thinking.

1. **State the existing event or condition.**

   A friend has a headache.

2. **Create a cause-effect network indicating the possible causes of the event or condition.**

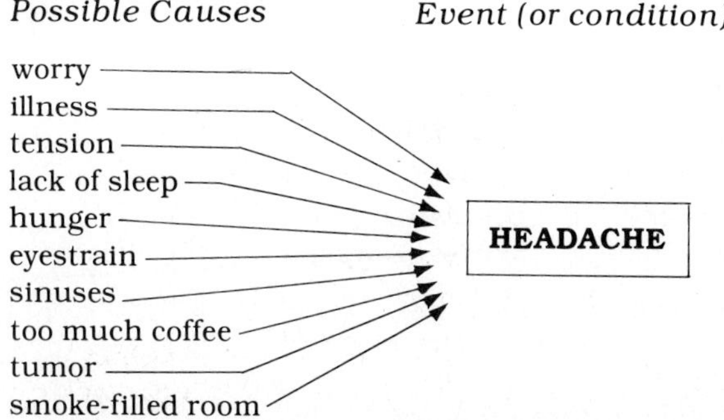

3. **Rate the causes on a certainty scale.**

unrelated	*unlikely*	*maybe*	*probably*	*most likely*
illness; tumor	sinuses; smoke-filled room	eyestrain	hunger	tension; worry; lack of sleep; too much coffee

4. **Decide if any of the "most likely" causes are responsible for one another.**

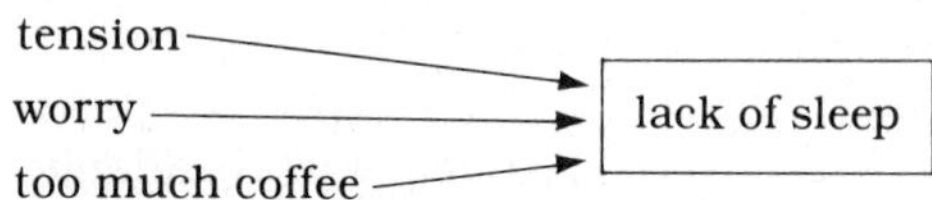

The following list contains some of the vocabulary that you will need to tell "this caused that." You will not necessarily use all of this vocabulary in any one piece of writing, but it is a helpful list to have.

LOGICAL CONNECTIVES AND VOCABULARY FOR TELLING "THIS CAUSED THAT"

To express causes

because
since
is due to
causes
the reason for
purpose

To express effects

as a result
consequently
therefore
is the effect of

To express causes and effects

if _____ , then _____
One effect of _____ is that _____

To express degrees of certainty

unrelated
unconnected
unlinked

unlikely
improbable

maybe
possibly
at first glance

probably
in all likelihood

certainly
clearly
necessarily

■ Warm-ups: "This caused that."

WARM–UP 24: Write a paragraph telling how "this caused that" using the information from the list of skills on pages 631–632.)

WARM–UP 25: Distinguishing kinds of relationships. A **chronological relationship** exists when two events are connected in time. One event does not cause the other; they just happen in sequence.

Linda finished writing her letter.
Linda mailed her letter.

The guru promised that world peace would come.
The war ended.

A **cause-effect relationship** exists when one event is the known cause for the events that follow.

The pedals of the bicycle were broken.
Eugene could not bicycle to work.

Indicate which kind of relationship is expressed in the pairs of sentences below: (a) a chronological relationship or (b) a cause-effect relationship.

1. Jonathan broke a glass. He picked up the pieces.
2. There was a drought. The crops failed.
3. I stared at the television. The picture began to roll horizontally.
4. Blanche walked up to the stage. She received an award.
5. It began to pour. The baseball game was postponed.

WARM–UP 26: Making a cause-effect network. Make a cause-effect network for one of the following conditions, listing as many possible causes as you can. (Review Step 2 on page 631.)

a. famines in Africa (or starvation in the world)
b. earthquakes in Iran
c. drug problems in the United States

Now evaluate the causes you have listed by placing them on a certainty scale (see the preceding page).

WARM–UP 27: Using a certainty scale. Place on a certainty scale the following statements about why animals become extinct.

1. Certain species of animals naturally die out.
2. Humankind is responsible for the plight of endangered species.
3. There is not room on earth for both people and animals.
4. The Blue Whale, the largest animal in all history, may die out because it is too large.
5. An animal's inability to adapt to a changed environment is the main cause of extinction.
6. Larger and stronger animals hurt and destroy smaller ones.
7. Animals become extinct if their brains are too small.
8. Pollution endangers some species of animals.
9. Changes in climate conditions cause extinction.
10. The domestication of animals causes extinction.

WARM–UP 28: Using cause-effect vocabulary. Use the logical connectives and the other special vocabulary listed on page 632 to write one statement about each of the following items. Each statement should express a cause or an effect or both.

a. the desalinating (desalting) of water
b. the disposal of chemical wastes
c. air pollution
d. human life expectancy
e. soil erosion

Pattern Practices: "This caused that."

Now you will move beyond writing single sentences about causes and effects into writing a paragraph or a series of paragraphs that explain "this caused that." It may seem natural to order your cause-effect paragraphs chronologically—that is, beginning with cause and ending with effect. At times, though, you will want to emphasize the effect, if only because it seems so mysterious. If such is the case, discuss the effect (or the result of the condition) at the beginning, consider various causes, and conclude with the most likely cause or causes.

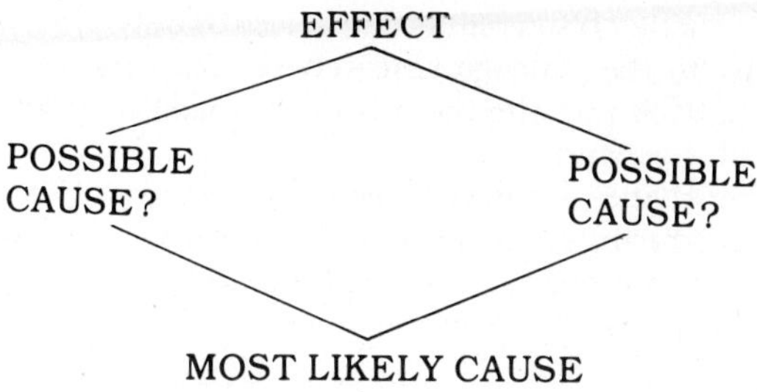

At other times, for other topics, you may wish to alternate paragraphs, first explaining a cause, then an effect, then another cause, and so on.

PATTERN PRACTICE 17: Writing myths; writing science. Each of the following questions can be answered in at least two ways: (1) You can give an imaginative, mythlike answer, which may be very satisfying to a young child who likes to hear magical stories. (2) You can do research in science books and prepare an explanation of cause and effect that will satisfy older people (who are not specialists in science). Pick one of the questions, and write two explanations that tell how "this caused that." One explanation should be a story for a child; one should be a report for an adult.

1. What makes clouds?
2. What makes boats float?
3. Where do waves come from?
4. How and why do tree trunks form rings?
5. Why do the seasons change?

Revise and edit your work. See the checklists in 11.h and 11.i.

PATTERN PRACTICE 18: Fact finding. The following article offers a brief explanation of one of the causes of heat loss in a home and suggests a possible remedy.

> As much as 31 percent of the house heat that normally escapes through windows in winter can be saved by keeping window shades lowered, according to scientists at the Illinois Institute of Technology. When outdoor temperatures ranged between 20 and 50 degrees F, a light-colored shade decreased heat loss through a test window by 24 to 31 percent, whereas a drape

and a venetian blind reduced heat loss by only 6 to 7 percent, according to the Chicago researchers. The shades work by reflecting back into the room heat that would otherwise escape through the window.

The shades are most effective in reducing heat loss in the evening, during the night and in the early morning. However, when the sun shines, the shades should be up to let in sunlight that can help warm the home.

—*New York Times*

Write a report in which you explain the causes of one of the following items and then offer a remedy.

1. waste of electricity
2. waste of food
3. waste of trees
4. waste of people
5. waste of gasoline

Revise and edit your work. See the checklists in 11.h and 11.i.

PATTERN PRACTICE 19: "Proverbial" cause-effect. Choose one of the following proverbs (from William Blake's *The Marriage of Heaven and Hell*) and develop an essay in which you separate the cause from the effect and explain how the two elements are related.

1. Always be ready to speak your mind, and a base man will avoid you.
2. To create a little flower is the labor of ages.
3. He who desires but acts not, breeds pestilence.
4. Expect poison from standing water.
5. If others had not been foolish, we should be so.

Revise and edit your work. See the checklists in 11.h and 11.i.

THE EXPOSITORY ESSAY

13 The Expository Essay

An **expository essay** is a composition that explains or clarifies a subject or otherwise instructs the reader.

The expository essay is probably the most frequent form of writing that you will do in school and in some job settings. The individual patterns of thinking and writing examined in Section 12 can be used in various combinations when writing an expository essay.

13.a SELECTING AND LIMITING A TOPIC

Even if you have a choice in selecting the topic of an expository essay, you must narrow the topic so that you can handle it in the length requested (often, but not always, five hundred words, or two typed pages). Here are some guidelines that may help you to select and narrow a topic.

1. *Select a topic that interests you.* The topic that interests you may be a very limited one. You may, for example, be interested in how to tune a tenor saxophone with your left hand. On the other hand, your interest may be very general—the whole field of music, for example, or band music. If you have a very limited topic in mind, you can begin to think about developing your topic at once. If, however, your interest is broad—say, nutrition—you will need to think about your *experience* and your *purpose* before you begin to write.

2. *Ask yourself which aspect of the topic you are best qualified to discuss based on your experience.* In an expository essay—as opposed to a research paper (see Sec-

tion 16) — you are expected to draw briefly upon personal experience: what you have experienced yourself or have seen others experience and what you have read about the topic. Assume for the moment that your most recent experience and thoughts about nutrition involve dieting. You have seen crash-dieting fail and have subsequently gained respect for the effects of well-balanced dieting. Make a list of the experiences and main ideas that you can use in writing your essay. Make notes freely as thoughts occur to you. Here is a list of possible notes about dieting:

NOTES

- story about what happened when my teen-age brother switched from his junk-food diet to a more balanced diet
- description of some of the physical results and emotional side-effects in a person who is not practicing habits of good nutrition
- description of the "healthy glow" of someone who does practice good nutrition habits
- how to stay healthy on a limited-budget diet while away from home
- decline of good eating habits: advertising pressure for sugar-coated foods and for high-carbohydrate foods
- how food fads and some ill-considered diet books prove harmful: giving impression that people can overeat now and lose weight later

3. *Relate your broad interest in a topic and your experiences to a specific purpose and to a specific audience.* In an expository essay you are usually expected to be informative. You cannot, however, inform your readers about the whole topic of nutrition or even the whole subtopic of dieting. You would need several years and several volumes to do so. You certainly could not cover the question of dieting in an essay that can be read conveniently in one sitting. You must begin to identify a clear purpose. Just what do you want to explain about dieting? Just what do your readers need or want to know? What can you assume they already know? Consider the list of experiences and ideas that you have made (see 2, above), and try to express your purpose in a single sentence.

   Statement of purpose: I want to explain that crash-dieting is not as healthful or as rewarding as a constant well-balanced diet.

4. *Convert your list of experiences and ideas to an outline* (see 13.b and 13.c).

5. *Convert your statement of purpose* (see 3) *to a thesis sentence, which you can use to begin your essay.* The **thesis statement** is vital to a successful expository essay because it states the main point of the paper and your attitude toward the topic. A thesis statement is also called a controlling statement. Wherever possible, use a strong action verb in the thesis statement rather than just a form of *be.* A strong action verb generally prepares your reader for your main point better than a form of *be.* Notice how the statement of purpose is reworded below to a thesis statement:

   Statement of purpose: I want to explain that crash-dieting is not as healthful or as rewarding as a constant well-balanced diet.

   Thesis statement: A constant, well-balanced diet offers a better chance for a healthful and rewarding life than crash-dieting.

   In framing the thesis statement for an expository essay, keep the following formula in mind. It will help you to remember that your interest plus your experience plus your purpose leads to your thesis statement.

   Regarding ______ (interest), what can I say, based on my own *experiences*, that will *inform* my reader?

6. *Be prepared to develop each item on your outline by using the patterns of thinking and writing that you learned about in Section 12.* (See 13.d in this section for more information about how to develop your expository essay in this manner.)

EXERCISE 1. Select one of the following broad topics and apply Steps 1, 2, and 3 from 13.a. That is, (1) select a topic that interests you; (2) list experiences and ideas related to the topic; and (3) write a statement of purpose.

energy	ballet
hobbies	superstars in sports
music	recent American films
summer jobs	college

13.b THE WORKING OUTLINE

A **working outline** will guide you as you think, plan, and gather any additional information that you may need.

Once you have determined the purpose of your essay, you should go back to the list of experiences and ideas, combine the items if appropriate, and decide on an order in which to present them. Prepare a working outline. (A working outline may also be called a preliminary outline.) The following example shows how the experiences and ideas listed as notes in 13.a can be combined and ordered into a working outline. For the working outline, begin with your statement of purpose and then list—using Roman numerals—each major item that you plan to explore. Notice that complete sentences are not necessary in a working outline.

EXAMPLE

Purpose: to explain that crash-dieting is not as healthful or as rewarding as a constant well-balanced diet

I. How the advertising of certain foods and how the promotion of some diet books have affected American eating habits
II. How poor eating habits affect the physical appearance and emotions of some people versus how good eating habits contribute to a person's overall well-being
III. True story of a teen-age brother who changed his diet and, as a result, his whole life
IV. Description of healthful, inexpensive, easy-to-fix lunches—at home, at school, at work

Then, with the working outline as your guide, add further thoughts and details that logically belong in each major category. Remember that any generalization must be supported by details. Here are some of the details that belong under Point IV on the working outline.

EXAMPLE

IV. Healthful, inexpensive, easy-to-fix lunches

Low-cost, low-calorie foods available in school cafeteria: salads (with lemon-juice dressing), yogurt, sandwiches on whole-wheat bread

Inexpensive and healthful lunches at home: fruits and cheese, soups with leftovers

Quick but heathful lunches at work: fruits and cheese bought from a nearby store or chef's salad in a coffee shop, rather than pizza or hot dogs on the run

EXERCISE 2. Use the list of experiences and ideas that you prepared for Exercise 1 to prepare a working outline. Copy over your statement of purpose and then present the experiences and ideas in three or four categories in the order in which you would like to take them up.

EXERCISE 3. Add your own ideas and experiences that can be used to fill out Points I, II, and III of the working outline given in 13.b, or fill in the details that belong in the working outline that you prepared for Exercise 2.

13.c THE FORMAL OUTLINE

A **formal outline** will guide you in writing your first draft.

Once you have added details to your working outline, you can write up a formal outline—either a topic outline or a sentence outline. You will probably find that merely listing topics and subtopics and sub-subtopics is sufficient, but if you find it easier to write complete sentences in your outline, do not hesitate to do so. Sometimes your teacher will specifically request you to prepare one kind of formal outline or the other. With either the topic outline or the sentence outline, there are certain conventions to follow, which are discussed below.

Guidelines for formal outlines

1. *Numbering:* Do not number the title of the essay. Do not use the terms *introduction, body, conclusion* on the outline itself.

   There is a preferred order of numerals and letters to designate main topics and various levels of subordinate topics: Use Roman numerals for each main topic. Use capital letters for each subtopic. Use Arabic numerals for the next level of subtopics. Use lowercase (small) letters for the next lower level.

You should never have only one subtopic in any category; there must be at least two subtopics. If you find that you have only one subtopic, the chances are that you have a main topic that is too weak to develop properly.

2. *Indenting:* Line up all Roman numerals under one another; line up all capital letters under one another; line up all Arabic numerals under one another; and so on.

I. (Main topic)
  A. (Subtopic of I)
  B. (Subtopic of I)
    1. (Subtopic of I.B)
    2. (Subtopic of I.B)
      a. (Subtopic of I.B.2)
      b. (Subtopic of I.B.2)
II. (Next main topic)
  A. (Subtopic of II)
    1. (Subtopic of II.A)
    2. (Subtopic of II.A)
    3. (Subtopic of II.A)
  B. (Subtopic of II)
    1. (Subtopic of II.B)
    2. (Subtopic of II.B)
III. (Next main topic)

3. *Capitalization and punctuation:* Begin the first word of each entry on an outline with a capital letter. In a topic outline you do not need a period at the end of an entry.

4. *Parallelism:* In preparing a topic outline, try to use the same kind of phrasing at the same levels of heads. For example, within a given Roman numeral head, if you use nouns in A.1, use nouns in A.2, A.3, and so on. If you use participial phrases in B.1, use participial phrases in B.2, B.3, and so on. Your phrasing within one Roman numeral head may be different from your phrasing within other Roman numeral heads. The following example shows how Parts III and IV of the working outline in 13.b can be presented in a *parallel* formal outline.

Partial formal outline

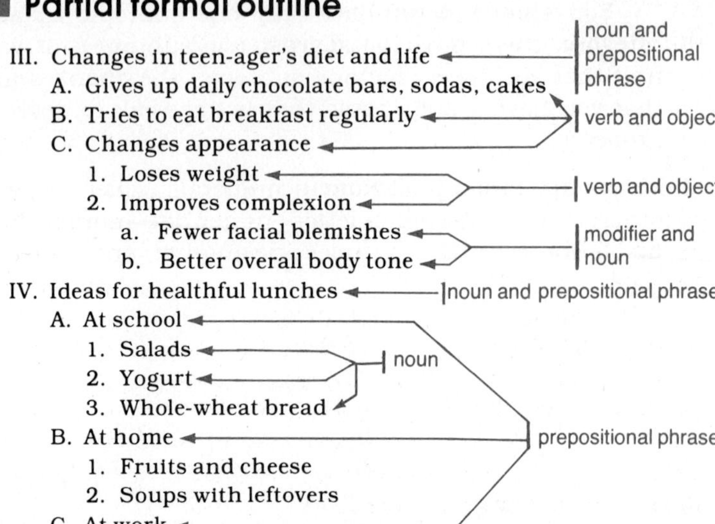

III. Changes in teen-ager's diet and life
A. Gives up daily chocolate bars, sodas, cakes
B. Tries to eat breakfast regularly
C. Changes appearance
1. Loses weight
2. Improves complexion
a. Fewer facial blemishes
b. Better overall body tone
IV. Ideas for healthful lunches
A. At school
1. Salads
2. Yogurt
3. Whole-wheat bread
B. At home
1. Fruits and cheese
2. Soups with leftovers
C. At work
1. Fruit and cheese from store
2. Chef's salad at coffee shop
noun and prepositional phrase
verb and object
verb and object
modifier and noun
noun and prepositional phrase
noun
prepositional phrase

EXERCISE 4. Correct the following faulty topic outline. Change sentences to topics, and make sure that the phrasing of equally important items is parallel. You may also add or eliminate topics. If you have trouble, review the Guidelines for Formal Outlines on pages 642 – 643.

I. How to take the SATs
II. How to prepare for the SATs
  A. Mental preparation
    a. Review math books
    b. Practice careful reading techniques
    c. Going through a study booklet
  B. Be physically prepared
    1. Sleep
    2. Have a good breakfast
III. Taking the SATs
  A. Answering the questions
    1. Work quickly and carefully
    2. Double-check answers
  B. Guessing
    a. Only guess if you can eliminate one or two answers
IV. Conclusion

EXERCISE 5. Write a formal outline replacing the working outline that you prepared for Exercise 2.

13.d DEVELOPING AN EXPOSITORY ESSAY

As you have seen, an expository essay usually has the purpose of informing readers about some aspect of a topic, such as diet, by drawing on the writer's own experiences and ideas. Each of the experiences and ideas must be developed into one or more paragraphs. Each experience or idea will suggest using a particular pattern of thinking and writing, as presented in Section 12. You should review those patterns and perhaps practice them before writing the first draft of your expository essay. Below you will see how any experience or idea from the outline can be written up according to one of the patterns of thinking and writing.

Outline items	Patterns of thinking and writing
I. Effects of advertising and certain diet books	"This caused that" (cause and effect), page 629
II. Health and appearance of people as determined by kind of diet	"This is the look of something" (description), page 589; "This is unlike that" (contrast), page 600
III. Changes in teen-ager's diet and life	"This is what happened" (narration), page 579
IV. Ideas for healthful lunches	"This is how to do something" (process), page 620

EXERCISE 6. Determine which pattern of thinking and writing you can use to develop each main topic on a formal outline. Use either the formal outline that you prepared in Exercise 5 or the formal outline that you corrected in Exercise 4.

13.e WRITING THE ESSAY

Using the formal outline as a guide, write a first draft of your essay. Do not worry at this point about a strong introduction or conclusion for your essay. Basically, concern yourself with the body of the essay. You may want to think of each main topic on your formal outline as forming one paragraph, but sometimes you will need more than one paragraph, especially if the main topic has many subtopics beneath it. You do not have to remain tied to the outline.

13.f TRANSITIONS BETWEEN PARAGRAPHS

Transitional devices make the movement from one paragraph to another clear, smooth, and easy to follow.

As you move through your outline from topic to topic or from subtopic to subtopic, you will probably end one paragraph and begin another. See Section 11 for a review of paragraphing if necessary. You can help your reader understand the relationship of one paragraph to another if you build in careful transitions between the paragraphs. In general, you should try to use one of three common transitional devices: determiners, repeated key terms, logical connectives.

Determiners

The common determiners *this, that, these*, and *those* are good devices for connecting the first sentence in one paragraph with the preceding paragraph. Assume that each of the sentences in the examples below is the first sentence of a paragraph. You can readily understand how the determiner in each sentence refers to an idea already introduced and now about to be discussed further.

> **This** approach to healthful lunches can be carried out at the office, too.
>
> **These** changes in eating habits were soon reflected in changes in my brother's appearance.

Repetition of key terms

Another transitional device is the repetition in the first sentence of a new paragraph of a word or expression from the preceding paragraph.

> . . . In fact, he gave up all forms of junk food.
>
> **Giving up junk food** alone would not have been enough. In addition, my brother made a dedicated attempt to eat a full breakfast regularly.

Logical connectives

Most of the connectives that you have used to link sentences can also be used as transitions between paragraphs. (See Section 12 for detailed instruction on logical connectives.) Here is an example of an effective transition from one paragraph to the next through the use of a logical connective.

> . . . Numerous cookbooks specialize in soup recipes and will supply you with endless suggestions for using those leftovers.
>
> **Similarly,** lunches at the office can be healthful and inexpensive . . . .

EXERCISE 7. Write a first draft of an expository essay. You may write an essay (a) from your own formal outline prepared in Exercise 5; (b) from the outline corrected in Exercise 4; or (c) on the topic of diets, as developed in preceding sections. (Do not concern yourself with an introduction or conclusion at this point.)

13.g THE INTRODUCTION TO THE ESSAY

After you have written the first draft of the essay, you can pay particular attention to writing a strong introduction because now you know exactly what you want to introduce. Consider the suggestions listed below, and adapt any one, or a combination, to introduce your essay.

1. Give background information on the subject—for example, what has recently been said about Americans' eating habits.
2. State the importance of the topic—for example, how important your physical and mental well-being is to happiness or success in life.
3. Begin with a question or quotation—for example, ask your readers their opinions on the topic.
4. Give a startling fact or statistic—for example, find out how many diet books are published every year.
5. Relate an anecdote—for example, tell something interesting about the teen-ager whom you plan to describe in detail later.

EXERCISE 8. Choose two of the methods for writing introductions suggested on preceding page. Then write two different introductions for the expository essay you began in Exercise 7.

13.h THE CONCLUSION TO THE ESSAY

The concluding paragraph should contribute to a feeling that the essay is complete. Consider the following methods, and select a combination that seems most effective.

1. Write a summary or summary statement that restates the central idea of the essay.
2. Use word signals: *finally, in conclusion*.
3. Make suggestions, or offer solutions.
4. Show the significance of the topic by relating it more directly to your readers.
5. Conclude with an anecdote or question.

EXERCISE 9. Write a concluding paragraph for the expository essay that you began in Exercise 7.

13.i REVISING

Once you have gotten your ideas on paper, you will need to examine your work carefully. If possible, set aside the first draft for some time—five minutes, an hour, a day. When you pick it up again, you will have a more objective eye. As you read the essay over, think about the questions on the Checklist for Revising an Essay.

Checklist for revising an essay

1. Does this essay accomplish my stated purpose? (See 13.a.)
2. Are the ideas developed in a logical order? (See 13.c.)
3. Do all of the elements in each paragraph contribute to the main idea? (See 11.b and 11.c.)
4. Do the ideas build upon one another from paragraph to paragraph? (See 13.e and 13.f.)

Your response to these questions will probably prompt some rewriting—a second draft. You may want to delete unnecessary information, reorder your ideas, and put related information together.

13.j EDITING AND PROOFREADING THE ESSAY

Once you have completed the revisions, you are ready to check the paper to make certain that no sentence contains an error in spelling, capitalization, punctuation, or grammar. A paper that shows careful editing and proofreading will represent you favorably.

A paper containing careless errors is everyone's loss. Use the following Editing and Proofreading Checklist. The cross references in parentheses indicate where you can look for review if necessary.

When proofreading a paper you might divide your task into steps. Check sentences first (points 1 through 7 below). Then look at key words to see if they can be improved. Then make sure that words are spelled and punctuated correctly.

As you edit and proofread, you may use Editing Signals, such as those below, from Section 9.

Editing and proofreading checklist

1. Are all sentences complete? (See 2.a.) *frag*
2. Are varied sentence structures used? (See Section 3.)
3. Have you used the voice (active or passive) that is the most effective in each sentence? (See 1.b.20.) *voice*
4. Are verb tenses consistent? (See 1.b.11.) *tense*
5. Do subject and verbs agree? (See 2.c, 2.e, and 2.f.) *agree*
6. Do pronouns agree with antecedents? (See 1.d.1 and 1.d.7.) *ref*
7. Is parallel construction used where appropriate? (See 3.k.) *not parallel*
8. Is vocabulary precise but varied? (See Section 4.) *vocab*
9. Are words spelled correctly? (See Section 5.) *sp*
10. Is punctuation correct? (See Section 7.) *cap, p*

13.k CHOOSING AN EFFECTIVE TITLE

Although you may have chosen a working title before beginning to write, you should select a final title only after you have completed your essay. In choosing an effective title, think of aspects of your topic that will catch your readers' attention and make them want to read your essay. For example, the titles "Crash-Diets Are Bad" or "How to Eat Right" are too dull and vague and are not likely to make your reader want to read your essay on nutrition. Do not choose too broad or general a title. For example, "Nutrition" or "Good Eating Habits" is too broad for the narrow topic of crash-diets. Make sure to convey the stated purpose of your essay in the title. The titles "Crash-Diets: Friend or Foe?" and "You Are What You Eat" may be appropriate for the expository essay discussed in preceding sections.

14

ARGUMENTATION AND LOGIC

14 Argumentation and Logic

Argumentation is a process by which you present support for a particular proposition.

The support takes the form of evidence or reasoning. A **proposition** is the thought, idea, or point of view that you want others to accept.

Almost every day you are faced with opportunities to argue a point on one topic or another. Whenever you try to convince someone that your proposition is correct, you engage in argumentation.

Logic refers to the clear and organized thinking that guides you to a reasonable conclusion. Correct and effective argumentation demands that language be used logically in support of a proposition. This section will explain the process of logical argumentation, focusing on two powerful tools: inductive reasoning and deductive reasoning.

INDUCTIVE REASONING

14.a DEFINITION OF INDUCTIVE REASONING

In **inductive reasoning** you gather a sample from a specific population and then use the sample to arrive at a conclusion about the population at large.

When you see a number of dogs with tails and conclude that all dogs have tails, you have used inductive reasoning. To understand how this process works, it will be helpful to examine the three basic concepts just mentioned in defining inductive reasoning — population, sample, and conclusion.

Population

Population refers to the whole class of events, objects, people, and so on, about which you are going to draw a conclusion. Populations can be just about anything at all: all the apricots in New Jersey, French-speaking individuals, walnuts, dwellings in Africa, ginkgo trees, or teen-agers. However, once you have defined your population, be sure to keep its borders firmly in mind. In each study your samples must be limited to the members or objects in the particular population that you have decided to investigate. If, for example, you have defined your population as Chicago stockbrokers and then included in your sample *London* stockbrokers, your process will be inaccurate, and your conclusion may be far off the mark.

Sample

The part of the population that you study or examine is called the **sample.** The sample can be as small as only one member or object from the entire population. Since the size of the sample that you use can dramatically affect the reliability of your conclusion, however, you should try to select as large a sample as possible.

If, after seeing one bird fly, you were to conclude that all birds fly, you would come to a false conclusion. One sample from the bird population is not sufficient. The likelihood of coming across a nonflying bird — like a penguin or an ostrich, for example — increases in direct proportion to the number of birds that you observe.

It is true that you could observe ten thousand birds and never come across one that does not fly. A large sample does not guarantee an accurate conclusion. Still, the larger the number sampled, the greater the probability of guessing correctly. Since inductive reasoning is really a sophisticated form of guessing, you want to give the process as much validity as possible. Do so by taking as large a sample as you can, thereby increasing the probability that your conclusion is correct.

Stating a conclusion

The statement that you make about the population that you have studied based upon your observation of the sample from that population is called the **conclusion** (or **generalization**). In the course of an argument, a well-researched and thoughtful conclusion may prove to be invaluable in support of a proposition.

EXERCISE 1. Read this selection and answer the questions.

Carmen, Sharon, and Theresa are taking their first trip from New York to Paris. Upon arriving in Paris, they hail a cab for the ride to their hotel. The driver charges them 65 francs for this ride. After dropping their bags off, Carmen, Sharon, and Theresa walk to the American Express office. The representative there, whose statements are reliable, says, "Your cab driver must have driven you all over the city. That ride should only have cost you 20 francs." Upon hearing this, the three visitors open their notebooks and record their conclusions as follows.

CARMEN: In Paris, the people are crooks.
SHARON: In Paris, the cab drivers are crooks.
THERESA: In Paris, some cab drivers are crooks.

1. Each of the three conclusions is the result of inductive reasoning. Name the particular population of Parisians to which each conclusion refers.
2. Which of these three conclusions would seem closest to the truth to the American Express representative?

EXERCISE 2. Each of the following numbered items represents a theoretical sample from an unstated population. For each item, name a possible population and one conclusion that you might draw about the population from the sample given. NOTE: Choose the smallest population in completing this exercise. (For the example below, the population *animals* or even *domesticated mammals* is too broad.) Remember that your conclusion need not be *correct*. It is a possible conclusion based upon the limited sample provided.

EXAMPLE Sample—a Dalmatian chewing a bone, a terrier chewing a bone, a mongrel chewing a bone

ANSWER Population—dogs
Conclusion—Dogs chew bones.

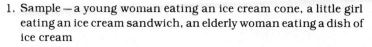

1. Sample—a young woman eating an ice cream cone, a little girl eating an ice cream sandwich, an elderly woman eating a dish of ice cream
2. Sample—an apple tree, a pear tree, an orange tree, a peach tree, all laden with fruit
3. Sample—a toothbrush, a hair brush, a shoe brush, a clothes brush
4. Sample—a pair of sneakers, a pair of oxfords, a pair of laced boots
5. Sample—a large church, a large temple, a large mosque

14.b THE INDUCTIVE LEAP

An **inductive leap** is the jump that you make from an observation about the sample to a conclusion about the whole population.

The inductive leap is a necessary component in inductive reasoning. You can get into trouble, however, if you try to jump too far on too little information.

EXERCISE 3. State five conclusions and give three facts that may have led to each. Be sure that your facts come from an observation of the samples and are not simply statements of opinion.

14.c THE OVERGENERALIZATION

An **overgeneralization** is an inductive leap from an observation about a small sample to an incorrect conclusion about the whole population.

The conclusion is incorrect because it applies to elements that you have not sampled. If you see ten birds fly and conclude that all birds fly, you are overgeneralizing.

Overgeneralization is a common danger in inductive reasoning, and examples of it abound in writing and in daily conversation: *Dogs chase cats; apples are red; nurses wear white dresses.* Overgeneralizations are untruths that seriously weaken our arguments.

14.d THE LANGUAGE OF CONCLUSIONS: LIMITERS

Limiters are qualifiers, or words and phrases that are used to restrict the scope of the conclusions.

Without limiters, some conclusions are so broad that they become unreliable overgeneralizations. If you state the conclusion that many people eat when they get depressed, you are expressing a probable relationship between eating and depression. When you say that something is probable, you suggest that it might be true according to the sample you have taken but that you cannot be sure enough to make an absolute statement. The limiter *many* can help keep your conclusion reliable. Notice the difference in the following:

People eat when they get depressed.
Many people eat when they get depressed.

You cannot be sure that all people eat when depressed. In fact, you can be fairly certain that this is not absolutely true.

Choose carefully the words that state your conclusion. Be sure that your conclusion thoroughly covers the observations that you have made and does not introduce unnecessary details. The language of your conclusion should provide a maximum amount of information and no misinformation.

There are a great many qualifying words or phrases that can be used to limit a conclusion so that it gives as much information and as little misinformation as possible. Words used as limiters of number and frequency increase the accuracy of conclusions. If you do not use them in your conclusions, you are making absolute statements concerning things about which you do not have absolute information.

EXAMPLES

as a rule
few
frequently
hardly ever
in most (many) cases
less than half of all
many
more than half of all
most
mostly
nearly all
nearly always
not all
occasionally
often
rarely
seldom
several
some
sometimes
usually

When expressing conclusions, remember that the truth of a conclusion is partially determined by the language used to express it. Since your readers do not know how you arrived at your conclusion, you should not misrepresent the sample of the population in wording your conclusion.

Carefully examine the following conclusion, and notice how the connotation of the word *destroys* affects the message of the conclusion: *Television destroys imagination.* In the context of this statement, *destroys* is a loaded word. Both the implication and the accuracy of the conclusion would change if, in the place of the word *destroys*, you were to use a word such as *dulls, inhibits, influences,* or *alters.* Also, the meaning of *imagination* is unclear in the context of the conclusion; the word can refer to a creative power, an intellectual capacity, or the ability to dream. Because of the broad meaning of *imagination* and the possible connotations of *destroys,* the entire conclusion may need limiters to prevent overgeneralization.

EXERCISE 4. Decide which limiting word or phrase can be added to each of the following conclusions. The conclusions are either based on limited observations or are intentionally distorted. Try to rewrite each statement so that it delivers as much information and as little misinformation as possible. Some sentences will use more than one limiter.

EXAMPLE Flowers smell sweet.
ANSWER Many flowers smell sweet.

1. Snakes are poisonous.
2. Dogs make better pets than fish.
3. Sports are competitive.
4. Dentists have bad teeth.
5. Men are better at hiding their emotions than women.
6. College graduates make more money than high school graduates.
7. Mexicans live in the United States.
8. People need haircuts.
9. Words read the same backward and forward.
10. Soloists play from memory.

EXERCISE 5. Which words in each of the following conclusions are likely to cause confusion? Read them carefully and then decide how each of the conclusions can be reworded to eliminate the confusion.

1. Men are stronger than women.
2. Alcohol kills.
3. Drugs corrupt.
4. War is useless.
5. Artists are temperamental.

14.e HASTY CONCLUSIONS

A **hasty conclusion** is a conclusion that does not hold up under the weight of subsequent additional sampling and that, therefore, is untrue.

You will come to a hasty conclusion if you jump to a conclusion about all the members or objects of a population *before* giving adequate consideration to enough samples from the population. You will also often be guilty of coming to a hasty conclusion if you make a statement based solely upon first impressions. Hasty conclusions are similar to overgeneralizations.

14.f STEREOTYPES

A **stereotype** is a conclusion that you arrive at if you are not careful in your use of inductive reasoning.

A stereotype is a kind of overgeneralization. Stereotypes are usually the result of accepting other people's opinions without a thorough examination of a large, representative sample. Suppose you wrote *New York City is dirty.* Such a stereotype would fail to do justice to the many New York City neighborhoods that are clean and attractive.

EXERCISE 6. There is no factual basis for each of the following stereotypes. Change each statement so that it no longer is a stereotype.

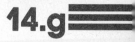

1. Rock musicians are talented.
2. Americans are happy.
3. Hockey players are rough.
4. Marines are insensitive.
5. Long-haired males are troublemakers.

DEDUCTIVE REASONING

14.g DEFINITION OF DEDUCTIVE REASONING

In **deductive reasoning** you start with a generalization, you state a related truth or fact, and then you arrive at a further conclusion about that truth.

The generalization that you start with in deductive reasoning *may* actually be a conclusion arrived at through inductive reasoning. You should see that inductive reasoning and deductive reasoning are opposites. The following diagram may help you to understand this relationship by illustrating both reasoning processes.

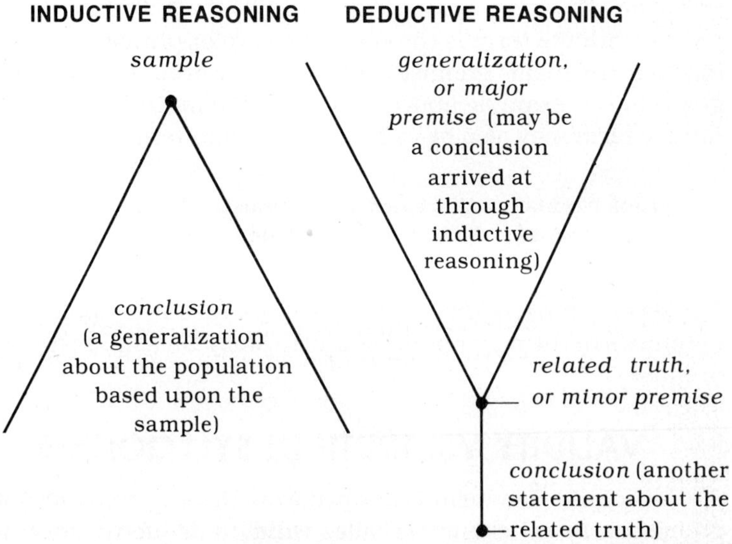

INDUCTIVE REASONING

sample

conclusion (a generalization about the population based upon the sample)

DEDUCTIVE REASONING

generalization, or major premise (may be a conclusion arrived at through inductive reasoning)

related truth, or minor premise

conclusion (another statement about the related truth)

You are using deductive reasoning when you (1) state the generalization *All women are mortal,* (2) state the related truth *Chris Evert Lloyd is a woman,* and (3) arrive at the conclusion *Therefore, Chris Evert Lloyd is mortal.* This example of deductive reasoning is stated in a form known as a syllogism.

14.h THE SYLLOGISM

A **syllogism** is a formal statement of a deductive argument.

A syllogism consists of three parts—a major premise, a minor premise, and a conclusion—and may be set up formally.

EXAMPLE

MAJOR PREMISE: All whales are mammals. [This is the generalization.]

MINOR PREMISE: Moby Dick is a whale. [That Moby Dick is one of the group "all whales" is a related truth.]

CONCLUSION: Therefore, Moby Dick is a mammal. [The conclusion *Moby Dick is a mammal* is deduced from the two premises.]

The **middle term** is the common word or phrase that ties together the major premise and the minor premise of a syllogism. In the example above, *whale* is the middle term. The middle term may also be called the common term.

MAJOR PREMISE: All **whales** are mammals.
MINOR PREMISE: Moby Dick is a **whale.**
CONCLUSION: Therefore, Moby Dick is a mammal.

The term *whale* is the middle term because it is applied to mammals in the major premise and to Moby Dick in the minor premise.

14.i VALIDITY VS. TRUTH IN SYLLOGISMS

If a logical conclusion is drawn from the major and minor premises, the conclusion is called **valid.** In deductive reasoning *validity* does not have the same meaning as *truth.* To call an argument valid is to indicate only that the reasoning method of the argument is correct. An argument may be valid even if the conclusion is not true.

EXAMPLE

MAJOR PREMISE: All whales are green.
MINOR PREMISE: Moby Dick is a whale.
CONCLUSION: Moby Dick is green.

The reasoning method in the above syllogism is correct, and therefore the conclusion is valid. The conclusion is not true, however, because it is based upon an untrue major premise. This example shows that the underlying premises of your argument must be true if you want your conclusion to be true.

EXERCISE 7. Each pair of statements below gives the major premise and the minor premise of a syllogism. For each pair first identify the middle (or common) term and then complete the syllogism with a conclusion that follows logically from the two premises.

EXAMPLE Major premise: Unjust laws should be revoked.
Minor premise: This is an unjust law.
ANSWER Middle term: unjust law(s) or law(s)
Conclusion: Therefore, this law should be revoked.

1. Gymnasts are athletes.
   Jane is a gymnast.
2. Honest persons should be rewarded.
   This person is honest.
3. Barbiturates are habit forming.
   This drug is a barbiturate.
4. A coleus plant needs water to grow.
   This is a coleus plant.
5. Birds that destroy insects should be protected.
   This bird destroys insects.

EXERCISE 8. This exercise will show you that *true* premises will lead to a conclusion that is both *valid* and *true*, whereas *untrue* premises lead to a conclusion that may be *valid* but that will be *untrue*. Each numbered item contains one major and one minor premise. Decide whether the major premise is *true*. Then identify the middle (or common) term. Finally draw the logically *valid* conclusion from the two premises, and indicate if that conclusion is true or untrue.

EXAMPLE All flying things have wings.
The helicopter is a flying thing.

ANSWER Major premise is untrue.
Middle (or common) term: flying thing(s)
Valid conclusion: The helicopter has wings. *(untrue)*

1. All birds can fly.
A penguin is a bird.
2. Every elephant has a trunk.
This animal is an elephant.
3. Every car has a steering wheel.
This is a car.
4. All light sources have a bulb.
The sun is a light source.
5. All monarchs are kings.
Queen Elizabeth is a monarch.

14.j THE MAJOR PREMISE: THE IF–THEN STATEMENT

The major premise of a syllogism can be phrased as an *if-then* statement.

EXAMPLES

MAJOR PREMISE: All bears have fur.
IF-THEN FORM: *If* something is a bear, *then* it has fur.

MAJOR PREMISE: Dictionaries contain definitions.
IF-THEN FORM: *If* something is a dictionary, *then* it contains definitions.

MAJOR PREMISE: Bone china breaks when dropped.
IF-THEN FORM: *If* something is bone china, *then* it will break when dropped.

MAJOR PREMISE: All wheels are round.
IF-THEN FORM: *If* something is a wheel, *then* it is round.

The *if-then* statement sets up a condition in its *if*-clause and then states the result in its *then*-clause. Converting a major premise to an *if-then* statement can help your reasoning.

EXERCISE 9. Change each of the following major premises into an *if-then* statement.

EXAMPLE All bears like honey.
ANSWER If something is a bear, then it likes honey.

1. All mammals use oxygen.
2. All copper pennies shine when polished.
3. All citizens can vote.
4. Everyone who officially runs in the marathon wears a number.
5. All bees can buzz.

14.k THE MINOR PREMISE

In order to arrive at a logically valid conclusion, the minor premise following the *if-then* statement (or major premise) can do only one of two things: It can either affirm the *if*-clause, or it can deny the *then*-clause.

Affirming the if-clause

Here are two examples of syllogisms in which the *if*-clause is affirmed. In this context, *to affirm* means "to fulfill the condition."

EXAMPLES

MAJOR PREMISE: If dinnerware is bone china, it breaks when dropped.
MINOR PREMISE: That cup is bone china.
CONCLUSION: That cup will break when dropped.

MAJOR PREMISE: If something is a bear, then it has fur.
MINOR PREMISE: This animal is a bear.
CONCLUSION: This animal has fur.

In each case above, the minor premise affirms the *if*-clause by saying that the condition has been fulfilled. Therefore, the result (or conclusion) must agree with the *then*-clause.

Denying the then-clause

Here are two examples of syllogisms in which the *then*-clause is denied. Here, *to deny* means "to reject the result."

EXAMPLES

MAJOR PREMISE: If something is a dictionary, then it contains definitions.
MINOR PREMISE: This book does not contain definitions.
CONCLUSION: This book is not a dictionary.

MAJOR PREMISE: If something is a wheel, then it is round.
MINOR PREMISE: This object is not round.
CONCLUSION: This object is not a wheel.

In each syllogism above, the minor premise denies the *then*-clause. Therefore, you must conclude that the condition set forth by the *if*-clause is not fulfilled.

EXERCISE 10. For each of the following major premises, construct a minor premise that affirms the *if*-clause. Then give the valid conclusion for the syllogism.

EXAMPLE If a car is an average car, then the car runs on gasoline.

ANSWER *Affirming the* if-*clause:* The Zebra is an average car.
Conclusion: The Zebra runs on gasoline.

1. If this is a circle, then it is round.
2. If this is ice cream, then you can eat it.
3. If a plant is a cactus, then the plant needs little water.
4. If something is a pencil, then it contains lead.

EXERCISE 11. For each of the following major premises, construct a minor premise that denies the *then*-clause. Then give the valid conclusion for the syllogism.

EXAMPLE If a car is an average car, then the car runs on gasoline.

ANSWER *Denying the* then-*clause:* The Gazelle does not run on gasoline.
Conclusion: The Gazelle is not an average car.

1. If it rains hard, then the river floods.
2. If you chop down the tree, then it will die.
3. If she wears strong boots, then her feet will stay dry in the puddles.
4. If something is a horse, then it has hooves.

14.1 FALLACIES IN SYLLOGISTIC ARGUMENTS

Fallacy is the term used to refer to faulty reasoning or a faulty premise.

The following fallacies can make a syllogistic (or deductive) argument invalid: (1) denying the *if*-clause, (2) affirming the *then*-clause, (3) using an ambiguous middle (or common) term, and (4) constructing a major premise.

Denying the if-clause

If you deny the *if*-clause, you arrive at a questionable conclusion.

EXAMPLE

MAJOR PREMISE: If something is a horse, then it has hooves.
MINOR PREMISE: This animal is not a horse.
CONCLUSION: Therefore, it does not have hooves.

This conclusion is nonsense. A goat is not a horse, but it has hooves—as do many other animals. If the minor premise states that the *if*-clause does not apply, the major premise becomes irrelevant and cannot be used for drawing a valid conclusion.

Affirming the then-clause

In the following examples, you will see that if you affirm the *then*-clause, you arrive at a conclusion that is either ridiculous or misleading.

EXAMPLES

MAJOR PREMISE: If something is human, then it is mortal.
MINOR PREMISE: My rattlesnake is mortal.
CONCLUSION: Therefore, my rattlesnake is human.

MAJOR PREMISE: If dinnerware is bone china, then it breaks when dropped.
MINOR PREMISE: This cup broke when it dropped.
CONCLUSION: Therefore, this cup was bone china.

The second of these syllogisms may sound less ridiculous than the first, but it is just as fallacious. The cup could have been made out of some other breakable material such as glass. A major premise states that a certain class of things or actions always has one particular feature or result. You must remember that other classes of things or actions may have the same feature or result.

The ambiguous middle term

The middle term (or common term) is the word or phrase that is common to the major and minor premises. The middle term is said to be **ambiguous** when it does not have the same meaning in both premises. An ambiguous middle term severely affects the validity of the conclusion.

EXAMPLES

MAJOR PREMISE: *Eggs* give a cake a delicious flavor.
MINOR PREMISE: This cake contains frogs' *eggs.*
CONCLUSION: Therefore, this cake will have a delicious flavor.
[Ambiguous middle term: eggs]

MAJOR PREMISE: *Beds* are the best place to sleep.
MINOR PREMISE: The ocean has a *bed.*
CONCLUSION: Therefore, the ocean is a good place to sleep.
[Ambiguous middle term: bed(s)]

In the first major premise *eggs* obviously refers to chickens' eggs, not the same product as the frogs' eggs of the minor premise. In the second syllogism the middle term *bed* has two entirely different meanings.

A fallacy from an ambiguous middle term may be less obvious than the examples above show. Advertisers sometimes use an ambiguous middle term in a more subtle way.

EXAMPLE

MAJOR PREMISE: *Experts* give you good advice.
MINOR PREMISE: Jack, here, is an *expert.*
CONCLUSION: Therefore, Jack gives you good advice on microwave ovens.

The above advertisement would follow legitimate reasoning and argumentation processes if Jack were an expert on microwave ovens. As it happens, Jack is a soccer star, or soccer expert. No matter how good he is at soccer, he is not thereby qualified to give advice on microwave ovens. You can see that the word *expert* does not mean the same thing in both premises.

The faulty major premise

A major premise is faulty when it is untrue. When you use a generalization as the major premise at the beginning of a syllogism (as the basis of your reasoning), you assume that the generalization is true. If the major premise is not entirely true, then the conclusion will be untrue.

Sometimes you may use a limiter with a generalization to make it true. You cannot, however, use a limited generalization *as a major premise* and come up with a reliable conclusion.

EXAMPLE

MAJOR PREMISE: Most birds can fly. [*Most* is a limiter.]
MINOR PREMISE: Penguins are birds.
FAULTY CONCLUSION: Therefore, penguins can fly.

EXERCISE 12. Identify the middle (or common) trm in each of the numbered syllogisms. Then show how it is ambiguous by stating what it means in the major premise and what it means in the minor premise.

1. Great art should be moving.
   Statues do not move.
   Therefore, statues are not great art.
2. Even major faults can be corrected.
   The San Andreas Fault is a major fault.
   Therefore, the San Andreas Fault can be corrected.
3. Antiques are worth a lot of money.
   This garbage can is an antique.
   Therefore, this garbage can is worth a lot of money.
4. If you have had a few drinks, you should not drive.
   You have had six cups of tea to drink.
   Therefore, you should not drive.
5. A gentle person would not hurt you.
   The doctor hurt you with the hypodermic needle.
   Therefore, the doctor is not a gentle person.

EXERCISE 13. State which of the following statements cannot be used as a major premise in a syllogism. Remember, a major premise must itself be true to be useful in an argument.

1. Politicians are dishonest.
2. Students do not like English.
3. Dinosaurs lived millions of years ago.
4. Watching television has replaced reading books.
5. Insects destroy crops.

EXERCISE 14. The following are sets of major and minor premises. For each set (a) decide whether the major premise is true; (b) if the major premise is true, decide whether the middle (or common) term is ambiguous; and (c) if the middle term is not ambiguous, state a valid conclusion you could draw based upon the premises. *Note:* If the major premise is false, or the middle term is ambiguous, do not complete the syllogism. Either condition will lead to a false conclusion.

1. If a film is sad, then some people will cry.
   People are not crying.
2. If the sun shines, then it will be very warm outside.
   It is not warm outside.
3. People who have committed a crime are in jail.
   Clarissa is not in jail.
4. Human beings have the ability to speak.
   Frederick does not speak to me.
5. Giraffes have long necks.
   This animal is a giraffe.

EXERCISE 15. Accept the major premise in each of the following syllogisms as true. Then decide whether each of the conclusions is valid. If you identify a conclusion as fallacious or illogical, indicate whether the error comes from denying the *if*-clause or from affirming the *then*-clause.

1. If she likes me, then she will call me.
   She doesn't like me.
   Therefore, she will not call me.
2. If the rain continues to fall, then the dam will burst.
   The rain continues to fall.
   Therefore, the dam will burst.

3. If red is green, then blue is yellow.
   Blue is yellow.
   Therefore, red is green.
4. If we win the game, then we will have a party.
   We did not win the game.
   Therefore, we will not have a party.
5. If it is a giraffe, then it will have eight neck bones.
   It has eight neck bones.
   Therefore, it is a giraffe.

14.m THE ENTHYMEME

The **enthymeme** is a shortened form of a syllogism.

With its three-step construction, the syllogism is too long for daily conversation and most writing. The enthymeme, on the other hand, suppresses (or holds back) the major premise and thereby condenses the syllogism. It is helpful to remember that the word *enthymeme* is derived from the Greek term that means "in the mind." In an enthymeme the major premise is understood, or is in the mind of the arguer, and only the minor premise and the conclusion are stated.

An enthymeme is the form that your arguments usually take. You should always be able to reconstruct a complete syllogism, however, to check the validity of your enthymeme.

EXAMPLE

Syllogism

MAJOR PREMISE: Whales are mammals.
MINOR PREMISE: Moby Dick is a whale.
CONCLUSION: Therefore, Moby Dick is a mammal.

Enthymeme

Moby Dick is a whale; therefore, Moby Dick is a mammal.

Enthymemes are not formal structures of logic and can be worded in various ways. The enthymeme *Moby Dick is a whale; therefore, Moby Dick is a mammal* is written as a compound sentence that has a conjunctive adverb as a tie between the two main clauses. The enthymeme can also be constructed with one of the sentence elements shown on the following page.

- *With an adverb clause:* Because Moby Dick is a whale, it is also a mammal.
- *With a prepositional phrase:* As a whale, Moby Dick is also a mammal.
- *With a participial phrase:* Being a whale, Moby Dick is also a mammal.
- *With an appositive:* Moby Dick, a whale, is a mammal.

When the premises are true and the reasoning is valid, then an enthymeme can be a very useful tool of argumentation. Consider the following, for instance: *She must be a good worker. She has excellent references from former employers.* Here, the suppressed major premise is *People who get good references are good workers.* This premise is a true enough generalization upon which to base a conclusion.

In argument, then, take the time to identify the suppressed major premise and determine whether or not it is true. If the suppressed major premise is untrue, the enthymeme will be untrue.

EXERCISE 16. Change the following syllogisms into enthymemes. In each case use a sentence structure that clearly presents the conclusion as a result of the conditions given.

EXAMPLE *Major premise:* Unjust laws should be revoked.
Minor premise: This is an unjust law.
Conclusion: Therefore, this law should be revoked.

ANSWER *Enthymeme:* This is an unjust law; therefore, it should be revoked.

1. *Major premise:* Clowns make people laugh.
Minor premise: Harry is a clown.
Conclusion: Therefore, Harry makes people laugh.
2. *Major premise:* Summers in the Midwest are hot.
Minor premise: Kansas is in the Midwest.
Conclusion: Therefore, summers in Kansas are hot.
3. *Major premise:* Hard and green apples are sour.
Minor premise: This apple is hard and green.
Conclusion: Therefore, this apple is sour.
4. *Major premise:* Chalk is brittle.
Minor premise: This is a piece of chalk.
Conclusion: Therefore, this piece is brittle.

5. *Major premise:* Spiders have eight legs.
   Minor premise: This insect has more than eight legs.
   Conclusion: Therefore, this insect is not a spider.

EXERCISE 17. Restate each of the following enthymemes using a different sentence structure.

EXAMPLE This animal is a giraffe; therefore, it has a long neck.

ANSWER This animal, a giraffe, has a long neck.

1. This animal is a cheetah; therefore, it has long legs.
2. The maple is a deciduous tree; therefore, its leaves will fall in the autumn.
3. Because this animal is a deer, it will shed its antlers.
4. Since he is a minor, Geraldo cannot vote in the election.
5. As a judge, Diane Schwartz was expected to remain impartial in the argument.

14.n ERRORS IN THE USE OF ENTHYMEMES

An enthymeme can have the same errors that a syllogism can: a faulty major premise, an ambiguous middle term, denying the *if*-clause, and affirming the *then*-clause. Since your writing will usually contain enthymemes rather than syllogisms, you must be on the lookout for hidden errors in reasoning.

For example, consider the following enthymeme: *Since you arrived late, I can only assume you missed the train.* The argument may sound reasonable, but the suppressed major premise is *If someone misses the train, that person arrives late.* The error in this enthymeme is that it affirms the *then*-part. True, the person arrived late, but the person may have been at the railroad station on time and may have caught the train. There are other reasons that could explain a person's failure to arrive on time—a delay on the way, for example.

Consider this enthymeme: *Since the story has two endings, I can only assume that this writer was indecisive.* This enthymeme is based on a suppressed major premise that is faulty. A "decisive" writer may purposely write more than one ending to a story.

EXERCISE 18. Write each of the following numbered enthymemes in the form of a complete syllogism. Identify the error in each argument.

EXAMPLE Because she gets the most rebounds, she is the best player.

ANSWER *Major premise:* The player who gets the most rebounds is the best player.
Minor premise: She gets the most rebounds.
Conclusion: Therefore, she is the best player.

This argument has a flawed major premise. A player who gets rebounds may be valuable, but the best player may be the one who scores the most points *or* takes the most foul shots *or* has the most playing time.

1. He must be a good student; he spends a lot of time in school.
2. I know what I am talking about; I saw the whole game.
3. Lots of people smoke; therefore, smoking must be all right.
4. Tracy must have won the contest; I see her standing by the trophy.
5. Vince did not send me a birthday card; therefore, he must not like me.

LIBRARIES AND INFORMATION

15 Libraries and Information

Today's libraries are hardly the musty, silent mazes of dusty volumes that some people imagine. They are busy storehouses of information, places where you can explore every aspect of the real world or rummage through the many imaginary worlds other people have created.

Libraries offer a wide variety of public services. Your neighborhood library may be among an increasing number that provide—in addition to general reading and research facilities—such special services as screenings of classic films, loans of records and paintings, day care for children, and recreational activities for senior citizens. Because of this diversity of services, modern libraries are sometimes called "learning resource centers."

Libraries have been changing and growing ever since they were first set up. Although historians disagree as to when and where they first appeared, no one denies that libraries are among the oldest human institutions.

15.a THE CARD CATALOGUE

The **card catalogue** is an alphabetical arrangement of individual file cards listing each of the books owned by a library.

To determine whether or not a library has the materials you need, look through the card catalogue. Usually the cards are kept in the drawers of special cabinets in the circulation or reference section. A few very large libraries have their card catalogue in the form of a series of paperback volumes, computer printouts, or microfiche.

BOOKS AND LIBRARIES: A TIME LINE

about 1230 B.C.	Hieroglyphic texts are collected in the library of Ramses II of Egypt.
about 700 B.C.	Administrative and commercial records are collected in Phoenicia and Babylonia.
about 500 B.C.	Libraries are established in China.
First century A.D.	The *codex* (the book form as we know it) is invented.
Early Middle Ages	The first monastic libraries in Europe are established.
about 770	Woodblock printing is used to print books in China and Japan.
Late Middle Ages	The first university libraries in Europe are established.
1450	Modern printing begins with the invention of movable type by Johann Gutenberg.
1638	The first university library in the United States is established at Harvard University; the first movable-type printing press in the United States is set up in Cambridge, Massachusetts.
1876	The first public library in the United States is established; the Dewey Decimal System of book classification is introduced.
1904	The Library of Congress System of book classification is introduced.
Today	More than 35,000 libraries exist in the United States and Canada.

If you cannot find the title of the book you need in your library's card catalogue, look in the *National Union Catalog* (usually found near the library's own card catalogue or in the reference section) to find out if the book is available at any other library in the United States. The *National Union Catalog* is a card catalogue printed as a series of books listing the holdings of the Library of Congress and four hundred other libraries in the United States. If another library has your book, you may be able to obtain it or copies of parts of it for a small fee through interlibrary loan.

The card catalogue contains three kinds of cards that give information about books. Examples of this information can be found on the *author card* and the *title card* (found in the Author/Title Index) and the *subject card* (found in the Subject Index).

Author (or editor) card

The main entry on this card is the author's or editor's name, last name first. That is, Gwendolyn Brooks would be entered as *Brooks, Gwendolyn*, and the card would be filed under *B*. If no author or editor is given credit in the book, the name of a place, institution, or corporation may be given instead; for instance, the U.S. Government Printing Office is listed as the "author" of such works as *A Short History of Benjamin Franklin* and *Simplified Spelling.* Some books have more than one author or editor, in which case there is usually a separate card for each person.

Cards for each book by an author will be filed together in alphabetical order according to the first important word of their titles (excluding *a*, *an*, and *the*). For example, the author card for F. Scott Fitzgerald's *The Last Tycoon* follows the card for *The Great Gatsby* but precedes the card for *Tender Is the Night.*

Title card

The main entry on this card is the title of the book, alphabetized by the first letter of the first important word (excluding *a*, *an*, and *the*). For example, Norman Mailer's novel *The Armies of the Night* would be listed under *A*, not *T*.

■ Subject card

The main entry on this card is the general topic of the book. In the Subject Index each general subject card is followed by a card for every book in the library dealing wholly or in part with the topic in question.

Author, Title, and Subject Cards for the Same Book

```
973.9
M4641
        Mead, Margaret, 1901-1978
             And keep your powder dry; an
        anthropologist looks at America.
        New York, Morrow, 1965.
        xxx, 340 pp. 21 cm
   Bibliography: pp. 333-340.
   1. National characteristics, American.
     I. Title.
```

Author Card (filed under *M*)

```
973.9
M4641
        And keep your powder dry; an
        anthropologist looks at America.
             Mead, Margaret, 1901-1978
        New York, Morrow, 1965
        xxx, 340 pp. 21 cm
   Bibliography: pp. 333-340.
   1. National characteristics, American.
```

Title Card (filed under *A*)

```
973.9
M4641   National characteristics, American.
             Mead, Margaret, 1901-1978
             And keep your powder dry; an
        anthropologist looks at America.
        New York, Morrow, 1965.
        xxx, 340 pp. 21 cm
   Bibliography: pp. 333-340.
   I. Title.
```

Subject Card (filed under *N*)

NOTE: Examples are taken from the card catalogue of Columbia University's Butler Library.

Catalogue card information

Catalogue cards offer information that you will find useful. The author card reproduced below provides an example:

Author Card

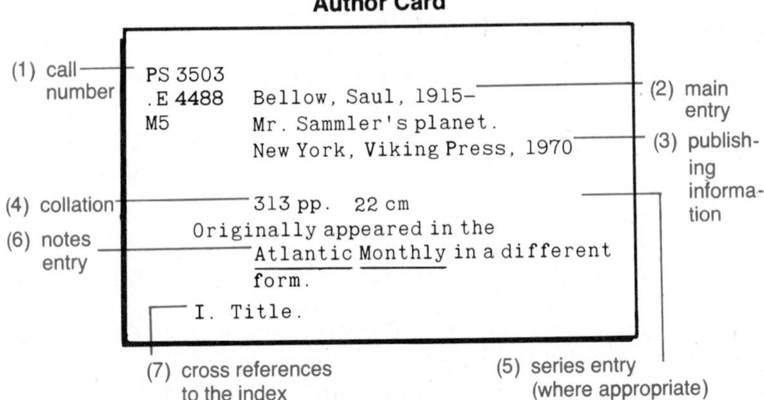

1. **Call number.** The **call number** is used to locate the book in the library. The number on the card corresponds to the number on the spine of the book. The call number, found in the upper left corner of the catalogue card, is based on the Dewey Decimal System, the Library of Congress System, or the library's own classification system. (The number on the sample catalogue card above is a Library of Congress call number.) If the book is a reference book, *Ref* will appear at the top of the call number.
2. **Main entry.** The **main entry** is the primary heading on a catalogue card.
3. **Publishing information.** This entry gives the location and name of the publisher and the date of publication.
4. **Collation.** The **collation** gives the number of pages (or the number of volumes) and the physical dimensions of the book. Sometimes it also indicates whether or not there are illustrations.
5. **Series entry.** If the book is part of a sequence of related publications, there is a series number in parentheses on the catalogue card.
6. **Notes entry.** The **notes entry** tells whether a book has any special features, such as a bibliography, and gives any special publication information.

7. **Cross references to the index.** Cross references to the Author-Title Index or to other subjects in the Subject Index are listed at the bottom of the card. The cross reference in the above example indicates that you will find a title card for the same book in the Author-Title Index.

Cross references

A ***see*** card simply tells you that the catalogue is using a different entry heading for the title, author, or subject that you are investigating. For example, if you look in the Subject Index of Columbia University's Butler Library for material on American Indians, you will find no titles listed. Instead, a *see* card filed under "American Indians" will direct you to look up (or "see") "Indians," "Indians of North America," or "Indians of South America." Likewise, if you look in the Author-Title Index for books by Mark Twain, a *see* card will direct you to look up "Samuel Langhorne Clemens," which is Mark Twain's real name.

See also cards direct you to material in addition to that filed under the heading that you look up. For instance, if you look under the subject entry "Women artists" in Columbia University's Butler Library, you may find several cards followed by a *see also* card directing you to more information under the subject headings "Women engravers," "Women painters," and "Women sculptors."

DECIDING WHICH BOOKS TO CONSULT

In looking through the Subject Index, you may come across a number of books dealing with a topic of interest to you. How do you decide which books will be the most useful to you? A good rule to follow is to find the most recent books, books with bibliographies (lists of other related books), and books with titles that sound broad and general. Once you locate these books, look through their tables of contents and indexes to determine whether or not they will indeed help you in your research.

15.b CLASSIFICATION OF BOOKS

Use the call number from the catalogue card to locate the book in the library.

Depending on the size of the library, the book that you are looking for may be right next to the card catalogue or on another floor of the building.

The two most common systems for classifying and arranging library materials are the Dewey Decimal and Library of Congress systems.

15.b.1 The Dewey Decimal System

The Dewey Decimal System organizes books by subject into ten very broad categories designated by three-digit numerals. Each category is then broken down into another ten subdivisions also designated by three-digit numerals. The general outline of the Dewey Decimal System follows (one of the sections, the six hundreds, is presented in detail).

OUTLINE OF THE DEWEY DECIMAL SYSTEM

000	General Works	600	Technology
100	Philosophy	610	Medicine
200	Religion	620	Engineering
300	Social Sciences	630	Agriculture
400	Language	640	Home Economics
500	Pure Sciences	650	Business Administration
600	Technology	660	Chemical Engineering
700	The Arts	670	Manufactures
800	Literature	680	Other Manufactures
900	Geography and History	690	Building Construction

Within each of the preceding categories, the use of decimals allows even greater refinement of classification—hence the name Dewey *Decimal* System. For example, in Columbia University's Butler Library 621.338 is the Dewey Decimal call number for the book *Telecommunications Reports.* The numerals after the decimal points for any given book may vary from library to library, but the general classification will remain the same.

Novels are not usually classified under the Dewey Decimal System (although some libraries do classify them in the eight hundreds). They are arranged alphabetically according to the last name of the author. To find the novel that you want, you can often go directly to the fiction section. (If you do not know the author of the novel, you will first have to look up the title of the book in the card catalogue.)

15.b.2 The Library of Congress System

The Library of Congress System classifies both fiction and nonfiction. Whereas letters of the alphabet occur rarely in Dewey Decimal call numbers,[1] letters are an essential part of the Library of Congress System.

OUTLINE OF LIBRARY OF CONGRESS SYSTEM

A	General Works, Polygraphy[2]
B	Philosophy–Religion
C	History–Auxiliary Sciences
D	History and Topography (except America)
E–F	America
G	Geography, Anthropology
H	Social Sciences
J	Political Science
K	Law
L	Education
M	Music
N	Fine Arts
P	Language and Literature
Q	Science
R	Medicine
S	Agriculture
T	Technology
U	Military Science
V	Naval Science
Z	Bibliography and Library Science

[1] Letters are used in the Dewey Decimal System when two books are on identical topics. The call number then includes the first letter of the author's last name.

[2] Polygraphy includes works too general to be classified under any particular subject—for instance, collections of essays in foreign languages.

Subdivisions of the broad-lettered categories are designated by using two letters; for example, *PQ* indicates Romance literature. Even greater refinement is achieved by adding numerals and more letters.

EXERCISE 1. Use the sample catalogue cards on page 677 to answer the following questions.

1. What is the Dewey Decimal call number of the book?
2. When was this edition of the book published?
3. How long is the bibliography?
4. Under what subject heading can the book be found?
5. Who wrote the book?

15.c REFERENCE MATERIALS

A reference section can range in size from a corner of a library to a huge collection housed in a separate building. The most frequently consulted reference materials are indexes to newspapers and periodicals, encyclopedias, almanacs, biographical reference books, and general language and literature reference books.

15.c.1 Indexes to newspapers and periodicals

An **index to a newspaper or periodical** lists, in alphabetical order, all the articles published in the issues under consideration.

If you want to find newspaper or periodical articles on a specific topic, you should look in the following indexes under an appropriate heading. In these indexes you will find a list of the newspapers or periodicals that have articles on your topic, complete with date, page number, and author information.

Essay and General Literature Index: an index to essays and collections in the humanities and the social sciences and to collections of literary criticism

General Science Index: an index to articles on astronomy, biology, botany, chemistry, physics, and zoology

Humanities Index: an index to articles that are published in scholarly journals; a useful source for tracking down scholarly or technical articles on such subjects as archaeology, art, folklore, history, literature, music, performing arts, philosophy, and religion

Social Sciences Index: an index to articles on anthropology, economics, law, political science, psychology, and sociology

New York Times Index: an index to all articles published in the *New York Times;* a useful source for tracking down articles on either current events or history

Readers' Guide to Periodical Literature: an index to articles published in 180 periodicals throughout the United States and Canada; a useful source for tracking down articles in general interest magazines, such as *Time* or *Scientific American;* not useful for locating articles in special-subject journals and quarterlies, such as the *Mark Twain Journal* or the *Texas Quarterly.*

The next page shows a sample column from the *Readers' Guide to Periodical Literature* and explanations of entry elements. Notice that most names of periodicals are abbreviated. Look in the front of the *Readers' Guide* for a list of the abbreviations used in the entries.

DECIDING WHICH ARTICLES TO CONSULT

In looking through indexes to newspapers and periodicals, you may come across a large number of articles dealing with your topic. How do you decide which articles will be the most useful to you? A good rule to follow is to find the most recent articles; articles with titles that sound broad and general; articles written by a recognized expert in the field (for example, Gloria Steinem writing on women's rights or Peter Bogdanovich writing on film techniques); and articles published in mature and responsible publications (such as *The New Republic, Harper's,* or *U.S. News and World Report).*

PHILADELPHIA

Hospitals

Climbing into the hospitals' bed: firing of D. Marston and the Hahnemann building program. E. Marshall. New Repub 178:12-14 F 11 '78

Music

Debuts & reappearances. il Hi Fi 28:MA30-1 F '78

See also

Opera—Pennsylvania

PHILBIN, Tom

Tips on installing foam-back carpeting. il Fam Handy 28:30+ Ja '78

—and Branson, Gary

Painting secrets from the pros. il Fam Handy 28:32-4 Ja '78

PHILIP II, King of Macedonia

Grave digging; discovery of Philip II's tomb. S. V. Roberts. New Leader 61:4 Ja 2 '78 *

PHILIPPINES

See also

Industry and state—Philippines

PHILIPPINO authors. See Authors, Filipino

PHILLIPS, Henry J. See Mullaney, J. jt auth

PHILLIPS, Thomas L.

Reluctant banker. por Forbes 121:71 Ja 23 '78 *

PHILOSOPHY

See also

Cosmology

Optimism

Political philosophy

Quotations, maxims, etc.

Feast of reason; Great treasury of Western thought. D. McDonald. Center Mag 11:56-9 Ja '78

PHIPS family

Phips coat of arms. H. K. Eilers. il Hobbies 82:150-1 F '78

PHOBOS (satellite) See Satellites

PHOENIX Resources Company. See Fuel industry

PHONOGRAPH

Pickup

New equipment reports:

Ortonfon's M-20FL Super: a sound that appeals. il Hi Fi 28:39-40 F '78

Testing

Julian Hirsch audio reports:

Garrard model GT25 automatic record player. J. Hirsch. il Pop Electr 13:27-9 F '78

Turntables

Turntable drive systems. J. Hirsch. il Pop Electr 13:21+ F '78

PHONOGRAPH record industry

Gems and curios from the International Piano Archives. H. Goldsmith. Hi Fi 28:82-3 F '78

Sire's Seymour Stein fathers American punk. C. Flippo. il por Roll Stone p25 Ja 26 '78

PHONOGRAPH records

Classical discs and tapes. il Stereo R 40:84-6+ Ja '78

Going on record. J. Goodfriend. il por Stereo R 40:60 Ja '78

People picks & pans. See issues of People

Recordings (cont) A. Goldman. Esquire 89:26+ F '78

Records (cont) D. Hamilton. Nation 226:62 Ja 21 '78

Records. A. Rich. N Y 11:66+ Ja 9; 91+ F 6 '78

Arias

Price meets Ariadne. M. A. Gurewitsch. il New Leader 61:26-7 Ja 16 '78

Awards, prizes, etc.

First chorus; down beat Student Recording Awards. C. Suber. Down Beat 45:6 Ja 12 '78

(a) subject heading

author heading (co-author)

(b) name of article

(c) *see also* reference

(d) author of article

(e) *see* reference

(f) subheading

(g) source of article (name of periodical, volume number, page numbers, month and year)

EXERCISE 2. Use the *Readers' Guide* excerpt on page 684 to answer the following questions.

1. Who wrote the article on phonograph records entitled "Going on Record"?
2. In what magazine will you find the article on T. L. Phillips?
3. To what other subject entry does the entry "Philippino authors" direct you?
4. What are the date and volume number of the *Nation* article entitled "Records"?
5. On what pages of the *New Leader* will you find an article under the subject entry "Phonograph records"?

EXERCISE 3. Use indexes to newspapers and periodicals to find the following information. You may use either the *Readers' Guide* or some of the more specialized indexes listed on pages 682 – 683 if they are available.

1. Find and give the publication information on three recent periodical articles on Chinese-American relations.
2. Find and give the publication information on three recent articles on food additives.
3. Find and give the publication information on three recent periodical articles on home computers.
4. Find and give the publication information on three recent articles on the actress Liv Ullmann.

15.c.2 Encyclopedias

Encyclopedias are alphabetically arranged collections of articles on almost every general topic.

Most encyclopedia entries are relatively brief; however, they can often direct you to more detailed information in other books. The following is an annotated list of the most frequently used encyclopedias.

Encyclopedia Britannica: by far the most sophisticated and comprehensive general encyclopedia; recent edition divided into three parts: the one-volume *Propaedia*, an outline of knowledge consisting of ten outlines of various broad topics, such as "Matter and Energy," "Human Life," "The Earth," and "The History of Mankind"; the nineteen-volume *Macropaedia*, in which individual topics are treated in full detail; and the ten-volume *Micropaedia*, in which short articles are arranged alphabetically and direct you to more detailed information in the *Macropaedia*

Encyclopedia Americana: thirty volumes of articles focusing primarily on American subjects

Collier's Encyclopedia: twenty-four-volume encyclopedia; detailed bibliography included in Volume 24

Merit Students Encyclopedia: twenty-volume encyclopedia for young adults

World Book Encyclopedia: twenty-two-volume encyclopedia for young adults; research guide included in Volume 22

Lincoln Library of Essential Information: two-volume desk encyclopedia, heavily illustrated, with bibliography

New Columbia Encyclopedia and ***Random House Encyclopedia***: one-volume desk encyclopedias

EXERCISE 4. Use one or more encyclopedias to find answers to the following questions.

1. Where was Irving Berlin born, and what is his real name?
2. What was Lillian Russell's profession, and what is her real name?
3. Who invented the bowie knife?
4. What are the names of Jupiter's twelve moons?
5. What are the modern names of each of the following: Abyssinia, Ceylon, Gold Coast, Persia, and Siam?

15.c.3 Almanacs

Almanacs are annual collections of information on history, vital statistics, and current events.

Use an almanac to look up such subjects as geography, population, weather, recent sports events, and famous people. In an almanac you will find lists of Nobel Prize winners, lists of noteworthy Americans, population and marital statistics, and capsule biographies of the Presidents.

EXERCISE 5. Use one or more almanacs to find answers to the following questions.

1. What language is spoken in the country of Qatar?
2. What was the population of Georgia in 1970? Of Wisconsin? Of New Jersey? Of Vermont? Of Oregon?
3. Who won the Pulitzer Prize for fiction in 1973? For what book did the author win the prize?
4. What director, leading actress, and film won Oscars in 1977?
5. Who won the women's singles competition in tennis at Wimbledon in 1959 and 1960?

15.c.4 Biographical references

Biographical references contain capsule biographies of noteworthy persons.

Following is an annotated list of the most comprehensive biographical reference books. Look in the *Biography Index* for listings of additional books and periodical articles that supply biographical information.

Current Biography: a monthly periodical containing biographical information on contemporary personalities

Dictionary of American Biography: contains capsule biographies of noteworthy deceased Americans

Dictionary of National Biography: contains capsule biographies of noteworthy deceased British subjects

New Century Cyclopedia of Names: contains biographies and illustrations of famous people, places, works of art, and monuments

Webster's Biographical Dictionary: contains capsule biographies of contemporary and historical personalities from all over the world

Who's Who books: With some exceptions, these books give basic biographical information about noteworthy *living* persons. Look in the *Who's Who* books to find information about such a person's parentage, place and date of birth, relations' names, occupations, awards, achievements, writings, club memberships, religious and political affiliations, and present address. These books include *Who's Who* (dealing mainly with British subjects); *Who's Who in America; Who Was Who in America* (dealing with deceased Americans); *International Who's Who; Who's Who of American Women;* etc.

EXERCISE 6. Use the biographical reference books cited in parentheses in each item below to help you answer the following questions.

1. In what state was Willa Cather born? Name three of her books. *(Dictionary of American Biography, Webster's Biographical Dictionary)*
2. What is the French author Colette's full name? Name two of her books. *(New Century Cyclopedia of Names, Webster's Biographical Dictionary)*
3. Who was Murasaki Shikibu? What did she write? *(New Century Cyclopedia of Names, Webster's Biographical Dictionary)*
4. Where was Betsy Ross born? What was her occupation? *(Dictionary of American Biography, Webster's Biographical Dictionary)*
5. For whom was the Taj Mahal built? *(New Century Cyclopedia of Names)*

15.c.5 General language and literature reference books

The following is a selected list of the most useful language and literature reference books.

LANGUAGE

American Usage: The Consensus, Roy H. Copperud
Dictionary of American-English Usage, Margaret Nicholson
Dictionary of Contemporary American Usage, Bergen Evans and Cornelia Evans
Roget's Thesaurus: provides lists of synonyms and sometimes antonyms
Webster's Dictionary of Synonyms

LITERATURE

Bulfinch's Mythology
Dictionary of Phrase and Fable, Brewer

Dictionary of Pseudonyms, Andrew Bauer

Reader's Encyclopedia, edited by William Rose Benét: The *Reader's Encyclopedia* is a compendium of biographical and descriptive information on authors, composers, painters, film directors, historical figures, literary genres and circles, literary symbols and allusions, and works of literature, art, and music. In the *Reader's Encyclopedia* you will find plot summaries of novels, poems, plays, operas, and films; descriptions of musical compositions and paintings; portraits of famous people; and personality sketches of characters in literature.

Reader's Guide to Literary Terms, Karl Beckson and Arthur Glanz

EXERCISE 7. Use the general language and literature reference books cited in parentheses in each item below to help you answer the following questions.

1. Find five synonyms for each of the following nouns: *start, end, attention, warfare,* and *vigor. (Roget's Thesaurus, Webster's Dictionary of Synonyms)*
2. What were Benjamin Franklin's pseudonyms? *(Dictionary of Pseudonyms)*
3. According to Greek mythology, what was the fate of Daphne? Of Europa? Of Philomela? *(Bulfinch's Mythology)*
4. In what book does the character Clarissa Dalloway appear? Who wrote the book? *(Reader's Encyclopedia)*
5. In what book does the character Miss Havisham appear? Who wrote the book? *(Reader's Encyclopedia)*

REVIEW EXERCISE. Use the entire range of reference books to answer the following questions. The kinds of reference books cited in parentheses will help you answer each question.

1. Find and give the publication information on three periodical articles on skiing. (indexes to periodicals)
2. What is the original name of the holiday Halloween? (encyclopedias)
3. Who won baseball's Most Valuable Player award in the National League in 1965? In the American League in 1965? (almanacs)
4. What is Elizabeth Bishop's occupation? (biographical reference books)

5. In which culture's mythology will you find the god Loki and the maidens called the Valkyries? (general language and literature books)

15.d OBTAINING LIBRARY MATERIALS

The card catalogue, indexes, and general reference books refer you to certain material that may help you in your research. You must then actually obtain the material to examine for yourself.

Circulating books (and other materials) are those that you may check out and take home from the library. By showing personal identification or a library card you may borrow fiction and nonfiction books, records, tapes, or any other circulating materials for periods usually ranging from seven days to a month. In university and special-subject libraries the loan period may vary from twenty-four hours to six months, depending upon the kind of material. If you keep the material past the due date, you will probably have to pay a fine.

Not all library materials circulate. Periodicals, microforms, reference books, and special-collection items are usually restricted to use within the library.

Circulating materials are usually checked out and returned at the circulation desk. If a book you want is off the shelves, ask a person at the circulation desk for help in locating it. Large, modern libraries often have data-retrieval terminals or computer printouts to tell you whether a book has been checked out, by whom it has been checked out, and when it is to be returned.

■ Using open and closed stacks

The shelf areas in which most circulating books and other materials are kept are called the **stacks**. Once you have a list of books and their call numbers, see if you can go to the stacks. The stacks are said to be *open* if patrons are allowed to enter them. The stacks are said to be *closed* if they are restricted to library staff. When the stacks are closed, you must ask a librarian to locate and obtain the books you need. Most public libraries and some college and university libraries have open stacks. Closed stacks are common in government libraries, special-subject libraries, and extremely large research libraries.

Obtaining newspapers and periodicals

Libraries store daily and weekly local newspapers, newspapers of national significance like the *New York Times* and the *Washington Post*, and foreign language newspapers. Current issues of newspapers are usually arranged alphabetically by their country or city of origin. Back issues of newspapers are usually placed on microforms (see below).

Current periodicals include recent issues usually no more than a few months old. Most libraries arrange the issues alphabetically by title on shelves or racks.

Past issues of periodicals are usually bound together in hardcover volumes containing six months' or a year's issues. Bound periodicals are usually shelved in a separate section of the library, arranged alphabetically or according to call numbers. Most likely you will not be able to check out either current or bound periodicals. If you need a copy of an article, you may be able to copy it on a photocopier.

Using microforms

Microforms are reduced photographic images of printed pages. Because of today's information explosion, no library can possibly store and keep track of all the books or periodicals published each year. Microforms make it possible to store a vast amount of material in a very small space. The most common microforms are microfilm and microfiche. **Microfilm** comes on reels and is made up of 35-millimeter strips of varying length, with two or four pages per frame. The film must be threaded onto a microfilm reader—a projector that restores the tiny images to their normal size and casts them on a lighted screen. A **microfiche** is a transparent plastic card, usually four by six inches in size. The cards hold from sixty to ninety-eight reduced images in horizontal rows. Like microfilm, the microfiche requires a special projector to magnify and illuminate it. The reading projectors are relatively simple, although you will probably need a demonstration before operating one on your own.

15.e PARTS OF A BOOK

Below is a chart on the various parts of a book in their usual order.

PARTS OF A BOOK

If you want to find:	*Look for the:*
(1) a photograph, painting, or drawing pertaining to the book's author, title, or subject	frontispiece
(2) information for footnotes or a bibliography (complete title, full name of the author or editor, edition number, name of the publisher, place of publication, date of publication)	title page, copyright page
(3) information for footnotes or a bibliography (date of copyright, name of copyright holder, book's number, Library of Congress Catalog Card Number, previous editions)	copyright page
(4) dedication epigraph (quotation at the beginning of the book)	dedication/epigraph page
(5) material explaining the nature, purpose, and scope of the book; a list of persons to whom the author is indebted	preface foreword introduction acknowledgments
(6) a list of the complete contents of the book and the page numbers where the contents are found	table of contents
(7) a list of the book's illustrations (maps, charts, diagrams, figures, or plates)	list of illustrations
(8) a list of any tables in the book	list of tables
(9) additional explanations and elaborations not essential to the text itself (diagrams, texts of documents and laws, charts and tables, long quotations)	appendix
(10) an alphabetical list of foreign, technical, or unfamiliar terms (with their definitions) used in the text	glossary
(11) a list of the sources used by the author; a list of additional readings suggested by the author	bibliography (may also follow each chapter)
(12) an alphabetical list of the subjects, names, and terms used in the book, given with all of the page numbers where they are found	index

16

THE RESEARCH PAPER

16 The Research Paper

The research paper is an informative essay of moderate length (usually 2,000–3,000 words, or 8–15 typed pages, or whatever length your teacher specifies) on a fairly narrow topic. It is easily identified by its use of scholarly footnotes and a bibliography, which call attention to the writer's research. To see what a research paper looks like, turn to pages 711–720 and 727–729.

In this section you will see how two research papers developed from ideas to final products. One paper is "Shakespearean Staging Techniques," and the other is "The Telephone in 1995." The first of these papers is based solely on print sources; the second uses firsthand personal interviews as well as supplementary print sources.

In planning a research paper, you should first organize your schedule so that you will have enough time to do a good job of researching. Next, you must select a specific topic. Then, with a stack of note cards and a formal outline in front of you, you can write a first draft, edit the draft, and prepare the final version of the paper. The steps involved in planning, researching, and writing are thoroughly outlined in sections 16.a. through 16.j.

Doing research is in some ways like taking a long trip across the country. It is an ambitious undertaking—a major expedition into parts unknown. You will surely get lost unless you take the time to plan a route and to estimate the time needed to move from your original idea to the finished product. As a general rule, assume that researching a topic for a ten-page paper will take you as long as a month, working evenings and weekends. Avoid the temptation to delay starting out until three days before the deadline.

16.a SELECTING A TOPIC

Selecting a topic for research requires considerable thought. Sometimes, of course, you are assigned a topic, but often you must find one for yourself. If the topic is too broad (such as "The Plays of William Shakespeare" or "The History of Communication"), it will take years to research. If it is too narrow (such as "Costumes for Lady Macbeth" or "The Symbols of the Morse Code"), you will search in vain for information that gives you anything new or interesting to say. To choose an engaging and manageable topic, think first of your own personal interests.

You might choose one particular interest and then try to relate it to a general topic from literature or contemporary society. For instance, combining a personal interest (animals) with an American writer you may have studied (Emily Dickinson) can result in a manageable topic: "The Function of Animals in Emily Dickinson's Poetry." Combining another personal interest (acting and directing) with a playwright you have probably studied (Shakespeare) can also result in a manageable topic: "Shakespearean Staging Techniques."

EXAMPLE

Elizabeth Dakelman, the writer of the research paper "Shakespearean Staging Techniques" (pages 711 – 720), had an excellent reason for researching Shakespeare's staging techniques. She had a personal interest in the theater and had acted in several high school plays, observing firsthand the difficulties of putting together a dramatic scene on stage. She explained her reasons to her teacher: "I thought it would be fascinating to see how William Shakespeare staged his plays and what kinds of materials he worked with."

16.b FINDING A BACKGROUND SOURCE

Having selected a possible topic, go to the library and locate one or two books or other sources that will give you a broad overview of your subject. Your goal now is to get an idea of the general dimensions of the subject before beginning the demanding task of taking detailed notes. You want to make sure that you are on the right track. Do not be surprised if you find that you have to adjust your topic somewhat. Researching is an ongoing process, and change is to be expected.

To locate a helpful book on your topic, check the Subject Index of the card catalogue (see 15.a). For a newspaper article look perhaps in *The New York Times Index* (see 15.c.1). For a periodical article look at appropriate headings in the *Readers' Guide to Periodical Literature* or in a special subject index related to your topic.

EXAMPLE

Elizabeth Dakelman went to the card catalogue searching for a general overview of her topic. The titles listed under the heading "SHAKESPEARE" were too numerous and bewildering. She therefore looked under the specific category "STAGING TECHNIQUES" and discovered that the library had three books on the subject, one specifically related to Shakespeare. She selected the book *Shakespeare and His Players* (which also contained a short bibliography) and spent several hours skimming the most pertinent chapters.

16.c PREPARING A WORKING OUTLINE

A **working outline** will guide you in your reading and note-taking.

After you have gained a general overview of your topic from a background source, put together a working outline. Write down four or five major topics that you wish to treat in your paper. Place them in a logical order. Each of your note cards should bear one of these topic headings (see 16.f).

EXAMPLE

After reading through *Shakespeare and His Players* Elizabeth Dakelman prepared a working outline that looked like this:

Shakespearean Staging Techniques

I. Scenery
II. Costumes
III. Entrances
IV. Stage Directions

Compare this working outline with Elizabeth Dakelman's final outline on pages 711 – 712 to see how she added to and rearranged her topics before writing her paper. See page 701 for an example of Dakelman's note cards that bear the topic headings from the working outline.

16.d FINDING ADDITIONAL SOURCES

Once you have reviewed your background source and prepared your working outline, you have to move on to additional source materials, which can be found in books, magazines, scholarly journals, newspapers, and the minds of experts. You will probably use both *primary sources* and *secondary sources* in your research paper. A primary source is an original work, such as a Shakespeare play, the letters and papers of Eleanor Roosevelt, or a personal interview. A secondary source is one that is written after the primary source and that deals with some aspect of the primary source. Examples of secondary sources are a book of critical essays on *Hamlet* or a biography of Eleanor Roosevelt.

It is your job as a researcher to locate the different sources that relate to your topic, to take detailed notes, and then to work from these notes, creating a paper that thoroughly explores the topic. Remember that you must research your topic completely and make yourself an expert. Become interested yourself; only then will you be able to interest your readers.

Compile a lengthy list of sources that seem to relate to your topic. Helpful lists of books and articles can be found in indexes, in books with bibliographies, and at the ends of encyclopedia articles. Write down the authors and titles of all works that might be helpful. Check the card catalogue in your library for all books and periodicals on your list. (See "Libraries and Information," pages 673 – 692, for more advice on getting your research project started in the library.)

EXAMPLE

Elizabeth Dakelman needed more materials. She examined a lengthy article on Shakespeare in the *Encyclopedia Britannica*, at the end of which was a list of sources. She wrote down the authors, titles, and publishing information for the books that seemed to bear most directly on her subject. She supplemented this list of books with a list of articles on Shakespeare's theater that she found in the *Essay and General Literature Index*, located in the reference section of the library. Dakelman looked through the stacks and in the periodicals section for the source materials. Eventually, she located five books and three scholarly articles that seemed appropriate — enough for the time being.

16.e PREPARING A WORKING BIBLIOGRAPHY

A **working bibliography** is a list of books and other source materials that you will consult.

After obtaining your sources — but before you begin serious reading — identify each one fully on a 3 x 5-inch index card. These cards, which form your working bibliography, contain the information that you will need later when writing your footnotes and final bibliography. Include the following information (from the title page and the copyright page) for each book:

- the full name of each author
- the complete title
- the name of the publisher
- the place of publication
- the date of publication

For either a magazine article or a newspaper article copy the following:

- the author of the article (if given)
- the title of the article
- the name of the newspaper or magazine
- the date of the issue
- the page numbers of the article

For an article in an encyclopedia, in addition to the article's page numbers, title, and author (if given), copy from the title page the volume number and the date of the edition of the encyclopedia.

It is essential that you use a separate card for each source. Be sure to number each card in the upper left-hand corner. This number will serve as a short identification of the source, so that you can save time later when you write up your note cards with information from each source.

EXAMPLE

Copying from the title page of her sources, Elizabeth Dakelman produced working bibliography cards like these:

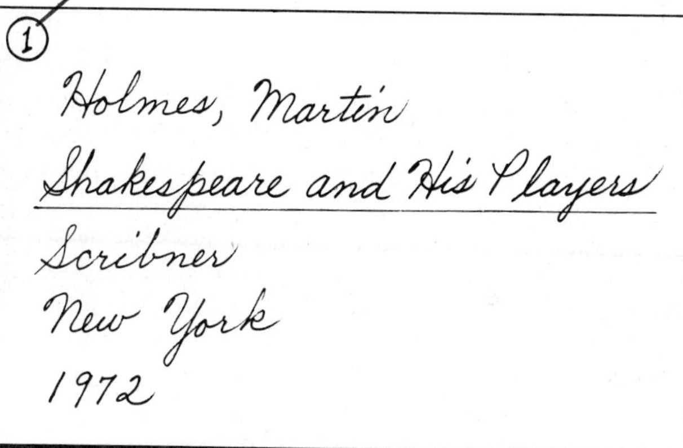

number to
identify this source
1
Holmes, Martin
Shakespeare and His Players
Scribner
New York
1972

number to
identify this source
2
Nicoll, Allardyce
"Theatre"
Collier's Encyclopedia
Vol. 22 p. 249
1969

16.f TAKING NOTES

After you have filled out your working bibliography cards, begin to read or scan the assembled materials. Scanning involves looking carefully for information that you can use in your paper.

As you discover a potentially useful idea or piece of information, write it down on a large-sized note card (4 x 6 inches). At the top of the card, write in a short heading taken from your working outline so that you will later be able to group together all of the note cards on the same topic.

In the midst of your thinking, searching, and discovering, you must remember to take notes carefully. It is easy to make a factual error if you are careless in taking notes. Also, you may make the worst error of all: plagiarizing (using someone else's words as if they were your own).

If you copy a sentence, phrase, or paragraph, make sure that all words and punctuation marks are copied *exactly* as written in the source. Copying word for word may *seem* easy, but, in fact, it requires great concentration and double-checking to avoid careless errors. Make sure to place quotation marks around the copied material. Otherwise, when you write your paper, you may forget that these words were originally written by someone else, and you may unintentionally plagiarize. Except when a direct quotation is particularly strong, it is much better to summarize or to restate ideas in your own words. Even if you use your own words, though, you must acknowledge that the *idea* was thought of by someone else.

One final touch is needed before putting down one note card and picking up another. On your note card indicate the number of the source (from the information on your working bibliography cards) and the exact page number on which the information or quotation that you plan to use appears. Then give the note card its own number in the upper right-hand corner.

EXAMPLE

While reading the article "Acting" in the 1969 edition of *Collier's Encyclopedia*, Elizabeth Dakelman produced many note cards including the one on the facing page.

number of source from working bibliography cards

aspect of the topic covered by note card

number of this note card

(3) Costumes 13

p.90 Even in Shakespeare's historical plays, actors were clothed in 17th-century costumes (the clothing of Shakespeare's day). For example, in Julius Caesar togas and ancient Roman dress were not worn.

page number on which information is found

summary of information in student's own words

16.g WRITING A FORMAL OUTLINE

A **formal outline** will guide you in writing your first draft.

After you have accumulated fifty to seventy-five cards, ask yourself the following questions:

- Have I gathered enough information to stop note-taking and to begin writing?
- Do I know enough about my subject?

If you think you have enough material, read over all of your notes and think about ways to arrange them in a logical order.

You will probably find that you have covered four or five major aspects of the general topic. The following steps are generally helpful:

1. Sort your note cards into piles, one pile for each major idea.
2. Remove from these piles three or four cards that, in your judgment, express particularly interesting ideas that might give strength and punch to the opening paragraph of your paper.

3. Remove and set aside those cards that are not at all helpful.
4. Finally, before sitting down to write, create a formal outline, following the form given on page 643. Key your numbered note cards to the outline.

EXAMPLE

See outline of the model Shakespeare research paper on pages 711–712.

16.h WRITING A FIRST DRAFT

Begin writing with your outline in front of you. Refer to your piles of note cards, but avoid copying from them unless you wish to copy a direct quotation. Each time that you use a note card, put its number right into the sentence so that you will know which ideas you took from which cards.

Write fairly rapidly, not pausing *at this point* to correct awkward phrasing. Nobody will read what you are writing now. It is only a rough attempt to put down the necessary information in the proper order. Keep moving from one part of the outline to the next. Write a concluding paragraph that ties together the major points in your paper. Then congratulate yourself, stand up, and walk away. Do not look back at what you have written for several hours or even a whole day. Allow sufficient time to review your writing later with a more critical eye.

16.i EDITING THE PAPER

Sit down and evaluate your first draft, page by page, line by line. Ask yourself the following questions:

1. Does my paper flow smoothly from one idea to the next?
2. Will a reader be able to follow my line of thought?
3. Have I made clear what I intend to cover in this paper, and do I indeed manage to cover these points or prove my case successfully?
4. Have I included enough specific examples and details?
5. Does my paper have a clear beginning, middle, and end?

If you are dissatisfied with your paper, try one or more of the following strategies:

1. Rewrite each problem paragraph until it flows clearly from one sentence to the next. (Review 11.d.)
2. Reword awkward sentences. Delete unnecessary words and eliminate monotony. (Review 3.h – 3.l.)
3. Insert smooth transitions between paragraphs. (Review 13.f.)
4. Shift the order of the sentences, if necessary.
5. Do not be afraid to cut out paragraphs that are not developed. Do not be afraid to cut the paper apart and rearrange sections.

After you have edited and revised your paper, you must credit with footnotes all direct quotations and ideas borrowed from other people. Place a raised number, or *superscript,* at the end of every sentence that contains either a direct quotation or a borrowed idea. Number the footnotes consecutively throughout the paper. See 16.k for instructions on the proper form for the footnotes and bibliography.

16.j THE FINAL FORM

After you have edited your paper, it is ready to be typed or rewritten in neat longhand. The footnotes and bibliography give a research paper a formal appearance and an authority that other kinds of essays lack. A research paper is very impressive if presented carefully, as follows:

1. Type (or neatly write) the title page, centering the title and your own name (see model Shakespeare paper, page 713).
2. When typing, leave a one-inch margin on all sides of the paper, and double space. Type (or neatly write) the body of the paper, inserting superscripts. (Note: Allow room at the bottom of a page for footnotes if your teacher advises you to place them there.)
3. Number each page in the top right corner, beginning with the first page of the paper (not the title page).
4. In typing the footnotes and bibliography, follow with great care the forms illustrated in 16.k. Single space foot-

notes and the bibliography, but leave a double space between individual items.

Proofread your paper at least twice. Make corrections (see Section 7, "Capitalization and Punctuation"). Then at last it is finished: a remarkable accomplishment.

16.k FOOTNOTES AND BIBLIOGRAPHIES

A **footnote** gives additional information, including source information, about a statement in your paper.

A **bibliography** lists all sources.

If you quote someone else's words *or* use someone else's ideas in your paper, you must cite the exact source in a footnote. The footnote serves two purposes: (1) to give the original thinkers and writers their due; (2) to direct your readers to the exact sources in case they want to do some research of their own.

Place a *superscript*, or raised numeral, at the *end* of a quotation or borrowed idea. This numeral refers the reader to a numbered footnote citing the source of the quotation or idea. The older style is to place footnotes at the bottom, or "foot," of each page. The modern style, recommended by the Modern Language Association, is to list footnotes on a separate page entitled "Notes" directly following the body of the paper. If you use one primary source consistently throughout your paper (such as a collection of Shakespeare's plays or a Faulkner novel), you have to cite the edition only once. Cite it in a footnote after the first quotation from that edition; the footnote should indicate that all following quotations will be from the same edition. In subsequent quotations from the edition, do not use a footnote, but indicate in parentheses the act, scene, and line numbers (for a play) or page numbers (for a novel or a short story). See page 716 for an example from the model Shakespeare paper.

A bibliography listing, which follows the Notes page, is an alphabetical arrangement by last name of author of all of the sources used in writing the paper. If the author of a source is not known, the first important word of the title figures in the alphabetical arrangement of the bibliography.

Footnotes and bibliographies include, in a specific and defined order, the author's name, the title of the work, the place of publication, and the date of publication. Different kinds of sources are cited in different ways. Footnote form is very different from bibliography form. Be alert to the differences. Carefully examine the Style Chart for Footnotes and the Style Chart for Bibliography on pages 706 – 709. First, study the categories of source material. Then, examine the differences in format between the footnote entry and the bibliography entry. The basic differences between footnotes and bibliographies follow:

1. **Indention.** In footnote format the first line is generally indented five spaces, and the second line (if any) is typed flush left. In bibliography format the indention is exactly the reverse—that is, the first line is typed flush left, and the second line is indented five spaces.

2. **Author's name.** In the footnotes the author's first name is written first; in the bibliography the author's last name is written first.

3. **Punctuation.** In the footnotes most of the information is set off by commas; in the bibliography most of the information is set off by periods. Also, parentheses are used in the footnotes but not in the bibliography.

4. **Page numbers.** Page numbers are always given in the footnotes but rarely given in the bibliography, with the exception of periodicals and collections of essays. A single page is abbreviated *p.;* two or more pages are abbreviated *pp.*

The Style Chart for Footnotes and the Style Chart for Bibliography show the corresponding footnote and bibliography entries for a variety of research sources. In all cases the citations in the charts and throughout this section follow the style recommended by the Modern Language Association in its *MLA Handbook for Writers of Research Papers, Theses, and Dissertations* (New York: MLA, 1977). For guidance on how to cite less common sources (unpublished manuscripts, films, musical compositions, etc.), consult this excellent handbook.

STYLE CHART FOR FOOTNOTES

• Book with one author

[1]Annie Dillard, *Holy the Firm* (New York: Harper & Row, 1977), p. 55.

• Book with more than one author

[2]Lynn Z. Bloom, Karen Coburn, and Joan Pearlman, *The New Assertive Woman* (New York: Dell, 1975), pp. 102–04. [NOTE: Use the name of the first author followed by the words *et al.* or *and others* if the book (or article) has more than three authors.]

• Multivolume work — same title for all volumes

[3]Paul M. Angle and Earl Schenck Miers, *Tragic Years, 1860–1865* (New York: Simon and Schuster, 1960), II, 42.

• Different titles for individual volumes

[4]Will Durant, *The Renaissance*, Vol. V of *The Story of Civilization* (New York: Simon and Schuster, 1953), pp. 222–24.

• Essay within a collection of pieces by different authors

[5]Katherine Anne Porter, "Notes on Writing," in *The Creative Process*, ed. Brewster Ghiselin (New York: New American Library, 1955), p. 125.

• Essay within a collection of pieces by the same author

[6]Malcolm Cowley, "Hemingway in Paris," in his *A Second Flowering: Works and Days of the Lost Generation* (New York: Viking, 1973) pp. 58–60.

• Edition of a work of literature

[7]Herman Melville*Moby Dick*, introd. Leon Howard (New York: Modern Library, 1950), p. 122.

• Translation of a work of literature

[8]Tacitus, *The Annals of Imperial Rome*, trans. Michael Grant (Baltimore: Penguin, 1959), p. 71. [NOTE: Even though the full name of the publisher is *Penguin Books*, a shortened form of the publisher's name may be used.]

STYLE CHART FOR BIBLIOGRAPHY

• Book with one author

Dillard, Annie. *Holy the Firm.* New York: Harper & Row. 1977.

• Book with more than one author

Bloom, Lynn Z., Karen Coburn, and Joan Pearlman. *The New Assertive Woman.* New York: Dell, 1975.

• Multivolume work — same title for all volumes

Angle, Paul M., and Earl Schenck Miers, *Tragic Years, 1860–1865.* New York: Simon and Schuster, 1960. Vol. II.

• Different titles for individual volumes

Durant, Will. *The Renaissance.* Vol. V of *The Story of Civilization.* New York: Simon and Schuster, 1953.

• Essay within a collection of pieces by different authors

Porter, Katherine Anne. "Notes on Writing." In *The Creative Process.* Ed. Brewster Ghiselin. New York: New American Library, 1955, pp. 120–29.

• Essay within a collection of pieces by the same author

Cowley, Malcolm. "Hemingway in Paris." In his *A Second Flowering: Works and Days of the Lost Generation.* New York: Viking, 1973, pp. 48 – 73.

• Edition of a work of literature

Melville, Herman. *Moby Dick.* Introd. Leon Howard, New York: Modern Library, 1950.

• Translation of a work of literature

Tacitus. *The Annals of Imperial Rome.* Trans. Michael Grant. Baltimore: Penguin, 1959.

(The Style Charts continue on the next two pages.)

• Article in an encyclopedia or other reference work

[9]Michael Kraus, "Roosevelt, Eleanor," *Collier's Encyclopedia*, 1952 ed.

[NOTE: Also cite the page number in the footnote if the citation refers to only one page of a multipage article.]

• Article from a weekly magazine

[10]Ada Louise Huxtable, "Mirrors of Our Time," *The New York Times Magazine*, 25 Feb. 1979, p. 22.

• Article from a monthly magazine

[11]Janet L. Hopson, "We May Follow Our Noses More Often Than Is Now Realized," *Smithsonian*, Mar. 1979, p. 78.

• Article from a daily newspaper

[12]"Consumer Prices Rocket Past Carter Projections," *Los Angeles Times*, 24 Feb. 1979, p. 1.

• Review of a film, book, or play

[13]Jack Kroll, "Woody's Big Apple," rev. of *Manhattan*, by Woody Allen, *Newsweek*, 30 Apr. 1979, pp. 78–81.

• Repeated reference or author

[14]Kroll, p. 80.

[NOTE: The older style is to use the Latin abbreviations *ibid.* (for a work cited immediately before) and *op. cit.* (for a work previously cited). The modern style of using the author's last name and the page number is now preferred. If there is more than one work by the same author, in repeated references use the author's last name, a shortened form of the title, and the page number.]

• Interview

[15]Personal interview with John Wright, Director of Planning, Independent Telephone, 22 Jan. 1979.

• Repeated reference (interview)

[16]Wright interview.

• Radio or television program

[17]"The Mind Machines," *Nova*, WNET, 25 Jan. 1979.

STYLE CHART FOR BIBLIOGRAPHY

• Article in an encyclopedia or other reference work

Kraus, Michael. "Roosevelt, Eleanor." *Collier's Encyclopedia.* 1952 ed.

• Article from a weekly magazine

Huxtable, Ada Louise. "Mirrors of Our Time." *The New York Times Magazine,* 25 Feb. 1979, pp. 22–30.

• Article from a monthly magazine

Hopson, Janet L. "We May Follow Our Noses More Often Than Is Now Realized." *Smithsonian,* Mar. 1979, pp. 78–85.

• Article from a daily newspaper

"Consumer Prices Rocket Past Carter Projections." *Los Angeles Times,* 24 Feb. 1979, p. 1.

• Review of a film, book, or play

Kroll, Jack. "Woody's Big Apple." Rev. of *Manhattan*, by Woody Allen. *Newsweek*, 30 Apr. 1979, pp. 78 – 81.

• Repeated author

________. "Altman's Apocalypse." Rev. of *Quintet* by Robert Altman. *Newsweek,* 12 Feb. 1979, p. 88.

[NOTE: References are not repeated in the bibliography. If a different work by the same author is included, however, use a straight line to represent the author's name.]

• Interview

Wright, John. Personal Interview. 22 Jan. 1979.

• Radio or television program

"The Mind Machines." *Nova.* WNET, 25 Jan. 1979.

EXERCISE 1. Assume that the five footnotes below are for a paper entitled "Edison's Phonograph and Its Impact on American Life, 1880–1920." Each citation contains several serious errors of form. Rewrite all five footnotes, making the necessary corrections.

[1]Gelatt, Roland. *The Fabulous Phonograph* (Houghton Mifflin, Boston, 1965) pp. 15–16

[2]*From Tin Foil to Stereo* by Oliver Read and Walter L. Welch published in 1959 by Columbia University Press (New York). pp. 122.

[3]Roland Gelatt (same source as above), page 132.

[4]*From Tin Foil to Stereo.* Pages 44–46

[5]*American Heritage,* July, 1961, "Music Machines, American Style" by Cynthia Hoover, p. 89.

EXERCISE 2. Devise a mock bibliography consisting of ten sources: five books, three magazine articles, and two newspaper articles. If possible, cite sources that you have on your bookshelves and magazine rack at home. Select sources that are at least thematically related—for example, sources on music or on sports. Make sure to list the ten sources in the correct alphabetical order.

SAMPLE RESEARCH PAPER (WRITTEN SOURCES)

The following pages contain the final outline and the partial text of Elizabeth Dakelman's research paper entitled "Shakespearean Staging Techniques." The paper uses only written sources. As a contrast, later on in the section, you will find the sources and partial text of a research paper that uses primarily oral sources in the form of interviews.

The portions of the paper covering parts I, II, IV-C., and V of the outline may be found on pages 714–719.

Portions of the paper itself have been omitted because of space considerations. These portions are indicated by ellipses.

OUTLINE

Shakespearean Staging Techniques

I. Special staging techniques because of limited stage facilities

II. Techniques used to indicate setting

   A. Scenery

      1. Lack of scenery on Elizabethan stage (note card 10)
      2. Dialogue indicating setting (note card 3)

   B. Costumes

      1. Contemporary costumes worn (note card 13)
      2. Customary costumes indicating setting
      3. Costumes emphasizing use of disguise
      4. Locale associated with character (note card 8)

   C. Stage directions

      1. Stage directions indicating setting (note card 1)
      2. Stage directions indicating change of scene (note card 2)

III. Techniques used to indicate passage of time

A. Progression of scenes (note card 16)

1. Quick passage of time

2. Slow passage of time

B. Simultaneous staging

C. Grouping (note card 6)

IV. Techniques used to indicate personality

A. Entrances

B. Different kinds of entrances (note card 17)

1. Mid-conversation entrance

2. Commanding entrance

3. Summoning entrance

4. Emotional entrance

5. Processional entrance

6. Soliloquy entrance

C. How entrances indicate personality (note card 18)

V. Shakespearean staging techniques useful to modern directors

title (not underlined)

Shakespearean Staging Techniques

by

Elizabeth Dakelman

author

course name Shakespeare

instructor Dr. George

date January 8, 1979

1

Those who read or attend Shakespeare's plays will better appreciate his scripts if they consider the practical problems that Elizabethan directors faced in staging a play. Playwrights had to work with limited stage facilities. To indicate setting, the passage of time, and a character's personality, they had to rely on dialogue, costuming, stage directions, and well-planned entrances. An understanding of how Shakespeare adapted his scripts to the limitations of the Elizabethan stage may also provide modern directors with additional ideas for staging.

The first paragraph directly states the focus and intent of the paper. Notice how the writer has avoided writing in the first person (using *I* and *we*) and thus has given a more objective and scholarly tone to her paper.

Theaters in Elizabethan England used very little scenery and mainly natural lighting. They were equipped with hangings of tapestry or painted cloth but no specific local background against which the actors played. Some stage furniture was used, such as stools, arbors, thrones, statues, and other small props that could easily be set up and taken away.[1] Many plays were performed in open-air theaters in the afternoon sunlight. There was no way to adjust the lighting on stage to suggest nighttime or a stormy setting. Therefore, dialogue had to indicate the setting.[2]

Descriptions in dialogue were the easiest and most effective way to let the audience know where the action was taking place. An excellent example of oral description is found in Lear's monologue in Act III of King Lear. Lear has been thrown out into the storm after being harshly scolded by his daughter Regan. His speech tells us where he is and what the weather is like.

> Blow, winds, and crack your cheeks. Rage, blow.
> You cataracts and hurricanoes, spout
> Till you have drenched our steeples, drowned the cocks.
> You sulph'rous and thought-executing fires,
> Vaunt-couriers of oak-cleaving thunderbolts,
> Singe my white head. And thou, all-shaking thunder,
> Strike flat the thick rotundity o'th' world;
> Crack Nature's moulds, all germains spill at once,
> That make ingrateful man.[3] (King Lear III.ii. 1–9)

Notice in the citation on the previous page that quotation marks are not needed for a quotation that is indented and set off from the rest of the paper. Notice, also, that the superscript placed after this quotation (which is the first time the source is cited) refers the reader to the edition being used. When referring to lines from Shakespeare, indicate in parentheses the play, act number, scene number, and line numbers as shown here.

It is obvious that Lear is in the midst of a raging storm. No dark gloomy scenery could better show his whereabouts. The audience may not actually see the storm that is being described, but—they see Lear experiencing the storm. A character's reactions are, of course, more important than scenery.[4]

Another example of how Shakespeare sets the scene in dialogue is in _Hamlet_, Act I. Note how the dialogue in the following two excerpts indicates the time, the place, and the weather condition.

Hamlet: Upon the platform, 'twixt eleven and twelve
I'll visit you. . . . (_Hamlet_ I.ii. 252–53)

Hamlet: The air bites shrewdly; it is very cold. . . .
Horatio: It is a nipping and an eager air.
Hamlet: What hour now?
Horatio: I think it lacks of twelve.
Marcellus: No, it is struck. (_Hamlet_ I.iv. 1–4)

Along with the use of dialogue to express time and place, Shakespeare made use of visual effects. The physical appearance of his characters was of great importance, and customs of the times often determined the sorts of costumes that the characters wore. Shakespeare's players always appeared in contemporary wigs and costumes. This practice was followed regardless of the play being presented. Even in a historical play, such as Julius Caesar, the characters were clothed in doublet and hose, rather than in the toga.[5]

According to descriptions of Venice in Shakespeare's time, it was the custom for a Venetian gentleman to appear in public gowned in black, keeping his finer clothes for wear at home. Senators and doctors wore scarlet gowns. These costumes were well known to the people of London and were important in the staging of Shakespeare's plays. The Merchant of Venice, for instance, contains many changes of scene between Venice and Belmont. Shakespeare used a simple but effective technique in this play to show his audience where the action was taking place. When Bassanio and his companions wore black gowns and little black hats, they were at home in Venice. When they later appeared in doublet and hose, it was clear that they were now in Belmont....

Shakespeare also made skillful use of stage directions to overcome the limitations of the sixteenth-century stage. For example, when Duncan arrives at Macbeth's castle in Act I, scene vii, of Macbeth, the directions indicate that "divers servants with dishes and service" should pass over the stage before Macbeth enters and delivers his soliloquy.[8] The sight of the head servant leading a small procession of less important servants across the stage gives the impression that an elaborate dinner is going on in the next room....

Entrances are of extreme importance because the manner in which characters enter tells a great deal about their personalities. If a character appears only when summoned, he or she is obviously less important than other characters. The processional entrance suggests a character of great importance —one powerful enough to deserve a following. In a solo entrance, which occurs just before a soliloquy, all of the audience's attention is focused upon one person. Thus, the character speaking is usually a main character or, perhaps, a minor character with information about one or more of the main characters. . . .

The concluding paragraph restates the major themes of the paper.

As the previous examples demonstrate, descriptions in dialogue, costumes, stage directions, and entrances all had very special meaning for Shakespeare's audiences. Thus, to understand Shakespeare's plays today, we must read both between the lines and beyond the lines, keeping in mind the special theater for which Shakespeare was writing. Shakespeare did not direct his plays haphazardly but, rather, used very definite techniques in staging. What Shakespeare can teach modern directors is that certain devices will focus the audience's attention on the setting, the action, the passage of time, and the personalities of the characters. A director should keep these devices in mind when considering how to create a powerful and believable production.

Notes

[1] Martin Holmes, Shakespeare and His Players (New York: Scribner, 1972), p. 112.

[2] Allardyce Nicoll, "Theatre," Collier's Encyclopedia, 1969 ed., p. 249

[3] Alfred Harbage, gen. ed., William Shakespeare: The Complete Works (Baltimore: Penguin, 1969). All subsequent references to the plays will be taken from this edition. Act, scene, and line references, enclosed in parentheses, will follow each quotation.

[4] Holmes, p. 113.

[5] Harold Clurman, "Acting," Collier's Encyclopedia, 1969 ed., p. 90.

[8] Holmes, p. 122.

Footnotes 6, 7, 9–16 are omitted because the corresponding parts of the paper are not shown.

Bibliography

Clurman, Harold. "Acting." Collier's Encyclopedia. 1969 ed.

Harbage, Alfred, gen. ed. William Shakespeare: The Complete Works. Baltimore: Penguin, 1969.

Holmes, Martin. Shakespeare and His Players. New York: Scribner, 1972.

Kernar, Alvin. "Place and Plot in Shakespeare." Yale Review, Oct. 1977, pp. 48–56.

Nicoll, Allardyce. "Theatre." Collier's Encyclopedia. 1969 ed.

Speaight, R. "Shakespeare on the Stage." Nation, 30 March 1974, pp. 405–06.

16.1 USING ORAL SOURCES IN RESEARCH

When you are writing about Shakespeare, books and scholarly articles are the most helpful sources. On the other hand, suppose that, instead of a literary or historical topic, you are curious to know about future changes in technology —for instance, the probable changes in the telephone between now and 1995. For such a topic, library research will still be helpful — but not conclusive. Changes in technology occur rapidly, and books on the subject are likely to be outdated almost as soon as they are published. Even current articles listed in the *Readers' Guide* may not tell you as much as a lengthy discussion with someone like an electronics engineer. When investigating a contemporary issue of any kind (pollution of a nearby lake, home computers, the future of the telephone), it is extremely helpful to conduct personal interviews with experts.

Arranging an interview

Arrange interviews with at least two people. It is risky to base a research paper on the opinions of a single expert. Like all human beings, experts have their limitations and biases as well as their particular knowledge on a particular subject. Most likely, one expert's views will differ in some respects from another's. Also, by the second interview, you will have become better informed and therefore more prepared to ask probing and pertinent questions. It does take courage to pick up a phone or write a letter to ask for an interview. Remember, however, that most people are flattered to be considered experts on a subject and will usually be eager to help you with your project. Make sure to identify yourself, the school you attend, and your reason for requesting the interview. Then allow the expert to suggest a convenient time and place for the interview.

EXAMPLE

Steven Lee chose to investigate the telephone as one aspect of a class project on the broad theme "The Way It Will Be in 1995." As part of his research, Lee interviewed an executive of a telephone company and a consultant to communications firms. He located these experts by checking with friends and family.

Preparing for an interview

Prepare for your interviews by obtaining background information on your topic. Find a book in the library that treats the subject in general terms. The information and ideas it contains may be slightly out of date, but you need to start somewhere. For more current information, consult the *Readers' Guide* and *The New York Times Index* and read at least three articles on your subject. Take notes on the book and articles. (See Section 15, "Libraries and Information," for advice on doing library research.) Then draw up a list of questions of a general nature that will help to guide the interview.

EXAMPLE

After doing several hours of research in the library, Steven Lee decided to base his interviews on the following questions:

- What changes have occurred in telephone technology over the past ten years?
- What changes are we likely to see in the next ten years?
- Can we be certain that these changes will indeed happen?
- What will be the effect of these changes on people's daily lives?

Conducting an interview

Bring to the interview a note book and (if possible) a tape recorder. Unless you know shorthand, a battery-operated cassette tape recorder is the only way you can hope to record the exact words used during the conversation. Ask permission to use the machine, which often makes people uncomfortable at first. After two or three minutes, though, you and the expert will both relax, forget the machine, and talk naturally. Do not rely on the tape recorder to do all of the work, however. Take thorough notes, as if the machine were not there. Note taking gives encouragement to the speaker, letting him or her know that you value what is being said. Also, the notes will help you locate on the tape the most useful parts of the interview. (Of course, if no tape recorder is available to you, you will have to rely entirely on your written notes.) Let your prepared questions guide you, but be prepared to take the interview in a different direction if the expert's answers suggest a new angle.

After the interview, ask for suggestions of printed materials (books, pamphlets, articles) on your topic. You may be given free brochures or photocopied documents.

Completing your research

After the interview, carefully review your notes. Reading your notes at home, you may find gaps or puzzling passages. If so, call the expert and ask for clarification. Never misquote or misrepresent the expert. Complete your research in the library by taking notes from the articles or books suggested by the expert or by going over your notes from your earlier reading. You may also find source material in other nonprint forms — for example, on a television program. When you are ready to write your paper, refer to sections 16.a – 16.j.

SAMPLE RESEARCH PAPER (WRITTEN AND ORAL SOURCES)

On the following pages you will find parts of the transcribed interviews and the partial text of Steven Lee's research paper entitled "The Telephone in 1995," which uses primarily oral sources.

You will see that information is presented in a random, almost haphazard manner in the interviews, The writer, however, found a way to make the information fit into a neat, logically organized pattern. You should also notice where quotations and ideas from the interviews are used in the paper.

FIRST INTERVIEW: LARRY ROTH, independent consultant to communications firms (January 21, 1979)

Be clear about who you are and what you want.

(1) **LEE:** What I want to talk to you about today, Mr. Roth, is aspects of the future. You know that I am a member of a team from my school that has studied different aspects of the future, and I've been assigned to talk to you about the telephone. To begin with, I'd just like to talk in general about how you think the average family is going to be affected by changes in the telephone in the next ten to fifteen years. What is going to be different about how telephones are used in the home?

(2) **ROTH:** Well, Steve, phones are changing rapidly today, and I think that, in ten years, if you walked into a home, you would

probably see many differences in the number of telephones, the way they are used, and the appearance of those phones. For example, we see today a profusion of decorator phones. There are many interesting variations on decorator phones: French, traditional, Mickey Mouse, Snoopy, and even Superman phones will make an appearance pretty soon. Beyond decorator phones, the manufacturers are working very hard to develop phones that offer real conveniences for consumers. For example, phones are being made that incorporate microprocessor technology, which enables the user to store up to thirty-five numbers in the phone itself. Then, when the user wants to retrieve and use a number, all it takes is the touch of one button. Phones are being made today that will redial at the touch of a button if the number that you reach either doesn't answer or is busy. The latest development is a phone that will redial a busy number every forty seconds. In addition to the kinds of phones that add decorative characteristics to the home and give many conveniences that weren't available before, we have to look at the whole area of answering machines and speaker phones and cordless phones. . . .

Make written notes as you go: perhaps "decorator phones" and "new technology."

(3) **LEE:** Do you want to discuss that now?

(4) **ROTH:** Yes . . . . An answering machine is a device that makes the phone more than a phone. It allows the user to take calls all day and all night.

(5) **LEE:** Can you find out what the messages were without being back at your phone machine?

(6) **ROTH:** . . . With the use of a small, hand-held transmitter that beeps tones into any phone anywhere in the world, you can actually call your own number, key the transmitter, and play back any messages from your remote location. In the future this particular capability will probably be extended so that you can change your outgoing message on the machine and then record messages for people calling . . .

Introduce a new topic.

(7) **LEE:** I read somewhere that something called the picture phone was on display back in, oh, 1930, and I've heard of attempts to introduce picture phones. Is this true?

(8) **ROTH:** I think what you're referring to is the picture phone trial tests conducted by AT&T a number of years ago for residential use. The trial was not successful, and the marketing of that service was discontinued. There are picture phone facilities used in business today that are quite expensive, however, and I believe that you have to go to a telephone company business office in order to use their facilities. You cannot bring them

directly into your office at this time. There is no home use now. I think that the day will come when we will see the return of the picture phone in some shape or form, and, of course, it will have to be offered on a cost-effective basis to make it an economical service for residential users . . .

(9) **LEE:** All this makes me wonder about other products and services that you can foresee.

(10) **ROTH:** Well, I think what you are alluding to is the development of things like electronic mail, electronic transfer of funds, and electronic or automated retailing. There are many, many services that will be developed and offered to both businesses and homes that are not available today. Rather than writing out our checks to pay all of our bills, we will be able to go either to our telephone or to a keyboard that is connected to a computer and put in all of the necessary coding for paying all of our bills and our checks. Our checks would be in the form of digitally coded pulses that we will activate and that will go out over the wire cable going from our house . . .

(11) **LEE:** How will we order merchandise?

(12) **ROTH:** Well, let's say you want to buy a new toaster. You will go to your telephone or keyboard after consulting some sort of a coding catalogue at home. Then you'll translate "toaster" into the system and obtain information, displayed on a cathode ray tube or your own television, that will show toasters from the ten local suppliers of toasters, listing their prices and availability so that you don't have to go to ten different stores. In addition to that, there will be a method whereby you can order a toaster directly through the home shopping system, and two or three days later it will be automatically delivered to your home . . .

(13) **LEE:** Mr. Roth, thank you very much for your time today.

Make sure that you express your thanks.

SECOND INTERVIEW: JOHN WRIGHT, a planning director with a large telephone company (January 22, 1979)

(1) **LEE:** . . . The general public thinks of the telephone as one thing and the computer as another, but these two are obviously coming together. Is it possible that the computer is going to be able to handle ordinary language, and that, therefore, you will pick up the phone and be able to use the computer without going through a keyboard?

(2) **WRIGHT:** They do currently have systems that enable you to converse with the computer as if it were a person. But these systems have a limited vocabulary.

They're up to about two thousand words, and it's hoped that in the future this capacity can be expanded. In fact, someone has plans for doing completely computerized operator assistance. You just spell the name, and the computer gives you back the phone number.

(3) **LEE:** Let's take one of the most important aspects of the world—medicine. In the future will we be able to pick up a phone and call a doctor to get medical information?

(4) **WRIGHT:** Well, of course we do that now when we communicate by telephone with doctors. Once you have a connection to a computer, you have a connection to a computer memory. Anything a computer can do, you can more or less have it do over the telephone. In particular, if it has some diagnostic library that can record symptoms and come up with a set of possible diagnoses, then you can get information by either sitting at the computer or communicating via high-speed telephone lines . . .

(5) **LEE:** Many of the things that we've talked about today hinge on the computer terminal. Now, would you give us some idea of what this means? How much would it cost to put such a thing in your home?

(6) **WRIGHT:** Although many things connected with computers have been decreasing rapidly, the home terminal might still cost something like $1,000. The terminal is very similar to an ordinary typewriter, and the computer system that you connect it to determines what you can type into it . . .

(7) **LEE:** Do you think the computer will help simplify in any way our complicated world, or make it more complicated?

(8) **WRIGHT:** The computer certainly has the potential to make things simpler . . . There has been a tendency to let things get more complicated, but maybe as it becomes more widely used, the computer will simplify life.

. . . .

(9) **LEE:** If I were a high school student in 1995 doing a research paper, how might the telephone help me to write my paper?

(10) **WRIGHT:** I have two comments on that. One is that students, I think, who are doing homework often call up a student in the same town and discuss it. The cost of telephone calls is becoming less and less dependent upon distance. If they go via satellite, it doesn't make much difference if it's to California or if it's ten miles away. So you may be able to discuss your school work with a friend very far away. The second point is that a telephone linked to a sophisticated computer will help with research. There are already systems, typically in colleges and currently very expensive, by which you can look up references and get resources that usually aren't found in small libraries. . . .

Portions of a research paper, "The Telephone in 1995" by Steven Lee, appear on the following pages. This excerpt covers only one part of Steven's paper: applications and effects of home telecommunications systems.

. . . In the field of medicine, for example, computers will serve as diagnostic libraries that store lists of symptoms and provide instant diagnoses.[11] A woman suffering from nausea and chest pains will dial or type her symptoms into a computer hooked up to her telephone and learn immediately from her home terminal whether or not the condition is serious. Medical specialists from all over the country will feed their knowledge into a central computer system that will, as a result, contain knowledge and experience more extensive than any one doctor's.[12] The new telecommunications system will even help in medical examinations. Doctor and patient will have a consultation while television lenses focus on the patient's body.[13]

The benefits of this vast electronic network will be great. The network will save time in making decisions. People from all parts of the country will have equal access to the most up-to-date information from renowned specialists. . . .

Neither will there be any reason in 1995 for people to leave home to go shopping. The new home telecommunications systems will make shopping a relaxing experience. Imagine, for example, that you want to buy a toaster (1995 model). All you have to do is to reach for the telephone (or keyboard) and a coding catalogue. According to the prediction of one expert:

> Then you'll . . . obtain information, displayed on a cathode ray tube or your own television, that will show toasters from the ten local suppliers of toasters, listing their prices and availability . . . you don't have to go to ten different stores.[14]

Note the ellipses (. . .) used in the above quotation. See Roth transcript, page 725, and observe the words that have been omitted. For advice on the use of ellipses, see 7.q.

If you want to review different store catalogues before deciding which model to buy, you will simply dial the appropriate catalogues and watch them flash on the screen—together with consumer information. In addition, as you place your order electronically, the cost of your purchase will be automatically deducted from your bank account.[15]

Notes (excerpt only)

[11] Personal interview with John Wright, Director of Planning, Independent Telephone Company, 22 Jan. 1979.

[12] "The Mind Machines," Nova, WNET, 25 Jan. 1979.

[13] James Martin, Future Developments in Telecommunications, 2nd ed. (Englewood Cliffs, N.J.: Prentice-Hall, 1977), p. 320.

[14] Personal interview with Larry Roth, Independent Consultant, 21 Jan. 1979.

[15] Martin, p. 324.

Bibliography

Bergland, G. D. "Looking Forward . . . ." Telco-Digest, Aug./Sept. 1978, pp. 35–44.

"Innovation Is Key to A.T.&T.'s Future." New York Times, 16 July 1979, p. D1.

Martin, James. Future Developments in Telecommunications. 2nd ed. Englewood Cliffs, N.J.: Prentice-Hall, 1977.

"The Mind Machines." Nova. WNET, 25 Jan. 1979.

Roth, Larry. Personal Interview. 21 Jan. 1979.

Strauss, Lawrence. "Telephone Comes of Age: A Retail Survival Kit." Consumer Electronics, Dec. 1978, pp. 44–87.

Waterford, Van. All About Telephones. Blue Ridge Summit, Pa.: TAB Books, 1978.

Wright, John. Personal Interview. 22 Jan. 1979.

16.m A RESEARCH PAPER CHECKLIST

After you have completed your paper, make a final check to see that it includes the following:

- a major idea carefully stated and well-supported with facts
- a clear and logical organization
- information drawn from many sources, not just one or two standard works
- ideas and direct quotations borrowed from a book, article, or other source properly credited in the footnotes
- a title page and bibliography, each of which follows a standard form

17

THE BUSINESS LETTER

17 The Business Letter

The purpose of a business letter is to give information or to get action in an efficient and courteous manner. Whenever possible, a business letter should be typed because a letter that is easy to read gets the quickest attention.

Every business letter follows certain conventions of format, style, and content. This section examines various kinds of letters in detail and includes a sample letter.

A business letter always has the following six parts:

- the heading
- the inside address
- the salutation
- the body
- the closing
- the signature

17.a THE HEADING

The heading is important because it is generally used as the return address and indicates when the letter was written. It is best not to use abbreviations; if you use any, however, use them consistently. Type the heading, single-spaced, to the right of the center of the page.

EXAMPLE

34 Oakwood Avenue
Benchville, Illinois 60106
January 27, 19—

If you are using stationery with a letterhead that gives your address, your heading will include the date only.

17.b THE INSIDE ADDRESS

The inside address identifies the person or organization to whom the letter is written. It is included to make sure that the letter reaches the right person even if it is separated from its envelope. Type the inside address flush with the left margin, and be sure that it is in the same form in which it will appear on the envelope.

■ Titles of respect

The person's full name is preceded by a title of respect. The titles *Mr., Ms., Mrs.,* and *Dr.* may be abbreviated, but other titles, such as *Professor* or *Rabbi,* should always be spelled out.

If a business title is used, it follows the person's name. It is generally typed next to the name, but if it is too long, it may be placed on a second line.

EXAMPLES

Ms. Carol Coles, President
Peress Productions
4025 Garfield Street
Metairie, Louisiana 70001

Mr. Robert H. Walzer
Assistant to the Dean
Fairfield Community College
Fairfield, California 93405

17.c THE SALUTATION

The salutation, or greeting, is placed two spaces below the inside address and flush with the left margin. It is generally followed by a colon.

The salutation will vary according to the person to whom you are writing, as is illustrated in the following examples.

1. When writing to a man whose name is known, generally use *Mr.*

   EXAMPLE
   A letter to:
   Mr. Charles Harris
   Salutation:
   Dear Mr. Harris:

2. When writing to a woman whose title is unknown, use *Ms.*

   EXAMPLE
   A letter to:
   Ms. Joyce Langley
   Salutation:
   Dear Ms. Langley:

3. When writing to a woman whose title is known, use *Ms.*, *Miss*, or *Mrs.* as she prefers.

   EXAMPLE
   A letter to:
   Miss Maria Velez
   Salutation:
   Dear Miss Velez:

4. It is also possible to address people by first and last names.

   EXAMPLE
   A letter to:
   Ms. Carol Bonasia
   Salutation:
   Dear Carol Bonasia:

5. When writing to a specific person whose name is unknown, generally use *Sir or Madam.*

   EXAMPLE
   A letter to:
   The Personnel Manager
   Salutation:
   Dear Sir or Madam:

6. When writing to a company, organization, or box number generally use *Sir or Madam.*

   EXAMPLE
   A letter to:
   The Wallace Corporation
   Salutation:
   Dear Sir or Madam:

For the correct salutations when writing to government officials, see below.

CORRECT WAYS OF ADDRESSING GOVERNMENT OFFICIALS

President of the United States

The President
The White House
Washington, D.C. 20500

Dear Mr. President:

United States Senator

The Honorable (full name)
The United States Senate
Washington, D.C. 20510

Dear Senator (surname):

United States Representative

The Honorable (full name)
House of Representatives
Washington, D.C. 20515

Dear Mr., Ms., Mrs., or Miss (surname):

Governor

The Honorable (full name)
Governor of (name of state)
City, State ZIP CODE

Dear Governor (surname):

17.d THE BODY OF THE LETTER

The body of the letter begins two spaces below the salutation. It should be single-spaced, with double spaces between paragraphs. The body of a business letter may be written in either block style or semiblock style. In a block-style letter the paragraphs are not indented. (See the sample of a semiblock letter on page 739.)

The body of the letter contains three parts:

- the beginning: makes clear your purpose for writing
- the middle: communicates your information
- the end: requests action or expresses appreciation

17.e THE CLOSING OF THE LETTER

Type the closing to the right of the center of the page, two spaces below the last line of the letter. Use a closing that is appropriate to the tone of your letter.

VERY FORMAL	Respectfully yours, Yours respectfully,	**LESS FORMAL**	Sincerely yours, Sincerely,
FORMAL	Very truly yours, Yours truly,	**PERSONAL**	Cordially yours, Cordially,

17.f THE SIGNATURE

The signature appears below the closing. It includes both the pen-written signature of the person writing the letter and that person's typed name and official position, if any. On handwritten business letters it is a good idea to print the name beneath the signature. The printed or typewritten name is necessary because the signature may be unclear.

Sincerely yours,

Flavia Barbosa

Flavia Barbosa
Senior Editor

Sincerely,

Trudy Radziewicz

(Miss) Trudy Radziewicz

Note that a woman may indicate how she wishes to be addressed by including *Ms.*, *Mrs.*, or *Miss* before her signature or, more frequently, in her typewritten name.

EXERCISE 1. Write the appropriate inside address, salutation, and closing for letters to the following parties. Using your home address, write a heading for the first letter only.

1. Dean of Admissions, University of California, Davis, California 95616
2. Personnel Department, Bloomingdale's, 1000 Third Avenue, New York, New York 10022
3. Someone with information about the Grand Canyon, The Sierra Club, 530 Bush Street, San Francisco, California 94108
4. Laura Ryan, The Holiday Lodge, P.O. Box #78, Block Island, Rhode Island 02807
5. The National Geographic Society, 17 Street NW, Washington, D.C. 20036
6. David Fein, Fein & Fein Insurance, Inc., 111 Kellogg Square, St. Paul, Minnesota 55101
7. The President, The White House, Washington, D.C. 20500

8. Mrs. Carolyn Strandberg, Vice-President of Production, Rodale Press, Inc., 33 E. Minor St., Emmaus, Pennsylvania 18409
9. A United State senator from your state, The United States Senate, Washington, D.C. 20501
10. Peter's Coffee, Tea, & Spices, 1391 West 33rd Street, Amarillo, Texas 79109

17.g THE ENVELOPE

The name and the address of the party to whom the letter is going are placed just below center and to the right on the envelope. In general, the return address goes in the upper left-hand corner of the envelope.

Always include the ZIP code with both addresses. The correct ZIP codes for local areas can be found in the telephone directory. If you need the ZIP code of an address outside your area, check the ZIP-code directory at the post office or library.

```
Ned Taylor
22 Ames Street
Hilton, Ohio 44748

                         Mr. Milton Rogers, Registrar
                         The New School
                         66 West 12th Street
                         New York, New York 10011
```

17.h KINDS OF BUSINESS LETTERS

Although there are many kinds of business letters that are used in a variety of situations, most people use the following few kinds for their personal needs: letters requesting information or services, letters of adjustment, letters of application, and letters to the editor. The following pages discuss the characteristics and requirements of each of these kinds of letters.

Letters requesting information or services

When you write a letter requesting information, you should do the following:

- Identify yourself.
- State a specific request.
- Explain your need for assistance.
- Tell why you have chosen your reader.
- Close courteously with a request for action.

Letters of adjustment

A letter of adjustment is written to register a complaint and to request that an error be corrected. It is a good idea to assume that your reader will want to remedy the situation. A positive tone will usually win more help than a negative one. When you write a letter of adjustment, be firm but fair and be sure to do the following:

- Explain the problem courteously.
- Give all necessary information.
- Assume that the problem will be solved.
- Request action.

Letters of application

A letter of application is frequently the first step toward getting a job or admittance to a school. If you hear of a job opening from a friend or read about one in the newspaper, it is appropriate to send a letter of application. Since the letter must create a favorable impression, pay careful attention to form, appearance, and correctness. In a letter of application you should do the following:

- Tell how you heard about the job.
- Explain your interest in the job.
- State your qualifications and experience.
- Summarize your education.
- Provide references.
- Request an interview.
- Specify where you can be reached.

A Letter of Application (*semiblock style*)

979 Scotland Road
Ann Arbor, Michigan 48104
March 12, 19—

Mr. James Emery, Director
Camp Merrimac
Woodberry, Michigan 47123

Dear Mr. Emery:

Bob Eastman, who is a counselor at Camp Merrimac, told me that you are looking for a counselor for the coming summer. I would like to be considered.

How he heard about the job

I am a senior at Lakeview High School in Ann Arbor and will be attending Michigan State College in the fall. For the past two summers I worked as a junior counselor at Camp Regis in Lake Hills. There I supervised crafts activities for six-year-olds and assisted the director of the sports program.

Qualifications and experience

At Lakeview High School I have been a member of both the dramatics club and the swimming team. I was president of my class in my junior year. I have maintained an overall B average.

Education

You may write or call the following people for references.

References

Mr. John Lieber, Director
Camp Regis
Lake Hills, Michigan 47125
(313) 721-2121

Ms. Stacy Morgan, Principal
Lakeview High School
Ann Arbor, Michigan 48104
(313) 662-6770

I will be happy to come for an interview. My phone number is (313) 247-9875. I hope to hear from you.

Interview request; Where he can be reached

Sincerely yours,

John Reilly
John Reilly

Letters to the editor

If you are writing to your local paper, examine the letters it prints to get an idea of the style and length that are favored by that paper. In general, though, follow these guidelines:

- Send your letter to one publication only.
- Choose a timely subject with reader appeal.
- Provide accurate factual information.
- State your points briefly and clearly.
- Include your full name and address. (Newspapers will, if requested, withhold names or print them as initials only.)

EXERCISE 2. The exercises below ask you to write letters of various kinds. Use your home address and today's date in each heading.

Request for information or service

1. Write to a college or university requesting a copy of its catalogue.
2. Write to your representative in Congress requesting his or her voting record on some recent legislation concerning public education.

Letters of adjustment

3. Assume that you subscribe to a monthly magazine and have not received your copy for the past two months. Write a letter asking for an adjustment on your bill and better service.
4. Your school board has decided to discontinue school plays for the year. As president of the drama club, write a letter requesting that the decision be changed.

Letters of application

5. The local swimming pool is hiring junior lifeguards for the summer. Write a letter applying for the job.
6. Select an advertisement in the local newspaper for a job for which you are qualified. Write a letter applying for the position.

Letters to the editor

7. Assume that your school has been receiving negative treatment from the local newspaper—for example, for vandalism, poor reading scores, or a bad football season. Select one such issue and write a letter to the editor requesting fair reporting.
8. Find a feature in the local newspaper that is of interest to you. Write a letter to the editor commenting on the issue.

18

TEST TAKING

18 Test Taking

This section explains how standardized tests are designed and how you can best prepare for them. Specifically, it discusses the following college-entrance examinations: the Scholastic Aptitude Test (SAT); the English Composition Test (ECT), one of the College Board Achievement Tests; and the American College Testing Program (ACT) Assessment test. The verbal (or language) portion of each of these exams is discussed in detail.

All examples and sample questions in this section are taken from previous standardized tests. Because you will practice reading the directions and answering the questions from actual tests, you will know what to expect when you take one of these standardized tests. The general advice in this section will also be helpful for licensing, certifying, and other career-oriented tests. The basic principles of test taking are the same whether you are trying to get into a school, become a real estate broker, or open an accounting office.

18.a STANDARDIZED TESTS

Most of the **standardized tests** you will take are of two kinds—aptitude tests and achievement tests. An **aptitude test** is designed to measure general abilities and knowledge. It is used to predict future performance in an activity that is broad in scope. For example, the Scholastic Aptitude Test

---

Sample questions in this section (except for ACT questions) are from *Taking the SAT: A Guide to the Scholastic Aptitude Test and the Test of Standard Written English* and *About the Achievement Tests.* Reprinted by permission of the College Board and of Educational Testing Service, copyright owner of the sample questions.

(SAT) predicts general future performance in college by measuring your ability to handle two systems of symbols — words (in the verbal section) and numbers (in the math sections). An **achievement test,** on the other hand, is designed to measure knowledge gained by studying a specific subject area. Two examples of achievement tests are the English Composition Test (ECT) and the College Board Achievement Test in Biology. Achievement tests tell more about how much you have learned than about your general ability to learn.

Most students are already familiar with some of the kinds of questions used in aptitude tests—for example, antonyms, analogies, and reading-comprehension questions. These are all multiple-choice questions. It is to your advantage, however, to understand how these and other questions work and what they really test.

Remember that standardized tests like the SAT, the ECT, or the ACT reveal nothing about your character, personality, motivation, or ambition. Your test scores tell only how you compare with other students in specific measures of certain intellectual skills and knowledge.

Strategies for standardized tests

1. Read the directions carefully for each section of the test. (Most tests are broken up into different sections, each with its own set of directions.) Then, before beginning, glance over the entire section so that you can see the number of questions and get an idea of their range of difficulty.

2. In multiple-choice questions be sure to read all the choices for a question before you decide on the best answer.

3. Pay very close attention to the way a question is worded and to each of the choices offered. Be aware of key words, such as *chiefly, only, most importantly, least, except,* and *not*. Often, recognizing these words in the question itself and in the answer choices can guide you to the right answer.

4. Skip any question on the SAT or a College Board Achievement Test (but not on the ACT) that you cannot answer

quickly. Be sure to skip the same numbered space on your answer sheet. If you have time later on, return to the questions skipped and give them further thought. On the ACT answer *every* question even if you have no idea of the correct answer.

5. Be sure that you know whether you will be penalized for guessing. On the SAT and the College Board Achievement Tests you are penalized for guessing; therefore, guess the answer only when you feel certain that at least two or three of the choices are wrong. If you can reduce the number of possible right answers to two or three, you have a better chance of choosing the correct answer. On the ACT, however, you are *not* penalized for guessing. It is therefore to your advantage to make even a wild guess at an answer.

6. Remember that you are not expected to answer all the questions correctly on an aptitude or an achievement test. Very few people can answer every question correctly. Rather, to obtain an average score, you generally must be able to answer slightly more than half of the questions correctly.

7. Try not to get nervous or flustered while taking the test. Relax. Most tests begin at 9:00 A.M. and last for two or three hours. It helps to get a good night's sleep and to eat a good breakfast before you begin.

What your test scores mean

Answer sheets for standardized multiple-choice tests are scored by machines. The number of right answers, the number of wrong answers, and the number of omits are added up. On the SAT and the College Board Achievement Tests, a "raw" score is calculated. This raw score is based on the number of right answers minus one fourth of the number of wrong answers. You are not penalized for the questions that you omitted. The reason for subtracting a fraction of the number of wrong answers from the number of right answers is to correct for guessing. On these tests, therefore, guess only if you can do so intelligently.

The *opposite* situation is true for the ACT. On the ACT no correction is made for guessing, and it is to your advantage to guess the answer to a question even when you have no idea what the question means. Some of your guesses are bound to be correct just by the laws of chance.

An important feature of these standardized tests is that the scores are converted to a common scale so that all students' scores can be compared. There are no passing or failing scores; there are only relative scores. On the SAT and the College Board Achievement Tests raw scores are converted to a scale that runs from 200 to 800. Such a broad scale provides a wide spread of scores and allows many distinctions to be made among scores. The average score on the verbal portion of the SAT is about 429. Scores on the ACT are reported on a scale that runs from 1 to 36. The average score is about 18. In addition, ACT, SAT, and College Board Achievement Test scores are also reported as percentile ranks. For example, if you have an SAT score of 450, your score report might show a percentile rank of 76 for the National High School Sample and a percentile rank of 58 for the College-Bound Senior Sample. These percentiles mean that you scored higher than 76 percent of the high school seniors who took the test and higher than 58 percent of those high school seniors who are applying to college.

Remember that your test scores are only one indicator of your accomplishments to date and of your probable success in college. Your high school grades and class rank are often more important than your test scores.

SCHOLASTIC APTITUDE TEST (SAT)

The verbal portion of the SAT contains four different kinds of questions: antonyms, analogies, sentence completions, and reading-comprehension passages. These kinds of questions correlate well with performance in college; that is, a relationship exists between how well you do on these test items and how well you will perform in college.

In addition, the SAT contains a thirty-minute Test of Standard Written English (TSWE). The TSWE contains some of the same kinds of questions found on the English Composition Test (see page 756)—that is, grammar and usage questions and sentence-correction questions (see 18.f and 18.g).

18.b ANTONYM QUESTIONS

The word *antonym* means "the opposite word." Antonym multiple-choice questions found on the SAT consist of a word in capital letters followed by five lettered words. You are to choose the *one* word that is the *most nearly opposite* in meaning to the given word.

Strategies for antonym questions

1. Read *all* of the choices given. Do not stop at the second or third choice just because it seems to be an antonym of the given word. One of the later choices may be a *better* antonym.

2. There are few words that have *exactly* opposite meanings. You are to find the word that is the *most nearly opposite* in meaning.

3. Try different ways of thinking about the given word. It may help to use the word in a sentence. Words in sentences often take their meaning from their use in the sentence; that is, their meaning depends upon whether they function as a noun, a verb, an adjective, or some other part of speech. In antonym questions the words stand alone. Using the given word in a brief imaginary sentence, first as a noun and then as a verb, may help you to determine the choice most nearly opposite in meaning.

Sample antonym questions

Try these sample antonym questions, and think about the explanations given after each one.

SAMPLE QUESTION A

CONCEAL: (A) examine (B) recognize
(C) expose (D) pronounce (E) arise

If you were working quickly, you might stop at Choice (B), thinking that *recognize* means "see" or "notice," and that something that can be seen is not *concealed.* If you read and think about all the choices, however, you will see that (C) is the best choice. *Conceal* means "hide," and *expose* means "reveal" or "show." Choice (C), *expose,* is more nearly opposite in meaning to *conceal* than Choice (B), *recognize.*

SAMPLE QUESTION B

PARTISAN: (A) commoner (B) neutral
(C) unifier (D) ascetic (E) pacifist

Since the noun *partisan* means "one who strongly supports one side in a fight," you might at first think that (E), *pacifist*, is the correct choice. A pacifist, after all, is one who believes in peace above all and would not fight on either side of a cause. "One who does not fight," however, is not directly opposite in meaning to "one who strongly supports one side." The adjective *neutral*, meaning "taking *no* sides," is the correct choice because it is most nearly opposite in meaning to the adjective *partisan*, meaning "strongly supportive of one side in a fight."

SAMPLE QUESTION C

ENIGMATIC: (A) exceptional (B) explicable
(C) exportable (D) expedient (E) exorbitant

This question illustrates that a wide general vocabulary is important on verbal tests. Unless you know something of the root meanings of words and are able to recognize prefixes (separable and inseparable) and suffixes, you will be forced to guess at or omit a number of questions. *Enigmatic* means "puzzling" or "obscure." *Explicable* means "able to be explained." The correct choice is (B), *explicable.* (See 4.i–4.l for a discussion of roots, prefixes, and suffixes.)

EXERCISE 1. Each question below consists of a word in capital letters, followed by five lettered words or phrases. Choose the lettered word or phrase that is most nearly *opposite* in meaning to the word in capital letters. Since some of the questions require you to distinguish fine shades of meaning, consider all the choices before deciding which is best.

1. ACCENTED: (A) unaccustomed (B) unstressed (C) infamous (D) invalid (E) irrelevant

2. HOARD: (A) misplace (B) miscalculate (C) spend freely (D) deal honestly (E) regard indifferently

3. CONGEAL: (A) lose (B) melt (C) confine (D) refresh (E) disappear

4. DISCREPANCY: (A) decision (B) attribute (C) restriction (D) clarification (E) concordance

5. LOUTISH: (A) dreamy (B) urbane (C) careful (D) courageous (E) impassive

18.c ANALOGY QUESTIONS

The word *analogy* refers to "a resemblance in certain aspects between things otherwise unlike." Analogy questions test your skill in identifying the relationship between a pair of words, understanding the basis of that relationship, and identifying the same or a similar relationship in another pair of words. Here is a simple example from the SAT.

RIVER : CREEK:: (A) street : alley
(B) hill : tunnel
(C) path : sidewalk
(D) hedge : fence
(E) island : peninsula

Read an analogy question in this manner: **River** *is to* **creek** *as* **street** *is to* **alley** . . . *as* **hill** *is to* **tunnel,** *etc.*

The first step is to figure out the relationship between the given pair of words, *river* and *creek*. Both are waterways, but a river is larger than a creek. Choice (A) is the correct answer because the relationship between *street* and *alley* is similar or parallel to the relationship between *river* and *creek*. A street and an alley are both roadways, but a street is larger than an alley. If you examine the other choices, you will see that none of them has the same kind of relationship to *river* and *creek* as does Choice (A).

Strategies for analogy questions

1. Think of the kind or quality of relationship that exists between the given pair of words—that is, large to small, small to large, action to doer, cause to effect, part to whole, worker to article made, class to species, etc.

2. Pay careful attention to the order of the words given in the analogy. In Choice (A) above, it is important that *street* is given first and *alley* second. *Street* is the larger of the two roadways, as *river* (also given first) is the larger of the two waterways.

3. Make up a sentence that expresses the relationship between the two given words. For the above example your imaginary sentence might be *A* **river** *is wider and longer than a* **creek.** Then insert the lettered choices in place of *river* and *creek*, and see which pair fits the best.

Sample analogy questions

Try these sample analogy questions, and study the discussion that follows each one.

SAMPLE QUESTION A

SONG : REPERTOIRE :: (A) score : melody
(B) palette : artist
(C) corn : garden
(D) benediction : church
(E) suit : wardrobe

The relationship between *song* and *repertoire* can be stated as follows: *Several songs make up a repertoire*. Of the choices, only (E) offers a relationship that is similar or parallel to the part-to-whole relationship of *song* and *repertoire*. Several songs make up a repertoire as several suits make up a wardrobe.

SAMPLE QUESTION B

FLURRY : BLIZZARD :: (A) trickle : deluge
(B) rapids : rock
(C) lightning : cloudburst
(D) spray : foam
(E) mountain : summit

A *flurry* is lighter and shorter than a *blizzard*. The relationship in this analogy is one of degree: light to heavy. Among the choices, this relationship appears only in Choice (A). A *trickle* of rain is lighter and shorter than a *deluge* of rain.

SAMPLE QUESTION C

EUPHONIC : LISTENER ::
(A) conspicuous : witness
(B) melodramatic : actor
(C) studious : pupil
(D) prosaic : reader
(E) savory : diner

The word *euphonic* is an adjective referring to a desirable quality that a *listener* appreciates. Choice (E) expresses the same kind of relationship. The word *savory* is an adjective referring to a desirable quality that a *diner* appreciates.

EXERCISE 2. Each question below consists of a related pair of words or phrases, followed by five lettered pairs of words or phrases. Select the lettered pair that *best* expresses a relationship similar to that in the original pair.

1. WHEEL : BALANCED ::
(A) guitar : tuned
(B) nail : rusted
(C) automobile : driven
(D) distance : measured
(E) piano : played

2. INVENTORY : SUPPLIES ::
(A) vocabulary : volumes
(B) vote : members
(C) outline : novel
(D) census : population
(E) catalogue : sales

3. SPATULA : ICING ::
(A) trowel : mortar
(B) knife : bread
(C) sieve : flour
(D) spoon : bowl
(E) straw : milk

4. IMPREGNABLE : AGGRESSION ::
   (A) imperfect : revision
   (B) invincible : defense
   (C) inequitable : criticism
   (D) indivisible : separation
   (E) immutable : preservation

5. BARREN : PRODUCTIVITY ::
   (A) torrid : warmth
   (B) innocuous : harm
   (C) aberrant : change
   (D) prodigal : reform
   (E) random : originality

18.d SENTENCE – COMPLETION QUESTIONS

A sentence-completion question consists of a sentence that is missing one or two words. You are to select the appropriate missing word or words from five choices offered.

Your understanding of the incomplete sentence will help you to fill in the blanks. There are key words within the sentence that control the possible words that can be substituted for the blanks. This kind of question is designed to test your ability to understand logical relationships and the interplay between word meanings and grammatical structures.

Strategies for sentence-completion questions

1. See if certain key words in the sentence control the meaning of the words that can be substituted for the blanks. These key words may be determiners, adjectives, or adverbs.
2. If there are two blanks in the sentence, try to understand how the missing words are related to each other. Are they similar in meaning? Are they opposite? Do they represent different stages of an event?

Sample sentence-completion question

Try the following sentence-completion question, and think carefully about the discussion that follows.

SAMPLE QUESTION

In the nineteenth century the relationship between the fields of mathematics and theoretical physics began to manifest itself in _____ developments rather than in direct _____.

(A) superfluous . . . theories
(B) parallel . . . interactions
(C) overlapping . . . interventions
(D) competitive . . . rivalries
(E) coordinated . . . communications

The key phrase in this sentence is *rather than*. This phrase implies that the two terms you will use to fill in the blanks will be somewhat opposite in meaning. The terms of (A), (C), (D), and (E) are not directly opposite in meaning and make no sense in the sentence. The correct choice is (B).

EXERCISE 3. Each sentence below has one or two blanks, indicating that something has been omitted. Beneath the sentence are five lettered words or sets of words. Make the choice that *best* fits the meaning of the sentence as a whole.

1. Engineers have long _____ that magnetic tape would _____ standard phonograph records, since it wears longer and is difficult to scratch.
   (A) predicted . . . replace
   (B) warned . . . destroy
   (C) admitted . . . ruin
   (D) lamented . . . surpass
   (E) charged . . . outsell
2. It is not enough for our rulers and administrators, who hold the world in their hands, to have no more than _____ intelligence; since they promise more, so they _____ more.
   (A) an unusual . . . arrange
   (B) a customary . . . organize
   (C) a remarkable . . . assure
   (D) an ordinary . . . owe
   (E) a modern . . . present
3. Art worth its name is never a _____ experience; it always _____ viewer and artist in some kind of active exchange.
   (A) foreseeable . . . excites
   (B) normal . . . steeps
   (C) forgettable . . . designates
   (D) passive . . . involves
   (E) fortuitous . . . employs

4. Immigrants to the United States are made to promise that they will refrain from subverting the Constitution, a precaution which seems to imply that the bomb-laden _____ will be _____ of telling a lie.
   (A) communist . . . confident
   (B) revolutionist . . . suspected
   (C) foreigner . . . relieved
   (D) anarchist . . . incapable
   (E) scientist . . . cognizant
5. The questions raised by our aspirations and wonderments, our creativeness, desires, and appetites, are _____, the answers relatively few.
   (A) legion
   (B) rhetorical
   (C) academic
   (D) inscrutable
   (E) bizarre

18.e READING-COMPREHENSION QUESTIONS

If you have learned to read well and enjoy reading, you will have little trouble with reading-comprehension questions. These multiple-choice questions are based on your understanding of a given passage. If you seldom read books, magazines, or newspapers, you cannot expect to find the reading passages on tests to be easy, but you can still do well on reading-comprehension tests if you keep in mind the following advice.

Strategies for reading-comprehension questions

1. Before you read the passage, skim through the questions at the end to get an idea of what you should look for—for example, the main idea, supporting facts, style, and tone.

2. In reading through the passage, concentrate carefully on *what* is being said and *how* it is being said.

3. Underline passages or points that you think are important.

There are four or five reading passages on the SAT, consisting of different kinds of prose and varying in length from 150 to 450 words. One passage may be from a novel or a short story. Another may be on a broad scientific topic, such as an explanation of some principle of chemistry or psychology. A third passage may be on a historical subject, such as the general causes of the Civil War. A fourth passage may be devoted to a logical argument in which the author states a point of view. One reason for the variety is so that no student will have an advantage over any other; another reason is that the reading matter on a test that measures scholastic aptitude should reflect the varied reading that students do in school.

There are four general kinds of questions asked about the passages. One kind tests your understanding of the *main idea* or central point of the passage. Some questions test your skill at identifying *supporting facts*. Others test your ability to *make inferences* (interpretations) using either inductive or deductive logic (see 14.a and 14.g). There are also questions that ask you to evaluate the *style* or the *tone* of the language that the author uses.

■ Sample reading-comprehension question

The following reading passage and questions are from a previous SAT exam and represent the kind of question that you will find on the exam. Read the passage carefully, and then study the questions and discussion that follow.

SAMPLE QUESTION

That Plato's *Republic* should have been admired, on its political side by decent people, is perhaps the most astonishing example of literary snobbery in all history.

Let us consider a few points in this totalitarian tract. The main purpose of education is to produce courage in battle. To this end, there is to be rigid censorship of the stories told by mothers and nurses to young children; there is to be no reading of Homer because that degraded versifier makes heroes lament and gods laugh; the drama is to be forbidden because it contains villains and women; music is to be only of certain kinds, which, in modern terms, would be military bands playing "My Country 'Tis of Thee" and "Stars and Stripes Forever."

Main Idea

1. The main point of the passage is to
   (A) cast contempt on the kind of music advocated in Plato's *Republic*
   (B) describe the content of Plato's *Republic*
   (C) discuss the positive and negative aspects of Plato's *Republic*
   (D) show how Plato's *Republic* influenced the lives of people at the time
   (E) criticize the political philosophy contained in Plato's *Republic*
2. Which of the following would be the most appropriate title for the passage?
   (A) The Perfection of Plato's *Republic*
   (B) Why Plato's *Republic* Has Been Censored
   (C) Plato's *Republic:* A Totalitarian Tract
   (D) The Heroes of Plato's *Republic*
   (E) Plato: The Moralist

Both of the above questions require that you understand the main point, which the author indicates in the first two sentences. In Question 1, the statement in (A) mentions one of the supporting points, not the main idea. Choice (B) mentions the content of the passage, but the main argument of the passage is much more negative than the statement in (B). Choice (C) is inaccurate because the author does not admit that the book has any positive aspect. Choice (D) makes a statement that is not supported in the passage. Only (E) adequately describes the main idea.

For Question 2, (C) is the answer.

Supporting Facts

3. According to the passage, which of the following are statements of Plato's beliefs?
   I. Drama should expose the weaknesses of villians.
   II. Only those parts of Homer dealing with the heroes and gods may be used.
   III. Stories told to children should be strongly censored.
   (A) I only
   (B) II only
   (C) III only
   (D) II and III only
   (E) I, II, and III

Statement I is inaccurate because no drama is permitted, and Statement II is inaccurate because no parts of Homer may be read. Only Statement III is accurate; the correct answer is (C).

Inference

4. The passage suggests that all of the following are forbidden in Plato's *Republic* EXCEPT
   (A) dance music
   (B) patriotic music
   (C) plays about villains
   (D) portrayals of the amusements of the gods
   (E) stories about poor people stealing to feed their families

Question 4 asks you to identify which of the choices is not forbidden in Plato's *Republic*. Since the author mentions only that songs played by military bands are permitted, the suggestion is that patriotic music is allowed. This is reinforced by the titles of the songs given as examples. The correct answer is (B).

Evaluation of Style and Tone

5. The author's attitude toward Plato's *Republic* is one of
   (A) quiet concern
   (B) cautious acceptance
   (C) reverent admiration
   (D) outraged disapproval
   (E) total indifference

Question 5 requires you to determine the author's attitude toward Plato's philosophy. A strong attitude of disapproval is evident in almost every sentence, but is most obvious in line 4 where the author refers to Plato's *Republic* as a "totalitarian tract." The correct answer is (D).

ENGLISH COMPOSITION TEST (ECT)

The English Composition Test (ECT) is one of the College Board Achievement Tests. It contains three different kinds of multiple-choice questions: grammar and usage questions, sentence-correction questions, and construction-shift questions.

Once a year this examination is administered with a twenty-minute essay question. This essay is used to predict each student's writing potential (see 18.j).

18.f GRAMMAR AND USAGE QUESTIONS

The kind of grammar and usage question that appears on the ECT does not require you to define a grammatical term such as *gerund* or *noun* or *predicate*. Nor does it test for spelling or punctuation knowledge. It tests only for your ability *to recognize errors* in grammar and usage in the sentence.

The error is either in one of four underlined parts of the given sentence, *or* the sentence may have no error. If the sentence has no error in any of the four underlined parts, mark your answer sheet (E). Many students mistakenly think that all of the sentences have errors; in fact, about one fifth of the sentences have no error.

Sample grammar and usage question

Try the following question, and study the discussion after it.

SAMPLE QUESTION

Every one of the city's newspapers have urged (A) its readers to vote (B) in (C) the special election to be held (D) on Tuesday. No error. (E)

The error lies in Choice(A).The verb does not agree with its subject in number. The subject of the verb phrase, the pronoun *one*, is third person *singular*. Hence, *Every one* **has urged** *its readers* would be correct (see 2.c).

Many students are confused by the noun *newspapers* coming just before the verb; they think that *newspapers* is the subject of the verb *have urged*. A closer look at the sentence reveals that *newspapers* is the object of the preposition *of* and therefore cannot be the subject of the sentence. Watch carefully for prepositional phrases that come between the subject of the sentence and its verb. Read the sentence without the prepositional phrase, and you will immediately see whether or not the subject and verb agree (see 2.c).

EXERCISE 4. The following sentences may contain problems in grammar and usage. Some sentences are correct. No sentence contains more than one error.

You will find that the error, if there is one, is underlined and lettered. Assume that all other elements of the sentence are correct and cannot be changed. In choosing answers, follow the requirements of standard written English.

If there is an error, select the *one underlined part* that must be changed in order to make the sentence correct.

1. A housing crisis developed (A) when (B) farm workers which were seeking (C) economic security came to the city looking for (D) jobs. No error. (E)

2. To have performed the trick so smoothly, (A) the dealer would have to know (B) the order (C) of the cards in advance. (D) No error. (E)

3. Rescue workers were severely hampered with (A) the freezing weather that gripped (B) the region even before (C) the flood waters had begun (D) to recede. No error. (E)

4. There are several places in Yellowstone National Park where (A) fish can be caught (B) in a freshwater pool and then (C) cooked in a hot spring close by. (D) No error. (E)

5. Few people outside of (A) botanists realize how indebted (B) North America is to (C) the Old World for (D) its cultivated vegetation. No error. (E)

18.g SENTENCE – CORRECTION QUESTIONS

Sentence-correction questions are designed to test your skill in using the most concise and logical syntactic structures in a given sentence. Sentence-correction questions differ from grammar and usage questions in that they also deal with faults of logic and structure.

A typical sentence-correction question contains an underlined element that may be wordy, awkwardly phrased, or illogical. You are to select from five choices a replacement for the underlined element that correctly completes the sentence. If there is no error in the original sentence, select the first choice; it always repeats the underlined element.

Sample sentence-correction question

Try the following question, and study the discussion.

SAMPLE QUESTION

Though a chronicle of actual events, the story of the survivors is an extraordinarily well-written book, it reads like an exciting tale told by a master storyteller.

(A) book, it reads
(B) book, and reading it
(C) book that reads
(D) book being that it reads
(E) book reading it being

The problem with this sentence is that it is a run-on sentence. In a run-on sentence a comma alone is used to separate two main clauses rather than a semicolon or a comma plus a coordinating conjunction (see "Avoiding Errors with Run-on Sentences," page 178). Choice (C) uses a relative pronoun *(that)* to subordinate the second idea to the first and to create a complex sentence out of the run-on sentence. Therefore, no commas are needed. See the list below for cross references that explain the choices.

(A) run-on sentence (see "Avoiding Errors with Run-on Sentences," page 178)
(B) faulty parallelism (see 3.k)
(C) correct
(D) incorrect use of *being that* (see Section 8)
(E) incorrect use of *being* (see Section 8)

EXERCISE 5. In each of the following sentences some part of the sentence or the entire sentence is underlined. The underlined part presents a problem in the appropriate use of language.

Beneath each sentence you will find five ways of rewriting the underlined part. The first of these repeats the original, but the other four are all different. If you think the original sentence is better than any of the suggested changes, you should choose Answer (A); otherwise you should select one of the other choices. Use your judgment and select the answer that seems best to you.

This is a test of correctness and effectiveness of expression. In choosing answers, follow the requirements of standard written English; that is, pay attention to acceptable usage in grammar, diction (choice of words), sentence construction, and punctuation. Choose the answer that produces the most effective sentence—clear and exact, without awkwardness or ambiguity.

Do not make a choice that changes the meaning of the original sentence.

1. It is still quite common in rural areas for a person to be born and then you spend your whole life in the same community.
   (A) then you spend your whole life
   (B) then they spend their whole lives
   (C) to spend their whole lifetimes
   (D) to spend his whole life
   (E) then he would spend his lifetime

2. Books like *Gulliver's Travels* and *Robinson Crusoe* were written for adults, but also becoming children's classics.
   (A) also becoming children's classics
   (B) a children's classic is what they have become too
   (C) since they have become children's classics
   (D) they have become children's classics
   (E) having become children's classics too

3. According to linguists, the Hopi language is unlike any other in that it does not have verb forms.
   (A) unlike any other
   (B) unlike any others
   (C) opposite to the others
   (D) opposite of the others
   (E) opposite of any other

4. To deal with the problems raised by the women's liberation movement, it demands basic changes in our assumptions about the organization of society.
   (A) it demands basic changes
   (B) basic changes are what it demands
   (C) there are basic changes demanded
   (D) people must make the basic changes
   (E) we must make basic changes

18.h CONSTRUCTION – SHIFT QUESTIONS

In a construction-shift question you must mentally rewrite a sentence according to instructions. You are told to substitute one expression for another in the sentence, making any other additional changes that are called for.

Sample construction-shift questions

Try the following question, and study the discussion.

SAMPLE QUESTION

Although Simon and Garfunkel began singing in 1957, they did not become famous until 1965, with their recording of "Sounds of Silence."

Insert *but* before *they*.

Your rewritten sentence will begin with which of the following?

(A) They began
(B) Beginning their singing
(C) Despite their beginning to sing
(D) That Simon and Garfunkel
(E) Simon and Garfunkel

When you insert *but* before *they*, the word *although* must be omitted if the meaning is to be retained. If you start the sentence with (A) you would have to delete the names of the two singers or else use a clumsy parenthetical expression. Choices (B), (C), and (D) create problems of repetitiveness and wordiness. Choice (E) is correct. The revised sentence reads as follows: *Simon and Garfunkel began singing in 1957, but they did not become famous until 1965, with their recording of "Sounds of Silence."* This revised sentence is compound in structure and retains the main idea of the original sentence.

EXERCISE 6. Revise each of the following sentences according to the directions that follow it. Rephrase the sentence mentally to save time. Although the directions may at times require you to change the relationship between parts of the sentence or to make slight changes in other ways, *make only those changes that the directions require.*

Below each sentence and its directions are listed words or phrases that may occur in your revised sentence. When you have thought out a good sentence, look in the Choices (*A*) through (*E*) for the word or entire phrase that is included in your revised sentence.

Of course, a number of different sentences can be obtained if the sentence is revised according to directions, and not all of these possiblities can be included in only five choices. If you think of a sentence that contains none of the words listed in the choices, rephrase the sentence again to include a word or phrase that *is* listed.

1. Poetry, like all the other arts, is to a very large degree a mode of imitation.
   Begin with Poetry and all the other arts.
   (A) has to be
   (B) have to be
   (C) has always been
   (D) are
   (E) is

2. A catalogue of all the species of plants and animals of a district represents its flora and fauna in the same way as a list of all the items of the general life of a people represents its culture.
   Begin with Just as.
   (A) like a list
   (B) so a list
   (C) therefore a list
   (D) in the same way a list
   (E) while a list

3. He was enthusiastic because of his recent success; therefore, he continued the project.
   Begin with Enthusiastic.
   (A) successful, and he
   (B) success, so he
   (C) success; therefore, he
   (D) successful; therefore, he
   (E) success, he

4. Certainty that the actors alone were to blame for the poor performance caused the theater board to retain the director.
   Change Certainty to Sure.
   (A) was retained
   (B) retaining
   (C) retained
   (D) has been retained
   (E) will have retained

5. Whether an essay is formal or informal depends upon the spirit in which it is written.
   Begin with The spirit.
   (A) depends on
   (B) is dependent upon
   (C) is determined by
   (D) determines whether
   (E) will determine when

ACT ASSESSMENT TEST

The ACT Assessment test is another college entrance examination. The English Usage Test, one of the four parts of the ACT Assessment, consists of seventy-five multiple-choice questions. The questions test your knowledge of grammar, usage, punctuation, sentence structure, word choice, style, logic, and organization.

18.i ACT ENGLISH USAGE QUESTIONS

The questions on the ACT English Usage Test are based on prose passages that contain underlined words, phrases, and clauses. You must decide if the underlined item is correct as is or, if it contains an error, which of the suggested alternative wordings is the best. You have to think about such matters as agreement, pronoun case, wordiness, and appropriateness of vocabulary.

The test lists four choices for each underlined item. The first choice is always NO CHANGE; the other three choices offer revisions of the underlined word, phrase, or clause.

Strategies for ACT English Usage questions

1. Read quickly through the passage before trying to deal with any of the underlined items. This quick reading will help you to grasp the author's ideas, tone, general style, and point of view. As a result, you will not have to concentrate on reading comprehension while you are thinking about the underlined elements.
2. Go back and read the passage again slowly, stopping to consider each underlined item and its four choices.
3. If you think there is an error in the underlined element, try substituting each of the three alternatives. Check each for sense, grammar and usage, and punctuation. The substitution must fit correctly within the *entire* sentence in which the underlined element appears.

Below you will find part of a passage that has ten underlined items. Skim the passage first, and then read it again carefully as you select the correct choice for each numbered item. A discussion of the first three items follows the sample.

Sample ACT English Usage questions

Thor Heyerdahl became famous for a unique sailing expedition, which he later described in *Kon-Tiki*. Having developed a theory that the original Polynesians had sailed or drifted to the South Sea Islands from South America, it then had to be tested.[1] After careful study he built a raft that was as authentic as possible. Using only primitive equipment, he and five other men sailed into the South Seas from Peru, which he judged to be[2] in the same general

1. A. NO CHANGE
   B. he set out to test it.
   C. it was decided that it must be tested.
   D. the theory was then to be tested.

2. F. NO CHANGE
   G. Peru, being judged as
   H. Peru, which had been
   J. Peru judged as being

area as the land of the original Polynesians. As a result, his group and him will long be
3

3\. A. NO CHANGE
B. him and his group
C. his group and himself
D. he and his group

remembered not only as thorough scientists but also as courageous men.

Heyerdahl's courage was first tested in Ecuador. His search for trees that was large enough for the expeditionary raft sent
4

4\. F. NO CHANGE
G. which would be of sufficient size
H. of adequate size
J. of certainly sufficient size

him to Quito, a city high in the Andes. There, he and his companions were warned about headhunters and bandits on the trail. Feeling undaunted, they hired a driver
5

5\. A. NO CHANGE
B. trail. Undaunted, they
C. trail, but they were undaunted, and
D. trail; undaunted they

and jeep from the U.S. Embassy, going on with their dangerous task.
6

6\. F. NO CHANGE
G. Embassy; and went on with
H. Embassy and proceeded with
J. Embassy, and kept on

After the raft was done, Heyerdahl
7

7\. A. NO CHANGE
B. When the raft was ready.
C. The raft was speedily completed and
D. The raft having been constructed.

made final preparations for the expedition. Even before his crew came aboard, the courage which Heyerdahl possessed (8)

8. F. NO CHANGE
G. Heyerdahls' manly courage
H. Heyerdahl's courage
J. the courage of this man

was tested again. As the raft was being towed out of the harbor, it drifted under the stern of a tug. Heyerdahl had to struggle to save it. Dangers at sea (9) were present, but

9. A. NO CHANGE
B. (Do not begin new paragraph) At sea, dangers
C. (Begin new paragraph Dangers, at sea
D. (Begin new paragraph) At sea, dangers

Heyerdahl and his men did not show fear. Instead they developed games that were actually tests of courage. Although man-eating fish were nearby, the men swam to relieve their tension, maintaining (10) that the fish were not dangerous unless a man had already been cut or scratched.

10. F. NO CHANGE
G. tension. Maintaining
H. tension. He maintained
J. tension, because it was maintained

In Item 1 the underlined element is a clause that, by itself contains no error. The clause, however, is the final element in a lengthy sentence that begins with the participle *having developed*. . . . The participle should modify Thor Heyerdahl, not the pronoun *it*. The problem is that the use of *it* creates a dangling participle (see "Avoiding Errors with Participles and Participial Phrases," page 118, and "Avoiding Errors with Participial Phrases," page 273.) Of the choices offered, (B) is the only one that begins with the pronoun *he*, meaning Heyerdahl. The sentence should read as follows: *Having developed a theory . . . he set out to test it.*

In Item 2 the participles *being judged* and *judged as being* in (G) and (J) would introduce an unnecessary passive construction: The author knew that it was *Heyerdahl* who did the judging, and could say so. The clause that results from (H) would make nonsense of the sentence as a whole. The correct choice is (F), NO CHANGE.

In Item 3 the problem is one of case: Should the pronoun in the sentence be *he, him*, or *himself*? Since the pronoun in the sentence is to function as the subject of the verb phrase *will be remembered*, the pronoun must be in the nominative, or subjective, case: *He* is the nominative case pronoun. Therefore, (D) is the correct answer (see 1.d).

Try to answer Items 4–10 either on your own for later checking by your teacher or as a class activity along with other students. The following list points out the sections of this book that you may refer to for help on each of the items:

4. subject-verb agreement (2.r.2); wordiness (3.l)
5. wordiness (3.l)
6. word choice; appropriateness (Section 8)
7. word choice; appropriateness (Section 8)
8. wordiness (3.l)
9. paragraphing (Section 11)
10. participial phrases (1.l); (3.f)

ESSAY TESTS

Many of the tests that you take in school are probably essay tests. Some standardized tests also require you to write an essay. For example, you must demonstrate your writing ability if you take an examination in Advanced Placement English, and you must write a twenty-minute essay if you take the English Composition Test (a College Board Achievement Test) at the December administration.

Your ability to reason logically, to argue persuasively, to organize ideas, and to analyze problems clearly all may be tested in an essay test, and what makes this test so useful is that you must demonstrate these skills directly in writing.

18.j WRITING ESSAY ANSWERS

When you write essays for national examinations such as the English Composition Test, keep in mind the following.

Strategies for essay tests

1. Be careful not to deviate from the question you are given to answer. Read it carefully, and note what it asks you to write and how you are to write it. Your essay will be scored only if it responds to the question.
2. The actual essay questions are not difficult. They are specifically designed to be general enough so that any student will be able to write some kind of response. Frame your essay around a definable beginning, middle, and end. Begin with an introductory statement on the topic. Support the statement with concrete examples and specific references, elaborating as necessary on your point of view. Then conclude your essay with a restatement of the main idea. Be sure to observe the guidelines for good expository prose, paying particular attention to unity and coherence. See Section 13 for detailed advice on writing an expository essay.

Sample essay questions

The essay questions below have all appeared on the English Composition Test. Choose one or two of the questions and write the required essay for each. Be sure that each essay has a clear beginning, middle, and end. Allow yourself only twenty minutes to plan and write each essay. Do not overlook planning: Think before you write, and put your ideas into an informal outline so that you will not forget a point.

SAMPLE QUESTION A

Some possessions, like a mink coat, a particular kind of car or dog, or membership in a particular club, by seeming to confer upon their owners a particular status, influence the average person more than he realizes.

Assignment: Choose one of these status symbols, or another that you think of, explain the reasons for its appeal, and show how that symbol has been a force for both good and ill.

SAMPLE QUESTION B

"Adventure movies, romantic tales, science fiction, and detective stories are often the means of escaping from reality. Such escape is irresponsible. It is also harmful, both to the individual and to his society."

Assignment: Comment upon this statement, using your reading, study, or observation as the basis for your opinion. In your discussion, state to what extent you think the statement is correct or incorrect. Use illustrations to support your opinion.

SAMPLE QUESTION C

"Growing up requires the acceptance of limitations."

Assignment: Do you agree or disagree with this statement? What evidence can you find in your own observation, reading, and study to support your point of view? Be sure in your discussion to make clear your interpretation or definition of *limitations*.

18.k SCORING ESSAY ANSWERS

Essays are scored by people, not by machines. To give you an idea of how essays are scored, three responses to an essay test are printed below. Study the general directions, the assignment, and the three student essays. The scores for the three essays—categorized as "high," "middle," and "low"—can be found on page 772. See whether you can place each essay in the same general category as the original scorers did.

The sample essays are printed exactly as the students wrote them. While some writing problems do exist, some of the errors in the papers are the result of haste rather than of ignorance and could have been eliminated by careful proofreading (see 13.k).

Directions: You will have twenty minutes to plan and write the essay assigned below. You are expected to express your thoughts carefully, naturally, and effectively. Be specific. Remember that how well you write is much more important than how much you write. DO NOT WRITE ON A TOPIC OTHER THAN THE ONE ASSIGNED BELOW. AN ESSAY ON A TOPIC OF YOUR OWN CHOICE WILL RECEIVE NO CREDIT.

You must fit your essay on the answer sheet provided. You will receive no other paper on which to write. You will find that you have enough space if you write on every line, avoid wide margins, and keep your handwriting to a reasonable size.

First, consider carefully the following statement. Then read and follow the directions that are given in the assignment that follows the statement.

"We must live in the present. If we dwell on the past, we will lose the present."

Assignment: To what extent and in what ways do you agree or disagree with this statement? Explain and illustrate your answer from history, literature, observation, or experience.

ESSAY A

I do not agree with this statement. It shows a non-thinking attitude on the part of the speaker. Living only for today without any thought about prior events is senseless. Intelligent people must, in their actions and decisions, remember events from the past and analyze, injest, and understand them in order to better understand and deal with the same problems in their current sitituation.

Any historian would deplore this statement. History is the study of the past. The aim of history is by understanding and learning from the past to better deal with the present. For example, the atom bomb was first employed in a war in World War II. We did not really know of its awful and often lingering effects. But in the 1970's we have looked back into the past and have realized our mistake. We will not use the bomb against a people ever again.

ESSAY B

Most of the older generation of today and also the younger tend to dwell on the past. The old people dwell on it because not to many of them agree with what's going on in the world today.

They also go back to the past so as to relate things also it brings them happiness and peace with themselves. It also causes them great pain and regret but yet they look to the past.

Most of them seem to forget about what's happening now and do not realize that if they forget about the future they will miss out on everything around them such as their family and friends also what is happening with them. We all need to know about the life we live in so as to understand it better. If we keep looking to the past and comparing we will not know ourselves and the past is not going to help us overcome our everday problems and give us a better education it will be more likely to help you lock yourself away from the future and the only way to do that is to stop living.

We need everything around us and if we dwell in the past the future is lost.

ESSAY C

It is harmful to live exclusively in the past, for then no progress will be made—yet it is always important to heed the past and learn from it. It is obvious that many feel it is important to forget the past and concentrate on the present, and many of our sayings reflect this.

Living in the past is detrimental to the progress off the world. If people constantly think about the past nothing will be done about the future. If Alexander G. Bell did not think of the then present need for faster and easier communication, but rather of the old ways of communicating, perhaps we would never have heard of the telephone today.

Yet on the other hand, one must think about the past at times and analyze what happened and why. One can learn a great deal from the past, why something went wrong, what was forgotten, etc. After the Wright brothers first invented their plane, the many people who went on to develope the plane did not forget all that they had done. Those developers went back and examined what the Wright brothers had done, where they had gone wrong, and what they themselves could do to improve the plane.

It is impossible to live solely in the present, discounting the past, and it is impossible dwell only on the past and not consider the present. There must be a happy medium between living the past and living for the present.

How essays are scored

The essays on the English Composition Test are hand scored by high school and college English teachers who are trained in the "holistic" scoring method. The philosophy of holistic scoring is that students are rewarded for what they have done well in their essays; they are not penalized for what they have done badly. Holistic scoring is based upon the assumption that a piece of writing as a whole is greater than the sum of its parts. Put another way, any composition combines in a unique way the writing skills of diction, language control, style, clarity, grammar, logic, and organization.

Holistic scoring evaluates the total effect of these skills in a given essay.

The method employed in scoring the essays is complex yet standardized so as to insure the greatest objectivity possible. The standards are not arbitrary, and essays are not judged against some imaginary ideal essay. The readers first study the topic and agree on what it requires of the student. They determine what kinds of papers are to be considered off the topic. Each group of about eight readers has a leader whose major function is to reread scored papers and to question any score that varies from the standards established by the group. Every possible effort is made to insure fair and accurate scoring.

Answer Keys

Exercise 1.

1) B 2) C 3) B 4) E 5) B

Exercise 2.

1) A 2) D 3) A 4) D 5) B

Exercise 3.

1) A 2) D 3) D 4) D 5) A

Exercise 4.

1) C 2) B 3) A 4) E 5) A

Exercise 5.

1) D 2) D 3) A 4) E

Exercise 6.

1) D 2) B 3) E 4) C 5) D

ACT English Usage questions

4) H 5) B 6) H 7) B 8) H 9) D 10) F

Scored sample essays

Essay A—Middle

Essay B—Low

Essay C—High

ADDITIONAL EXERCISES

Additional Exercises

1. Nouns

PART A: Identify each common noun in the following sentences. Each sentence has more than one common noun. The number in parentheses at the end of the first five sentences indicates the number of common nouns you should find in that sentence. (Review 1.a and 1.a.1.)

1. Preservation of food was once a tedious chore. (3)
2. In late summer, women cooked and stored fruits and vegetables in jars and cans for consumption during the wintertime. (8)
3. Then, a change in the way tin was made into cans created a new industry. (5)
4. In the early nineteenth century a skilled tinsmith made one hundred cans a day by hand. (5)
5. About seventy years later, J. D. Cox of Bridgeton, New Jersey, invented a machine that greatly speeded up the production of cans. (4)
6. Cox's device enabled an unskilled crew to produce thirty thousand cans daily at a low cost.
7. Large companies began to sell industrially canned foods to the American public.
8. Further improvements have now pushed production to 100 billion cans per day.
9. A larger variety of foodstuffs has become available to the average family.
10. The evolution of American technology has produced giant corporations that manufacture countless canned products, ranging from peanuts to pineapple to chow mein.

PART B: Examine the common nouns that you identified in Part A. Decide which common nouns are concrete (like a pineapple) and which ones are abstract (like taste). (Review 1.a.)

PART C: Reexamine the common nouns from Part A. Indicate which of these common nouns are compound nouns. Remember that compound nouns can be written as two words, as one word, or as a hyphenated word. (Review 1.a.2.)

PART D: Reexamine the common nouns from Part A. Now indicate which ones are collective nouns. Remember that a collective noun names a group. (Review 1.a.4.)

2. Verbs

PART A: Identify the verb or verb phrase in each of the following sentences. (Review 1.b.)

1. An ancient Chinese emperor built an underground tomb for himself.
2. He was preparing for a life after death.
3. In an underground chamber of the tomb, the emperor placed six hundred clay statues of soldiers and horses.
4. The clay statues look very real.
5. Each soldier appears unique.
6. A number of the soldiers are driving chariots.
7. Until recently, few foreigners had seen the tomb.
8. Some American tourists have now seen the emperor's tomb.
9. Before long, other visitors will probably be flocking to the site of this tomb.
10. Perhaps this tomb will one day become one of the world's greatest tourist attractions.

PART B: Reread the sentences, paying attention to those with action verbs. Decide whether each action verb is transitive or intransitive. (Review 1.b.2.)

PART C: Reread the sentences. Now decide in which of the following categories each verb belongs. (Review 1.b 11–1.b.19.)

1. present
2. present progressive
3. past
4. past progressive
5. present perfect
6. past perfect
7. future
8. future progressive

3. Adjectives

PART A: Identify all the adjectives in each of the following sentences. (Do *not* identify the *proper* adjectives at this point. Also, do not identify articles as adjectives.) Some sentences may contain more than one adjective. (Review 1.c.)

1. Everyone who was ever young knows how wonderful it is to ride a carousel.
2. No carnival is complete without a festive merry-go-round.
3. Joyous children fly by on swift horses, ferocious lions, and magical gazelles.
4. Little girls with bright eyes command brighter Arabian horses.
5. It is not often that an American child gets the opportunity to travel on a sleek panther.
6. On such a fearless beast the youngest rider becomes more powerful than the mightiest king.
7. Maturer riders sit back comfortably in their Roman chariots.
8. Riders of all ages try their best to catch the brass ring and win a free ride.
9. Eager horses gallop to the squeaky but cheerful music of the organ.
10. Generations of enthusiastic children, all playful and happy, go around and around on the carousel.

PART B: Reread the sentences. For each adjective, indicate whether it is in its *basic* form, in its *comparative* form, or in its *superlative* form. (Review 1.c.3 and 1.c.4.)

PART C: Reread the sentences. Now identify all the proper adjectives. (Review 1.c.6.)

4. Pronouns

PART A: Identify all the pronouns in each of the following sentences. (Review 1.d.)

1. What is more romantic than a windmill working with the wind?
2. That is, indeed, a beautiful site, which is returning to the American landscape.

3. The windmills that followed colonists to America were primarily sources of power for them.
4. Windmills were popular here for a long time, but the steam engine led to their disappearance.
5. The problem with windmills, as it has always been, is their unreliability.
6. After all, what happens when the wind itself dies down?
7. The windmills that are part of America's past are now portrayed on five postage stamps.
9. The first is a post mill, which was built by William Robertson, who was from Virginia.
10. Everyone has to decide for himself whether he prefers the stamp of his windmill or the stamps of windmills from Rhode Island, Massachusetts, Illinois, or Texas.

PART B: Look at the pronouns that you identified in Part A. Decide in which of the following categories each pronoun belongs: (Review 1.d.1–1.d.7.)

1. personal
2. demonstrative
3. interrogative
4. relative
5. indefinite

5. Pronouns

PART A: Select the appropriate pronoun from the parentheses in each of the following sentences. (Review 1.d.1 and 1.d.6.)

1. Each player paused before (he/they) made a move.
2. No one would predict (who/whom) the winner would be.
3. Both contestants anxiously hoped that (he/they) would win.
4. After a while, Peter Winofsky did not hear as many people applauding (him/himself) as before.
5. The crowd was cheering more for Nilda Vargas than (he/him).
6. After all, the title was (her's/hers), and he was just a hopeful challenger.

7. The lights and noise overwhelmed Peter and made (he/him) feel dizzy.
8. The crowd held (its/their) breath as they watched.
9. Would the winner be (he or she/him or her)?
10. It turned out to be Nilda, (who/which) won the U.S. Scrabble Championship once again.

PART B: Look at the pronouns that you selected in Part A. First decide whether each pronoun is a *personal pronoun* or a *relative pronoun*. Then, for each personal pronoun indicate whether it is in the *nominative case* or in the *objective case*. (Review 1.d.1 and 1.d.6.)

6. Adverbs

PART A: Indicate which of the following sentences have adverbs. Identify each adverb. (Review 1.f.1.)

1. Then suddenly he saw the ridiculous side of the situation.
   —Aldous Huxley, "The Gioconda Smile"
2. He afterwards gathered the books and hurled them on the fire.
   —Emily Brontë, *Wuthering Heights*
3. It was an absolutely perfect obstacle.
   Ernest Hemingway, *In Our Time*
4. It was always snowing at Christmas.
   —Dylan Thomas, "A Child's Christmas in Wales"
5. Laura was terribly nervous.
   —Katherine Mansfield, "The Garden Party"
6. Occasionally she glanced anxiously over her shoulder toward her shining kitchen, with a black and white linoleum floor in big squares, like a marble pavement.
   —Willa Cather, "Old Mrs. Harris"
7. Annabel and Midge did, and completely, all that young office workers are besought not to do.
   —Dorothy Parker, "The Standard of Living"
8. Now and then the most legitimate business runs out of luck.
   —O. Henry, "The Man Higher Up"
9. I'll think about it all tomorrow, at Tara. . . . After all, tomorrow is another day.
   —Margaret Mitchell, *Gone with the Wind*

10. Nessim appeared in tunic and fez, but Mountolive instantly recognized in him a person of his own kind.

—Lawrence Durrell, *Mountolive*

PART B: Look at the adverbs that you identified in Part A. Decide in which category each adverb belongs. (Review 1.f.1.)

1. adverb of time
2. adverb of place
3. adverb of manner
4. adverb of degree

7. Prepositions and Conjunctions

PART A: Identify each of the italicized words in the following sentences as either a preposition or a conjunction. (Review 1.g and 1.h.)

1. An American was visiting Germany *during* World War II.
2. The woman carried a large amount *of* money *inside* her luggage *for* the local underground.
3. The woman was a well-known writer; *therefore*, she was *under* police scrutiny.
4. *Nevertheless*, she managed to make contact *with* an underground agent.
5. *Neither* she *nor* the agent knew *if* they were being observed.
6. The agent was a porter *at* at a station where the writer's train stopped *for* a short while.
7. The writer left an attaché case *near* a pile of luggage *and* quickly returned *to* her compartment *on* the train.
8. She did not breathe easily *until* the train crossed the border *into* France.
9. *After* the war ended, the writer found out that the money had reached the proper people *in* Germany.
10. She felt thankful *and* proud, *for* she had helped.

PART B: Look at the conjunctions that you identified in Part A. Indicate what type of conjunction each is, as follows. (Review 1.l, 1.n, 1.p.)

1. coordinating conjunction
2. correlative conjunction
3. subordinating conjunction
4. conjunctive adverb

8. Verbals

PART A: Each of the following sentences contains one verbal. Identify the verbal and indicate whether it is a gerund, a participle, or a infinitive. (Review 1.j–1.p.)

1. Nature's greatest talent may be merely surviving.
2. Centuries ago glaciers destroyed all plant life on the Appalachian mountains, but warmer weather permitted plants to grow there once again.
3. The first plant life to appear was lichen, a primitive plant that can grow on solid rock.
4. Consisting of both algae and fungi, the lichen is a natural oddity.
5. The algae produce food for both parts of the plant, while the fungi act to protect the more delicate algae.
6. Growing is then a process whereby the lichen breaks down the rock chemically.
7. In the Appalachians this process served to create a very thin layer of soil.
8. Another plant covering the soil in dark and moist areas is moss.
9. Enriched further by moss, the soil can produce lovely white mountain flowers.
10. Flowering shrubs returned years later, and eventually fir trees grew again on the once-bare slopes.

PART B: Reread the ten sentences. Seven of the sentences contain a verbal phrase—a gerund phrase, a participial phrase, or an infinitive phrase. Identify those phrases. (Review 1.l, 1.n, 1.p.)

9. Subjects and Predicates; Subject-Verb Agreement

PART A: Identify first the complete subject and then the simple subject in each of the following sentences. For now, do not pay attention to the words in parentheses. (Review 2.b.)

1. Cemeteries (does/do) not always call forth emotions of sadness or fear.

2. Some cemeteries (offers/offer) delightful country landscapes.
3. One in particular (has/have) always been a popular place for a Sunday stroll.
4. Green-Wood Cemetery in Brooklyn, New York, (covers/cover) 478 parklike acres.
5. Its grounds (includes/include) rolling hills, green woods, and several small lakes.
6. Ducks and swans (swims/swim) serenely in the lakes.
7. There (is/are) no sign of the nearby city.
8. Looking from the top of the hill, however, a visitor (has/have) a spectacular view of the Manhattan skyline.
9. *The Sights of New York* (lists/list) this cemetery among recommended attractions in Brooklyn.
10. There (is/are) a number of people buried in Green-Wood Cemetery.
11. The abolitionist Henry Ward Beecher (lies/lie) there.
12. Currier and Ives (is/are) buried there in a setting similar to one of their paintings.
13. "Boss" Tweed, politician and one-time ruler of New York, (rests/rest) there also.
14. Every grave, no matter how humble, (has/have) a history.
15. Many of these histories (remains/remain) unknown, of course.
16. One statue of a young woman in an evening gown (marks/mark) the grave of a seventeen-year-old girl.
17. She (was/were) killed in 1845 in an accident with a horse-drawn coach.
18. Most of the half-million graves at Green-Wood (features/feature) elaborate gravestones and monuments.
19. Taking photographs or making rubbings of the older gravestones (interests/interest) some people.
20. Many a visitor to Green-Wood (returns/return) again and again.

PART B: Select the appropriate form of the action verb, linking verb, or auxiliary from the parentheses in each of the preceding sentences. Your choice must agree in number with the subject of the sentence. (Review 2.c–2.e.)

10. Compound Subjects; Compound Verbs; Prepositional Phrases

PART A: Identify each compound subject and each compound verb in the following sentences. Not every sentence has compound parts. (Review 2.d and 2.g.)

1. Many American homeowners chop firewood and burn it as fuel.
2. Wood-burning stoves and chain saws sell briskly in the colder parts of the United States.
3. A lightweight person can cut trees of several hundred pounds with a chain saw.
4. Oak, ash, and hickory are cut, stored, and dried for a year.
5. One woodcutter and newspaper reporter advises her readers to cut only dead trees.
6. Seasoned wood weighs surprisingly little and burns extremely well.
7. The writer herself fells trees, cuts logs, and splits firewood.
8. Many city dwellers avoid such work and buy their firewood.
9. Every able-bodied man or woman can learn to use a chain saw, however.
10. Learning and doing are, of course, two very different things.

PART B: Identify all the prepositional phrases in each of the above ten sentences. Indicate whether each phrase is part of the subject or part of the predicate. Not every sentence has a prepositional phrase. (Review 2.h.)

11. Subjects; Predicates; Complements

PART A: Identify the complete subject and the complete predicate in each of the following sentences. (Review 2.b.)

1. Citizens of Winooski, Vermont, may build a dome over their town.
2. The idea seems odd to some people.
3. Such a project does suggest science fiction.
4. The town of Winooski has two sections with bad pollution.
5. A clear plastic dome could cover the whole city or just those two sections.

6. The enclosure might save residents millions of dollars in heating costs.
7. One kind of dome is retractable for sunny days.
8. Engineers consider that particular plan desirable and feasible.
9. The protection of the dome would be over many houses.
10. Umbrellas and rain boots may soon be unnecessary in Winooski, Vermont.

PART B: Reexamine each of the predicates that you identified in Part A. Identify the following items in each of those predicates. (Review 2.j–2.m.)

direct objects (d.o.)
indirect objects (i.o.)
predicate nominatives (p.n.)
predicate adjectives (p. adj.)
predicate adverbs (p. adv.)
object complements (o.c.)

12. Main Clauses

PART A: Identify each main clause in the following sentences. (Review 2.o.)

1. Each of the two sides of the human brain performs different functions.
2. The left side of the brain controls the right side of the body, and the right side of the brain controls the left side of the body.
3. Our eyes are linked to both hemispheres, but the actual visual fields of each are divided.
4. Information from the left half of each eye's visual field goes to the right side of the brain, and information from the right half of each eye goes to the left side of the brain.
5. Language and arithmetic are processed in the left hemisphere; art and music are managed in the right.
6. Some people consider the right side responsible for hopes and dreams and the left side accountable for practicalities.
7. The reality is actually more complex, for the brain seems to be rather changeable.

8. The sound "bee," for example, is processed in the left side to mean the alphabetical letter but in the right side to mean the insect.
9. We use the right side of our brain to read fiction but the left side to read technical material.
10. The left side controls innovation, and the right side works on cooperation.

PART B: Decide whether each of the preceding sentences is a simple sentence or a compound sentence.

PART C: Reexamine each of the main clauses that you identified in Part A. Identify the simple subject and the verb in each main clause. (Review 2.o and 2.c.)

13. Main Clauses; Subordinate Clauses

PART A: Identify each clause in the following sentences and tell whether the clause is a main clause or a subordinate clause. (Review 2.n–2.p.)

1. Coral is a limestone formation that is created by tiny animals in the sea.
2. The animals that form coral belong to the same animal group that includes jelly fish.
3. These animals, which are known as polyps, have round bodies with many tentacles.
4. What we know as coral is actually limestone skeletons that are left by colonies of polyps.
5. A large mass of the limestone skeletons form a coral reef, which is a ridge of coral near the surface of the sea.
6. Coral islands appear when these masses rise above the water; many Pacific islands were formed in this way.
7. Reefs are found mostly in warm and tropical seas, for coral cannot live in cold water.
8. Many colorful sea animals live among corals, and so people sometimes think that the reefs look like sea gardens.
9. The Great Barrier Reef of Australia, which is more than 1,250 miles long, is magnificent.

10. Whoever wishes to dive for coral should look for it in the Mediterranean Sea or the Pacific Ocean.
11. Black corals are found a few hundred feet underwater, but red and gold corals grow 1,150 feet below the surface.
12. Although scuba divers can harvest black coral, submersible vehicles are necessary to get the red corals.
13. Because coral is beautiful and long-lasting, it is popular for jewelry.
14. Most of the coral that grows in shallow reefs is too soft for jewelry, however.
15. Precious coral is the species that is used in jewelry, for it has a hard core that can be polished to bring out hues of red.
16. Gorgonian corals, which are yellow, rose, or purple, often look like bushes or fans.
17. Some say that these corals look like sea gardens as they wave on the reefs.
18. Coral is now plentiful, but the coral beds could one day become depleted.
19. The early 1960s saw terrible exploitation of coral beds after huge deposits were discovered near Japan.
20. Hawaii has passed laws that prevent young coral from being harvested.

PART B: Reexamine each subordinate clause that you identified for Part A. Decide whether each one is an adjective clause, an adverb clause, or a noun clause. (Review 2.p–2.s.)

PART C: Reexamine the sentences and identify each one as a compound sentence, a complex sentence, or a compound-complex sentence. (Review 2.u.)

14. Coordination and Subordination; Kinds of Sentences

PART A: Look at the italicized words in the following sentences. Classify each one according to the following list. (Review 2.p–2.s.)

a. coordinating conjunction joining words or phrases
b. coordinating conjunction joining main clauses
c. subordinating conjunction introducing an adverb clause
d. relative pronoun or other subordinate introducing an adjective clause
e. subordinator introducing a noun clause

1. Archer reddened, *and* his heart gave a leap of surprise.
   —Edith Wharton, *The Age of Innocence*
2. *What* recommends commerce to me is its enterprise *and* bravery.
   —Henry David Thoreau, *Walden*
3. The boys began to laugh at their mother *because* she flushed so red, *but* she stood her ground *and* threw up her head.
   —Willa Cather, "Neighbor Rosicky"
4. I've noticed *that* the conversation of grown-ups is always the same.
   —Elizabeth Bishop, *The Diary of Helena Morley*
5. The conversation, *which* was at a high pitch of animation *when* Silas approached the door of the Rainbow, had, as usual, been slow *and* intermittent *when* the company first assembled.
   —George Eliot, *Silas Marner*
6. Millicent Bruton, *whose* lunch parties were said to be extraordinarily amusing, had not asked her.
   —Virginia Woolf, *Mrs. Dalloway*
7. I am always drawn back to places *where* I have lived, the houses *and* their neighborhoods.
   —Truman Capote, *Breakfast at Tiffany's*
8. The Frenchmen flung their laughter *and* light words over their shoulders, *and* often Jimmy had to strain forward to catch the quick phrase.
   —James Joyce, "After the Race"
9. They were both in white, *and* their dresses were rippling *and* fluttering *as if* they had just been blown back in after a short flight around the house.
   —F. Scott Fitzgerald, *The Great Gatsby*
10. There is no doubt *that* Marley was dead.
    —Charles Dickens, *A Christmas Carol*

PART B: Reexamine each of the sentences. Now identify each one as a simple sentence, a compound sentence, a complex sentence, or a compound-complex sentence. (Review 2.u.)

15. Restrictive and Nonrestrictive Adjective Clauses

PART A: In each of the following sentences, categorize the italicized adjective clauses as restrictive or nonrestrictive. Notice that commas have intentionally been omitted from around adjective clauses. (Review 2.r.1.)

1. Jane Goodall *who is an English zoologist* studies the behavior of chimpanzees.
2. Her research *which has contributed a great deal to zoology* is conducted in Gombe Stream National Park.
3. The park *which is a Tanzanian game reserve* serves as a living laboratory for Goodall and her staff.
4. In her research each chimpanzee becomes an individual *whom Goodall can recognize*.
5. It was she *who first observed chimpanzees using tools*.
6. She was also the first scientist *who observed chimpanzees hunting insects and animals for food*.
7. This discovery surprised other scientists *who had believed fruits and vegetables to be chimpanzees' only food*.
8. One of the most important discoveries *that Goodall has made* was of murder among chimpanzees.
9. She was the first to observe chimpanzees *who systematically killed other chimpanzees for no obvious survival reason*.
10. Goodall *whose theories and observations are recorded in In the Shadow of Man* is considered a world authority on chimpanzees.

PART B: Reread the ten sentences in Part A. Provide commas around any adjective clauses that require them. (Review 2.r.1.)

Index

The boxed material in Sections 1, 2, 3, and 7 is indexed here under three heads: "Avoiding Errors," "Punctuation," "Spelling."

AVOIDING ERRORS

PUNCTUATION

SPELLING

LIST OF REFERENCE KEYS

There are several ways for you to become familiar with the content of each section of this book. First, there is the Table of Contents. Second, there is the title page of each section, listing all the main divisions of the section. Third, there is the following list of reference keys.

Each main head within a section is marked by a reference key. Each subhead is marked by another key. The main keys are also used as tabs on the top of right-hand pages to help you locate material.

SAMPLE FROM SECTION 7, "CAPITALIZATION AND PUNCTUATION"

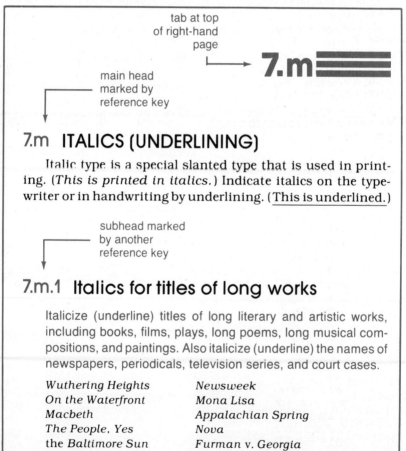

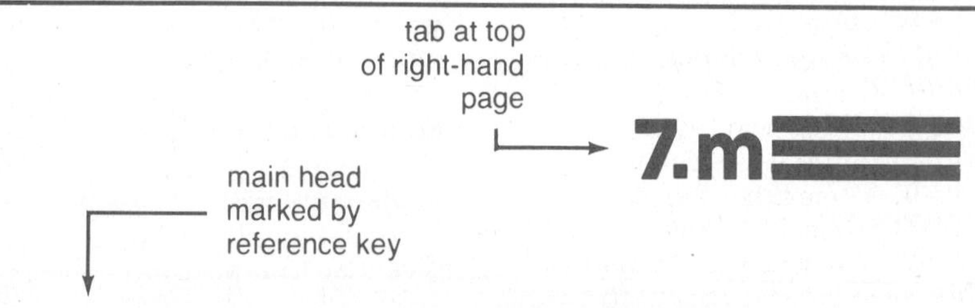

7.m ITALICS (UNDERLINING)

Italic type is a special slanted type that is used in printing. (*This is printed in italics.*) Indicate italics on the typewriter or in handwriting by underlining. (This is underlined.)

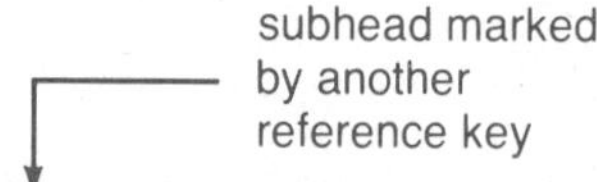

7.m.1 Italics for titles of long works

Italicize (underline) titles of long literary and artistic works, including books, films, plays, long poems, long musical compositions, and paintings. Also italicize (underline) the names of newspapers, periodicals, television series, and court cases.

Wuthering Heights	*Newsweek*
On the Waterfront	*Mona Lisa*
Macbeth	*Appalachian Spring*
The People, Yes	*Nova*
the *Baltimore Sun*	*Furman* v. *Georgia*

PARTS OF SPEECH

PARTS OF A SENTENCE

WRITING SENTENCES

VOCABULARY

SPELLING

THE DICTIONARY

CAPITALIZATION AND PUNCTUATION

PATTERNS OF THINKING AND WRITING

THE EXPOSITORY ESSAY

ARGUMENTATION AND LOGIC

LIBRARIES AND INFORMATION

THE RESEARCH PAPER

THE BUSINESS LETTER

TEST TAKING

EDITING SIGNALS AND REFERENCE KEYS

	Editing signal	See Editing Chart
Editing for grammar and clarity		
Error in subject-verb agreement	*agree*	510–511
Error in case	*case*	511–512
Error with pronoun reference	*ref*	512
Error with the negative	*neg*	513
Error in noun plurals	*pl*	513
Error in possessive	*poss*	513
Error in verb tense	*tense*	513–514
Error in comparative, superlative	*adj*	514
Error in reflexive pronoun	*pro*	515
Error with *this* or *them*	*pro*	515
Error with *-ly* adverb	*adv*	515
Unnecessary preposition	*prep*	516
Using commas instead of end marks	*run-on*	516
Incomplete sentences	*frag*	516
Misusing conjunctions	*conj*	516
Shift in voice	*voice*	517
Dangling elements	*dangling*	517
Misplaced elements	*misplaced*	517
Sagging sentences	*sag*	517–519
Lack of parallelism	*not parallel*	519
Wordiness	*wordy*	520

	Editing signal	See Reference Key
Editing for spelling	*sp*	5.a–5.f
Editing for capitalization	*cap*	7.a.1–7.a.7
Editing for punctuation	*p*	7.b–7.q
Editing paragraphs and compositions		
Weak topic sentence	*t.s.*	11.a.1
Topic sentence poorly supported	*support*	11.b.1–11.b.3
Lack of unity	*unity*	11.c
Lack of coherence	*cohere*	11.d
New paragraph	¶	11.e
Weak introduction	*intro*	13.g
Weak sequencing of details	*seq*	12.a, 12.b, 12.e
Weak transitions	*trans*	12.a–12.f, 13.f
Weak conclusion	*conclusion*	13.h